A REVIEW

OF

THE POLITICAL CONFLICT IN AMERICA,

FROM THE COMMENCEMENT OF THE ANTI-SLAVERY AGITATION TO THE CLOSE OF SOUTHERN RECONSTRUCTION;

COMPRISING ALSO A

Resumé of the Career of Thaddeus Stevens:

BEING A SURVEY OF THE STRUGGLE OF PARTIES, WHICH DESTROYED THE REPUBLIC AND VIRTUALLY MONARCHIZED ITS GOVERNMENT.

Quando imperium tenent pravi, plorat populus.

By ALEXANDER HARRIS.

NEW YORK:
T. H. POLLOCK, Publisher, 37 Park Row.
1876.

STEREOTYPED BY
J. & T. A. RAISBECK,
Stereotypers & Electrotypers.
No. 74 Beekman Street.

PREFACE.

THE undersigned proposes to present to the public a history, to be entitled "A REVIEW OF THE POLITICAL CONFLICT IN AMERICA." He does so, in obedience to monitions that were ever reminding him, since the close of our civil war, that duty demanded of this generation, that it write the truth concerning the origin and progress of the conflict, through which the nation has passed. The work will also comprise a "Resume of the Career of Thaddeus Stevens," who conspicuously figured, as the leading revolutionist of the American Congress; and who towered as the unconcealed contemner of law and the Federal Constitution. Until the work was completed, it had been the design of the undersigned, to entitle it "The Life and Times of Thaddeus Stevens;" because it was believed, that the prominence and admitted intellectual capacity of the man being treated, would secure attention from all classes of readers. But his career had been mainly selected, in order to embody therewith, the history of the times in which he lived; and because also he of all American Statesmen, appeared as the typical representative of the destructive revolutionary movement, which the work is designed to illustrate and unfold. Upon its completion, however, the originally conceived title, appeared not to harmonize with what, it might have seemed to have imported; and therefore, after some reflection, it was changed to what has been adopted. The plan thus followed, in the treatment of the work, notwithstanding the change of title, will allow of a clearer light being reflected (as is believed) upon the development and progress of the revolution, as it passes scenically before the vision.

The work will trace the conflict to its inception, deducing it from inherent principles. It will thence follow the progress of the anti-slavery agitation, from its commencement to its full development in one of the political parties of the country, and its complete seizure of power, in the election of Abraham Lincoln, in 1860. The movement intended to check the progress of sectionalism will also be sketched, until the final effort to do so, resulted in the secession of the Southern States; and the bloody collision of arms followed. During the progress of the civil war, the ideal conflict in Congress and throughout the nation, which animated and sustained the armed combatants upon the fields of battle, is alone viewed and depicted. The Presidential and Congressional acts which had reference to the prosecution of the war, and the motives influencing these, are presented in historical delineation of the political struggle, as it progressed. The breach of President Johnson with his party, is detailed in appropriate compass, and the conflict of parties which followed, until the reconstruction legislation of Congress, insured the Africanization of the South.

No asperity or bitterness, should be aroused in the breasts of those, who may honestly differ with the author, as to the causes which led to our late conflict. He claims, as a free citizen, the right to present the reasons, which ever induced him to condemn the war against the South and its prosecution. He has presented these openly and fearlessly ; records for all time his conviction, that the war was wholly unwarranted by the Federal Constitution ; and he believes the time will come, when the majority of the American people, will be fully convinced that coercion was an unwise policy, adopted to preserve republican government. Not only unwise, will they come to see it to have been, but wholly suicidal to the institutions, it was meant to preserve. The ship of state, which, under republican steersmen, had sailed on a calm ocean, no sooner came under the management of those of contrary principles, than it was driven upon the shoals and quicksands of political disorder, from which it is even problematical if it can ever be rescued.

Though the work, to the unreflecting, may appear as if written to subserve partisan politics, the author disclaims all such motives, as in anywise, having influenced his undertaking. And, before being so accused, those thus charging him, should inquire, what selfish interest he could promote, by advocating views unpopular in both parties, in his state and section. Nay, the truth is the pole star by which he is guided, and, albeit he may be (as he has been heretofore) subjected to reproach and bitter vilification, for the maintenance of his opinions, he hesitates not to defend them, believing, that though covered with the darkness of midnight, the dawn of morning is approaching. Our Union has sustained a long and arduous struggle, with the foes of her own household, but patriotism, like a deity seated upon some Olympian summit, has been from the first viewing the combat, and expecting every true Amer can to do his duty. Should none have the boldness to break the silence, the slumber of truth, might at times, be the sleep of death ; but she has ever by her couch, her faithful sentinels to arouse her, and messengers to go forth amidst terror and gloom, to proclaim her immutable laws, to sound her clarion and arouse her hosts to victory.

Fully trusting, that the deductions of the work now to be submitted to the public, are the inspiration of truth, the author invokes for them no leniency of criticism ; and, if able to be controverted by truth, logic and sound ratiocination, let them fall and forever perish ! For the author only desires to know the truth, and, if fully convinced that the opinions which he has steadily defended, since the commencement of the civil war, were erroneous, he should himself be one of the first to disavow them. But until proven false, in the forum of reason, he claims the right to defend and publish them to the reflective world. Careful, however, as the author has endeavored to be, historical inaccuracies, no doubt, will have eluded his scrutiny, and he is not so presumptuous as to conceive, but that his work, will disclose many literary errors to the critical eye. He entertains, nevertheless the hope, that it may in a slight degree help to pacify turbulent passion, and correct mistaken views ; and, so believing, he commits it to the judgment and criticism of ages.

ALEXANDER HARRIS.

CONTENTS.

CHAPTER XXV.

CHAPTER XXVI.

CHAPTER XXVII.

CHAPTER XXVIII.

CHAPTER XXIX.

CHAPTER XXX.

CHAPTER XXXI.

CHAPTER XXXII.

CHAPTER I.

BIRTH, EDUCATION, ADMISSION TO THE BAR AND EARLY LEGAL SUCCESS OF THADDEUS STEVENS.

THADDEUS STEVENS was born at Danville, Caledonia County, Vermont, April 4th, 1792. His parents were persons in limited circumstances, being possessed of nothing save a poor farm, upon which they were enabled to rear their children with the most pinching and parsimonious economy. His father, named Joshua Stevens, was a shoemaker by occupation, but as he was a man of rather dissipated habits, he contributed little to the support of his family. He was well built, strong and muscular, and quite an athlete, bearing the reputation of being the best wrestler in his county. He enlisted as a soldier in the war of 1812, and in the attack upon Oswego, received a bayonet wound in the groin, of which he shortly afterwards died. His mother, whose maiden name was Sarah Morrill, was a women of strong native sense, and of an unconquerable will and resolution. On account of the loose and irregular life of his father, the management of the farm and the rearing of the family devolved upon his mother; and being a woman of shrewdness and penetration, she determined to afford her children (as all she could give them) the advantages of an education. The school system of Vermont, at that time being very similar to that of the other Eastern States, Thaddeus was placed, as soon as old enough, under tutelage in one of these New England seminaries of the people, where he soon acquired the rudiments of an English education. Being the youngest of the family, and besides, lame and sickly in youth, he obtained advantages in the way of schooling over and above his brothers. He was the favorite and pet of his mother, as is often the case with the mothers of deformed children; and she spared no pains to provide that he should be in constant attendence at school, in order to prepare him as she fondly hoped, to make his way in life by some means not demanding manual exertion. She was not slow in perceiving his rare powers, in the acquisition of the ordinary branches of an education; and the thought occurred to her that one who could so thoroughly, and in so short a time, master reading, writing and arithmetic, should have an opportunity to try his strength in the higher departments of knowledge. In a word, it was quietly resolved that Thaddeus should be sent to college; and perhaps he might be able to carve his way to one of the professions, at that time the goal of the ambition of every intelligent New England mother. But the path of life from the cradle to the grave, is beset with thorns; and the smart of these young Thaddeus must also feel. On account of his lameness, being unable to sport around as briskly as other boys of his age, he came somewhat to be regarded as a youth of great sedateness and sobriety; nor was he able to escape the taunts and jeers of his youthful school companions, who would at times mimic his limping walk, and otherwise annoy and vex him. These petty anoyances to his proud and sensitive nature, were very galling; and in their oft repetition his stern and sedate character may originally have received its earliest impression. But although his young classmates were ready to gibe him because of his deformity, he had the sweet satisfaction of knowing that he could far outstrip any of them, so far as class standing was concerned.

The following anecdote is related by Mr. Stevens of his school days, and whether narrated to create amusement, or to delineate character and the condition of the country at that early period, it at least deserves rehearsal in this connection: "At one time," said Mr. Stevens, "the schoolmaster was a broad shouldered Irishman. During a severe winter, the bears encroached on the settlement, and it became the duty of all good citizens to enlist in a war of extermination. The teacher marshalled his pupils, and at their head ventured to obstruct a noted bear-path, he being armed with a long rifle, well loaded and primed, and the boys with clubs and a miscellaneous assortment of weapons. The baying of the dogs soon indicated that the game was up, and the cracking of the bushes, that the bear was approaching. He came on within a few feet of where the army was posted, and leaping up, his fore feet resting on a large log, he hesitated, while he snuffed the danger ahead. The teacher sounded the charge, saying to the boys: 'Now I'll show you a rale specimen of bear hunting.' But his impetuosity," added Mr. Stevens, "overcame his discretion, and rushing on the astonished animal he demolished him with the butt end of his rifle. When laughed at by the boys, and rallied on his forgetfulness by myself, the spokesman of them, he replied, 'an what's the use of powder and ball when the thing itself made sich an *illegant shelalah.*'"

The first time that young Thaddeus was introduced to a knowledge of the world, as he himself related, was in the year 1804, when he accompanied his parents on a visit to Boston, to see some of their relations. It is inferred from what he remarked of this visit, that he then made up his mind to endeavor to procure riches, that he might be able to live as did the wealthy people, whom he there for the first time met. This resolution of one so young shows his remarkable perceptive capacity, and his strong intellect; and as this was his first knowledge of the power of money, it was natural that he should feel prompted to strive for that which he learned supplied so many of the wants of life.

The desire for the accumulation of wealth, was that which first fired his youthful genius, and the sight of any other admitted excellence, might have produced a similar resolve in his mind. Does not history record the names of several of the eminent ancients, whose ambition was excited by hearing a distinguished poet recite his verses at the Olympic games, or an orator thunder forth his eloquent harangues at the forum, or in the Senate chamber? Although in the present case, our visitor to Boston would seem very young to have formed such high resolves; yet it is quite certain that at that time he first determined that no efforts should be wanting on his part, to ascend the ladder of life set before all who make the proper efforts.

The following year, after his parents had returned from Boston, the spotted fever prevailed to an alarming extent in his native County of Caledonia. For miles around his home, there was scarcely a family that escaped the attacks of this very dangerous disease. In some families all were sick at one time, and it was next to an impossibility to procure any assistance. In this condition of affairs Mrs. Stevens became a ministering angel, as it were, to the sick of her acquaintance, visiting from family to family and relieving their needs in every capacity in which she was able to help them. In these visits amongst her sick neighbors, she took young Thaddeus with her, and on these circuits of mercy, he obtained another glimpse of life which left an impress upon his memory that never forsook him. His heart was then tender, and the sights of suffering which he witnessed, so operated upon his sensibilities as to make him ever afterwards kindly disposed to the sick and poor of every class. To such, to the end of his life, he was ever ready to extend a helping hand.

Mr. Stevens' estimate of his mother we give in his own words, detailed shortly before his death. Speaking of his efforts in the Legislature in behalf of the Free School system of Pennsylvania, and in reference thereto, he said: "That is the work that I take most pleasure in recalling, except one perhaps. I really think the greatest gratification of my life resulted from my ability to give my mother a farm of 250 acres, and a dairy of 14 cows, and an occasional bright gold piece, which she loved to deposit in the contribution box of the Baptist Church which she attended. This always gave her great pleasure, and me much satisfaction. My mother was a very extraordinary woman. I have met very few women like her. My father was not a well-to-do man, and the support and education of the family depended on my mother. She worked night and day to educate me. I was feeble and lame in youth, and as I could not work on the farm, she concluded to give me an education. I tried to repay her afterwards, but the debt of a child to his mother, you know, is one of the debts we can never pay. Poor woman! the very thing I did to gratify her most, hastened her death. She was very proud of her dairy, and fond of her cows, and one night going to look after them, she fell and injured herself so that she died soon after."

As his father was a shoemaker, Thaddeus had an opportunity to pick up so much knowledge of this trade, as to enable him to make the shoes of the family, and perhaps a few for the neighbors. This he did at least after the death of his father. In his younger years, when first a candidate for the legislature, he used to boast that he was a shoemaker; and this gave birth to the numerous stories that circulated all over Pennsylvania, after his fame as a great lawyer was fixed, that he first came to York as a shoemaker and worked at the business for some time before he studied law. These stories were purely mythical, as are many that are usually retailed concerning distinguished personages; and have their origin in the deception and credulity of mankind:

> "Magnas it Fama per urbes
> Fama malum, quo non aliud velocius ullum
> Mobilitate viget, viresque acquirit eundo."

When a boy, Thaddeus Stevens was a diligent reader and, like Benjamin Franklin, not having a great supply of books, he perused everything that came within his reach. Books at that early day, were not so plenty as at the present time, and particularly not within the reach of one so situated as he then found himself. His fondness for books, it is said, induced him at the early age of fifteen to essay the experiment of starting a library; but whether this be one of the stories that accompany fame, we are not prepared to say. The example of Franklin, whose life by this time no doubt had been perused by him, might have very readily suggested such an idea in the mind of an intellectual youth of New England. At least, it was not long after this time, that he began to teach school as a means of supply to aid him in his course through college; for his parents were not able to provide in every particular for his subsistence and expense whilst passing his collegiate career. The clothing, board, text-books and tuition of a college pupil, to a poor Vermont family, was no light burden; but by his teaching and other industry, he greatly alleviated his parents, and enabled him to provide himself with some additional books by which he might store his mind with useful information. The first part of his classical course was made in Burlington College, Vermont, where he continued for a considerable period. "On September 11th, 1814, he was a student at Burlington College, for on that day he saw with a spy-glass the fight between McDonough and the British fleet, on Lake Champlain. For some reasons he did not graduate at this college, but at Dartmouth, in the following year."*

The following anecdote of his college life whilst at Burlington is from Alexander Hood's sketch of Mr. Stevens: "The campus at Burlington College was not enclosed, and the cows of the citizens used to enjoy it as a pleasant pasture ground. Before commencement it was usual to give the people notice to keep their cows away until after commencement was over. The grounds were then cleared up, and everything kept in complete order, until the exercises were ended and the students gone to their homes. It happened that among the citizens of Burlington was a man, "a stubborn fellow, whom," as Stevens said "we shall call Jones." He would take no steps to keep his cows off the campus. One

*Hood's Sketch in Harris' Biographical History of Lancaster County, pp. 571-2.

night, about a week before the commencement, Stevens and a friend were walking under the trees in front of the college, when they saw one of Jones' cows within the prohibited lines. They knew the cow belonged to Jones; they knew Jones let her go there in a spirit of defiance to the students. After some discussion it was agreed to kill the cow.

"Among the students was a young man who kept himself aloof from most of the others. In a word, he had the reputation of being decidedly pious. This young man had a room in an outhouse belonging to the college, where in spare moments he manufactured many things out of wood, which he sold to the people of the town, and to others. Among other tools he was known to have an axe, and Stevens and his companion determined to use it in the execution of the cow. The axe was procured, the cow was slain, the axe returned, and the two avengers of the college dignity retired to rest. The next morning Jones was with the President making complaint about the death of his cow. An investigation was at once begun; blood was found upon the axe of the pious, well-behaved student; he denied the charge, but as there was no evidence against any other person, he was threatened with a public reprimand on the day on which he had expected to graduate with high honor. No doubt the young man suffered much, but Stevens and his associate suffered much more. They dare not inform against themselves, yet they could not see an innocent person punished for their misconduct. What was to be done. After many conferences, without any result, Stevens suggested that Jones was not a bad man, but rather a high-spirited fellow, who would help them out of the scrape, if they would throw themselves upon his mercy. This they resolved to do. It was the night before commencement day, when they had the interview with Jones. They made a clean breast of it, and offered to pay twice the value of the cow whenever they should be able to do so. Jones listened kindly; told them not to distress themselves about the price of the cow, and said he would fix it all next morning. True to his word, about nine o'clock Jones appeared, just before the proceedings were to begin; told the professors that he was all wrong about the death of his cow, and that she had been killed by soldiers who were going down the river on a boat, and had no time to dress and remove the meat. This made all things right; the pious young man was not expelled, but honorably acquitted of the charge. Stevens and his friend were never suspected. Some years afterwards, when Stevens was rising in the world, Mr. Jones received a draft for the price of the best sort of cow in the market, accompanied by a fine gold watch and chain by way of interest. A year or two afterwards there came to Gettysburg, directed to Mr. Stevens, a hogshead of the best Vermont cider, and this was the end of the killing of Jones' cow." *

Which of the professions Mr. Stevens may have made up his mind to study, in his passage through college, is not known. On one occasion, in an argument with an Arminian, concerning predestination, he evinced such an intimate acquaintance with the writers and arguments of the Calvinistic school, that a friend was induced to put to him the inquiry: "Mr. Stevens, did you ever study with a view to the pulpit." The answer was: "Umph! I have read the books." But no further information on that point was he able to elicit from him.

After taking his degree at Dartmouth College, he prepared and set out in quest of employment, and at length found himself about the close of the year 1815 in York, Pennsylvania. Here he obtained a situation as assistant teacher in an academy taught by Dr. Perkins. Amos Gilbert, a very noted teacher, then residing at York, afterwards remarked of Mr. Stevens, that he was at that time "one of the most backward, retiring and modest young men he had ever seen," and besides spoke of him as being a very close student. Soon after his arrival in York, he began reading law, both morning and evening, when not engaged in teaching, under the instruction of David Casset, a prominent York County lawyer, and prosecuted its study with great zeal, utilizing thus the scraps of his time to a valuable purpose. During the period he was in this manner preparing himself for future life, an effort was made by the members of the bar to thwart the fulfilment of his designs, by the passage of resolutions, providing that no person should be recognized as a lawyer who followed any other vocation whilst preparing himself for admission.† The young student, however, never took any concern as regards the protest, but pursued the even tenor of his way, until he felt that he had mastered his studies. He therefore repaired quietly

*Harris' Biographical History of Lancaster County, pp. 512–13.
†Forney's Press, August 12, 1868.

to Bel Air, the county seat of Harford County, Maryland, while the court was in session, and made application to be examined. At that time Maryland admitted all applicants to the bar who, upon examination, were found to be qualified. The Court, Judge Chase of impeachment notoriety, appointed a committee, the chairman of which, was Gen. Winder. The following is Mr. Stevens' description of the examination as given in Mr. Hood's sketch of him:

"Supper was over, the table was cleared off, and the clock said it was half-past seven. Stevens was of course punctual to time, and shortly after, the Judge and the committee took their seats. 'Are you the young man who is to be examined?' asked the Judge. Stevens said he was. 'Mr. Stevens,' said the Judge, 'there is one indispensible pre-requisite before the examination can proceed. There must be two bottles of Madeira on the table, and the applicant must order it in.' The order was given, the wine brought forward, and its quality thoroughly tested. Gen. Winder began with: 'Mr. Stevens, what books have you read?' Stevens replied, 'Blackstone, Coke upon Littleton, a work on pleading, and Gilbert on evidence.' This was followed by two or three other questions by other members of the committee, the last of which required the distinction between a contingent remainder, and an executory devise, which was satisfactorily answered. By this time the Judge was feeling a little dry again, and broke in saying: 'Gentlemen, you see the young man is all right, I'll give him a certificate.' This was soon made out and signed, but before it was handed over, two more bottles had to be produced. These were partaken of by a large number of squires and others, who were there attending court, who, as soon as the examination was concluded, came in and were introduced to the newly made member of the bar. 'Fip-Loo' was played then for a good part of the night. Stevens was then a green hand at the business. To use his own words, when he paid his bill the next morning, he had but $3.50 left out of the $45 he began with the night before."*

He left Bel Air early next morning, directing his course for Lancaster, and narrowly escaped a watery grave in crossing the McCall's Ferry Bridge, not yet completed. His horse became frightened and would have fallen with its rider into the river, but for the presence of mind of one of the workmen who was engaged

Harris' Biographical History of Lancaster County, pp. 574-5.

upon the bridge. The same day he reached Lancaster by noon and dined at Slough's Hotel, then one of the headquarters of the old inland city; and while his horse was resting he reconnoitered the place, and walked from one end of King street to the other. He had concluded, should Lancaster please him, to select it as a location for the practice of his profession. Not believing that the place suited one whose pocket was so near empty, he next determined upon Gettysburg and started the same day for York, which he reached in the evening. The following day he arrived at the county seat of Adams County where he began his legal career, with but few friends and little money.

Mr. Stevens had now embarked in that career, in which to one devoid of amability and captivating address, time, patience and ability are all required to obtain marked success. Being unendowed in a high degree, with either of the former traits of character that pave the way in most instances to ordinary success, he had to depend upon patience and ability with whatever slight auxiliary fortune might interpose to aid him in his early struggles. But with all the force of intellect he could command, his patience was well nigh exhausted before anything turned up to assure him that his profession would afford him the ladder of life-ascent, which he had hoped to meet in it. It is very certain, at least, that the quality for which Job was distinguished had in his case nearly all become exhausted before he met with any success commensurate with his anticipations; as he stated to a confidential friend at a dance at Littlestown, that he could hold out no longer, and must select a new location. Destiny, however, had resolved, that in his case, though reduced to the lowest depths of despair, the profession of the law, with its political accompaniments, should make up his career; as the darkest hour of night is that before day-break, so it was with him. A day or two after the despondency of his condition had led him to ruminate in his mind a new location, a horrible murder was committed; and none of the prominent lawyers felt inclined to undertake the defense of the accused. Mr. Stevens was retained and exerted his powers to the utmost in behalf of his client, although without being able to acquit him; yet he brought to the trial of the cause such an array of legal learning, so marshalled and arranged; and he handled the evidence with such masterly adroitness, that the court, the bar, the jury, and the citizens were taken by surprise.

His speech before the jury evinced a mind of such logical acuteness, that the trial ended with his reputation fixed as possessing the elements of an able lawyer. This trial, and the masterly defense, became at once the subject of conversation throughout the whole country. His client was found guilty of murder and executed, but the case brought Mr. Stevens a fee of $1,500, which was the beginning of his fortune. He had already ascended the first step of the ladder of life. From this period there was no occasion that he must content himself with cases that the other lawyers saw proper to decline. He now began to receive a different class of clients than those to whom the other attornies semi-sneeringly had remarked, "there is a young man in town by the name of Stevens who may, perhaps, be willing to attend to your case."

Persons were no more fearful to employ the club-footed lawyer, as he thenceforth came to be known by those who were not yet much acquainted with him. But his success must depend upon his own efforts, for the seemingly instinctive jealousy of lawyers precluded his receiving any favor from which they could debar him. Regarded as an interloper by most of them, he was thrust aside from all the favors which bars have in their power to exhibit, and their reflection was that if he succeed it must be by dint of superior ability and application to business. But Mr. Stevens was one of those who could, in a remarkable measure, divest himself of all appreciation of the petty and contemptible jealousies of human nature. He could afford to despise all such, and yet give no exhibition of his feelings. As, however, he felt that his success must depend upon the impression he would continue to make upon the people, he studiously applied himself and, to the best of his ability, to the preparation for trial of every case with which he was entrusted. It was soon perceived by the people of the county that he was able to try a case with as much success as any lawyer at the Gettysburg bar. His reputation all the time was spreading, and his business increasing. His great candor in everything he said, or undertook, made at once a favorable impression upon those with whom he came in contact. Besides, his freedom from all affectation and pride procured for him the confidence of the German citizens of Adams County, although unable to converse with them in their vernacular language, a confidence which he ever afterwards was able to retain. The ready humor he could make use of in his intercourse with the people or his brethren of the bar, and his sallies of wit, with which he could often disconcert an opposing attorney in the trial of a cause, were additional weapons which in his setting out in legal life were of incalculable service to him.

His legal business rapidly increased on his hands, and by the year 1821 he made his first appearance in the Supreme Court, holding its session at Chambersburg, then one of the five places at which the highest Court of Pennsylvania sat. It is somewhat remarkable, in view of his latter political course, that his first case in that court should have been a suit *de homine replegiando*, in which the liberty of a colored woman and her children were concerned. But as lawyers have not the choice of sides in a case, in this instance, Mr. Stevens found himself compelled to dispute the claim for freedom. Henry Butler and Charity his wife, and their children had brought suit for their liberty, and Stevens was employed for the defense. Their claim grew out of a contract between the owner of Charity and a man named Cleland, both Marylanders. Cleland again entered into another contract with a Mr. Gilleland, living in the same State, concerning the services of Charity. Gilleland having deserted his wife, the latter was obliged to turn seamstress, and went occasionally into Pennsylvania, taking Charity with her. After returning to her mother's domicil in Maryland, she sent Charity back to her original master, being then eleven years of age. It became a question of fact for the jury to determine upon the trial, whether Charity had ever, at one time, been kept six months in Pennsylvania. If she had been so detained, she was then entitled to her freedom, as also her children. The jury returned a verdict against her freedom. The case was taken to the Supreme Court, but Mr. Stevens succeeded in sustaining the verdict of the court below.* At this period he was established in a profitable practice. From the year 1823, he was engaged on one side or the other, of all the important suits of his County, of which fact the report books of the period afford abundant evidence.

By 1827, he was become a man of influence and standing in his county, and owned therein considerable real estate. His fame had now far passed the bounds of Adams County, and he was henceforth employed in the trial of important causes, in the neighboring

*7 Sergeant & Rawle, pp. 379.

counties of Cumberland, Franklin and York. His business now almost engrossed his whole attention, but he was not unmindful of the necessity of exercise. He was in the habit of riding much upon horseback, and became known as one of the most skilled equestrians in his section of country. He was fond of attending the races in Maryland, then one of the customary amusements of the day. His contiguity to Maryland and the numerous suits in which he was concerned, involving the liberty of colored persons claimed as slaves in the State of Maryland, had no doubt much to do in giving him his strong bias in opposition to the institution of African Slavery. As far as can be gathered, he always seemed to sympathize with the colored race, and was ready to assist them in gaining their freedom when in his power to do so.

CHAPTER II.

RISE OF THE ANTI-MASONIC PARTY. ELECTION OF MR. STEVENS TO THE LEGISLATURE OF PENNSYLVANIA.

We have seen that Mr. Stevens, first selected in his mind the County of Lancaster for the practice of his profession, but after visiting it, came to the conclusion to go to Gettysburg. Both these choices would seem to imply that he was not altogether unmindful of political considerations in choosing a location. But belonging to a party, whose principles had become generally unpopular throughout the nation, we do not find him participating in political affairs for many years after his settlement in Adams County. He was not the man to change his principles for the sake of success; and it was only when new questions began to be discussed that he stepped forward upon the political arena.

The excitement aroused, throughout the Northern States, against the Masonic order, occasioned by the abduction and execution of William Morgan, in the Autumn of 1826, had the effect of reorganizing parties upon a new basis in many States of the Union. Morgan, a citizen of Batavia, New York, had prepared for publication, a work detailing the secrets of the three first degrees of masonry, and had the same in press, when the fact became known amongst the members of the Masonic order. As subsequent developments seemed to indicate, steps were concerted in the New York lodges to thwart the exposure of the secrets of an order, to which many of the most influential and respectable men of the nation had united themselves. Morgan was accordingly seized by members of the Masonic order in broad daylight, and borne by conveyance to the northern part of the State of New York, where all trace of him was lost. It was believed that he was sunk in Lake Ontario. The news of this transaction was soon spread throughout the country, but it was in Western New York where the highest degree of excitement prevailed. Committees of investigation and safety were appointed to ferret out the mysteries of a transaction that impressed the people with the conviction that a vital stab was inflicted upon American civil liberty. Prosecutions were also instituted against the conspirators in the Morgan tragedy, but these resulted in the acquittal of all except Bruce and Whitney, who were imprisoned for their participation in the affair.

The trials that took place, perhaps more, even than the abduction of Morgan itself, intensified the excitement. The courts were crowded when the trials were in progress, and although many of the witnesses were masons of admitted respectability and standing, it was believed by the people, that they testified falsely in order to shield their brother masons from punishment. This was the allegation that they would do so, and the boasts of certain masons were retailed, who had declared that their friends would not be allowed to suffer. In America, then, as it was charged, was an institution that dared in the light of day to arrest a citizen and execute him, and the civil law was powerless to prevent the wicked and diabolical deed. What more could the *Invisible Tribunal* of Germany, or the *Spanish Inquisition* do, than was now witnessed in Republican America? Was an order to be permitted to exist in the United States, that would dare the perpetration of such high handed iniquity as was enacted in this instance? The excitement diffused itself from the locality of the occurrence of these scenes throughout the whole North. A party arose, styling themselves Anti-Masons, in the following year, which cast 33,000 votes in New York State for their candidate for Governor, and in 1828 this number was increased to 70,000. In this last named year, the party had obtained some foothold in Pennsylvania; newspapers being established in this State in favor of Anti-Masonic principles. Men from both the old political parties attached themselves to the new organization, though it is not to be denied, that the greater number by far were Federalists, whose party was become quite defunct.

Amongst the foremost in Pennsylvania, to espouse the principles of the Anti-Masons, was Thaddeus Stevens, who saw in the new party, the means of rising in political life. He no doubt hated an institution that had rejected, as is said, his admittance as a member; and besides he saw that it might be combatted with advantage to his party. He began to denounce the Masonic order as an *imperium in imperio*, a power that set the laws of the land at defiance, and nullified the system of the civil tribunals. If Masonry be permitted to endure, argued he, how can a member of the order be brought to trial, when one Mason in accordance with his obligations, is required to support another, in all difficulties, "whether right or wrong," and hold his secrets inviolable, "murder and treason not excepted." He declared that it was impossible to remain in doubt as to how he should act when American liberty was subjected to such peril from an institution, the power of which he perceived to be governed and supported by the credulity of ages. The courts of justice, trial by jury, the sanctity of the witness stand were all able to be set at naught, as he averred, by men who felt that the obligations of Masonry were more binding upon their consciences than the judicial oaths of the land. In co-operation, therefore, with others, he used all his efforts to consolidate the Anti-Masonic opposition in Pennsylvania into a political organization, that might prove effective in overthrowing a society of oath-bound enemies of the body politic. In the year 1829, the opposition to the Democrats, was united as the Anti-Masonic party, and supported Joseph Ritner for the gubernatorial chair of Pennsylvania. He was defeated, but in some counties of the State, the party was strongly in the ascendant.

The war of opposition, that was henceforth waged against the Masonic institution, was a severe and trying one. Books exposing the secrets of the order were in great demand. Bernard's Light of Masonry, Morgan's Illustrations, and other works of like character, obtained a wonderful circulation. Masonry soon sunk below par. By the year 1830, it was ascertained that over one thousand Free Masons had withdrawn from the order, and exposed the secrets of initiation. The seceding masons fully corroborated what was contained in the books divulging the secrets of Masonry, and averred that the oaths therein set forth, were the same identically as those which the initiated were required to accept. This was fully made out in the Le Roy convention of seceding masons, held in July, 1828, in the State of New York. Men of the highest respectability and social standing deserted the order like a sinking ship, and proclaimed that youthful curiosity had induced them to unite with it, (as is the case with most intelligent young men entering it) but that they had not visited a lodge for many years. John Q. Adams, William Wirt, Moses Stuart, of Andover, Caldwallader Colden, and a host of the first men of America, expressed publicly, their disapprobation of the order. The lodges all over the country were closed, and so continued for years. Masonry was required to pass through a searching ordeal. Its history was examined to the foundation by able scholars, and its claims of antiquity shown to rest upon the assertions of credulous members, but for which truth furnished no basis. The origin of speculative Masonry, was traced to the year 1717 in England, and the averments of a more ancient deduction, were proved to be entirely fabulous.

Mr. Stevens, having the sagacity to perceive that Free Masonry and all other secret societies were of anti-republican tendency, denounced the same as such. In his denunciation of these he was not far astray. These societies had derived their birth under monarchial governments, and seemed to exhibit the natural inclination of mankind to recur back in principle to the ancient form of policy, which republics should seek to overthrow. Deducing their principles from the aristocratic feelings of superiority which one class of people entertain towards another, it was apparent that Masonry was but laying the foundation for kingly rule, and the ruin of republican liberty. Even the names of the officers in the lodges, indicated this fawning after the titled appellations of monarchial rulers. As our republic prohibited its countrymen from the assumption of titles, that are conferred by the crowned magnates of Europe., secret societies afforded to the aristocratic fawner that which his heart craved, but which the laws of his country prevented his assuming in the light of day. All this Mr. Stevens saw with clearness, and hence believed that the outside prejudice could be united with admirable effect as to himself against the initiated.

Entertaining these notions, and conscious of the antagonism which the new movement would be compelled to encounter in the battle against Masonry, Mr. Stevens, from the organization of the Anti-Masonic party in Pennsylvania, actively labored to consolidate, and give it national strength and diffusion. In September, 1831, he was a member of the Baltimore National Convention of the Anti-Masonic party, which placed Wm. Wirt and Amos Ellmaker, in nomination for the Presidency of the United States. But the election of 1832, resulted disastrously to the hopes of the Anti-Masons, but one State casting its electoral votes for their candidates, Mr. Stevens' mountain home of Vermont. It was now believed by many, that the party could never succeed as a national organization. The Southern States had kept aloof from it, and the North was unable to unite upon Anti-Masonic principles. Five years had elapsed since the excitement occasioned by the Morgan abduction was first aroused; and yet the party had so far been unable to achieve any substantial victory. Large numbers of individuals, who had united with the new organization, merely from political motives, now became apathetic, as regards its future permanency, and were ready to attach themselves to any other that would show indications of greater success. Like vultures, the politicians are endowed with remarkable nasal organs for scenting the official carcass. But, four years must now elapse before another presidential struggle could take place; and in the meantime each State must manage its political affairs in accordance with the judgment of their respective leaders. In Pennsylvania, the Anti-Masonic organization was kept up perhaps better than in most others; and yet here many visible signs existed that the seeds of party dissolution were not confined alone to the other States of the Union. It is believed that Anti-Masonry, as a party organization, was prolonged in Pennsylvania through the influence of Thaddeus Stevens more than that of any other man that could be named.

In the fall of 1833, Mr. Stevens was elected to the lower House of the Pennsylvania Legislature, taking his seat in December of that year. The legislative session of 1833–4, was a most important one, insomuch as the system of free schools was first introduced into Pennsylvania in its enactments. The free school bill passed at this session, and which was approved by Gov. Wolf, April 1st, 1834, received the warm support of Mr. Stevens. The measure itself was the outgrowth of the intelligent thought of the age, striving for the discovery of the best method by which to enlighten the masses, and fit them for citizenship in a free republic. It was but the expression of the united intelligence of the patriotic public citizens of Pennsylvania, who desired the welfare and improvement of the people of their State.

The American system of free schools is of New England birth, and dates its origin to an early period in the history of the Eastern States. Massachusetts and Connecticut are rivals for the honor of its discovery. Pennsylvania was slow in accepting the system, although her people were far from being averse to education. In their efforts for the advancement of general intelligence, her statesmen, with that deliberation and caution, which are characteristics of the people of Pennsylvania, sought for the best system of schools that could be obtained, and which had as yet been tried. When the Constitution of 1790 was adopted, it was made an article of that charter, that "*the Legislature as soon as may be, shall provide by law for the establishment of schools throughout the State, in such manner that the poor may be taught gratis.*" In accordance with this constitutional provision, it was early enacted, that the tuition of all poor children attending school should be paid out of the public treasury. But this plan did not seem to meet the necessities of the demand for general instruction, as most persons needing assistance had a reluctance to being enrolled as paupers upon the school lists; and the question how to remedy the defect, became more and more a matter of discussion amongst educated men. The attention of philanthropists in all parts of the country was directed to this subject shortly after the close of the war with Great Britain; and the best methods of education were discussed. Improved schools were in the year 1817, established in many of the principal American cities, and their influence did much to educate the public up to a knowledge of the advantages of a general system of free education.

The Governors of Pennsylvania, being men of cultivated minds, and surrounded by such, seeing the current of advancing intelligence in other States and countries, were in their messages, in the habit of calling the attention of the Legislature of the State to the necessity of providing means for a more general system of public instruction. Gov. Wolf was particularly distinguished as the advocate of a free school system, and in his message of 1833, he urged the measure in the strongest terms. The subject was taken up in both houses of the Pennsylvania Legislature, and the result was, that a free school bill was passed in both, and received the sanction of the Executive. The law went into operation, but met with furious resistance in many sections of the State; indeed, in all parts, a party arose in opposition to the law of 1834. The majority of the heavy tax-payers in all quarters of the State were opposed to a law that abstracted money from their pockets, as they conceived, without any justice or right, save the enactment of the Legislature. The advantages of elevating communities to a condition of intelligent citizenship were overlooked. Again, the law was opposed by many, because the system severed religious from intellectual instruction; and withdrew the education of the youth from the supervision of the clergy and other church authorities. It was this latter objection, that induced the heavy opposition on the part of the German counties of the State, a resistance that required years to overcome.

When the legislature therefore of 1834–5, assembled, petitions began to pour in from all parts of the State, urging the repeal of the school law that had been passed the year before. On the 17th of March, 1835, it was reported in the House of Representatives, that 558 petitions, signed by 31,988 names were before that body, asking that the school law of 1834 be repealed, whereas but 49 petitions with 2,575 signers were in its favor. All the outside pressure seemed to demand the repeal. A bill, revoking the school law of the last year, was introduced into the Senate, passed that body, and was transmitted to the House for its concurrence. Speech after speech was now made in the House, in favor of what seemed almost the universal sentiment of the people. Many short-sighted members, who had even favored the free school law, were ready to vote for its repeal, as they feared to place themselves upon record as supporters of a law which the public, in their petitions, seemed so emphatically to have condemned. Politicians are timid, and fear to support a measure, that their constituents have reprobated, much as their judgment, might approve it. Thaddeus Stevens was this year a member of the Legislature of Pennsylvania. His New England birth and training made him naturally inclined to favor the free school system. He had the sagacity likewise to perceive that it would receive the support of the poorer classes, much as it might be combatted by the wealthy. It belonged to the equalizing movements of the age, which seemed to harmonize with American ideas. Mr. Stevens therefore boldly resisted the repeal, in a speech of great ability and force, delivered in the House. It was a fine opportunity to become the champion for the elevation of the masses at the expense of the monied classes. Such championship, in America, ever secures for the demagogue high applause, whether deservedly or otherwise. Mr. Stevens espied his own gain in his strong defense of the free school system, as he perceived that he was thus making himself the leader of the people, in opposition to the opulent few.

In him, the people and the timid free school men found a leader. His speech had a magical effect upon the sentiments of members. Such a masterly, argumentative, and convincing array of thought, as they conceived, had not been heard in the Pennsylvania halls of legislation for years. A master intellect had simply defended the growing popular sentiment. All without distinction, whether enemies or friends, acknowledged the overpowering superiority of the speech. Many who had determined to favor the repeal, changed their opinions, and voted to sustain the law of 1834. The House decided to non-concur in the action of the Senate, and thus the common school law was saved to the commonwealth. This speech ranked its author, henceforth, as one of the first intellects of Pennsylvania.

CHAPTER III.

MASONIC INVESTIGATION. STAR CHAMBER COMMITTEE. CHARTER OF THE UNITED STATES BANK OF PENNSYLVANIA. MEMBER OF STATE REFORM CONVENTION.

The political tide of Anti-Masonry was somewhat broken in the Presidential election of 1832. But this, instead of weakening, seemed rather to have had the effect of enhancing the force of the moral onslaught which was made against the institution of Masonry, and which, through the courage and intellectual superiority of Thaddeus Stevens, became more intense in Pennsylvania, perhaps, than in any other State of the Union. The legislative warfare in this State was begun in March, 1828, in the presentation in the House of Representatives, by a Mr. Diesbach, of three memorials from sundry citizens of the Commonwealth, setting forth that the society of Free Masons had become dangerous to the free institutions of the Commonwealth, and that men who are members of the order, are wholly incompetent to act as jurors and arbitrators, in cases wherein a Free Mason and another citizen are parties. The memorialists prayed for some legislation that would afford the requisite relief in such cases. Other petitions of like character were also presented, all of which were laid upon the table. In this manner, the people, year after year, sent their petitions to the Legislature, asking for some law to remedy the evils of Masonry.

When Mr. Stevens took his seat as a member of the lower House of Representatives at Harrisburg, the Anti-Masons found a leader competent to marshall the party in the Legislature, and cope with the ablest opponents that might be arrayed against it. He was but a short time in the House, until he had an opportunity of proving his capacity for leadership, in a speech delivered by him in which he took occasion to review the course of the Jackson party, and the men who molded its principles. As the antagonist of Masonry, on February 10, 1834, he introduced the following resolution:

"*Resolved*, That a committee be appointed to inquire into the expediency of providing by law for making Free Masonry, a good cause of peremptory challenge to jurors in all cases, where one of the parties is a Free Mason, and the other is not, and on the part of the Commonwealth, in all prosecutions for claims and misdemeanors, where the defendant is a Mason; and also, where the judge and one of the parties are Free Masons, to make the same provisions for the trials of causes as now exist where the judge and either of the parties are related to each other by blood or marriage, and to make the same provison relative to the summoning and return of jurors, where the Sheriff and either of the parties are Free Masons, as now exists where they are related to each other by blood or marriage, and that said committee have power to send for persons and papers."

On the second reading, on the question shall the resolution as offered pass, the vote was yeas, 34, nays, 45. By this vote the Anti-Masons were shown to be incapable of effecting any legislation of a party nature. Mr. Stevens, as chairman of the committee appointed to investigate Masonry, on the 27th of March, 1834, submitted the following report:

"*Whereas*, Numerous petitions, signed by a large number of highly respectable citizens of this Commonwealth, have been presented to the Legislature, stating their belief that the masonic fraternity is associated for purposes inconsistent with the equal rights and privileges which are the birth-right of every freeman; that they are bound together by secret obligations and oaths, illegal, immoral and blasphemous, subversive of all public law, and hostile to the full administration of justice. They ask for a legislative investigation into the truth of these charges, and, if supported, a legislative remedy; and for the purpose of obtaining authentic proof, they ask for the appointment of a committee to send for persons and papers.

"In pursuance of what was supposed to be the prayer of the petitioners, a committee was appointed and the petitions referred to them. The committee met and organized, and, supposing it to be their duty to proceed to investigate the charges made against the Masonic institution thus referred to them, they gave a precipe for a subpœna for witnesses to the Clerk of the House, to be by him issued in the usual way, signed by the Speaker. The committee would not deny their right to inquire into the the truth of the charges, for the investigation of which they had been specially appointed. Nor did they suppose they had been commanded by the House to perform that duty without being clothed with the power asked for by the petitioners, and indispensably necessary, and incident to its faithful and intelligent discharge. The Clerk and Speaker of the House thought otherwise, and declined issuing the subpœna. The committee appealed to the House to grant explicitly the questioned power. It was objected to, on the ground (among others) that it would subject refractory witnesses to punishment for contempt if they refused to testify; a power which the House seemed disposed not to pursue towards masonic witnesses. To obviate this objection, the committee consented to modify the resolution, so as to give them power to take the testimony of such witnesses only as would appear to testify voluntarily before them. But the House, by a vote of every member present, except two, of all parties, not politically opposed to Masonry refused the request. The committee were thus prohibited from ascertaining by legal testimony the true character of Free Masonry as practised in Pennsylvania. Nor could they fail to view that decision as a plain intimation by the House of their unwillingness to have the secret designs, principles and practices of that institution established and made known to the people. Feeling themselves bound by that intimation, and trusting it with the respect which is always due to the wish of this body, the committee feel themselves constrained not to make use of the proof within their power, taken in other States to develope its alledged iniquities. Such proof might and would be met with the allegation, that it "*might be New York, but not Pennsylvania Masonry*." To establish the identity of Pennsylvania and New York Masonry by a legislative committee, vested with adequate power, is left to a future time and other hands. To suppose that this will not soon take place, would be a foul and unwarranted libel on the intelligence and firmness of the freemen of this Commonwealth.

"To show the necessity of the power asked for, and to justify their failure to make a more extended report on the subject confided to them, the committee will briefly state the nature and quality of the testimony which they had intended to submit to this House. That the evidence might be above suspicion, they had determined to call before them none but adhering Masons who could not be suspected of testifying out of hostility to the institution. To leave no doubt as to the character of the witnesses, it was proposed to examine the Masonic members of this House and the Cabinet. It was particularly desirable and intended that the Governor of this Commonwealth should become a witness, and have a full opportunity of explaining under oath, the principles and practices of the order of which he is so conspicuous a member. It was thought that the papers in his possession might throw much light on the question how far Masonry secures political and executive favor. This inspection would have shown, whether it be true that applications for offices have been founded on Masonic merit and claimed as Masonic rights; whether in such applications the "significant symbols" and mystic watch words of Masonry have been used, and in how many cases such applications have been successful in securing executive patronage. It might not have been unprofitable, also, to inquire how many converted felons, who have been pardoned by the present Governor, were brethren of the "mystic tie," or connected by blood or politics with members of that institution, and how few of those who could boast of no such connection have been successful in similar applications. The committee might have deemed it necessary, in the faithful discharge of their duty, to have called before them some of the judges, who are Masons, to ascertain whether, in their official character, the "grand hailing sign" has ever been handed, sent or thrown to them by either of the parties litigant, and if so, what has been the result of the trial. This would have been obviously proper, as one of the charges against Masonry is its partial and corrupt influence in courts of justice. Who the witnesses were to be, was distinctly announced to this House by the chairman of the committee on the disscussion of his resolution. The House decided that no evidence should be taken; every member of the Masonic institution present voting in the negative. The committee have deemed this brief history of legislative proceedings necessary to justify them for failing to make a report which is anxiously looked for by the people. The committee are aware that most of those who opposed the power to send for "persons and papers," did it on the avowed grounds that it was unnecessary, as the principles of Masonry were fully disclosed and known. For themselves, the committee have no hesitancy in saying, that Masonry is no longer a secret to any but those who wilfully make it so, and that its principles and practices are as dangerous and atrocious as its most violent opponents have ever declared. They take pleasure, however, in saying that a great majority of its members reject its doctrines, habitually disregard its principles, and in honesty, honor and patriotism, are inferior to none of their fellow-citizens. It is the duty of government, while it looks with charity and forbearance on the past, to take care that in future none of our respectable citizens should be entrapped into such degrading and painful thraldom. To effect this object and give those who profess to be morally opposed to Masonry an opportunity to record such opposition, the committee report a bill "*to prohibit in future the administration of Masonic, Odd Fellow, and all other secret extra-judicial oaths, obligations and promises in the nature of oaths.*"

As parties were constituted in the legislature, Mr. Stevens had no further object in the submission of the above report than to place upon record the demands and views of the Anti-Masonic party. In the session of 1834–5 the AntiMasons were again in the minority in the legislature. Mr. Stevens being a member of the House at this session also, considerable discussion took place and there was the usual display of partizan tactics regarding the question of Masonry. Mr. Stevens submitted a motion in the House, prefaced by a lengthy preamble, detailing in varied items the evils of Masonry and which contained a resolution "*that the Committee on the Judiciary be instructed to bring in a bill effectually to suppress and prohibit the administration and reception of Masonic, Odd Fellow and all other secret extra-judicial oaths, obligations and promises in the nature of oaths.*" This resolution was without delay laid upon the table and authority to publish the same was denied by a vote of 38 yeas to 58 nays.

During the controversy waged throughout the country over the question of the removal of the deposits by President Jackson, Joseph R. Ritner was nominated for the governorship of Pennsylvania, distinctly as an Anti-Mason, and through the division of the Democratic party was elected. A majority was chosen to the House of Representatives favorable to the same principles as the Governor was supposed to represent. Mr. Stevens was again returned as a member from Adams County. Governor Ritner, in his inaugural, expressed the sentiments of his party upon the Masonic question, and spoke of his election as an endorsement of Anti-Masonic principles. He said:

"The supremacy of the laws, and the equal rights of the people, whether threatened or assailed by individuals, or by secret sworn associations, I shall so far as may be compatible with the constitutional power of the Executive, endeavor to maintain as well in compliance with the known will of the people, as from obligations of duty to the Commonwealth. In these endeavors I shall entertain no doubt of zealous co-operation by the enlightened and patriotic legislature of the State. The people have willed the destruction of all secret societies, and that will cannot be disregarded."

At the legislative session of 1835–6, on motion of Mr. Stevens, a committee was appointed to investigate the evils of Free Masonry and other secret societies. This was that to which the Free Masons and their allies gave the name of the "*Star Chamber Committee*," because of the attempt to extract information from the Masons themselves, which as was believed, would be prejudicial to the order. Subpœnas were accordingly served upon Gov. Wolf, Geo. M. Dallas, Francis R. Shunk, Joseph R. Chandler, and a number of the other distinguished lights of Masonry, citing them to appear before the committee and answer such questions as might be asked them touching their knowledge of Masonry. The questions as agreed on in committee to be propounded to the parties subpœnaed were the following:

1. "Are you, or have you been a Free Mason? How many degrees have you taken? By what lodge or chapter were you admitted?"

2. "Before or at the time of your taking each of those degrees, was an oath or obligation administered to you?"

3. "Can you repeat the several oaths or obligations administered to you, or any of them? If so, repeat the several oaths, beginning with the entered apprentice, and repeat them literally, if possible, if not, substantially; listen to the oaths, and obligations, and penalties, as read from this book (Allyn's Ritual) and point out any variation you shall find in them from the oaths you took. Is there a trading degree?"

4. "Did you ever know the affirmation administered in the lodge or chapter?"

5. "Are there any other oaths or obligations in Masonry than those contained in Allyn's Ritual and Bernard's Light on Masonry?"

6. "Is Masonry essentially the same everywhere?"

7. "State the ceremony of initiation in the R. A. degree, and particularly whether any allusion is made to the scripture scene of the burning bush. State fully how that scene is enacted in the lodge or chapter."

8. "Are you a K. T.? If so, state fully the obligations and ordinances of that degree. In that degree is wine administered to the candidate out of a human skull? State fully the whole scene. Listen to the account of it as read from this book (Allyn's Ritual), and point out whether it varies from the genuine oath or ceremony."

Most of those subpœnaed sent to the committee written replies, declining to appear and answer in obedience to the writ; some of them appeared in person before the committee and read their reasons for refusing to answer any questions concerning Masonry, and their connection therewith. Their reasons for declining to answer, as gathered from their several replies, embraced substantially the following. They claimed that the House of Representatives possessed no constitutional authority to institute an inquiry concerning any organization within its borders, or its secrets, that violated no law of the land. If their society, or any other, was proved to have become injurious to the rights of the commonwealth, in that event, the paramount superiority of the State must subordinate all others. But until this be shown, the State had no more right to interfere than would it have to institute an inquiry concerning any private family affairs. Masonry existed when the constitution of the State was first formed, and no objection was made against it; and they claimed it, as one of those natural and indefeasible rights which men possess, to unite together in the pursuit of their own happiness. Again, were it conceded that the Masons had been guilty of any infraction of law, the proceedings contemplated the compulsory crimination of the accused, a principle violative of constitutional privileges. Enact, however, a "constitutional law," as Joseph R. Chandler remarked in his reply to the committee, "prohibiting the existence of Masonic institutions, and I shall be the first to withdraw from all communion with the order, without reference to the weight of penalties, and shall feel bound to bear testimony in a court of justice against any Mason who might, within my knowledge, violate the statute."

The committee asked authority of the House to commit those subpœnaed for contempt, but this, after considerable disputation, was refused. The cowardice of some who professed Anti-Masonic principles, and the influence and standing of the parties charged with the contempt, shielded the recusant witnesses from the imprisonment which some, and amongst those Mr. Stevens, were ready to inflict. Thaddeus Stevens was the soul and leader of this movement, and in it showed himself equal to any emergency when his party should summon his services. For his participation in this undertaking, he subjected himself to great obloquy and abuse from the members of the Masonic order and their adherents. But the movement, on the part of Mr. Stevens, was in itself sufficient to stamp him as a man of wonderful mental stamina and courage; and were nothing else of his public services extant, this itself would record him among the famed names of history. One man in this case, by the potent strength of his intellectual superiority, sets up an investigation to overthrow an order that claimed an existence from the building of Solomon's Temple, and which the whole power of the Roman Catholic Hierarchy and Priesthood had essayed in vain to destroy. Had public opinion been a little more ripe for the attempt, it is unknown what results the investigation might have had. Secret societies are never too strongly entrenched in public sympathy to escape censure. The exclusive (never popular), in a free country, must ever find itself an exotic, and be ranked with that wholly anti-republican in its nature. Its development displays the aristocratic feelings of humanity, severs the people into classes, and ultimately fits nations for governmental changes. Had the associate partisans of Mr. Stevens, who espoused the Anti-Masonic cause, done so with equal ardor as himself, Free Masonry in Pennsylvania, and perhaps in America, would in the main have ceased to exist. It does not, however, seem to have been high moral reasons that caused his opposition to Free Masonry; but rather because deformity had precluded his initiation into the mysteries. But as it was, the order met a shock that will not soon be forgotten. And while Free Masonry in the United States is altogether likely to continue to be molded by the spirit of our institutions, in order that it may still defer the crusade, which (if our republic be resurrected) seems destined, in the march of ages to eradicate it, with all the other relics of superstition and monarchy.

The session of the Pennsylvania Legislature of 1835–6, was an important one in more respects than one. The charter of the United States Bank would expire on the 4th of March, 1836. The political contest, regarding this institution, had been one of violent and impassioned intensity. From the first intimation by President Jackson, in his message in 1829, of his doubt as to the constitutionality of the bank, the people were divided in sentiment regarding it. Upon the appearance of the President's Message, the stock fell six dollars per share, but when Congress expressed a contrary opinion, the stock rose to a higher figure than before. The affairs of the bank moved smoothly as before, but in view of the expiration of its charter in 1836, its stockholders in 1832 applied for a renewal of national banking privileges. The bill for the re-charter of the bank passed both Houses of Congress, but met resistance in the veto of President Jackson. This action upon the part of the Executive had the effect of arousing in Pennsylvania (where the bank was located and was popular) a furious resistance against the national administration; and it was for a time believed that the President's policy would not be sustained by the people of this State. A very large meeting was held in Philadelphia, in July, 1832, soon after the veto of the bank bill, which was composed of the President's former political friends, at which resolutions were adopted disapproving of his course, with regard to the bank, and deprecating his reelection to the Presidency as a national calamity, against the occurrence of which, they pledged themselves to use their utmost efforts.

The hostility thus arrayed against the President had the effect of embittering him against the bank and its supporters. In view of the uncertain financial condition of the bank, the President, in his Message of December, 1832, recommended the withdrawal of the public funds from the institution. Congress, on the contrary, by resolution expressed its entire confidence in the solvency of the bank. William J. Duane, the Secretary of the Treasury, in whose province it was to see to the removal of the deposits, if in his judgment necessary, declined removing them, and he was accordingly removed from the Secretaryship, and Roger B. Taney appointed in his stead. The deposits were now removed, and a period of financial stringency set in, which greatly embarrassed the trade and business of the country. All this, in the opinion of the President and his friends, was the result of the improper conduct of the managers of the United States Bank.

The bank question remained for years one of the great subjects of national politics, and by it, perhaps, parties then were more molded than by any other. It was a fruitful theme of discussion for many years.

When it was fully discovered at length, that a national charter for the United States Bank could not be secured, its friends conceived the idea of a State incorporation, in order to save the expiring bank from impending dissolution. Thaddeus Stevens was the admitted Achilles of the bank party in the Pennsylvania Legislature. He was accordingly selected by the stockholders as the man to champion in the Legislature the application for a State charter of the United States Bank. On the 19th of January, 1836, he presented in the House of Representatives a bill for the charter of the bank, with a capital of $35,000,000, which met violent opposition from the Jackson party in Pennsylvania and all over the country. It nevertheless passed both Houses of the Legislature, and having received the approbation of the Governor, became a law. A leading inducement with the advocates of the charter was, that the State was to receive a bonus of several million dollars from the stockholders for internal improvements. The resistance to the State charter manifested itself not only in the denunciations of the Jackson press, but even in the legislation of some of the States. Ohio passed a law in March, 1836, prohibiting within the limits of the State any branch of the Pennsylvania United States Bank. The institution thus chartered, purchased the assets, assumed the liabilities of the old United States Bank, and continued its business under the same roof. But the new bank was unable to resist the adverse tide of financial affairs, that was gradually approaching to a crisis. This set in fully by 1837. All the banks in the Union, with few exceptions, suspended specie payments. A resumption was attempted in 1839, but was only persevered in by the banks of New England and New York. This new suspension, however, was not generally followed by contraction of the currency in Pennsylvania until 1841, when another attempt was made to resume, which proved fatal to the United States Bank of Pennsylvania. It was now obliged to go into liquidation.

In the fall of 1836, Mr. Stevens was returned a member of the Reform Convention, which was fixed by the Legislature to be chosen in November, the same time as the Presidential electors.

The calling of the convention to amend the constitution of Pennsylvania, had been for years a question of discussion, and was decided in 1835, by a majority of 13,000 in favor of the call. In 1825 the people had voted in opposition to a convention by a majority of 15,000. Among the members chosen to the body, were some of the ablest intellects of Pennsylvania. Some of these made lasting reputations from the part they bore in the deliberations of that body. The convention assembled at Harrisburg, May 2nd, 1837, and entered upon its duties of amending the fundamental charter of the State. Mr. Stevens took a seat in this convention, in the fullness of his intellectual vigor, and with a reputation as one of the ablest men in the commonwealth. At the opening of the deliberations, he assumed the position that his consciousness of ability dictated as his place, and should a larger share of hypocricy been part of his character, he would no doubt have been able to wield much more influence in the workings of the convention than he found it in his power to do. Jealousy soon manifested itself on the part of several members, who were ready to measure swords with him, as regards intellectual superiority. His readiness to express his opinions proved a source of weakness to him, and oft exposed him to thrusts from his competitors, which otherwise he might have avoided. Unlike most politicians, his nature prompted him to avow what he sincerely believed; and this trait made him appear to those who have no convictions singular and erratic.

He was placed by the president of the convention as chairman of one of the principle committees; but his great readiness to assert his opinions, and some sweeping measures of reform, which he was prepared to advocate, alarmed those even of his own political party, so that he soon sunk from the rank of a deviser and arranger of reforms, to be simply the disputant of those already submitted. Much weaker men than he were those, as a consequence, who suggested and carried through, by their mildness and amiable manners, the reforms that were adopted by the convention. Radical men like Mr. Stevens, are never popular in any body; and though they may do at times what none else could accomplish, it is because they happen to be in entire accord with the sentiments of those whose influence and votes they require. The agitator is mostly in the minority, and so it was with Mr. Stevens in the convention of 1837–8. It is not, therefore, in any particular measures that he proposed and caused to be adopted, that he made his mark in this body, but rather in the bold stand he in the main assumed, in the defense of what he regarded as right.

Although belonging to the party in opposition to the Democrats, he was too violent an Anti-Mason to be popular with the Whigs, now risen to considerable political importance in the country. This branch was the rising sun of the opposition party, whereas Anti-Masonry was that which was setting. No cordial affiliation had as yet taken place between the two wings, and as a consequence Mr. Stevens was far from being popular with the Whigs of the convention; indeed some of his most bitter assailants belonged to this branch of the party. In the advocacy of his plan of representation, which would limit the largest city to six representatives, he reiterated Jefferson's sentiment, that cities are "*sores of the body politic*," and strongly advocated his views before the convention. This induced a severe attack from Wm. M. Meredith, of Philadelphia, wherein he applied to him some cutting remarks, and though conceding his great ability, yet designated him as the "*great unchained of Adams*," and attached to him other slurring appellations. Mr. Stevens' reply upon this occasion evinces his power of rejoinder, and as indicating this is inserted:

"The extraordinary course of the gentleman from Philadelphia has astonished me. During the greater part of his concerted personal tirade, I was at a loss to know what course had driven him beside himself. I could not imagine on what boiling cauldron he had been sitting to make him foam with all the fury of a wizzard who had been concocting poison from bitter herbs. But when he came to mention Masonry, I saw the cause of his grief and malice. He unfortunately is a votary and a tool of the '*Handmaid*,' and feels and resents the injury she has sustained. I have often before endured such assaults from her subjects. But no personal abuse, however foul or ungentlemanly, shall betray me into passion, or make me forget the command of my temper, or induce me to reply in a similar strain. I will not degrade myself to the level of a blackguard to imitate any man, however respectable. The gentleman, among other flattery, has intimated that I have venom without fangs. Sir, I needed not that gentleman's admonitions to remind me of my weakness. But I hardly need fangs, for I never make offensive personal assaults; however, I may, sometimes, in my own defense, turn my fangless jaws upon my assailants with such grip as I may. But it is well that with such great strength that gentleman has so little venom. I have little to boast of, either in matter or manners, but rustic and rude as is my education, destitute as I am of the polished manners and city politeness of that gentleman, I have a sufficiently strong native sense of decency not to answer arguments by low, gross, personal abuse. I sustained propositions which I deemed beneficial to the whole State. Nor will I be driven from my course by the gentleman from the city, or the one from the county of Philadelphia. I shall fearlessly discharge my duty, however low, ungentlemanly and indecent personal abuse may be heaped upon me by malignant wise men or gilded fools."

When upon the presentation by Mr. Denny, of a petition from sundry free citizens of color of Pittsburg, remonstrating against the adoption of any clause in the new constitution, depriving the free colored citizens of the right of suffrage, and when objection was made to its reception, Mr. Stevens spoke as follows:

"I maintain that those who have petitioned this body, whether white or black, have a right to be heard, whether on this or any other subject relative to the business of the convention. We have a right, then, to give the prayer of the petitioners a respectful consideration."

The question of suffrage before the convention, gave rise to considerable discussion. The constitution of 1790, had confined suffrage to freemen; and as slaves then existed in Pennsylvania, it was generally held that colored persons were not intended to be included under the expression of freemen. However, as time advanced, and the spirit of hostility to slavery grew stronger, there were those in the State who claimed that all free persons were meant, and even in some few counties negroes were permitted to vote, though in the most of them this was not attempted. In large cities the attempt would have been attended with danger. The question had been already decided by some of the courts that the constitution of 1790 limited suffrage to the white race.

When, therefore, this subject came up in the convention, it was moved to incorporate the word *white* in the section, fixing suffrage, which led to an animated debate, the convention being somewhat, though not entirely, divided on this point by party lines. The Democrats were almost a unit in opposition to negro suffrage. But not all of the other party favored it. Wm. M. Meredith, a Whig, remarked: "That he knew no good reason why they (the negroes) should be admitted into the political class. They never had been admitted into it. * * * The right of suffrage ought to be the privilege of white citizens alone." Mr. Stevens, though a bitter opponent to the word white, yet took no special part in the discussion. It was at that time a very unpopular question; petitions were pouring in from all quarters of the State in opposition to negro suffrage, and the strong supporters of such a measure would have become marked men. This Mr. Stevens seemed to recognize, and may have acted upon the reticent list in view of public opinion. If on this occasion he played politician, it was, no doubt, under the strong rebukes of conscience, for his firm faith in human equality would have prompted him to be the staunchest resistant to the introduction of the word white in the suffrage section. When the first discussion on this question was before the convention, he was present, but was absent in January, 1838, when the first vote was taken introducing the discriminating word. Mr. Stevens, in this instance, evinced much of his real nature; for while he desired to be regarded as the bold defender of principle, he had that much of corrupted nature as to keep an eye upon his future political success.

During the last days of the convention, he attended the sittings of the Legislature at Harrisburg; having been elected to the Lower House in October, 1837. And when the new Constitution was completed, he declined to append his signature to it, because of the incorporation of that distinction of suffrage which, for some reason, contrary to his nature, he had not the boldness to battle. Thus far, ambition alone can be supposed as that which triumped over principle, othewise he should have pronounced some philippics that might have enhanced his reputation as an agitator, but which in that event might forever have bolted against him the doors of the National Congress.

Not long after the adjournment of the Legislature in 1838, Gov. Ritner appointed Mr. Stevens one of the Board of Canal Commissioners, John Dickey and a Mr. Pennebaker being the other two members. One of the enterprises that drew upon

Mr. Stevens much odium as a member of the Canal Board, was his advocacy of the Gettysburg Railroad, which he was charged by his political opponents as favoring, because of its passing his furnace in Adams County. It was a measure, however, that had received the warm support of Gov. Ritner; but with the Democrats this in no wise shielded Mr. Stevens, as he was regarded upon all hands as the controlling spirit of the Ritner administration. The Governor was viewed simply as a puppet in his hands, and his messages as but the dictations of the power behind the throne. The Gettysburg Railroad was designed to unite with the Baltimore and Ohio Railroad, then in process of construction. The tortuous route that it was necessrry to take in order to unite the points contemplated by railway, was what gave this road the nickname of the "*Tape-worm.*" An appropriation was secured, and the route was surveyed, and considerable sums of money expended upon its construction. The road was inspected by the committee during the legislative session of 1837–8, one from the House of Representatives, and the other from the Senate. Both committees reported adversely to the completion of the road. The Senate, at that time, had a majority of its members of Mr. Stevens' own party. John Strohm, a Whig Senator, was Chairman of the Senate Committee, from whose report some extracts are submitted:

"The Gettysburg Railroad, commencing at Gettysburg and extending to a point at or west of Hagerstown, in the State of Maryland, is but an isolated link which can never become useful or profitable until the Baltimore and Ohio road, to be extended to Pittsburg or Wheeling, and the Railroad from Gettysburg to the Columbia Railroad at Wrightsville are completed. That portion of the latter which lies between Wrightsville and York, about twelve miles is in progress. Between York and Gettysburg an experimental survey has been made, but no permanent location fixed; and it is the opinion of many that an early completion of the said road by the company need not be expected.

"It is evident, therefore, that no certainty can be attained, either in regard to the location or time of completing the Baltimore and Ohio Railroad. Would it, then, be consistent with cautious prudence and sound policy to persevere in expending millions in constructing a work, the utility of which is dependant on such precarious and doubtful circumstances?"

The Committee reported that, in their opinion, the objects sought for by the Gettysbur Road, would much more advantageously be obtained by adopting the route through the Cumberland Valley, by way of Chambersburg. The Gettysburg Road, in crossing the South Mountain, was obliged to select such a meandering line, that it was not strange that it secured its surname of the "*Tape-worm.*" On the aspect of this road the committee say:

"But on the latter (the Gettysburg road) for about twenty-five miles, the traveler is either ascending or descending at the rate of fifty feet to the mile, a rugged, solitary and barren mountain, uninhabited and almost uninhabitable; on the one hand he sees perpendicular cliffs rise like towering steeples above his head, covered with projecting rocks which threaten him with instant death for his temerity; on the other, he perceives a frightful precipice, over which he is in eminent danger of being hurled into the abyss below, with the certain prospect of being dashed to pieces by the fall. Now he is whirled over a ravine, or an embankment of some fifty or sixty feet in height, and now engulphed in an excavation from which he can scarce see the sun; or immured in a tunnel where daylight may enter but cannot penetrate. The slightest accident must expose him to danger of life, limb and property, from which nothing but a miracle can save him."

Near half a million of dollars were expended upon this road through the influence of Mr. Stevens, as was charged by his enemies, and as it from the first concentrated the hostility of the Democratic party when David R. Porter came into power, the road was abandoned. It, however, was one of those projects that clung to Thaddeus Stevens throughout life, and like the poisoned spirit of Nessus, would have proved a fatal tunic to a weaker man, or, perhaps, to any other than himself.

CHAPTER IV.

THE BUCKSHOT WAR.

The event that will ever be known in the history of Pennsylvania as the "Buckshot War," and in the scenes of which Thaddeus Stevens bore a conspicuous part, to be understood must be traced from its inceptive causes. At the general election, held on the second Tuesday of October, 1838, the people of the County of Philadelphia voted for two Senators and eight Representatives, besides other officers. The highest Democratic candidate for the senate, C. Brown, received 10,036 votes, while W. Wagoner, the highest on the Whig ticket, had but 9,490 votes. On the representative ticket the Democrat who polled the lowest vote had a majority of 385 over the highest Whig candidate.

Charles J. Ingersol, the Democratic candidate for Congress, had run several hundred votes behind his ticket, and as the vote in his district was counted, he was defeated. It was averred, on the part of him and his friends, that vast frauds had been perpetrated in the district of the Northern Liberties. Articles immediately began to appear in the public journals and in handbills, calling upon the people to be ready to assert their rights, and urging upon them to attend at the meeting of the return judges, at the State House, in Philadelphia, on Friday after the election, in order to see that justice be done them and their friends. This at once aroused public attention, and at the meeting of the return judges, Mr. Ingersol and his friends appeared and demanded that they be heard in defense of his claims. The board of return judges numbered seventeen, representing the same number of districts: ten Democrats and seven Whigs. Mr. Ingersol claimed the privilege of proving that certain irregularities had taken place at the polls in the Northern districts, and after considerable discussion this right was granted by a party vote of the return judges. Having proved that the law had been violated at one of the polls in the Northern Liberties; and as this whole district voted in one building, it was demanded by Mr. Ingersoll and his party friends, that the whole vote of the Liberties be excluded. This vote amounted to about 5,000, and its rejection would have the effect of electing the Democratic candidate for Congress, but in no wise altered the result as regards the candidates for tho Senate and House of Representatives, save that it increased the Democratic majorities. The Democratic return judges, having the majority of the board, decided infavor of Mr. Ingersol's claim, and the vote of the Northern Liberties was rejected. The Whigs entered their protest against this action of the majority, but were powerless to prevent it. They contended that the board of return judges had no legal authority to exclude the vote of any district, and that this power was vested in other tribunals. But as the majority thought otherwise, duplicate returns were made out and signed by the ten judges, which elected the two Democratic Senators and the eight Representatives, one copy of which was deposited in the Prothonotary's office, as the law required, and the other was placed in the post office, directed to the Secretary of the Commonwealth. After this the six Whig return judges, in conjunction with the one from the city of Philadelphia, met in another room of the State House, and they also prepared and signed duplicate returns of the votes polled in seven of the seventeen election districts of the County of Philadelphia. The one of these returns they in like manner deposited in the Prothonotary's office, and the other they handed to the Sheriff, who sent the same by express on a steam engine to the Secretary of the Commonwealth. This last return came first into the hands of the secretary; and on this account, induced it would seem by partisan logic, he chose to consider as the only legal one.

The Whigs assumed to believe that the Democrats, in casting out the vote of the Northern Liberties, were guilty of a fragrant outrage, and that dissenting as they did from the majority return, no other remedy was left them save to act as they had done. The Democrats, on the other hand, claimed that the minority return was intended to force into the Legislature, as sitting members, ten defeated Whig candidates from the County of Philadelphia; and by their votes before they could be removed by contesting their election, to pass laws, to elect the Canal Commissioners, a United States Senator, and other officers. The fear was even expressed that they would contest the Governor's election and declare Ritner re-elected for three years longer, and thus set the will of the people at defiance. That the honorable leaders of either party desired anything but what was fair, is hardly presumable, much as the partisans of each may have desired to advance their own interests. But it was about this time in the history of Pennsylvania, when the most daring displays of political corruption first began to be witnessed. The corruptionists of each party were ready to advance their cause by any means whatsoever, and the upright and conscientious men of either organization were made to believe that the fraud all attached to their opponents. As the election of 1838 had been warmly contested, and as both parties had felt confident of victory, and had wagered large sums of money on the result, it was not reasonable to suppose that the defeated would yield the contest, when fraud was believed to have contributed to their overthrow. Accordingly, Thomas H. Burrows, the Secretary of State, and who was also chairman of the Whig State Committee, no doubt, after conference with his party counsellors, issued on the 15th day of October, a few days after the election, the following address to the friends of Joseph Ritner:

"FELLOW CITIZENS:—The general election has resulted in a manner contrary to all our reasonable calculations and just expectations. The opponent for the office of Governor appears to be elected by at least 5,000 majority. This is an event to which, if it had been fairly produced, we, as good citizens, would quietly, if not cheerfully, submit. But there is a strong probability of malpractice and fraud in the whole transaction that it is our duty peacefully to resist it and fully to expose it.

"The election has been characterized by features altogether unparalleled in the history of our State politics. A few of those of a more general nature may be here instanced.

"When the returns from all the counties shall be received, it will probably be found that the whole vote given for Joseph Ritner, on the 9th instant, is greater than that which he received in 1835 by a number at least equal to the natural, regular and legal increase of votes in the whole State in three years. It will also be found that his friends in nearly every county polled fully as many votes as they before the election expected to do, upon the strength of which expectation a reasonable estimate gave him a majority of 10,000. Then grave questions arise. Whence came the majorities returned for his opponent? And how can he be defeated who has so well sustained himself with the people and so largely increased his vote? It will be discovered that in the districts where the friends of Joseph Ritner had the control of the elections, a moderate increase of votes for him, arising from sufficient and well-known causes, took place; while in the same districts his opponents had fair play and polled their full number of legal votes. On the other hand, it is known to all that in the districts in which the inspectors and judges were the friends of Mr. Porter, not only were the friends of Joseph Ritner in many cases wholly excluded from voting, but his opponents admitted without shadow of right, thus swelling the majorities of Mr. Porter even beyond the wild expectations and extravagant calculations of his own friends. Is it right that this state of things (the existence of which each voter will determine by facts known to himself) should be submitted to in a free country?

"Finally it is known that in several counties in which our opponents had the control, the votes of whole districts, favorable to our candidate, were without shadow of law or justice, wholly rejected, and false and partial returns made. Can there be any safety under republican institutions if such high-handed oppression be tolerated? No! We owe it to ourselves as free men and good citizens, to examine into this matter, and if fraud be detected to expose and resist it. We owe it to our country and posterity.

"On behalf, therefore, of the State Committee of Correspondence and Vigilance, the propriety is suggested of taking measures at once for investigating the manner in which the election was conducted and the result produced. Now is the time to make the examination while the facts are fresh and the outrage recent. Let it be done then peacefully, determinedly and thoroughly. But let it be commenced with an honest resolution to submit to the result whether it be favorable or unfavorable to our wishes. This is the duty of all who contend for equal rights and the supremacy of the laws.

"*But, fellow citizens, until this investigation be fully made and fairly determined, let us treat the election of the 9th instant as if we had not been defeated, and in that attitude abide the result.*

"In the meantime your State Committee will take all proper measures on the occasion, and when the whole facts are known and the returns received, will probably address you more at length."

This address, issuing from such authority, was accepted by the Democrats as a threat of revolution, and taken in connection with the return of the minority judges of Philadelphia, had the effect of arousing partisan passion to its highest pitch of intensity. From that time till the meeting of the Legislature in December, the anticipated action of each party at that period was a subject of discussion in the party journals, and preparation was made by each for the probable colision that (as was believed by many) would take place. As the time approached for the meeting of the Legislature, the active partisans began to flock to Harrisburg to be witnesses of the scenes that were about to transpire, and also to see that their party friends obtained their constitutional rights. By Deecmber 3d all the hotels were crowded, and bullies and roughs of both parties were parading the streets of the capitol, loudly boasting what they would do in case their respective parties were unjustly treated. Thaddeus Stevens, all this time, was the centre of influence with his party friends, and the principal object of malediction with the Democrats. The Whigs and Anti-Masons looked to him for advise in all their movements, while their opponents could see in him nothing but the incarnation of all iniquity, fraud and corruption, against which they were compelled to contend. The chief of the fallen angels himself, was almost as honorable a character in the estimation of the violent Democratic partisans, as was Thaddeus Stevens at this time. He, the contriver of the whole plan for revolutionizing the State goverment and securing ascendancy for his party, could be nothing better than an arch-fiend, and many a threat escaped the mouth of a swaggering politician that he should bite the dust for his treasonable designs against the rights of the people.

The memorable morning of the 4th of December, 1838, the day fixed by law for the assembling of the Legislature, found the adherents of both parties anxiously waiting the hour for the House to assemble. The hour of meeting was 11 A. M. Long before this time the hall, the galleries, aisles and lobbies were crammed with members and spectators almost to suffocation, waiting the time for the organization of the House. Bowie knives and pistols were in the pockets of a large number, who had come from Philadelphia and the public works, in order, as they fancied, to see justice done to their party friends. The matter in dispute seemed well understood, not so well the cause of it. All, however, recognized that the diffculty was concerning the Philadelphia County delegation to the Senate and House of Representatives. This was about all that was generally understood; the merits of the dispute had dot yet been closely inquired into. When the hour of eleven struck, the Clerk called the House to order, and Thomas H. Burrows, Secretary of the Commonwealth, stepped forward and handed that officer the Philadelphia returns, which, contrary to custom, he had up to this time failed to deliver. This was the occasion for some manifestation of disapprobation in the galleries. Mr. Charles Pray, one of the Democratic contesting members, from Philadelphia, rose and handed the clerk a certified copy of the returns made by the majority of the return judges, and desired also that it might be read. Mr. T. S. Smith, another Philadelphia member, protested against the reading of a document thus irregularly presented. The law prescribed the officer by whom all returns must be made; and coming from any other they were illegal and void. After some discussion, both returns were allowed to be read, and afterwards the returns from the east of the State were read without opposition. The contesting members of both political parties were thus, as it were, admitted; and the House was now ready for organization. Counting the eight contesting members, each party had a majority. Thos. B. McElwee, of Bedford, next rose and moved that the House proceed to elect a Speaker, which motion was adopted. All this time great confusion reigned. Scarcely was the voice of the clerk, when calling the names of the members, audible above the din that prevailed through the whole hall. Wm. Hopkins, of Washington County, was now nominated for Speaker, and the tellers were appointed. Hereupon, Thaddeus Stevens arose and named as Speaker, Thomas S. Cunningham, of Beaver, and having appointed tellers, immediately put the motion and declared his candidate elected, who proceeded to the speaker's stand and took the chair. He was greeted by his partisans with tumultuous applause when he reached the speaker's seat. A like election on the part of his partisans declared Mr. Hopkins Speaker of the House, who mounted a chair and began to address the multitude. Thos. B. McElwee advanced to him and escorted him to the speaker's platform, and gently removing Cunningham with his elbow, placed the Democratic Speaker in his seat. This in turn was greeted by vociferous cheering by those who saw in this act the advantage gained by their party. Both Speaker's were now sworn by their partisans, and thereupon Mr. Cunningham assumed to adjourn the House till 2:30 P. M. next day. The Cunningham members now retired, and afterthe transaction of some unimportant business, the Hopkins House also adjourned until next day at 10 o'clock. The crowd now gradually dispersed; the Democrats, however, took the precaution to leave some trusty guards in possession of the capitol, in order to retain possession of the advantage they had gained.

Both parties now returned to their several hotels and boarding houses, some chagrined and others jubilant over what had transpired. After dinner had been partaken of and the all-engrossing subject for a short time discussed, the leading politicians began to wend their way to the Senate chamber, which body was to organize at 3 o'clock. Like the hall of the House had been, when the clock struck three, the Senate chamber was a perfect jam. When the clerk called the Senate to order, Mr. Burrows, the Secretary of the Commonwealth, handed to him the return of the minority judges from the Connty of Philadelphia. At this point the crowd gave vent to some tokens of disapprobation, after which the roll was called and the Senators answered to their names. A Mr. Hannah was one of the Senators from Philadelphia who was returned by the Whig judges as elected. When his name was called and he was about to be sworn, the utmost confusion prevailed. The crowd broke over the lobbies, and some of them mounted chairs and began to speak. Charles Brown, one of the contesting Senators from Philadelphia, attempted to address the Senate, but was called to order as not being a member of the body. This excited his partisans in the crowd, and the shout was raised: "Hear him," "Brown," "Brown," "You shall hear Brown." These and similar outbursts of excitement now for a moment rent the hall. For a time all single voices were drowned in the universal clamor and confusion which prevailed. Gen. Rodgers, of Bucks, a member of the Senate, rose and moved that Mr. Brown be permitted to address the Senate. Brown now addressed it and the crowd at considerable length, and all the while the tumult remained unabated. All this time Penrose, the Speaker, kept his seat and endeavored to preserve order to the best of his ability, but to no purpose. It was now near seven o'clock in the evening. During all this time Stevens had been in the hall, and was regarded by his political enemies as the spirit that animated and inspired confidence in the hearts of his partisans. Penrose, finding his efforts to preserve order fruitless, beckoned to Gen. Rodgers to take the chair, he retiring behind the desk. About this time, Stevens perceiving that the waves of faction already resistless were still surging with greater intensity, desired to make his way out through the crowd, but was unable to do so. He went back to the fire-place and while standing there, was told by a friend that it was intended to kill him if he went out by the door. It was then suggested that he and Burrows should leave by the window of the room, near the fire. As it was too perilous a descent to leap out of the window, they crept out by means of a lamp lighter's ladder, which had been obtained by some of their friends, and secured against the back wall of the Senate Chamber. While going out of the window the door of the room, opening at the end of the lobby stood open, and they were seen by some of the crowd. "Three persons, one of them with a long bowie knife in his hand, ran out through the crowd, swearing he would kill the ——— scoundrel yet." * Had not these roughs mistaken the direction of the window they might, in the intensity of the excitement, have imbued their hands in blood. Penrose, about the same time, also made his escape. Shortly after the retreat of Stevens, Penrose and Burrows, the Senate adjourned.

By this time the people of Harrisburg were in the midst of the greatest excitement and terror. Every moment it was now expected that a collision between the parties might ignite the flames of civil war in their midst. Stevens, Penrose and Burrows were the triumvirate that received all the abuse of their political opponents for what had happened, or was likely to take place. As the preponderance of plebeian influence was possessed by the Democratic party, it was already apparent that the Whigs had so far been necessitated to yield to its influence. Perhaps, even in this case, the *vox populi* was *vox dei*, much as reason might utter its dissent. Passion and patriotism now had free scope for display. A mammoth meeting of Democrats was held the same evening at the Court House in the Borough of Harrisburg, presided over by Gen. T. C. Miller, of Adams County, assisted by a large number of vice-presidents. A number of stirring and inflamatory addresses were delivered at this meeting by Col. J. J. McCahan, of Philadelphia, George W. Barton, of Lancaster, and others. A committee was appointed to wait upon Thomas H. Burrows, and request him forthwith to furnish to the clerks of the Senate and House of Reprentatives, the full and legal returns of the election for the County of Philadelphia, held on the 9th of October, 1838. A Committee of Safety was also appointed, of which Gen. Adam Diller, of Lancaster County, was made Chairman. The meeting then adjourned until next morning at half-past eight o'clock.

After the adjournment of the Senate, Gov. Ritner issued the following proclamation:

---

* Biographical History of Lancaster County, pp. 582.

Pennsylvania, ss: In the name and by the authority of the Commonwealth of Pennsylvania, by Joseph Ritner, Governor of the said Commonwealth:

"WHEREAS, A lawless, infuriated armed mob, from the Counties of Philadelphia, Lancaster, Adams, and other counties, have assembled at the seat of Government with the avowed object of disturbing, interrupting and over-awing the Legislature of this Commonwealth, and of preventing its proper organization, and the peaceable and free discharge of its duties. And

"WHEREAS, The said mob have already, on this day, entered the Senate Chamber, and in an outrageous and violent manner by clamoring, shouting and threatening violence and death of the members of that body and other officers of the Government, and finally, by rushing within the bar of the Senate Chamber, and in defiance of every effort to restrain them, compelled the Senate to suspend business. And

"WHEREAS, They still remain here in force, encouraged by a person who is an officer of the General Government from Philadelphia, and are setting the law at open defiance and rendering it unsafe for the legislative bodies to assemble in the Capitol.

"THEREFORE, This is to call upon the civil authorities to exert themselves to restore order, to the utmost of their power, and upon the military force of the Commonwealth to hold themselves in readiness to repair to the seat of Government; and upon all good citizens to aid in curbing this lawless mob, and in re-instating the supremacy of the law.

"Given under my hand and the great seal of the State, at Harrisburg, this 4th day of December, in the year of our Lord, one thousand, eight hundred and thirty-eight, and of the Commonwealth the sixty-third. By the Governor.

"THOMAS H. BURROWS,
"Secretary of the Commonwealth."

The Democratic citizens met pursuant to the adjournment at the Court House meeting at 8:30 o'clock A. M., of December 5th, and were again addressed at some length by the eloquent Col. J. J. McCahan. He exhorted them to use all peaceful measures, in order to secure their rights. The Committee on Resolutions submitted the following:

"*Resolved*, That we recommend to the citizens generally to pursue a prudent and calm course, waiting the events of the day with that firmness which freemen in a free country have resolved upon.

"*Resolved*, That neither those in power, who endeavor to perpetuate their reign through unlawful and fraudulent returns, as citizen soldiers, who have the same feelings and interests with us, will intimidate people resolved upon having their rights."

At 10 o'clock, on Wednesday, December 5th, the Hopkins House met pursuant to its adjournment, in the hall of the House of Representatives, and elected their officers; and after the transaction of some unimportant business, adjourned. About the time the House was adjourning, a rumor was afloat that the Whigs had taken possession of the arsenal with a large body of armed men. Some of the members, going to ascertain the truth of the rumor, found a large collection of men around the arsenal. Armed men were seen parading in the arsenal, with fixed bayonets. Gov. Ritner had issued orders that a special guard should be detailed for the defense of the State property in the arsenal. The Democrats who surrounded the arsenal had a field-piece and acted under the orders of the Committee of Safety, of which Gen. Adam Diller was chairman. As they viewed affairs, the occupation of the arsenal was but part of a plan to coerce them into the relinquishment of their rights; and to this they determined to interpose whatever resistance the occasion might demand. The proclamation of the Governor, calling for troops, had now become known, and this now added fresh fuel to the flames. The Democrats demanded either the evacuation of the arsenal, or that it should be guarded by equal numbers of both parties. This latter demand was refused, and as the parleying had already lasted for a considerable time, it was feared by many of the Whigs that unless some compromise were effected a collision might ensue. At this point, George Ford, of Lancaster, and Joseph Henderson, called upon the Committee of Safety and represented themselves as deputed by Stevens, Ritner & Co. to confer in reference to the arsenal and the public property of the Commonwealth. Messrs. Ford & Henderson pledged themselves, "that as men of honor, no ordinance, arms, muskets, or amunition, should by any order of the Governor, or any other authority whatever, be taken from the arsenal for the purpose of arming any forces that might collect in obedience to the proclamation of the Governor, and that if any use of them should be made they would hold themselves personally responsible for the consequences."

The Committee of Safety thereupon despatched three of their number to advise the citizens of the pledge that had just been made, and the arsenal guard shortly afterwards consented that if the citizens would withdraw, they would evacuate the premises. Room being now made for the retreat, the garrison sallied forth at full run for Gleims' Hotel, the headquarters for the Ritner party. In the chase, one of the fugitives, a known bully, was overtaken by a Philadelphian of like character, prostrated, and severely handled. As soon as the arsenal was evacuated, an immense crowd gathered in front of Gleims' Hotel, in which it was rumored that five hundred muskets were deposited. These muskets, it was averred, had been purchased in Philadelphia by Stevens and Burrows after the October election, and deposited in a room of this hotel for service on the present occasion. It was now past noon, and rain was falling in torrents upon the crowd, now swollen to an immense size, in the streets and around the hotel. Col. Lewis Corryel and Col. Piolett addressed the multitude and calmed them by assurring them that no immediate danger of a collission now existed. The crowd after this, gradually began to disperse.

As soon as Mr. Stevens had heard of the negotiation made with the Committee of Safety, concerning the arsenal, by Ford and Henderson, he disclaimed, in a public letter addressed to the editor of the Pennsylvania *Telegraph*, as far as he was concerned, having authorized the parties to so negotiate. The following is the copy of the letter:

"HARRISBURG, Dec. 6th, 1838.

"*To the Editor of the Pennsylvania Telegraph:*

"SIR:—I understand that a publication, issued by authority of the rebel forces, who for two days past have had possession of the seat of government and the State Capitol, states that while such forces surrounded the arsenal, yesterday, and were threatening to force it open, a committee, consisting of Messrs. Ford and Henderson, sent by Ritner, Stevens, Burrows & Co., pledged their honor, that if the people would disperse no arms should be taken out of the arsenal by any persons, either in behalf of the government or others. I desire to contradict this statement, so far as it concerns myself. What Messrs. Ford and Henderson may have done, I know not; but no man had any countenance from me, in either making or listening to any suggestions from the rebels on any subject; nor do I believe that either of the gentlemen named authorized any such communication. I have uniformly said that I should deem it disgraceful to treat with the rebels on any subject, or do any act, either now or hereafter, on their demand. Such acts I should consider as disgraceful to myself, personally, and an infamous surrender of the rights of the people of the Republic.

"Your obedient servant,

"THADDEUS STEVENS."

The hall of the House of Representatives was securely guarded by the Democrats, during the whole of the 5th of December. The Cunningham House had completed its organization in a room of Wilson's Hotel, in the City of Harrisburg, now the Lochiel

House. As Cunningham had adjourned his House when the two parties on the 4th divided in their organizations, until half-past two P. M. on the 5th, he directed a Mr. Spackman, of Philadelphia, to proceed to the hall of the House of Representatives, and again adjourn it till the next day. Meeting Thomas B. McElwee, Spackman was asked by his political opponent, where he was going. Spackman replied, "to adjourn the House." McElwee told him he had no right to do so, as there was no House to adjourn, and started immediately for the Speaker's stand. Some one in the House (for the hall was again densely crowded) said to him, "you will get a ball through your head if you attempt to keep Spackman from the Chair." Spackman advanced to the platform. McElwee the second time demanded of him what he wanted, and the reply was, "to adjourn the House." The interrogator remarked that there was no House to adjourn. Spackman said, "the Cunningham House," to which McElwee told him he would not be permitted to do so. Great agitation now prevailed throughout the hall. Some, supposing a collision iminent, raised the windows to make their escape if danger arose. Some cried out, "Spackman, adjourn the House from where you are." McElwee immediately remarked to some of the bystanders, "gentlemen, remove this man from the hall." He was at once seized by the men, and led to the door. While he was being conveyed out, he remarked to one of those leading him, that "he would adjourn the House from a member's chair." The gentleman assured him that if he attempted to do so he would not be responsible for his safety. Spackman then retired from the hall. In the interval a rush was made, and the folding doors between the hall and rotunda were burst from their hinges, and many individuals leapt from the windows. Great confusion reigned for a short time, some attempting to speak, in order to quell the disorder. After some time the citizens again quietly dispersed, and the hall was once more almost deserted.

Gov. Ritner, on the 5th of December, addressed a letter to E. V. Sumner, Captain of the United States Dragoons, at Carlisle, urging him "forthwith to march the troops at your command to Harrisburg, for the protection of the constituted authorities of the Commonwealth, for the suppression of the insurrection, and for the preservation of our Republican form of Government, agreeably with the Constitution of the United States." Captain

Sumner, on the same day, replied to the Governor as follows:

"As the disturbance at the Capitol of this State, appears to proceed from political differences alone, I do not feel that it would be proper for me to interpose my command between the parties. If this riot proceeded from any other cause, I would offer you the services of my command before you will receive this letter."

On Friday, December 7th, Gov. Ritner addressed the following letter to the President of the United States:

HARRISBURG, PA., December 7th, 1838.

"SIR:—It is my exceedingly unpleasant duty, officially to inform you, that such a state of domestic violence exists at this place, as has put an end for the present to all the regular functions of the State Government. The Senate of the State has been compelled, by imtimidation, to break up in confusion. The duly appointed presiding officer of the House of Representatives was prevented from calling the House to order, to which it stood adjourned, and was ejected from the hall by violence. The State Department is closed, and I have not deemed it safe or prudent to proceed to the Executive Chamber since the first disturbance, which took place on the 4th instant.

"Under this state of things, I have thought it my duty, to the good citizens of this Commonwealth, and to law and order, to lay the foregoing fact before you, and to request you, in accordance with the Fourth Section of the Fourth Article of the Constitution of the United States, to take measures to protect this State against the effects of the domestic violence which is now in existence.

"That there may be no doubt, in your mind, as to the propriety of some interference at the present moment, without an application of the Legislature, it is only requisite to say that I have been officially informed that neither branch of the Legislature can with freedom and safety meet for the transaction of business; and further, that though the Legislature of this State annually convenes on the first Tuesday in December, I have not yet been officially informed, in the usual manner, of their organization. I, therefore, do not believe that the Legislature can be convened or that it is already in session. On yesterday I made a formal application to Captain E. V. Sumner, commanding the United States Dragoons, and other forces at Carlisle, for the assistance of his command, of which the accompanying papers will exhibit a copy of his reply.

"For the full information of your Excellency, I enclose the copy of a proclamation which I have issued on the occasion, together with the published statements of the facts connected with the riot in the Senate Chamber, signed by a majority of the Senators, and the material facts of which have been sworn to by the Speaker and other members of the Senate, and other published documents.

"I have the honor to be, sir, with great respect,

"Your obedient servant,

"JOSEPH RITNER.

"To his Excellency, Martin Van Buren,

"President of the United States."

The above letter of the Governor of Pennsylvania, was referred by the President to the Secretary of War, J. R. Poinsett, who under date of December 11th, replied to the application for troops, a portion of whose reply is here inserted:

"The commotion," says the Secretary of War, "which now threatens the peace of the Commonwealth of Pennsylvania, does not appear to arise from any opposition to the laws; but grows out of a political contest between the different members of the Government, most, if not all of them, admitted to be the legal representatives of the people constitutionally elected, about their relative rights, and especially in reference to the organization of the popular branch of the Legislature. To interfere in any commotion growing out of a controversy of so grave and delicate a character, by the Federal authority, armed with the military power of the Government, would be attended with dangerous consequences to our republican institutions. In the opinion of the President, his interference in any political commotion in a State could only be justified by the application for it, being clearly within the meaning of the Fourth Section of the Fourth Article of the Constitution, and of the Act of Congress passed in pursuance thereof, and while the domestic violence brought to his notice, is of such a character that the State authorities, civil and military, after having been duly called upon, have proved inadequate to suppress it."

Gen. Patterson, of Philadelphia, marched about one thousand troops from that city to Harrisburg, arriving with them at the State Capitol on Sunday morning, December 9th. A number of troops were also marched from Carlisle by Gen. Alexander, and companies prepared themselves to march in different sections of the State, but were informed that their services were not required. By Thursday, the 6th of December, the greatest of the excitement had subsided; and the Senate was again in session at the close of the week transacting business. All the soldiers were dismissed, and had reached their homes on Saturday, December 22nd. The expenses occasioned by this attendance of the citizen soldiery, amounted to the sum of one hundred and forty-seven thousand dollars.

The Cunningham House of Representatives continued to meet regularly in a room of Wilson's Hotel, and it was believed by the Democrats for a time that the Senate would recognize this body as the legally constituted House. The majority of the Senators were Whigs, and as politicians usually stand by their party, it was supposed that this case would present no exception to the general rule. But after the whole truth, as regards the election in Philadelphia County, came to be fully understood, many of the Whigs doubted the propriety of resisting the fairly expressed will of the people at the ballot box. Much as they were entitled to the organization upon the return made by the Secretary of the Commonwealth, yet it was gravely questioned by many of them if that official had not transcended his authority in discriminating between the two returns, and deciding upon a matter which was by the constitution entrusted to the House of Representatives itself. In this they agreed with their political opponents. Accordingly, on Monday, December 17th, three members of the Cunningham division, Messrs. Butler and Sturdevant, of Luzerne, and Montelius, of Union, came into the Hopkins' House and offered to be and were sworn in as members. This gave the Hopkins' House a majority of the members whose seats were uncontested. Mr. Micheler, a Whig Senator from Northampton, on the 25th of December, offered a resolution to recognize the Hopkins House of Representatives, as containing a majority of the legally elected members; and this resolution was adopted, 17 voting in the affirmative, and 16 in the negative. The Whig Senators who supported this resolution, in addition to the eleven Democrats, were: Messrs. Fullerton, Case, Strohm, Micheler, McConkey and Miller. Two days after the passage of this resolution in the Senate, a large number of the Whig members presented themselves to the recognized House of Representatives, and after being qualified took their seats. Wm. Hopkins on the same day resigned the Speakership, in order to accord to the acceding members their choice in the selection of a Speaker. He was, however, immediately re-elected, and the remaining Whigs, one after another, except Mr. Stevens, whose spirit was too proud to yield, came in, and after having been sworn, took their seats. He who had been the soul of his party in its struggle, was too spirited to succumb when defeated and even deserted by all his followers; and he chose rather to absent himself during the remainder of the session.

In view of the adoption of the new Constitution, it was found necessary, for certain reasons, to convene a special session of the

Legislature, on May 7th, 1839. The political friends of Mr. Stevens in Adams County, regarding themselves as entitled to full representation in the Legislature, held a meeting and passed resolutions requesting him to assume his seat in the House of Representatives at the coming special session. A committee was appointed to convey to Mr. Stevens the wishes of his constituents. To this committee he replied as follows:

"GETTYSBURG, May 3d, 1839.

"GENTLEMEN:—I have received your letter of the 27th ult., inclosing resolutions of a county meeting held in my absence, approving of my conduct in having refused to take my seat in the House, and suggesting as the opinion of the meeting, that I could be of service to the Commonwealth by going into it at the adjourned session; containing also flattering expressions of confidence reposed in me by the meeting.

"My opinion of the legality of the body called the 'Hopkins' House,' remains unchanged. I believe it to be an usurping body, forced upon the State by a band of rebels who have shaken to their fall the pillars of our Constitution. But I owe too much to the kindness and steady confidence of the people of Adams County to disobey their wishes, however delicately intimated. I shall therefore conquer my repugnance to it and enter the House at the adjourned session. I shall feel happy if contrary to my expectations, I should be able to be of any service to you, the Commonwealth at large, and the liberty of the people which I fear is doomed to a short existence. Accept gentlemen for yourselves my most cordial thanks for the kind manner in which you have discharged the duties of your appointment.

"To James Cooper, R. S. Paxon and M. C. Clarkson, Esq's, Committee.

"THADDEUS STEVENS."

Mr. Stevens presented himself at the special session of the House on May 7th, 1859, and offered to be qualified as a member. It was the occasion for the manifestation of intense hostility towards him. Thomas B. McElwee offered the following resolution:

"WHEREAS, Thaddeus Stevens, a person elected from Adams County, claims a seat in this House; And Whereas, if even the said Stevens has had a right to sit as a member on this floor, he has forfeited this right by acts in violation of the law of the land, by contempt of this House, and by a virtual resignation of his character as a representative of Adams County, therefore

"*Resolved*, That his admission as a member be postponed for the present, and that a committee of five be appointed to investigate the claims of Stevens to a seat in the House of Representatives of Pennsylvania, and whether he has, if duly elected, forfeited his seat by malconduct."

The above resolution called forth considerable discussion, but the committee was finally appointed and the following notice served upon Mr. Stevens:

"HARRISBURG, Saturday Morning, May 11th, 1839.

"SIR: The committee appointed by the House of Representatives 'to inquire whether Thaddeus Stevens, a member elect from Adams County, has forfeited his right to a seat in the House,' will meet for that purpose in the committee room of the House, on Monday next at 4 o'clock, or at an earlier period if you desire it, where you may attend and be heard.

"To Thaddeus Stevens, Esq.

"CHARLES M. HEGINS, Chairman."

To this notice Mr. Stevens sent the following reply:

"HARRISBURG, May 13th, 1839.

"SIR:—I received your letter of the 11th instant, informing me that the committee 'to inquire whether Thaddeus Stevens, a member elect from Adams County, has not forfeited his right to a seat in the House,' will meet on Monday next, when I may attend and be heard.

"I decline to appear before the committee, because I will not consent to a palpable violation of the Constitution and laws. If, as on recent occasions, I am compelled by force to witness such scenes, I can at least withhold from them my sanction, both express and implied.

"The resolution admits the legality of my election and return, but proposes to inquire whether I have not forfeited my seat before my admission into the House. The grounds of such forfeiture are not specified in the resolution, and I can only infer them from the remarks of the original mover of the resolution, T. B. McElwee. As set forth by him, they consist in *non user*, *misuser*, contempt of the House, by calling it an illegal body—the offspring of a mob; and for sundry personal improprieties. No *constitutional* disqualification was or is alleged, and for none other can the House, without an illegal exercise of arbitrary power, prevent a member elect from taking his seat. Expulsion for good cause, after admission, stands on different grounds, and is authorized by the Constitution.

"I think it will trouble the committee to find a precedent of the declared forfeiture for *non user* of an elective representative office. For two whole sessions the minority in the House of Parliament absented themselves from the House, yet neither the King, the Speaker, nor the majority dared to exercise the high-handed tyranny now attempted by what is called the House of Representatives of Pennsylvania.

"That certain public executive or ministerial offices may be forfeited for *non user* in England where no written paramount Constitution exists, is true. The business of several departments of government could not otherwise be transacted. But it must be a continuing *non user*. It would be too late to declare the forfeiture after the officer had taken possession of his office, and was ready to discharge its duties. The forfeiture is a remedy against public inconvenience, and not a punishment for an offender. But in Constitutional Governments no such forfeiture takes place, except for the causes and in the mode pointed out in the Constitution itself.

"In the present case, the majority did not seem to consider the public business as suffering by my absence, nor claim a right unknown to the Constitution, to forfeit my seat; else they would have declared it vacant before the adjournment, and given my constituents a new election during the vacation, so that they might be represented in the present session. No intimation of a vacancy, no step to supply it was taken until I appeared to take the oath and use the office. The House, therefore, seems rather anxious to create than supply a vacancy.

"I need hardly notice the allegation of *misuser* of an office, which I have been prevented from using at all.

"The right to exclude a member elect for speaking or writing contemptuously of the House or its proceedings is a novel and dangerous position. Until a member elect has taken the requisite oaths he can no more participate in the proceedings of the House, nor is he any more subject to its jurisdiction than a private citizen. Individuals may be punished by the House for corrupt attempts upon its integrity by attempting to bribe its members, or for disturbing or interrupting its proceedings, as in the case of the December mob, but not for any written or printed comments on its proceedings however severe. The Sixth Section of the Ninth Article (the Declaration of Rights) of the Constitution declares that "*the printing press shall be free to every person who undertakes to examine the proceedings of the Legislature or any branch of the Government, and no law shall ever be made to restrain the right thereof.*" Anything I may have published, therefore, is not subject to your supervision, if the Constitution be yet considered as existing.

"If I were an admitted member, and should demean myself indecorously and disorderly towards that body, the House has the power of expulsion. And if calling it 'an illegally organized body, the offspring of a mob,' as was contended in debate, be sufficient cause for expulsion, I think I may safely promise to furnish an excuse for that act soon after my admission. I do consider the 'Hopkins House' a usurping body, but like all other usurpers, having possession of the Government *de facto*, its acts will be binding for good or evil on the State. Hence, my constituents have thought proper to ask me to take my seat and attempt to moderate an evil which is now without remedy.

"If the committee should occupy the ground pointed out by the mover of the resolution, and sit in judgment upon decency and morality, I must still further object to the tribunal. I mean no disrespect to the committee for the majority of them I feel a high regard; but the whole question on their report will be again in the power of the majority of the House, and I cannot agree to admit the intellectual, moral or habitual competency of Thomas B. McElwee, his compeers, coadjutors and followers to decide a question of decency and morals.

"For myself, personally, I feel no anxiety for the result of this inquiry or the reasons which may be given for it, and to put which upon the Journal, I presume was the chief object of the proceeding. My only anxiety is that the Constituti n may not be further violated, and that the people may yet have some ground to hope that Liberty, although deeply wounded, may not expire. I owe my acknowledgments to the committee for their prompt attention to this business, and trust it may be speedily finished. With proper respect, your obedient servant,

"To Charles Hegins, Esq., "THADDEUS STEVENS.

"Chairman of Committee, &c."

After the committee had submitted their report, a resolution was adopted by a strict party vote of 58 to 34, declaring the seat of Mr. Stevens vacant in the House, and ordering a new election, to take place on the 14th of June. At the special election, Mr. Stevens was re-elected, and on the 19th of June he appeared in the House, and having subscribed the requisite oath, took his seat. The Legislature adjourned on the 27th of the same month. The following is his address when presenting himself as a candidate at the special election:

"FELLOW CITIZENS:—In accordance with your wishes, I presented myself to the body now exercising the duties of the House of Representatives of this Commonwealth, and desired to have administered to me the oath prescribed by law. A majority of that body, using the same unconstitutional and unlawful means which invested them with official authority, refused to allow me to occupy that seat to which I had been called by the free choice of my fellow citizens. Under the most shallow, hypocritical and false pretences, they have declared my seat vacant and imposed upon you the expense of a new election, to be held on the 14th of June next. In doing so they have committed an unprecedented outrage on the rights of the people. If submitted to by the people, Liberty has become but a mere name. Already is the Constitution suspended and the most sacred contracts between the State and individuals are violated with the most daring and reckless audacity. The tyrants who have usurped power, have determined to oppress and plunder the people. It is for you to say whether you will be their willing slaves. If they are permitted finally to triumph, you hold your liberty, your lives, your reputation, and your property at their will alone.

"I had hoped that no circumstances would occur which would render it necessary for me to be again a candidate for your suffrages. Both my inclination and my interest require me to retire from public life. But I will not execute that settled intention, when it will be construed into cowardice or despondency. To refuse to be a candidate now would be seized upon by my enemies as evidence that I distrust the people, and am afraid to entrust to them the redress of their own wrongs. I feel no such fear—no such distrust. Without intending any invidious comparison, I have always said what I still believe, that the people of Adams County have more intelligence, and not less honesty, than the people of any other county of the State. To such a people I can have no fear in appealing against lawless aggression. To them I appeal to restore to me that which was their free gift, and therefore my right, and of which I have been robbed by those who 'feel power and forget right.'

"I present myself to you as a candidate to fill that vacancy which was created to wound my and your feelings. I do not want to receive a party nomination from my friends. The question now to be decided is above party considerations, and would be disgraced by sinking it to the level of a party contest. Every freeman must be impelled to resist this public outrage as a personal wrong to himself. Every thing dear to him in his country, his liberty, the liberty of his children and the title to his property admonish him to rise above every paltry personal consideration, and rebuke tyranny at that great tribunal of freemen—the ballot box.

"While, however, you are determined, resolute and energetic, let me implore you not to imitate the example of our oppressors, but do everything calmly and temperately. This admonition is hardly necessary to the orderly citizens of Adams County, but when oppression is so intolerable, as at present, it is difficult for the most peaceable and quiet men to control their indignation.

"With respect and gratitude, I am,

"Your obedient servant,

"THADDEUS STEVENS,"

Harrisburg, May 25th, 1839.

A number of prosecutions for riot were instituted against the leading Democrats who participated in the scenes at Harrisburg during the 4th and 5th of December, 1838, and true bills of indictment were found by the Grand Jury, at the Dauphin County January Sessions, 1839, against Gen. Adam Diller, Charles Pray, George W. Barton, and others. These bills were quashed by the Court at the April Sessions, for reasons presented by the attorneys for the defendants. Mr. Stevens was one of the counsel for the prosecution in these riot cases.

When Mr. Stevens retired from the Legislature in June, 1839, it was with the determination that it should be his last service in the State Legislature; but at the solicitation of friends he allowed himself to be prevailed upon once more to become a candidate, and he was returned again to the House in 1841. On the organization of the Legislature he was placed upon the Judiciary Committee of the House, a position for which he was known to possess rare qualifications. In February, 1842, the resolutions of Mr. Rumford, suspending executions between the banks and their debtors while the banks remained in suspension, came up on third reading. Mr. Stevens obtained the floor, and moved to go into Committee of the Whole, for the purpose of substituting in the place of the bill then pending, one which he caused to be read at the Clerk's desk. "He supported," says the reporter, "his motion in a powerful speech—such a speech as only Thaddeus Stevens can make—which cast into insignificance the attempts at oratory which are daily made here. The bill provides for an immediate resumption of specie payments, under specified penalties, amongst which is that during the time of suspension the pay of all the officers of the institution shall be suspended. The matter was postponed without any action upon it, as it was desirous to get rid of a troublesome subject."

During the same session, Mr. Stevens offered a resolution to amend the Constitution by limiting the State debt to forty millions of dollars. The resolution passed in the House by a large majority.

A large number of petitions being presented to the Legislature at this session, asking for the abrogation of the death penalty in cases of murder, and these being referred to the Judiciary Committee, the latter through their Chairman, Mr. McElwee, reported against the requests of the petitioners. George Sharswood and Thaddeus Stevens, two members of this committee, submitted a minority report, setting forth their reasons for favoring the abolition of the death penalty, and concluding as follows:

"How imperfectly then, does the example of this punishment operate to deter men from the commission of this crime (*murder*), accompanied as it is with so many multiplied chances of escape. Indeed, in the present constitution of society, we repeat, no crime is so likely to escape its due and proportionate punishment as that highest one, to which our law has affixed the severest penalties.

"Let the punishment be commuted to solitary imprisonment at hard labor for life, and these chances of partial or entire immunity will no longer exist. The terror of the doom, joined to the moral certainty of its infliction, will be ample to deter offenders. The natural horror felt for the crime will not be lost in the minds of prosecutors, witnesses, jurors and judges in sympathy for the accused. The mercy of the Executive will not be extended, except in those cases in which from after discovered evidence the innocence of the convict has been made apparent, or when after the probation of years, his moral reformation and repentance are placed beyond a reasonable doubt."

The following review and estimate of Mr. Stevens as a member of the Pennsylvania Legislature, from the pen of one of his own partisan contemporaries, is appended as the conclusion of his career as a State Legislator. It is from the Harrisburg *Telegraph:*

"We are aware that our columns have been accused of a blind devotion to Thaddeus Stevens; and those whose aim it has been to detract from his reputation, have sought to brand the sincere praises inspired by his talents and eloquence, as the favoring sycophancy of the parasite. But the writer of the present article has never had the pleasure before this session (1?4) of hearing Mr. Stevens in a deliberative body; and he has been too deeply impressed with the commanding influence of his talents, the well trained tone of his mind, and with his blended graces of the orator and rhetorician, that he is no longer at a loss to discover why it is that all the invective which partisan spleen could suggest, all the ribaldry which political malice could engender, all the scurrility which a corrupt press could procreate, and all the venom which was spit out under the protection of a 'previous pardon,' have been high heaped upon him.

"So inveterate have been these attacks, so untiring the activity of his assailants, that a portion of the very party with which he acts politically, has caught the tone of their opponents denunciations, and look on him with distrust. It would be difficult for any who adopt this course to explain their reasons. We look in vain through the public career of Mr. Stevens to find in what particular he has been unfaithful to the cause of democracy, unless we are to mistake for the pure fountain of truth the poluted streams of partisan malignity. Whenever the destructive tendencies of his political enemies seek to make inroads on our constitutional safeguards, or batter the muniments of our chartered liberty, there is he found contending for the letter and spirit of Freedom's *magna charta*. When the illiberal policy of those who would fetter the minds and hold in thrall the intellects of our rising generation exhibits itself, then is he found exerting his giant powers in favor of an universal spread of education, which, like the light-giving sun, shall shine on all alike and gild with equal brilliancy, the yeoman's cottage and the demagogue's stately mansion. If the acts of those who are recreant to the true interests of the free labor of the North, for the purpose of strengthening their unwholly alliance with the slave drivers of the South, at any time aim a deadly blow at agriculture and manufacturing prosperity, he will be found throwing himself into the breach, and with fervid eloquence, pointing to the lights of the world's experience and calling on all, to use them as beacons to avoid the rocks on which thousands have foundered, or the quicksands in which they have been engulphed.

"To judge of the varied powers of Thaddeus Stevens, it is only necessary to review his course during the brief limit of the present session. In this review would be included his powerful argument on the right of petition, even from a meeting of repudiators, his cogent appeals on the necessity of placing a constitutional limit to the State debt, and taking from any future legislature the power of continuing the present system of wasteful expenditure without any provision to meet liabilities incurred thereby; his able and practical remarks on the vital importance of the protective policy to the interests of our nation, showing how the flood of commerce poured into England under the Navigation Act; how Holland, once the commercial carrier of the whole world, was paralyzed under the influence of free-trade doctrines, and how the first principles of legislation demand that home labor should be fostered and protected. Whoever has heard Mr. Stevens, at this session or at any other, cannot hesitate to accord him the most commanding abilities and sound constitutional sentiments. Hence it is, standing as he does, a giant among his pigmy opponents, that every shaft of malice and invective is hurled at him by every *puny whipster*, who, like the fool of Crete, exposes his waxy softness to the fervid glow of his eloquent reply.

"It is not so much our wish to eulogize Mr. Stevens as to direct the public attention to the position he has assumed, and so well maintains. We want the eyes of the Commonwealth directed towards him. We want him judged of by his acts, and not through the false medium of political vituperation. We desire to see his course scanned with impartial discrimination, and on its issue we want our Commonwealth to pronounce its judgment. If he be found to swerve a point from the true cynosure of democracy, or if he varies a line from the most matured principles of legislative economy, let that judgment be of condemnation; but if he pass the trial, justice demands that the praises be awarded to him which are the meed of every public servant who has labored long and faithfully for the best interests of the Commonwealth."

CHAPTER V.

THE ANTI-SLAVERY AGITATION.

The anti-slavery struggle in America, in which Mr. Stevens bore a conspicuous part, is necessary to be somewhat considered in order to have a more perfect understanding of his character, as an individual and as a statesman, than otherwise could be obtained. Born and educated in New England, where anti-slavery sentiments first developed themselves in the United States, it is not strange that he should have manifested at an early period of his life an opposition to the southern institution. Besides, he belonged to the party that had led the resistance to the admission of Missouri as a slave State into the Union; and from that period all whose convictions became fixed in that memorable struggle remained unchanged, and were rather strengthened than weakened as time progressed and the opposition to slavery as a movement became more consolidated.

Human slavery has been one of the established forms of the social organization of the ancient, mædieval and modern world. Its establishment was based upon the assumed inequality of men, as indicated by the clearest proofs of experience and reason in all ages and nations. This manifest inequality, as witnessed in all creation, was sufficient to satisfy the philosophers and legislators of ancient nations that a system of subordination was necessary to maintain that law and order which the constitution of society and government seemed to require. Hence flowed those systems of enslavement, that from the earliest periods of history caused the feelings of humanity to enter their protest, but which in modern times have overborne the logic of reason and proclaimed a universal jubilee to all races of mankind throughout the civilized countries of the earth. But in the institution of slavery is witnessed simply, as it were, the construction of all the social forms of existence, as they obtained from the earliest periods of time, with rare exceptions, down to the protestant reformation, itself the first united remonstrance against mental and ecclesiastical domination. Ancient policy was based upon subordination, while the effort of modern times is to make speech, thought and action, free. Freedom was first fully born when the Wittemberg monk attached his theses to the castle gate of the city, and it has been growing from that period until the present, branching in all directions. Every movement, religious or civil, from the sixteenth century, owe their impulse to that which was then set in motion.

But the American movement of anti-slavery is that alone, after having glanced at its paternity, which concerns our attention at this time. This protest of the Anglo-American mind against the enslavement of the African race, had its immediate birth in the sympathetic feelings, which were entertained by the philanthropists of the 19th century for a race that they hoped to elevate, by placing it in a system of legal equality with themselves. It was about the year 1833, that the agitation first set fully in, although individual protests against the institution of slavery had hitherto been numerous. What, more than all else, gave an impulse to that movement at this particular time, was the result of British agitation, which was crowned with success in August 1833, by Parliament decreeing the emancipation of all the slaves on the West India plantations. No event could have occurred so gratifying to the wishes of the abolitionists, as that enactment which proclaimed freedom to the West India negroes and raised them to the rank of equality with the whites. At this time, however, the number of decided abolitionists were comparatively few, and such as they were, persons of humble condition and insignificant influence. Many there were whose feelings were repugnant to slavery, but they had been taught to believe that it was legal and based upon the words of revelation, and hence they were unwilling to interfere with it. The influence that set the agitation on foot was germinated in free thought and promulgated by reformers who recognized a higher than any written code. It was that of which universal humanity was the recipient, and of which Voltaire, Rousseau and Montesquieu were the ablest apostles.

The enemies of negro slavery, about the period of the American Revolution, were those chiefly who had imbibed the doctrines of the French writers, who prepared the way for the scenes that drenched the soil of France with blood in the convulsion of 1789 and '93. This species of abolitionism was quiet and sympathetic, but entirely unaggressive in its character, and yet potential in its effects. It made its way through all the States of the North, obliterating in each, one after another, the traces of slavery that existed in them. It bore with it likewise the quickening influences that helped to kindle the flame of aggressive anti-slavery agitation which began as above stated. Benjamin Lundy, Charles Osborne, Elihu Embree, humble yet sincere workers in the cause of freedom, were early fanning the flame of anti-slavery agitation, and arousing the American mind to its own consciousness of the evils which the Southern blacks endured. The first named of these by 1815 had organized the Union Humane Society, consisting of but five or six persons, and in the following year issued an appeal to the philanthropists on the subject of slavery. Osborne, not long after this, began the publication of the *Philanthropist*, and the *Emancipator* also started by him, was afterwards issued for a time near Jonesville, Tennesee. The first American Abolition Convention was held in Philadelphia in the winter of 1823–4, which was attended by men prompted by the love of humanity. William Lloyd Garrison became a convert to the cause of abolitionism in the year 1828. These various influences and movements, like the different branches of a stream, were thus uniting themselves, and by 1833 a swollen stream, with an active current was visible, and one that attracted from this point considerable attention.

The movement up to this time had been chiefly philanthropic in its character, and like the Colonization Society, met with supporters in both sections of the Union, South as well as North. Already, however, the New England Anti-Slavery Society had been organized, and the year, 1833, saw one instituted in New York City, and a National Anti-Slavery Convention asssemble in Philadelphia, consisting of sixty members, and representing ten States of the Union. Every newspaper established in the interest of anti-slavery, and every society which was organized and the proceedings of whose meetings were published gave, as it were, new impetus to the movement. But now it was that resistance began to be encountered by the Abolitionists, and from this period the agitation had a steady and increasing influence upon the reorganization of the parties throughout the country. Up to

1833, the Abolitionists drew recruits from both of the old political parties of the North; but it is undeniable that by much the larger proportion came from the Federal party, and its successors as comprising the majority of the men of wealth, culture and social position. The Democratic party, from its earliest organization, had been that to which the bulk of the people had been attached. The reasons for this division of parties, it concerns us not, on the present occasion to investigate.

The character of the earliest resistance to the anti-slavery agitation, showed itself in the mobbing of abolition lecturers in the North, the dispersal of assemblages and the burning of halls erected for the holding of liberty meetings, and the destruction of newspapers published in that interest. The period of these mobs and riots extended from 1833 up to about 1841, when they mostly ceased. When these disturbances were first inaugurated, they were participated in by men of character, and belonging to both political parties; but the preponderance of participants in these demonstrations being usually composed largely of the party of the people, and the majority of the lovers of law and order belonging to the opposite one, it was not long till this division itself arrayed a diversity of sentiment on this question amongst the people of the North. It was reasonable to expect that the Democratic party should become the staunchest advocates of the rights of the southern people under the constitution. The principles of that party were fixed and well understood both North and South; its creed founded upon the Virginia and Kentucky resolutions of 1798, had been time and again proclaimed and re-affirmed in State and National Conventions; and its organization from the days of Jefferson was complete and entrusted with the management of the General Government. The Federal party, though originally comprising in its ranks the leading minds of the nation, had forfeited the confidence of the country; and after the late war with Great Britain, it gradually disappeared as a national organization. Anti-Masonry, which in the Northern States took its place, never was able to attain to position in the South, and as a consequence soon expired. Another reason why the Democracy from the first were the attached defenders of southern institutions, was that the party had national leaders in the South who were slave-holders, and it was natural that the party should defend these and their rights as their own. Wher the anti-slavery agitation first began fairly, Gen. Jackson, a slaveholder, was the President of the United States, and the most honored man in the Republic. An institution defended by him and other eminent southern statesmen, would not be likely to be viewed as odious by the masses of the people, and one deserving of the abuse that the Abolitionists were in the habit of applying to it. On the part of the Federalists and Anti-Masons the same attachment was not felt for the President and his policy; and from political antipathy it is easy to perceive how a feeling of sympathy for the negro slaves could gradually ripen into intense opposition to the southern institution. And thus it was that the Abolition ranks, secret and avowed, were swelled chiefly by enlistments obtained amongst the opposition to the Democracy.

From the year 1833, the varied evolutions of the contesting parties in the interest of and opposed to slavery, would require volumes to fully detail. Only the leading features, therefore, can be expected to be grouped in a work of this character ; and such as most fully illustrate the current of American opinion as it shaped itself in both sections of the Union. In the mob resistance of the North, to the spread of abolition sentiments, is seen simply an exhibition of the deep-seated conviction of the people of the inferiority of the African as compared with the Caucasian race ; an inferiority stamped by the hand of creative power, and which history and experience had demonstrated to reflecting minds in all ages. But the principle of the mob being altogether adverse to the rules of social order, could not but sink to its normal level, as the work of the lawless element of the body politic. Its aim, though heartily approved by the respectable and influential classes of society, could not long receive their open and sanctioning encouragement; and it soon, as a conse, quence, became the work of the vulgar and degraded in society. Not that the mob did not still continue to be inspired by the leading minds of the different localities where it showed itself in resistance to anti-slavery agitation; for it may be accepted as a truth that the turbulent members of society in such lawless advances as above alluded to, ever receive their orders, or at least their sanction, from higher authority than themselves. They are in a sense, therefore, the expression of the public opinion of their localities, and are, as it were, minor revolutions for the overthrow or removal of grievances that are felt by society. The spirit of tumultuous resistance are but premonitions of the diseased condition of existing society, which the laws of social being are essaying to remedy by all possible efforts in order to its preservation. The mobbing of Lovejoy, of Illinois, the seizure and dragging of Wm. Lloyd Garrison through the streets of Boston, and the burning of Pennsylvania Hall in Philadelphia, were but manifestations of the antagonism that the northern people exhibited towards the new ideas of the radical Abolition school. But the Abolitionists, although in a miserable minority, had as against mob resistance every moral advantage. They were the champions of free speech and a free press, cardinal principles of republicanism; and all the elements of social order must naturally cling to these as the landmarks of freedom. As it was impossible for any to justify lawbreaking, mob interposition must gradually retire into the background.

But there was another form of resistance to anti-slavery agitation, germinated by the same influences that also began about 1833; and which, to properly comprehend the period, must be considered. This was the moral dislike that showed itself to the aggressions of abolitionism, and which was exhibited by the educated and refined part of the northern people. The vastly preponderating weight of intelligent public opinion in the North, from the commencement of the anti-slavery agitation, was altogether in opposition to the innovating doctrines of the radical reformers; and this preponderance was early manifest in both the secular and ecclesiastical American northern press. In the *Literary and Theological Review* for December, 1835, published in the City of New York, the position was boldly assumed and ably argued that the Abolitionists were "justly liable to the highest civil penalties and ecclesiastical censures." This sentiment expressed the current opinion as held by a large number of the leading men in America at that time, and, as a consequence, it escaped all censure amongst the patrons of the journal, or even from the organs of the rival theological party. In unison with the sentiment as expressed in the above-named *Review*, a Grand Jury of Oneida County, N. Y., a short time prior to the Utica riot made a presentment, in which they declared that those who form Abolition Societies are guilty of sedition, that they ought to be punished, and that it is the duty of all citizens, loyal to the Constitution, to destroy their publications wherever found. In the same year, the Hon. William Sullivan issued a pamphlet in Boston, in which the following desire was expressed: "It is to be hoped and expected that Massachusetts will enact laws declaring the printing, publishing and circulating papers and pamphlets on slavery, and also the holding of meetings to discuss slavery and abolition, to be public indictable offences, and provide for the punishment thereof in such manner as will more effectually prevent such offences."

The intense indignation that inflamed the Southern people against the anti-slavery agitation of the country may in a large measure be considered as instrumental in producing the strong conservative sentiment in the Northern States, which declared itself in favor of the guarantees of the Federal Constitution. The people of the South had been most ardent advocates of constitutional liberty, and had ever shown a steady attachment to republican principles of Government. They had declared themselves as ready to make any honorable sacrifice that might be required of them, in order to secure the perpetuity of the Union and the Constitution as it had been transmitted by its framers. The institution of slavery, they claimed as one of the vested rights that they, as a people possessed, and over which neither the General Government nor any branch thereof had any authority to interfere, either for the emancipation of the Southern slaves or the amelioration of their condition. All this, they insisted, was a matter over which the people of the several slave States alone had jurisdiction. The attacks of the Northern Abolitionists upon the institution of slavery had the effect of deeply incensing the southern people, and they loudly protested against the unjust interference, as they denounced it, and demanded that their rights should be observed and their opinions respected. Public bodies and legislative assemblies of the South offered rewards for the rendition of northern agitators, and southern Governors called upon northern officials to supress the anti-slavery discussion, as calculated, unless checked, to disrupt in the future the American Union. The whole southern people seemed a unit in favor of this demand upon the North. The clergy of that section from the first, with one accord, sanctioned the justice of the request, and sought by every means in their power to help to stifle the rising fire that might envelope the fair fabric of the Republic in its flames. Rev. Thomas S. Witherspoon, of Alabama, thus wrote to the *Emancipator:* "Let your emisaries dare to cross the Potomac, and I cannot promise that your fate will be less than Haman's. Then beware how you goad an insulted but magniminous people to deeds of desperation."

Rev. William S. Plummer, of Richmond, Virginia, in 1835 expressed the following sentiments: "Let them (the Abolitionists) understand that they will be caught if they come among us, and they will take good care to keep out of our way. If Abolitionists will set the country in a blaze, it is but fair that they should receive the first warming at the fire."

Governor McDuffie, of South Carolina, in December, 1835, called the attention of the Legislature to the subject of abolition agitation at the North. On the 16th of the same month, both Houses of the legislature adopted the following:

"*Resolved,* That the Legislature of South Carolina, having every confidence in the justice and friendship of the non-slave-holding States, announces her confident expectation, and she earnestly requests that the Government of these States will promptly and effectually suppress all those associations within their respective limits purporting to be abolition societies."

On December 19th, 1835, the General Assemby of North Carolina resolved as follows:

"*Resolved,* That our sister States are respectively requested to enact penal laws prohibiting the printing within their respective limits, all such publications as may have a tendency to make our slaves discontented."

January, 7th, 1836, the Alabama legislature adopted the following resolve:

"*Resolved,* That we call upon our sister States and respectfully request them to enact such penal laws as will finally put an end to the malignant deeds of the Abolitionists."

February 10th, 1836, both Houses of the Virginia Legislature adopted the following:

"*Resolved,* That the non-slave-holding States of the Union are respectfully but earnestly requested promptly to adopt penal enactments, or such other measures as will efficiently suppress all associations within their respective limits, purporting to be, or having the character of Abolition Societies."

Resolutions were passed in the Georgia Legislatureof the following import:

"*Resolved,* That it is deeply incumbent on the people of the North to crush the traitorous designs of the Abolitionists."

The above resolutions were officially communicated to the

Governors of the Northern States, and by them laid before their respective Legislatures. It was quite apparent by this time that the leaven of abolitionism was principally confined to the Whig and Anti-Masonic party of the North, for reasons as before stated. The Democratic Governors and Legislatures were ready to lend their influence for the repression of the agitation; whereas, many influential members of the Whig party were differently disposed. George Wolf, the retiring Democratic Gov ernor of Pennsylvania, in his last Annual Message in December, 1835, expressed his disapprobation as regards the movements of the Abolitionists in the free States; and predicted the consequences unless checked, and a reign of reason re-inaugurated. But on the other hand, Joseph Ritner, the Anti-Masonic successor of the last named executive, stigmatized all such sentiments as had been expressed by his predecessor in his Message as a "bowing of the knee to the dark spirit of slavery." It was believed, from the influence known to be exerted by Thaddeus Stevens upon the mind of the Anti-Masonic Governor of Pennsylvania, that the sentiment thus expressed in his inaugural as regards slavery, was the inspiration of the former, who was already an avowed opponent of the southern institution. Whilst the leaven of abolitionism was confined in the main to the ranks of the Whig party, there was nevertheless a strong section of it that in no wise so sympathized. Edward Everett, the Whig Governor of Massachusetts, in his Message communicating the southern documents, held the following language:

> "Whatever by direct and necessary operation is calculated to excite an insurrection among the States, has been held by highly respectable and legal authority, an offence against the peace of the Commonwealth, which may be prosecuted as a misdemeanor at Common law."

William L. Marcy, the Democratic Governor of New York, in his Message in January, 1836, upon the same subject, spoke as follows:

> "Without the power to pass such laws, the States would not possess all the necessary means for preserving their external relations of peace among themselves."

But in 1835 the movement of the anti-slavery agitation had already become of such importance as to claim the attention of President Jackson, who, in his Message of December in that year, accused the Abolitionists of "unconstitutional and wicked attempts," menacing the stability and perpetuity of the Federal Union, and recommending as follows:

"I would, therefore, call the special attention of Congress to the subject, and respectfully suggest the propriety of passing such a law as will prohibit, under severe penalties, the circulation in the Southern States, through the mail, of incendiary publications intended to instigate the slaves to insurrection."

The attention of the President had been called to this subject by the tumultuous occurrences that had taken place, occasioned by the transmission through the mails of Abolition documents to citizens in the Southern States. On the 29th of July, 1835, a riot, headed by the influential citizens of Charleston, had broken open the post office in that city and destroyed the incendiary Abolition matter. From this time, Southern postmasters, and even some in the North, assumed the authority of determining what should not be transmitted through the mails. Samuel L. Gouverneur, the postmaster of New York, urged upon the Anti-Slavery Society "voluntarily to desist from attempting to send their publications into the Southern States by the public mails." Finding that his request was not heeded, he addressed Amos Kendal, Postmaster General, for instructions on this point, who, under date of August 22d, replied as follows:

"I am deterred from giving an order to exclude the whole series of Abolition publications from the Southern mails, only by a want of legal power, and if I were situated as you are, I would do as you have done."

Gen. Jackson's recommendation for the enactment of a law for the repression of incendiary matter through the mail was referred by the Senate to a Select Committee, of which John C. Calhoun was Chairman. The report of this committee, as submitted, expressed the convictions of the southern people, and also of the great majority of those of the North, as regards the agitation of the slavery question. On this point, the report speaks as follows:

"The inevitable tendency of the means to which the Abolitionists have resorted to effect their object, must, if persisted in, end in completely alienating the two great sections of the Union. The incessant action of hundreds of societies, and a vast printing establishment throwing out daily, thousands of artful and inflammatory publications, must make, in time, a deep impression on the section of the Union where they freely circulate, and are mainly designed to have effect. The well informed and thoughtful may hold them in contempt, but the young, the inexperienced, the ignorant and thoughtless, will receive the poison. In process of time, when the number of proselytes is sufficiently multiplied, the artful and the profligate, who are ever on the watch to seize on any means, however wicked and dangerous, will unite with the fanatics and make their movements the basis of a powerful political party, that will seek advancement by diffusing, as widely as possible, hatred against the slave-holding States. But as hatred begets hatred and animosity, these feelings would become reciprocal till every vestige of attachment would cease to exist between the two sections, when the Union and the Constitution, the offspring of mutual affection and confidence, would forever perish. Such is the danger to which the movements of the Abolitionists expose the country. If the force of the obligation is in proportion to the magnitude of the danger, stronger cannot be imposed than is at present on the States within whose limits the danger originates, to arrest its further progress—a duty they owe not only to the States whose institutions are assailed, but to the Union and Constitution, as has been shown, and it may be added, to themselves."

But Mr. Calhoun, as a States right Democrat, clearly perceived that the General Government had no right to legislate upon a subject of this character, save by claiming authority not delegated in the Federal Constitution. The assumption of such power would end in that consolidation of the Government, which he and the other leaders of his political school had so persistently battled, from the earliest organization of the Jefferson Republican party. On this point, in the same report, he reasoned as follows:

"Nothing is more clear than that the admission of the right of Congress to determine what papers are incendiary, and as such, to prohibit their circulation through the mail, necessarily involves the right to determine what are not incendiary, and enforce their circulation. If Congress may this year decide what incendiary publications are, they may next year decide what they are not, and thus laden the mails with real or corrupt abolitionism. It belongs to the States, and not to Congress, to determine what is or what is not calculated to disturb their security."

It was thus proposed that it should be within the province of each State, to say for itself, what kind of reading it would deem incendiary, and that Congress should prohibit the transmission of such matter to that State. A bill for this purpose was submitted as follows:

"Be it enacted, etc., that it shall not be lawful for any deputy postmaster in any State, Territory or District of the United States, knowingly to deliver to any person whatsoever, any pamphlet, newspaper, handbill, or other printed paper or pictorial representation touching the subject of slavery, where, by the laws of the said State, Territory or District their circulation is prohibited; and any deputy postmaster who shall be guilty thereof, shall be forthwith removed from office."

The above bill was ordered to a third reading in the Senate by the vote of 18 yeas to 18 nays, Vice-President Van Buren giving the casting vote in the affirmative; but it failed on the final vote, and, as a consequence, never became a law. And thus ended the effort to exclude the abolition literature of the age from passing through the Federal mails. The moral victory thus gained by the Abolitionists was of incalculable advantage to them and their cause in all their subsequent movements, for they seemed to stand forth before the world as the champions of free speech and a free press, which all the power of President Jackson and his followers were unable to suppress. The *eclat* of the victory resounded far and wide, and became as it were the watchword in other conflicts of like character.

The first great battle of abolitionism had been fought in the Halls of the National Congress. Others of equal importance were soon to be decided, but upon a less august arena; but in all the same principles were in dispute. The demand of the Southern States that discussion should be suppressed on the slavery question, was one altogether in seeming disharmony with the generally received principles of republican liberty. On the 2d of February, 1836, a bill was reported in the Legislature of Rhode Island for the purpose of repressing slavery agitation in the borders of the State. The attempt thus to muzzle free speech appeared to liberal-minded men, an effort as it were, to turn back the dial of the age, and as this was impossible, the Abolitionists had, as allies, the advocates of progressive and independent free thought. The small State of Rhode Island, accordingly, arrayed itself through the efforts of George Curtis and Thomas W. Dorr, in opposition to southern demands. In New York a report was adopted by the Legislature in May, 1836, responding to the sentiments of Governor Marcy's Message, already cited, and pledging the faith of the State to enact such laws whenever they shall be requisite. But it is doubtful if even then, or at any subsequent time, such legislation could have been secured, for the belief in free speech is one of the cardinal principles of all who believe in the democratic form of government.

But of all the Legislative collisions between those favoring the repression af anti-slavery agitation, and the friends of free speech, that which took place in Massachusetts in 1836, was the most fiercely contested, and arrayed in opposition to each other, the ablest and most eloquent opponents. A joint committee of both

Houses of the Legislature had been raised to report upon the Southern demands, and of this committee Senator Lunt was chairman. The anti-slavery committee at Boston were notified to appear and make their defense on March 4th. A few prominent men appeared on the side of the Abolitionists, and were heard by the committee in defense of their principles. Those who spoke took the ground that free speech was one of the unalienable rights of every citizen of the old Commonwealth. Prof. Charles Folen in the course of his remarks alluded to some outrages that had recently been perpetrated against the Abolitionists, and averred that any legislative interposition of the kind proposed, would simply invite a repetition of what had occurred. The chairman of the committee at this point silenced the speaker, as reflecting offensively upon the legislative body of the State, and terminated the interview. Such proceeding could have but one effect upon minds conscious of rectitude of intention, and attached to American freedom. Much as they might dread slavery agitation in its effects, they could not consent to see the right of free speech frustrated. A Boston editor in giving an account of the proceedings contended that the Abolitionists were entitled to a fair hearing. During the next two days they issued their defense in a pamphlet of over forty pages; and a copy of this was soon in the hands of every member of the Legislature, and scattered throughout the whole country. The committee was directed by the Legislature to allow the Abolitionists to complete their defense on the 8th of March. The adjacent country was now aroused, and the Hall of the House of Representatives where the committee sat was crowded at the hearing. Prof. Folen concluded his defense and was followed by William Lloyd Garrison and others. William Goodel, one of the speakers, charged upon the Southern States a conspiracy against the liberty of the free North. He was repeatedly called to order; but alluding to the documents from the South, lying on the table, he styled them fetters and remarked: "Mr. Chairman! are you prepared to attempt putting them on?" He was interrupted by the Chairman and ordered to take his seat. He sat down amidst the great agitation of the assemblage. The bold words of freedom had already produced their effect upon the crowd of spectators. The dauntless divine, William E. Channing, was one of that assembly, and though not identified with the Abolitionists, yet in the battle for free speech, he could not be an indifferent spectator. His countenance alone served to indicate the side he espoused, and his presence on this occasion, more than all else perhaps, gave weight and respectability to the abolition cause. After the last named speaker had been silenced, all was in considerable confusion for a time, when a couple of independent spectators rose, one after the other, and remarked, that "*the freedom of speech and of the press could never be surrendered by the sons of the Pilgrims.*" The committee then adjourned, but the victory was again complete with the Abolitionists. And thus ended in Massachusetts all attempts to legislate adverse to the demands of freedom.

One of the methods pursued by the Abolitionists to arouse the attention of the American people to the enormity of slavery, was the petitioning of Congress for its abolition in the District of Columbia, in the National Territories, and also for the suppression of the inter-State slave trade. At an early period in the history of the Government, it had been solemnly determined that Congress had no jurisdiction over the question of slavery, as it existed within the States. But as regards its existence in the Federal District and the Territories, it was believed by many that Congress had the right to interfere. The points of attack for the agitators were therefore limited; and even as to these it was a matter of divided opinion whether Congress had the moral right to interpose its authority. The main object, however, of petitioning Congress, was to keep alive the agitation of the slavery question, in order to educate public opinion up to an opposition to the southern institution, and in that manner create a sentiment that would effect its overthrow. For this purpose, in 1835 and 1836, Congress was flooded with petitions praying for the abolition of slavery in the Federal District, in the Territories, and also for the suppression of the inter-State slave commerce. These, taken in connection with the excitement that had already been aroused by the transmission of incendiary publications through the national mails, were the occasion of great commotion in Washington, the seat of the General Government. The number of the petitioners and the zeal manifested by them in such a cause, had the effect of alarming men both North and South as to the safety of the Federal Union. The right of petition for a redress of grievances, was one which existed by constitutional warrant, and any abridgment of this privilege should be cautiously and only after full deliberation, adopted. As the right generally was viewed, it was one that authorized the citizens to petition for the removal of evils affecting themselves, and their section of country. In the case of the Abolitionists, they were asking for the abridgment of the constitutional and vested rights of citizens equally entitled to the protection of the Government as themselves. They were demanding the suppression of slavery, where it existed by virtue of law and the constitution; and in this view, Congress considered that the petitioners had transcended their rights.

It became a matter of long and animated discussion what disposition should be made of these petitions. The presentation by James Buchanan, in 1836, of the memorial of the Caln Quarterly Meeting of Friends asking for the abolition of slavery in the District of Columbia, brought the question of these petitions prominently before Congress. As far as can be gathered from the debates in the Senate at that period, no member of this body appears to have favored the sentiments of the memorialists. The question, however was, how to dispose of the petitions. John C. Calhoun expressed the southern view, upon this occasion, in the following language:

> "We must not permit those we represent to be thus insulted on this floor. He stood prepared, whenever petitions like these were presented, to call for their reading, and to demand that they be not received. His object was to prevent a dangerous agitation which threatened to burst asunder the bond of the Union. The only question was, how was agitation to be avoided? He held that receiving these petitions encouraged agitation, the most effectual mode to destroy the peace and harmony of the Union."

Mr. Buchanan held the conservative attitude on this question, and whilst opposed to the sentiments of the petitioners, he denied that Congress had the right to refuse their reception, and insisted that the true method was to act upon and reject them. His plan was adopted in the Senate by 34 yeas to 6 nays. Substantially the same manner of disposing of these petitions was pursued in the House of Representatives. In 1836, on motion of H. L. Pinckney, of South Carolina, a resolution was adopted to refer all anti-slavery memorials now before the House, or that might come before it, to a Select Committee, with instruction to report against the prayers of the petitioners, and the reasons for so doing. On the 18th of May, 1836, the committee, through Mr.

Pinckney, its Chairman, unanimously reported a series of resolutions, the last of which was as follows:

"*Resolved*, That all petitions, memorials, resolutions, propositions or papers, relating in any way or to any extent whatever to the subject of slavery or the abolition of slavery, shall, without being either printed or referred, be laid upon the table, and that no further action whatever shall be had thereon."

The above resolution was adopted by 117 yeas to 68 nays, the latter being chiefly Whigs from the free States. Resolutions to control or allay the abolition excitement were adopted annually by nearly similar votes to the above until 1840, when the substance of these was incorporated amongst the standing rules of the House of Representatives. The rule known as the twenty-first, which excluded the abolition petitions remained in force until December, 1845, when through the persistent efforts of John Quincy Adams it was finally rescinded.

The northern Whigs, in the main, had opposed these resolutions as too strongly violating the right of petition. Many of the Whigs from the free States were hostile to the avowed principles of the Abolitionists; but they became their allies, so far as to strive for their right of petition, an invaluable advantage to them at this stage of the controversy. The privilege became a shield, under the cover of which many an unavowed Abolitionist, was able to make assaults upon southern institutions. The division of parties upon this question serves to show why it was that the Abolition element of the North still clung to the Whig instead of the Democratic party.

On this question, Thaddeus Stevens, though not yet become a national legislator, was one of the most ardent advocates of the constitutional right of petition; and that such was his position he during these congressional contests, gave frequent testimony in his speeches in the Pennsylvania Legislature and elsewhere. Whilst a member of the Legislature, at Harrisburg, so enthusiastically did he champion the abolitionists right of petition, and their free mail privilege with other citizens, that the contest on these questions for a time would have seemed as if transferred from the Halls of the National Congress to those of the Pennsylvania Assembly. And in this manner it was that he had much to do in imparting tone to the northern Whig members of Congress in their resistance to the demands of the South. Thus the propriety of incorporating, in a work treating of Mr. Stevens, a view of the anti-slavery movement, that preceded his entry into Congress is seen, when his influence as a molder of public sentiment is considered. But for such as he there would have been no movement to call forth the action of Congress and of State Legislatures as we have observed took place. Mr. Stevens could with truth have remarked of the great social convulsion and gathering revolution of his country, "*quorum pars magna fui.*"

CHAPTER VI.

REMOVAL OF MR. STEVENS TO LANCASTER. HIS SUCCESS AS A LAWYER AND HIS MOVEMENTS AS A POLITICIAN.

Notwithstanding Mr. Stevens, up to 1842, had mingled considerably in politics, having been repeatedly elected, as we have seen, to the Pennsylvania House of Representatives, yet more fortunate than most politicians, he was able to retain a firm grasp upon his legal practice. Before his entry upon public life at Harrisburg, he had laid the foundation of a fine legal practice, and this (though absent at the State Capitol during the winter months) rather continued to increase than diminish. The obstacle with many lawyers, who would willingly enter into politics is, that doing so breaks up their business, and having little or nothing to fall back upon, they choose rather to keep out of the entanglements of political life. Not many American statesmen have ever been distinguished as lawyers, and this because but few possess the varied talents that are adapted for these different careers. A man may be admirably suited for the politician, and yet would find himself unable to cope with the weighty men who try the important causes in our civil and criminal courts. And on the contrary, not every successful lawyer would shine upon the floors of Congress, or even in the Halls of our State Legislatures. A peculiar structure of mind is needed for each of these pursuits; and he whose qualities fit him for the one, often finds something lacking when he enters upon the other. Mr. Stevens, however, had qualities that enabled him to attain a front position, whether at the bar or in the halls of legislation, and yet it cannot be denied that he most of all towered at the bar. It was in this calling that his best energies were expended; and here also many of his most intellectual victories were achieved.

After the termination of his services in the Pennsylvania Legislature, several motives contributed to induce him to remove from Adams and locate in Lancaster County. His practice at the

Gettysburg bar could in no probability ever become so profitable as he might secure in a county so wealthy and populous as Lancaster. Besides the fine field offered in this latter place for the practice of his profession, it was a county strongly of his political sentiments, and this was a consideration in his view not to be overlooked. These, no doubt, were amongst the leading motives that induced his removal from Gettysburg to Lancaster City. It was in August, 1842, that he reached this latter place, and he immediately opened an office and began the practice of the profession in his new home. Some time prior to his arrival, it had become known that he intended to change his location, and certain articles appeared in the Lancaster papers, eulogizing Mr. Stevens as a man of towering abilities, and as a lawyer of rare sagacity and shrewdness. His arrival soon became known amongst the people of Lancaster County, and it is related that many of them came to the County-seat to obtain a sight of the man of whose fame they had already heard so much. He was kindly received in his new location by the citizens generally, although in the main bearing the reputation of being a tricky and unscrupulous politician. His extraordinary talents were upon all sides conceded; and this reputation procured for him kind and courteous treatment amongst all classes. He was, most of all, viewed with suspicion by the members of the bar, who are never disposed to look with favor upon new arrivals in the profession, and such as may divide business with themselves. But in Mr. Stevens they saw more than an ordinary additional attorney who was come to secure amongst them his living at the bar. In him they recognized a man ready and competent to cope with the ablest of them in litigious warfare; and one who might even be disposed to wrest the sceptre of superiority from the most distinguished of their number. It is not strange, therefore, that his arrival in Lancaster was anything but agreeable to the wishes of the members of one of the oldest and most renowned bars of Pennsylvania. But gifted as he was with the sagacity needed in situations such as he was then placed, he did not seem to observe the jealousy of his brother barristers, but simply attended to his own business, as if altogether unconcerned for their opinions regarding himself. The jealousy was most intense on the part of the older lawyers, those who had taken the lead in business prior to his arrival. With the younger members of the profession, he was rather an object of esteem; for as they did not feel themselves able to compete with him, they were disposed to admire him rather than those who were jealous of his superior ability.

Samuel Parke, Reah Frazer, William B. Fordney and John R. Montgomery were amongst the leading Lancaster lawyers of that period. There were besides, many others of considerable legal ability. The Lancaster bar had for years held the rank of one of the first in the State of Pennsylvania. Many names of wide repute had practiced in the old inland city—James Hopkins, Molton C. Rodgers, Jasper Slaymaker, William Jenkins, James Buchanan, Amos Ellmaker and George B. Porter, had all gained their reputations, as practitioners, at this old bar of German Pennsylvania. These last named had chiefly retired from practice when Mr. Stevens made his appearance in his new location. Benjamin Champneys was upon the bench, but shortly afterwards resigned this position, having been nominated by his party for the State Senate, to which he was also elected. His place was filled shortly after his resignation by the appointment of Ellis Lewis, a lawyer of deep reading, and withal, a man of rare native sagacity.

At the August Sessions, in 1842, the first at which Mr. Stevens made his appearance, he volunteered his services in behalf of a colored man from Columbia who was indicted for assault and battery with intent to kill. This was the first case in which he appeared before a Lancaster County jury, and he handled it with great ability, but the evidence being too clear, his client was convicted and sentenced to an imprisonment for five years. His fixed reputation immediately brought him business, and it was not long till he had an opportunity of grappling with the leading men of the Lancaster bar. Their first encounters with him exhibited most intense feeling, and their weapons not always hurled with courtly grace, sped as if impelled with savage malignity. One of the first who met the new Achilles of the bar, in an important civil case was Benjamin Champneys, who, before his elevation to the bench, had ranked as one of the ablest lawyers of the State. Those who relate the circumstances of this trial, and the fierce combat of words it elicited, have likened it to the fatal scene between Hector and the conquering Pelides. The contest was warm, vigorous and spirited; the dexterous combattants hurled and counter-hurled, parried and counter-parried the weapons, that flew across the arena of forensic strife; but the superior prowess of the adventurous knight, though in the territory of his antagonist, soon convinced all observers that whilst victory might not in this encounter perch upon his banner, yet that the claim of dominion would surely pass to the invading chevalier of the bar. This first encounter but gave assurance that others to follow would be with like result, for one after another, of the old knights of the Lancaster bar were met and stript of the fame they had long worn with credit, and the exultant warrior rode triumphant over the new field of his conquests and future fortune. In six months after Mr. Stevens arrived in Lancaster, there was no member of that bar that dared to dispute his intellectual and legal kingship. He was crowned by common consent, and wore the diadem to his grave.

At the first session of the Supreme Court, held at Harrisburg in May, 1843, after his location in Lancaster, he appeared in four of the six cases from Lancaster County, that were tried at that time. He was also engaged with Meredith, of Philadelphia, at the same term, in the important case of the Commonwealth vs. the Pennsylvania Canal Commissioners. A success such as this has scarcely a parallel in history. A new lawyer locating in a strange county, without friends or social influence, and taking the lead at a bar where there were several able, experienced and accomplished members of the profession, is one of those events of history that have rarely transpired, and which will be as seldom repeated. Such marvelous success, more than all else, stamps him who has accomplished it as one of the prodigies of creation. In May, 1844, at the following session of the Supreme Court held in the same place, out of eight cases from Lancaster County Mr. Stevens appeared in six of them, besides being employed in two from Adams and also one from Franklin County. His practice was now become very large and lucrative, and ranged for years from twelve to fifteen thousand dollars per year. He was employed in many of the most important suits tried in different parts of the State.

The custom of making lengthy speeches before the court and jury, was one of long standing with the Lancaster lawyers, before Mr. Stevens located in their midst. When a cause was to be tried, they were in the habit of bringing into the court room, law books by the wheelbarrow load and piling them upon the tables, and reading one authority after another for the support of the plainest and most common principles of the science. Sometimes a case would consume a day or more in the arguments of legal points, that were little illuminated by the long and tedious discussion. The custom was an old one and inherited from their predecessors; and the lawyer who should not have conformed to it, would have lost, in the opinion of his client, the credit of possessing the requisite legal knowledge for the trial of an important case. It remained for the new dictator of the bar to abolish the pernicious habit of speech-making by the day, and long-winded arguments. After Ellis Lewis was appointed to the bench, Stevens having a case for trial came into court one morning and observed the tables stocked with law books, and his legal adversary busily engaged in looking them over and preparing them for citation. Judge Lewis was already upon the bench, but the court had not yet been formally opened. Stevens remarked, loud enough to be distinctly heard, "What are all these books for?" Lewis replied, that he believed they were to be used on the trial of the case now before the court. Stevens rejoined that He "did not know who wanted to listen to the reading of all those books." Lewis then remarked: "Mr. Stevens, you are something of my opinion; that a lawyer should carry the law in his head and not always depend on his books." The opposing counsel heard all this conversation, and its effect was magical. It was the last time the tables were crowded with law books upon the trial of a case. Afterwards only such books were produced as contained authority directly applicable to the points at issue before the court in the case then being tried. Mr. Stevens never made lengthy speeches before either the court or jury in the trial of cases in which he was concerned; and in this he was also imitated by the other members of the bar. The making of long speeches soon disappeared, and no regrets were ever felt for the departure.

Mr. Stevens was gifted with a remarkable memory. In the trial of a cause he very rarely wrote down any of the evidence, as is customary with ordinary lawyers, trusting to their memory for the remembrance of all the important facts required in their arguments before the court and jury. He possessed the rare faculty of being able to perceive, as if by intuition, the real point of every case; and all his efforts in the elicitation of evidence was to support this view of it. Instead of wasting his time in drawing out of the witnesses all the possible evidence, and exhausting his energies in writing down the same, Mr. Stevens, having a clear conception of the point to be supported, simply sought for evidence for this purpose. He rarely or never took notes of the evidence, but often made a few strokes to induce the opposing counsel to suppose that he was doing so. But his memory was so powerful that often when a dispute arose among counsel, as to the exact language used by a witness, he would appeal to the judge's notes; and in such instances he was found almost invariably accurate in his recollection of the evidence. Had his memory not been so powerful as it was, he should surely have proved a failure as a lawyer, for he neither wrote with rapidity nor was his chirography even to himself, much less to others, always legible.

In his legal arguments he likewise confined his attention, in the main, to the turning point of his case, and brought it out in all the clearness which his great ability was capable of doing; and to this method he was more indebted, perhaps, for his splendid success in his profession than to any other reason that might be named. In this particular, his legal sagacity may in a sense be compared with the strategy of the great Napoleon who was in the habit of concentrating all the force of his assaulting columns upon one point of the enemy's lines, and this being broken, rout and disorder followed. Stevens, in like manner, as it were, by being able to see the point upon which a case must turn, and by so shaping the testimony as to make it bear directly in support of that position, was able to carry the victory over an opponent less dexterous than he, in the marshalling and argumentation of the evidence. Hence, though a remarkably successful lawyer, he never wearied the court with his arguments, nor the jury by a tedious recapitulation of useless evidence.

Upon one occasion, on the trial of a cause, one of his witnesses had detailed important testimony consisting of a statement of facts that had transpired many years in the past. This witness was subjected to a rigid cross-examination by the opposing counsel, with the view of impairing his testimony, by showing his deficient recollection of facts altogether of no consequence, and having no bearing upon the trial of the case, and only intended to perplex the witness, and produce the impression upon the jury that his evidence was unreliable. Mr. Stevens, seeing the delusion that was attempted to be produced, utterly discomfited his legal antagonist by simply propounding in his humorous tone, (itself revealing his design) the following question: "Mr.———, had you a pin in your coat collar that morning?" The court and jury at once saw the hit, and the effect was damaging to his adversary. His ability to disconcert an opposing attorney, in a trial, by some witty remark, as by asking a witness a question eliciting laughter, was of incalculable value in his professional career. Ridicule, which is often more potent than argument, he had entirely at his command. All these appliances of his intellectual ability gave him an advantage over other men equally able and learned as himself, but unendowed with mental traits of this nature.

As regards the knowledge of law Mr. Stevens was not so remarkable. There were other lawyers in Lancaster who were quite as well if not better read in their profession than he; his great strength was with the jury in being able to present the strong points of a case in a more powerful manner than it was the faculty of most other lawyers to do. Before the Supreme Court of Pennsylvania, he could scarcely be said to be more successful than any other able well-read lawyer. His consciousness of ability gave him confidence in himself, and he was ready to express an opinion upon almost any case without examination. Owing to this disposition he allowed careful lawyers, who examine their cases before giving an opinion upon them, the opportunity of entrapping him and carrying cases against him, often with ease. There have been instances where, having no confidence in a case, he allowed the whole management of it in the Supreme Court to a colleague, and the latter was successful in opposition to his opinions. His great power as a lawyer, consisted in his being able to influence ordinary minds and control them to his advantage.

Some of Mr. Stevens' finest and most eloquent speeches as a lawyer, were those made on trials in defense of fugitive slaves. Even before his arrival in Lancaster, he was widely known as a most violent opponent of southern institutions; and from his settlement in Lancaster County, he was almost uniformly retained in the defense of the fugitives. It was not every lawyer, at that period, that desired to be employed in the defense of a case of that character. The slave master was fortified by legal enactment; and the Constitution guaranteeing the surrender of fugitives from service, public opinion generally sanctioned the enforcement of the law. It was only the extreme Abolitionists who dared to resist the claims of the master; but these, as yet, had little influence, neither of the great political parties of the country having espoused even their moderate principles as national organizations. On one occasion, a negro had been brought before Judge Lewis in Lancaster, under the Pennsylvania Act of 1826, and there being no evidence to show that he was a slave, he was discharged. Mr. Stevens was employed in this case by the friends of the negro. After the discharge, the claimant was advised to have the negro re-arrested under an old Act of Congress, which required no evidence except the oath of the owner of the slave. As soon, therefore, as he was discharged, an officer took him in custody upon a writ issued by Alderman Osterloe. Stevens, having been informed of this, went before the magistrate; and his speech before this officer is said to have been one of the finest gems of eloquence ever delivered by him in Lancaster. The negro, however, was discharged by the magistrate, after official evidence of the former trial before the court had been certified to him.

But it is as a politician that Mr. Stevens is most widely known; and of his actions in this particular it remains for us to speak, since the period of his removal from Gettysburg to Lancaster. As soon as he had settled in his new home, a circle of politicians gathered around him and deferred to him at once as their counsellor and adviser. Those who flocked to his standard were politicians for the most part of the Anti-Masonic persuasion, who had chiefly lost position in their party, and who wanted a leader to make head against those who controlled the affairs of the country. Anti-Masonry had for years been simply a name, the great majority of those who had once rallied under its banner were attached to the Whig party, now risen to national importance and respect, under the leadership of Clay and Webster. Stevens himself had for years been nominally attached to the Whig party, and had, in 1840, supported Harrison for President.

"In the great campaign of 1840, Mr. Stevens took a decided stand in favor of the 'Hero of the Thames.' For months before the nomination of Harrison, it was understood throughout Pennsylvania, that Mr. Stevens was to have a seat in the Cabinet. That Harrison had selected him for Post-Master General is known with certainity, but through the open opposition of Clay and the wavering of Webster, the appointment was given to Granger. Stevens never forgave Webster for the part he took in this transaction."*

But though united to the Whig party, Mr. Stevens found himself powerless in this organization. Having showed himself an ardent Anti-Mason, he encountered violent antipathies amongst the Whigs on account of old animosities aroused by his course against the ancient order. He was besides, viewed by the great body of the Whig leaders as too violent and impracticable a man to be entrusted with the management of the party affairs. Even before leaving Adams County, this was the opinion generally entertained of him by the leading minds of his own party. He was able to control in a measure the party organization in Adams County, but he met with strenuous resistance amongst his political friends as soon as he attempted to influence beyond the bounds of the county. But for this resistance there is little doubt but he would have appeared in the State Senate of Pennsylvania, and also in Congress, whilst a citizen of Gettysburg. No sooner, therefore, had he appeared in Lancaster than the same Whig opposition met him, and was potential in keeping him in the political background of his party. By the fall of 1843 a sufficient nucleus of strength, however, had gathered around him, as to induce him to believe that he might inaugurate the political game with his Whig friends for the control of Lancaster County. He dared not to stand idle. He must act unless he chose to remain a zero upon the chess-board of political strategy. Having no strength in his own party, his first aim was to secure such. Most of those who operated with him were equally ignored by the Whig leaders, and, therefore, there was nothing to be lost in making an effort to obtain that recognition which they sought.

It was resolved, at the suggestion of Mr. Stevens, to make an effort to revive the Anti-Masonic party in the county. It cannot be supposed that a man of his sagacious mind, could have believed that this was possible, at a period when the old organization had years ago sunk into obscurity, and was already well nigh forgotten. But it served in this case as the basis of a movement to divert

Biographical History of Lancaster County, pp. 582.

votes from the Whig party in the county. The object hoped to be gained by this, was to withdraw sufficient strength from the controlling Whig party, so as to permit the Democrats to carry the victory in the county. Could the Stevens wing effect this they were then in a condition to dictate the terms of compromise. Accordingly, a ticket was placed in nomination, but the Democrats of the county having been beaten for so long a time, failed to rally in their strength at the October election of 1843, and the Whigs again carried the victory by a considerable majority. The new movement polled about 1,400 votes, but falling short of securing a Democratic triumph, the leaders were prostrated beneath the power of their opponents. Stevens was now fully shorn of any political strength he might have had, and was forced for a time to content himself to be simply a voter of the Whig party, if he chose to remain in it, or to make choice of a new organization with which to act.

The Whig party of Lancaster County was almost a unit for Henry Clay for President in 1844. About the time that Mr. Stevens and his associates were planning the resuscitation of Anti-Masonry in the county, a monster Whig meeting was held in Lancaster City, July 29th, 1843, for the purpose of recommending their favorite Clay as the Whig candidate for President in 1844. William Hiester presided over this meeting, and speeches were made by Morton McMichael, Abraham Herr Smith and others; but Mr. Stevens had no invitation to participate in this movement. When Clay was made the nominee of the party it was deemed by the leaders politic to have all their partisans to unite in support of the candidate; but Stevens being inimical to the great orator of Kentucky, Harmar Denny was entrusted with the task of reconciling him with the nomination. Denny assured him that he was authorized by the Whig candidate to say that in case of his election, "atonement would be made for past wrong." It could not be claimed, however, that Mr. Stevens entered into the support of Henry Clay with any enthusiasm, although giving him his public endorsement upon the rostrum and elsewhere. Political success was clearly his guiding star; and it is necessary for politicians to shape their craft so as to sail as much as possible with the breeze, otherwise their hopes of fortune would soon end in disappointment and despair. He made some speeches in the campaign of 1844, and in these placed himself fairly upon the platform of the National Whig party. During the campaign he was invited with Webster and other distinguished leaders of the party, to address the great Whig meeting in Philadelphia; and the assemblage being very large, whilst Webster was speaking to the people, another stand was erected at some distance from the main platform, and Mr. Stevens was invited thence to address his fellow-citizens. He mounted the newly erected rostrum, and being gifted with those indispensable qualities of the popular orator, wit and anecdote, he is said to have been able upon that occasion to attract to his speaking most of those who had been listening to the great Massachusetts statesman. But ardently as was Henry Clay supported by his party throughout the country, the election resulted in the choice of James K. Polk as President of the United States.

Although Stevens and his followers supported Clay for President in 1844, the division in the party in the county was nevertheless kept up. There are generally two factions in each party in every county; and that Mr. Stevens was able from the first to become the dictator of the one of these in the Whig party, is evidence of his power as a political manipulator. Although greatly in the minority at first, it was the foundation of what afterwards obtained the control of Lancaster County, and which placed Mr. Stevens upon the highway of his political success. But the weakness of his influence in the county in 1844, was apparent in the nomination of John Strohm for Congress, in that year. Mr. Strohm had for years ranked as one of the principal leaders of the Whig faction opposed to Stevens. As Senator from Lancaster County, he was one of those who in December, 1838, failed to sympathize with Mr. Stevens in his course at Harrisburg, during the period of the "Buckshot War;" and who also voted for the recognition of the Hopkins' House of Representatives. To see one with these opinions nominated to Congress, was galling to Mr. Stevens in the extreme; but John Strohm was a man of unimpeachable reputation; and whose high regard for probity had become proverbial. His course at Harrisburg in the winter of 1838, had at first subjected him to considerable censure from his political friends, even in his own county; but a reaction soon set in, as the facts became better understood, and his action was at length fully endorsed by the majority of the Whig party of Lancaster County. His nomination for Congress in

1844, was generally, therefore, viewed as an attestation of that fact; as also an evidence of the entire approval by his party of his whole previous career as a public man.

Mr. Stevens, in this condition of affairs, could do little else than attend to his legal business and gradually strengthen himself amongst the citizens of the county. His ability as a lawyer gradually introduced him to a wide circle of acquaintances; and this had the effect of enhancing his political power. An element of political strength, in favor of Mr. Stevens, not to be overlooked, was found in the large number of young men who studied law in his office and under his instructions. A greater number of young men studied the elements of the profession under his instruction, than with any other member of the bar who ever before practiced in the inland City of Lancaster. Although not all of these were members of his own political party, yet the majority naturally being such, and these being greatly devoted to him and his success, were ready upon any occasion to buckle on their armor and march to the conflict when the interests of their tutor were at stake. But few men have ever had the faculty of securing more devoted and more ardent followers than he. His students were almost equally attached to him, as children to a father; at least, this was the case with a great majority of them. This was not altogether unnatural. Young men in the selection of a legal preceptor, generally endeavor to choose one whose reputation may enhance their own prospect of success by a kind of radiation of fame, as it might be termed. Although in the main delusive, yet the impression has its weight in the choice of the man with whom the profession is, as a rule, studied. In the case of Mr. Stevens, the rule also obtained; and as advantage was anticipated by originally selecting him as their instructor, the more they could add to his reputation by their efforts, would still extend, as they conceived, that reflection of fame that might illumine themselves. Of students who had studied with Mr. Stevens, or who became associated in legal practice with him, and whose influence perhaps more aided him in his after political career than any other individuals, were Alexander H. Hood and Oliver J. Dickey, both men of admitted native capacity. Both of these men were ardently attached to Mr. Stevens. The former, a political editor, and also a member of the Legislature, had studied law with him, having entered his office as a student shortly after his arrival in Lancaster; and the latter was the son of one of his old political associates as a member of the Board of Canal Commissioners of Pennsylvania, and who as a leader in the Anti-Masonic party, had been strongly attached to him. Mr. Dickey visited Lancaster in 1846 and became associated with Mr. Stevens in the practice of the profession; and this union proved the foundation of a life-long attachment between them.

By 1848, Mr. Stevens, having extended his acquaintance in all parts of the county, felt himself strong enough to aim at the nomination for Congress in the Lancaster District. Although he had many friends attached to him, he nevertheless had a powerful opposition to combat. The old Whig leaders were mostly opposed to his nomination for Congress, as were also the principal organs of the party, the *Examiner*, published by E. C. Darlington, and the *Volksfreund*, a German newspaper. But both factions of the Whig party in the county had endorsed the nomination of Gen. Taylor for President, as the most available candidate that could be presented. This endorsement seemed for the time to indicate the complete union of the Lancaster County Whigs; and Stevens was sufficiently sagacious to see the advantage to be gained in this lull of the storm. A large Whig meeting was held in Lancaster for the purpose of endorsing the nomination of Zachary Taylor for the Presidency. Stevens and his friends were the strong advocates of the objects of this meeting. Emanuel C. Reighart, an influential Whig, a man of high social standing, and one who had never openly committed himself to the interests of Mr. Stevens, assumed at this meeting, in the name of the party, and in view of the subsisting harmony of all factions, to publicly nominate him as a candidate for Congress. This had the effect of directing public attention to him, as an aspirant for Congressional honors.

But the leaders of that part of the Whig party which hitherto opposed Mr. Stevens were not ready to acquiesce in that kind of nomination for a Congressional candidate. It was altogether an unusual manner of placing a candidate before the party for this office, and besides, there were individuals in their section of the party whom they preferred to see elected to Congress. It was not to be supposed, therefore, that they would tamely submit to a nomination in which the choice of the people had not been consulted; and especially, where the candidate was a stranger in the county, and one who a few years before had been engaged in an effort to defeat the nominees of their party. Abraham Herr Smith, a young lawyer of promise, belonging to one of the oldest and most influential families of the county, who had served with credit for two sessions in the Pennsylvania House of Representatives, and was just closing a term in the State Senate, was induced to become a candidate for the Congressional nomination in opposition to Mr. Stevens. Candidates at that period were generally nominated in conventions of their party, the delegates to which were elected by the party votes in the different districts. Primary elections were, therefore, in accordance with this recognized rule of the party, held all over the County of Lancaster, and the respective friends of one or the other candidate returned to the convention. In several of the districts special instructions had been given to the delegates for which one of the two candidates they should cast their votes. By the returns from the several districts, Mr. Smith appeared as having received a clear majority of the delegates of the county, and his nomination before the assembling of the convention was by himself and his friends regarded as quite certain. The balloting in the convention, however, disappointed the anticipations of all parties, and Mr. Stevens was nominated by one of a majority. Some of the delegates in the convention from one or more of the districts, violated their instructions by voting for Mr. Stevens, thus giving him the Congressional nomination, according to the accepted rules of the party.

What peculiar agencies contributed to this first nomination of Mr. Stevens for Congress, it is not within the reach of history definitely to determine. The trait of character, as given by Alexander H. Hood in his sketch of Mr. Stevens, in the Biographical History of Lancaster County, may have somewhat contributed to the result: "Beggars of all grades, high or low, are very quick in finding out the weak points of those on whom they intend to operate; and Mr. Stevens was always, but more particularly when he was a candidate, most unmercifully fleeced. This trait was the cause of injury to the politics of this country. Before he was nominated for Congress, no one here thought of spending large sums of money in order to get votes. Now, no man, whatever his qualifications, can be nominated for any office, unless he answers all demands made upon him, and forks over a greater amount than any one else will, for the same office. It is a most deplorable state of things, but the fact is not to be denied."*

Some reflections, are in this connection submitted, as explanatory of conduct that has attached odium to the character of Mr. Stevens, but which rather flowed from the spirit of the times in which he lived. All truthful history, is but subsidiary to the development of higher forms of culture, and a more enlarged comprehension of the mysterious design of creative power. So it is believed a delineation of the errors of men and nations but lead to a clearer apprehension of the truth, that all are anxiously seeking. Men's mistakes, whether wilfull or otherwise, demonstrate the necessity for settled rules of action. The world and its intelligence are advancing. Perfection in civilization is being more nearly approximated, but perhaps will never be fully realized. Government is the form of social organism, that has from the earliest ages, engaged much of man's attention. Whether the product of reason or of divine dispensation is not determined; neither of its primary forms, pure monarchy, aristocracy or democracy seem to satisfy the advancing intelligence of the human race; and an eclecticism of these has in modern times amongst civilized nations given the most general satisfaction. But that form which is most condusive to the interests of a true civilization, seems as yet, to be but faintly realized. The admirable system of government adopted for the United States, by our republican ancestors, proved for a period the noblest heritage of reason for the management of society, that perhaps the world has ever seen. The Government, however, presented by our revolutionary forefathers, was itself a combination of the original forms, and in such proportions as was then believed would, if properly observed, perpetuate liberty, justice and equity to the most distant posterity.

But there is less real difference between the forms of government, as regards their practical working, than is popularly supposed. In absolute monarchies, no one man, though nominally so, is entirely supreme. The influence of other intelligent men, besides the monarch, control the government. In democratic or republican forms of government, on the contrary, the intellectual men of the State are those again in whose hands the power chiefly resides. The mass of the people may or may not be

*Biographical History of Lancaster County, pp. 589.

voters, and their power in either case is not far from being equally balanced. In the one case they may be made the instruments of ambitious men for their own advancement and success, and perhaps even to the ruin of liberty. As Aristotle and Plato taught, society, like the human body, has its various members, and in both instances the directive power centers in the head. The intellectual men of a nation, under whatever form of government that may be adopted, are those who form the head of the State. The great aim in government is that a people be able to obtain wise and virtuous rulers, and the form under which these can be secured is of less consequence.

After the adoption of the Federal Constitution, although universal white suffrage was generally accepted, yet an intellectual supremacy obtained in the selection of the rulers which almost ignored the popular voice, save as by way of ratification so considered. High toned honor ruled this intellectual conclave of both political parties of the Union, and he who was unworthy of initiation into this unorganized circle, was unable to secure the objects of his ambition, and hence was an outcast of the body politic. The highest principles of chivalry formed the foundation stones upon which the edifice of rule had been erected, and a worthy applicant could scarce fail to receive that recognition to which his merits entitled him. As the nation grew and expanded, and wealth was accumulated, the people still kept insisting upon greater privileges and power, and the rulers gradually yielded to their demands. Large numbers of offices, that in the early history of the government had been filled by appointment, were subjected to popular elections. All this was more nearly meeting the popular demand, and abandoning the conservative attitude of the framers of our Republic. Popular education, it was urged, by those advocating the innovation, was the great anchor of free representative government, and that upon this the safety of a nation depended. But this refuge itself was based upon the assumed equality of men, which, however, all the observation and experience of ages had disproved. Equality before the law, and equality in fact, are quite different assumptions.

The seeming effort of modern advance, is entire freedom from all restraint, save what is self-imposed. Whether the world in the future will attain to this is unknown, but at this time it seems not yet prepared for it; and till such period of perfection arrives, government must be perpetuated. For minds capable of devising rules of social order, they should, as it would seem, be a rule to themselves. The more, therefore, power is shifted from the hands of the natural rulers and given into the possession of those requiring a subjecting influence, though this be but nominally, to such an extent, is the order of creative design reversed, and the principles of corruptive political life thence germinate. Herein, then, we have the causes which about the period that Mr. Stevens was first nominated to Congress, induced the introduction of the elements of political corruption. Political power was found in the possession of the people more than at any former period of history. To obtain political position, it was no longer essential to secure the recognition of that chivalric intellectual body of men, that had hitherto so largely wielded the power of the nation. Other means about this time came to be effective in securing power. Wealth had become the most influential agent in society. Honor only influences intellectual and refined minds ; but that which now proved the most potential with the mass of society, was that which the aspirants for official place must employ.

The last years accordingly, of the history of the American Republic, have been submitting volumes of testimony as to the capacity of man for self government. The people are being surfeited with political power, but the mountains of iniquity and corruption that are arising amidst the vast upheaval of ages, are shocking the innate moral convictions of the race. But reason and right, those stern guides of the world, will yet be called upon to render their verdict upon the last phases of republican government, and remove the obstructions that still impede humanity's, progress, to a higher and a purer civilization.

CHAPTER VII.

AMERICAN POLITICAL PARTIES AND THEIR PRINCIPLES.

The Anti-Slavery movement in the northern States has already been adverted to, and the excitement occasioned thereby, considered in a preceding chapter at some length. It was not long after the agitation began until the Abolitionists conceived that it was necessary to unite the Anti-Slavery strength into a distinct political organization, and this was accomplished in the year 1840. As early as 1834, William Lloyd Garrison, speaking in the *Liberator* of the necessities of co-operation for the purpose of overthrowing slavery, remarked that, "a christian party in politics" was most of all things required. Prof. Charles Folen, two years afterwards, suggested the utility of a new political party of progress, the leading object of which should be the abolition of slavery. A distinctive party for the purpose of securing the cherished objects of abolitionism, was in 1839 urged by Alvan Stewart upon the Executive Committee of the New York State Anti-Slavery Society. All these expressions indicated what was becoming a somewhat prevalent opinion amongst the Abolitionists, that if they wished ever to be successful in the eradication of American Slavery, they must abandon all connection with the old parties, and organize a new one of different principles. As before stated, most of those who became avowed Abolition ists, came originally from the Whig party, or at least that one which was in opposition to the National Democracy.

All parties that have as yet existed in America, have belonged to one or other of two antagonistic schools, the founders of which were Thomas Jefferson and Alexander Hamilton. Hamilton was a member of the convention, which in 1787 formed the Federal Constitution; and in that body had the honesty and boldness to propose a form of government, copied after that of Great Britain, which he ever regarded as the most perfect model of political polity which the world had discovered. There were several other able and intellectual members of the convention, who entertained sentiments similar to those of Hamilton, but who, for prudential reasons, chose not to avow them too publicly, especially as in the state of public opinion that then obtained, it was believed that anything but a republican form of government was impossible to be established. The great majority of those who sat in the convention, were Republicans in sentiment themselves and besides they perceived that the demands of the age would not permit a monarchical constitution to be fixed upon the American people. They permitted themselves, therefore, to drift with the current of popular opinion, and did so, even in cases where their judgment entered strong protests to much that was done. But as in the natural, so also in the political world, there are only two poles of aniagonistic opinion, those of monarchy and democracy; aristocracy being a mere compromise of the extremes. Metaphysical philosophy teaches us that every man is either a Platonist or an Aristotelian; and of Americans, it can with truth be averred, that every citizen is either a follower of Hamilton or of Jefferson in political opinions. The one strove for the adoption of a strong, and the other for a liberal Government, based purely upon human consent.

Alexander Hamilton, and those who sympathized politically with him in the Federal Convention, did not obtain that form of government which they desired, but having secured what was preferable to the old articles of Confederation, they favored its adoption as the best that was then attainable. Jefferson was in France during the sittings of the convention, and had no immediate share in the adoption of the instrument of Union that was agreed upon, and which was sanctioned for the Confederation of the States. His opinions, however, were well known, and were similar to those of perhaps a majority of the members of the Convention of 1787. The dividing line of party sentiment was that which separated between those favoring and those opposing a monarchical or strong form of government. The Hamiltonian party, in the formation of the Constitution, opposed every liberal aspect that was given to the instrument, whilst the Jeffersonians equally strenuously resisted the incorporation of every thing of a centralizing character. When the Constitution was at length completed by its framers, it received the support of all the Hamiltonians, because of the advantages secured in it over the old form of union; and it also found friends in the Jeffersonian school, amongst those who believed it the best form of government that could be secured; and also on account of the generally received interpretation that (as was agreed upon all sides) should be applied to it. It cannot be denied, however, that the leading opponents to the Constitution were members of the Jeffersonian school. Their animosity was aroused against it, because of the concession of certain powers to the Federal Government, which were not possessed under the Articles of Confederation; and such as many of them apprehended might undermine the liberty of the States at some future period. With the original reasons for the division of the early American parties borne in mind, it will be less difficult at any period to discover the descendants of each, notwithstanding slight intermixtures may have been constantly taking place. The distinguishing features of each of these early schools of political opinion have from that time been clearly discernible in all the different periods of our history.

Those giving the Constitution their hearty support were entitled Federalists, and those opposing the same were known as Anti-Federalists. Jefferson on account of his duties abroad, was not involved in the disputes which arose upon the adoption of the Constitution. Although friendly himself to the instrument, from the known views of its framers, yet the large majority of his political followers exerted themselves to their utmost to defeat its adoption. But the Constitution was adopted, and as was natural, those who had championed it before the people would be those who would first be chosen to put it into operation. Gen. Washington had been its friend in the Convention, and also before the people; and he was now chosen by a unanimous vote to be the first who should pilot the new vessel upon the ocean of conflicting American opinion. With that sagacity for which he was in a high degree noted, he strove to calm the antagonistic sentiments that he knew prevailed throughout the country, by forming his cabinet out of the opposing political schools. Hamilton and Jefferson were accordingly placed as the heads of different departments of the government; but this, instead of allaying the strife, may be viewed as rather having hastened the full development of parties, which followed the first election of Washington as President of the United States. It was not long till Jefferson and his party friends discovered, as they believed, that the aim of the Hamiltonian leaders was to secure by Constitional interpretation what they had failed to obtain in the original adoption of the Federal pact. Power was claimed for the general government that had never been granted to it, and which had been reserved alone to the States and people, as in the words of the charter itself was expressed. But the Federal, was the party of character, wealth and influence, and it required a considerable period to divest it of that position of strength and power which it had secured in the young Republic. At length, upon the enactment of certain obnoxious laws, Jefferson and the other Southern leaders who had always sympathized with him, and who were the warm friends of liberal governmental views, succeeded in grasping the reins of the general government. Federalism sunk at once, never again to rise in its own name; but not so its principles. These lived and continued with modifications to form the elements of vitality of every organization that was arrayed against the Jeffersonian party from that period.

So complete was the overthrow of the Federalists, that many years elapsed before any organization was able to make a stand against the old party of Jefferson, or the National Democracy. In 1824, all the candidates for President ran as members of the Democratic party, but the election of John Q. Adams had the effect of attracting together the disunited elements of Hamiltonianism, and laying the foundation for that structure which became, in a sense, the National Whig party. This party was somewhat the expression of that resistance, that must of necessity manifest itself in opposition to the ruling organization; but whose animating spirit was caught from its Federal ancestors. This was true, rather as regarded the Northern Whigs; for in the Southern States, the peculiar Hamiltonian principles being exotic, never took deep root. In the South the Whig party may be viewed as the embodiment of the personal opposition that was marshalled by Clay and other distinguished leaders against the administrations of President Jackson, Van Buren and others; and in which principles, though loudly heralded, were ever of minor significance. It was owing to this fact that only a seeming harmony ever existed between the northern and southern sections of the Whig party; and also, that in South Carolina no organization of this name, for many years had any political strength whatever. Anti-Masonry, another daughter of Federalism, had its home in the North, and in its missionizing tours in the South met but a cold reception. The Anti-Slavery political party, which took its rise in the Liberty organization in 1840, with Birney as its Presidential standard bearer, was also the growth of the centralizing principles and the germination of Federalism.

The leading feature of distinction which characterized the Democratic party of Jefferson, was its advocacy of the doctrine of State sovereignty, in opposition to the principle of centralization. The Democrats contended that the States were the sovereigns that had framed the general government, and that they remained so, although they had delegated specified powers to the Federal head, but only such as were clearly enumerated. The Virginia and Kentucky resolutions of 1798–9, the former drafted by Madison, and the latter by Jefferson, explicitly set forth the doctrine that the general government was one of limited powers, and that the States would not be bound to yield acquiesence in the enactments of the Federal authority in an instance where the power assumed, was clearly usurped, and did not come within those delegated in the Constitution. This doctrinal assertion of principles, from the two leading statesmen of the old Republican party, was made at a time when it was charged that the Federal party had violated the Constitution in the passage of certain obnoxious measures; and the principles thus enunciated in those resolutions from that time forward became the recognized democratic creed, which was affirmed and re-affirmed in nearly every State and National Convention of that organization that was afterwards held. The doctrine was boldly anounced, as the general understanding of all parties, who had participated in the formation of the Federal Constitution, and at a period when the principal actors who had taken part in its formation and adoption were yet living, and able to controvert any assertions thus made had they been false and unsupported by facts. But the doctrines so set forth remained uncontradicted, an incontestible evidence in itself that they were sustained in historical verity; and especially, as all this occurred at a time when it was in the power of a party whose principles the resolutions opposed, to have disproved their assertions had they been able to have done so.

The concession in the Constitution to the general government of the power to execute its own enactments upon the citizens of the States, was that feature of the Federative compact, which rendered it so vastly superior to the articles of Confederation that preceded it. This, in the words of De Tocqueville, was: "A wholly novel theory, which may be considered as a great discovery in modern political science. In all the Confederations which preceded the American Constitution of 1789, the allied States, for a common object, agreed to obey the injunctions of a Federal Government; but they reserved to themselves the right of ordaining and enforcing the execution of the laws of the Union. The American States, which combined in 1789, agreed that the Federal Government should not only dictate but should execute its own enactments. In both cases the right is the same but the exercise of the right is different; and this difference produced the most momentous consequences."* But, in the clear and express enumeration of these powers, over which the general government was alone to exercise authority, the Jeffersonian State right Republicans felt that their safety rested. They willingly conceded that within these prescribed limits, the Federal power was supreme over the States, but not beyond those bounds. The various limitations of power had been agreed upon with great care and deliberation; and the several boundaries of authority, both National and State, were intended to be steadily and scrupulously observed.

The institution of slavery was one over which the general government had no authority. It was altogether a matter for State regulation, and was so conceded by the early statesmen of all political parties. The movement of Abolitionism in the North, with the consequent rise of the Liberty party in 1840, although engendered in humanitarian motives, was nevertheless a direct avowal that all constitutional rights of the southern people must yield to the behests of the new party, as soon as it should be able to grasp the reins of the Federal Government. It was thus a threat made against all constitutional government, in which the danger did not alone consist in the determination to wrest from the southern people so much property as was invested in their negro slaves. If national compacts and plighted faith must bend before the will of majorities, then constitutional governments become a failure, and a despotism of numbers is installed in their stead.

*De Tocqueville's Democracy in America, Vol. I, pp. 481.

A constitutional government is based upon the will of the people at the time of its adoption, and if any alteration is at any time sought to be made therein, this must be accomplished in accordance with the provisions of the original charter. Any other method of change is revolutionary, equally as if produced by the might of armies. The abolition movement, for the overthrow of slavery, was the commencement of the revolution for the obliteration of slavery from the United States. The insignificant vote of a little less than 7,000 for Birney for President, in 1840, seemed to the unreflecting as unworthy of notice; it was only to the deep comprehension of John C. Calhoun and such as he, that the real danger was fully felt and appreciated. It was the means by which the object to be attained was proposed to be accomplished, quite as much as the result itself, that was felt as so threatening to the principles of free government. It was, in short, the announcement of the right of reducing government to chaos, and out of the anarchy, reconstructing it in accordance with the passions of the multitude. In principle and essence, the avowal of the Abolitionists was equally as alarming in one section of the Union as in the other. The only difference was, that in the South, with abolition success, together with the overthrow of constitutional government, the rights and privileges of the people of that section must likewise perish in the flames of social convulsion. The Liberty party asserted the right of the people of the North to interfere with slavery in the southern States, a doctrine before unheard of and in utter violation of the compacts that had formed part of the Constitution. The States were separate independent Republics, that for valid reasons had formed a central authority, entrusted with certain specified powers, the better to promote the interests of all amongst each other, and with foreign nations. The people of the northern States, had therefore, no more legal or constitutional right to intermeddle with the affairs of those of the South than in the concerns of foreign nations. They might condemn slavery in the South or elsewhere, but when they assumed to dictate to the southern people, or to organize a party of aggression against the constitutional rights of any of the States, they became revolutionists equally as had they rose with arms in their hands to overthrow the existing constitution. But the Abolitionists chose to confine their warfare within the moral arena; and thus they escaped the perpetration of the crime of treason, of which an armed assault would have made them guilty.

The whole Anti-Slavery movement in all the various channels in which it flowed, took its rise in Hamiltonian principles, which demanded the subordination of all the States to the Federal Government. One supreme central authority was demanded, which should dictate what institutions and laws should, and what should not exist in the several States. That system would inaugurate a national government of strength, one having unity of purpose and efficiency in its administration. Such had ever been the fond hope of the old Federal leaders, and of all such as believe that the principles of monarchy are essential for the government of men and nations. But, besides the attitude and action of the pure Anti-Slavery party, which was organized in 1840; in order to see the revolutionary movement as it progressed, it is necessary to follow, in connection therewith, the course of the Whig party, until its final overthrow as a national organization. On the question of slavery, the Whig party, North and South was never harmonious; and it was alone upon other questions, that it was able to unite in opposition to the Democracy, the party of unadulterated States right sovereignty. The Southern Whigs, from the earliest agitation of the slavery question, were about in sentiment with the National Democratic party, save that as politicians, on unimportant questions, they would at times veer into seeming opposition to the slavery interests in their section; and they did so in order to bring themselves more into harmony with their northern brethren, already dominated by abolition sentiment.

The annexation of Texas was one of those questions that severed the Whig party into a sectional division. John Q. Adams, a Whig Member of Congress, was one of the first to sound, as early as 1837, the bugle of northern anti-slavery opposition against the project of annexing the new Republic of Texas to the United States. Texas had secured her independence in the memorable battle of San Jacinto, fought April 21st, 1836. In March, 1837, the United States recognized the independence of the new sister Republic. Daniel Webster, in his speech of March 15th, 1837, at Niblo's Garden, expressed his entire disapprobation to the annexation of Texas, basing his opposition to it on the ground that it would be extending the boundaries of slavery. Avowed Abolitionists had first sounded the note of opposition on the Texas question, and it was taken up by the Whig politicians of the North for the purpose, mainly, of securing political capital from northern sentiment on the slavery question, as had happened in the interests of Federalism during the contest on the admission of Missouri into the Union. The resistance thus early manifested in the North against the annexation of Texas, had the effect of delaying operations for some years, for the consummation of the measure. It was only when the anti-slavery agitation had advanced to such a stage as almost to have divided the country into two sectional parties, indicated by the Mason and Dixon boundary, that annexation began again seriously to be discussed. That such a division had taken place between the North and South was undeniably true as regards the Whig party, for although Harrison had been elected President by the Whigs, yet this was more owing to the great personal popularity of the candidate, than because of any unity of sentiment amongst his partisans.

It was during the administration of John Tyler, the successor of William Henry Harrison, that the incorporation of Texas into the Union was fully resolved upon by southern statesmen, who saw in this measure how they could perpetuate the balance of power between the northern and southern sections of the Union. Leading members of the Whig party in the South were equally ardent for the admission of Texas as the Democrats, although well aware of the antagonism generally entertained towards the measure on the part of their political brethren of the North. The question came to be one of importance in the Presidential election of 1844. It, and the tariff, were the leading questions of that political struggle. Aspirants for Presidential honors had a delicate task, therefore, in dealing with these national questions; and in this struggle the strength of parties was so equally balanced that the writing of a letter, it is believed, turned the scale of victory from one side to the other. Martin Van Buren clearly sealed his defeat as the candidate of the Democratic party by his letter written to William H. Hammet, of Mississippi, in which he took grounds against Texan annexation. The crafty Statesman of Lindenwald thought to secure his nomination by catering to the northern sentiment of opposition to the spread of slavery; but found himself entrapped by his letter, and which forever sealed his hopes of future Presidential promotion. The Democratic party, in its National Convention, which met at Baltimore on May 27th, 1844, boldly announced its principles on the annexation question in the following resolution :

"*Resolved*, That our title to the whole Territory of Oregon is clear and unquestionable ; that no portion of the same ought to be ceded to England, or any other power ; and that the re-occupation of Oregon and the re-annexation of Texas, at the earliest practicable period, are great American measures which the convention recommends to the cordial support of the Democracy of the Union."

The effects of anti-slavery agitation upon northern opinions by 1844, were conspicuously visible. The body of the public men in the North, of both political parties would, as a matter of choice, have voted that no more slave States be admitted into the Union. They were aware that the enlightened sentiment of the age, both in Europe and America, was averse to the institution as it existed in the Southern States; and free from all party trammels they would have voted against its extension. There is little doubt but that this was the prevailing sentiment of the enlightened classes of both political parties. Unlike certain Abolitionists, however, they did not regard slavery as a sin, but the steady discussion of the question for years had at length produced its influence, and they in general looked upon it as somewhat repugnant to their moral convictions. In the Democratic as well as in the Whig party, this feeling had considerable strength ; and the above resolution of the Baltimore convention, endorsing the annexation of Texas, met with opposition from men who upon no other question had ever been found unfaithful to party principles. Silas Wright, a prominent Democrat from New York, had conspicuously opposed annexation in the United States Senate; and knowing that the measure would be endorsed by his party in the Presidential campaign of 1844, he declined the nomination for Vice-president on the ticket with James K. Polk. Mr. Wright nevertheless became the candidate of his party for Governor of New York the same year, and in a canvassing speech at Skaneateles, he referred to his opposition as unabated, and declared that he never could consent to annexation. This sentiment was loudly applauded in a large Democratic convention held in Herkimer, in the autumn of that year. Messrs. George P. Barker, William C. Bryant, John W. Edmonds, David Dudley Field and Theodore Sedgewick united in a letter, urging their fellow-democrats, while supporting Polk and Dallas, to repudiate the Texan resolution, and to unite in supporting for Congress Democratic candidates hostile to annexation.*

Henry Clay was the great Southern leader and idol of the Whig party, and had been long pressed by his ardent admirers for the Presidency. But for the division on the slavery question that had made its way into the Whig party, he would have been nominated for the highest office in the Republic in December, 1839. The following extract from the *Emancipator*, an abolition journal, explains the condition of the Whig party at that period:

THE HARRISBURG CONVENTION.

"Well, the agony is over, and Henry Clay is laid upon the shelf; and no man of ordinary intelligence can doubt or deny that it is the anti-slavery feeling of the North which has done it, in connection with his own ostentatious and infamous pro-slavery demonstrations in Congress—Praise to God for an anti-slavery victory! A man of high talents, of great distinction, of long political services, of boundless personal popularity, has been openly rejected for the Presidency of this Republic on account of his devotion to slavery. Set up a monument of progress there—let the winds tell the tale! Let the slave-holders hear the news. Let foreign nations hear it. Let O'Connell hear it. Let the slaves hear it. A slave-holder is incapacitated for the Presidency of the United States. The reign of slaveocracy is hastening to a close. The rejection of Henry Clay by the Whig Convention, taken in connection with all the circumstances, is one of the heaviest blows the monster slavery has ever received in this country."

The remarks of Garrison on the rejection of Clay by the Whig Convention are to the same purport: "All the slave States went for Clay. Had it not been for abolitionism, Henry Clay would undoubtedly have been nominated."

In the National Whig Convention, held at Baltimore in 1844, the party nominated Henry Clay for President by acclamation. His political letters on the Texas question, published in the *National Intelligencer*, in which he expressed his disapprobation to the admission of Texas, had the effect of uniting in his support the northern Whigs; and his real opinions known to his southern friends, served to retain them likewise. In his letter intended for northern circulation he dextrously struck the key-note to northern resistance to annexation in the following language:

"I do not think Texas ought to be received into the Union, as an integral part of it, in decided opposition to the wishes of a considerable and respectable portion of the Confederacy. I think it far more wise and im-

*Greeley's Conflict, Vol. 1, p. 166

portant to compose and harmonize the present Confederacy as it now exists, than to introduce a new element of discord and destruction into it. In my humble opinion it should be the earnest and constant endeavors of American statesmen, to eradicate prejudices, to cultivate and foster concord, and to produce general contentment among all parts of our Confederacy."

This letter of Clay upon annexation was found not to give entire satisfaction to all his southern friends, and he was urged to make a further statement of his views upon the Texas question. Accordingly, on the 16th of August, a letter appeared in the *North Alabamian*, which had been written by him to friends in Alabama. In this letter occurred the following language:

"I do not think it right to announce in advance what will be the course of a future administration, in respect to a question with a foreign power. I have, however, no hesitation in saying, that far from having any *personal* objection to the annexation of Texas, *I should be glad to see it*, without dishonor, without war, with the common consent of the Union, and upon just and fair terms."

This last letter was at once seized upon by the Democrats as well as the Abolitionists, as an entire change of base upon the part of Clay, and which had no doubt considerable influence upon the result of the election. Many have ever believed that this letter caused his defeat as President of the United States. James G. Birney, the Presidential Abolition candidate of the Liberal party, in the same canvass made a handle of Clay's Alabama letter, to abstract from him anti-slavery votes, and he was successful in polling upwards of 60,000. James K. Polk, the Democratic nominee, was elected President of the United States, and this victory was fairly interpreted as the national endorsement of the policy of Texan annexation. Congress, acting in obedience to the public sentiment, as thus expressed, passed resolutions for the admission of Texas, and John Tyler affixed thereto the Presidential signature March 1st, 1845.

On the 3d day of March, 1845, President Tyler despatched a messenger to deliver to Mr. Donelson charge d' affaires of Texas, the joint resolutions of Congress for its admission into the Union, and instructing him to communicate the same to the Texan officials. The resolutions admitting the Republic as a member of the Union, were submitted by the President of Texas to a convention of delegates called for the purpose of forming a State Constitution, and were assented to by that body in behalf of the people on the 4th of July, in the same year; and thus one more State was added to the number of the existing sovereignties of the American Union. The Convention of Texas, thereupon requested the President of the United States, to occupy and establish posts without delay upon the exposed frontier of the Republic, and to despatch such forces as might be deemed requisite for the defence of the territory and people of the newly-admitted State. In accordance with this request, an "army of occupation" was despatched by order of President Polk, under command of General Taylor, and on the 26th day of July, 1845, the American standards were unfurled over Texan soil. This movement, with the measures of annexation transacted between the United States and Texas, were regarded by the Mexican government as acts of hostility towards the latter, and preparations were made by the Mexican Republic for an appeal to arms. On the 5th of March, Gen. Almonte, the Mexican minister at Washington, protested against the resolutions of the Federal Congress providing for the annexation of Texas, and demanded his passports, which were granted him; and on the 3d of April the Government of Mexico refused to hold further diplomatic intercourse with the United States, and informed the American Minister that such intercourse was irreconcilable with Mexican honor, in view of the annexation of Texas. The President of Mexico, here upon, on the 4th of June, 1845, issued a proclamation declaring that the annexation of Texas did not change the relations of Mexico towards that Republic, and that she was resolved to maintain them by force of arms. Under these circumstances, the diplomatic relations were of necessity suspended between the two countries, and this state of affairs so continued until the commencement of hostilities in 1846. On the 11th of May, 1846, the American Congress declared that war existed between the United States and Mexico, by act of the latter—the President having announced that the Mexicans had "at last invaded our territory and shed the blood of our fellow citizens on our own soil."

Congress, two days after the reception of this message from President Polk, responded by the passage of an act calling out 50,000 vounteers, and appropriating ten millions of dollars for the prosecution of the war with Mexico. The annexation of Texas had thus resulted in what from the first had been the repeated prediction of the Whig party; and although towards the prosecution of the war, the Whigs in Congress, in the main, voted for men and money, yet did so with the greatest reluctance, at the same time, stigmatising it as an unjust invasion of Mexican rights, and an infringement of inter-national comity. Congress remained in session until the 10th of August. In the meantime, the encounters between the American and Mexican forces, gave assurance that the war could not be of long duration, as a series of victories had crowned the American standards from the first commencement of hostilities. President Polk believed a treaty of peace might be negotiated with the Mexican Government, and that by the payment of a sum of money, not only the boundary of the Rio Grande, but a considerable acquisition of territory might be secured. He accordingly sent a special message to Congress on the 8th of August, two days prior to the time fixed for the adjournment, asking that an amount of money be placed at his disposal for these purposes. A bill was immediately reported in Committee of the Whole, making appropriations of $3,000,000 for the expenses of the negotiation, and $2,000,000 to be used at the discretion of the President in making such a treaty. The bill seemed on the point of passing through all its various stages without serious opposition. After a hasty consultation with some friends, David Wilmot, a democratic Member of Congress from Pennsylvania, introduced his celebrated proviso, and moved to add it to the first section of the bill now pending, and which was to the effect *that no part of the territory to be acquired should be open to the introduction of slavery.*

The introduction of the above *proviso*, proved a new firebrand cast into the American Congress, as might have been readily surmised by its author, had he but chosen to remember occurrences of no remote date. Equity demanded that the people of the South be treated as equal members of the Conferation, the same as those of the North; and that no discrimination should be adopted to exclude them from their equal and constitutional rights. Besides, the proviso was in direct violation, if not of the words, at least of the spirit of the Missouri Compromise, a compact in harmony with justice and sectional equality.

When the proviso was first offered, it met with the almost universal favor of the Representatives from the North, doubtless (as was likewise the case in the commencement of the Missouri struggle) without any intention upon the part of most of those from that section, of violating the rights of their southern brethren. So much discussion, however, had at one time and another taken place with reference to the power of Congressional legislation over the territory now possessed, or hereafter to be acquired, that it came about this time to be generally believed in the North that slavery in the national domain was subject to the same control. Quite a different opinion, however, had ever prevailed in the South, as regards the power of Congress; and in view of the intense feeling that had already been engendered in the minds of the Southern people on account of the known intention of the Abolitionists, the proviso was at once seized upon by them as the greatest possible outrage that could be inflicted upon them. The first vote on the proviso in the House, was 80 ayes and 64 nays, only three Democrats from the North opposing it. The North and the South had now fully divided on this question, the sectionalizing of representatives having become complete upon any issue affecting the institution of slavery.

The 10th of August, the time for the adjournment of Congress arriving, put an end to further discussion, and the appropriation sought by the President was not granted. The turbulent scenes of the two days, however, that Congress was in session, after the introduction of this apple of discord by Mr. Wilmot, was sufficient to communicate the inflamation to the people of all the Southern States of both political parties, and, in the Legislatures of several of these, conditional disunion resolutions were passed. "Everywhere in the slave States the Wilmot proviso became a Gordon's head—*a chimera dire*—a watchword of party, and the synonym of civil war and the dissolution of the Union." *

The application of the Executive was renewed at the next meeting of Congress, with this difference that instead of two he now asked for three millions of dollars. A second bill was now prepared and introduced into the House, and the proviso being again incorporated into it, this passed by a vote of 115 to 105. The bill being now sent to the Senate, the proviso was stricken out by the vote of 31 to 20, and in this shape was returned to the House of Representatives where, upon a reconsideration, the action of the Senate was concurred in by 102 yeas to 91 nays. Thus, after a violent contest in both Houses of Congress, the

*Benton's Thirty Years View. Vol. 2, p. 695.

appropriation was granted without any anti-slavery restriction. The excitement occasioned by the discussion that grew out of the introduction of this proviso, was perhaps the most fiery and intense that had ever yet taken place in Congress, and served more than all else to inflame the public mind in both sections of the Union.

After a series of brilliant victories, the conquest of Mexico was effected, and the American standards waved over the Spanish Republic. The conquest of Mexico was speedily followed by the flight of Santa Anna, its President, and peace between the two countries was concluded February 2d, 1848, by the treaty of Gaudaloupe Hidalgo, by which Upper Calfornia and New Mexico were ceded to the United States. This treaty received the ratification of the Mexican Congress May 29th, 1848. The acquisition of this new scope of country still increased the national domain, and served to add additional complication to the already unadjusted difficulties between the North and South, as regarded the government of the national territories. The organization of the territories from this period became one of the difficult questions before Congress, and this because of the division of sentiment on the slavery question which had sundered the two sections, as it were, into antagonistic parties.

But, although the leaven of Abolitionism had already caused somewhat of fermentation in the Democratic party, it yet remained thoroughly national in its principles, and decided in its efforts to resist aggressions upon southern rights. A small wing of the party in the North had allowed itself to be led captive by free soil principles, which were producing discord in the old Jeffersonian ranks. In the State of New York, these principles had already produced a schism of the party into two factions, the one of which was styled *Hunkers*, and the other *Barn-burners*. In the Democratic Convention, which nominated Gen. Lewis Cass and William O. Butler, for President and Vice-president, in May, 1848, both factions of the party from New York, appeared by their delegates, and claimed seats in that body; and with the desire of harmonizing the differences both were admitted to seats in the convention, each being authorized to cast half the vote to which the State was entitled. This served the Barn-burners with the excuse which they desired; and declaring themselves unwilling to be bound by the decision of the convention, retired therefrom. After the Free Soilers, Radicals or Barn-burners had withdrawn, the convention adopted a platform of principles, national in its character, and very similar to those of previous conventions of the same party. But as to the power of Congress over the question of slavery in the territories, which had recently come into prominence, the convention declined to commit itself. On this question William L. Yancey, of Alabama, submitted the following resolution:

"*Resolved,* That the doctrine of non-interference with the rights of property of any portion of the people of this Confederacy, be it in the States or Territories thereof, by any other than the parties interested therein, is the true Republican doctrine recognized by this body."

This resolution was rejected—nays 216, to yeas 36. Its rejection was the work of the northern leaders of the party, although not so indicated by the vote in the convention. This was the first manifest wavering that the Democratic party had shown before the abolition sentiment of the North; and much as the leaders of both sections believed in the justice of non-intervention, those in the Northern States feared to meet their constituents, should this be endorsed as a cardinal principle. It was a cowardice, however, of which no political party should ever be guilty. If the principle was right, the resolution should have been endorsed, even at the risk of party defeat.

The Whig National Convention assembled at Philadelphia, on the 8th of June, 1848, and selected Zachary Taylor and Millard Fillmore as its candidates for President and Vice-President. Gen. Taylor was made the nominee of his party purely because of his supposed availability as a candidate and the great personal popularity he had gained in the Mexican war. As he was a slaveholder, he was far from being acceptable to the northern Whig leaders, but circumstances compelled them to acquiesce in his nomination. The disintegration and dissolution of the Whig party were already nearly complete, and but time was wanting to render it a finality. In this convention the party was unable to agree upon a platform of principles. Repeated efforts were made to endorse the principle of the Wilmot proviso, but without success, the motions made for this purpose being successfully tabled. The ardent Abolitionists of the party on this account took little interest in the election, but feeling themselves powerless in the party, they permitted themselves to drift with the political current. Several members of the convention declared their utter dissatisfaction with the candidates; and so great, indeed, was the smothered opposition that the nominations could not be made unanimous, according to custom. All this opposition was stimulated by anti-slavery zeal. Mr. Allen, a delegate to the convention from Massachusetts, said that the Whig party was that day dissolved. Mr. Bingham, of Ohio, offered a resolution that the nominations should be unanimous provided Gen. Taylor would pledge himself to the non-extention of slavery over free territory. Such a pledge was never obtained; and if it had been, that moment the Whig party would have dissolved. Gen. Wilson, of Massachusetts, declared that he would do all in his power to defeat the nominee of the convention. "Gen. Taylor, though an excellent soldier, had no experience as a statesman, and his capacity for civil administration was wholly undemonstrated. He had never voted; had apparently paid little attention to, and taken little interest in politics; and though inclined towards the Whig party, was but slightly identified with its ideas and its efforts. Nobody could say what were his views regarding Protection, Internal Improvement, or the Currency. On the great question—which our last acquisitions from Mexico had suddenly invested with the greatest importance—of excluding slavery from the yet untainted Federal Territories, he had in no wise declared himself; and the fact that he was an extensive slaveholder, justified a presumption that he, like most slaveholders, deemed it right that any settler in the Territories should be at liberty to take thither and hold there as property, whatever the laws of his own State recognized as property."*

But the strength of the Abolition sentiment of the North was still advancing to more prominent recognition. The schism of several of the leading churches into Northern and Southern communions, beginning with the Methodist Episcopal in 1844, had already given an importance to the anti-slavery movement, that it had not before possessed. And although the two great parties of the country had their Presidential candidates in the field before the nation, harmony no longer reigned in the ranks of either. The Liberty party had supported candidates for President and Vice President in 1840, and in 1844, but was able to draw but a comparatively feeble vote.

*Greeley's Recollections, p. 211.

For the purpose of showing the rise of the Free Soil party from Abolition authority, the following extract is submitted:

"In the midst of these exhortations, the National Convention of the Liberty party assembled at Buffalo, October 20th, 1847. Gerrit Smith, still a member of the Liberty party, was proposed as a candidate for the Presidency. His nomination would have secured the co-operation of the Liberty League in his support. But the course marked out by the leading men in the convention beforehand, required the nomination of a different man from Gerrit Smith. The Liberty party for the first time adopted the policy of going out of its own ranks for a Presidential candidate. After debating awhile the question of nominating at all till next year, they nominated Hon. John P. Hale, United States Senator from New Hampshire, an independent Democrat, who had certainly done himself honor in refusing to do homage to the slave power, and who had drawn off a portion of the Democracy of New Hampshire to his support." * * * "But the nomination of Mr. Hale was only a temporary one, and answered its temporary purpose. Gentlemen active in making it united with others of other parties in calling another convention, which was held at Buffalo, August 9th, 1848, composed of the opponents of slavery extension, irrespective of parties and including of course, as was designed, large numbers who did not intend to be committed to 'the one idea' of abolishing slavery. On that occasion was organized the *Free Soil party*, in which the Liberty party was designed to be wholly absorbed."*

The Liberty party was thus, in 1848, metamorphosed into that named Free Soil, through the machinations of Martin Van Buren and his friends out of revenge to General Cass, who had been largely instrumental in 1844, in causing the defeat of the former before the Democratic Convention of that year Although the North was not yet fully ripe for the organization of a purely sectional party, yet the free soil vote in 1848 indicated that the abolition movement would take that direction. Horace Greeley, speaking of the National Democratic nominations in 1848, says:

"This ticket was respectable, both as to character and services, yet its prospects were marred by the fact, that that faction of the New York Democracy, which had been known as Barn-burners or Free Soil men, resenting the admission of their competitors to seats in the convention had bolted, and refused to be governed by the result. Ultimately, they united with the Abolitionists and with sympathising Democrats in other States in holding a *National*† Convention at Buffalo, which nominated Martin Van Buren, of New York, for President, and Charles F. Adams, of Massachusetts, for Vice-president. This ticket, though it obtained no

*Goodel on Slavery, p. 478. †Mr. Greeley should more properly have said a Sectional rather than a *National* Convention, for there were no delegates in it except from the Northern States, and the most of those who figured in it were secret Abolitionists, whom policy deterred from the expression of their honest sentiments.

single electoral vote, blasted the hopes of General Cass and the regular Democracy." *

The distinctive feature of the platform of the Free Soil party was opposition to slave institutions, and a desire to abolish or restrain slavery wherever this could be constitutionally accomplished. These three principles were laid down: First, that it was the duty of the General Government to abolish slavery wherever it could be done in a constitutional manner. Second, that the States within which slavery existed had the sole right to interfere with it; and third, that Congress can alone prevent the existence of slavery in the Territories. By the first of these principles, it was the duty of Congress to abolish slavery in the District of Columbia; second, to leave its regulation to the States where it existed, and third, to abolish it in territory now free.

In the sectional aspect of this party lay its danger. Thomas H. Benton speaks thus of the Buffalo Convention that nominated Van Buren and Adams:

"It was an organization entirely to be regretted—its aspect was sectional—its foundation a single idea—its tendency to merge political principles in a slavery contention. The Baltimore Democratic Convention had been dominated by the slavery question, but on the other side of that question, and not openly and professedly; but here was an organization resting prominently on the slavery basis. And, deeming all such organizations, no matter on which side of the question, as fraught with evil to the Union, this writer, on the urgent request of some of his political associates, went to New York to interpose his friendly offices to get the Free Soil organization abandoned. The visit was between the two conventions, and before the nominations and proceedings had become final; but all in vain. Mr. Van Buren accepted the nomination, and in so doing placed himself in opposition to the general tenor of his political conduct in relation to slavery, and especially in what relates to its existence in the District of Columbia. I deemed this acceptance unfortunate to a degree far beyond its influence upon persons or parties. It was to impair confidence between the North and the South, and to narrow down the basis of party organization to a single idea; and that idea not known to our ancestors as an element of political organizations. The Free Soil plea was that the Baltimore Democratic Convention had done the same; but the answer to that was that it was a general convention from all the States, and did not make its slavery principles the open test of the election; while this was a segment of the party, and openly rested on that ground."†

The election of 1848 resulted in the choice of Gen. Taylor for President of the United States, and Millard Filmore for

* Greeley's Recollections, p. 213. †Benton's View, Vol. II, p. 723.

Vice-President. In the Congress that assembled in December, 1848, after the election, the question on the organization of the Territories came up, and was debated with great warmth and at considerable length. A majority of the House of Representatives were desirous of excluding slavery from New Mexico and California, but the Senate being unwilling that this principle should be incorporated, no bill, as a consequence, for the organization of these Territories was passed at this session. The territorial question was now become the great subject of dispute between the North and South; and its discussion was the cause of increasing bitterness and alienation between the two sections. When it became manifest that no organization of these Territories could take place at this session, the members of Congress from the slave States united in an address to their constituents, which was a clear resume from the pen of John C. Calhoun of what the South regarded as their constitutional rights. Thus ended the administration of James K. Polk, and with it the Thirtieth Congress.

CHAPTER VIII.

COMPROMISE MEASURES OF 1850.

The 31st Congress assembled in December, 1849. Thaddeus Stevens made his first appearance at the beginning of this Congress as a Whig member of the National House of Representatives, having been elected during the campaign which bore Gen. Taylor into the Presidential chair. Questions of the greatest importance for the harmony of the States and for the peace and prosperity of the Union, were awaiting the decision of the new Congress; and the American people were looking to it with fond hopes for the adoption of measures that might avert the threatened dissolution of the Confederacy. The territorial controversy was that which, most of all, was arousing the passions of sectional hostility; and which had now raged with intensity for a considerable period. Repeated efforts had already been made to solve the territorial problem between the North and the South, but all in vain. Tho 30th Congress had adjourned after fruitless attempts to terminate the increasing difficulties.

California, New Mexico and Utah were awaiting the action of the Federal Legislature to clothe them with their republican regalia, which the exigencies of their several conditions required; the first already having formed a State Constitution, was asking to be received as a member of the Union. The great question to be determined was the status that should be given to the new Territories as regards the institution of slavery. For the first time in the history of the Republic, a small body of Representatives from the North, took their seats in Congress upon the platform of opposition to the extension of African Slavery. Besides these, the large majority of northern Representatives, whether Whigs or Democrats, were likewise in sentiment averse to the spread of the institution over States and Territories, now deemed free. With these latter Mr. Stevens was identified. This state of opinion being well understood at the South, it is but reasonable to suppose that a high degree of excitement would prevail in that section.

"Never had any Congress convened under so much excitement or under so great responsibility as did the one on which then devolved the disposition of this (slavery) question, under all the circumstances attending it. The embarrassments of the period were increased from the fact that for the first time Southern Senators and Members were greatly divided as to the proper course to pursue, in view of the question with all its bearings. Some believed the time had come for a separation of the States, and that everything should be done with a view to effect that result. Others believed that the Union might still be preserved upon constitutional principles, and that the object was worth the most earnest and patriotic efforts. This class believed, however, that the time had come for a total abandonment of all old party associations, and that the united South should act in party organization with those of the North only, who would maintain the system as it was established by the Constitution."*

The storm that had almost driven the Ship of State upon the shoals of disunion and civil convulsion was still raging, and showed no signs of abating. It was the Æolus of abolitionism that had let fly the winds of strife, and all was in commotion. Many of the Nothern States were arrayed in bitter antagonism to their Southern sisters, and through their Legislatures assailed the institution of slavery in the most harsh and offensive terms. Vermont, Connecticut and other Eastern States had passed resolutions declaring that "the existence of slavery and the slave trade in the District of Columbia is a national disgrace, &c.;" and that their Senators and Representatives in Congress "are hereby strictly instructed" to vote in every possible case for what is called the Wilmot proviso; and "to vote always, and in every state of the question, for the abolition of slavery in the District of Columbia, and against the admission of another slave holding State into the Federal Union." These resolutions and others of like character, were sent to the Governors of the different States and to their representatives in Congress. As giving the tendency of such resolutions and their transmission to the Southern States, the following extract from the *National Intelligencer*, the leading organ of the Whig party is inserted:

"In the substance of these resolutions, as in that of the Vermont resolutions on kindred subjects at an earlier period of the session, we find the fruitful cause of much of the excitement that within the last few months

* Stephens' War between the States. Vol. 2, p. 177.

manifested itself in the Legislatures of the Southern States; the exemplification of a practice reprehensible in itself, inconsistent with friendly intercourse and justly offensive to those who are the objects of it. It is an idle pretence, that it is from any motive of courtesy that copies of such resolutions, as these are forwarded to the Governors of the States whose feelings, more than their interests, they are calculated deeply to wound; they can be so addressed with no other intention than to incense and irritate those whose known opinions and convictions they wilfully assail. The practice is at best an invidious and ungenerous one, and ought to be reformed altogether. The States are in all matters of opinion at least sovereign and independent of each other, and no one of them has a right to invade (so to speak) the domesticity of another. What does the reader suppose would be the consequence were one of the governments of Europe to address such a missive to another with respect to its peculiar institutions? Suppose, for example, the Government of France were to send its compliments to the Government of Russia, with a message that the Emperor's holding of Serfs, or permitting them to be held in his dominion, was (in the language of the Vermont resolutions) a *crime against humanity*—a *national disgrace*, and demanding the abolition of that feature of government. True or false, what answer could Russia be expected to make to such a proposition, but a declaration of war, or war without a declaration? And in matters of internal government, what more right has one of our States to address such language to another in a matter of constitutional right, than one European Government would have to do it to another government on the same continent, and not more remote or distinct from it than the Government of Vermont is from half of the States on this continent."*

But another grievance much complained of by the South, was the disposition of the people of the North to interpose obstructions to the surrendering to their masters of fugitives from labor. This change of sentiment from what it was formerly, had been the result of the Anti-Slavery agitation that had almost severed the nation into two hostile parties. In the early history of the Republic, such a spirit of comity reigned between the North and South, that laws were enacted in near all of the Northern States which permitted citizens from the Southern States to sojourn in their midst with their slaves, and return home without loosing the right to their services. In the year 1826, Pennsylvania, at the request of the people of Maryland, passed a liberal law to aid in the recovery of fugitive slaves, entitled, "An Act to give effect to the Constitution of the United States in reclaiming fugitives from justice." Other Northern States acted in a disposition of like liberality. However, after Anti-Slavery ideas rose to power in the North, all this friendly legislation in behalf of

*Editorial in *National Intelligencer*, February 23, 1850.

Southern rights underwent a change. In the case of Prigg vs. the Commonwealth of Pennsylvania, decided in 1842, the Supreme Court of the United States affirmed the constitutionality of the fugitive slave act of 1793. This act of Congress had imposed upon the State magistrates the duty of arresting the fugitives from labor and returning them to their owners. This duty the Supreme Court in the above decision, declared not to be binding upon the State magistrates, and whether they would aid Southern masters in the recapture of their slaves, was left entirely to their own discretion. Under this decision of the highest tribunal, it became competent for the State Legislatures to prohibit their own functionaries from aiding in the execution of the Fugitive Slave Act.

"Then commenced a furious agitation against the execution of this so-called '*sinful and inhuman*' law. State magistrates were prevailed upon by the Abolitionists, to refuse their agency in carrying it into effect. The Legislatures of several States, in conformity with this decision, passed laws prohibiting these magistrates and other State officials from assisting in its execution. The use of the State Jails was denied for the safe keeping of the fugitives. Personal Liberty Bills were passed, interposing insurmountable obstacles to the recovery of slaves. Every means which ingenuity could devise was put in operation to render the law a dead letter. Indeed, the excitement against it arose so high that the life and liberty of the master who pursued his fugitive slave into a free State were placed in imminent peril. For this he was often imprisoned and in some instances murdered."*

Even the conservative State of Pennsylvania, by her Act of March 3d, 1847, repealed her Sojourning Act of 1780, and also the Act of 1826, and therein forbade her judicial authorities to take cognizance of fugitive cases; granted a habeas corpus remedy to any fugitive arrested, and denied the use of her jails for their confinement. Thomas H. Benton thus speaks of the Pennsylvania Act of 1847:

"Such had been the just and generous conduct of Pennsylvania towards the slave States, until up to the time of passing the harsh Act of 1847. Her legal right to pass that Act is admitted; her magistrates were not bound to act under the Federal law; her jails were not liable to be used for Federal purposes. The Sojourning Law of 1780 was her own, and she had a right to repeal it. But the whole Act of 1847 was the exercise of a mere right against the comity, which is due to States united under a common head, against moral and social duty, against high national policy, against the spirit, in which the constitution was made, against her own previous conduct for sixty years; and injurious and irritating

*Buchanan's Administration on the Eve of the Rebellion, p. 17.

to the people of the slave States, and parts of it unconstitutional. The denial of the intervention of her judicial officers and the use of her prisons, though an inconvenience, was not insurmountable, and might be remedied by Congress; the repeal of the Act of 1780 was the radical injury, and for which there was no remedy in the Federal legislation."*

Testimony might be indefinitely amplified as regards the injustice done the southern people by northern legislation, and the unwillingness of the citizens of the North to acquiesce in the requirements of the Constitution, but unwilling to overburden with extracts, the following from Webster and Clay are alone added:

'But I will state these complaints, especially one complaint of the South, which has, in my opinion, just foundation, and that is that there has been found at the North, among individuals and among the Legislatures of the North, a disinclination to perform fully their constitutional duties in regard to the return of persons bound to service who have escaped into the free States. In that respect it is my judgment that the South is right and the North is wrong. Every member of every Northern Legislature is bound by oath to support the Constitution of the United States, and this Article of the Constitution which says to these States they shall deliver up fugitives from service, is as binding in honor and conscience as any other Article. No man fulfills his duty in any Legislature who sets himself to find excuses, evasions, and escapes from their constitutional duty. I have always thought that the Constitution addressed itself to the Legislatures of the States, or the States themselves. It says that those persons escaping to other free States shall be delivered up, and I confess I have always been of opinion that it was an injunction upon the States themselves. When it is said that a person escaping into another, and becoming therefore within the jurisdiction of that State shall be delivered up, it seems to me the import of the passage is, that the State itself, in obedience to the Constitution, shall cause him to be delivered up. That is my judgment, I have always entertained, and I entertain it now."†

"MR. PRESIDENT.—I do think that that whole class of legislation, beginning in the Northern States, and extending to some of the Southern States, by which obstructions and impediments have been thrown in the way of the recovery of fugitive slaves is unconstitutional, and has originated in a spirit which I trust will correct itself, when those States come calmly to consider the nature and extent of their federal obligations. * * * * I know full well, and so does the honorable Senator from Ohio know, that it is at the utmost hazard and insecurity to life itself, that a Kentuckian can cross the river and go into the interior to take back his fugitive slave to the place from whence he fled. Recently an example occurred, even in the City of Cincinnati, in respect to one of our most respectable citizens. Not having visited Ohio at all, but Cov-

*Benton's View, Vol. II, p. 775.
† Webster's 7th of March Speech, 1850, in *National Intelligencer*.

ington, on the opposite side of the river, a little slave of his escaped over to Cincinnatti. He pursued it; he found it in the house in which it was concealed, and it was rescued by the violence and force of a negro mob from his possession, the police of the city standing by, and either unwilling or unable to afford the assistance which was requisite to enable him to recover his property."*

During the last days of Mr. Polk's administration, the veteran statesman of South Carolina, John C. Calhoun, became more than ever convinced that a crisis was approaching in the affairs of America, that would, unless checked, prostrate the South and her institutions, and with them the liberty of self-government. With this foreboding, he urged more thorough union amongst the Southern States, and in accordance with this advice, a large number of Senators and Representatives from that section united in an address to the people of the South, setting forth a statement of wrongs on the part of the North that demanded redress. This address was responded to by a convention of delegates of the people of Mississippi, chosen without distinction of party, which assembled in October, 1849, and recommended that "a convention of slave holding States should be held at Nashville, Tennessee, on the first Monday of June, 1850, to devise and adopt some mode of resistance to the aggression of the non-slave holding States." Several Southern States appointed delegates to the Nashville Convention, but the movement was not popular with those who believed that a compromise of the pending difficulties between the two sections was still possible. The convention, nevertheless, met in June, but was not largely attended. It issued an address enumerating a statement of southern complaints.

Notwithstanding the grievances alleged by the South against the North were manifold, that which more than all else caused the present excitement, was induced by the opposition that existed to permitting the extension of slavery into the Territories or States hereafter to be admitted into the Union. The Northern Representatives had shown their unwillingness to either permit the application of the Missouri compromise to the new Territory, acquired from Mexico, or to acquiesce in any settlement which would permit slavery to enter it. This was claiming the lion's share, surely. If the principle of the Missouri compromise was to be only valid, as regards one section of the Union, the com-

*Clay's 6th of March Speech, 1850, in *National Intelligencer.*

pact had become a nullity. And such was the veritable fact, as the votes in Congress for some years had shown. Whenever its application served the interests of anti-slavery proscription, the compromise was made use of; but when the reverse was the case, other means were then resorted to without scruple.

Such was the attitude of affairs when the 31st Congress assembled. The first significant movement at the opening of this body that arrested the attention of the country, was made by those known as Southern Whigs.

"They set the ball in motion by refusing to act further with the Whig organization, as it was then constituted, when the party met in caucus to nominate a Speaker of the House. A resolution previously prepared was submitted to this meeting, which in substance was, that Congress ought not to put any restriction upon any State institution, in the Territories, and ought not to abolish slavery, as it then existed, in the District of Columbia. Upon the refusal even to entertain this proposition, this class retired from the meeting, and would not act with the Whigs in the organization of the House." * Howell Cobb, of Georgia, was the Democratic candidate for the Speaker's Chair, and Robert C. Winthrop, of Massachusetts, was placed in nomination for the same position by the Whigs. Fourteen independent Free Soilers, composed of Whigs and Democrats, refused to support either of these nominees. Thaddeus Stevens and many other extreme anti-slavery men acted with the regular Whigs, and supported Mr. Winthrop for Speaker. But neither of the two great parties, as matters then stood, having a majority in the House, the election for Speaker was a long and fierce contest, and attracted the attention of the country as one that boded no future good. Nearly a month was consumed before a Speaker was elected, an event then unprecedented in the history of American legislation. As parties were divided, no election would have been possible, under the rules, but for the passage of a resolution declaring that a bare plurality of votes cast for any one candidate, instead of a majority of the whole, should constitute an election.

In the midst of the election for Speaker, Robert Toombs, one of the leaders of the Southern Whigs, made a speech in the

* Stephens' War. Vol. 2, p. 178.

midst of great excitement, in which the following language occurs:

"The difficulties in the way of the organization of the House are apparent and well understood here, and should be understood by the country. A great sectional question lies at the foundation of all these troubles. * * * * I do not, then, hesitate to avow before this House and the country, and in the presence of the living God, that if by your legislation you seek to drive us from the Territories of California and New Mexico, purchased by the common blood and treasure of the whole people, and to abolish slavery in the District, thereby attempting to fix a national degradation upon half of the States of this Confederacy, I am for disunion; and if my physical courage be equal to the maintenance of my convictions of right and duty, I will devote all I am, and all I have on earth to its consummation." *

That the sentiments of the Southern people at this period were equally as intense as those of their leaders in Congress, the following extract from a conservative Southern journal is evidence:

"The two great political parties of the country have ceased to exist in the southern States, so far as the present issue is concerned. United they will prepare, consult and combine for prompt and decisive action. With united voices (we are compelled to make a few exceptions, but they will, we hope, soon cease to be so) contend—with united voices they proclaim in the language of the Virginia resolutions, passed a few days since, *the preservation of the Union if we can, the preservation of our rights if we cannot.* This is the temper of the South; and this is the temper becoming the inheritors of rights acquired for freemen by the blood of freemen. Thus far shalt thou come and no further—or else the proud waves of northern aggression shall float the wreck of the Constitution.

"We only love a Confederacy of equals; for as equals we entered the Union, and we will remain in it upon no other condition. This is the deliberate conclusion of the Southern people. There is no hesitancy, no reservation, no escape. The Southern man should die who would accept for his State any other condition."†

The period was altogether alarming. The threatening clouds of disunion were gathering thick and fast along the Southern horizon; and everything betokened a collision of the elements as rapidly approaching. The dashing waves of abolition fury indicated that the storm was almost equally terrific in the northern as in the southern sections. The Vessel of State was in danger of being borne upon the billows of the uniting tempest, and sunk beneath its blasts. The exigency called for one who was able to say to the troubled waters, "Peace, be still!" He came in the person of the Sage of Ashland, the great Pacificator of

***Congressional Globe*, 31st Congress, 1st Session, p. 27.

†Richmond *Inquirer*, Feb. 12th, 1850.

his country, Henry Clay, of Kentucky, who on former occasions had guided the rocking bark of the Union, as between the roarings of Scylla and Charybdis, and moored her in the harbor of safety and peace. But now, silvered with the locks of honored wisdom, gained in a long and faithful public service, he returned to the United States Senate, to do the last service for his country in clutching her from the grasp of fratricidal convulsion, which the condition of her nature had been long preparing. Coming back thus in the far spent evening of a useful life, he was the admired of all the patriotic lovers of the constitution, who believed in the cardinal principles of republican government, that all just authority rests upon the consent of the governed. His watchword of safety for his countrymen was that which had laid the foundation, cemented, and for upwards of sixty years preserved the Republic. It was the watchword of freemen, *compromise.* All petty partisan malignity retired before the honored chief; and his advise is anxiously sought as the Nestor of his age and country. His illustrious compeers of other days, Webster and Calhoun, were still in the Senate, anxious to aid in saving the nation from the dangers that were surrounding it. The above intellectual trio were surrounded by Cass, Benton, Berrien, King, Bell, Mangum, Douglas and other gifted statesmen, all glowing with zeal for the preservation of the Union from impending disaster and dissolution.

On the 29th of January, 1850, Henry Clay introduced his celebrated resolutions which were intended to embrace all the questions involved in the sectional controversy. It having been announced that Clay would address the Senate on this occasion, it was filled with a dense mass of spectators, attracted to catch the words of wisdom and peace as they flowed from the golden mouthed orator of America. But thousands, anxious to hear the words of pacification that might calm the ocean of strife, were necessitated to retire in disappointment, being unable to penetrate within the hearing of the speaker. This, of all the scenes, that American history has yet unfolded, was most worthy the powers of a Raphael or Michael Angelo. It was America's greatest orator, prompted by the noblest motives of his nature, speaking before the most august and intellectual body of the world, in behalf of the grandest object of human conception, the preservation of the most complete system of free government that the wisdom of man had yet devised, and urging for that purpose those measures by which alone it could be perpetuated, conciliation and compromise.

Mr. Clay's compromise proposed the admission of California under the Constitution she had adopted, although irregularly framed; the adjustment of the boundary between New Mexico and Texas by negotiation with the latter; the organization of Utah and New Mexico without any restriction as to slavery; the enactment of an efficient fugitive slave law, and the abolition of the slave trade in the District of Columbia. This plan, as a whole, satisfied very few members, either in the House or Senate. The great majority from the North desired the exclusion of slavery from the Territories, and many of the same number were equally unwilling to permit the enactment of a fugitive slave law. With this latter division Mr. Stevens may be numbered. He, and those of intense anti-slavery notions, were likewise disinclined to accept alone the suppression of the slave trade in the District, but insisted upon its entire abolition. On the southern side, an overwhelming majority resisted the admission of California, because of the irregularity that had obtained in the adoption of the Constitution without an Act of Congress warranting it. Those styled Southern Whigs were ready to waive this irregularity, but demanded that in the organization of Utah and New Mexico, no exclusion of slavery should be allowed, but that the people of all the States should be at liberty to emigrate thither with their property of every kind; that the citizens of the said Territories should be permitted to form such State Constitutions as they chose; and that they should be admitted into the Union, when making applications therefor, whether their Constitutions established slavery or otherwise. Thus was Con gress divided upon these perplexing questions.

On the 18th of February, a resolution was offered in the House by James D. Doty, of Wisconsin, which had for its object the admission of California, without any settlement of the other questions. A large majority of the House was in favor of its admission, but of this number the Southern Whigs desired as a preliminary, the settlement of the territorial question. By a concerted arrangement, these with others thwarted action on Mr. Doty's resolution by means of dilatory motions.

In the Senate the intellectual giants, one after another, exerted themselves in efforts to effect some form of compromise that would allay the sectional passions and the excitement then raging. The veteran statesman of South Carolina, too feeble to mingle in the strife as once he had done, submitted his last views on the crisis in a speech read for him on the 4th of March, in which he warned his countrymen of the danger that was menacing free government. He was followed on the 7th of March by Webster, who took decided grounds against Congressional restriction in the Territories. "This speech made a profounder sensation upon the public mind throughout the Union than any one delivered by him before. The friends of the Union under the Constitution were strengthened in their hopes and inspired with renewed energies by its high and lofty sentiments."* On the 18th of April, a resolution submitted by Henry S. Foote, of Mississippi, an ardent friend of compromise, was passed in the Senate to raise a Select Committee of Thirteen, to whom the resolutions of Mr. Clay were to be referred. The selection of this committee was made by ballot, and the Chairmanship of it was by almost unanimous consent awarded to Mr. Clay. On the 8th of the following month, the Chairman of this Committee reported to the Senate what was afterwards known as the "*Omnibus Bill*," covering all the matters contained in his resolutions heretofore submitted. An amendment added by the majority (without Clay's approbation, as he stated) seemed to southern members generally, to imply a positive Congressional exclusion of the South from the Territories.

On the 11th of June, Mr. Doty's bill for the admission of California, came up in the House, it having been referred to the Committee of the Whole on the 27th of the preceding February. His first resolution, instructing the Committee on Territories to report the bill, had miscarried. Mr. Green, of Missouri, now rose and moved as an amendment the recognition of the Missouri line through all the newly acquired territory. This was rejected by a large majority. Mr. Stanton, of Tennessee, on the 13th of June, offered the following amendment:

"*Provided*, However, that it shall be no objection to the admission into the Union of any State which may be hereafter formed out of the territory lying south of the parallel of latitude of 36°, 30′, that the Constitution of said State may authorize African slavery therein."

*Stephens' War, Vol. II, p. 211.

This proposition was rejected, 78 yeas to 89 nays, the vote being almost a sectional one. After this vote had been taken, Robert Toombs spoke as follows:

"We do not oppose California on account of the anti-slavery clause in her Constitution. It was her right, and I am not prepared to say that she acted unwisely in its exercise; that is her business; but I stand upon the great principle that the South has the right to an equal participation in the Territories of the United States. I claim the right to enter them all with her property and securely to enjoy it. She will divide with you if you wish it;* but the right to enter all, or divide, I shall never surrender. In my judgment, this right involving as it does political equality, is worth a thousand such Unions as we have, even if they each were a thousand times more valuable than this. * * * Give us our just rights and we are ready as ever heretofore to stand by the Union, every part of it and every interest. Refuse it, and for one I will strike for independence."†

"This speech of Mr. Toombs delivered on the 15th of June, produced the greatest sensation," says Alexander H. Stephens, "in the House that I ever witnessed by any speech in that body during my congressional course. It created a perfect commotion. Several Southern Whigs who had not before sympathized with the class above alluded to,‡ now openly took sides with them. The House adjourned without coming to any further vote. The excitement in the House increased that in the Senate. It extended to the city, and the subjects discussed in the House, become the topics of heated conversations on the streets and at the hotels. This was Saturday. Monday, Mr. Doty made another effort to get a resolution passed requiring the Committee of the Whole to report his bill. The effort failed."§

In the Senate the excitement was equally as intense as in the House. At this stage of the proceedings, Mr. Soule, of Louisiana, arose and offered the following amendment to the first section of Mr. Clay's compromise, which related to the Territorial Government of Utah:

*By this remark Mr. Toombs expressed his willingness to abide by the Missouri compromise, provided its principle would be applied to all the new Territories, but as just seen that had been rejected in the vote last taken in the House. His proposition must ever be considered as equitable, and embodied that principle by which alone equals can at all negotiate.

†*Congressional Globe*, 31st Congress, 1st Session, p. 1216.

‡He means those Southern Whigs who refused to co-operate with the remaining Whigs in the election of a Speaker and otherwise, after the resolution presented by them to the Whig caucus had been rejected.

§Stephens' War, Vol. II, p. 217.

"And when the said Territory, or any portion of the same, shall be admitted as a State, it shall be received into the Union, with or without slavery, as their constitution may prescribe at the time of their admission."

This amendment presented the issue squarely between the North and the South, and become thenceforth "the *turning point*, upon whose adoption every thing depended, so far as concerned Mr. Clay's compromise."* Many a heart beat with anxiety as to the result of the vote upon this question in the Senate. Its rejection in this august body of the nation, would have terminated all hope of a satisfactory adjustment of the slavery question between the two sections. The interest was greatly enhanced from the uncertainty and doubt which existed as to the attitude of several Northern Senators. Prior to this time, the Wilmot proviso had received the support of several of these, who had given no indication as to how they would vote upon the question of leaving to the people of the Territories the determination of this question when framing their State Constitutions. Of this number was the great Senator from Massachusetts. Just before the question was put, and when anxiety had risen to its highest pitch, this renowned statesman of New England arose to address the Senate. The momentuous occasion aroused the dormant virtues of the powerful defender of the Republic, and forgetful of self or sectional interests, he proclaimed himself the advocate of the rights of all under the Constitution. The amendment he declared should receive his support. He concluded his masterly effort in the following language:

"Sir, my object is peace—my object is reconciliation. My purpose is not to make a case for the North, or to make a case for the South. My object is not to continue useless and irritating controversies. I am against agitators, North and South; I am against local ideas, North or South, and against all narrow and local contests. I am an American and I know no locality in America. That is my country. My heart, my sentiments, my judgment, demand of me that I should pursue such a course as shall promote the good, the harmony, and the union of the whole country. This I shall do, God willing, to the end of the chapter."

"Daniel Webster resumed his seat," says the reporter, "amidst the general applause of the gallery." The anxiety seemed immediately to subside. The great statesman of the North had thrown his weight in the scale of the amendment. "The friends of the measure felt that it was safe. The vote was taken—the

*Stephens' War, Vol. II, p. 218.

amendment was adopted. The result was soon communicated from the galleries, and finding its way through every passage and outlet to the rotunda, was received with exultation by the crowd there; and in less than five minutes, perhaps, the electric wires were trembling with the gladsome news to the remotest parts of the country. It was well calculated to make a nation leap with joy, as it did, because it was the first decisive step taken towards the establishment of that great principle upon which this territorial question was disposed of, adjusted and settled in 1850."*

Mr. Clay's bill continued the subject of discussion in the Senate until the 31st of July, when it was so mutilated and altered as to leave nothing but that portion providing for a government for the Territory of Utah, with the Soule amendment incorporated in it, as stated. In this shape it passed the Senate and was then sent to the House. In this way, Clay's "Omnibus Bill" went to pieces. The Senate, however, immediately took up the parts, embodied them in separate bills, which, after being passed, were transmitted to the House for concurrence.

But the anti-compromise party of the Thirty-first Congress, was far from being one of insignificance, either numerically or intellectually. Being the result of the long anti-slavery agitation, it comprised in its ranks men of large scholastic attainment, and such as were imbued with pure humanitarian impulses, but whose minds partaking too largely of the reformatory bent, are never safe counsellors in legislative capacities. For the establishment and perpetuation of government, men of logical minds and philosophical comprehensions are needed, rather than those devoted to assumed conceptions which no rational considerations could induce them to modify or abandon. The legislator and the reformer † are widely variant characters, whose spheres of

*Stephens' War, Vol. II, pp, 219 and 220.

† The reformer is the enthusiastic advocate of moral, social or religious change as he conceives; for the alteration he aims to effect may be a dire calamity to mankind. He is the honest innovater upon the past who is guided by his feelings more than by his judgment. His aspirations are too intense to allow reason to enter, and hence he gives way to the most extravagant excesses that prostrate law and social order. Peter Munzer and John of Leyden, were quite as sincere reformers as Martin Luther and John Calvin; and so as social reformers, Robespierre, Danton and Mirabeau were as sincere and enthusiastic champions of human equality as the world ever saw. But intolerance, proscription and zealous hate more frequently accompany the character of the reformer than that Pauline charity which even nature instills. That such should be the case

duty dare never be intermingled, save at the risk of constant turmoil and governmental disquietude. The sentiments of this reformatory party on the subject of compromise between the North and South were expressed in the following extract of a speech made by Thaddeus Stevens on May 20th, 1850:

"It is proper, then, to inquire whether the thing (*slavery*) sought to be forced upon the Territories, at the risk of treason and rebellion, be a good or an evil. I think it is a great evil which ought to be interdicted; and that we should oppose it as statesmen, as philanthropists, and as moralists, notwithstanding the extraordinary position taken by the gentleman from Alabama (Mr. Hilliard) to the contrary.

"While I thus announce my unchangeable hostility to slavery, in every form and in every place, I also avow my determination to stand by all the compromises of the Constitution and to carry them into faithful effect. Some of these compromises I greatly dislike; and were they now open for consideration, they should never receive my assent.* But I find them in a Constitution formed in difficult times, and I would not disturb them.

"By those compromises, Congress has no power over slavery in the States. I greatly regret that it is so; for if it were within our legitimate control, I would go regardless of all threats, for some just, safe and certain means for its final extinction. But I know of no one who claims the right, or desires to touch it within the States. But when we come to form governments for Territories acquired long since the formation of the Constitution and to admit new States, whose only claim for admission depends on the will of Congress, we are bound to so discharge that

---

arises from the nature of his character; for as he conceives himself and those agreeing in opinion with him, as the only divinely illumined beings on earth, he desires that all others shall either be converted to his views or exterminated, so as to prevent their errors from proving the destruction of themselves and others. The fires of Smithfield, the Inquisitorial flames of Spain and the Italian peninsula, and the blazes in which Servetus expired, were all kindled by the excessive zeal of the reformatory spirit.

*As regards the principle of compromise, we think Mr. Stevens was radically wrong, assuming that he was a believer in the principles of republican government. No general government for the States could ever have been formed in America but for this principle. It lies at the basis of all democratic government, and so soon as it is repudiated the monarchical principle takes its place. In accordance with this principle, the Confederated American Republic was formed and perpetuated until the breaking out of the war between the Northern and Southern States. As evidence of what is thus affirmed as regards the principle of compromise, the Supreme Court in the case of Prigg vs. the Commonwealth, speaking of the Fugitive Slave Clause in the Constitution, say: "Historically, it is well known that the object of this clause (the above clause of the Constitution) was to secure for the citizens of the slaveholding States, the complete right and title of ownership in their slaves as property, in every State of the Union into which they might escape from the State where they were held in servitude. The full recognition of this right and title was indispensable to the security of this species of property in all the slaveholding States; and indeed was so vital to the preservation of their domestic institutions, that it cannot be doubted that it con-

duty as shall best contribute to the prosperity, the power, the permanency and the glory of this nation."*

In the House the great sectional contest was fought on the Soule amendment offered by Mr. Boyd, of Kentucky, to the bill establishing the Territory of New Mexico. During this contest, which lasted from the 28th of August until the 6th of September, the discussions were of the most animated character, and partisan tactics were made use of with the greatest skill and adroitness. In this fierce strife of the sections, the debates seemed to open on every succeeding day with renewed intensity, and in the war of sentiments destiny seemed as but arousing the combatants, and preparing them for the trials that awaited them in the future. In this and similar encounters, unless the verdict of universal history be reversed, the American Republic received her first fatal stabs; and it is for time to determine whether she can outlive those already received, and those which, from the nature of her being, the enemies of her own household in future as in past collisions, will have it in their power to inflict. On the last direct vote, on the Boyd amendment, the bill passed by 108 ayes to 98 nays. The anti-restrictionists had won the day at last. The hall was in a general uproar. This was the kernel of the compromise of 1850. The other associated measures depended upon this one, and with it formed the compact of settlement between the North and South. After the passage of this first bill, the others came up in order, and were likewise passed. The fugitive slave bill, like that embracing the Territorial compromise, met with a stubborn resistance from the Northern Anti-Slavery men with whom Mr. Stevens acted.

The compromise measures were heartily accepted by the masses North and South, as a settlement of the difficulties between the two sections. It had received the support of the distinguished leaders of the Whig and Democratic parties; and the people are ever ready to abide by the words of those possessing their confidence. Although the Anti-Slavery men in the North, and the Southern extremists had opposed the compromise, this was

stituted a fundamental article, without which the Union could not have been formed. Its true design was to guard against the doctrines and principles prevalent in the non-slaveholding States, by preventing them from intermeddling with, or obstructing or abolishing the rights of owners of slaves."

*Appendix to *Congressional Globe,* 31st Congress, Part 1st, p. 141.

not considered at the time as alarming. It was clear to all observing men, however, that the dissolution of the Whig party was near at hand, as it was within the ranks of this organization that most of the Free Soil and Abolition element of the country found itself. But it was also evident that the Democratic party of the North was not, by any means free from the same element, and the Southern leaders began to consider the propriety of a reorganization of parties. It was this which induced Henry Clay, Howell Cobb, and many other Southern leaders, at the close of the compromise session, to unite in a manifesto to the country declaring that they in future would support no man for office either State or Federal, who would not agree to stand by and support the principles established by these measures. But in the Southern States efforts were made to succeed under party banners opposed to the compromise, all of which, however, proved failures; and the same was true where it was tried in the North.

Mr. Stevens was nominated for Congress in the year 1850, while the compromise measures were yet pending, and his party having an immense majority in Lancaster County, he was elected. But his action in Congress as regarded the compromise arrayed in 1852 a powerful opposition against him in Lancaster County, and he failed to receive the nomination of the party in that year. Isaac E. Hiester, a young and rising lawyer, was selected as the Congressional standard-bearer in his stead. No other opposition was urged against his nomination, except that of his having opposed the compromise of 1850. His intellectual superiority over all other aspirants in the county was generally conceded; but he was then regarded by the majority of his party (as he ever was by the Democrats) as partaking too much of the character of the agitator, one dangerous to the perpetuity of free institutions.

The great unanimity with which the Northern Whigs in Congress had opposed the compromise, made it a matter of uncertainty, whether the party would be able to unite as a National organization in the Presidential election of 1852. The Whigs in some sections of the North, fought the compromise with straightforward boldness, and arrayed themselves under banners inscribed with its condemnation. In 1851, the Whig State Convention of Ohio passed resolutions repudiating the compromise as a measure of their party, and nominated Samuel F. Vinton for Governor, who, while in Congress, had opposed it. The New York State

Convention of the Whig party, shortly after Millard Fillmore assumed the Presidential chair, refused to endorse his policy, because he had sanctioned the Fugitive Slave Law. For the purpose, therefore, of testing Northern sentiment on the Slavery question, before the assembling of the party conventions for the nomination of candidates for the Presidency, Mr. Jackson, of Georgia, on the 5th of April, 1852, submitted in the National House of Representatives the following resolution:

"*Resolved*, That we recognize the binding efficacy of the compromises of the Constitution, and believe it to be the intention of the people generally, as we freely declare it to be ours, individually, to abide by such, and to sustain the laws necessary to carry them out—the provisions for the delivery of fugitive slaves, and the act of the last Congress, for that purpose included; and that we deprecate all further agitation of questions growing out of that provision of the questions embraced in the acts of the last Congress, known as the compromise, and of questions generally connected with the institution of slavery, as unnecessary, useless and dangerous."

This resolution was opposed by all the Northern Whigs in the House of Representatives except seven. The Whig Congressional caucus met on the 20th of April, 1852, in the Senate Chamber, to consider matters of political interest to the Whig party, at which Mr. Marshall, of Kentucky, submitted the following resolution:

"That they regard the series of Acts known as the Compromise Measures, as forming in their mutual dependence and connection, a system of Compromise, the most conciliatory and the best for the whole country, that could be obtained from conflicting sectional interests and opinions; and therefore they ought to be observed and carried into faithful execution, as a final settlement in principle and substance of the dangerous and exciting subjects which they embrace."

This resolution was ruled to be out of order, and the decision of the Chair was sustained by a vote of 46 to 21. The members who voted to sustain the decision of the Chair were from the North, and in principle opposed to the compromise. Thereupon a number of Whigs from the Southern States seceded from the caucus and published an address to the party throughout the United States.

The Whig National Convention assembled at Baltimore June 16th, 1852, and exhibited a division in its ranks without precedent in party annals. The Northern Whigs, who had opposed the passage of the compromise measures in Congress, and had never since acquiesced in their justice, (especially the fugitive slave law) presented as their candidate for the Presidency General Winfield Scott, who was believed to be opposed to the institution of Southern slavery; and on the other hand, the Southern Whigs were favorable to the nomination of Fillmore, who had approved the compromise measures of 1850. A few delegates from the Northern States were desirous that Daniel Webster should be made the party nominee. The Southern and the Northern anti-slavery wing of the party held their respective conclaves in a spirit of the most bitter hostility towards each other. Sectionalism had severed the Whig party. All that remained of it was the form; and yet it was hoped that a Presidential campaign might be made with a popular nominee, and that thus the lifeless trunk might be galvanized into a brief vitality. A platform of principles for the party had been agreed upon by the Southern delegates and the Northern friends of Webster prior to the meeting of the convention, which endorsed the compromise of 1850 as a measure of Whig policy. It was clearly understood, that unless the party in convention affirmed this measure as a final settlement between the North and South, the Southern delegates would take no part in the proceedings. The Southern delegates, with the Webster wing from the North, formed a majority of the convention, and the compromise was endorsed by 164 ayes to 117 nayes. The resolution affirming the measure, as a principle of the party, was in these words:

"The series of acts of the Thirty-first Congress, commonly known as the Compromise, or the adjustment, (the act for the recovery of fugitives from labor included) are received and acquiesced in by the Whig party of the United States as a final settlement in principle and substance of the dangerous and exciting questions which they embrace; and so far as these acts are concerned, we will maintain them and insist upon their strict enforcement until time and experience shall demonstrate the necessity of further legislation to guard against the evasion of the laws on the one hand, and the abuse of their power on the other; not impairing their present efficiency to carry out the requirements of the Constitution; and we deprecate all further agitation of the questions thus settled as dangerous to our peace; and we will discountenance all efforts to continue or renew such agitation whenever, wherever, or however made; and we will maintain this settlement as essential to the nationality of the Whig party and the integrity of the Union."

General Winfield Scott and William A. Graham were nominated for President and Vice-president of the United States.

After the enactment of the compromise, in 1850, the Democratic party manifested its approval of this series of measures, and its determination to abide by the same. In the year 1851, the convention of this party for the State of Pennnsylvania, met at Reading and adopted resolutions condemning the Act of 1847, passed by the State Legislature, which denied the use of her jails for the detention of fugitive slaves, and also approving of the compromise measures of 1850. The State Convention of Ohio nominated Reuben Wood for Governor in 1851, and after his election, in his inaugural address, speaking of the compromise, he said:

"Under all the circumstances which surround us, it (the compromise) should remain undisturbed, and this fruitful source of agitation and excitement be forever closed."

The Democratic National Convention assembled on the 1st of June, 1852, and adopted a platform of principles which was strictly national, and reaffirmed its ancient position on the slavery question. As regards the compromise of 1850, the convention declared its purpose to "adhere to a faithful execution of the acts known as the compromise measures, settled by the last Congress—the act for reclaiming fugitives from service or labor included; which act, being designed to carry out an express provision of the Constitution, cannot with fidelity thereto be repealed or so changed as to impair its efficiency." "The Democratic party will resist all attempts at renewing, in Congress or out of it, the agitation of the slavery question, under whatever shape or color the attempt may be made." The nominees of this convention were Gen. Franklin Pierce and William R. King, of Alabama.

The Free Soil party, which had supported Van Buren and Adams in 1848, assembled again in 1852, and nominated for President John P. Hale, of New Hampshire, and for Vice-President George W. Julian, of Indiana. It was then, as now, styled the "Free Soil Democracy." The platform of this party is quite elaborate in words, and yet it narrows itself down substantially to a denunciation of the institution of slavery. It declares slavery a sin against God and man; pronounces the Fugitive Slave Law repugnant to the Constitution of the United States; advocates the policy of recognizing the Independence of Hayti, and says that "The Free Democratic party is not organized to aid either the Whig or Democratic wing of the great slave-compromise party of the nation, but to defeat them both." This party received the support of the radical abolitionists of the Northern States. The number of votes polled by this party was not so large in 1852 as it polled in 1848.

The Democratic party obtained a triumphant victory in the campaign of 1852, utterly routing their Whig opponents in every State of the Union, save four. After his inauguration, Franklin Pierce as President of the United States, took occasion in his first annual message to the 33d Congress to announce his determination to conform to the pledges given in his behalf by those who had elected him to the Presidency. He said:

"It is no part of my purpose to give prominence to any subject which may be properly regarded as set at rest by the deliberate judgment of the people, but whilst the present is bright with promise, and the future full of demand and inducement for the exercise of active intelligence, the past can never be without useful lessons of admonition and instruction. If its dangers serve not as beacons, they will evidently fail to fulfill the objects of a wise design. When the grave shall have closed over all who are now endeavoring to meet the obligations of duty, the year 1850 will be recurred to as a period filled with anxious apprehension. A successful war had just terminated. Peace brought with it a vast augmentation of territory. Disturbing questions arose, bearing upon the domestic institutions of one portion of the Confederacy, and involving the constitutional rights of the States. But, notwithstanding differences of opinion and sentiment which then existed in relation to the details of specific divisions, the acquiescence of distinguished citizens, whose devotion can never be doubted, had given renewed vigor to our institutions and restored a sense of repose and security to the public mind throughout the Confederacy. That this respose is to suffer no shock during my official term if I have the power to avert it, those who placed me here may be assurred."

The career of the Whig party was now terminated. The Presidential canvass of 1852 was the closing contest in which it participated. Clay and Webster, its renowned leaders, had descended to their graves and their party speedily followed them. The last cohesive elements that had still united it, dissolved in the demise of these patriotic and intellectual men, the noblest productions of the American Republic. With these great statesmen, broad, liberal, National ideas were cherished; but with those who rose to take their places, sectional views were fostered as of paramount importance to confederated integrity. Only an opportunity was now wanting to develop, to evident observation, the existing schism that had rent the Whig party into sectional extremes.

CHAPTER IX.

RESISTANCE TO THE FUGITIVE SLAVE LAW. CHRISTIANA RIOT, &C.

The disinclination of the Northern people to surrender fugitive slaves to their masters, when they had made their escape amongst them, originated in that humanitarian feeling which recognizes all men as equals and brethren of the same great family. The equality of mankind, from its popular announcement in the Declaration of Independence and its constant repetition in the newspaper press and elsewhere, had become in the estimation of most Americans an accepted opinion, even amongst the intelligent classes; and one that reason has difficulty to contradict. Its repetition and belief was agreeable to the feelings of the masses, and proved in the possession of demagogues, an admirable charm by which to seduce the unreflecting into the support of their selfish interests and schemes. In its earliest promulgation, it was thrown out simply as a declaration that seemed to comport with Democratic theories, rather than as expressing existing truth. In the estimation of the thinking world, it could never have imported what it expressed; for inequality is clearly stamped upon the whole face of creation. The proposition that "all men are born equal," is a sheer absurdity. "All men are born unequal. Their education is unequal. Their associations are unequal. Their opportunities are unequal. And their freedom is as unequal as their equality. The poor are compelled to serve the rich, and the rich are compelled to serve the poor by paying for their services. The political party is compelled to serve the leaders, and the leaders are compelled to scheme and toil in order to serve the party. The multitude are dependent upon the few who are endowed with talents to govern. And the few are dependent on the multitude for the power, without which all government is impossible. From the top to the bottom of the social fabric the whole is thus seen to be inequality and mutual dependence. And hence, all mankind, from the hightest to the lowest are subject to that imperative necessity, the slavery of circumstances," *

But even truth itself, is for a time impotent to resist the seductive insinuations of the feelings, as the demonstrations of history and experience abundantly prove. The opposition to the surrender of Southern fugitives to their masters, which for years had been increasing in intensity in the North, was germinated amongst the masses in both social and ecclesiastical views. In the latter aspect the position taken by the Northern Methodist, Baptist and other protestant churches, had largely contributed to increase in the minds of innocent and pious Christians their dislike of Southern slavery and their detestation to the rendition of human chattels. Overlooking the fact that slavery opposition had taken its rise in the schools of free thought, and in the rationalistic churches of England and America, the zealous of the other sects, marched blindly to the advocacy of principles that have done more to subvert biblical christianity and ecclesiastical truth, than any other that could have been adopted. The daring assumption of infidel teaching, that law and social order must yield to private opinion as the most holy and sacred conservator of truth, was loudly re-echoed by the Northern churches; and the doctrines avowed with unblushing effontry, that no enactment of Congress could impose it as a duty, to aid the Southern master in the reclamation of his escaped property. The angel's mandate to Hagar, and St. Paul's conduct towards Onesimus, together with the action of the Christian church in all anterior ages, were entirely forgotten. The modern churches had so far exchanged the principles of the bible for the infidel moral codes of latter ages; and blindly permitted their new teachers to exercise the chief influence in their synagogues, and consecrate those filling the highest seats in the nation.

In the case of those entertaining views as thus stated, it would be resonable to suppose that the fugitive slave law could impart no obligation to yield acquiescence in its provisions. No sooner was it, therefore, enacted in 1850, as part of the great compromise between the States of the Union, than meetings were held in various sections, and resolutions adopted by the rationalistic high priests of the Northern sanctuaries and their neophite church followers, denouncing the act as wicked and inhuman.

*Hopkins' Bible View of Slavery, p. 23 and 24.

Of the rationalistic American churches, none had shown so early and determined an opposition to the institution of slavery as the Quakers; and this, because of the character of its membership and remarkable freedom from all faith domination. In its organization, as an ecclesiastical body, it had divested itself of every conceivable appendage of biblical belief, for which reason was unable to interpose a solution; and therefore it was not difficult for it, in addition to all this, to accept as Christian teaching, what had been conceived in the schools of French and British free thought. The Quakers, as a people, originally belonged, in the main, to the humble and unpretentious classes: and a simplicity marked their conduct and character, even to the eschewing of the higher grades of intellectual culture and advanced education. A plain, unadorned and unobtrusive manner pervaded the every-day life of Quaker society, which seemed to present a cognate affinity with the ascetic orders of history. It is not strange, therefore, that that church should be the first to denounce slavery as unchristian, which was able to set aside all the historical verity of the world's existence; and conceive that society, with its attained development could subsist without the resistant power; and that national life could endure without that highest coercive of humanity, legalized warfare.

"Upon the organization of the anti-slavery societies throughout the Northern States, it was to be expected that the Quakers should figure prominently in these efforts to abolish slavery. All that the Quakers and the other anti-slavery organizations could effect was to keep up an agitation of the slavery question, and thus endeavor to educate the public conscience up to their principles. In this, they were to a very great degree successful. Their opinions entered others of the American churches, and divisions of the same followed, marked by the Mason and Dixon boundary. The American Union, in the eyes of many of the leading statesmen of the nation, was again rocking in the throes of disunion or civil convulsion; and another compromise, headed by Clay and Webster, was sanctioned by the National Congress in 1850, which made it the duty of the Northern States to surrender fugitive slaves to their masters, where the proper legal demand was made for them. Against the compromise of 1850, and especially against the fugitive slave law, the Northern conscience at length fully revolted. Slavery being regarded as a sin by a large portion of the intelligent citizens of the North; that they should be compelled to render aid in capturing the fleeing fugitive from labor, was altogether incompatible with their sense of duty. In their view they would rather bear the penalty of the law as aid in its execution. No law could justly, as they believed, compel them to violate conscience."

"In no section of the whole North was there a more determined feeling of opposition or disinclination to the execution of the fugitive slave law than in the eastern part of Lancaster County, where the citizens were mostly either Quakers or their descendants. For years fugitive slaves had found among the people of Sadsburg and Salisbury townships kind treatment, and quite a colony of them had been congregated and settled in the vicinity of Christiana. It was natural to suppose that the fleeing fugitive would direct his steps to a retreat amongst the friends of his liberty, rather than amongst those who were ready to surrender him for pelf, or out of hatred to his race." *

Some of the slaves of Edward Gorsuch, a highly respectable citizen of Maryland, had made their escape into the eastern part of Lancaster County, and were living amongst others of their race in that section. Mr. Gorsuch, having ascertained the locality of his slaves, set out for Pennsylvania in search of the absconded property. He called upon and made the requisite affidavits before Edwaad D. Ingraham, Commissioner of the United States, appointed under the fugitive slave law of 1850. That officer issued four warrants dated September 9th, 1851, directed to Henry H. Kline, as Deputy Marshall, by virtue of which he was authorized to arrest Joshua Hammond, George Hammond, Nelson Ford and Noah Buley, four fugitive slaves, believed to be living in Lancaster County. The facts of the issuing of the writs became known to a colored tavern keeper in Philadelphia by the name of Samuel Williams, who with another colored man preceded the official party to the neighborhood where the slaves resided, and where the arrests were to have been made, and gave notice to the negroes of the vicinage that officers would shortly visit them for the purpose of capture. Word was at once circulated amongst the negroes of the colony, and such white persons as were known to sympathize with them, and it was resolved that

*Harris' Biographical History of Lancaster County, pp. 148 and 149.

united resistance should be made to all attempts to recapture the fugitive slaves. The negroes were emboldened to this resolution by the known views of a large number of the influential citizens of the neighborhood, who in their hearing had frequently expressed their disapprobation of slavery and the fugitive slave law. Meetings of the citizens in that locality even had been held after the enactment of that law, condemning it as wicked and unjust; and that the Northern people owed no obligation to aid in its execution. Besides, there is little doubt but the negroes had the quiet approbation of some of their influential neighbors, by whom, perhaps, in all probability, the first suggestion of resistance to capture may have been made.

As soon as the warrants for the arrest of the fugitives were placed in the hands of Deputy Marshal Kline, arrangements were made for executing the writs as speedily as possible. Edward Gorsuch was accompanied by Dickinson, his son, Dr. Thomas Pearce, a nephew, and Joshua Gorsuch; besides two neighbors, who had come to assist in making capture of the fugitives. Deputy Marshal Kline and the Maryland capturing party set out for Lancaster County, taking different modes of conveyance, and arrived at Christiana early on the morning of September 11th. Having secured the service of one acquainted with the locality, they started on hunt of the fugitives; and when they had neared a tavern kept by a negro named Parker, about two miles from Christiana, they espied one of the slaves coming down the lane from Parker's house. As soon as the slave saw them, he returned and fled to the house, pursued by the party; but he succeeded in eluding their grasp. He made his way up stairs, and the party in search of him immediately surrounded the house so as to prevent escape.

But it was soon apparent that resistance to the execution of the writs was determined upon, for as the party was approaching the house, a horn was distinctly heard, which proved to be a signal for the collecting of their friends. Edward Gorsuch, the owner, and the Deputy Marshal, now entered the house and, discovering that several blacks were up stairs, they demanded of them that they surrender, which they promptly refused and began loading their guns, showing the utmost determination of resistance. Mr. Gorsuch, addressing his slave by name, said: "Come down, Nelson, I know your voice; I know you," and after a pause added: "If you come down and go home with me, without any trouble, we will overlook the past." One of the negroes answered, "If you take one of us you must do so over our dead bodies!" The Marshal now read his warrant aloud, and assurred the negroes that he was clothed with the legal authority to make the arrest. Mr. Gorsuch now called upon the Deputy Marshal to ascend the stairs and arrest the fugitive; and in attempting to do so he was struck at with a sharp instrument and compelled to desist. Mr. Gorsuch, in the meantime, stepped outside and called to his slave and endeavored to persuade him to surrender himself peaceably to his authority; and while doing so was shot at by one of the negroes from a window, but the shot failed to take effect. The Marshal again read his warrant, and advised the negroes of the peril of resisting the authority of the Government; and added, that if it became necessary, he would call upon additional assistance to aid him in making the arrest. He told Parker, the keeper of the house, that he would hold him responsible unless he surrendered the negroes, as the law required. Parker replied that he was a Pennsylvanian, and did not care for the law, but asked for a few moments for reflection, that they might determine what course to pursue.

During this period, two white men named Castner Hanway and Elijah Lewis, the former on horseback and the latter on foot, suddenly appeared upon the ground. This was seen to have the effect of inspiring enthusiasm into the negroes in the house, who immediately set up a cheering. Whether any previous secret understanding had existed between these whites and the negroes, may perhaps never be fully ascertained; but the cheering raised upon their appearance had a very suspicious aspect. Edward Gorsuch requested the Marshal to ask these white men to assist in making the arrest. He approached the one on horseback, Hanway, and politely addressed him, without receiving any recognition of his salutation. He then asked him if he belonged to that neighborhood, and received as the reply, "it is none of your business." He next inquired of him his name, and was told, "you will have to find it out." The Marshal next informed him who he was, and of his authority for making the arrest, at the same time handing him his warrant. Hanway read the warrant, and returned it to the officer. He also handed it to Lewis, the other white man, who read it in like manner, and afterwards returned it. The Marshal now called upon them, by virtue of his authority, to assist him in executing his writ. Hanway replied, that "he would have nothing to do with it; he would not assist at all; the negroes had a right to defend themselves." By this time a considerable number of negroes had made their appearance near the lane armed with double-barrelled guns, pistols, corn-cutters, scythes and clubs. The organization had been complete; and soon as the horn was sounded, as above indicated, the negroes began to assemble from all directions. Lewis told the Marshal that he had better desist from attempting to make the arrest, otherwise blood would be shed. All this time the negroes were gathering, and evinced by their manner a spirit of the most determined resistance, and some of them were already standing with their guns cocked, and near enough to hear the conversation of the officer with Hanway and Lewis. The Marshal, seeing the number of the negroes and the threatening demonstrations made by them, asked Lewis to influence the negroes not to fire upon them, and he would withdraw his party, but was told by him that "the negroes might defend themselves." The blacks in the house, seeing their friends gathered in such abundance, came out and mingled with them. "Hanway walked his horse up to where the crowd of negroes were, and he spoke something low to them, and they gave one shout; he walked his horse about twenty or thirty yards, and looked towards them, and they fired up where Mr. Gorsuch was." *

Edward Gorsuch immediately fell, and his son Dickinson, running to his assistance, was also shot in the breast and lungs, and fell to the ground. Dr. Pearce was likewise shot in several places, but succeeded in making his escape. Deputy Marshal Kline, Joshua Gorsuch, and the other two individuals, Nelson and Hutchins, who formed part of the capturing party, all speedily made their escape as best they could. Edward Gorsuch was mutilated by the negroes, his pockets rifled of about $300, and left lying dead where he fell. His son Dickinson was rescued from death through the interposition of an old colored man, who begged of the murderers to spare his life, and he was shortly afterwards removed by some white persons who visited the scene, to the house of Levi Pownall, where he lay a considerable time before he could be removed.

* Evidence of Marshal Kline in Report of Christiana Tragedy, p. 7.

As soon as the news of this ocrurrence reached Lancaster, John L. Thompson, the District Attorney, and J. Franklin Reigart, an Alderman, accompanied by some of the most resolute citizens, repaired at once to Christiana, and after taking certain legal steps, proceeded to arrest the suspected parties. Nine were taken in less than two hours. Castner Hanway and Elijah Lewis, hearing of the warrants, surrendered themselves without resistance. All were committed by Alderman Reigart, and conveyed to the Lancaster Jail for a preliminary hearing. The United States Marshal, the United States District Attorney and the Commissioner, with a strong force of Marines and a detachment of Philadelphia police, arrived shortly afterwards at Christiana, and lent their aid in making arrests of those supposed to be implicated in the transaction. Both parties proceeded to make arrests, and in a short time every section of country was pretty well scoured. A large number of additional prisoners were brought in, and among them two whites, one named Scarlet, and the other Hood.

It became a question of considerable dispute between the State and national authorities, as to the disposition of the prisoners. District Attorney Thompson contended, that the prisoners had been guilty of the highest crime known to the law of Pennsylvania, wilfull and deliberate murder, and that as this had occurred in Lancaster County, the prisoners should be taken to Lancaster for trial. John W. Ashmead, the United States District Attorney, on the contrary, insisted that the prisoners had been guilty of the crime of treason, in levying war against the United States authorities. In this he was sustained by the Commissioner, E. D. Ingraham, and finally a compromise was effected, by which each party was allowed to dispose of its own arrests. A preliminary hearing of the prisoners was held before Alderman Reigart, at which several witnesses were examined. At this hearing, J. W. Ashmead, Robert J. Brent and William B. Fordney, appeared for the prosecution, and Thaddeus Stevens for the prisoners. Castner Hanway, Elijah Lewis, John Morgan, Henry Sims and Jacob Moore, were committed to answer the charge of treason, and delivered into the custody of A. E. Roberts, United States Marshal for the Eastern District of Pennsylvania.

No event, scarcely, could have occurred that would have aroused a more profound excitement throughout the country than was occasioned by this riot at Christiana. Political rancor was in this occurrence fanned to its highest pitch. The newspapers gave full scope to the rehearsal of the facts as they were reported; and these in many cases grossly exaggerated, as has become usual with the modern newspaper press. The deed was as variantly viewed as were the creeds of the different parties. Even in Pennsylvania, partisans condemned or exculpated the act of the rioters as their political proclivities dictated. Shrewd observers fully comprehended the nature of the transaction, and where the fault originated; but this did not appear upon the surface; and hence the widely different reports that were circulated. Blame was sought to be attached to the Whig Governor of Pennsylvania, because of believed indifference shown by him in taking steps to aid in arresting the rioters. It was not till the fourth day after the riot that he issued his proclamation, offering a reward for the capture of the murderers of Mr. Gorsuch. And even this was delayed until a letter, signed by John Cadwallader, C. Ingersoll, John W. Forney, and others, had demanded of him that he take measures to "vindicate the outraged laws of the Commonwealth."

The division in sentiment in Pennsylvania that chiefly obtained as regards the riot, was seen to be marked very considerably by party lines. It was not forgotten that the fugitive slave law had met with almost universal opposition from the Northern Whigs in Congress; and the condemnation of the act of the rioters was not believed to be sincere upon the part of many of that party, who were loud in its denunciation. But with many Whigs it was so; for, as before seen, by no means all of this party had become tainted with abolition principles. Being a Whig at that time, however, subjected an individual even in Pennsylvania to suspicion, and something was needed to remove it. But it was in the South that this negro riot created the greatest commotion. In this section it was viewed as an illustration of the Northern resistance to the compromise of 1850, which might still be expected to display itself in one form or other; and which would thus render it a dead letter upon the statute books. A lingering faith, however, that the majority of the people of Pennsylvania and of the North, were still friends of the Federal Constitution and the laws made thereunder, induced the South to hope that the insulted authority of the nation would yet vindicate itself in the Northern tribunals of justice.

On Monday, November 24th, 1851, the trial of Castner Hanway, for treason, was commenced in the United States Circuit Court before Judges Grier and Kane. The counsel who appeared for the United States were, John W. Ashmead, James R. Ludlow and George W. Ashmead; also, James Cooper and Robert W. Brent for Maryland. The counsel for Castner Hanway were John M. Reed, Thaddeus Stevens, Joseph J. Lewis and Theodore Cuyler. The trial lasted fifteen days, and was handled on both sides with masterly ability. Although, without doubt, Mr. Stevens was the brain of the defense in this trial, yet because of his known anti-slavery sentiments, it was deemed prudential that to John M. Read should be entrusted its principal management. After the arguments of counsel on both sides had been made and the Court had submitted their views of the law, the Jury upon retiring from the box, returned after an absence of ten minutes and reported a verdict of "Not guilty." Castner Hanway and Elijah Lewis were then brought to Lancaster to answer any charge that might be preferred against them. An indictment was laid before the Grand Jury for murder, but the Jury ignored the bill, and thus ended the Christiana Riot Case.

This trial, in a measure, illustrated the inutility of attempting, under our form of government, to convict an offender when a respectable and influential party openly espouses his cause. Members of the Anti-Slavery Society were present in court during the time of this trial, openly manifesting their sympathy for the accused; also for the other prisoners, black and white, that were implicated with him in the transaction. When "Harvey Scott, a free negro, who had thrice testified—once at Christiana, once at Lancaster, and once at Philadelphia—to the fact of being an eye witness to the murder of Mr. Gorsuch; and now on this trial, influenced by bribes, or some other corrupt consideration, when placed on the stand by the United States, openly confessed that he had thrice committed perjury, and then swore on this trial that he was not present and knew nothing about the affair; this perjury was received with open applause in the court room. Again, the counsel for the defense applied to the Court for an order to bring out some twenty-four of the negroes in prison to see which of them could be identified as participants in the treason, by Henry H. Kline (the Deputy Marshal), a material witness for the prosecution. At the opening of the court, on the next day, these negroes were seen sitting in a row, supported on each side by white females, who, to the disgust of all respectable citizens, gave them open sympathy and countenance; each of the negroes appeared with new comforts around their necks—their hair carefully parted and their clothing in every respect, so as to present one uniform appearance to the eye as far as possible—all done doubtless for the double purpose of giving "aid and comfort" to the accused murderers of a white man, and of confusing so important a witness as Kline, in respect to their identity. And this was manifestly done with the privity, sufferance and consent of the officers having charge of the prisoners, and passed unrebuked."* Such a degree of sympathy did the members of the Anti-Slavery Society manifest for those accused of participation in the Christiana riot, that on Thanksgiving Day they caused a banquet dinner to be prepared for the prisoners, and A. E. Roberts, the United States Marshal, confessed in open court "that he had not only assisted at the dinner but had sat down and partaken sparingly."†

The decisive points ruled by Judge Grier, and which proved fatal to the prosecution, were in the following words:

"Without desiring to invade the perogatives of the jury, in judging of the facts of this case, the Court feel bound to say, that they do not think the transaction with which the prisoner is charged with being connected rises to the dignity of treason, or a levying of war—not because the number or force was insufficient, but first—for want of any proof of a previous conspiracy to make a general and public resistance to any law of the United States; second—there is no evidence that any person connected in the transaction knew that there were any such Acts of Congress, as they were charged with conspiracy to resist by force and arms, or had any other intention than to protect one another from what they termed kidnappers—by which slang term, they included not only actual kidnappers, but all masters and owners seeking to recapture their slaves, and the officers and agents assisting them." ‡

Southern hopes, in the above trial, were once more disappointed. The tempting cup of promise which had been carried to the lips in the compromise of 1850, was thus again rudely dashed to the earth; and nothing save chagrin and mortification were left to console those south of the Mason and Dixon parallel. The South was an integral portion of the Confederacy, the Con-

*Report of Robert J. Brent on the Christiana Treason Trial to the Governor of Maryland, p, 5.
†Report of R. J. Brent, p. 4.
‡ Report of R. J. Brent, p. 7.

stitution recognized their rights of property, and the National Congress, in clearly defined terms, had guaranteed them these; and yet all as they felt to no purpose. Their citizens were treated as culprits and assassins when going North to lay claim to their escaped property; yea, even in the event which had but just occurred, the soil of Pennsylvania (without any redress being accorded) had drunk the blood of a most respectable citizen of Maryland, who had dared to cross the threshold of his State to seek his fugitive slaves. Another bond of confidence between the North and South was again snapped asunder, and still more feeble became those yet remaining. The fugitive slave law became virtually a dead letter in most of the Northern States, and the feelings of each section grew more and more estranged towards the other. And all this was but leading the North and South up to that pinnacle of mutual hate, from which both to free themselves, voluntarily plunged into the gulf of revolution and civil convulsion, which a near future had in store for them.

CHAPTER X.

THE KANSAS-NEBRASKA BILL, WITH THE REPEAL OF THE MISSOURI COMPROMISE. ORIGIN, RAMIFICATION AND ASPECTS OF THE REPUBLICAN PARTY.

The 33d Congress assembled in December, 1853. Mr. Stevens not being a member of this Congress, again devoted his attention to the practice of his profession, a career in which he was always remarkably successful. After the close of his second Congressional term, he found his legal business by no means diminished; and for the next six years he was little heard of outside of Lancaster County, as mingling in political strife. These years were for him a period of great professional activity; and in many of the most important suits tried in the courts of Pennsylvania, he was during this period the leading counsel. He nevertheless remained no indifferent spectator of public events, as they were then transpiring. And all this time he held himself in readiness to act his part when public sentiment might warrant his participation.

Upon the opening of Congress in December, 1853, it was found that certain portions of the public domain, embraced in the Louisiana cession, were already sufficiently populated to require local governments. Two delegates had been chosen by the people of this Territory who were awaiting admission into the National Legislature, and seeking local organizations for their constituents. On the 4th of December, 1853, Mr. Dodge, of Iowa, introduced a bill into the Senate for the organization of a Territorial Government for Nebraska, which was referred to the committee on Territories, of which Stephen A. Douglas was chairman. On the 4th of the following January, Mr. Douglas reported back this bill, with amendments so changing its language, as to make it accord with the language of the Utah and New Mexico Bill of 1850, on the question of slavery. This Bill was accompanied with an elaborate report, stating fully the reasons that had induced the Committee to change its phraseolgy in these particulars. The principle aimed at by the Committee was expressed in the following words:

"In the judgment of your Committee, those measures (compromise of 1850) were intended to have a far more comprehensive and enduring effect than the mere adjustment of the difficulties arising out of the recent acquisitions of Mexican territory. They were designed to establish certain great principles, which would not only furnish adequate remedies for existing evils, but in all time to come avoid the perils of a similar agitation, by withdrawing the question of slavery from the Halls of Congress and the political arena, and committing it to the arbitrament of those who were immediately interested, and alone responsible for its consequences."

The report concluded with these words:

"The substitute for the bill which your Committee have prepared, and which is commended to the favorable action of the Senate, proposes to carry these propositions and principles into practical operation in the precise language of the compromise measures of 1850."

Senator Douglas, speaking of the report of the Committee, said:

"We were aware that from 1820 to 1850, the abolition doctrine of Congressional interference with slavery in the Territories and new States, had so far prevailed as to keep up an incessant agitation in Congress and throughout the country, whenever any new Territory was to be acquired or organized. We were also aware that, in 1850, the right of the people to decide this question for themselves, subject only to the Constitution, was substituted for the doctrine of congressional intervention. The first question, therefore, which the Committee were called upon to decide, and indeed the only question of any material importance, in forming this bill was this: Shall we adhere to and carry out the principle recognized by the compromise measures of 1850, or shall we go back to the old exploded doctrine of congressional interference, as established in 1820, in a large portion of the country, and which it was the object of the Wilmot proviso, to give a universal application not only to all the territory which we then possessed, but all which we might hereafter acquire? There were no other alternatives. We were compelled to frame the bill upon the one or the other of these two principles. The doctrine of 1820, or the doctrine of 1850, must prevail. In the discharge of the duty imposed upon us by the Senate, the Committee could not hesitate upon this point, whether we consulted our individual opinions and principles or those which were known to be entertained and boldly avowed by a large majority of the Senate. The two great political parties of the country stood solemnly pledged before the world to adhere to the compromise measures of 1850 in principle and substance. A large majority of the Senate, indeed every member of the body, I believe, except the two avowed Abolitionists (Mr. Chase and Mr. Sumner,) profess to belong to the one or the other of these parties, and hence were supposed to be under a high moral obligation to carry out *the principle and substance* of those measures in all the new territorial organizations. The report of the Committee was in accordance with this obligation."*

The original bill as amended and reported by the Committee, was received in some parts of the country as effecting the repeal of the Missouri Compromise Act, whilst in others it was differently construed. In order that all ambiguity as regards this point might be removed, Archibald Dixon, a Whig Senator from Kentucky, on the 16th of January, gave notice that when the Nebraska Bill should come up for consideration, he would offer an amendment repealing the Eighth Section of the Missouri Act, as being inconsistent with the Compromise of 1850. On the following day, Sumner introduced into the Senate a memorial against slavery generally, and at the same time gave notice that when the bill to recognize the Territory should come up for consideration, he would offer an amendment re-affirming the old Congressional restriction of 1820. A manifesto was issued from Washington on the 19th of January, denouncing the repeal of the Missouri Compromise, signed by the following Senators and Representatives, viz: S. P. Chase, Charles Sumner, J. R. Giddings, Edward Wade, Gerrit Smith and Alexander De Witt. This remonstrance appeared in all the Abolition papers of the country, and again roused the monster of sectional agitation from his slumber. The remonstrants spoke of the old Missouri line as a "*sacred pledge*," never to be violated. It became in their estimation a "solemn compact" when its endorsement favored their principles. "Three thousand New England Clergymen, assuming to speak in the name of the Almighty God, joined in the chorus. But when did these men, or any of their class, singly or collectively, ever before acknowledge any binding obligation of the now and so-called "solemn compact?" Was it when Missouri was denied admission by them under it? Was it when the admission of Arkansas was opposed by them? Was it when the provision was made for the admission of Texas? Was it when a government for Oregon was organized? Was it when this line was voted down for the last time in the House on the 13th of June, 1850?"†

The Committee on Territories, in view of the extent of domain

*Appendix to *Congressional Globe*, 33d Congress, 1st Session, p. 336.
†Stephens' War, Vol. II, p. 248.

to be organized, deemed it expedient to divide it into two separate Territorial Governments, one to be named Kansas, and the other Nebraska. Accordingly a substitute organizing two Territories instead of one was reported in the Senate by Mr. Douglas on the 22d of January. The language in each upon the subject of slavery was identical, with that in the first Nebraska Bill with the exception of that clause which in express words declared the Eighth Section of the Missouri Act inoperative. This was in the following words:

"Except the eighth section of the Act prepatory to the admission of Missouri into the Union, approved March 6th, 1820, which being inconsistent with the principle of non-intervention by Congress, with slavery in the States and Territories, as recognized by the legislation of 1850, commonly called the Compromise Measures, is hereby declared inoperative and void; it being the true intent and meaning of this Act not to legislate slavery into any Territory or State, nor to exclude it therefrom, but to leave the people thereof perfectly free to form and regulate their domestic institutions in their own way, subject only to the Constitution of the United States."

Senator Douglas, speaking of the Missouri Compromise, showed by whose dereliction it had originally been violated, and that this violation of it had necessitated the abandonment of the principle it had established, and a recurrence to that of non-intervention. In his speech of Jan. 30th, he said:

"True, the express enactment of the 8th section of the Missouri Act, (now called the Missouri Compromise) only covered the Territory acquired from France; but the principle of the Act, the objects of its adoption, the reasons in its support required that it should be extended indefinitely westward, so far as our Territory might go, when new purchases should be made."*

When Texas was admitted into the Union, on motion of Stephen A. Douglas, then a member of the House, the principle of the Missouri Compromise was applied to it without open opposition, doubtless lest abolition breach of faith would appear too palpable. He also in 1848 made an effort as Senator, to have the same principle applied to the newly acquired Mexican Territory. Of this effort he speaks as follows:

"Then, sir, in 1848, we acquired from Mexico the country between the Rio del Norte and the Pacific Ocean. Immediately after the acquisition, the Senate, on my own motion, voted into a bill a provision to extend the Missouri compromise indefinitely westward to the Pacific Ocean, in the same sense and with the same understanding with which it was

National Intelligencer, February 2d, 1854.

originally adopted. That provision passed this body by a decided majority—I think by ten at least—and went to the House of Representatives and was there defeated by Northern votes.

"Now, sir, let us pause and consider for a moment. The first time that the principles of the Missouri compromise were ever abandoned, the first time they were ever rejected by Congress, was by the defeat of that provision in the House of Representatives in 1848. By whom was that defeat effected? By Northern States with free soil proclivities. It was the defeat of that Missouri compromise that re-opened the slavery agitation with all its fury. It was the defeat of that Missouri compromise that created the necessity for making a new compromise in 1850. Had we been faithful to the principles of the Missouri Act in 1848, this question would not have risen. Who was it that was faithless? I undertake to say it was the very men who now insist that the Missouri compromise was a solemn compact and should not be violated and departed from. Every man who is now assailing the principle of the bill under consideration, so far as I am advised, was opposed to the Missouri compromise in 1848. The very men who now arraign me for a departure from the Missouri compromise are the men who successfully violated it, repudiated it, and caused it to be superseded by the compromise measures of 1850. Sir, it is with rather a bad grace that the men who proved false themselves should charge upon me and others, who were ever faithful, the responsibilities and consequences of their own treachery.

"Then, sir, as I before remarked, the defeat of the Missouri compromise in 1848 having created the necessity for the establishment of a new one in 1850, let us see what that compromise was.

"The binding feature of the compromise of 1850 was Congressional non-intervention as to slavery in the Territories; that the people of the Territories and of all the States were to be allowed to do as they pleased upon the subject of slavery, subject only to the provisions of the Constitution of the United States.

"That, sir, was the leading feature of the compromise measures of 1850. Those measures, therefore, abandoned the idea of a geographical line as the boundary between the free and the slave States; abandoned it because, compelled to do it from an inability to maintain it; and in lieu of that substituted the great principle of self-government, which would allow the people to do as they thought proper."*

Speaking of the inconsistency of the Abolitionists as regards the Missouri compromise, Senator Douglas further said:

"Did not every Abolitionist and Free Soiler in America denounce the Missouri compromise in 1820? Did they not for years hunt down, ravenously for his blood, every man who assisted in making that compromise? Did they not, in 1845, when Texas was annexed, denounce all of us who went for the annexation of Texas and for the continuation of the Missouri compromise line through it? Did they not, in 1848, denounce me as a slavery propagandist, for standing by the principles of the Missouri com-

*Speech of Douglas of Jan. 30th, 1854; in *National Intelligencer* Feb. 2d, 1854.

promise, and proposing it to be extended to the Pacific Ocean? Did they not themselves violate and repudiate it then? Is not the charge of bad faith true as to every Abolitionist in America, instead of being true as to me and the Committee and those who advocate this bill."*

Mr. Douglas and those co-operating with him, hoped by the passage of the Kansas-Nebraska Bill, that the question of slavery might be removed from the Halls of Congress, and left with the people of the Territories themselves. This legislation was but re-introducing first principles which had been abandoned when the Missouri Compromise was adopted, and which the Southern people accepted with reluctance as being an unjust discrimination against their equality as integral members of the Confederacy. Alexander H. Stephens, the philosophic statesman of the South, whilst in Congress, in a speech delivered in the House, February 17th, 1854, said:

"It (the Missouri Compromise) was literally forced upon the South as a disagreeable alternative by superior numbers." †

The Kansas-Nebraska Bill asserted, upon its face, that its true intent and meaning was that the question of slavery should be left to the people of the Territories to determine for themselves whether they desired it, and subject only to the Constitution of the United States. Stephen A. Douglas, the author of the bill, was violently assailed as false to his own democratic faith which execrated all slavery agitation; but he justified his course by affirming his entire conformity with the compromise measures of 1850. His object, as he contended, was simply to free the Territories from all unconstitutional legislation, and to leave the question of slavery where the framers of the government had designed, that is, with the people of the territories themselves. The bill was not only discussed with great violence in Congress, but was taken up by the abolition press in all sections of the North, and contrary to expectation, the slavery agitation was aroused in all its strength and intensity throughout the whole country. The discussion produced one of the most terrific political storms that had ever yet raged upon the American continent. The very flood-gates and windows of abolition fury seemed now for the first time to have been fully opened. The abolition Whigs embraced this opportunity to retrieve their fallen political

*Speech of Douglas January 30, 1854; in *National Intelligencer*, February 2d, 1854.

†*National Intelligencer*, February 24th, 1854.

fortunes, and unite the North in a sectional contest against the South. Public meetings were held in the Northern States, denouncing the repeal of the Missouri Compromise, and remonstrances to the same effect flooded the National Legislature. Large numbers of both political parties participated in these meetings who had given their hearty adhesion to the Compromise of 1850, and a monster meeting at Boston, was presided over by Samuel S. Elliot, the only Whig representative from New England, who had favored that last national adjudication of the slavery question.

The Bill, however, passed both Houses of Congress, and became a law by receiving the signature of the President on the last day of May, 1854. It was clearly the refusal of the Abolitionists of the North to yield a fair and full acquiescence in the Missouri Compromise, in letter and spirit, which led to its final repeal in 1854. And it is also undeniable that this repeal simply restored to its original normal position, the doctrine of popular sovereignty, as it was designed to obtain from the foundation of the government. But it must also be accepted as true, that whilst the repeal of the Missouri Compromise, in strict interpretation, may have been effected by the principle adopted by the Compromise measures of 1850; yet no averment was made at the time that such was really so; and it remained for the year 1854 to disclose it. The Compromise of 1850, applied to the Territory acquired from Mexico, whilst that of 1820 included the Louisiana purchase; and therefore entirely distinctive and separate portions of the territorial domain were embraced by these two famous National settlements. The Compromise of 1850 did not expressly repeal that of 1820, and although it had in spirit been repudiated by the North, yet in view of the intense opposition that existed to the spread of slavery, over any of the Federal territory, policy seemed to dictate that the South should only claim what the clear letter of the Constitution and the national contracts accorded them. That this was the opinion of a considerable number of the leading statesmen both North and South, is undoubted; and even of those voting for the repeal of the Missouri Compromise were some who regarded the act as impolitic, and likely to entail in its train sad consequences. Gen. Lewis Cass, whilst sustaining the Kansas-Nebraska Bill thus expressed himself regarding the measure:

"I should have been better content had the whole subject been left as it was in the bill when it was first introduced by the Senator from Illinois, without any provision regarding the Missouri Compromise." *

James Buchanan was another of those statesmen who viewed the repeal of the Missouri Compromise, as in itself altogether impolitic and injudicious. "The Compromise measures of 1850 had his hearty adhesion, as in these he seemed to recognize the settlement of the only question that could perhaps for ages jeopard the national integrity. With the greatest anxiety and dread was it, therefore, that he heard, whilst in Europe, of the repeal of the Missouri Compromise in 1854. In a letter written to a leading statesman of his party, about the time that the repeal began to be mooted, he uttered solemn words of warning, and strongly remonstrated against the abrogation of this time-honored compact. He depicted in strong colors the dangers he apprehended would result should this unwise attempt be consummated. From an intimate knowledge of the feelings of the people of the North, he predicted the terrible storm that would be aroused throughout the country by such an opening up of the slavery agitation as this would occasion."†

Mr. Buchanan, in the History of his administration on the eve of the rebellion, page 28, speaks in this manner of the repeal of the Missouri Compromise:

"After a careful review of the history of the Anti-Slavery party from its origin, the candid inquirer must admit that up till this period it had acted on the aggressive against the South. From the beginning it had kept the citizens of the slave-holding States in constant irritation, as well as serious apprehension of their domestic peace and security. It is true, they had denounced the assailants with extreme rancor and many threats, but had done nothing more. In sustaining the repeal of the Missouri Compromise, however, the Senators and Representatives of the Southern States became the aggressors themselves, and thereby placed the country in an alarming and dangerous condition from which it has never since been rescued."

The repeal of the Missouri Compromise afforded to the Abolitionists the opportunity that was required to unite the North in a sectional organization against the South. Many of the Northern Whigs of free soil proclivities had desired to see a party constituted upon principles adverse to the further spread of slavery, and pledged to its final extinction, could any means be devised

* *National Intelligencer*, March 7th, 1854.
† Harris' Biographical History of Lancaster County, pp. 105–6.

for that purpose. The following extracts from addresses made by R. C. Winthrop, of Massachusetts, and Thomas Corwin, of Ohio, both distinguished leaders of the Whig party, attest this fact:

"Why, my friends, how long is it since it was distinctly declared by some of the leaders of the Republican party, that the great remedy for existing evils was the formation of a party which should have no Southern wing; yes, that was the phraze—*no Southern wing;* for it was added that as long as there was a Southern wing there must be complainers and concessions to the South, and compromises would be the order of the day."*

Thomas Corwin, speaking of the repeal of the Missouri Compromise, said:

"And do you not see how gladly it was seized upon by those who have been trying to form a Northern party for years, and how the war-cry they raised went up through the whole North. And yet they are the very men who had long denounced the compromise as an infringement of right and freedom."†

It was understood by the leading Whigs that their party was composed of elements altogether too inharmonious to remain united after the demise of Clay and Webster. The divisions of the party, which had for years disclosed themselves in Congress, was ample proof of this fact; and it was clear that the disharmony was every year becoming more apparent and decided. After the defeat of Gen. Scott for President, in 1852, crafty leaders availed themselves of the American sentiment, by means or which to rear an organization that might take the place of the old Whig party; and early in 1854 the movements for this purpose were in active operation. The sentiment upon which this new effort to construct a party was based, had repeatedly shown itself in the United States, especially in the large cities; and owing to the social elements of the country, it is one that is likely, more or less potentially, ever to make itself felt. An antagonism to Catholics and foreigners is somewhat natural to the bulk of the Protestant population of America; and this will be always greatly manifested when party spirit is dragged into the arena. This was the effort in 1854, and the prospect seemed for a time as if it might be successful. It was at that time, familiarly characterized as the Know Nothing movement, and it achieved temporary triumphs in several States of the Union, and

*Speech of Gov. Winthrop, in *National Intelligencer*, Oct. 30, 1856.
†*National Intelligencer*, Oct. 23d, 1856.

even stoutly battled for ascendancy in the old Commonwealth of Virginia. The elections in 1854 in the Northern States, were largely influenced by the operations of this party; to it was James Pollock indebted for his election as Governor of Pennsylvania. The success achieved by this organization was no doubt largely due to the fact that it assumed the shape of a secret order; and curiosity (as is ever the case with secret associations) induced elements of the most incongruous character to enter it. But, because the order was made up of men of radically incompatible views and purposes, its dissolution become simply a question of time. The Whigs who joined the order remained such, and so did also the Democrats; and it became soon apparent that no views so discordant could long remain united.

The Know Nothing breeze became one of the currents that served to confuse parties, as they existed in Lancaster County, and enabled Mr. Stevens and his political wing to grasp hold of the reins of power. He permitted himself to be initiated into a secret order, in which he recognized political power looming up for himself in the distance; and for the time he forgot the opposition that he had years before waged against the Masonic fraternity. The American movement was for Mr. Stevens a very important one, so far as his future prospects were concerned. It served to prostrate his principal antagonists amongst the Silver-Grey Whigs, and left him prospectively the master of the field. Although unable to secure the Congressional nomination for himself in 1854, yet he manipulated affairs so adroitly that A. E. Roberts, an intimate and confidential political friend, was made the party choice. This was a near advance to the goal of his own ambition. He had now become the power behind the throne.

But what served most to unite a Northern sectional party, was the opposition which arrayed itself against the repeal of the Missouri Compromise and the further extension of slavery. The Whigs in the Free States in 1854, were almost unanimously opposed to the repeal, as were likewise a considerable number of Democrats.

In the meetings that were held to denounce the measure, men of both political parties participated, but by far the larger proportion was made up of Whigs. The Abolitionists sought at once to form a party of fused elements, united in opposition to the spread of the hated Southern institution; but this met with a spirited resistance from those who still preferred the Whig organization. The Whigs, in their State Conventions held in the Northern States, repudiated the repeal of the Missouri Compromise; but many of the trusted leaders of this old National party resisted its abandonment for what they clearly saw would become a sectional one, and which would doubtless endanger the perpetuity of the American Union.

The old party of Jefferson had a difficult task in the North during the campaign of 1854. The party being virtually committed to the principles of the Kansas-Nebraska Bill, found that these would prove a heavy burden in the Free States. Stephen A. Douglas, the author of the bill, upon his return home from Congress, met in Chicago a storm of opposition, for which he was not prepared. Those, who on former occasions, had listened with delight to the glowing eloquence of the Illinois Senator, refused now to hear him; and as often as he attempted to speak in his defense, they drowned his voice with their hisses and groans. Little more favorable receptions were accorded to him in some other sections of his State. Democratic meetings addressed by him, would as soon as adjourned, extemporize a new one, and pass resolutions condemning his action as a Senator in Congress, and denouncing the Kansas-Nebraska Bill. In every State of the North, the repeal of the Missouri Compromise, proved a cause of disturbance in the Democratic party. The majority of the party sustained the principles of the measure; but so intense and powerful was the opposition in some States, that the party conventions refused to endorse it. In many States the conventions split upon this all engrossing question. The party leaders in the North strove to meet the threatening catastrophe by endeavoring to prevent the measure from being made a party test. A number of leading Democrats of Michigan, in 1854, issued a circular urging as follows:

"We respectfully submit, that every consideration, both in principle and policy, appeals to us to stand firmly against the Kansas-Nebraska Bill as a party test. It is a measure which is strongly disapproved of by a large portion of the Democracy of the nation. Unwisely introduced, it has already done infinite mischief, and if made a party test it will inevitably divide the Democratic party, and let loose a storm of the wildest agitation."

The Democracy of the Empire State of New York were divided into the Hards and Softs, the latter having largely the preponderance. Resolutions demanding the restoration of the Missouri Compromise passed both Houses of the New York Legislature by great majorities, and in Massachusetts, such were adopted in the Senate by a unanimous vote, and in the House, consisting of 400 members, with only thirteen negative votes. In all parts of the North the repeal made an instantaneous impression, and the Democracy, as never before, began to stagger under the unendurable burden. W. B. S. Moore, Chairman of the Maine Democratic Committee on Resolutions in the Convention held in June, 1854, remarked:

"We came into power eighteen months ago with an unprecedented majority in the nation; and in the State we had a great moral power—perhaps too much. Since then, changes have come over the aspect of and the prospect of the Democracy. We have lost Maine, Rhode Island, Connecticut, and it is nearly a draw game in New Hampshire, that ought to stand firm as her granite hills."

Skelton, an Anti-Nebraska Democratic Representative of New Jersey, said:

"The party was strong and united until the passage of this bill. Now it is divided in every Congressional District. It was introduced as a measure of Peace, but it has rent the party and renewed the slavery agitation."

The Charleston *Mercury*, seeing the coming storm that was rising in the North, in its issue of June 21st, 1854, said:

"The spectacle presented by the North and South at the present moment is well calculated to arrest the attention of thoughtful men. In the former we find society convulsed; all the slumbering elements of sectional bitterness roused and slavery agitation awake again, after its brief and delusive sleep, strengthened by new accessions and eager for the onset. Never before have the Northern press approached so near to unanimity in the cause of abolition. Never before were all other issues so far buried, and the sentiment and voice of the whole section so united in war upon the South."

The fall elections of 1854 in the Northern States, one after another swept from power the party which was held responsible for the repeal of the Missouri Compromise. Maine, that had remained firm to her democratrc moorings since 1840, was carried for the new party by an immense majority. The other Eastern States followed in the same line; and New York wheeled under the banner of Anti-slavery extension. Not a single Congressman from the Empire State that had supported the repeal, was re-elected, and the Keystone State gave a congressional delegation strongly Anti-Nebraska. Ohio rallied by an immense majority to the Anti-Slavery standards, electing all Anti-Nebraska Congressmen. The People's party triumphed in Indiana, and the strong oaks of the Democracy bent beneath the blasts of the opposition. The members of Congress throughout the whole North, who had supported the repeal of the Missouri Compromise, were almost all defeated, and Anti-Slavery ideas rose at once to ascendancy and power. The revolution passed like a hurricane over the North; and the new party in most sections styling itself Republican, bore the banner of victory. The fruits of the long Anti-slavery agitation had ripened; and a sectional Northern organization was the result of the struggle. The agitators had at length gained the prize; the Northern States were now united against the South and her institutions in clear and unmistakable opposition; and time alone could determine the result of the conflict.

CHAPTER XI.

THE STRUGGLE FOR ASCENDENCY IN KANSAS. THE DEVELOPMENT OF CONFLICTING VIEWS INTO SECTIONAL ANTAGONISM AND THE ULTIMATE TRIUMPH OF REPUBLICANISM.

The repeal of the Missouri Compromise opened the Territories to all the social institutions of the different States of the Union. It was believed that this would terminate the national conflict on the question of slavery by removing it from the Halls of Congress, and leaving it for disposition with the people of the Territories themselves; but in doing so, the public interest was only the more aroused and intensified. The repeal of the compromise appeared to the Northern mind such a flagrant violation of everything that was sacred in compact, that it was prepared to interpose every obstacle to the introduction of slavery into the new Territories, which might in any wise baffle the friends of the institution. Even Kansas, the most Southern Territory, belonged to that part of the public domain which had been consecrated to freedom; and now that this should be snatched from its heritage and offered as a prize to the fleetest occupant, was to Northern sentiment offensive in the highest degree. The views and policy of statesmen could not be expected to countervail the feelings of the masses, that had for upwards of two decades been influenced by Anti-Slavery agitation; and which was every year evincing greater opposition to the spread of the hated institution of the Southern States. Northern sentiment on no former occasion rose in such unanimity and earnestness to utter its protest against the introduction of slavery into the Territories, as it did when Kansas and Nebraska were organized and laid open for settlement.

An Emigrant Aid Society was accordingly incorporated in Boston in the year 1854, by the Legislature of Massachusetts, for the purpose of encouraging settlers to emigrate to Kansas, who would be pledged to resist the introduction of slavery into the new State. In the repeal of the Missouri Compromise, the

Southern people, on the contrary, seemed to recognize simply the removal of all unjust discrimination against them in the common Territories of the nation; and the restoration of those rights which they had originally enjoyed prior to the year 1820. The movement of the Abolitionists in Massachusetts, therefore, had the effect of arousing in the Southern mind a determination of resistance; and societies were speedily organized in Missouri and elsewhere, pledged to promote the interests of settlers from the South and those who favored the pro-slavery cause. These acts of the antagonistic parties, so different from what had before occurred in the settlement of the Territories, displayed the wonderful zeal of the contestants; and at once attracted public attention to Kansas as the prize which should reward for his skill and prowess the conquering gladiator of his country. The contest for Kansas thus rose immediately from State to national importance; and the removal of the question from Congress, served but to light the flames of strife between the North and South in all parts of the country. The removal, therefore, was fatal to the peace of the Republic, and proved also fatal to the hopes of any man in the North, who had anticipated applause and position from his instrumentality in its accomplishment.

Settlers from the South and emigrants from the North were hurried into the new Territory, all more or less eager to win Kansas for their party. The enthusiast and the fanatic, the adventurous and the daring, all moved to this inviting El Dorado of their political hopes, and the mixture was a sample of democratic society in its native compound.* Anarchy and misrule held high carnival in the new Territory, and for a time marauding bands of partisan settlers were the only legislators who dispensed law as their passions and prejudices dictated. Both of the political parties who were struggling for ascendency in the new region, were amply represented by correspondents, whose chief aim was to depict that which would meet the warmest reception in the circle of their readers. The truthful chronicler, never popular, was especially unadapted to such a state of society. Partisans must have the food they desire, and such as will minister pleasure

* The democratic society, here meant, is that form of the body politic where the government is assumed to reside in the corporate mass; and it is not intended to designate any political party which may at any time have borne that designation.

to their corrupted appetites. An admirable field was presented in Kansas for the Eastern and Southern press; indeed, the narrative of the same event, from different pens, appeared as altogether separate occurrences, and only at times could the identity be discovered from a similarity of names. But the party readers who are content to receive one version of a story, could not but be incensed to the highest degree by the iniquity and injustice that were perpetrated as they conceived upon their friends in the new Territory. Section was thus aroused against section, and this chiefly effected through the instrumentality of the party press, one of the great evils of republican institutions.

A. H. Reeder was appointed Governor of the new Territory, and he, with such other officers as the territorial condition required, arrived in Kansas in the fall of 1854. It being too late to organize the full machinery of the Territory, no election was held except for a delegate to Congress, which resulted pro-slavery, in the choice of John W. Whitfield. Early in 1855, a census having been taken, an election for a Territorial Legislature and County officers was ordered on the 30th of March. This resulted in a Southern victory, and as the Free State men charged, by the aid of Missouri invaders. In such a state of society, nothing else should have been expected, for the kind of voters who flock to new Territories are not those who weigh scruples when partisan interests are at stake. That their opponents were unable to counteract all the frauds committed by the Missourians, was not because greater conscientiousness interposed, but rather, that no opportunity afforded the means. It was, in truth, the lawless elements of society in conflict, and only somewhat restrained by the subordination to which the General Government had subjected them. Murder, bloodshed and rapine will always be the concomitants of such states of the body politic.

But the Legislature as elected, was convened by the Governor, and proceeded to enact a code of laws, molded by the most intense pro-slavery feelings, and drafted in the interests of party views. The formation of Kansas as a Slave State, was the animating motive of every legislator who favored the adopted code. The enactments of this Legislature was water upon the abolition mill. The Northern press teemed with denunciations of an assembly that was held up as representing Southern sentiments and views. The Kansas settlers were amongst the extremes of their parties.

Whilst the one party became extreme in its legislation, the other was equally so in its resistance. Instead of waiting until they might disposses the Southern party at the ballot-box, the Free State men showed the utmost lawlessness in organizing at Topeka, an independent government in opposition to that first elected, and which had the regularity of law in its favor. Having framed a Constitution, elected a Governor, Legislature and other County officers, they applied to Congress for admission into the Union, but were justly rejected, if for no other reason than that they lacked that formal and legal status which entitled them to make application. Between two antagonistic territorial organizations, one defying the other, disturbances must necessarily occur; and it was only owing to the interposing authority of the General Government that the territory was not precipitated into a party collision, that might have engulphed the whole Union in the flames ot civil war. The contestants were rapidly preparing for a clash of arms; and the outposts first met on the plains of Kansas, and fought their initial sectional conflict.

The General Government nobly strove to hold the balance of justice even between the parties of Kansas; but law and order demanded that no other authority should be recognized than that which was created by virtue of the original charter. When, therefore, the Legislature chosen under the Free State Constitution, adopted at Topeka, determined to assemble on the 4th of July, 1856, they were dispersed by Col. Sumner with a force of regulars, by the orders of President Pierce. The spring and summer of 1856 was the principal period during which the Kansas war raged; and which formed a fertile theme for the abolition papers of the North in the Presidential campaign of that year. The war, in itself, was of little consequence, save as a means of inflaming Northern and Southern sentiment. One of the principal conflicts was the battle of "Black Jack," wherein twenty-eight Free State men, led by old John Brown, fought a somewhat superior number of Southerners and defeated them. But the Republican papers were glutted with the stories of *bleeding Kansas;* some of these possessing a grain of truth, but largely fictitious, and retailed for partisan circulation in the campaign then pending. It was the discussion of this fertile subject, the difficulties in Kansas, that served largely to solidify the Republican party into symmetrical proportions, and give it that strength and full sectional importance which it obtained in the year 1856.

Although the opposition to the repeal of the Missouri Compromise in many parts of the North, had united itself in 1854 into a party styled Republican; yet in Pennsylvania the resistance was unorganized. No steps had been taken in Lancaster County, the home of Thaddeus Stevens, for the organization of the new party until the year 1855; and when it was first suggested to him by a political friend that something should be done to organize such a movement in the county, the project, instead of meeting his approbation, was rather discouraged. Political advancement was the goal upon which Mr. Stevens had fixed his eye; and knowing the character of the people of his district, he trusted not to commit his fortunes to an untried bark, that had not yet been fairly launched upon the waters of American conservatism; and which had but made its passage in the smaller bays of radical innovation. Not forgetful that his course in Congress, as regards the Compromise of 1850, had bolted the doors of the National Assembly against him, he chose to pursue the path which policy dictated and watch the political gales before he would permit his vessel to be trimmed. But the movement of Republicanism was onwards, and the Keystone State was unable to remain aloof from its influence; and finally a meeting of those favorable to the cause was announced to meet in Fulton Hall, in the City of Lancaster. and organize the new party in the county. Those who assembled upon this occasion did not exceed seventeen persons in all; the great body of the Whig leaders absented themselves until they might see what success the future promised. Consistency, however, compelled the attendance of Mr. Stevens at this meeting. Republicanism was the movement in which the principles he cherished had ultimated; and it was necessary that he should obtain the control over it in his district; otherwise he would be washed into political retirement. He was present and addressed the small meeting, and thus placed himself as its leader in that field over which his influence extended. At a subsequent meeting he was selected to represent the Republican party of Lancaster County in the Philadelphia Convention of 1856 for the nomination of candidates for President and Vice-President of the United States.

The 34th Congress assembled in Washington, December 3d, 1855, and then began the great contest in which the sectional

Republican party strove for ascendency in the Halls of National Legislation. This was the long struggle for the election of Speaker in the House of Representacives, which lasted over two months, and ended in the election of Nathaniel P. Banks, the candidate of sectional ideas. In this triumph of Northern opposition to the spread of slavery, the Republican party saw the clearest omen of its future victory and triumph; and the leaders now exerted themselves to the utmost of their ability, to cement and unite the organization in all the States of the North. The first convention of this party from the Northern States, assembled in Pittsburgh in February, 1856; and this was followed by that of June 17th; which met in Philadelphia and nominated candidates for President and Vice-President of the United States. John C. Fremont and William L. Dayton were the candidates of the Philadelphia Republican Convention. Thaddeus Stevens was a member of this convention, although he took no very prominent part in the proceedings. The adopted platform placed the party in open and avowed resistance to the further extension of slavery; and made the organization the expression of the anti-slavery sentiment of the Northern States. One of the resolutions of the Philadelphia Convention declared:

"That the Constitution confers upon Congress, sovereign power over the Territories of the United States for their government; and that in the exercise of this power, it is both the right and the duty of Congress to prohibit in the Territories, those twin relics of barbarism, polygamy and slavery."

It was clear to all discerning men, in view of the composition of the Republican party, that its objects as expressed in its platform were simply secondary to the one idea, the entire abolition of slavery throughout the Southern States. The announcement of the real design of the party leaders would, however, have been fatal to their prospects of success; for much as the people of the North were opposed to slavery, they were not yet prepared for an unconstitutional attack upon the rights of their Southern brethren. But the leaders adopted the whole argument of the Abolitionists for the purpose of educating public sentiment up to the highest demands of the radical school; and at the same time announced their objects to be simply the confinement of slavery within its bounds. The growing national corruption was fully evinced in this attitude of the new party, which was so organized that it might gain power under false colors. The crafty argument was likewise made use of, that the exclusion of slavery was not opposed for the sake of the negro, but because it was desired that the Territory be preserved for the free settlers of the North—"free homes for free men."

The people of the South, and the calm and considerative of the North saw, with the greatest alarm, the advances of the new party threatening the peace and prosperity of the Union. The maxims of the Republican creed promulgated the doctrine dangerous to free institutions, that the will of the majority may determine the constitutional and vested rights of minorities. The principle thus announced was revolutionary in itself, destructive of all constituted authority, and engendered in the Red Republican teachings of the old world. Patriotic men of all sections, dreaded the consequences likely to ensue to liberty, should the revolutionary party of the North succeed in grasping the control of the Federal Government, and many of them admonished their countrymen of the dangers that threatened the integrity of the Union, and earnestly advised them to beware of the principles of sectionalism. Millard Fillmore, who had just returned from Europe, when he saw the aspect which the Republican party occupied in 1856, spoke as follows:

"But this is not all, sir. We see a political party presenting candidates for the Presidency and Vice-Presidency, selected for the first time from the Free States alone, with the avowed purpose of electing these candidates by the suffrages of one part of the Union only, to rule over the whole United States. Can it be possible that those who are engaged in such a measure can have seriously reflected upon the consequences which must inevitably follow in case of success? Can they have the madness or the folly to believe that our Southern brethren would submit to be governed by such a Chief Magistrate? Would he be required to follow the same rule prescribed by those who elected him in making his appointments? If a man living south of Mason and Dixon's line be not worthy to be President and Vice-President, would it be proper to select one from the same quarter as one of his Cabinet Council, or to represent the nation in a foreign country, or, indeed, to collect the revenue or administer the laws of the United States? If not, what new rule is the President to adopt in se'ecting men for office that the people themselves discard in selecting him? These are serious but practical questions, and in order to appreciate them fully it is but only necessary to turn the tables upon ourselves. Suppose that the South, having the majority of electoral votes, should declare that they would only have slave-holders for President and Vice-President, and should elect such by their exclusive suffrages to rule over us at the North; do you think we would submit to it? No, not for one moment! And do you believe that your

Southern brethren are less sensitive on this subject than you are, or less jealous of their rights? If you do, let me tell you that you are mistaken. And, therefore, you must see that, if this sectional party succeeds, it leads inevitably to the destruction of this beautiful fabric, reared by our forefathers, cemented by their blood, and bequeathed to us as a precious inheritance."

The disruption of the Whig party, occasioned by the slavery question, induced many of the Southern Whigs to unite with the Democracy, as the only party professing national principles, that gave evidence of ability to cope with the new enemy. In attaching themselves to their former political rival, they in no wise compromised their early principles, for the old Whig and Democratic parties equally favored the constitutional rights of all sections of the Union, in the States as well as in the national Territories. A small portion of the Northern Anti-Slavery Democrats had united with the Republicans; but the large body of the party in that section remained attached to the old principles of a former period. The Democracy of all the States having met in convention at Cincinnatti, June 2d, 1856, reaffirmed the ancient doctrines of the party on the slavery question; and besides, announced their recognition of the principles embodied in the Kansas-Nebraska Bill. James Buchanan and John C. Breckenridge were next placed in nomination for President and Vice-President of the United States.

A small portion of the Whig party, North and South, united in the nomination of Millard Fillmore and Andrew J. Donaldson for the Presidency and Vice-Presidency. This movement being entirely the product of attachment to the old organization of Clay and Webster, gave no evidence of any ability to counteract the dangerous principles which it assumed to oppose. The Democratic party was the only one that possessed the semblance of ability to defeat the sectional Republican organization of the North. Patriotism would have demanded that any sacrifice should be made for the welfare of the country; but party spirit interposed. This spirit, regardless of constitutional guarantees, had organized the Republican party upon a basis of sectionalism that arrayed one-half of the Union against the other. Ambitious leaders, destitute of political principle, flocked to the rising party, who could not but see that the success of the new principles would entail civil war upon the country or a dissolution of the Union. The want of principle in party leaders was at this time apparent upon all sides; and to this cause was it mainly owing that sectional organizations were permitted to obtain a dangerous control in the nation.

But the result of the campaign of 1856 was one more triumph of national principles and the election of the Presidential candidates of the Democratic party. Sectionalism was simply stayed by this victory, but by no means overthrown. The banner of abolitionism waved in triumph over eleven States of the North; and the powerful vote indicated to a certainty the success of Republican principles in the near future. Southern statesmen now clearly perceived that their institution was doomed so soon as Northern ideas would obtain permanent control of the General Government. The antagonism of the North to slavery had produced its counterpart in the South, which had become a unit in defense of their inherited rights. In Southern estimation, therefore, the election of Buchanan and Breckenridge simply granted a respite of four years to the Constitutional Republic.

James Buchanan was inaugurated President of the United States, March 4th, 1857. Shortly after his elevation to the highest seat in the gift of the people, the Supreme Court in the Dred Scott case, announced the important decision that the Missouri Compromise had been an unconstitutional act of Federal legislation; that slavery existed in all the Territories by virtue of the Constitution; and that neither Congress nor a Territorial Legislature could terminate its legal existence. It was only the people of a Territory, when forming a Constitution, who were competent to determine whether slavery should exist or not, in the new State. This decision of the highest judicial tribunal of the nation, affirmed the doctrine on the slavery question, that had always been held by the South, and also by the Democratic and Whig parties; and that which was the dictate of reason and of a sound and enlightened public policy.

The people of Kansas had determined in the regular Territorial Legislature, to call a convention for the purpose of forming a State Constitution. Accordingly on the 20th of May, 1857, F. P. Stanton, then acting Governor of the Territory, published his proclamation commanding the proper officers to hold an election on the third Monday of June, 1857, for the choice of members to this Convention, as the Act of the Legislature directed. The election was legally held as directed, and the Convention assembled at Lecompton, according to law, on the first Monday of the following September. Having framed a Constitution, the Convention adjourned on the 7th of November, 1857. Only that clause of the Constitution respecting slavery, which seemed to be the principle question in dispute between the parties in the Territory, was directed by the Convention to be submitted to a vote of the people for ratification or rejection. This submission took place on December 21st. The Free State men, having chiefly absented themselves from the polls, the vote resulted as follows: For the Constitution, with slavery, 6,226; for the Constitution, without slavery, 567. By the new Constitution it was directed, that an election should be held on the 4th of January, 1858, for a Governor, Lieutenant-Governor, Secretary of State, State Treasurer, Members of the Legislature, and also a Member of Congress.

At the election held in October, 1857, the Free State party participated, and the result was that a Territorial Legislature of their selection was chosen, and also a Delegate to Congress. Acting Governor Stanton convened, by proclamation, an extra session of the Free State Legislature, for which act he was removed from office by the President, and Governor Denver appointed in his stead. The Territorial Legislature, when assembled in extraordinary session, also authorized an election to be held on the 4th of January, 1858, at which the Lecompton Constitution should be submitted *de novo*, to a popular vote of the people of Kansas, for acceptance or rejection. Of this election, ordered by the Territorial Legislature, James Buchanan, in in his Message of February 2d, 1858, said:

"This electionwas held after the Territory had been prepared for admission into the Union, as a Sovereign State, and when no authority existed in the Territorial Legislature, which could possibly destroy its existence or change its character."

The election ordering the Lecompton Constitution to a new vote of the people, resulted in its repudiation by over ten thousand majority. The Pro-Slavery party declined to vote, inasmuch as they contended that the Constitution had been already submitted in a legal manner, and, consequently, adopted. But both parties participated on the same day in the general election appointed as before stated in the Lecompton Constitution, and the result was a great triumph for the Free State party. The Anti-

Slavery men were thus placed in the ascendant, and the political power of the Territory was in their hands.

Afterwards, on the 30th of January, President Buchanan received a copy of the Lecompton Constitution, with a request from the President of the Convention that it might be submitted to the consideration of Congress. This was done by the President, in his Message of February 2d, 1858, in which he recommended the admission of Kansas, and the termination of the pending territorial difficulty. He urged the admission of Kansas because its Constitution had been adopted in a regular and formal manner; and, although the one party had declined to vote either for the election of delegates to the Convention, or on the question of slavery, when the same was submitted to the people for adoption or rejection; this, in his opinion, was no reason why the Constitution as adopted was not valid. Mr. Buchanan further contended in his Message, that no other course would so speedily terminate the slavery agitation as the admission of the new State; and he also showed, that the people of Kansas had it in their own power immediately to take steps for changing their Constitution and abolishing slavery if the majority of the citizens so desired. In this Message he said:

"The people of Kansas have in their own way and in strict accordance with the Organic Act, formed a Constitution and State Government; have submitted the all-important question of slavery to the people, and have elected a Governor, a Member to represent them in Congress, Members of the State Legislature, and other State officers. * * * For my own part I am decidedly in favor of its admission, and thus terminating the Kansas question."*

"This message occasioned a long, exciting and violent debate in both Houses of Congress, between the Slavery and Anti-Slavery members, which lasted nearly three months. It was but the re-echo of the storm that was raging throughout the land. Mr. Buchanan was bitterly denounced as truckling to the slave power, and as lending the weight of his high office towards fixing upon the people of Kansas the curse of slavery against their will. Members of Congress were classified during this controversy as Lecompton and Anti-Lecompton, as they favored or opposed the admission of Kansas. A wing of his own party separated from Mr. Buchanan on this point, and among these Stephen A. Douglas, of Illinois. Kansas was not admitted under the Lecompton

*Buchanan's Administration, p. 42.

Constitution and was only admitted a short time before the close of Mr. Buchanan's administration, with a Free Constitution."*

During the administration of James Buchanan, a permanent schism developed itself in the Democratic party, which rendered the triumph of Republicanism in the next Presidential election almost a certainty. The discord which rent the old party of Jefferson, was itself produced by Anti-Slavery agitation; and emanated from the conflicting opinions that existed as to the power of the people of a territory to legislate concerning slavery whilst in a territorial condition. In the year 1847, Gen. Cass, in his celebrated Nicholson letter, had given utterance to sentiments that seemed to imply such power in the inhabitants of a Territory; and from this period the question was more or less discussed in Congress and in the public journals. The great object of the leading statesmen at that time appeared to be the removal of the question of slavery from the Halls of Congress and leaving it with the people, who were themselves directly interested in it. It soon became evident that Southern Democrats viewed the doctrine of squatter sovereignty, as an innovation upon the ancient creed; and from its earliest advocacy they determined to resist its incorporation into the platform of the party. In 1854 the Richmond *Inquirer*, speaking of General Cass, said:

"The concerted efforts of the Washington *Union* and other journals in his interest, to run him a second time (for President) and incorporate squatter sovereignty into the Democratic creed, will provoke a resistance which may possibly end in a disruption of the party."

That Gen. Cass had been rightly understood as favoring the disputed doctrine, seems clear from remarks made by him in the Senate in May, 1856, as follows:

"He held, however, that after Congress had enabled a Territory to assume legislative powers, it was not competent for Congress to restrain any legislative act of such Territorial Government under the Constitution of the United States; and amongst such acts he held the *admission or exclusion* of slavery. This was a necessary deduction of popular sovereignty."†

The Cincinnati Convention of the Democratic party in 1856, did not determine in its platform the disputed question as regards the power of a Territorial Legislature, but left it for future decision. James Buchanan, speaking of this convention, says:

*Harris' Biographical History of Lancaster County, p. 108.
†*National Intelligencer*, May 13th, 1856.

"It is altogether silent in regard to the power of a Territorial Legislature over the question of slavery. Nay, more; whilst affirming in general terms the provisions of the Kansas-Nebraska Act, it specifically designates a future time when slavery may be rightly dissolved, not by the Territorial Legislature but by the people. This is when '*acting through the legally and fairly expressed will of a majority of actual residents, and whenever the number of their inhabitants justifies it (they assemble), to form a Constitution, with or without domestic slavery, and be admitted into the Union upon terms of perfect eqality with the other States.*' Before this period the Cincinnati platform is silent on the subject."*

The Congressional struggle over the Lecompton Constitution was potential in widening the breach that already existed in the Democratic party. Stephen A. Douglas, in view of the Anti-Slavery storm that had been prostrating the ancient structures of his party, deemed it necessary to find refuge for his own safety in some of the modern edifices that were rearing their domes around him. The contest for the admission of Kansas offered the Illinois Senator an admirable opportunity to redeem his sin-stained head from the impending destruction with which he was menaced by the Anti-Slavery spirit of the North. He had seen the terrific overthrow which the Democracy suffered in 1854, and even had witnessed by his side the fall of his Senatorial colleague; and all this the product of his own conjuration in the repeal of the Missouri Compromise. He must make peace with the aroused demon, and obtain atonement for the deeds of the past. In uniting with his former enemies in opposing the admission of Kansas under the Lecompton Constitution, Senator Douglas hoped again to so re-instate himself in Northern confidence as to assure his return to the United States Senate in 1859. Some of the high priests of Republicanism were ready to clothe him with sacred robes for his able defense of their cause. Horace Greeley says:

"It seemed to me that not only magnanimity but policy dictated to the Republicans of Illinois that they should promptly and heartily tender their support to Mr. Douglas, and thus insure his re-election for a third term with substantial unanimity." †

This opposition of Senator Douglas and his friends to the admission of Kansas, proved the entering wedge that distracted the National Democratic party. But it was in the famous Illinois contest which took place between Stephen A. Douglas and

*Buchanan's Administration on the Eve of the Rebellion, p. 55.
† Greeley's Recollections, p. 357.

Abraham Lincoln, that the former revealed himself as the politician, who sought to secure his election at the risk of disrupting that party, to which he was indebted for all his substantial honors, and upon whose harmony the union of the States perhaps depended. Although as touching the slavery controversy he had obligated himself to acquiesce in the decision of the Supreme Court, yet when this was rendered in 1857, he, with the Republicans, strove to evade its effect, in his pandering to the abolition sentiment of the Northern masses. He declared in his Illinois speeches, that it was within the power of any Territorial Legislature, by a species of "unfriendly legislation," to exclude slavery from the new Territories—and though conceding the Supreme Court to have declared that the Constitution carried slavery into all the public domain, and that neither Congress nor a Territorial Legislature were authorized to exclude it—yet Senator Douglas argued that it could not exist, unless certain favoring enactments of the Legislature were passed for its protection. In this manner he endeavored to conciliate the Anti-Slavery opposition of his State, and to show that his attitude was equally antagonistic to slavery extension as that of the Republican party.

Such subterfuges of the politician, however, are miserable to contemplate. What a death of demoralization does the position of Senator Douglas assume? His plan for excluding slavery from the Territories pre-supposed that every Territorial legislator was ready to perjure himself in order to accomplish his political schemes. Does not every legislator swear to support the Constitution of the United States? How then could the legislator, who believed with Senator Douglas, that the Constitution guarantees the right to hold slaves in the Federal Territories, free himself from his oath, unless he favored such legislation as would enable the slaveholder to enjoy his property after transporting it to his new settlement? Does an oath to obey the Constitution, permit a legislator to support laws violative of rights established by that National compact? Is he a supporter of the Constitution, who, knowing or believing there is a right established under it needing specific legislation, would refuse the required enactments? Would he not, by such refusal, violate the solemn oath he had taken to support the Constitution? And yet such "unfriendly legislation," received the approbation of Senator Douglas. He would have the members of a Territorial Legislature, who were sworn to support the guarantees of the Constitution, and which they themselves accepted as genuine, assist in legislation intended to defeat those rights. This was, in plain words, to counsel the repudiation of legislative obligations. It is not surprising that the period of political corruption had fully set in, when a prominent leader of one of the great American parties could be guilty of such a breach of moral conviction; and yet at the same time, not alienate from him his partisan followers.

If the principles of the Democratic party were wrong, neither Senator Douglas, nor any other man, should have advocated them; but if right, as he professed, then it was his duty to battle for them before a corrupted public opinion, even if he must fall in the contest. The Republicans challenged the truths of the Democratic doctrines; resisted openly the extension of slavery into the Territories; and planted themselves in opposition to the former principles upon which the Government from its origin had been conducted. In the estimation of all men of clear perception, they were the revolutionists who strove for the overthrow of the old social status and the inauguration of a new one. But, Stephen A. Douglas and his followers avowed themselves as Democrats; as friends of the existing order of government and its institutions; and yet they did nothing to avert the revolution which was threatening the country. Instead of presenting themselves as a breakwater to the flood that was rising, they simply added the squatter sovereignty current as a cumulative force to the deluge, and permitted it, unobstructed, to beat with still greater impetuosity against all the landmarks of ancient order and constitutional guarantee. The Illinois Senator was therefore no true man for the crisis. He was the sunshine patriot whose voice was loudest when prosperity covered with her wings the party to which he was attached; but when adversity advanced, the ingrate was soon found a deserter in the enemy's ranks.

But besides all this, the Congressional struggle over the Lecompton Constitution, added new strength, as was anticipated, to the Republican revolutionists of the North; and the election of 1858 resulted for them in another triumph. Thaddeus Stevens was in this year returned from Lancaster County to the 36th Congress, which assembled on Monday, December 5th, 1859. He again took his seat in that body, of which he continued a member during the remainder of his life, a period of the most eventful interest in his own and the history of the Republic. The elements of discord were at no former time so threatening, as at the opening of this Congress. The country had but just recovered from the shock produced by the raid into Virginia, led by the fanatical John Brown and his deluded followers. In the opinion of every reflecting man, a crisis was near at hand. The portents indicating such were visible on all sides. The whole period of James Buchanan's administration up to this moment, was like a diseased body, one pustule appearing after another, indicating the putrefying condition of the whole. The Southern mind was highly alarmed with the state of affairs, and unity of interest had cemented their States into an attitude of resistance to Northern sectionalism. The Republican nominee for Speaker of the House, was John Sherman, of Ohio, who had made himself especially odious to the South, by publicly recommending in connexion with sixty-eight other members of Congress, a document called "Helper's Book," the doctrines of which were of the most fanatical and revolutionary character. But political madness and insanity ruled the hour; and although the entire Southern delegation gave warning that they would regard the election of Sherman, or any other man with his record, as an open declaration of war against the South, the Republican revolutionists defiantly continued to vote for him for nearly two months, giving him a majority lacking but a few votes upon every trial of his strength.* He was finally withdrawn and William Pennington, from New Jersey, a member of the same party, was elected.

The Republican party, openly pledged to oppose slavery extension, was already dominant in the Northern States. The Douglas Democracy of the North also advocated sentiments that in Southern estimation would circumscribe slavery within its present bounds; indeed, this was the secret of their reception amongst that wing of the party, tinctured with anti-slavery views. The anti-slavery agitation had raged with such intensity, and for so long a period, that the Northern people were seduced by the arguments of the Abolitionists into the belief that slavery was a great social and moral evil, and repugnant to the instincts of a refined humanity. But few remained unconverted to the

*Pollard's First Year of the War, pp. 29.

sentiments of the abolition reform, save those who were competent to think and reason for themselves. The leading intellects of the South were not slow in detecting the state of Northern opinion upon the slavery question; a vigilant statesman of the South took occasion to denounce the Douglas defection as "a short cut to all ends of Black Republicanism." Whilst the "Helper Book" controversy was agitating the country, one of the Georgia Senators was so bold as to denounce, in his place in Congress, the entire Democratic party of the North as unreliable and rotten.

Jefferson Davis, on the 2d day of February, 1860, offered in the Senate a series of resolutions, expressive of Southern opinions, as regards the relation of the States of the Union, and the power of Congress, or of a Territorial Legislature over slavery in the Federal Territories. The resolution defining the Democratic position on the slavery question, denied to Congress or a Territorial Legislature the power "to annul or impair the Constitutional right of any citizen of the United States to take his slave property into the common Territories, and there hold and enjoy the same while the territorial condition remains." These resolutions were adopted in the Senate by nearly a two-thirds vote; the Republicans, however, opposed their passage with unanimity as conflicting with the principles of their party.

The States Right party of the South had in 1856 at Cincinnati, united with the Northern Democracy upon a platform of principles which received different interpretations in the two sections. In the North it was believed by one wing of the party (the followers of Douglas) to express the doctrine of popular sovereignty for the government of the Territories; and in the South a contrary interpretation obtained. The popular sovereignty doctrine of the North claimed for the people of a Territory, the right to determine the slavery question for themselves. Those favoring this view, asserted that this was the principle established by the Kansas-Nebraska Act. This assertion James Buchanan refutes in the following language:

"If the Douglas construction of the act be correct, it is morally certain that the Southern Senators and Representatives who were warm advocates of its passage, could not possibly have so understood it. If they had, they would then have voluntarily voted away the rights of their constituents. Indeed, such a construction of the act would be more destructive to the interests of the slaveholders than the Republican doctrine of Congressional exclusion. Better, far better, for him to submit the question to Congress, where he could be deliberately heard by his representatives, than to be deprived of his slaves after he had gone to the trouble and expense of exporting them to a Territory, by a hasty enactment of a Territorial Legislature, elected annually, and freed from all constitutional restraints. Such a construction of the Kansas-Nebraska Act would be in direct opposition to the policy and practice of the Government from its origin. The men who framed and built up our institutions, so far from regarding the Territories to be sovereign, treated them as mere wards of the Federal Government. * * * It was not then foreseen that any political party would arise in this country claiming the right for the majority of the first settlers of a Territory, under the plea of popular sovereignty, to confiscate the property of the minority. When the population of the Territories had reached a certain number, Congress admitted them as States into the Union, under the Constitution framed by themselves, with or without slavery, according to their own discretion."*

The dual Democratic interpretation obtained, regarding that part of the Cincinnati platform, which adopted the principles of the Kansas-Nebraska Act; and it was agreed amongst the leaders of the party that the subject should be referred to the Supreme Court for adjudication. But when the Dred Scott decision was promulgated, so violent was the clamor which was raised against it by the revolutionary Republican party, that Stephen A. Douglas and those agreeing with him in sentiment, were intimidated from that defense of it, of which the high character of the Court should have rendered it worthy. And, even though some of the principles decided might strictly not have been before the Court, yet they disclosed what the judges regarded as law, and were indicative of what would be affirmed when the point in technical accuracy might arise. In this view of the question, the Dred Scott decision was a positive affirmance of the Southern interpretation of the Cincinnati platform. In this decision, all Democrats, both North and South, should willingly have acquiesced; it was only for that party to dispute it whose principles of policy were based upon the doctrine that no law or decision of any court could justify the existence of Slavery in the States, and much less its extension into the Territorial domain. Supported by the decision of the highest Federal Court; by the unanimous opinion of their own section and a respectable portion of the Northern Democracy; and also in the historical practice of the country as regards the manner of governing the Territo-

*Buchanan's Administration on the Eve of the Rebellion, pp. 54–5.

ries, the Southern people determined to insist upon their rights and defend their honor as integral members of the Confederacy. In view of the assembling of the Democratic party for the purpose of nominating candidates for President and Vice-President, the people of several of the Southern States defined the conditions upon which their delegates should hold seats in the National Convention, appointed to meet at Charleston, April 23d, 1860. The Democracy of Alabama was first to move in this direction. A series of resolutions were passed, affirming the Southern doctrine that neither Congress nor a Territorial Legislature were authorized to interfere with Slavery in the Federal Territories; and also directing their delegates to see that these principles be incorporated as part of the National Democratic creed, or that they retire from the convention. Similar resolves formed the credentials of the delegates from other Southern States.

The Democratic Convention which assembled at Charleston, was composed of discordant elements, representing the unharmonious condition of the only remaining organization that formed a tie between the Northern and Southern portions of the American Union. The Democracy now met as did the old Whig party in 1852, when nothing remained of it save the name; for as to principles, a full separation had taken place between its antagonistic sections. It was soon apparent that the party would be unable to harmonize upon a platform of principles satisfactory to both divisions of the Union; and this because such a spirit of compromise was wanting as the exigency of the hour would have demanded. Patriotism required that the Democrats of the North should meet their brethren of the South in fraternal amity, and accord them in a public platform of principles the recognition of those rights which the Constitution guaranteed. This was all they demanded, and whilst the constitutional compact endured, equity suggested the fulfillment of its stipulations. The revolutionists were in serried array; the alarming decree had gone forth that the will of the majority must triumph, and that the accorded rights of the minority must yield; and yet the Democrats of the North stood stubbornly upon a principle in which it was impossible for the South, as she conceived, to acquiesce without a sacrifice of her honor as a member of an equal Confederation. After the convention had been in session for several days, the South was out-voted in the adoption of the platform;

and this ultimated in the disruption of the assemblage by the withdrawal of the cotton States; and an adjournment to Baltimore followed. The border Slave States still remained in the convention in the hope of effecting some ultimate settlement of the difficulty. But the breach, instead of being closed, widened. The re-assembling of the convention at Baltimore resulted in a final and embittered separation of the opposing delegates. The majority still clinging with uncompromising tenacity to their position; Virginia and the other border States, except Missouri, withdrew from the convention and united with the representatives from the cotton States, then assembled at Baltimore, in the nomination of candidates representing their views. A portion of the Northern delegates also retired from the convention and united with them. Their nominees were John C. Breckenridge, of Kentucky, for President, and Joseph Lane, of Oregon, for Vice-President. The Northern Democracy placed in nomination Stephen A. Douglas, of Illinois, for President, and Herschel V. Johnson, of Georgia, for Vice-President

The Constitutional Union party, being the remnant of the old Whig and American organizations, met in Baltimore May 9th, 1860, and nominated for President and Vice-President, John Bell, of Tennessee, and Edward Everett, of Massachusetts. The platform of this party was a vague and undefined enumeration of their politcal principles summed up in the following words:

"The Constitution of the country, the union of the States, and the enforcement of the laws."

The Democracy was at length sundered, the Whig party was virtually defunct, and nothing seemed now able to interpose resistance to the triumphant march of the revolutionists to victory. This party met in Chicago in June, 1860, and placed Abraham Lincoln, of Illinois, in nomination for the Presidency, and Hannibal Hamlin, of Maine, for the Vice-Presidency, and at the same time adopted a platform declaring freedom to the normal condition of the Territories. Sectionalism had now chosen its captains for its last struggle with the principles of representative democratic government. Its Anti-Slavery and Non-Compromise banners floated over the hastily constructed wigwam in which the leaders had assembled, and the nominations as made were received with an eclat which seemed to portend triumph as about to crown their standards. But reason was lost sight of in an assembly, which was intoxicated with the contemplation of negro emancipation upon the Western continent.

The weakness and incapacity of men for self-government was fully exemplified in the campaign of 1860. The people of both sections of the country, in opposition to the admonitions of the framers and ancient patriots of the American Republic, permitted themselves to be seduced by false leaders into a hostility of sections, which could not but carry with it revolution and constitutional overthrow. Party success and partisan triumph, were the motives of the politicians in a campaign which, of all others, should have produced instances of pure disinterestedness and patriotic self-devotion. But the contrary was everywhere apparent. Men adhered to their parties, although in doing so, they were consciously adding firebrands to the Federal Republic, soon to be ignited in the flames of civil convulsion. The campaign resulted as all reflecting men must have anticipated, in the election of the revolutionary candidates, Lincoln and Hamlin. Republicanism, save in New Jersey, triumphed throughout the entire North. Sectional antagonism, which an Anti-Slavery agitation of many years had been preparing, was at length fully complete. Destiny, however, had in store for the American people the fruits of officious interference and impolitic reform.

CHAPTER XII.

SECESSION OF THE SOUTHERN STATES, AND THE EFFORTS AT COMPROMISE.

The Southern people correctly interpreted the import of Northern ascendency in the election of Lincoln and Hamlin, on the 6th of November, 1860. The composition of the Republican party, the utterances of its orators and press, and the resolves of its conventions, left no doubt as to the *animus* of the organization, much as this, for political reasons, might be concealed. The most violent Abolitionists of the North were the most ardent champions of the new combination, and the entrusted chiefs in all party manipulations, provided they displayed sufficient sagacity as not to disclose the esoteric doctrines of the initiated. The enunciated principles of simple opposition to the extension of slavery, were far from being those which raised the enthusiasm of the sincere Abolitionists, and attracted them to the standards of Republicanism. The same secret which attached to the rising party, the enemies of slavery, aroused the friends of the institution, and, as it were, admonished them of the adder in the grass, whose poison was to be avoided. This antagonism resulted from the existence of slavery in the Southern States, and although the Republicans avowed no intention to interfere with the institution where it existed, yet this addition to the creed was simply a matter of time, and the education of Northern public opinion.

Southern institutions were doomed to a short existence under the Federal Government in the hands of the Republican party. This, leading statesmen of the South had often predicted, should Northern sectionalism succeed in gaining control of national affairs. It had been determined, therefore, by the controlling minds in the slave States, that if their constitutional rights were to be preserved, resistance would become necessary when a sectional party should come into power with principles known to be violative of the guarantees of the Federal compact. In the election of Abraham Lincoln, as they conceived, that period had at length arrived. The predictions of Calhoun, Clay, and other leading statesmen of the South were verified; Northern Abolitionism, under the false name of Republicanism, had triumphed; and the Southern people would simply be conceded such rights as the new rulers would see proper to accord. The only question in the South, was the remedy to be adopted, in view of Northern ascendency upon a basis of hostility to their institutions.

A number of prominent South Carolinians had met on the 25th of October, 1860, and had determined upon the secession of their State, in case the Republican party, as was anticipated, should triumph in the pending campaign. This determination of the influential men of the Palmetto State, was shared very generally by the controllers of public opinion in the remainder of the cotton States. The Legislature of South Carolina, being convened by Gov. Gist, on Monday, November 5th, the day before the Presidential election, for the purpose of choosing electors; the State politicians had an opportunity of perfecting their plans, should Republicanism in the North triumph. The Governor, in his proclamation, and other prominent men of the State, who were serenaded on the evening of the 5th, expressed the opinion that in the event of Abraham Lincoln being chosen President of the United States, duty demanded that South Carolina should inaugurate the movement of separation from the Union; and set in motion the ball of resistance to the Northern despotism.

The morning of the 7th of November, 1860, announced to the people of the South the unwelcome news that the hated party of the North had won its crowning victory. Abraham Lincoln and Hannibal Hamlin were elected to the highest offices in the gift of the people; and by a party pledged in its platform to prohibit Slavery extension; and animated with the resolve to weaken the institution at all points, and ultimately effect its entire extinction. William H. Seward, the life and soul of the Republican party in 1848, thus spoke at Cleveland:

"Correct your own error that Slavery has any constitutional guarantees which may not be released, and ought not to be relinquished. Say to Slavery, when it shows its bond (the Constitution) and demands its pound of flesh, that if it draws one drop of blood, its life shall pay the forfeit." * * * "Do all this and inculcate all this, in the spirit of moderation and benevolence, and not of retaliation and fanaticism, and you will soon bring the parties of the country into an effective aggression upon slavery. * * * Slavery can be limited to its present bounds; it can be ameliorated. It can be and must be *abolished*, and you and I can and must do it. The task is as simple and easy as its consummation will be beneficent and its reward glorious."

Henry Wilson, another of the shining lights of Republicanism, expressed himself in the following manner:

"We shall triumph in the end; and we shall overthrow the slave-power of the Republic; we shall enthrone freedom; we shall abolish slavery; we shall change the Supreme Court of the United States, and place men in that Court who believe that our prayers will be impious to heaven while we sustain and support human slavery."

The diabolical and fiendish principles of the Helper Book, which had been endorsed by 69 Republican members of Congress, could never be forgotten by the people of the Southern States. As soon, therefore, as the triumph of Abolitionism was made known, secession was very generally determined upon by Southern Statesmen as the remedy for evils which threatened the overthrow of that form of Constitutional Government under which their States had prospered, and to which they were devotedly attached. The Legislature of South Carolina being at this time in session, joint resolves were passed in both Houses calling for the election of a convention on the 6th of December, and which should meet on the 17th of the same month, to take into consideration the question of separation from the Union. Steps leading in the same direction were taken throughout the whole section of the cotton States; and the influential leaders in most of the remaining slave States prepared themselves so to act as the current of a united Southern sentiment might dictate. By general consent it seemed now recognized that the period had arrived which demanded harmony of counsel amongst the slave States, in order that they might be able by united action to countervail Northern sectionalism, and defend their constitutional rights as equal members of the American Confederacy.

The South Carolina Convention, assembled at Columbia, the Capitol of the State, on the day determined upon; and on the 20th of December, 1860, proceeded to pass by an unanimous vote an Ordinance of Secession, dissolving their connection with the Federal Union. The secession of South Carolina was received by the dominant party in the North as a matter of light consequence; as only another nullification affair which would scarcely create a ripple upon the ocean of American life. Indeed, a studied system of deception had characterized the utterances of the organs of this party from its organization in 1854. During the whole of the campaign of 1860, the declarations of Northern and Southern Conservatives that the election of Abraham Lincoln would produce revolution and civil war, were scouted by the Republican orators and press, as simply election threats, intended to intimidate the dough faces of the North; and that as soon as the election was over the Southern braggarts, as they were termed, would tame down as on former occasions. This system of deception was simply a part of the programme to enable the party to gain power. The objects to which they were leading the Northern people, and the dangerous course over which the passage led, must all be concealed from the eyes of the people, otherwise these were unattainable. The Northern masses were neither prepared for the abolition of slavery, nor for civil war with their countrymen of the South; both of which were logical results of the success of the Republican party.

But the eyes of the Northern masses were partially opened as one after another of the cotton States followed in the wake of South Carolina secession. Mississippi was the first to imitate the example of the Palmetto State, and enrol herself under the banner of Southern resistance, having passed an ordinance of secession January 9th, 1861. Florida buckled on the secession armor in defence of her inherited rights on the 10th of the same month, and on the day following, Alabama was by her side in similar warlike array. On three successive days, these last named States had in secession resolves, donned the martial outfit of Southern independence. Georgia, the old Empire State of the South, was next to take her stand by the side of her resistant sisters, and give character and weight to the movement of secession. This she did January 19th, in an ordinance asserting her State Sovereignty and independence of the Federal Government. Louisiana passed her act of secession January 25th, and on the 1st of February the Lone Star of Texas was added to the flag of the Southern Confederacy. On the 4th of February, 1861, a Congress of Delegates from the seven seceded States convened at Montgomery, the capitol of Alabama, adopted a Provisional Government, and elected Jefferson Davis, President of the Confederate States.

The deception that had been practiced began to show its lining through the clouds, and as many as caught the glimpse broke in all directions. Horace Greeley, the leading Abolition editor of the North, says:

"Every local election held during the two months succeeding our national triumph, showed great conservative gains. Conspicuous Abolitionists were denied the use of public halls, or hooted down if they attempted to speak. Influential citizens, through meetings and letters, denounced the madness of fanaticism, and implored the South to stay her avenging arm until the North could have time to purge herself from complicity with fanatics, and demonstrate her fraternal sympathy with her Southern sister."*

During all this period, the leading Republicans of Abolition faith exerted themselves to the utmost to turn the tide that had so strongly set in against them. The politicians, the journalists, and the infidel clergy of the North, had another difficult task to obscure the vision of the people and prevent them from seeing the yawning gulph of destruction to which they were conducting them. They were made to believe by these wolves in sheep's clothing, that the South was only blustering in order to terrify the timid conservatives and enable them to obtain further guarantees for Slavery. Efforts at compromise were discouraged by them because, as they assured the people, such would be vain and useless. Sentences from the speeches of Southern men were perverted from their connection; and these were made to utter sentiments which they never entertained. The papers teemed with the declarations of Clingman, Chestnut, Rhett, and other Southern statesmen, who were cited as asserting that no compromise would avail to arrest the revolution. But the reasons given by these men for believing and asserting that no compromise could heal the difficulties between the North and South, were carefully concealed from the Northern people. Had they told the whole story as it now stands revealed to history, and as shrewd men well understood at that time, such a demand for conciliation would have gone up, as would have almost rent the whole Northern heavens, and have driven the leaders from a platform of discord, which admitted no entrance for the Angel of Peace; but which was conducting the American people to the bloodiest chasm of civil war, that the annals of the world have

* Greeley's Recollections, p. 396.

ever recorded. It was the Chicago conclave that interposed and made harmony between the sections impossible. It was the resolves of the Lake City Convention, in 1860, together with the knowledge of the designs of these men, that induced Southern statesmen to declare that secession could not be arrested. To show that the people were somewhat aroused to the alarming dangers to which the Republican party had brought the country, the following Abolition testimony is submitted. Horace Greeley says:

"In fact the attitude of the North during the two last months of 1860, was foreshadowed in four lines of Collins' Ode to the Passions. * * * And the danger was imminent that if a popular vote could have been had (as was proposed) on the Crittenden Compromise, it would have prevailed by an overwhelming majority. Very few Republicans would have voted for it; but very many would have refrained from voting at all; while their adversaries would have brought their every man to the polls in its support, and carried it by hundreds of thousands."*

South Carolina and the other cotton States did not secede, as was averred by the Republican leaders, on account of any hostility to the Union, or the people of the North, but simply because they became fully satisfied that their rights were in jeopardy. Mutual interest had originally induced the people of the South to unite with those of the North; and while it was clear that it was to their advantage to remain in the Union, like all other people, they would do so. In the Union with their Northern brethren they had grown wealthy and powerful; and some valid reason existed to induce them to prefer a dissolution of the Union. The reason was no clearer to Southern than to Northern apprehension. It was the intermedling, fanatical disposition of the Abolitionists of the North which induced them to interfere in the affairs of others, and assume to be the rulers over all America and her institutions. This in short was the lion in the way of an amicable settlement of the National troubles. A party existed confined to the Northern States, whose doctrines were antagonistic to the interests of the Southern people; this party was soon to obtain control of the Federal Government; and as a consequence, the Union for them had no further attractions. Nations, as well as individuals, will ever seek such alliances as will redound, as they conceive, to their advantage. It was so in the case of the union of the States. But the long, bitter and intemperate Anti Slavery agitation, had antagonized the North into a sectional

*Greeley's Recollections, pp. 396–7.

attitude against the South and her institutions; slavery was clearly seen to be jeoparded in a longer association with a people who could be seduced into such a hostile aggression against the rights and interests of another people over whom they had no legal control; and therefore, reason and common sense dictated a dissolution of a once friendly and happy alliance; but which had now become dangerous and threatening to constitutional civil guarantees, and even to the perpetuity of free representative government itself. The men of the South would have been poltroons and worthy the doom of slavery themselves, had they ignobly yielded to the dictation of Northern fanaticism; and tolerantly permitted the inauguration of a policy that in the end was sure to lead to the subversion of their constitutional rights.

In the system of disimulation and deception, by which the Republican leaders blindfolded the Northern people in 1860 and 1861, there was no one more adroit than Thaddeus Stevens in the use of such instruments as were required for the purpose; and one who was able to distort Southern sentiment, and pervert it into the support of his own party position. An instance of this is seen in his speech in the House, delivered January 29th, 1861. He said:

"I regret, sir, that I am compelled to concur in the belief stated yesterday by the gentleman from Virginia, (Mr. Pryor) that no compromise which can be made will have any effect in averting the present difficulty." *

Mr Stevens fails to state in his speech (intended for circulation in the Northern journals of the Republican party †) what stood in the way of compromise; but this is seen in the speech of Mr. Pryor, to which he refers. The latter, in his speech of January 28th, spoke as follows:

"MR. SPEAKER, since the fatal 6th of November to the present hour, the Representatives of the South have invariably exhibited an accomodating disposition. The first day of our session was signalized by a proposition from a colleague of my own (Mr. Botteler), which contemplated a pacific adjustment of our difficulties. A similar movement, likewise originating with a Southern man, was initiated in the Senate.

**Congressional Globe*, p. 621.

†Hence flows one great evil of an unbridled press, which details all that is deemed favorable to the intests of party; but the antidote is rarely permitted to appear. Under such a system as now obtains with most party organs in America, the truth is with the greatest difficulty ascertained, even by investigators, but rarely by the masses. Some method would seem necessary to be devised which would better secure the dissemination of the truth than now exists.

Meanwhile, various schemes of settlement have been submitted in one or the other House of Congress, of which, without much regard to their intrinsic efficacy, we have uniformly avowed our support; while on the other side (the Republican), they have been as uniformly rejected with a contemptuous disdain of compromise. Thus, while the South are willing to remain in the Union with an assurance of their rights, the North declare, by a refusal of all concession, that they will destroy the Union rather than renounce their aggressive designs. In the perverted patriotism of the dominant party, the Constitution of Washington is substituted by the platform of Lincoln; and rather than be reproached with logical inconsistency, they chose to incur the guilt of civil war."*

Mr. Stevens, on the 14th of February, 1861, in replying to a Mr. Webster, of Maryland, who characterized his speech of January 29th as "a strong Anti-Compromise speech," admitted that instead of being *sorry*, he was gratified that compromise could not save the Union. He said: "I did not agree to go for compromise. I am opposed to compromise until there is something to compromise."†

Another illustration from the speech of Mr. Stevens of January 29th, is cited as an example of the illogical and clap-trap method made use of by the Republican leaders to parry Southern argument in favor of compromise, and by sophistry also, to arouse Northern pride and false patriotism against the people of the South. He spoke as follows:

" When I see these States in open and declared rebellion against the Union, seizing upon her public lands and arsenals, and robbing her of millions of the public property; when I see the batteries of seceding States blockading the highway of the nation, and their armies in battle array against the flag of the Union; when I see our flag insulted, and that insult submitted to, I have no hope that concession, humiliation and compromise can have any effect whatever..' ‡

Such was the pabulum that fed Northern venom during the period when patriots North and South were engaged in the holy mission of endeavoring to adjust the national difficulties, and shield the Republic from bloodshed and fratricidal strife. Much more worthily would the powers of Mr. Stevens have been engaged, if in true republican spirit he had employed his intellectual abilities in logically controverting the positions of Southern statesmen, and convincing them, in the forum of reason, that their rights would be better secured in the Union than out of it.

* *Congressional Globe*, p. 603.
† *Globe*, p. 907.
‡ *Globe*, p. 621.

That was the method by which the Union had been framed, and by no other could a republican Union be perpetuated. Instead, therefore, of parading the iniquity of Southern secession, why did not he and his party endeavor to prove that the reasons which induced it were groundless? The eloquent R. A. Pryor, of Virginia, (against whom, as has been seen, Mr. Stevens in a measure replied) submitted a resume of the causes that induced the Southern revolt which deserved an argumentative rather than a bitter, sneering reply. After recapitulating the non-execution of the fugitive slave law by the North, with many other violations of Southern rights, Mr. Pryor said:

"But the defence of the South rests upon still stronger grounds; and her secession from the Confederacy is justified by even higher principles than the right to vindicate a violated covenant. Absolute power is the essence of tyranny, whether the power be wielded by a monarch or a multitude. The dominant section in this Confederacy claims and exercises absolute power—power without limitation and without responsibility—without limitation, since all the restrictions of the Constitution are broken down, and without responsibility, because in the nature of things, the weaker interest cannot control the majority. Of all species of tyranny, the South is subject to the most intolerable. Under the rule of a despot we might hope something of his impartial indifference between the sections; but to be exposed to the unbridled sway of a majority adverse in interest, inimical in feeling, and ambitious of domination, is to be reduced to a condition more abject than that of the slaves whose emancipation is the pretext of all this controversy.

"It is against this sectional domination, this rule of the majority without law and without limit,—a rule asserted in subversion of the Constitution, and established on the ruins of the Confederacy,—it is in resistance to this despotic and destable rule that the people of the South have taken up arms. This, sir, is the cause of the South; and tell me if cause more just ever consecrated revolution? It is the cause of self-government against the domination of foreign power—the very cause for which our fathers fought in 1776. I repeat, it is against the rule of a sectional despotism that the South demands protection; and it is to assert the cause of civil liberty that she declares her independence. You of the North lavished your sympathy on the people of Hungary in their revolt against Austrian absolutism; but our cause is identical, in principle and in purpose.

"To-day, it is Southern interests which suffer from the overthrow of constitutional guarantees and the irresponsible reign of the majority. But the principle of absolute power, once ascendant in the Government, no interest is secure; and circumstances will determine against what object it may be directed. The only safeguard of American liberty is in maintaining the integrity and preserving intact the limitations of the Government. For that the South contends; and all are alike concerned in her cause.

"If, after the endurance of so many wrongs and the menace of others still more intolerable, were anything wanting to justify the South in the public opinion of the world, it would be supplied by her solicitude to avoid violence and redress her grievances within the Union. We are reproached, I know, with precipitancy in not waiting an *overt act* of hostility from the sectional administration. Sir, in our judgment, a proclamation of war is an overt act, and such proclamation we find in the election by an exclusively sectional vote of a President pledged to put our rights and our property '*in course of ultimate extinction*,'—a President who admonishes us in advance of his aggressive designs by the sententious but significant declaration that '*they who deny freedom to others do not deserve it themselves, and under a just God cannot long retain it.*' We could not agree to await, inactively, the development of the disposition of the President elect; for we claim to hold our rights by some higher and more solid tenure than the capricious temper of any individual. Indeed, the arguments of our opponents involves a concession of our case, inasmuch as it implies that the rights of the South are no longer secured by constitutional guarantees, but are suspended on the accident of an unfriendly administration.

"A more imperative consideration still determined the South to act at once and to act decisively. If negotiation might avail, we thought to strengthen this by a demonstration of our spirit. If the sword alone can reclaim our rights, we were resolved not to be unprepared for the issue."*

The united South and the Democracy of the North were all in favor of an adjustment of the dispute between the sections, without recourse to coercive measures. Even a considerable wing of the Republican party which had supported Lincoln for the Presidency, were likewise favorable to a peaceful solution of the national difficulties, in order to avoid a collision of arms that would endanger the Federal Union, and might ultimate in a total overthrow of republican institutions. Influential men of both political parties, in view of Southern demonstrations, felt that a crisis had arisen, that called for the efforts of patriots to exert their influence to ward off the dangers with which the country was threatened. Meetings were held in different sections of the North for the purpose of giving expression to public opinion; and also with the design of securing such a coincidence of sentiment as might lead to an amicable termination of the troubles that were threatening the peace of the country. One of the largest of these assemblages was that held in Independence Square, in the City of Philadelphia, and which, by the advice of the councils, had been summoned by Mayor Henry to counsel

**Globe* of 2d Session, 36th Congress, Vol. I, pp. 602–3.

together, in view of the apprehension that disunion was imminent, unless the "loyal people casting off the spirit of party, should in a special manner avow their unfailing fidelity to the Union, and their abiding faith in the Constitution and laws." This meeting—the spontaneous outburst of the purest patriotism that a people could exhibit—was of vast magnitude, and showed the interest that was felt by the masses who came in any wise to realize the maelstrom of civil war into which the Ship of State was rapidly descending. Addresses were made before this concourse of citizens by leading old line Whigs, Democrats and Conservative Republicans, evincing a desire of compromise; and that fraternal concord might again be restored between the States and the Union perpetuated without bloodshed. It was a clear indication that the Northern people wished the Union to be preserved by pacific remedies rather than risk its safety upon the hazard of the sword. But power had passed from the hands of those who desired that the Union should be perpetuated in the manner it had been formed. In compromise its foundations had been laid; in conciliation its structure had been reared; but this policy must now yield to that which can terminate the career of Slavery and end its existence as one of the institutions of the American Republic.

The second session of the Thirty-sixth Congress opened on Monday, December 3d, 1860, and President Buchanan on the next day transmitted to this body his fourth and last Annual Message. In this document, the President essayed the discussion of the national difficulties, and set forth as he believed the causes that had induced the troubles. He said:

"Why is it then, that discontent now so extensively prevails, and the Union of the States, which is the source of all our blessings, is threatened with destruction? The long continued and intemperate interference of the Northern people with the question of slavery in the Southern States, has at length produced its natural effects. The different sections of the Union are now arrayed against each other, and the time has arrived so much dreaded by the Father of his country, when hostile geographical parties have been formed. I have long foreseen and often forewarned my countrymen of the now impending danger. This does not proceed solely from the claims on the part of Congress or the Territorial Legislatures to exclude slavery from the Territories, nor from the efforts of the different States to defeat the execution of the Fugitive Slave Law."

In both the Senate and House of Representatives, committees were appointed to consider the state of the Union in view of the threatening aspect of national affairs. The Senate Committee, consisting of thirteen members, was composed of the most distinguished Senators, representing the different parties to which they belonged. It consisted of five leading Republicans, the same number from the slave States, and three Northern Democrats.* The latter were intended to act as mediators between the extreme parties of the Committee. The Committee of the House consisted of thirty-three members, one from each State, and was made up of sixteen Republicans, fifteen Southern men and two Northern Democrats. Horace Greeley, speaking of this Committee, says:

> "Mr. Speaker Pennington, who formed the Committee, was strongly inclined to conciliation, if that could be effected, on terms not disgraceful to the North; and at least six of the sixteen Republicans placed on the Committee, desired and hoped that an adjustment might yet be achieved. No member of extreme Anti-Slavery views was associated with them." †

The Committee of the Senate first met December 21st, and preliminary to any other proceedings, they "resolved that no proposition shall be reported as adopted, unless sustained by a majority of each of the classes of the Committee; Senators of the Republican party to constitute one class, and Senators of the other parties to constitute the other class." This resolution was adopted, because it was well-known that any report that might be submitted would be vain, unless sanctioned by at least a majority of Republican Senators. Few Southern men ever believed that these efforts at compromise would result in any amicable settlement of the difficulties between the sections; but they were willing to co-operate in any measures that promised the least hope of warding off from the country the calamities of civil war. On the 22d of the same month, John J. Crittenden, of Kentucky, submitted to the Committee his proposed amendments to the Constitution, which became popularly known as the Crittenden Compromise. This was designed as a compromise of conflicting claims, inasmuch as it proposed that the South should surrender their adjudicated right to take slaves into all the Territories, provided the North would concede this right in the Territory

*The five Republicans of the Committee were Messrs. Seward, Collamer, Wade, Doolittle and Grimes; the Southern Senators were Powell, Hunter, Crittenden, Toombs and Davis; and the Northern Democrats, Douglas, Bigler and Bright.

† Greeley's American Conflict. Vol. 1, p. 372.

south of the old Missouri Compromise line. It was the acceptance by the South of vastly less right in the Territories than she possessed under the decision of the Supreme Court, and showed Southern readiness to acquiesce in terms of reasonable compromise that might stay the flood-gates of civil outbreak between the States.

Of the vast existing Territory, all was conceded to the North by the proposition of Compromise, save New Mexico alone. And in regard to this section it was generally believed that it never could with profit be made a slave-holding State. At first it was thought by some that this amendment would be yielded by the North as a peace offering to the South. It was in truth, but an offer to restore the Missouri Compromise, against the repeal of which the Northern Anti-Slavery men had struggled so fiercely in 1854. It was hailed throughout the country as the rainbow of peace, promising perpetuity to the Union. James Buchanan thus speaks of this measure:

"Indeed, who could fail to believe that when the alternative was presented to the Senators and Representatives of the Northern States, either to yield to their brethren in the South, the barren abstraction of carrying their slaves into New Mexico, or to expose the country to the imminent peril of civil war, they would choose the side of peace and union? The period for action was still propitious. It will be recollected that Mr. Crittenden's amendment was submitted before any of our forts had been seized, before any of the cotton States except South Carolina, had seceded, and before any of the conventions which had been called in the remaining six of these States had assembled. Under such circumstances it would have been true wisdom to seize the propitious moment before it fled forever, and even yield, if need be, a trifling concession to patriotic policy, if not to abstract justice, rather than expose the country to a great impending calamity. And how small the concession required, even from a sincere Anti-Slavery Republican."*

In advocacy of this Compromise, Mr. Crittenden used the following language:

"The sacrifice to be made for its (that of the Union) preservation is comparatively worthless. Peace, harmony and union in a great nation were never purchased at so cheap a rate, as we now have it in our power to do. It is a scruple only, a scruple of as little value as a barley corn that stands between us and peace, reconciliation and union; and we stand here pausing and hesitating about that little atom which is to be sacrificed."†

---

*Buchanan's Administration on the Eve of the Rebellion, pp. 136–7.
†*Congressional Globe*, 3d January, 1861, p. 237.

As leading Southern statesmen however correctly apprehended, the Crittenden Compromise failed to receive the approbation of a single Republican member of the committee; and therefore it could not have been reported to the Senate as adopted, according to the resolution which they had agreed upon, though all the other thirteen members had voted for it. But because of the unanimity of the Republican opposition, neither Jefferson Davis nor Robert H. Toombs would stultify themselves by supporting a measure in which they were willing to acquiesce, but which they were satisfied the ruling party would not accept. In addition to this, Senator Davis, in view of the attitude of his State, had desired to be relieved from serving upon the committee when first named as a member of it. Senator Toombs, in his speech of January 9th, 1861, in enumerating the demands of the South, evinced that all he desired was a fair and honorable compromise. He said:

"We demand that the people of the United States shall have an equal right to emigrate to and settle in the present or any future acquired Territories, with whatever property they may possess (including slaves), and be securely protected in its peaceable enjoyment, until such Territory may be admitted as a State into the Union, with or without Slavery, as she may determine, on an equality with all existing States. * * * We have demanded simply *equality, security and tranquility.* Give us these and peace restores itself. * * * But although I insist upon this perfect equality in the Territories, when it was proposed, as I understand the Senator from Kentucky, now proposes that the line of 36°, 30′, shall be extended, acknowledging and protecting our property on the south side of the line, for the sake of peace, permanent peace, I said to the Committee of Thirteen, as I say here, that with other satisfactory provisions I would accept it."*

In addition to this, we have the testimony of Senator Douglas in his speech of January 3d, 1861, showing upon whom rested the responsibility of the failure to accept the Crittenden Compromise in the Committee of Thirteen. He said:

"If you of the Republican side are not willing to accept this [a proposition of adjustment offered by himself] nor the proposition of the Senator from Kentucky (Mr. Crittenden's), pray, tell us what you are willing to do. I address the inquiry to the Republicans alone, for the reason that in the Committee of Thirteen, a few days ago, every member from the South, including those from the cotton States (Messrs. Davis and Toombs), expressed their readiness to accept the proposition of my venerable friend from Kentucky as a final settlement of the controversy, if

Congressional Globe, p. 268–70.

tendered and sustained by the Republican members. Hence, the sole responsibility of our disagreement and the only difficulty in the way of an amicable adjustment is with the Republican party."*

In his reply to Mr. Pugh, of Ohio, Senator Douglas re-affirmed his former statement. He said:

"The Senator has said, that if the Crittenden proposition could have been passed early in the session, it would have saved all the States except South Carolina. I firmly believe it would. While the Crittenden proposition was not in accordance wi h my cherished views, I avowed my readiness and eagerness to accept it, in order to save the Union, if we could unite upon it. No man has labored harder than I have to get it passed. I can confirm the Senators declaration that Senator Davis himself, when on the Committee of Thirteen, was ready at all times to compromise on the Crittenden proposition. I will go further, and say that Toombs was also ready to do so."†

Although Mr. Crittenden's measure failed before the Committee of Thirteen, he did not despair of ultimate success with it. After this he could not expect to carry his compromise as an amendment to the Constitution, but believed it was possible to obtain a majority of each House in its favor so as to have it referred to a direct vote of the people of the States. He thought a portion of the Republican Members of Congress might be willing to favor a reference of the questions in dispute to the people themselves, as in this manner their party could relieve itself from its former committals to the Chicago platform. Besides, he scarcely conceived it possible that they would be willing to assume the responsibility of denying to the people of the States an opportunity of expressing an opinion at the ballot-box, on questions involving no less a stake than the peace and safety of the Union. It was quite manifest to any one observing the current of public opinion at that time, that the people of perhaps every State but one were ready to accept the Crittenden Compromise as a settlement of all difficulties between the North and South. Memorials in its favor poured into Congress from all sections of the North. One of these presented to the Senate was from the Mayor, members of the Board of Aldermen and Common Council of the City of Boston, and was signed by over 22,000 citizens of the State of Massachusetts, praying the adoption of the Compromise measures proposed by Mr. Crittenden. Another from the City of New York contained 38,000 names.

* *Congressional Globe*, 1860-61, p. 1391.
†Appendix to *Congressional Globe*, 1860-61, p. 41.

A greater number of persons petitioned in favor of the Crittenden Compromise than for any former measure that had ever been before the American Congress.

Mr. Crittenden made repeated efforts to bring the Senate to a vote upon his propositions, but was steadily baffled by the parliamentary tactics of Republican Senators. On the 14th of January, 1861, he made an unsuccessful attempt to have it considered, but it was postponed until the following day. On this day it was again postponed by the vote of every Republican Senator present, in order to make way for the Pacific Railroad Bill. He succeeded on the 16th, by a majority of a single vote, in bringing his resolution before the body; every Republican Senator voting against its consideration. A direct vote upon the resolution so earnestly desired by the country, now seemed inevitable; but Republican fertility was not lacking, and a new display of tactics once more, baffled the compromisers. Mr. Clark, a Republican Senator from New Hampshire, moved to strike out the entire preamble and resolution offered by Mr. Crittenden, and in lieu thereof insert those of a directly opposite character, and such as were in accord with the Chicago platform. This motion prevailed by a vote of 25 to 23, every Republican present voting in its favor. Six secession Senators declined to vote on the Clark amendment, being already firmly convinced that all efforts to compromise between the sections would prove abortive because of Republican obstinacy. Mr. Iverson, of Georgia, one of the six, who declined to vote, in his speech of December 11th, 1860, expressed his utter disbelief that compromise in any wise could effect a solution of the National difficulties. He said:

"Then, sir, is it proposed by Congressional legislation to appease the Southern States by the adoption of the doctrine of Congressional protection to Slavery in the Territories of the United States? Sir, I want to know who expects that such a remedy as that will ever be occorded by this Congress, or any other? We know that the Republican party, so far as they are concerned, are a unit against any such provision. It was the great Shibboleth, on which they fought the recent battle and won it. It is the great principle which stands as the very basis of their political organization that Slavery shall never advance one inch beyond its present boundaries, and shall never plant a footprint in any Territory of the United States.

"The Southern people now moving for secession, will never be satisfied with any concession made by the North that does not fully recognize not only the existence of Slavery in its present form, but the right of the

Southern people to emigrate to the common Territories with their slave property, and their right to Congressional protection while the Territorial existence lasts. The recent battle of the South was fought upon that very issue. The friends of Mr. Breckenridge put him upon the very grounds of Congressional protection to slave property in the Territories; and it was upon that ground that he carried the cotton States.

"The North, if they yield at all, yield from an apprehension that the South is going to dissolve the Union, and they yield from fear of the consequences. Of what value would any concessions, made under these circumstances, be to the South? None, as long as this vitiated public sentiment of Anti-Slavery exists in the hearts and minds of the Northern people. And, when is that ever going to be changed? Never, as long as the Union lasts. It is a part, not only of their literary education, but of their religious creed. It enters into all the complications of society. It pervades the pulpit, the halls of legislation, the popular assemblies, the school houses—all teach the doctrine of the '*irrepressible conflict*'; and how many arguments in favor of Slavery, its morality, its social and political advantages, ever reach the Northern eye and the Northern ear."*

Mr. Wigfal, of Texas, another of the six secession Senators who refused to vote on the Clark amendment, gave his reasons for so doing in a speech delivered by him January 30th, 1861. He said:

"What were the Clark resolutions? They were resolutions asserting that no amendments to the Constitution were necessary; and that the only matter of importance was that coercion should be used upon the sovereign States that had declared themselves out of the Union. When these resolutions came up as a substitute for the resolutions of the Senator from Kentucky, every Senator who belongs to the dominant party—the party that is to be entrusted with the reins of Government on the 4th of March next, voted for the Clark resolutions as a substitute for the Crittenden resolutions. What then was the use of our stultifying ourselves? What was the use of our sitting here and voting down resolutions, which expressed the opinion of the dominant party of the country, in order that the Senator from Illinois might write letters or telegraph to different States that the Union was about to be saved; that the Crittenden resolutions had been passed through the Senate. I did not intend to make myself a party to the fraud; and therefore, when the question came up between the Crittenden and Clark resolutions, I for one forbore to vote. I knew the Senators on that side of the chamber had the majority. We had appealed to them; we had begged them in God's mercy and for the good of their own people and for the peace of the country, to interpose and to settle this question upon some safe basis."†

All hope of a compromise that could save the Union was virtually abandoned, when the Senate of the United States declined to accept the Crittenden propositions, as the basis of an adjudi-

Congressional Globe of 1860–61, pp. 49–50.

†*Congressional Globe*, 1860–61, p, 665.

cation. The intense anxiety, however, that existed in the breasts of those who desired to avert the calamity of civil war, suggested one plan of conciliation after another, but all to no purpose. The General Assemby of Virginia, on the 19th of January, 1861, adopted resolutions expressing the opinion "that unless the unhappy controversy which now divides the States of the Confederacy shall be satisfactorily adjusted, a permanent dissolution of the Union is inevitable." For the purpose of averting this calamity, they invited all the States to appoint Commissioners to meet at the City of Washington, February 4th, 1861, in order that an earnest effort be made "to adjust the present unhappy controversies in the spirit in which the Constitution was originally framed." These resolutions expressed the belief that the Crittenden propositions with perhaps some modifications, would "be accepted as a satisfactory adjustment by the people of this Commonwealth."

Seven of the Southern States had already either seceded or were moving in that direction. Everything indicated the breaking up of the Union, with its consequent calamities of civil war, and the probable downfall of the Government. To avert these calamities, all classes were willing to unite, except those who were resolved to risk national disaster rather than compromise their party principles; and those, also, who were fully assured that no satisfactory settlement could be obtained. The former were the anti-compromise Republicans of the North, and the latter, the Southern secessionists and their allies in the border States. Commissioners were appointed to the Peace Conference from fifteen Northern and seven Southern States, although the movement was one which met with little sympathy in Republican circles. Some of the Northern States refused to appoint Commissioners, and those who did so, selected men of strong Anti-Slavery opinions, who were known to be opposed to any compromise whatsoever. Senators Chandler and Bingham telegraphed to the Governor of Michigan, urging him to send to the conference radical Abolitionists, in order that no compromise might be effected. A view of the composition of the conference, to one acquainted with the antecedents of the members from the North, was sufficient to satisfy the observer that little hopes could be based upon the actions of that body. What reasonable expectation of compromise could be anticipated from the deliberations of an assembly in which such men as Salmon P. Chase and David Wilmot exercised a leading control; and the majority of whose members were associated together in the same political organization? It was only in deference to public opinion, that the radical Republican leaders consented at all, to participate in the movements of the Peace Conference, for they never for one moment cherished the thought of acceding so far to Southern demands, as reason dictated it to be necessary, in order to avert the calamities of civil war. But the people demanded compromise, and it was necessary for the politicians, in view of the popular desire, to yield in appearance, and thus shield themselves from public condemnation. It was but a part, therefore, of that system of dissimulation which had secured abolition ascendency under another name, and which was now baffling the wish of the people, until the party of new ideas had firmly grasped the reins of the General Government.

But a compromise was adopted by the conservatives of the Peace Congress, which restored the old Missouri division of 36° 30′ to all the present territory of the United States. North of this line, slavery was to be prohibited, and south of it permitted; but this compromise was not to extend to future territorial acquisition. And even this diluted compromise was extorted with such grinding reluctance, that it failed altogether in its effect. Southern men, who had still cherished some lingering hope of a settlement of the difficulties, left the convention fully satisfied that the day of conciliation had passed. John Tyler, the President of the Peace Congress, however, in obedience to the resolution of that body, communicated February 27th to the Senate and House of Representatives, the result of their deliberations. In the Senate, on motion of Mr. Crittenden, this was referred to a Select Committee. The Committee, on the following day, reported it as an amendment to the Constitution, but the Senate was never able to be brought to a direct vote upon it. Failing in this effort, Mr. Crittenden made a motion to substitute the amendment of the Peace Congress instead of his own propositions. This was rejected by a very large majority, eight yeas to twenty-eight nays. Mr. Crittenden, on the 2d of March, 1861, after having been repeatedly thwarted, succeeded in getting a direct vote in the Senate upon his propositions of compromise, but they were defeated by a vote of nineteen in the affirmative to twenty in the negative. They were rejected by Republican votes alone.

In the House of Representatives, everything looking to compromise, met with resistance from Mr. Stevens and other leading Republicans. He, with 37 others, on the 1st day of the 2d session of the 36th Congress, voted against Mr. Botteler's resolution to refer the President's message to a Committee of one from each State. On the 7th of January, 1861, the Republicans of the House on a vote of yeas and nays, refused to consider certain propositions moved by Mr. Etheridge, of Tennessee, which were less favorable to the South than the Crittenden resolutions offered in the Senate. The Crittenden proposition in substance was submitted as the ultimatum of the South to the House Committee of thirty-three, by Albert Rust, of Arkansas, but was voted down, no Republican sustaining it. Mr. Stevens, and 64 radical Republicans of the House, even voted against Corwin's amendment to the Constitution, reported by a majority of the Committee of thirty-three, and which declared that no power existed to interfere with slavery in the States. Every act of the radical Republican members of the House, as well as the Senate, during the last session of the 36th Congress indicated, that the Abolition wing of the party had fully resolved upon permitting no concession to the South, such as might lead to a pacification between the sections. When a Conservative would offer in Congress, resolutions looking to a settlement of the National difficulties, some radical Republican would call for the regular order of business, and endeavor to exclude their presentation. Mason W. Tappan, a Republican Congressman from New Hampshire, and a member of the Committee of thirty-three, submitted February 5th, 1861, a minority report of that Committee, which declared that the provisions of the Constitution were ample for the preservation of the Union. Speaking of the Crittenden plan of compromise, he said:

> "It would be the adoption into the Constitution of the creed of the ultra portion of the Democratic party, who broke up the Charleston Convention, because the dogma of *protection* to Slavery was not inserted in the Democratic platform. Sir, the Free States will never concede these terms of settlement, let the consequences be what they may."*

Galusha A. Grow, Thaddeus Stevens, Hickman, Lovejoy, and

**Congressional Globe*, 1860–61, p. 760.

other Radicals of the House, on the 1st of March, co-operated in preventing the reception of the Memorial of the Peace Congress. They baffled its reception by refusing to allow the suspension of the rules of the House. Mr. Stevens, in voting to prevent the suspension, remarked:

"I think we had better go on with the regular order (of business). We have saved this Union so often that I am afraid we shall save it to death."*

The day of compromise was past and the new era had set in, with the advent of the Republicans to power. The Abolition portion of the party were fully resolved to stand by their principles. B. F. Wade, in a speech delivered by him in the Senate, December 17th, 1860, said:

"Sir, I know not what others may do; but I tell you that with the verdict given in favor of the platform upon which our candidates have been elected, so far as I am concerned, I would suffer anything to come before I would compromise that away. I say, then, that so far as I am concerned, I will yield to no compromise."†

A New England dinner was given in the City of New York on Saturday, December 22d, 1860, at which a number of Republican orators, including William H. Seward, made speeches, all of whom rejected the idea of a compromise with the South.‡ The New York *Tribune*, of the same date, contained the following declaration:

"We are enabled to state in the most positive terms, that Mr. Lincoln is utterly opposed to any concession or compromise that shall yield one iota of the position occupied by the Republican party; that the great North, aided by hundreds of thousands of patriotic men in the slave States, have determined to preserve the Union—peaceably, if they can—forcibly, if they must!"

The following sentiments, to the same purport, were quoted as emanating from Mr. Lincoln, by James H. Campbell, of Pennsylvania, a Republican member of the House, in his speech of February 14th, 1861:

"I will suffer death before I will consent or advise my friends to consent to any concession or compromise which looks like buying the privilege of taking possession of the Government, to which we have a constitutional right, because, whatever I might think of the various propositions before Congress, I should regard any concession in the face

Congressional Globe, 1860-61, pp. 1332-3.
†*Globe* of 1860-61, pp. 102-3.
‡New York *Herald*, December 24th, 1860.

of menace as the destruction of the Government itself, and a consent on all hands, that our system shall be brought down to a level with the existing disorganized state of affairs in Mexico." *

Following in the wake of the New York *Tribune*, the chameleon organ of New England Puritanism, the influential press of the North, with the exception of the Albany *Evening Journal*, decried compromise with the South as an ignoble surrender to the behests of the slave power. After the first alarm of secession had extorted from their leader the declaration that he *would resist all coercive measures to preserve the Union*, the whole radical journalistic fraternity gradually veered into an attitude that compelled their *Jupiter Tonans* of the press to change his base with them. *No compromise with traitors* was henceforth the standing utterance of the combined radical press of the North. Even whilst Senators and Members of Congress, in melifluous sentences and smooth words, spoke of fraternal affection and the blessings of the Union, the radical press was teeming with the most bitter denunciations of the Southern rebels and their institutions, and so far as they had the power, consigning them and the Northern compromisers to the lowest depths of Hadean darkness and seething perdition. Shielded by the press, those who hesitated elsewhere to utter their real sentiments, spoke with courage, and vented their spite in strains of malignity that cast into the shade the annals of all former history. The radical ecclesiastical as well as the secular press were in entire accord in this system of wholesale denunciation; and besides, the Abolition pulpit came in for its full share of credit in stemming the tide of compromise, and fanning the flames of the approaching revolution.

Were Southern statesmen then, mistaken, when they declared in Congress that no compromise could stay secession? Why, it was the stereotyped assertion of the radical press and pulpit of the North, that the era of conciliation and compromise had passed forever, and they all rejoiced to be able to say so. But, unlike the sincere Abolitionists of the Philippo-Garrison school, they lacked the honesty to declare manfully and openly the objects of their party. By fraud and deception they continued still to deceive the Northern people, and have them to believe that they were the only friends of the Union and free government.

* *Congressional Globe*, 1860–'61, p. 110.

Whilst the Garrisonians rejoiced in the dissolution of the Union, because they believed this event would overthrow slavery, the political Abolitionists pretended that they cherished unbounded love for the Constitution of the Republic. In opposing compromise, they felt assured that a collision of arms would supervene, which would end in the overthrow of Southern slavery. That, instead of the preservation of the Union, was what inspired their opposition to every proposition of settlement with the South. The mob philosopher of the *Tribune*, in his journal of the 26th of February, 1861, disclosed in somewhat oracular words, his genuine opinions. He says: "We are not willing to make every sacrifice for the preservation of the Union, because we value liberty and right more than we do the Union." Philosophers do not seek under dark expressions to hide their ideas; they express them fearlessly and accept the consequences. If slavery was an unendurable evil, it should have been battled with Garrisonian weapons and under genuine colors; and history will remove the philosopher,s cloak from the statue of every one who otherwise fought it. The stern arbiter of time ever consigns the agitating knave and hypocrite to the historic recesses of execration and contempt, where the shades of Robespierre, Danton and Marat are gathered.

CHAPTER XIII.

STATE SOVEREIGNTY AND CENTRALIZATION, OR THE OPPOSITE PRINCIPLES OF GOVERNMENT STRUGGLING FOR ASCENDENCY.

As stated in a former chapter, two schools of political opinions strove for mastery in the Convention of 1787, which framed the Federal Constitution. The same fundamental questions which divided the framers of our Government, have from that period continued to separate the American people into two antagonistic parties, each of which trace a lineal descent from revolutionary ancestors. The effort of the one party was to consolidate the States into a National Government, so as to give it that strength and durability which monarchies possess; but this was combatted and successfully resisted by those who were unwilling to merge the sovereignty of the States in any consolidated form. De Tocqueville says:

"When the war of independence was terminated, and the foundations of the new government were to be laid down, the nation was divided between two opinions which are as old as the world, and which are perpetually to be met with, under all the forms and all the names which have ever obtained in free communities—the one tending to limit, the other to extend indefinitely the power of the people.

"The party which desired to limit the power of the people, endeavored to apply its doctrines more especially to the Constitution of the Union, whence it derived its name of *Federal*. The other party, which affected to be more exclusively attached to the cause of liberty, took that of *Republican*. America is the land of Democracy, and the Federalists were always in a minority; but they reckoned on their side, almost all the great men who had been called forth by the war of independence, and their moral influence was very considerable. Their course was, moreover, favored by circumstances. The ruin of the Confederation had impressed the people with a dread of anarchy, and the Federalists did not fail to profit by this transient disposition of the multitude. For ten or twelve years they were at the head of affairs, and they were able to apply some, though not all their principles; for the hostile current was becoming from day to day too violent to be checked or stemmed. In 1801, the Republicans got possession of the Government: Thomas Jefferson was named President, and he increased the influence of their party by the weight of his celebrity, the greatness of his talents, and the immense extent of his popularity."*

Whilst the Federalists held the reins of the General Government, there were entrapped in the passage of the Acts of Congress known as the *Alien and Sedition* laws. These were seized upon as an exposure of the cloven-foot of their monarchical principles; and the people were aroused to the dangers that threatened free government from a further continuance of that party in power. The leaders of the Republican or Democratic party conceived that the liberty of the people was in jeopardy, if laws infringing the Constitution could be passed with impunity; and they determined to resist the illegal measures of the ruling faction and secure their condemnation by the verdict of American public opinion. For this purpose Jefferson, the prominent advocate of the Republican theory of Government, drafted a series of resolutions for the Kentucky Legislature; and similar resolves were sketched by Madison for the Virginia Assembly, both of which received the sanction of these legislative bodies. The resolutions were transmitted to the Legislatures of the other States for their approval or disapproval. The Democratic party throughout the Union endorsed the correctness of the doctrines enunciated in the Virginia and Kentucky resolutions of 1798; and these famous declarations of governmental principles formed in after years the political creed of the organization. The soundness of the principles of these resolutions was necessarily disputed by the Federalists as being directed against their own legislative measures. These resolutions formed the platform upon which the Democratic party triumphed in 1800, and succeeded in electing Thomas Jefferson to the Chief Magistracy of the Nation.

The cardinal principle was laid down in the Virginia and Kentucky resolutions, that the General Government was one of limited authority, granted originally by the States as the sovereign members of the Confederation, and that in case undelegated powers should be assumed, such became void and of no force, because unauthorized in the original constitutional compact. It was farther declared that the General Government was not the "exclusive or final judge of the extent of the powers delegated to itself, since that would have made its discretion and not the

*De Tocqueville's Democracy, pp. 187–8.

Constitution the measure of its powers; but as in all cases of compact among powers having no common judge, each party has an equal right to judge for itself, as well of infractions as of the mode and measure of redress."

The General Government, according to the above theory, was simply the representative of the delegated authority of the sovereign States of the Union, and was authorized to execute its civil mandates upon the people of every State, so far as its authority extended. It was, therefore, simply the agent of the States for the execution of certain general powers, which are necessary in all governments, and which alone, could properly be performed by a federal head. All the authority granted to the General Government was of a civil nature, and specified only civil modes for its execution. The union of the States was a Confederated Republic, and was different from all former leagues of this character, in the feature already mentioned, that it permitted the Central Government to execute the general laws upon the people of the States themselves. Under the articles of confederation, the laws of Congress could only be executed through the instrumentalities of the State organizations, and it was, in the main, to remedy this defect that the Federal Union was formed. All the power delegated to the Federal Government to be executed over the people of the States, was either of a civil character or such as the execution of civil law required. In the convention which framed the Federal Compact, the exertion of military power against the States or the people thereof, save as the Constitution expressed, had been explicitly refused.

We find by the proceedings of the Federal Convention of May 31st, 1787, that the adoption of a clause was defeated, "authorizing an exertion of the force of the whole against a delinquent State." This Mr. Madison opposed in a speech, in which he said:

> "The use of force against a State, would look more like a declaration of war than an infliction of punishment; and would probably be considered by the party attacked, as a dissolution of all the previous compacts by which it might be bound."

Upon Madison's motion, the consideration of this clause was unanimously postponed, and it was never again presented.

The following extract from No. 16 of the *Federalist*, combats the idea of the General Government being clothed with the right of coercing the States of the Union, as chimerical and absolutely preposterous:

"Whoever considers the populousness and strength of several of these States singly, at the present juncture, and looks forward to what they will become, even at the distance of half a century, will at once dismiss, as idle and visionary, any scheme which aims at regulating them or coercing them in their collective capacities, by the General Government. A project of this kind is little less romantic than the monster-taming spirit attributed to the fabulous heroes and demi-gods of antiquity. Even in those Confederacies which have been composed of members smaller than many of our counties, the principle of legislation for sovereign States, supported by military coercion, has never been found effectual. It has rarely been attempted to be employed against the weaker members, and in most instances attempts thus to coerce the refractory and disobedient, have been the signals of bloody wars, in which one-half the Confederacy has displayed its banners against the other. The first war of this kind would probably terminate in a dissolution of the Union."

That eminent patriot and statesman, Alexander Hamilton, who was a member of the convention which framed the Constitution of the United States, in a speech delivered by him in the year 1788, in the ratifying convention of the State of New York, used the following language in reference to the coercive power being entrusted to the General Government:

"The coercion of States is one of the maddest projects that was ever devised. A failure of compliance will never be confied to a single State. This being the case, can we suppose it wise to hazard a civil war? It would be a nation at war with itself. Can any reasonable man be well disposed toward a government that makes war and carnage the only means of supporting itself—a government that can exist only by the sword? Every such war must involve the innocent with the guilty. This single consideration should not be inefficient to dispose every peaceable citizen against such a government."

The Virginia and Kentucky principle of the sovereignty of States, and their non-coercion through military force by the General Government, was the only doctrine compatible with republican principles, which declare that *all government rests upon the consent of the governed.* And so signal was the overthrow of the antagonistic doctrine of the Federal party, that the Government was a consolidated union of the people of all the States in one National Republic, that from the election of Thomas Jefferson until that of Abraham Lincoln, no President was chosen upon the avowed principles of consolidation. But the principles of monarchy ever continued secretly to form the leading characteristics of the party, which at all times was arrayed in opposition to the National Democracy. On this point hear De Tocqueville, in his History cf Democracy, Vol. I, pp. 190–1.

"But when one comes to study the secret propensities which govern the factions of America, he easily perceives that the greater part of them are more or less connected with one or the other of those two divisions which have always existed in free communities. The deeper we penetrate into the workings of these parties, the more do we perceive that the object of the one is to limit and the other to extend the popular authority. I do not assert that the ostensible end, or even that the secret aim of American parties is to promote the rule of aristocracy or democracy in the country, but I affirm that aristocratic or democratic passions may easily be detected at the bottom of all parties; and although they escape a superficial observation, they are the main point, the very soul of every faction of the United States."

This penetrative writer elsewhere permits it clearly to appear that the Democratic was the party of the people, whilst its opponent was that which was ever influenced by aristocratic or monarchical principles.

Resistance to the efforts of the Federal party to enlarge the powers of the General Government led, as has been seen, to the enunciation of the principles of the Virginia and Kentucky resolutions, and to the utter prostration, for the time, of the Consolidationists. But, although the Federal party was overthrown, its principles as already noted still continued to live, and inhere in all the organizations which succeeded it in opposition to the National Democracy. The question of a protective tariff was germinated in the principles of Hamiltonianism; and after the Alien and Sedition Laws, was the next which caused serious alarm, and threatened danger to the Union. "Before 1816, protection to home industry had been an incident to the levy of revenue, but in 1816 it became an object." *

The tariff of 1816, having inaugurated the protective policy, the measure was seized upon by the politicians of the Hamiltonian school as one that might again re-instate their party in power. From this period, once in every four years, the question was brought up with the evident purpose of influencing the Presidential election. The tariff bills of 1816, 1820, 1824 and 1828, each succeeding the other in its degree of protection, became the regular appendages, as it were, of the Presidential canvas. The great debate on the tariff before Congress at the session of 1823

* Benton's View. Vol. 1, p. 266.

and 1824, was the commencement of that dispute which afterwards led to the nullification difficulties. Members of Congress, "divided (at this time) pretty much on the line which always divided them on a question of constructive powers. The protection of domestic industry, not being among the granted powers, was looked for in the incidental, and denied by the strict Constructionists to be a substantive power to be exercised for the direct purposes of protection; but by all, at that time, and ever since the first tariff 1789, to be incident to the revenue-raising power, and an incident to be regarded in the exercise of that power." * "After 1824, the New England States (always meaning the greater portion when a section is spoken of) classed with the protective States—leaving the South alone as a section against that policy." † The Southern States believed themselves impoverished under the protective policy, to enrich those of the North.

The Southern States were therefore almost a unit in opposition to a protective tariff. The Act of 1828 bore the most oppressively of all against the interests of the people of that section. South Carolina, North Carolina, Georgia, Mississippi, Alabama and Virginia, had all united in remonstrances against the principle of protection; declared over and over again its unconstitutionality, and passed resolutions condemning the system. The people of these and other Southern States pointed out the inequality and the injustice of a protective tariff, and showed that the one section of the country was enriched at the expense of the other. This they urged was altogether unjust, and sustained by no warrant in the Federal Constitution. But Southern remonstrance was in vain; and all efforts to secure a repeal of the odious tariff legislation proved useless and abortive. The election of Andrew Jackson was a triumph of constitutional principles over a protective policy; and the Southern people demanded that its true import be considered. After his second election as President of the United States, South Carolina, seeing no hopes for the attainment of their rights by a repeal of an ununjust tariff, determined to have recourse to those reserved rights which she, as a sovereign member of the Confederacy, possessed. A convention of her people accordingly assembled on the 19th

* Benton's View. Vol. 1, p. 32.
† Benton's View. Vol. 1, p. 97.

of November, 1832, and passed an ordinance of nullification, which declared the existing tariff "null, void and of no law, nor binding on this State, its officers and citizens." The duties imposed by the Federal law were forbidden to be paid within the State after the 1st day of February, 1833.

Matters had now approached a crisis; and great caution and sagacity were required in order to obviate a collision of authorities. Fortunately, statesmen at that period ruled America, if an exception did not exist as to the Presidential occupant. A philosophic foreigner's estimate of President Jackson will not be out of place in this connection:

> "Gen. Jackson, whom the American people have twice elected to be the head of their government, is a man of a violent temper and mediocre talents; no one circumstance in the whole course of his career ever proved that he is qualified to govern a free people; and indeed the majority of the enlightened classes of the Union have always been opposed to him."*

If nothing more existed to show that Gen. Jackson was devoid of the necessary judgment to conduct the Government of a free people, sufficient would be found in his Proclamation of the 11th of December, 1832, to the people of South Carolina. The whole scope and tenor of this proclamation to the nullifiers, were antagonistic to the principles of the party of which he professed himself a member; and if a body of prudent statesmen had not been found in the country, the Republic at that early day might have sunk beneath the waves of civil convulsion. For although South Carolina was alone in her nullification attitude, her Southern sisters sympathized with her in her demands, and would have resisted her forcible coercion upon the battle field. Even the patriotic statesman of Roanoke, though upon the brink of the grave, declared that should Gen. Jackson attempt to coerce South Carolina into the Union, he would cause himself to be buckled upon his old white charger, and that he himself would fight in defense of liberty and State sovereignty.

President Jackson recommended to Congress that additional power be granted to him to collect the revenue at Charleston, and that sufficient troops be placed at his command so as to enable him to enforce the laws against the people of South Carolina. A bill for this purpose was reported by the Judiciary

*De Tocqueville's Democracy, Vol. I, p. 316.

Committee in the Senate, which called forth an animated debate, and for a period produced great excitement throughout the country. Many feared that the days of the Republic were numbered, and different opinions were entertained as to the best method of averting the dangers that were threatening the peace and integrity of the Union. The North permitted itself to be seduced into the support of the monarchical measures recommended by President Jackson, one of which was the coercion by military force of a State by the General Government. This had ever been a cherished principle of the Federal Consolidationists, and in this instance was seized upon by Gen. Jackson as a weapon by which to defeat his political enemy, John C. Calhoun, the philosophic statesman of South Carolina, who was the ablest defender of State Sovereignty, and the admitted father of nullification. In enforcing the view of the General Government held by Webster and the other leaders of the Federal school, President Jackson placed himself in antagonism to the principles he had ever professed to advocate, and inflicted upon free government the severest blow it had ever been compelled to endure in America. Being a Southerner by birth, education and sympathies, a member of the Jeffersonian State Right party, and a man whose military career gave him a reputation with the whole people of the country; the President by the force of his position and influence, was able to carry to the support of his measures all except those who had carefully studied the character of the General Government, and who apprehended danger to liberty in the exercise of undelegated authority; and who, besides, had the boldness to defend their sincere opinions, even in the face of controlling authority. But the obsequious vassals of party are ever ready to truckle before the throne of power, and pay their obeisance to any despot who may for the time happen to fill it. It was so in this case. Power emenated from the Federal Executive, and obedience to his dictates was the surest method of securing power.

Besides humbling his bitter enemy, the great statesman of South Carolina, President Jackson, in asking power to enforce the laws against the nullifiers, doubtless desired nothing more than to be able to preserve the Union of the States. This was the opinion of the Northern people, and also of many in the South; but the real danger existed in the establishment of an unconstitutional precedent. Rome was perfectly safe when she called Cincinnatus from his plow, and clothed him with unlimited powers; but she had cause to grieve long when she gave the dictatorship to Sylla and Marius, whose legions overthrew the bulwarks of liberty, and rioted in the blood of their countrymen. But a resolute band of Southern statesmen, seeing the danger that threatened freedom, boldly arrayed themselves in opposition to the demands of Executive power, and though prostrated, placed upon record the unmistakable words of truth, which will live and be cherished whilst republics endure. They declined clothing President Jackson with power to coerce South Carolina, not because (as most of them declared) they favored nullification, but because the Constitution granted no authority for this purpose. All power granted to the Federal Government was of a civil nature, and it was never contemplated by the framers of the Government that the military authority should be exerted save as auxiliary to the civil, and in that case as the Constitution specified. In the debate upon that occasion, Judge Bibb, of Kentucky, spoke as follows:

"It seemed to him that a false issue was presented. The question of war against South Carolina is presented as the only alternative. The issue was false. The first question was between justice and injustice. Shall we do justice to the States, who were united with South Carolina in complaint, and remonstrance against the injustice and oppression of the tariff? Shall we cancel the obligations of justice to five other States, because of the impetuosity and impatience of South Carolina, under wrong and oppression? The question ought not to be, whether we have the physical power to crush South Carolina, but whether it is not our duty to heal her discontents, to conciliate a member of the Union, to give peace and happiness to the adjoining States which have made common cause with South Carolina, to compel her to remain in the Union? Shall we keep her in the Union by force of arms for the purpose of compelling her submission to the tariff laws of which she complains?

"My creed is, that by the Declaration of Independence, the States were declared to be free and independent States, thirteen in number, not one nation,—that the old articles of Confederation united them as distinct States, not as one people;—that the treaty of peace of 1783, acknowledged their independence as States, not as a single nation; that the Federal Government was formed by States; submitted by States; and adopted by the States as distinct nations or States; not as a single nation or people.

"He would like to know when and where South Carolina surrendered the right to secede from the Union in case of a dangerous invasion of her rights by the Federal Government."*

*Stephens' War between the States. Vol. 1, pp. 425-27.

John Tyler, of Virginia, said:

"The idea that ours is a National Government, has lately received much encouragement from high sources, The President in his proclamation, speaks of the people as one mass, and of the Government as forming us into one Nation. When were the States, he would ask, welded together? Was it before or since the revolution?"

Further speaking of the overthrow of the principles of Federalism, Tyler says:

"In the year 1798,* all these doctrines were, he had thought, put down completely and forever. He had not expected to be obliged to renew the contest. For thirty years they had now been in obscurity, but suddenly they are waived into life, and brought into daylight by the President's proclamation.

"The President of the United States had declared against the doctrines of secession. But the President should not decide that doctrine for him. The military power was called for, to support this foregone conclusion of the President of the United States. If South Carolina secede, he is to be armed with military and naval power to subdue her."

Mr. Tyler speaks of the dangerous precedent that would be established by acquiescing in the executive demands. He said:

"He had all proper confidence in the Executive, but he was not disposed to confer very great powers upon any Executive. If they should even be used by the present President for the common good, and our institutions should come out safe from the trial, the precedent would be left standing on the statute book, and other Presidents might not use the power so beneficially."†

Mr. Poindexter, of Mississippi, deduced the origin of the unconstitutional power claimed by Gen. Jackson, as follows. He said:

"But this extra official document (Jackson's proclamation to the people of South Carolina) owes its origin, in reference to the political heresies it contains, to the speech of the Honorable Senator (Mr. Webster) of Massachusetts, delivered in this body in 1830, on what were familiarly called "*Foot's Resolutions*," These principles have never before been avowed by any political party in this country. They leave the old Federal School far in the rear, in their utter consolidation tendencies, and were for the first time introduced to the notice of the American people, in the speech of the Honorable Senator to which I have referred."‡

Several other distinguished statesmen of the South, with John C. Calhoun, took the ground that no power had been delegated to the Federal Government to exert the military arm against a State in its sovereign capacity, the people of which had assumed

---

*He refers to the Kentucky and Virginia resolutions.
†*National Intelligencer*, Feb. 6th. 1833.
‡*National Intelligencer*, March 19, 1833.

either a nullifying or seceding attitude. Even the Virginia House of Delegates condemned the doctrines contained in the President's Proclamation, characterizing them as the product of Federal inspiration. John Floyd, Governor of Virginia, in his Message of December 13th, 1832, said:

"Many questions of deep import have heretofore agitated these States, but none have equalled this in importance, either in the interest it ought to excite among the people or the effect it may produce upon the Confederacy. A sovereign State has spoken her sentiments in relation to this subject, and has pronounced those laws unconstitutional. Should force be resorted to by the Federal Government, the horror of the scenes hereafter to be witnessed cannot now be pictured, even by the affrighted imagination.

"The genius and spirit of our institutions are wholly adverse to such a step, and ought not to permit the mind of any to look in that direction—for what safety has any State of her existence as a sovereign, if difference of opinion should be punished with the sword as treason? Surely, civil war is not a remedy for wrongs in a country where the people are recognized as sovereign, and each individual has the right to the full and free expression of his opinions."*

But, although the Force Bill became a law, reason and good sense still whispered that the only proper way to preserve the Republic, was by the removal on the part of the General Government of those features of the tariff, which had occasioned the discontent in South Carolina and the other Southern States. Measures introduced into Congress for that purpose, and which received the approbation of those bodies, satisfied the South Carolinians that it was the desire of the General Government to respect their rights, and without delay they yielded all further resistance to the national authority.

As soon as the storm of nullification had spent its strength, the Virginia and Kentucky resolutions became again the acknowledged creed of the Democratic party both North and South. Even President Jackson, through his political organs, attempted to satisfy public opinion, that no doctrine enunciated in his proclamation to the people of South Carolina was repugnant to the principles of Jeffersonian State Sovereignty. But all such attempts failed to convince the logical understanding of the small band of bold adherents of State rights, whom the popular storm had well nigh overborne, because of their firm defense of the principles upon which Republican Government rested. The

National Intelligencer, December 18, 1832.

staunch defenders of principle saw the fatal stabs that Jeffersonianism had received, and the danger that threatened liberty in the coercion precedent which had been established. The re-endorsement of the resolutions of 1798 by the Democratic party, was unable to give ample assurance of safety to the sincere believers in State Sovereignty, in view of the manner those doctrines had been trailed in the dust in obedience to the demands of impassioned excitement and popular phrensy.

A lesson had been learned by the friends of Free Government not soon to be forgotten. That little reliance was to be placed upon the declarations of politicians, when interest admonished their repudiation, was a demonstrated truth. It was also ascertained that the will of a people, expressed in times of great commotion, is not the utterance of convictions based upon reason and justice; but rather the effervescence of passion and vindictive hatred. The vast influence of position on such occasions was likewise clearly perceived; and it was observed that one man may have it in his power, to so arouse a whole people that the compacts of liberty afford no protection to guaranteed rights. What assurance of safety had those who dreaded consolidation, when the very party itself which came originally into power upon the principles of the Virginia and Kentucky resolutions, could be induced, through Presidential influence, to repudiate its cardinal doctrine; and the one of all others that distinguished it from its Federal antagonist. But the deed was done, the principles upon which the Constitution was founded were prostituted at the anarchical cry of national preservation; and it but remained for the enemies of the Federal Union, like the conquerors at Phillippi, to overwhelm in a general collision the defenders of constitutional republicanism.

It was not difficult for State Sovereignty in the forum of reason to maintain its ascendency, while statesmen were permitted to rule in the Halls of the nation. In peaceful times this principle triumphed, and no party in America could have sustained itself that would have openly endorsed the contrary opinion. It was only in the Northern wing of the Whig party that the Hamiltonian principles were still visible. But the Abolition party and its successor, the Republican, were based upon a pure monarchical creed, which stamped them as the legitimate deendscants of Federal ancestors. The avowed and leading principle of that party, which declared that no more slave States should be admitted into the Union, was itself a plain repudiation of the principles of Free Government, which assumes that all authority flows from consent. And even the agitation of slavery by the Northern people was an interference with the rights of those of the Southern States, over whom, under the Constitution, they had no control.

The known principles of the Republican party were sufficient to determine the people of the South, after the election of Abraham Lincoln in 1860, to seek their safety in the exercise of those reserved rights which they, as States, had never surrendered to the General Government. The preparations that from that period, began to be made throughout the whole of the Cotton States, again made the question of State Sovereignty a leading subject of discussion in all parts of the Union. That portion of the Democratic party in the North which still adhered to Jeffersonian principles, viewed the Constitution as a compact between the States, and that no power could be exerted against the States or the people thereof, save as had been already expressed and delegated. According to this view of the Constitution, in case one or more of the States should choose to secede from the General Government, no authority was believed to exist by which these seceding members of the Confederated Republic could be coerced back into the Union. James Buchanan, in his last Annual Message, gave the following opinion with reference to the coercion of the seceding States:

"The question fairly stated is: Has the Constitution delegated to Congress the power to force a State into submission, which is attempting to withdraw or has actually withdrawn from the Confederacy? If answered in the affirmative, it must be on the principle that the power has been conferred upon Congress to declare and make war against a State. After much serious reflection I have arrived at the conclusion that no such power has been delegated to Congress or to any other department of the Federal Government. It is manifest upon an inspection of the Constitution, that this is not amongst the specific and enumerated powers granted to Congress; and it is equally apparent that its exercise is not "necessary and proper for carrying into execution" any one of these powers. So far from this power having been delegated to Congress, it was expressly refused by the convention which framed the Constitution."

Mr. Buchanan had taken the precaution to consult Jeremiah S. Black, his Attorney-General, and one of the ablest lawyers of the nation, as to the powers of the General Government, with reference to the question of secession. The Attorney General in his reply to the President, showed clearly that military force could only be used to aid in the execution of civil powers, and only then, when the civil officers would be resisted in their duties, and the appropriale State official would call upon the President for assistance as the Constitution specifies. "But," says the Attorney-General, "what if the feeling in any State against the United States should become so universal that the Federal officers themselves, (including Judges, District-Attornies and Marshals) would be reached by the same influence, and resign their places? Of course, the first step would be to appoint others in their stead, if others could be got to serve. But in such an event, it is more than probable that great difficulty would be found in filling the offices. We can easily conceive how it might become altogether impossible. We are, therefore, obliged to consider what can be done in case we have no courts, judicial process, and no ministerial officer to execute it. In that event, troops would certainly be out of place, and their use wholly illegal. If they are sent to aid courts and marshals, there must be courts and marshals to be aided. Without the exercise of these functions, which belong exclusively to the civil service, the laws cannot be executed in any event, no matter what may be the physical strength which the Government has at its command. Under such circumstances, to send a military force into any State with orders to act against the people, would be simply making war upon them.

"If it be true that war cannot be declared, nor a system of general hostilities be carried on by the Central Government against a State, then it seems to follow that an attempt to do so would be *ipso facto* an expulsion of such State from the Union. Being treated as an alien and an enemy, she would be compelled to act accordingly. And if Congress shall break up the present Union by unconstitutionally putting strife, and enemity, and armed hostility, between sections of the country, instead of the *domestic tranquility* which the Constitution was meant to insure, will not all the States be absolved from their Federal obligations? Is any portion of the people bound to contribute their money or their blood to carry on a contest like that?"

Without a further attempt to specify the names of leading

Northern Democrats, who maintained the doctrine of State Sovereignty; and that the General Government was clothed with no power to exert the coercive arm against States in case of their secession, it can be affirmed with confidence, that this was the accepted doctrine of the great body of the party in the North, as well as in the South. This was the opinion of all who, in any wise, were conversant with the history of the formation of the Federal Constitution; and who were disposed to resist the monarchical tendency, which, from the origin of the Republic, had shown its workings; and which, to sagacious minds, seemed to threaten entire overthrow to the Constitutional Government. The American Union was, as they conceived, the product of the advanced intelligence of the age and founded upon the principle of consent alone. Experience had taught mankind to believe that republican institutions could endure in their simplicity only in the government of small countries and States; and that if they were to be extended over large territories, this must be accomplished by means of confederations amongst these, still permitting the several allied States to remain sovereign as to all power not expressly delegated to the Federal Union. That this was the character of the American Confederacy, had been the received and steadily avowed opinion of all who maintalned rank amongst the sound thinkers and statesmen of the Jefferson school of politics. Even publicists,* who were strictly members of neither political party, viewed the Government as a compact between the several States; and that as the Union was constituted, there was nothing to prevent a State from seceding, should she choose to assume and exercise her reserved powers.

But such a construction of the Constitution was never agreeable to that party, which strove to concentrate power and to dictate their opinions to the people of the whole country. That school of politics, which have ever striven to impose their views of social polity upon other States and people, would necessarily be the enemies of State rights, as declared in the Virginia and Ken-

*Judge Tucker, Professor of Law in the University of William and Mary, Virginia, in his edition of Blackstone's Commentaries, issued about 1803, and Mr. Rawle, an eminent Jurist of Pennsylvania, in his work upon the Constitution, published in 1826, took the view that the General Government was simply the result of a compact between the States; and that the right of secession was a sequence that necessarily flowed therefrom, should the States choose to exercise this denier remedy for experienced or apprehended evils.

tucky resolutions of 1798. And hence Puritanism from the first has been arrayed against them.

The doctrine of abolitionism could derive its support in no other principle than that of monarchy; even though slavery should be conceded to be a moral and social evil; for it was the effort of one people to interfere with the affairs of another and dictate how they shall manage them. The principle thus assumed was the same as had ever enchained the nations of the old world and bound them with the manacles of despotism; and again, not dissimilar from that which riveted ecclesiastical fetters upon independent thought, which modern ages have busied themselves in disrupting. The inquisitorial judges and the robed prelates of the Spanish Peninsula, made no other assumption than was claimed by the abolition band infidel priesthood* of the North, when they demanded the emancipation of the negro slaves in the Southern States. And all the blood that flowed on St. Bartholomew's night, and that in religious wars moistened the soil of Europe, was shed in obedience to that same dictatorial spirit, which would impose the conscientious convictions of one people upon the minds of another.

The peaceful and conservative policy of the Democracy was destined to yield to one of a different character upon the advent of Hamiltonianism to power in 1860, under the assumed name of Republicanism. Prior to this time, the utterances of the leading men of the party had been very guarded as regards their intentions, and those of them who had the honesty and courage to express their real sentiments, were popularly viewed as enthusiasts and fanatics, who would possess no influence under the new governmental regime. Even Thaddeus Stevens himself, was regarded as one of those extreme men whose opinions would never

* "Wherever the seed of Abolitionism has been sown broadcast, a plentiful crop of infidelity has sprung up. In communities where Anti-Slavery excitement has been most prevalent, the power of the gospel has invariably declined; and where the tide of fanaticism begins to subside, the wrecks of church order and of Christian character have been scattered on the shore. * * * The effect of abolitionism upon individuals is no less striking and mournful than its influence upon communities. It is a remarkable and instructive fact, and one at which Christian men would do well to pause and consider, that in this country, all the prominent leaders of abolitionism, outside of the ministry, have become avowed infidels; and that all our notorious abolition preachers have renounced the great doctrines of grace as they are taught in the standards of the reformed churches."—Sermon of Rev. J. Vandyke, of Brooklyn, New York *Herald,* December 10th, 1860.

become the rule of the Republican party. But the news of the election of Abraham Lincoln had scarcely flashed across the telegraphic wires until a greater boldness of utterance was discernible in the columns of the Republican press. This party had won the political battle, and henceforth, inspired with confidence, they assumed the attitute of masters that must be entreated rather than menaced. The exiled monarch that had wandered in disguise, and in varied habits, since the people had elected Thomas Jefferson to the Presidential Chair, at once returned and ascended again the throne of his federal ancestors. The fiat was immediately issued to the magnates of power, that the principles of compromise should be suspended, and the maxims of Empire substituted.

But, that the humble obeisance of the vassals might be secured, and a ready obedience to the orders of despotism guaranteed, a preliminary course of instruction was required. The subjects so long inured to the policy of peace and democratic leniency, must be indoctrinated into the principles of the new school, and this without delay was undertaken. In reference to the secession commotion, the Republican press of the North instead of discussing the reasons of Southern discontent, and the method to effect its allayment, spoke of the powers of the Government, craftily thereby endeavoring to inflame the enthusiasm of the unreflecting masses, in behalf of naticnal unity and the perpetuity of the Republic. How captivatingly were the people admonished, that *the first question to be decided, was, whether we have a Government or not.* The Union was dear to the people of the North, save to the abolitionists themselves, who had now succeeded in gaining power under the Republican banner. The first aim of the leaders of the triumphant party, was to arouse the people to the danger by which the Union was threatened from Southern secession. By the haranguing of an inflamatory press, Northern sentiment was soon made almost unanimous against this dogma of the State's Right School. No name at this period was so potential with the people as that of Andrew Jackson, whose famous declaration now formed the watch-word with the Constitution destructives, "*the Federal Union, it must be preserved.*" Those seeking to subvert the Constitution were now loudest in their cries for the preservation of the Union.

Gen. Jackson in the nullification excitement had given expression, as has been seen, to utterances for which he afterwards had cause sincerely to repent. No man ever filled the Presidential Chair, who was subjected to more malignant abuse by that party which comprised in its ranks the monarchical or consolidation element of the country; and yet when this same school succeeded in gaining political power in the government, the unstudied expressions of this much abused President, were rehearsed before his admirers, by those who despised and vilified all his actions; save the one in which he unfortunately erred, and which was contrary to the whole tenor of his political life, and to his subsequently expressed convictions. This same party whilst retailing the declarations of President Jackson, studiously avoided circulating the following extract from his farewell address to his countrymen:

"It is well known that there has always been those among us who wish to enlarge the powers of the General Government; and experience would seem to indicate that there is a tendency on the part of this Government to over-step the boundaries marked out for it by the Constitution. Its legitimate authority is abundantly sufficient for all the purposes for which it was created; and its powers being expressly enumerated, there can be no justification for claiming anything beyond them. Every attempt to exercise power beyond these limits should be promptly and firmly opposed. For one evil example will lead to other measures still more mischievous; and if the principle of constructive powers, supposed advantages, or temporary circumstances shall ever be permitted to justify the assumption of a power not given by the Constitution, the General Government will before long absorb all the powers of legislation, and you will have in effect but one consolidated government. From the extent of our country, its diversified interests, different pursuits, and single habits, it is too obvious for argument that a single consolidated Government would be wholly inadequate to watch over and protect its interests; and every friend of our free institutions should be always prepared to maintain, unimpaired and in full vigor, the *rights and sovereignty of the States*, and confine the action of the General Government strictly to the sphere of its appropriate duties."*

The excitement throughout the country had become intense upon the assembling of Congress in December, 1860. As soon as President Buchanan had submitted the views of the administration upon secession and coercion, the Republican press united in a general condemnation of the principles therein enunciated, and ridiculed the Executive as a coward and committed to the interests of treason. Assaults upon the peace policy of the administration, now became one of the means by which the Repub-

*Statesman's Manual, vol. 2, p. 952.

lican leaders strove to intensify Northern sentiment against the Southern people; and prepare the masses for that bloody strife of sections which they found it necessary to foment in order to strengthen their own political power and crush that of their adversaries. When South Carolina at length seceded, the auroral star of the millenium seemed to rise upon the vision of those who had for upwards of a quarter of a century prayed for a dissolution of the Union. Wendel Phillips and his associate band of open and avowed Abolitionists, were in exstacies over the event. The harbinger of the new epoch was announced. The emancipators shouted huzzas when the convention of South Carolina had proclaimed secession. "Deck her with garlands—lade her with jewels," cried they; "because she has gone, and God speed her on her journey."

But the unavowed Abolitionists, Republicans in name, Emancipationists in principle, Wade, Hale, Stevens, and others, now found a glorious opportunity to assault the South, the administration and the Democratic party in general. Compromise with traitors was ridiculed, and all members of the Republican party favoring a conservative policy were denounced as derelict to the principles of the Chicago platform. The strong current that set in shortly after the election of Lincoln, in favor of compromise, had the effect of intimidating all but the boldest Republicans from expressing freely their designs as regards the coercion of the Southern States. John P. Hale, of New Hampshire, was one of the first who permitted it clearly to appear that it was determined by the Republican leaders to declare war against the seceded States. This announcement in the United States Senate emboldened those editors of like opinions to utter their sentiments with less reserve; and the Republican press from this period teemed with threats of coercion and condign punishment of the rebels. As early as December 20th, 1860, the Springfield *Journal*, the presumed reflector of the views of Abraham Lincoln, the President elect, gave utterance to the following sentiments:

"She (South Carolina) cannot get out of this Union until she conquers this Government. The revenues must and will be collected at her ports, and any resistance on her part will lead to civil war."

The following extract from the New York *Herald*, seems very truthfully to portray the Republican attitude at the time of its appearance:

"Because Mr. Buchanan has adopted the peace policy, he is denounced by the Republicans as a dotard, an imbecile, a traitor, and a lunatic. * * * The Republican journals of the North, are daily becoming more and more bitter in the tone of their belligerent manifestations, and in their vituperative advocacy of the extremest measures to reduce the slave States to submission to the doctrines laid down in the Chicago platform. Appeal to the inexorable logic or grooved cannon, Sharpe's rifles, and the bayonet, takes the place of reflection and argument now, just as cant, abuse, calumny and diatribe did that of truth and facts while they were arousing their readers to that pitch of Anti-Slavery excitement which has produced the present crisis. They demand that Mr. Lincoln shall inaugurate his administration with blockades, bombardments and invasions, as flippantly and impudently as though the welfare of the country could be promoted by conformity to such diabolical fancies. They decree that the South shall be put down as glibly as if fifteen States were a vagrant to be arrested by the first policeman. With quasi authoritative language, they pretend to foreshadow the policy of the incoming administration as substituting the blood-red flag of civil war for the stars and stripes which float over the Capitol; and confidently predict that the '*irrepressible conflict*' will be carried out with a ruthless barbarity which John Brown himself would have hesitated to sanction.

"The transparent motive of so much furious clamor on the part of the Republican press, is to drive Mr. Buchanan into initiating aggressive measures against South Carolina and any other States that may secede, in order that he and his administration may be charged with beginning the war. He is denounced for not sending troops to Moultrie and surrounding Charleston with a naval cordon. Should Buchanan accede to them, they would be the first to turn upon him the full vials of popular indignation, and charge him as responsible for beginning the war."*

The tide of denunciation against President Buchanan and his peace policy, rose still higher and higher; and broke upon the public ear in all its vindictive fury and tumultuousness. The roar of the Abolition press resounded throughout the whole length and breadth of the North; a partisan malignity seemed as if ready to engulph all reason and sobriety beneath the opening waves of the social convulsion. Henry Ward Beecher regretted that destiny had not vouchsafed to America, at this time, an Oliver Cromwell for President; and the Republican journals urged that in the imbecile attitude in which the country found itself, owing to the treasonable dereliction of the administration, it behooved the loyal States of the North to act with reference to the emergency and prepare for the coming crisis. Some of the Republican Governors called attention to the condition of the country and urged upon their Legislatures to place the military

*New York *Herald*, Dec. 24th, 1860.

forces of their States upon such a footing as to be ready to respond when called upon by the Federal authority. All these movements in the North served to indicate what the proposed policy of the incoming administration would be, as regards the seceded States.

That it was the full intention of the Republican leaders after their elevation to power, to inaugurate coercive measures against such Southern States as might secede from the Union, admits of no reasonable doubt. And although William H. Seward and other members of the party, attempted to appear as conservative in their views, and willing to extend the olive branch of peace; yet all these vascillating manœuvres were simply designed to enable these diplomatists to veer between the Scylla of Abolitionism and the Charybdis of Conservatism. The New York Senator had been selected as the premier of the incoming administration; and yet in view of the opposition that existed against him in his own party, and the growing strength of the movement favorable to compromise, he esteemed it prudential to feign conciliatory sentiments; and at the same time avoid committing himself to any definite line of policy. By this means he sailed in the centre current of his own party and avoided touching the extremes. As regards personal popularity and promotion, he felt that this was altogether his safest method; and at the same time he was sufficiently astute as to perceive that in times of commotion, the extremists of party always lead the Conservatives. In sentiment he either was or had ever feigned himself an extremist; but he now chose to be led to that point, where in truth, he wished to conduct others. On the one hand his early radicalism allied him with the Abolition wing of his party; on the other, his sentiments as uttered in his speeches in the Senate and elsewhere, since the election of Lincoln, gained him the confidence of the Compromisers; and he therefore was prepared for leadership in the Cabinet, should public opinion even force a conservative policy upon the new administration.

Remembering that the Republican leaders almost unanimously resisted all compromise which might prove satisfactory to the Southern people, was it not apparent in view of events that one of two things must occur, either a dissolution of the Union, or civil war to prevent it? Must it not then be accepted as an undeniable truth that they preferred either of these results, rather than acquiesce in a compromise? And yet they sought to evade these logical inferences which necessarily flowed from their words and actions. But the popular mind was unable to detect the real aim of those who despised the old Union, and who simply sought to arouse the Northern people to fight in its defense, in order that they might effect its destruction.

An ominous silence was maintained by Abraham Lincoln as to the policy which would be pursued after the Government came into his hands. For over three months after his election not a word was spoken by the new President that served clearly to indicate what his future policy would be. This silence was maintained in order that he might be free to accept that guidance which the controling opinon of his party might indicate. It can not be doubted, but that he with other leaders of the party, had fully agreed upon a course of action after his accession to the Chair of State, and time simply was permitted to determine whether the proposed plan could be executed or not. And this silence was simply a part of the revolutionary programme, which from the organization of the Republican party it was impolitic and politically dangerous to disclose. It was not believed by the Southern leaders, and by many in the North, that there was doubt as to the course the new administration would pursue when once installed in power. The unanminity of the Republican party, favoring the coercion of the seceded States by military power, made it sufficiently clear what the policy of the Lincoln Administration would be. This unaminity was but the echo of the well understood views and expressions of Members of Congress and other leaders of Republican opinion. Any one, at all attentive to the discussions which took place in the Senate and House of Representatives during the second session of the Thirty-sixth Congress, would have shown remarkable obtuseness not to have discovered, that war was the policy determined upon by the Republican leaders. The following extract would seem to indicate that the sentiment on this point was almost unanimous:

"The Republican leaders and journalists, with one or two exceptions, insist upon holding the Chicago platform, the whole platform, and nothing but the platform, no matter what may be the consequences to the party, the country, or the human race. * * * * They declare they will maintain it to the bitter end, though civil war should be the consequence."*

* New York *Herald*, January 21st, 1861.

The great difficulty, with which the Repnblican leaders had to contend, was the growing current of conservatism that set in after the Presidential election in November, 1860, and which flowed in opposition to their wishes, and which they feared might bear their revolutionary bark upon the rocks of political disaster. This current showed itself in the numerous petitions that flooded Congress in favor of compromise with the South, in the manifest changes which marked the local elections in many sections of the North, and also in the breaking up of Abolition assemblages and John Brown demonstrations, which six months before had been popular and held without interruption. It was the general belief of all the conservative classes, that the troubles likely to burst upon the country had been produced by the fanatical agitation of the slavery question, and respectable citizens, in different places, aided in dispersing meetings of Abolitionists, believing that such were but gathering additional fuel for the flames of civil discord now threatening to consume the fair fabric of the American Republic. But this popular opposition only served the more to intensify the efforts of the whole radical school of the Republican party; unite the better in one compact band, the avowed and secret Abolitionists, and give this faction the leadership and entire control of the political machinery of the organization. Wendel Phillips, Beecher, Sumner, Hale, Hickman, Howard, Stevens, Lovejoy and others were compactly united together in a band of brotherhood, pledged by mutual consent to unite their forces in a general assault upon the citadel of State Rights and Southern Slavery. It was soon manifest that the radicals were master of the situation, and Thurlow Weed * and other Republicans who had advocated compromise were threatened with ostracism for the their opinions. Even the editor of the New York *Tribune*, the pretended staunch advocate of principle, after having declared in favor of peaceable secession, was compelled by the radical conclave to espouse the policy of coercion against the seceded States. And after permitting himself to be made the mere mouthpiece of the

* "Thurlow Weed has been denounced and his peace propositions repudiated by the journals and leaders of the Republican party." Movements were even made to start a new paper in Albany opposed to him, and which the leaders promise shall be conducted "*without temporizing concessions and vacillating expediencies.*"—New York *Herald*, December 17, 1860.

ruling faction, he, to whom the editorial fraternity gave the name of philosopher, became the bitterest amongst his countrymen in resisting a compromise with the Southern people, and the most ardent in hounding on the masses of the North to a conflict that must work the prostration of the principles of Free Govern ment, and the downfal of the Constitutional Union.

At length the pilgrimage of the new President, from his home in Springfield, Illinois, to Washington, began on the 11th of February, 1861; and the people of all sections of the country now looked with anxiety for a disclosure of the views of the man, who more than all others held the future destiny of the Union in his hands. But the country was sadly disappointed. At a time when double-dealing should have been laid aside, and when manhood and honor demanded a clear and explicit declaration of the future intentions of the Chief Magistrate, we find him in his speeches made to the crowds that flocked to see him, giving utterance to ambiguous expressions; and such as but served to conceal his real intentions. His home organ, the Springfield *Journal*, about the time of his departure for the Seat of Government, contained the following enunciation of policy, which doubtless expressed the intentions of the journeying President; but which State craft and perfidy would not permit him openly to disclose. The *Journal* said:

"The seceding States are in rebellion against the Federal Government, and it is the duty of this Government to put down rebellion. Away with compromises. We should not talk of compromises while the flag of traitors floats over an American Fort, and the flag of our country trails in the dust. Until that flag is unfurled over Moultrie and every other stolen Fort, Arsenal, Custom House and Navy Yard—until the laws of this Government are obeyed and its authority recognized, let us never talk of compromise. Let the stolen Forts, Arsenals and Navy Yards be restored to the rightful owners,—tear down your rattlesnake and pellican flags, and run up the ever glorious stars and stripes, — disperse your traitorous mobs and let every man return to his duty."*

But the only competency shown by the New President on his journey to Washington, was the proficiency he displayed in the science of Machiavelism, by which he was enabled to discourse to the people concerning the brewing troubles, and yet conceal from them his opinions. Otherwise his speeches gave no evidence of intellect; but were interspersed with the flimsey jests of the low

*Extracted in New York *Herald*, Feb. 14, 1861.

politician, altogether unbecoming the man that was chosen to succeed the honored statesmen, who, from Washington to Buchanan, had graced the Presidential Chair. In his harrangues to the crowds which intercepted him on his journey, at a time when the country was in revolutionary chaos; when commerce and trade were prostrated, and when starving women and idle men were among the very audiences that listened to him, he declared to them, in his peculiar phraseology, that "*nobody was hurt,*" that "*all would come out right,*" and that there was "*nothing going wrong.*" Nor was his rhetoric the only entertainment he afforded those who flocked to hear the new Sovereign.

His conduct and speeches disclosed the demagogue; and evinced his admirable adaptedness to be the President of the radical conclave, that was to dictate to him as a subaltern the duties required of him to be performed. As President, he was the creature of and for the occasion. He was chosen in revolutionary times, for revolutionary purposes, and by the revolutionary element of the country. Statesmanship was at a discount; the destructive in politics ruled, and reason and reflection must of necessity be laid aside. A conservative President was not wanted by the men who controlled affairs in the new party; and Lincoln was known to be of that pliable disposition which would allow himself and his policy to drift with the current.

In his Indianapolis speech, the touring President sufficiently disclosed his sentiments for esoteric ears, but which the uninitiated mass accepted simply as interrogatories. He said:

"If the United States should merely hold and retake its own Forts and other property, and collect the duties on foreign importations, or even withhold the mails from places where they are habitually violated, would any of these things be invasion on coercion? Would the marching of an army into South Carolina be invasion?"

By these and many other similar remarks, it was ascertained that coercion had been determined upon by the radical Republicans. Senator Chandler, during the last days of the Thirty-sixth Congress, declared that the Republican party *were ready to stand in blood.* Fessenden, of Maine, remarked "that if the time was coming to use force, he was perfectly ready to do it." Thaddeus Stevens, in the course of the debate upon the Navy Bill, expressed it to be the intention of his party to retake the Southern forts.* A volume might be filled with similar declara-

* New York *Herald,* February 22nd, 1861.

tions, all to the same purport, showing that civil war was the pre-determined policy of the radical school.

The first distinct enunciation by Abraham Lincoln of the course he would pursue was made in his inaugural address, wherein he says:

"It follows from these views that no State, upon its own mere motion, can lawfully get out of the Union; that resolves and ordinances to that effect are legally void, and that acts of violence within any State or States against the authority of the United States are insurrectionary, according to circumstances.

"I, therefore consider, that in view of the Constitution and the Laws, the Union is unbroken, and to the extent of my ability I shall take care, as the Constitution expressly enjoins upon me, that the laws of the Union shall be faithfully executed in all the States.

"In doing this there need be no bloodshed or violence, and there shall be none unless it be forced upon the national authority."

Did despot ever lay down more dogmatic and authorative dicta than are contained in the extracted portion of this inaugural? Without condescending to consider the alleged grievances of the Southern people, or recommend any terms of concession, as a wise and virtuous ruler, master of his own thoughts, would have done, the Republican President proceeds in one sentence to declare State Sovereignty, the cardinal doctrine of the Jeffersonian school of politics, as baseless and unfounded. Was greater presumption ever manifested? The matured thought of a whole school of distinguished American statesmen was not to be overthrown by the mere declaration of a man, whom accident rather than intellect had elevated to power. But presumptuousness and conceit were the characteristics of the party to which he was indebted for the position he occupied, and he must necessarily display a similar pretentiousness with that of his compeers.

He next declared that he would cause the laws of the Union to be faithfully executed, *as the Constitution expressly enjoins*, which to the American ear was more palatable, than to have told them what he meant, which was that he and his party had determined to conquer by military force the Southern States. But the Constitution did not permit, much less enjoin him to make war upon the seceding States in order to preserve the laws, and purposing to do so, as his party leaders had resolved, he falsely accepted his obligation to the Constitution, which he pretended to obey. But a part of the secret programme still remained to be performed. This consisted in sending a naval squadron, under the pretence of relieving the Southern garrisons, when in truth designed to provoke an attack upon the American flag, and thus obtain a pretext for declaring war against the South, under the plea of defending the Union. This scheme, which was craftily planned, was entirely successful, and on the 12th of April, 1861, the attack upon Fort Sumpter lighted up the flames of civil revolution, and the triumph of centralization was now assured.

CHAPTER XIV.

WAR FOR THE UNION.

The news of the attack on Fort Sumpter aroused the demon of the North, in all his ferocious hate and unreasoning madness. Revenge, deep and bitter, was resolved upon in every hamlet and village from the most remote corner of Maine to the furthest extremity of California. The Southern secessionists who had dared to question the National authority and fire upon the flag of the Republic, became at once in the public mind, the objects of malediction and of the most burning execration; and resolves of vengeance seemed for the time written upon nearly every countenance. Insanity, in truth, ruled the hour. It was a people at length fully awakened to a realization of the dangers, of which they had often been admonished, but which they as repeatedly had been assured, were groundless and without foundation. Like a mob destitute of that reflection by which it should weigh causes and consequences, the people were everywhere borne in blind zeal to oppose resistance to the immediate agent of their dread. The Government was threatened; the Southern people had turned their cannon upon a Federal Fortress and forced its evacuation; and all the sacred associations of the Union, Constitution and National integrity were jeoparded. At once they forgot the lesson of philosophy, that "the aggressor in a war is not the first who uses force, but the first who renders force necessary."*

Although the people of the North had been admonished by patriots and Statesmen, from Washington to Buchanan, that the formation and success of sectional parties could not but endanger the perpetuity of the American Republic; still all their counsel was rejected and their admonitions unheeded. Men had arisen who repudiated the wisdom of former generations; and who had succeeded in securing followers, a majority in the Northern

*Hallam's Constitutional History.

States. The most studied efforts had been made by leading Republicans, in their speeches and through their presses, to convince the people that the object of the Southern secessionists was to extort from a passive North, further guarantees for slavery, as they had succeeded in doing on former occasions. And they were also told that even should actual resistance occur; and the South be found to be in earnest in their determination to sever their connection with the Union by force of arms, the collision would prove one of short duration; and that a month, or at furthest, ninety days would end the struggle. Believing these declarations, the mass of both political parties in the North, regarded the suppression of the rebellion as an undertaking of no great difficulty.

Now was the opportunity for the deep, crafty schemes of Abolition consolidation; and with admirable adroitness was it seized. With a full knowledge of the delusion which reigned in the public mind, as regarded the rebellion, and for the purpose of still further strengthening this false impression, Abraham Lincoln, as President of the United States, on the 15th of April, 1861, issued his proclamation calling for seventy-five thousand men to suppress the insurrection in the seceded States. Assuming to treat the Southern revolt as mere insurrectionary resistance, he ordered the seceders to disperse in twenty days from the issue of his mandate. Will posterity ever give him credit for believing that the rebels would disperse at his bidding, or that his quota of soldiers would prove sufficient to overthrow the armed resistance of the South? If matured reflection shall satisfy coming ages that the *role* he played on this occasion was not an hypocritical one, then the only alternative to be accepted will be, that his party made a great mistake in selecting one of no superior sagacity for President of the United States.*

The idea promulgated at Washington of a ninety days' commotion was encouraged by the Northern press, with the same

*The great admirers of the Sage of Springfield, in justification of the call for seventy-five thousand men for three months, will attempt to defend him in asserting that he acted in accordance with the law of 1795, in calling out the militia and ordering the dispersal of the insurgents in a specified time. It is true that he did model his call for troops after an Act which contemplated simply the raising of armed *posses*, in aid of the civil authorities. In doing so, however, he disclosed the desperate length that he and his party were ready to go for the purpose of carrying out their designs.

design as had influenced the Executive Chief in the Federal Capitol. It was all done to continue the deception that had been practised from the organization of the Republican party. The rebellion was derided as a matter of mere insignificance, and belittled in language which no sane men but imposters could utter. The New York *Tribune*, the leading organ of the Republican party, declared that it was nothing "more or less than the natural recourse of all mean spirited and defeated tyrannies, to rule or ruin, making of course a wide distinction between the will and power, for th hanging of traitors is sure to begin before one month is over. The nations of Europe," it continued, "may rest assured that Jeff. Davis & Co., will be swinging from the battlements at Washington at least by the 4th of July. We spit upon a later and longer deferred justice."

The New York *Times* expressed the following confident opinion:

"Let us make quick work. The 'Rebellion,' as some people designate it, is an embryo tadpole. Let us not fall into the delusion, noted by Hallam, of mistaking a 'local commotion' for a revolution. A strong, active pull together will do our work effectually in thirty days. We have only to send a column of twenty-five thousand men across the Potomac to Richmond, and burn out the rats there ; another column of twenty-five thousand to Cairo, seizing the cotton ports of the Mississippi, and retaining the remaining twenty-five thousand included in Mr. Lincoln's call for seventy-five thousand men at Washington, not because there is need for them there, but because we do not require their services elsewhere."

The Philadelphia *Press* declared that no man of sense, could for a moment doubt, that this much-ado-about-nothing would end in a month. The Northern people were "simply invincible." "The rebels," it predicted, "a mere band of ragamuffins, will fly like chaff before the wind on our approach."

The people of the West in no wise flagged in their competency to depreciate the magnitude of the troubles that awaited the country. It was necessary for the political success of the Republican party to under-rate the impending evils that were threatening the nation; for had the people fully realized the magnitude of the undertaking they were entering upon, the Peace party would have been too potential to have permitted the inauguration of the carnage that was to drench the land in blood. The Chicago *Tribune*, the valorous sheet of the Lake City, insisted that alone and unaided, the West should be permitted to fight the battle through, since she was probably most interested in the suppression of the rebellion and the free navigation of the Mississippi. "Let the East," demanded this warlike organ, "get out of the way; this war is of the West. We can fight the battle and successfully, within two or three months at the furthest. Illinois can whip the South by herself. We insist upon the matter being turned over to us."

Horace Greeley, the editor of the New York *Tribune*, who skillfully performed his part in helping to deceive the masses of the North into the belief that the rebellion would melt away in sixty days, was willing, however, to be judged in history as an imposter rather than a fool. In his history of the war he says:

"The original call of President Lincoln on the States for 75,000 militia, to serve for three months, was a deplorable error. It resulted naturally from that obstinate infatuation which would believe in defiance of all history and probability, that an aristocratic conspiracy of thirty years standing, culminating in rebellion based on an artificial property valued at four thousand millions of dollars, and wielding the resources of ten or twelve States, having nearly ten millions of people, was to be put down in sixty or ninety days by some process equivalent to the reading of the Riot Act to an excited mob, and sending a squad of police to disperse it."*

After the fall of Sumpter, it was indeed esteemed disloyal to even intimate a doubt of the speedy overthow of the rebellion. Many a patriotic citizen was branded as a traitor, because his reason admonished him that the conquest of a people so united as were the Southern Confederates, would be an undertaking requiring years, and also vast outlays of blood and treasure. Many, who in other matters were endowed with excellent sense, either really agreed with the short-sighted rabble in believing that the South would soon be conquered, or for the sake of selfish interests permitted themselves to drift with the current of public opinion.

Such an apparent change of sentiment as took place upon the fall of Sumpter, perhaps never was before witnessed in any country. Newspaper editors, who up to this period had battled the positions of the Abolition party, and pointed out the dangers into which their anti-compromise policy would drift the country, shifted their positions without delay into the advocacy of war against the South. Notwithstanding they had contended that the coercion of the seceding States was altogether unconstitutional,

*Greeley's American Conflict. Vol. 1, p. 551.

yet in obedience to selfish aspirations, or induced by fears of mob violence, war for the Union was now urged by them with as much vehemence and zeal as before had been conciliation. Other leading citizens, who before had been prominent and influential members of the Democratic and old Whig parties; and who had never sympathised with the abolition movement, immediately changed positions; and permitted themselves to be made instruments of fanaticism to unite the North in a war against the Southern people and their institutions. Democratic ex-Governors, Mayors, Members of Congress and other influential men of the party, presided at war meetings, and thus lent their aid and encouragement to the war party. Daniel S. Dickinson, of New York, who had even enjoyed the reputation of a "Northern man with Southern principles," became one of the fiercest advocates of war, and consigned his former friends in the South to fire and sword. Edward Everett, the scholarly orator of New England, who a few months before declared that the Southern States should be permitted to secede in peace, became an apostle of coercion, and exhausted his beautiful rhetoric in proclaiming the new gospel of subjugation. The conversions of this character were remarkably abundant, indeed; and men of all professions and occupations received the outpouring of the war spirit, and became new creatures in their whole walk and conversation. No doubt their olfactories scented the sweet perfumes of power, and they forgot the past in anticipations of the future. So manifest and mighty was the change that had been wrought, that the unregenerate could but look with amazement upon the scenes in which their eyes and ears were unable to deceive them.

The crusade of passion, fury and blasphemy, which set in against the South is entirely undescribable. It would have seemed as if the fiends of Pandemonium had burst forth from their confines and were exciting the frenzied multitudes of the North to deeds of hate and cruelty. The infidel clergy of New England, and their *pious* brethern of the modern ecclesiastical schools, feasted their souls in the holy anticipations of humanitarian elevation, through the blood and carnage of their Northern and Southern countrymen. The holiness of the war was proclaimed from the pulpit as well as from the hustings. Dr. Tyng, a distinguished divine of New York, assembled certain ferocious cut-throats of that city, commonly known as "Billy Wilson's men," presented them bibles, and declared to them that in carrying fire and sword into the rebellious States they would propitiate Heaven, and would go far to assure the salvation of their souls. Were the dark ages ever guilty of more ungodlike and unchristian abomination? But this is but an illustration of the sentiments that were popular and lauded to the skies throughout the Northern States.

A like madness seized the people in their seeming adoration of the flag of their country. The national emblem was flung to the breeze in nearly every street of the Northern towns and cities; and floated from the house-tops and windows of the most intensely loyal of the people. When these signs of war ardor made no voluntary appearance from a residence, a committee of patriotic citizens often deemed it their duty to admonish the inmates that a token of loyalty should be displayed. Some few bold men, however, who claimed to have opinions of their own, and who believed that they still lived in a free country, refusing to be driven into an apparent endorsement of an inquitous and unconstitutional war, declined to display any other insignia of patriotism than the laws of their country demanded. But those manifesting such independence, in all cases did so at the risk of life, property, business and reputation; and were sure to be branded as sympathisers with treason and desirous of seeing the Government overthrown.*

Up to this period in the history of the country, one oath to support the Constitution of the United States was deemed sufficient; but this opinion also underwent a change at the outbreak of the rebellion. Men whose intelligence and self-respect should have shielded them from the commission of acts only designed to win popular applause, permitted themselves to assume the patriotic attitude of moving that all the members of their bar renew their official oaths, and swear, more firmly than ever, that they would support the Federal Constitution. An instance of this superflous swearing was enacted in the Court Room in Lan-

*The portraits of Isaac Toucey, of Connecticut, Secretary of the Navy under James Buchanan, of C. L. Vallandingham, and other eminent Democrats of the North, were placed in the Rogue's Gallery of New York with the design of blackening their reputations with the unthinking masses. And journals like the New York *Tribune* endorsed such malignant partisan conduct as highly becoming and creditable.

caster City, one morning after the reduction of Fort Sumpter; and done at the instance of Benjamin Champneys and seconded by Thaddeus Stevens. What a prostitution of the sacredness of an oath to attempt to render that more binding which was already sealed before Heaven as the holiest obligation which humanity is capable of attesting. The annals of the French revolution would be scanned in vain for an instance of greater mockery of sacred solemnities.

It is not strange, that with the prospect of a short war, given out from Washington and encouraged by the whole Republican press, the rage for volunteering would be immense. Going to the war for three months, under the first call of Abraham Lincoln, was viewed as a sort of holiday excursion; and had peculiar attractions for large numbers of the fast youth in the Northern cities. From this material it was boasted that the North could gather the most terrible and invincible army that ever enacted deeds of war. Some of these adopted the Zouave costume in order to gratify their desire for singularity, and add to their ferocious appearance; and a company of them even went through the ceremony of being sworn, in a public hotel in New York, to "cut off the head of every d—— secessionist in the war." Such exhibitions of ferocity were retailed with glee and devoured with the most gratifying satisfaction by the most saintly advocates of the war. These valiant defenders of liberty were extolled for their burning patriotism, after having plundered the stores of some sympathizers with treason; and prostrated the persons of others who presumed to question their inalienable right to act as they saw proper in the city of their birth. They were simply giving evidence of the manner they could handle Southern traitors; and these experiments upon Northern sympathizers afforded the greatest satisfaction to their admirers. These acts were retailed with the most fiendish pleasure by the Loyalists, as they termed themselves, and were cited as proof that the crusading army from the North would strike terror into the secession bands, and win the brightest and bloodiest laurels on the fields of battle.

But it was not the vagrant and unrully classes of the Northern cities alone that enrolled themselves in the war for the Union; the quiet and orderly young merchants, clerks, printers, farmers and others, entered the race for glory. The North was full of martial courage, and war ardor animated both rich and poor.

Gov. Dennison, of Ohio, telegraphed to Washington, tendering thirty thousand troops for the service. Weston, the Governor of Indiana, received assurances that a like number of soldiers was eager for enlistment in his State. A. G. Curtin, the Executive of Pennsylvania, was not to be outdone in his promises to the Washington authorities. Massachusetts and New York were pressing in their offers of men for "the three months war."

The deceptious conduct of Abraham Lincoln and his counsellors, gradually displayed itself as time advanced. The second call of the President of May 4th, 1861, for forty-two thousand volunteers, for three years or during the war, besides the twenty-two thousand called for at the same time for the regular army, and eighteen thousand seamen, would on its face seem to evince that the Federal authorities had rapidly changed their views as regards the magnitude of the conflict that was to be encountered. The truth, however, simply was that the administration feared to alarm the country by calling at first for a large force of volunteers, until the sections had become so far involved in the strife as to preclude all further efforts of the Peace party at accommodation. This is clear from the endeavors which were quietly made to induce the three months' soldiers, soon after their enrolment, to re-enlist for three years, even under pain of dishonorable dismissal from the army. The Lancaster *Express* correspondent of May 15th, 1861, says:

"The call was for three months, but we are now asked to serve for three years; should we decline the latter proposition, we are told that we will be discharged in such a way as not to leave the service with honor."

So great had been the willingness of the administration to enroll a large army, and one much greater even than its several calls would indicate that by the middle of June, 1861, it was estimated that the number of men already in the Government service amounted to 308,875.

But an administration that was inaugurating a policy in violation of solemn obligation and constitutional warrant, and striving for the utter overthrow of Republican Government, was not one to hesitate at any stage of perfidy, that might be required for the accomplishment of its designs. It was but in harmony, therefore, with a well-matured and pre-arranged programme when President Lincoln, in the presence of Gen. Scott and his Cabinet, and in conflict with his proclamation calling for 75,000 men, solemnly assured the Mayor of Baltimore and other leading men of that city, that the troops called for were simply for the protection of the Federal Capital. Of this assurance Mayor Brown said:

"The protection of Washington he (the President) asseverated with great earnestness, was the sole object of concentrating troops there, and he protested that none of the troops brought through Maryland were intended for any purposes hostile to the State, or aggressive as against the Southern States."*

That William H. Seward was well skilled in the tortuous ways of perfidious diplomacy, and admirably suited to be the colleague of a President who would deny his public record and intentions, no evidence from Judge Campbell was needed to determine. The Premier's letter to Governor Hicks, of Maryland, furnishes abundant testimony on this point. With reference to the passage of the troops through Baltimore, he wrote a letter to the Governor, April 22d, in which he says:

"The force now sought to be brought through Maryland is intended for nothing but the defense of the Capitol."

Horace Greeley, the editor of the *Tribune*, perceiving the bald untruth of the Secretary's declaration, and with reference to it, said:

"Is this true? Is it safe? It certainly is not very consistent with the President's Proclamation, which Governor Seward countersigned. The militia of the loyal States were called out to suppress combinations that defy the laws and obstruct their execution—not in Washington, but in the disloyal States. Having reached Washington, they are several hundred miles on their way to those States—not to speak of the rebellion that has suddenly broken out in Virginia and Maryland. Having drawn men enough to Washington to repel the apprehended attack, is it probable that they will be sent home without even attempting to effect the object for which they were expressly called out? And if not, will not the Government be accused of bad faith in giving the assurances embodied in Governor Seward's letter, and then acting in defiance of them?"†

The War against the seceded States was inaugurated by Abraham Lincoln and his party, for the purpose as they declared of preserving the integrity of the Union. But the maintenance of a Union and Constitution that guaranteed the existence of slavery could not be desired by any save a hyprocritcal member of a party, whose animating principle was opposition to the Southern institution. Every sincere and honest leader in the Republican

Annual Cyclopœdia, 1861, p. 717.

† New York *Tribune*, April 26th, 1861.

organization, had avowed the mission of his party to be the eradication of Southern Slavery, and it was left to state craft and deception to devise a policy which could carry to its support sufficient strength to accomplish the party aim. Had not Abraham Lincoln and the members of his Cabinet, repeatedly declared their antipathy to the institution of slavery, and that its existence was incompatible with republican institutions? And yet when war was proclaimed, did not these same statesmen avow that the object of the administration was simply to preserve the Union and the Constitution, and that the destruction of slavery was altogether out of their power and foreign from their intentions? On the contrary, however, the honest and manly avowals of Wendel Phillips, Gerrit Smith and others, proved that the administration was sailing under false colors in order to catch the popular gale. In his speech of April 27th, Gerrit Smith said:

"The end of slavery is at hand. If we suffer it to live, it may return to torment us. Let no Northern man henceforth propose, for any reasons whatever, the sparing of slavery. Such measure, such insult, such contempt of her interests and rights and honor, the North will stand no longer. Thank God! the spirit of the North is at last aroused at this point. She is determined to kill slavery, and she will be patient with no man who shall thrust himself between her and her victim."*

With the above compare the following words from Abraham Lincoln's inaugural:

"I have no purpose, directly or indirectly, to interfere with the institution of slavery in the States where it exists. I believe I have no lawful right to do so; and I have no inclination to do so."

Which of these two men, will posterity determine, expressed most sincerely and honestly his convictions? Which of them must forever bear the brand of *hypocrite* upon his brow, and be enrolled in the category of those who deserve the execration of mankind?

Influenced with the same design as President Lincoln, his Secretary of State, William H. Seward, in his letter of instructions, in April, 1861, to the Federal Minister in Paris, says:

"The condition of slavery in the several States will remain just the same, whether it (the rebellion) succeeds or fails. The rights of the States, and the condition of every human being in them, will remain subject to exactly the same laws and form of administration, whether the revolution shall succeed or whether it shall fail. Their Constitutions and forms and customs, habits and institutions, in either case will remain

*New York *Tribune*, May 3d, 1861.

the same. It is hardly necessary to add to this incontestible statement, the further fact that the new President, as well as the citizens through whose suffrages he has come into the administration, has always repudiated all designs whatever and wherever imputed to him and them, of disturbing the institution of slavery as it is existing under the Constitution and laws, The case however, would not be fully presented were I to omit to say, that any such effort on his part would be unconstitutional, and all his acts in that direction would be prevented by the judicial authority, even though they were assented to by Congress and the people."

But the political Abolition editor of the New York *Tribune* discloses the reason which detered the administration from allowing the war to appear as waged for the destruction of slavery. He says:

"This war in truth is a war for the preservation of the Union—not for the destruction of slavery; and it would alienate many ardent Unionists to pervert it into a war against Slavery."*

This humane editor and *would-be philosopher*, this *wise and sagacious statesman*, like the administration, through dread of antagonizing the conservatives of the country, declares that the war is prosecuted for the preservation of the Union; and yet, in an issue of four days earlier, he eulogizes Daniel S. Dickinson, who had advocated the extermination of the Southern people in order to eradicate slavery, the germinating root of the revolt. It was this *philosophic* editor who first of all the members of his party most clearly explained the policy of the administration war for the Union; and, calmed by the following arguments, the complaints of those who early demanded that it should be directed for the emancipation of the Southern slaves. The war for the Union, argued he, is sure to ultimate in the destruction of slavery, and therefore it behooves all Abolitionists to give it their support. Do not strive to have emancipation proclaimed, for by doing so many friends of the Union will be turned into enemies of the war, which will only procrastinate the overthrow of the Southern institution. Let those fight for the Union who will, for in doing so they likewise aid the cause of emancipation. Many patriots do not desire the liberation of the slaves, and it is necessary, therefore, that the war be waged in behalf of the Union and the Constitution; and in this manner the enemies of emancipation really aid the movement of abolition. We who perceive the results to follow the war, favor it because of these;

*New York *Tribune*, May 14th, 1861.

and hence both Unionists and Abolitionists can unite in its prosecution. This, in brief, was the whole secret and philosophy of the Abolition enthusiasm in the war for the Union.

The first acts of the Federal authority, in the prosecution of the war touching the institution of slavery, were made to conform strictly to the assurances that had been given. An extravagant zeal was shown by Federal officials to prove that the war was prosecuted alone for the restoration of the Union. Fugitive slaves were not only arrested within the Federal military lines and returned to slavery, but were taken in the streets of Washington and surrendered by judicial process to their masters. On the 26th of May, 1861, General McClellan issued an address to the people of Western Virginia, assuring them that not only would his troops abstain from any interference with their slave property, but that they were ready likewise to assist in quelling any efforts at servile insurrection. General McDowell issued an order prohibiting fugitive slaves from coming into, or being harbored within his lines. All these acts were permitted by the Federal administration, in order to disprove the assertion of the Southern people, and of those in the North who charged the Republicans as secretly designing the overthrow of slavery.

But the administration and the Republican leaders awaited with impatience for an opportunity to allow the commencement of that line of policy which was to ultimate in the entire overthrow of slave institutions. The war had been inaugurated for the avowed maintenance of the Union and the Constitution; but other aims animated most of the sincere friends of the coercive policy. The first opportunity which permitted a change of base for the administration, was furnished by General B. F. Butler, a former member of the Democratic party, and one high in its confidence. Some fugitives had made their way into the camp of General Butler at Fortress Monroe; and being demanded by an officer of a Confederate force in the neighborhood, Butler declined to surrender these; choosing to consider them contraband of war, as being the property of rebels. He placed the able-bodied negroes at work upon his fortifications, and immediately notified the War Department of his action as regards the fugitives. Other fugitives, men, women and children, shortly afterwards came to his camp, and he now chose to consult the War Department as to his duty under the circumstances. The administration felt itself safe in accepting and endorsing the views of a States Right Jeffersonian Democrat, who was fighting for the Union and the Constitution. Gen. Cameron, Secretary of War, under date of May 30th, 1861, replied to our Contraband General as follows:

"Your action in respect to the negroes who came within your lines, from the service of the rebels, is approved. The Department is sensible of the embarrassments which must surround officers conducting military operations in a State by the laws of which slavery is sanctioned. The Government cannot recognize the rejection by any State of its Federal obligations, nor can it refuse the performance of the Federal obligations resting upon itself. Among these Federal obligations, however, none can be more important than that of suppressing and dispersing armed combinations, formed for the purpose of overthrowing its whole constitutional authority. While, therefore, you will permit no interference by persons under your command with the relations of persons held to service under the laws of any State, you will, on the other hand, so long as any State within which your military operations are conducted, is under the control of such armed combinations, refrain from surrendering to alledged masters, any persons who may come within your lines. You will employ such persons in the services to which they may be best adapted, keeping an account of the labor by them performed, of the value of it, and the expenses of their maintenance. The question of their final disposition to be reserved for future determination."

This decision of the administration, which touched the slaves of rebels voluntarily seeking refuge within the Federal lines, was reached with great misgivings at the time as to the effect it might have upon public sentiment and the prosecution of the war. The aim of Abraham Lincoln and his Cabinet was to so conduct the Government policy, with reference to the slavery question, as to follow rather than lead popular opinion in the North; and which was steadily being shaped by abolition agitation. Aware that in civil convulsions the radical revolutionists ever triumph over the moderates, the same, it was believed by President Lincoln and his counsellors, would happen in the Republican party. They could, therefore, afford to permit events to dictate the varied changes of policy to effect the cherished objects; yet, nevertheless, aiding by every means in their power, to hasten the steps that would permit their open espousal of the changed schedule.

But Congress, at its extra session in 1861, aided the administration in making a new advance towards its destined goal, in the enactment of the first Confiscation Bill, which the President, with great hesitation, approved. This bill "limited the penalty of confiscation to property actually employed in the service of the rebellion, with the knowledge and consent of its owners; and instead of emancipating slaves thus employed, left their status to be determined either by the Courts of the United States or by subsequent legislation."* This was as bold a move, at so early a period in the history of the war, as dared be hazzarded; and was only engineered through the Senate and House of Representatives amidst the greatest misgivings upon the part of many Republicans, and after the defeat of the Federal army at Bull Run had aroused the country to the necessity of putting forth every effort that might weaken the rebellion. It was contended by the political Abolitionists, that the rebel property, including slaves, should all be confiscated, in order to aid in breaking the strength of their enemy in arms against the Government. Whilst really striving to effect in this way the emancipation of the slaves by confiscation, they strenously maintained that the object of the war was simply the maintenance of the Union; and that negro liberation was only one of the means to be made use of to put a termination to the conflict. This disguise was well made up, and prevented those who could not penetrate the veil from showing to the dim-eyed masses the naked skeleton of emancipation that stood in the background.

During the extra session of Congress in 1861, the conservative patriot of Kentucky, John J. Crittenden, on the 19th of July, 1861, asked the unanimous leave of the House of Represetatives to submit the following resolution:

"*Resolved*, By the House of Representatives of the Congress of the United States, that the present deplorable civil war has been forced upon the country by the disunionists of the Southern States now in revolt against the Constitutional Government, and in arms around the Capitol; that in this national emergency Congress, banishing all feeling of mere passion and resentment, will recollect only its duty to the whole country; that this war is not waged on our part in any spirit of oppression, nor for any purpose of conquest or subjugation, nor for the purpose of overthrowing or interfereing with the rights or established institutions of the States, but to defend and maintain the supremacy of the Constitution, and to preserve the Union, with all the dignities, equality and rights of the seceded States unimpaired, and that as soon as these objects are accomplished, the war ought to cease."

The most thoroughly consistent member of the Republican

*Letter of Joseph Holt, of Sepembter 12, 1861.

party in the House at that time, (Thaddeus Stevens) objected to the reception of the above resolution, and when it passed by an almost unanimous vote, he declined to allow his name to be recorded, either affirmatively or negatively. The cowards and hypocrites of his party in Congress, like Abraham Lincoln and William H. Seward, feared to disclose their real designs of emancipation, and supported a resolution which expressed sentiments contrary to their feelings, and by which they never meant to be obligated. That negro freedom was the darling goal of aspiration of the Republican party, the following from "Occasional" in the Philadelphia *Press* of August 31st, 1861, would seem to attest:

"Thousands who have recoiled from a mere Anti-Slavery war, now advocate emancipation as an imperative necessity."

Although Thaddeus Stevens, Owen Lovejoy, Charles Sumner, and a few other radicals, had somewhat partially disclosed the designs of the Republican party, it was altogether too soon for the Administration to show its hand upon the slavery issue. These men though the soul of their party, were represented by the crafty Republican leaders as extremists, whose views would never be adopted by any organization; and much less by the conservative administration of Abraham Lincoln. Such were the stereotyped reiterations of the Republican press of the North. But time disclosed whose sentiments really represented the heart of the party in power; and to what point the *highly Conservative* Republican administration was drifting.

On the 10th of August, 1861, the Secretary of the Interior, Caleb Smith, in an address to the citizens of Providence, Rhode Island, declared the policy of the Government in the following language:

"The minds of the people of the South have been deceived by the artful representations of demagogues, who have assured them that the people of the North, were determined to bring the power of this Government to bear upon them for the purpose of crushing out the institution of slavery. I ask you, is there any truth in this charge? Has the Government of the United States, in any single instance, by any one solitary act, interfered with the institutions of the South? No, not one. The theory of this Government is, that the States are sovereign within their proper sphere. The Government of the United States has no more right to interfere with the institution of slavery in South Carolina than it has to interfere with the peculiar institutions of Rhode Island."*

**Annual Cyclopedia*, 1861, p. 643.

But it remained for General Fremont to strike the key note of Republican sentiment, when in his proclamation of August 30th, 1861, he said:

"Real and personal property of those who shall take up arms against the United States, or who shall be directly proven to have taken an active part with their enemies in the field, is declared confiscated to public use, and their slaves, if any they have, are hereby declared free men."

From this period the famous explorer, in Abolition estimation, became the *beau ideal* of an Amèrican General and Statesman; and the laudations that were showered upon him by the Republican press, were almost bewildering. The chord of radical aspiration had been touched; and the harmony that followed showed the real motives of the revolutionists, much as they had endeavored to conceal them. But the border States and the conservatives of the North were yet an object that could not be dispensed with by the war party. Abraham Lincoln and his counsellors deemed it too soon to permit the aim of their party to appear before the vision of all; and the avowed emancipationists now had the bitter mortification of seeing the confiscation order of their favorite general rescinded. The President, under date of September 11th, issued to John C. Fremont the following order:

"Yours of the 8th, in answer to mine of the 2d, is just received. Assured that you, upon the ground, could better judge of the necessities of your position than I could at this distance, on seeing your proclamation of August 30th, I perceived no general objection to it; the particular clause, however, in relation to the confiscation of property, and the liberation of slaves, appeared to me to be objectionable in its non-conformity to the Act of Congress, passed the 6th of last August, upon the same subjects; and hence I wrote you expressing my wish that the clause should be modified accordingly. Your answer just received, expresses the preference on your part, that I should make an open order for the modification, which I very cheerfully do. It is therefore ordered that the said clause of the said proclamation be so modified, held and construed, as to conform with and not to transcend the provisions on the same subject contained in the Act of Congress, entitled, 'An Act to confiscate property used for insurrectionary purposes," approved August 6th, 1861, and that said Act be published at length with this order."

Events now sped with a rapid gait, and upon the assembling of Congress, in December, 1861, it was discovered that legislative timidity was being laid aside, and frank avowals were made by Thaddeus Stevens and other bold leaders, showing still more clearly the objects of the war. The session was a long and active one, and the administration gathered strength and confidence as one legislator after another expressed himself as regards the exigencies of the occasion. By the middle of February, 1862, the Marat of the revolution, the editor of the New York *Tribune*, was able to make the following announcement:

"Some of our readers will have noticed with interest, a recent prominently published despatch of a Washington letter writer, whose correctness has never been denied, announcing that President Lincoln had, in a conversation with Gen. Lane, declared that after much deliberation he had come to the conclusion that he could not recognize the existence of slavery in the seceded States. Slavery must be deemed to be abolished within those States by the very action of the State seceding; and of course there can be no return of the fugitives from those States nor any constitutional recognition of the institution."*

At length the bold attitude of the radical leaders in Congress, the tone of the radical press, and the recollection of the eulogistic praise which had been heaped upon Fremont by the Abolitionists, coupled with a *holy zeal* for negro freedom, induced General Hunter, commanding the Department of the South, to essay emanicipation in order that his name likewise might be enrolled, as one of the distinguished commanders of the world, along with the great California explorer. For this purpose, he issued an order putting the States of Georgia, South Carolina and Florida under martial law, and declaring that as slavery and martial law were incompatible, the slaves of those States should be forever free. If the exuberant commendations of the Republican press were sufficient to place General Hunter in the category of famed military heroes, then had he truly reached the height of his ambition, for his eulogists assigned the zealous foe of Southern serfdom to a rank with the Cromwells and Napoleons of history. With the patriot daughters of the North he was the valorous knight, *sans peur et sans reproche*, and far eclipsed all the Bayards of chivalry. But Abraham Lincoln was Commander-in-Chief of the American armies, and some glory was his due. Were he to permit his pragmatical subordinates one after another, to strike off the chains of slavery in their different departments, nothing would remain for himself, the Jupiter tonans of the abolition camp, to perform. He needed no council from Generals Fremont and Hunter; wiser and more cautious intellects supplied him with advice. No threats by infidel orators of New England of *encircling his brow with a slave hound wreath*,

*New York *Tribune*, February 12th, 1862.

would induce him to yield to the hasty behests of hair-brained enthusiasts who were unable to preserve their own secrets, much less dictate his governmental policy. When the omens gave assurance that a servile and degraded people would fully sustain his decree, the grand jubilee of freedom would be proclaimed. They did not as yet so admonish him. General Hunter's proclamation of freedom was accordingly set aside, and the officious commander rebuked.

But during all this time, the fruit was maturing, and the fields of abolition were rapidly ripening for the harvest. The long period of growth was ended. The husbandmen had watched and waited with patience, and the reapers would soon be called to finish the work, The call of the master was now looked for with longing anxiety.

CHAPTER XV.

EMANCIPATION DECREED.

The shock of war which aroused the nation from its slumber, had for a time a depressing effect upon abolition agitation and the utterances of the school. An upheaval of union aspiration arose in the Northern breast, all else being stifled in the general desire that the compact of the fathers should not be broken, and the leaders of the revolutionary sect found it necessary to retreat for a period from the public gaze, and discuss their sentiments in retirement. It was only in the secret chambers where these leaders dared any longer to give expression to opinions that were now perceived upon all hands as those which had plunged the nation into the throes of intestine strife and bloodly revolution. Gerrit Smith, an honest pioneer in the cause of emancipation, on the 30th of October, 1861, spoke as follows:

"For months the state of the public mind has not been such as to encourage me to speak or write as an Abolitionist." *

Thaddeus Stevens was one of the Members of Congress who were looked upon as the extemists of their party, and the mantle of power was but cautiously conferred upon him, and only when it was perceived that the night of contempt which had weighed upon the Abolitionists was beginning to depart, and their aurora of dawn to ascend the political horizon.

The agitating crew began again their movements with the design of influencing public thought, and preparing the nation for the reception of their views, which were the emancipation of the negro slaves in the Southern States, and their social and political equality with the whites. After the battle of Bull Run, a plausible pretext was afforded them to argue that slavery must be destroyed in order to weaken an enemy that had so contrary to all expectations shown such dexterity upon the battle-field. As the preservation of the Union was the sole object of the masses

* New York *Tribune*, November 9, 1861.

that had espoused the prosecution of the war, the agitators had the sagacity to perceive that they could now urge with safety a policy and measures that were calculated to weaken the Southern Confederates. The services of the political club, the abolition pulpit and the rostrum of the revolutionary lecturer were again brought into requisition to further emancipation, and intensify Northern hate against the Southern cause. The following extract from the New York *Herald* of July, 1861, shows the movement of the avowed abolition school of the Eastern States:

"The speeches delivered at Framingham, Massachusetts, on the 4th of July; the resolutions of Lovejoy; the epistolary manifesto of Gerrit Smith, from Peterboro; and the renewed vigor in behalf of Abolitionism of Wendell Phillips, Garrison, Chandler and Greeley, with their satellites, all prove that the deadly fear of consequences which frightened the revolutionary demagogues of the Northern States into silence, three months ago, is subsiding, and that they are renewing their mischievous attempts to undermine the Constitution and perpetuate the dissolution of the Union. They have commenced a simultaneous onslaught upon Mr. Lincoln, and abuse him openly for not having made the destruction of slave institutions and the confiscation of Southern property a part of his programme. Wendell Phillips, at Framingham, gives the President the choice of having '*slave-hound*' branded on his forehead, or being the liberator of four millions of bondmen."

The utterances of the radical Jacobins, simply betokened that the army of revolutionists were near at hand and ready to second their most violent demands. The New York Republican Central Club, an influential organization, petitioned Congress soon after the battle of Bull Run, to pass a law abolishing slavery; and letters began to come in inquiring why Government would not destroy the root of the evil to save the nation.* By the middle of September, the Northern Abolition pulpit was fully freighted for the crusade, and performed its full share of service in shaping opinion to subserve the objects of the timid political leaders that stood at the helm of Government. The following extract of a sermon of Dr. Cheever, preached in the Church of the Puritans, will show the boldness of the utterances that were by this time become current. Dr. Cheever said:

"The desire in England and in Europe, is to see in us a nation, honored, great and noble, by abolishing slavery and putting away the accursed thing from among us. This is it, which chills Christian sympathy and draws upon us instead, the rebukes of the English people. * * * There can be no peace—there must be none till this rebellion is

*New York *Tribune*, August 2d and 3d, 1861.

put down. * * * We say to England, give us your sympathy, for ours is a holy conflict, we are fighting the battle of ages; the battle of humanity and mankind against the most odious and wicked rebellion the world ever saw. But to the South we say, down with your rebellion, we do not object to slavery, we have never interfered with it. Why the newspapers load their columns with arguments to prove that we never intended to interfere against slavery, and that we do not mean to interfere. They say to the South, you may keep your slaves, and if you return to your allegiance we will assist you in keeping them. The declaration that you may keep your slavery in the Union! What an attitude to hold before the world! In God's name, the people demand emancipation, not only as an act of beneficence to the slaves, but as their right. Those only are traitors who refuse this; and the only treason that can destroy the Government, is the denial of this measure of righteousness. This measure can only save the country engaged against the most wicked and atrocious Confederacy of hell, We must not loose sight of the fact that this is God's war against slavery. He has given to us the means of putting an end to slavery, through the rebellion. * * * If the people are faithful and resolute, they will petition and memorialize the President until he issues a proclamation to all the bond of the country. The Church must do this. If the Church takes a lead in it, the masses will follow. There must be an uprising in the Church, in the demand for justice to the slaves, as there was an uprising when the booming of the first cannon was heard from Sumpter. It is said on all sides that the force of circumstances must be relied on for bringing about the emancipation of the slaves. This is a false, cowardly way of dealing with the great question."*

No man, perhaps, in the nation, since the outbreak of hostilities, had done more to strengthen the courage of the Abolitionists throughout the North, and add new fuel to the flame of agitation that set in after the battle of Bull Run, than Thaddeus Stevens. Although he himself labored under the suspicions of his party friends of being too outspoken in his views; yet he was an honored and influential member of a body that represented the voice of the Northern people. At the extra session of Congress even, called in July, 1861, he maintained the bold and independent attitude of one who had little desire to conceal that so far as he could influence events, the war should be engineered in the interest of emancipation and negro elevation. And when the distinguished John J. Crittenden, of Kentucky, offered his famous resolve in Congress, on the 19th of July, 1861, that "*when the Union should be restored by force of arms, the war ought to cease*," Mr. Stevens was the only member of his school who was unwilling to be enrolled as a hypocrite. In manly utterances he

*New York *Herald*, September 16th, 1861.

objected to the reception of a resolution which he could not approve; for with him the war meant something more than the simple restoration of the Union. Again, during the same session when the bill was before the House to confiscate property used for insurrectionary purposes, he had given utterance to the following sentiments, that by no means were heard with patience by his more cautions compeers. Mr. Stevens said:

"If this war is continued and is bloody, I do not believe that the free people of the North will stand by and see their sons, brothers and neighbors slaughtered by thousands and tens of thousands by rebels with arms in their hands, and forbear to call upon their enemies to be our friends, and help us in subduing them. I for one, if it continues and has the consequences mentioned, shall be ready to go for it, let it horrify the gentleman from New York or anybody else. That is my doctrine; and that will be the doctrine of the whole free people of the North before two years roll around, if this war continues.

"As to the end of the war, until the rebels are subdued no man in the North thinks of it. If the Government are equal to the people—and I believe they are—there will be no bargaining; there will be no negotiation; there will be no truces with rebels, except to bury the dead, until every man shall have laid down his arms, disbanded his organization, submitted himself to the Government and sued for mercy. And, sir, if those who have the control of the Government are not fit for the task and have not the nerve and mind for it, the people will take care that there are others who are—although, sir, I have not a bit of fear of the present administration or of the present Executive."

"I have spoken more freely, perhaps, than gentlemen within my hearing might think politic; but I have just spoken what I felt. I have spoken what I believe will be the result; and I warn Southern gentlemen that if this war is to continue, there will be a time when my friend from New York will see it declared by this nation, that every bondman in the South—belonging to a rebel recollect; I confine it to them—shall be called upon to aid us in war against their masters and restore this Union."

It was to be expected that speeches such as the above from men of the conceded capacity of Mr. Stevens, would embolden Abolitionists everywhere to utter their opinions with more freedom than they had as yet been able to do since the outbreak of the war. A writer in the New York *Tribune* in November, 1861, spoke as follows of the growing sentiment of the people, which in other words was simply abolitionism gradually withdrawing the mask which it had hitherto carefully worn. This writer says:

"We do not think we over-estimate the rapid march of public sentiment in this direction. Cautious and conservative men are going forward faster than they imagnine. All now conceive, "*if Slavery or the Union must fall, then let Slavery instantly perish.* And the number of those who believe that this alternative is close upon us is multitudinous, and increases with every reverse of our arms, and with every day that postpones a decisive victory of our forces.

"When the Confiscation of August last was passed, discharging from labor or service every slave who had been used by the rebels, directly or indirectly for carrying on the war, the President even hesitated to sign it. Weeks rolled on, our arms encountered reverses, the rebellion assumed gigantic proportions. At length Fremont's proclamation appeared. After a little breathing spell, and when the President resolved to modify it so as to make it conform exactly to the Act of Congress, these timid and conservative classes, who had stigmatised this law as an abolition scheme, rushed to the defense of the President, and eulogized the Act of Congress as a wise measure.

"And we recollect how cautiously the people received and how gingerly the administration handled the contraband proposition which General Butler let fly at the public from Fortress Monroe. The War Department, after much painful cogitation, and despite not a few misgivings in conservative circles, restricted the application of this novel doctrine exclusively to the slaves of rebels who voluntarily sought shelter within the walls of the fort, and were then to be set at work only in pacific employments. But we now find the department applauded in all quarters, while instructing commanders invading the South, not only to receive and arm them in companies to aid in crushing the rebellion—in a word, to convert them into military auxiliaries. This rule is to be applied not to the slaves of rebels only, but to those of loyal citizens, giving assurance to the latter that Congress will pay them for their losses."*

By the time the Thirty-seventh Congress assembled in December, 1861, the current of agitation had become quite rapid, and every day added to its velocity. Vast armies had been called from both sections of the country to meet each other in mortal combat, and many a field had been drenched with American blood without any decided advantage having been secured up to this period by either of the contestants. The flag of the North was, however, rather in the ascendant. Severe blows had been dealt to the Southern Confederacy in Missouri, Kentucky, and West Virginia; and the stars and stripes were floating over Hatteras and Port Royal on the Eastern coast.

The conflicting sentiments that had, from the formation of our Constitution, formed the basis of the two political parties of the nation, with the meeting of Congress, in December, 1861, were again brought forward in marked contrast. The unanimity of approval that the prosecution of the war for the Union seemed

*New York *Tribune*, November 12th, 1861.

to have secured, after the assault upon Sumpter, began now to disappear; and the leaders assumed in somewhat disguised bearings, before the country, the respective positions that marked their several views. The radicals of each of the divergent parties were the first to display their positions. Clement L. Vallandignam and George H. Pendleton, of Ohio, and ex Governor Wickliffe, of Kentucky, were conspicuous amongst those who undisguisedly maintained the old attitude of the Democratic party, that the war against the South was an encroachment upon the Federal Constitution, and an invasion of State rights and of the immunities of the Southern people. It was an unpopular position for a statesman to defend in the midst of the excitement of war; for the people, the large proportion of whom are incapable of reasoning and deducing logical conclusions, were already carried away by their zeal in behalf of the Union, as they conceived; and which they now regarded as in great jeopardy and danger of dissolution. It was indeed with the greatest difficulty that these men and the few who heartily co-operated with them, were able to unite all the Democratic Representatives of Congress in a phalanx of solid resistance to the unconstitutional measures of the dominant party. Their resistance, however, was but ciceronic and vain in its results. They simply could enter their protests against the behests of power sustained by the bristling bayonets of a hireling soldiery; and in doing so they periled their reputations and future political prospects before their several constituencies, to such an extent that most of them, by degrees, sunk beneath the waves of a boisterous political ocean. They, however, are the political patriots and martyrs whom truthful history will enroll on the same pages with Cicero, Brutus and Cassius; and with the patriots who sunk with Roman liberty on the field of Phillippi.

Civil war was no period for calm reflection, and for the successful display of considerative statesmanship, such as is needed to guide the affairs of States and Nations. But, upon the other hand, it was the epoch for bringing to the surface of the political caldron, the revolutionary and fanatical leaders whose mission in life would seem to be most appropriately characterized by styling it the *destructive*. Thaddeus Stevens, Charles Sumner and Owen Lovejoy arose to the ascendant, as leaders of their party, and displayed a disregard of inherited rights and of the mandates of the Federal Constitution, that find no parallel in American history; and to be equalled, must be found, if at all, on the dark and bloody pages of the French Revolution. These men came to Washington, all of them, for one reason or another, freighted with cargoes of gall and bitterness to pour upon the heads of the Southern people driven to rebellion; and now the opportunity was fully come for such a display of partisan tactics, as would enable them to triumph over their ancient foes, and ultimate the struggle in universal emancipation. Thaddeus Stevens, the dreaded extremist of his party, was at length harnassed by his coadjutors in the glittering armor of strength, being now the honored Chairman of the Committee of Ways and Means of the Lower House of Congress. Representing a constituency, in which his party could figure five thousand majority, he was the representative of all others who dared to be frank in his public expressions, and bold in his recommendations of measures to accomplish the objects of the revolutionary school.* And, instead of being, therefore, any longer the shunned Northern radical, he now towered in his strength as Achilles on the plain, and his blows were dealt with unerring aim upon slavery, his Hectorean antagonist. At the beginning of Congress, he was one of the first members of the House to open his batteries upon his foe, and indicate the aim of the war party. On the first day of the session, he submitted the following preamble and resolutions:

"WHEREAS, Slavery has caused the present rebellion in the United States; and whereas, there can be no solid and permanent peace and union in this Republic so long as that institution exists within it; and whereas, slaves are now used by the rebels as an essential means of supporting and protracting the war; and whereas, by the law of nations it is right to liberate the slaves of any enemy to weaken its power; therefore,

1st. "*Be it resolved,* By the Senate and House of Representatives of the United States of America, in Congress assembled, that the President be

*"Some of our public men do not hesitate to say, that rather than bring back the seceded Slave States into the Union, they would agree to a peaceful and prompt separation. They contend that in the event of a reunion, the slave despotism would rule by its unity and with the aid of the Breckinridge Democrats of the Free States; and by means of the divisions of the Republicans, the destinies of the future of our country will be completely controlled by traitors to the Federal Constitution. Although no open demonstration in favor of this theory has yet been made, it is undoubtedly sincerely entertained in certain influential quarters,"—"Occasional," in Philadelphia *Press,* January 21, 1862.

requested to declare free, and to direct all our generals and officers in command, to order freedom to all slaves who shall leave their masters, or who shall aid in quelling this rebellion.

2d. "Be it further resolved, That the United States pledge the faith of the Union to make full and fair compensation to all loyal citizens who are, or shall remain active in supporting the Union, for the loss they shall sustain by virtue of this Act." *

In the above resolutions, the *animus* of the Republican party was clearly betokened; yet the more cautious manipulators of partisan tactics contended that they expressed simply the views of the extreme Abolitionists; and that they would never be made the basis of the party creed.† Indeed so closely veiled had Abraham Lincoln and his esoteric advisers been able to keep their opinions, that the rash men of the Abolition wing of his party, came to suspect the head of the Government as lacking in zeal for the cause of emancipation. His zeal, however, was equally ardent with their own, as time at length disclosed. But he was surrounded with an array of counsellors who were sagacious enough as to perceive that the only way by which slavery could be destroyed, was to permit the administration to appear as if led by public opinion, to lay the axe to the root of the institution they were all seeking to extirpate. In one of the earliest caucuses held by the extreme Abolition members of Congress, after the assembling of that body in December, 1861, and convened for the purpose of considering the emancipation measures already submitted; Mr. Stevens, who was recognized as the leading radical spirit of the House, if not of his party at Washington, made an attack upon the President for refusing to acquiesce at once in the expediency of the emancipation programme. In that speech he is reported to have said:

"That the Republican party have been sold in the election of Lincoln to the Presidency; that the North West had deceived them by assur-

Congressional Globe, part 1 of Second Session of 37th Congress, p. 6.

†The manner in which the Republican papers deceived the country, is seen in the following, from "Occasional," of the Philadelphia *Press*, of June 16th, 1862: "In the campaign that is about to be opened against the administration and the war, powerful emphasis is to be laid upon the empty accusation that the friends of Mr. Lincoln favor unconditional emancipation and negro equality. Contemptible as this accusation is, it is frequently repeated by men who, in their heated partisanship, forget that they are intelligent and reasonable beings. * * * The men in the Free States who advocate unconditional emancipation, are very few in numbers; and in the Republican party they do not number one in five hundred."

ances that he was a true and sound Republican ; but that assurance had failed."*

Wendell Phillips and other ardent Liberators, had before this made repeated assaults upon the President, and accused him of a desire to perpetuate the institution of Southern Slavery. Mr. Phillips had even been so bold as to assert that the President had it in his own choice, either to wear a wreath of contempt or be enrolled in history as the destroyer of Southern serfdom.

The resolutions, tactics, and tone of the radicals of the Republican party in this Congress, disclosed that it had been fully determined that slavery should either perish in the national struggle then waging, or a restoration of the old Union be rendered impossible.. Indeed, Mr. Stevens from this period made little concealment that this, so far as he could influence public affairs, was his fixed and determined resolve. He and his zealous coadjutors should have been less severe upon Abraham Lincoln and the administration; for this official was not in a situation to give as free utterance to his opinions as others; and besides, he had dextrously disclosed in his message to Congress of December 3d, 1861, that he was in spirit, in full accord with the most outspoken radical of his party. In that message he disclosed, to an observant mind, his willingness to accept the most extreme results of the emancipating crusade, that is to say the social equality of the black race. He said:

"If any good reason exists why we should persevere longer, in withholding our recognition of the independence and sovereignty of Hayti and Liberia, I am unable to discover it. Unwilling, however, to inaugurate a novel policy in regard to them, without the approbation of Congress, I submit for your consideration the expediency of an appropriation for maintaining a *charge 'd affairs* near each of those new States."

The recognition of these States, and the appointment of gentlemen to fill the new posts of honor, was a clear and unmistakable recognition of the social equality of the negro with the white race.

One of the earliest measures submitted by the radical leaders of the Republican party, in this Congress, was the bill to punish officers and privates of the armies for arresting, detaining or delivering fugitive slaves to their masters. But this, at first, was feared by many of the party, as too plain a disclosure of their views; and one that might not meet with public approbation. The Fugitive Slave law stood yet unrepealed upon the statute

*New York *Herald*, December 10th, 1861.

books of the nation; and the bill now proposed, too clearly, had the appearance of conflicting with that law. Being stubbornly resisted by the Democrats, and also by some Conservative Republicans, it was defeated in its original shape; but it was afterwards in February, 1862, reported from the Military Committee as an additional article of war in the following words:

"All officers are prohibited from employing any of the forces under their respective commands, for the purpose of returning fugitives from service or labor, who may have escaped from any persons to whom such service or labor is claimed to be due. Any officer who shall be found guilty by court-martial of violating this Article, shall be dismissed from the service."

This bill, after having been resisted in its new shape by the Constitutional defenders in both Houses, was passed and received the sanction of the President on March 13th, 1862. Indeed, it seemed clearly apparent, almost from the beginning of this session of Congress, that one spirit, without any digested plan, animated the leading Abolitionists in these bodies, inasmuch as innumerable propositions one after another were submitted in the two Houses, all having one general aim, negro emancipation.

But the bill which, of all others, was intended as the real entering wedge for all subsequent emancipatory measures, was that prepared as early as December 17th, 1861, reported by Morrill, of Maine, on February 13th, 1862, and which was to free the slaves of the District of Columbia. The bill served its purpose of testing the sentiment of the country as regards this radical advance, and assured the extreme Republicans how far the moderate men of their party would follow them. They were determined to overleap all constitutional barriers in their way, and if a sufficient following in their ranks would permit the passage of this radical measure, the future seemed clear for them. This bold attempt to subvert the plain spirit of the Constitution, the Democrats and Border State Representatives battled with the most stubborn resistance; but their efforts, as on former like occasions, were futile; and they were obliged to witness another invasion of the constitutional immunities of their countrymen. The arbitrary assessment of $300 as the value of the slave of each loyal master in the District, was a most palpable infraction of the Constitution, which declared that no man shall "be deprived of life, liberty and property without due process of law." The rapid change of base by the Republican party, which the support of this measure indicated, did not escape the animadversion and severe reproof of Senator Davis, of Kentucky, who stood by the landmarks of the Constitution, and fought as an ancient Roman in behalf of his country's liberty. He said:

> "There is a very different spirit and there are very different purposes, now in the dominant party in relation to slavery, to what were declared a few months ago."

This bill was passed in both Houses by an almost strict party vote, and received the approval of the President April 16th, 1862. The abolition re-echoes of approval to the passage of this law, giving freedom to the few slaves in the District were heard throughout the whole North, as therein the fiery advocates of negro liberation recognized an assuring harbinger of their long anticipated millennium.

In the midst of the blows that were falling thick and fast upon the institution of slavery, it would have indicated great lack of ardor had not Abraham Lincoln, the Agamemnon of the Abolition host, shown some apparent readiness, at least, to do his full share in the great battle of emancipation. He must somewhat keep pace with his ardent chieftains, or all the honor of the victory might be borne away by others; and he left to pine in grief because of inactivity. Accordingly, on the 6th of March, 1862, he submitted in a special message the proposition that Congress should pledge the Government as ready to co-operate pecuniarily with any State, that might be willing to inaugurate measures for the emancipation of the slaves within its borders, His proposition, as he was well aware, could not fail to attract some agreeable perfume in the shape of abolition adulation to his olfactory sensibilities; and might in a measure compensate for some of a contrary character, to which he had been repeatedly subjected. It is true his proposition was not composed of the ingredients coveted by the Stevens wing of his party; for this leader of the House characterized it as "the most diluted milk and water-gruel proposition that was ever given to the American nation."

Mr. Stevens, however, who by this time had come more fully to realize the qualities of Darwinian development possessed by the head of the Government, moved and carried in the House, a reference of this message to a Committee of the Whole on the state of the Union. All the unconstitutional objections that were urged against the passage of this measure; and every lack of warrant shown to draw money from the National Treasury for the purpose of freeing slaves, were insufficient to swerve from their purposes the reckless leaders of the Republican party. Emancipation was the first goal they were bent upon reaching; and all obstacles that stood in the way of their passage must be removed at any cost. The object must be reached or the Union of the States must pay the forfeit. President Lincoln, before submitting this proposition of compensated emancipation, was well aware that no Southern State either desired, or could be induced under the existing circumstances voluntarily to emancipate its slaves. Honor and integrity, therefore, should have demanded of the President to declare what he really meant; *that if the Southern States declined to accede to the abolition demand, he would shortly relieve them of that necessity.* But the subject afforded the President an excellent opportunity to exhibit himself as disposed to be fair and generous to the loyal slave holders of the South; whereas, neither he nor his party ever meant that the proposition should be accepted. The measure, however, passed both Houses, and received the assent of its proposer, President Lincoln.

The abolition current was by this time become a rapid tide, and was washing away one constitutional embankment after another. Every day developed more clearly that the assurances which had been made by the Republican leaders and press, that they did not intend to interfere with slavery, were all deceptious and intended to blindfold the nation, until it became involved in fratricidal strife with the people of the Southern States. One Member of Congress after another was disclosing his secret views that the destruction of slavery with the zealous leaders had from the first been a deliberate and well matured resolve. Members no longer hesitated to declare upon the floor of Congress, that they would not vote a man or a dollar for the further prosecution of the war, unless it be made one for the emancipation of slavery, clearly expressed.

Even the attitude that the party had assumed in the 36th Congress, in the organization of the new Territories of Colorado, Nevada and Dacotah, was hypocritical and false. These Territories had been organized after the withdrawal of the Representatives from the Cotton States; and by Acts which maintained a profound silence as regarded slavery. These Acts were passed at a time when Abolitionism was rather at a discount, in view of the calamities it was bringing upon the nation. But as soon as its former strentgh was regained, and it became apparent that the nation was intoxicated with the fumes of blood and fratricidal strife, this territorial legislation must undergo a like metamorphose. For this purpose, Owen Lovejoy reported a bill at this session of Congress for the abolition or prohibition of slavery in all the Territories of the United States. This Bill after having passed the ordinary ordeal of resistance, as the other measures already alluded to, became a law in the Abolition sense, though stigmatized as unconstitutional.

Affairs were now nearing a crisis. Congress had shown itself ready to endorse the most extreme measures of the radicals of the Republican party. All the extreme measures seemed to emenate from the representatives of the people; and the President had hitherto been fortunate in being able to appear before the country as a Union man, with or without slavery. He and his advisers were sufficiently shrewd to have him preserve an equipoise amidst the extremes. While therefore, the President stood before the friends of the Union, as a Union man, Senator Sumner who could communicate with the inner recesses of his soul, was early in 1862, able to assure his Abolition friends in the East, that they need not be solicitous as to the views of the Commander in Chief. That personage was all right, as time would fully disclose. Time did precisely what the Senator had promised. The country was fully committed to the task of subjugating the Southern States. A people cannot reason amidst the strife of warfare. All this the President or his advisers knew; and the long anticipated opportunity seemed near at hand when the curtain could with safety be raised.

In an interview with the Representatives from the Border States, the President urged them to accept compensated emancipation for their several States; but these men, educated in schools in which a reverence for right and obedience to the Constitution had been taught, spurned an offer that they felt no other save a usurper of his country's liberty was able to tender. A fitting parallel to this proposition of the American President is found in the instance of that individual who escorted the Son of Man to the pinacle of the Temple, and temptingly proposed, "*all these will I give thee.*" Neither in the one case nor the other, was it in the power of the proposer to execute his promise; but in the modern instance it was designed to enable the deceiver the better to develope his contemplated programme.

Northern arms on the battle-field were still slowly penetrating the rebellion, and General Lee, the commander of the Southern invading army, had left the field of Antietam with no advantage. The President was buoyant with a victor's joy, and four days after this sanguinary contest, on the 22d of September, 1862, he issued his famous emancipation decree, to take effect with the beginning of the coming year. The edict of the master was at length issued; the goal of emancipation had been reached; and like death upon the pale horse of apocalyptic vision, the abolition fiend went forth conquering and to conquer.

CHAPTER XVI.

EXECUTIVE UNCONSTITUTIONALISM.

The declaration of war by President Lincoln against the people of the seceded States, was in conflict with the letter and spirit of the Federal Constitution; which was but the receptacle of such clearly specified powers, as the framers of that instrument, the States, through their Representatives, had deemed it expedient to delegate. But the party to which he owed his election as the Chief Magistrate of the nation was the legitimate successor of Federalism and its descendants; that party which during all the anterior history of the Government had struggled for a liberal interpretation of the Constitution, as it was termed, in opposition to the strict construction of the Democracy. Indeed, this principle of constitutional construction with the new party was a necessity, as otherwise the institution of slavery, whether in the States or Territories, was invulnerable. It came into power, therefore, bearing upon its front the clear and unmistakable evidence of Hamiltonian parentage; and the period now seemed to have arrived that promised verification to the anticipations of the ancient monarchist.

The leading patriots of the nation, Clay, Webster, Calhoun, Benton and Buchanan, had from the inception of the Anti-Slavery agitation, clearly perceived the tendency of the new school of theorists, should they ever succeed in grasping the reins of government. And now, when this at length had taken place in the election of Abraham Lincoln, the declarations of these philosophic statesmen were verified. The Constitution, as they had predicted, was trampled upon, and the laws of the Government set at defiance. This was worse than monarchy itself—it was the inauguration of the despotism that followed. The monarchical Alexander Hamilton, and these later American patriots, were equally logical and sagacious. Both perceived that the future of America was freighted with dangers to the perpetuity of free Constitutional Government; equally was it manifest to their logical visions that under republican institutions wild, turbulent and selfish leaders would be able to seduce the people, and ascend the seats of power; and fully conscious of these dangers, the one foresaw the eventual overthrow of the Republic, and the others, hoping against hope, still fondly clung to their darling favorite and strove in vain to battle the rising fanaticism that endangered it.

But the unconstitutional declaration of war against the seceded States, was simply the commencement of the despotic power of the party calling itself Republican. The great inheritance of English liberty, the culmination of individual rights, the famous privilege of *Habeas Corpus* that had been wrested by the staunch freemen of the mother country from the Sovereigns of Great Britain, was next to fall before the usurping despot, who had been chosen by a revolutionary party to trample upon the inherited rights of his countrymen, and give freedom to a race of men, whom history had shown to be incapable of building up or sustaining civilization But usurpers usually proceed with cautious steps, and it was so in this case. In the name of libery and clothed with the sanctimonious garb of humanitarianism, the ancient inheritance is invaded. The American President, without any legislative sanction,* directs the suspension of the

*The suspension of the *Habeas Corpus* by President Lincoln, was a bold undertaking for an American Executive to assume, and one that should have caused his arrest as an usurper of his country's liberties. Up to the outbreak of the war, all the expository writers on the Constitution, without exception; all the most eminent jurists of the country; and all the Members of the only Congress in which the question was fully discussed (during the Burr conspiracy), had agreed that this extraordinary power, the suspension of the *Habeas Corpus*, was lodged in Congress alone. It was regarded as a legislative power, but one which no former Congress deemed it expedient to exercise. The exertion of this power, by President Lincoln, from the first met with the steady and almost unanimous opposition of the best legal minds of the nation of both political parties; and it was only a few second-rate lawyers (anxious to support revolutionary principles) whose legal endorsement in this particular the President ever received. Attorney-General Bates, and the octogenarian, Horace Binney, of Philadelphia, were conspicuous amongst the President's defenders.

In the celebrated Merryman case, Rodger B. Taney, Chief-Justice of the Supreme Court, clearly enunciated the doctrine that the suspension of the *Habeas Corpus* by President Lincoln was unconstitutional and void. This same view was expressed by Chief-Justice Dixon, as the unanimous opinion of the highest Court of the State of Wisconsin. Judge Dixon says: "And first, I think the President has no power in the sense of the Ninth Article of the Constitution of the United States to suspend the privilege of the writ of *Habeas Corpus*. Upon this ques-

Habeas Corpus in a specified district, by virtue of which a citizen of Maryland was seized and incarcerated, who was guilty of no defined legal offence—and an inhabitant of this State was made the object of despotic power, because of the strong sympathy of its people with those who had raised the banner of revolt to abolition domination; and because, in phrenzied Northern opinion, the people of these States should be held in the strictest reins. The President and the powers behind the throne, felt assured that the abrogation of the privilege of the time-honored writ of *Habeas Corpus* in behalf of a citizen of Maryland, would be less resented in the condition of public opinion that then obtained, than were the like attempted in New York or Pennsylvania. This first essay of such power, was wholly experimental, but the result justified further advances. Sustained by his obsequious Attorney-General and a maddened public sentiment, President Lincoln was able to set at defiance the mandate of the learned and venerated Rodger B. Taney, the Chief-Justice of the highest court of the nation; and it was then apparent that no bounds

---

tion, it seems to me that the reasoning of Chief-Justice Taney, in *ex-parte* Merryman, is unanswerable."—*Annual Cyclopædia*, 1862, p. 515.

Judge Hall, in the Northern District of New York, in a case that came before him, expressed the same opinions and fortified the same by a vast array of legal learning. Judge Curtis, of Boston, one of the dissenting members of the Supreme Court in the Dred Scott case, published a strong argument combatting the position of President Lincoln in assuming the right to suspend the writ. Even the ablest Republican lawyers of Congress were unwilling to advocate a view of constitutional law which was repugnant to their legal understandings, and to all just theories of interpretation. Senator Sherman, of Ohio, in his speech of December 9th, 1862, said: "Our attention was called to this question at the extra session by the opinion of the Attorney-General, that the President had the power and by the actual exercise of it by his proclamation, of suspending the writ in certain cases. I formed and expressed the opinion, at an early period of the session, that this power was purely a legislative power, to be exercised by Congress with the approval of the President. This opinion has been strengthened by subsequent reflection, by the able criticisms of lawyers and statesmen, which the discussion has elicited and by the decisions of some of the Courts. It is apparent from the context in which this power is found, that the framers of the Constitution classed it with the delegated powers of Congress. In its nature it is a legislative power."

Senator Trumbull, in a speech of December 9, 1862, said: "The better opinion, as has been stated here to-day among judges, lawyers and constitutional commentators, surely is that the writ of *Habeas Corpus* was never intended by the Constitution to be suspended, except in pursuance of an Act of Congress."

John Merryman was the party arrested, and in behalf of whom Rodger B. Taney issued a writ of *Habeas Corpus*, but which, in pursuance of instructions from President Lincoln, was not obeyed. A full report of this case is found in the 9th Volume of American Law Register, p. 524.

could be placed to his usurpations. The renowned Massachusetts Senator's prediction was thus early fulfilled, that if ever the fanatical Abolition party came into power, the Constitution would perish, the Supreme Court be overthrown, and its decrees repudiated.

Another unconstitutional stretch of executive authority, was the Presidential Proclamation of the blockade* of April 19th, 1861, along the whole seceded coast, and which afterwards, upon the secession of Virginia, North Carolina, Tennessee and Arkansas, was enlarged so as to embrace the sea-coast of these latter States that had united their fortunes with the new Confederacy. In support of these infractions of the Federal compact, the tyrant's plea of necessity was omnipotent to refute every argument that could be urged against the President's illegal assumption of power. An observer, even at this early period, might have reflected in the following strain. The weakness of free government is strikingly exemplified in this convulsion, and this should seem patent to every reflecting mind. Here is a ruler elected in accordance with the letter, but in violation of the spirit of the Constitution of the country, and who has sworn to defend it, striking down that same Constitution, in order that he and his party may be able to grasp objects, which are unattainble as long as the old *Magna Charta* subsists. The friends of the Constitution are in banishment, in apparent array against the Government, though in truth fighting its battles, and Cataline holds the gates of the city. The people are in confusion; have mistaken their enemies for their friends; are crusading under the banners of duplicity, and fast digging the graves of constitutional republicanism and free government. But the elected ruler is guilty of no higher offence than all the other leaders, who have sworn allegiance to the governmental compact; but who like him were too cowardly to openly assail it, yet who gained control of affairs by falsehood

* Thaddeus Stevens was too able a lawyer to be willing to acknowledge that the General Government could blockade its own ports. In his speech of December 9th, 1862, in the House of Representatives, he said: "We, ourselves, by what I consider a most unfortunate act, not well considered—declared a blockade of their (the Confederate States) ports—have acknowledged them as a power. We can not blockade our own ports. It is an absurdity. We blockade an enemy's ports. The very fact of declaring this blockade, recognized them as a belligerent power entitled to all the privileges and subject to all the rules of war, according to the law of nations."

and fraud; and then, as matricides, stab the kind parent who nourished them and shielded their ascent to power. A people that can be seduced by such leaders, and induced to fight for principles they utterly abhor, neither deserve nor or they competent to preserve the inheritances of freedom. They evince this inability in disclosing the simplicity and weakness here presented, and time is but required to fasten the rivets of Imperialism upon their social structure.

But madness and fury had carried reason away, and the masses seemed bent upon their own downfal and destruction. The sacrifice of peace, liberty and prosperity were insignificant, provided only the subjugation of the Southern Confederates could be effected. This object in the general fanatical opinion, was worth all it might cost, though the Union and Free government itself should perish in the achievement. Even the breaches made by Lincoln and his administration in the walls of the Federal Constitution, were greeted with shouts of applause by an infatuated populace; and with still greater huzzas, should some honest defender of that ancient heritage, utter his feeble protest against the Presidential usurpation. The impotent friend of his country's liberty was execrated as a traitor; whilst the cool, calculating tyrant who had fraudulently seized the helm of State, was applauded as *Honest Abe.*

At the extra session of Congress, which assembled on the 4th day of July, 1861, little else was transacted save that men and money were freely voted to the Administration for the prosecution of the war against the South; and the infractions of the Federal Constitution were also condoned. A larger appropriation of money, and a greater number of soldiers even, were granted by Congress for the war, than Lincoln had asked for in his message; and a resolution was introduced in the Senate by Wilson, of Massachsetts, and pressed for a considerable time with the greatest zeal to legitimate the confessedly illegal acts of the President. But this body, although overwhelmingly Republican, was unwilling as yet to place itself upon record as openly endorsing the plainest violations of the Constitution, and such as no partisan justification would serve to exculpate. Public sentiment was not yet clear upon this point. The manner, however, in which the leaders of the Republican party in both Houses of Congress, chose in their conduct to excuse the unconstitutional acts of the President, demonstrated that instead of censure being intended for him, his whole course, since his elevation to power, met with their warmest approval. No necessity, therefore, dictated to him to be at all guarded in his further advances on the highway of despotism, and he, himself, was sufficiently shrewd as to perceive that a general Congressional permit was now granted to him to strike down without reserve the remaining liberties of his countrymen.

President Lincoln, as the Chief Executive of the Northern and of such Southern States as the Government had been able to retain in its military grasp, with the adjournment of this Congress, began through his Secretaries to order with less hesitation the arrest and imprisonment of prominent Democratic citizens; and those who disbelieved in the war against the seceded States. The hated bastile, that relic of barbarism, which had sunk amidst the upheaval of the French revolution, arose on the Western continent, and became the receptacle of those Americans who feared not a despot's oppression, because they loved the institutions of the country under which they had been reared and educated. Arbitrary arrests of prominent individuals in all sections of the country, subject to the Lincoln administration, were matters of common occurrence in nearly every community; and the little bell of Secretary Seward became an instrument of daily requisition in the overthrow of the people's inalienable rights. Instead of Americans being free, by virtue of a written Constitution, which guaranteed to all life, liberty, and the pursuit of happiness; the further enjoyment of these rights depended upon the individual will of a ruler and his satellites. Men who had ranked as eminent and worthy statesmen, were without warrant seized in the seclusion and sanctity of their homes, and dragged thousands of miles and immured in loathsome cells—yea, at times in dungeons, because, perhaps, they had given expression to some sentiment unpalatable to a member of the party in power. Judges, who for years had adorned the chairs of justice, were dragged from their seats by a ruthless and vulgar squad of soldiers, and often brutally wounded in the struggle that occasionally ensued on such occasions. Should the party to be arrested demand the authority for the arrest, and the accusation with which he was charged, he would in all probability be told that he was a *Democrat*, and that all such were traitors and deserved not only to be arrested but also to be hung. One of the incarcerated in Fort Lafayette, afterwards describing his condition of imprisonment, says:

'Here you would see men from almost all the States, the largest portion of whom were in the vigor of manhood. You would find men who had ably represented our Government at foreign courts, had adorned the United States Senate, been Governors of States, Judges of courts, Members of Congress, State Legislatures, doctors, lawyers, farmers, and indeed almost all departments of business were here represented, not one of whom was tainted with any crime."*

Forts Lafayette, Warren, McHenry, the old Capitol at Washington, and other places of confinement were crowed with innocent citizens who had been arrested without legal warrant in all sections of the North and in the border States; and these victims of Federal power were subjected to indignities and outrages, the recital of which yet fires a freeman's blood with honest indignation. Citizens of almost all ages and conditions of life were compelled to wear the chains of despotic power, such as Americans in their palmy days would have broken with vindictive fury; and consigned the destroyer of their country's peace and constitutional liberty to a felon's cell, there to await his doom on Haman's gallows. Persons who had the misfortune to be incarcerated in one of these filthy Federal fortresses, were for months not even informed of the accusations that had been alleged against them; and the most studied efforts seemed to be made by the despot and his minions to degrade the manhood of those in their custody.

The miserable wretches, clad in Federal uniforms, who acted the jailor's *role* in these bastiles, in guarding those who had resented a tyrant's will, conscious of their degredation, were but too anxious to reduce to their own level, the noble spirits they held in custody. But they found in their keeping those whose spirit no oppression could bend; and who chose to endure for months and years the prison and oppression of despotism, rather than gain their freedom by dishonorable concessions. Many a patriot was subjected to the rigor and petty tyranny of a shoulder-strapped turnkey who compelled them to submit to the taunts and insults of the sentinels placed over them by day and night. The prisoners were reprimanded, yea, even punished, should

---

American Bastile, p. 516.

they dare to retort or resent the scoffs of the boorish soldiers, who stood over them as guardsmen. They were not even permitted to leave their quarters to visit a fellow-prisoner, unless leave were granted them by some sergeant whose loyal uniform indicated his master's service. The wives and friends of the inmates, who came to visit them, were not allowed access until a pass were obtained from Secretary Stanton, or some other magnate of Federal authority. And even when admitted, the conversations of the prisoners with their relatives, were limited to an hour, and that in the presence of the Commandant.

The black inquisitorial system of incarceration was germinated in a desire to repress all critical investigation of the acts and conduct of the revolutionary party; and those especially were the victims of this species of despotism, who were perceived to be most likely to influence public opinion, and thus thwart perhaps the designs of the revolutionists. Can history determine aught, but that the man who wielded the whole executive power of the nation, and by whose sanction all these tyrannous outrages upon constitutional freedom were enacted, was anything save a demon incarnate, who, under the guise of humanitarian impulses, trampled upon the rights of his countrymen? His name, in spite of all party efforts to enshrine it in hallowed recollection, will be written upon the same darkened pages upon which those of Louis XI and Lucretia Borgia stand inscribed.

Besides the restrictions that almost totally precluded intercourse with the friends and relatives of the prisoners, the interposition of legal counsel, that agreeable solace in times of difficulty was peremtorily forbidden. In being thus precluded from securing the assistance of gentlemen learned in the law, to bring their cases before the judicial tribunals of the country, another Article of the Federal Constitution was trampled upon, which prescribed that in all criminal prosecutions, "the accused shall have the assistance of counsel for his defense." On the 3d of December, 1861, the commanding officer at Fort Lafayette came to the prisoner's quarters and read a document signed by a Federal satrap, in which was the following language:

"I am instructed by the Secretary of State to inform you, that the Department of State will not recognize any one as an attorney for political prisoners, and will look with distrust upon all applications for release through such channels, and such applications will be regarded as additional reasons for declining to release the prisoners."

Of all the States in the Union, Maryland suffered most from the tyranny of the Federal administration. In September, 1861, the Democratic Members * of the Legislature of this State were arrested by orders of the Government, and conveyed to Federal fortresses, because of their known sentiments which were hostile to the party in power. The pretence alleged was, that they were concerting a scheme to have the State secede, and unite its fortunes with the Southern Confederacy. But this excuse lacked all basis, as at the time of the arrest, the Northern Government had its tyranous heel upon the neck of a people who could not but revolt in sentiment against the invasion of its sister Southern States, and the inauguration of the despotism they witnessed.

The pretence of the Federal Administration was further destitute of foundation, because, that at the Special Session of the Maryland Legislature, called by Governor Hicks in April, 1861, the question of secession was fully disposed of and determined. The session opened on the 26th of that month, and on the following day a Select Committee of the Senate reported an address to the people of the State, in which occurs the following language:

"We cannot but know that a large portion of the citizens of Maryland, have been induced to believe that there is a probability that our deliberations, may result in the passage of some measure, committing this State to secession. It is, therefore, our duty to declare that all such fears are without foundation. We know that we have no constitutional authority

---

*The following is the statement of S. T. Wallis, Chairman of the Committee on Federal Relations, of the Maryland House of Delegates: "I was a member of the Maryland Legislature in 1861, and was arrested at midnight at my dwelling, in the City of Baltimore, about the middle of September, 1861; from which time until the 27th of November, 1862, I was confined in one or other of the fortresses of the United States, which have been appropriated by Mr. Lincoln for the use of State prisoners. I have never been informed of the grounds upon which I was arrested.

"The commission, consisting of Messrs. Dix and Pierrepont, which was created by the Secretary of War, for the examination of the cases of prisoners arrested and confined like myself, held a session at Fort Warren in May, 1862; but I was not vouchsafed any communication as to the charges against me or any opportunity of being heard in my own defense. The commissioners, in fact, took no notice of my existence. Counsel I was not permitted to employ, for as early as the 28th of November, 1861, the United States Marshal, at Boston, visited Fort Warren for the purpose of communicating to my fellow prisoners and myself an order from Mr. Seward, the Secretary of State, announcing that no one would be recognized by this Department (which then had charge of us) as attorney of any State prisoner; and that the employment of counsel by any of us, would be regarded by him as a sufficient reason for the prolongation of our imprisonment. On the 26th of November, 1862, I was released from Fort Warren without conditions or explanations of any sort. The authority for my discharge, as I suppose for my arrest, was a telegram."—*New York World, Dec.* 30, 1862.

to take such action. You need not fear that there is a possibility that we will do so."

In the House of Delegates, at the Special Session, the question of secession also came up, on the petition of 216 voters of Prince George County, asking of the Legislature of Maryland the passage of an Ordinance of Secession without delay. On the 29th of April, this petition was referred to the Committee on Federal Relations. This Committee submitted both majority and minority reports, in the former of which, the following language occurred:

"That in their judgment the Legislature does not possess the power to pass such an ordinance as is prayed for, and that the prayer of the memorialists cannot be granted."

The minority of this Committee begged leave "to report unfavorably to the prayer of the memorialists." From that period down to the forcible suppression of the Legislature by Mr. Lincoln's orders, the subject was never again mooted, but was considered on all hands as absolutely and permanently disposed of.

With personal liberty, the freedom of the press also sunk beneath the weight of the Lincoln despotism. As early as September, 1861, several of the leading Democratic newspapers of New York were suppressed by orders from Washington, and the editors conveyed to Fort Lafayette, where they were detained at the pleasure of the administration. Many independent presses in the border States and in other sections of the North, were compelled either to moderate their tone of hostility to the ruling powers, or suspend their publication. Some of the most resolute editors chose the latter alternative, which was generally accompanied with free ingress into a governmental bastile. To many the alternative was not presented; and the doors of a Federal fortress fastened upon them, before they were made aware of the charges that were preferred against them. The sum of all their sinning consisted in their belief in the principles of the Virginia and Kentucky resolutions; and in occasionally attempting to argue in their papers that the Constitution warranted no military coercive force for the maintenance of the Union. Many, indeed, known simply to entertain these views of the Constitution, were subjected to incarceration in a military fortress for the utterance of sentiments that in others would have escaped all animadversion.

"If a Democratic paper did not proclaim war with the zeal of a Mohamedan, and denounce all who opposed it with the approbrious epithet of "*traitors*," and recommend them as fit subjects for the "*rope and halter*," the editor himself was liable to receive these delicate attentions."* Should a paper contain sentiments severely reflecting upon the Administration, for the inauguration of the war, or otherwise condemning its policy, a crowd of excited citizens, instigated by some pimp of power, was likely to assemble and demolish the office from which the offending sheet made its appearance; and likewise maltreat the editor, should he be so unfortunate as to fall into their hands. Many papers in different parts of the North were destroyed by infuriated mobs of lawless citizens, who had been instigated in their conduct by men who stood high in the confidence of Republican leaders; and from whom a word of dissuasion would have been sufficient to prevent the outrage. Persons who desired to figure in community as respectable personages, would make remarks calculated to inspire the mob-element like the Eastern college President, who declared himself as "*opposed to tarring and feathering traitors*;" but who added that he "*was forced to admit that this act had at times been well done.*" It is apprehended that it would require no logician to deduce the intent of this loyal Puritan's remarks. And in scarce a single instance where the law had been violated, was adequate satisfaction able to be obtained; for prejudice ran to such extremes that Democrats, with the greatest difficulty, could secure justice at the hands of partisan courts and juries. Indeed, citizens of all grades of outspoken anti-war opinions, were villified with all kinds of abuse during the whole continuance of the rebellion; and the word traitor or copperhead would often be heard by them, whilst walking the streets and engaged in the pursuit of their daily avocations.

Early in 1862, an order was issued transferring the matter of arbitrary arrests to the War Department. From this department a proclamation emenated by order of President Lincoln, which in itself virtually subverted republican government, inasmuch as Mr. Stanton, the Secretary of War, was authorized to appoint a number of men to constitute a corps of provost marshals, clothed with authority, in addition to their military duties, to arrest any citizen throughout the country. These marshals were appointed

**American Bastile*, p. 119.

and proved an annoyance to peaceable citizens in all sections of the unrebellious States; they had it in their power, upon indefinite charges, to arrest any person against whom accusations might be alleged, and for this purpose they were warranted to call in military aid to sustain their authority. They were required to report to the central power at Washington, and hold prisoners in custody subject to its authority. In truth, these provost marshals were vested with imperial power in their respective districts, and could order the arrest of any citizen whatever, without dread that their conduct would be subjected to an investigation.

In Maryland, Missouri and other Southern States, commissioners were appointed, under military authority, who proceeded by a kind of illegal inquisitorial surveillance, to take cognizance of the acts and even sentiments of their fellow-countrymen; and those whom these judges determined to be sympathizers with treason, were arbitrarily assessed certain sums of money by way of assessments upon their property; and compelled under pain of confiscation to liquidate these assessments.* Assessments of this kind, purporting to be sanctioned by marshal law, but inflicted in districts where no authority warranted its proclamation, were palpable violations of the Constitution, which prescribes that no individual shall be "deprived of life, liberty or property without due process of law." And though the establishment of these extraordinary tribunals may in many instances have been the work of executive subordinates, still their existence could not escape the notice of the Washington authorities, or endure without their sanction.

But as the war against the Southern States and people was inaugurated in conflict with the plainest principles of republicanism, and in accordance with those of imperialism, it must of necessity be in the same manner sustained. There was no other way of sustaining a war which the framers of the Constitution never designed to be proclaimed. When the Northern armies had overrun portions of Tennessee, North Carolina, and other Southern States, and overthrown the State authorities, President Lincoln, without any constitutional warrant whatever, appointed Military Governors for those States, in order thereby to re-erect State authority. Andrew Johnson was appointed Military Gov-

*New York *World*, Sept. 20th, 1862.

ernor of Tennessee, and Edward Stanley of North Carolina; and others were again assigned as the Military Executives of other States. Thaddeus Stevens was too able a lawyer to be willing to stultify himself by claiming that such appointments found support in the Federal Constitution. He and his special school of radical followers ignored all restraint of the Constitution, averring that they acted outside of that charter, and in accordance with the law of nations; but seeing the absurdity and hypocritical audacity of President Lincoln, who assumed to be guided by that instrument, on the 9th of December, 1862, he spoke as follows:

"I see the Executive one day saying, *you shall not take the property of rebels to pay the debts which the rebels have brought upon the Northern States.* Why? Because the Constitution is in the way. And the next day I see him appointing a Military Governor of Virginia, a Military Govenor of Tennessee, and some other places. Where does he find anything in the Constitution to warrant that?

"If he must look there alone for authority, then all these Acts are flagrant usurpations, deserving the condemnation of the community. He must agree with me, or else his acts are as absurd as they are unlawful; for I see him here and there ordering elections for Members of Congress, wherever he finds a little collection of three or four consecutive plantations in the Rebel States, in order that men may be sent here to control the proceedings of Congress, just as we sanctioned the election held by a few people at a little watering place at Fortress Monroe, by which we have here the very respectable and estimable member from that locality."

But the culminating point of Executive despotic innovation on constitutionalism was reached, when President Lincoln issued his proclamation declaring the emancipation of the negro slaves in the rebellious States. If the ruler of a people was ever guilty of the violation of faith, solemnly plighted in his own and the declarations of his party, it was in this instance. From the origin of the Republican party in 1855, the only object to be obtained by this organization, as gathered from the declarations of its leaders, the utterances of its presses, and its *so-called* national platforms, was to prevent the further extension of slavery into free territory. During the campaign of Fremont in 1856, and again of Lincoln in 1860, the Republican leaders solemnly repudiated all designs of interfering with slavery in the Southern States. They were unanimous in their solemn declarations, that they neither possessed the power nor the inclination to meddle with the institution where it existed. The Constitution was pointed to as an obstacle to any apprehended designs they might be supposed to entertain, as to the eradication of slavery in the States where it already had a legal existence.

But revolutionary partisans do not stop for obstacles. They can readily find excuses (as in the instance of the wolf and the lamb) to abandon their assurances, and seize the objects which form the centre of their designs. It was so in the case of the Republican party. From the composition of their party, and the enthusiasm which it arroused in the breasts of the undissembling Abolitionists, it was apparent that the ultimate aim of the party was universal emanicipation, much as the leaders strove to conceal this. In this, Southern and Northern conservative statesmen were not deceived, as they repeatedly predicted. But the achievement of this object must depend upon circumstances. That it would surely be the result of Republican success in the nation could easily be affirmed, when the principles were considered. It was a necessary sequence. The poison lay in that dogma of their creed, that would give to the majority of the people of the United States, a right to determine questions in which those of the several States had constitutional interests. It was, in a word, to allow democracy to override constitutionalism. This itself, an efflux of centralization, the product of imperialistic rule, was subversive of all constitutional guarantee, and calculated to awaken serious alarm in the minds of thinking men both North and South. It was sure to overwhelm the ancient State-right landmarks, as soon as a party of these principles gained control of the General Government.

The emancipation decree of Abraham Lincoln was simply the legitimate fruit of Republican teaching, and an aim of the party that was striving for the social and political equality of the negro race. Though its promulgation had been from the first fully resolved upon, yet in the estimation of the President and his confidential advisers, its further postponement might have been judicious. Public opinion, as the President feared, was scarcely prepared for the measure. But the pressure of the ardent emancipationists, amongst whom Mr. Stevens ranked conspicuous, compelled the Executive, as it were, to issue a proclamation which but a few days before he had declared could prove of no utility to the Abolition cause. The Massachusetts Republican State Convention, however, had assembled some days prior to its issue; and this body had declined to give the President the usual resolution of confidence, which every Chief Magistrate expects of his party. Mr. Lincoln was deeply wounded by this indignity in the very citadel of Republicanism; and he must hasten to do penance for his transgression. He understood what the slight of his party betokened. A secret meeting of New England Governors had also been held which indicated no confidence in the Administration. The Republican State Convention of the Empire State was soon to assemble at Syracuse; and it behooved the President to endeavor to obviate a new animadversion upon his conduct, such as he had experienced in the Bay State.

Besides, the novelty of enlisting for the three months' war had subsided. The soldiers and the people had been deceived by the Republican orators and journals; and additional recruits were needed to fill up the depleted ranks of the Northern armies, held at bay by the Confederates. Additional deception was again required. Indeed, it was the constant pabulum of the soldiers, and the easily deluded people, during the struggle. The rebellion was always just upon the brink of yielding. Governor Andrews, of Massachusetts, and other radical statesmen, now predicted that so great enthusiasm would follow the promulgation of emancipation, that the roads would be crowded with soldiers who would flock to the national escutcheon to defend the cause of universal humanity.

Indeed, the deception practised by men in power during this time was of the very grossest character, and if for no other reason, the names of those who practised such fraud and imposition, should be written upon tablets of contempt, and handed down for execration to the remotest posterity. A worthy cause needs not such means for its execution. But the means employed have sown the seeds of such social and national demoralization, that Republican Government is no longer able to perpetuate liberty, honor and integrity, and but time is required to evolve a new order of things.

CHAPTER XVII.

LEGISLATIVE UNCONSTITUTIONALISM.

When the elements and fundamental principles of the Republican party is considered, it will not seem strange that the Constitution, after the inauguration of war against the South was found to interpose but a slight check upon the lawless invasion of civil rights. The enthusiastic, self-styled reformers, whose opinions of right can tolerate no contradiction; the Maine liquor advocates whose efforts to remodel society had for years been distracting social order; and the narrow ecclesiastical sectaries, who can only see moral evil in distorted visions; all these and others of like character had become consolidated into one aggregated mass of turbulent agitators. This agitating army of fanatical zealots, found its home in that political organization termed the Republican. Abraham Lincoln and the majority of the Thirty-seventh Congress, were the choice of that party of the American people largely composed of the enthusiastic classes, whose zeal ever surpasses their wisdom.

That the Republican President and the Members of Congress chosen on the same ticket with him, should be persons of the same characteristics as the partisans to whom they owed their election, was to be expected. The discussion of the slavery question had largely eliminated the zealous classes from the Democratic party, and attached them to the new organization that was combatting the institution of Southern slavery. These all were fired by the same zeal for the emancipation and elevation of the negro race, as had been Innocent III. and his coadjutors in the establishment of the Roman inquisition. The spirit of persecuting ecclesiasticism was again to be witnessed upon a new arena; and the maddened zeal that flamed forth as in fiery volumes from the North, was the result of the sincere desire upon the part of the ardent classes for the extirpation of the Southern institution. It was, however, in itself that same principle that ever destroys civil organism and leaves but a wreck of ruins in its path; and which, perhaps, prepares the minds of the reflecting classes for the disagreeable reception of imperialistic, when constitutional Republican Government has failed. The reformer and the statesman are designed to occupy very variant spheres in the world's life, and never can with safety be exchanged. The philosophic ruler holds the scepter even, between all conflicting opinions, and permits none to overstep the bounds of constitutional order; but the zealot becomes the mediæval iconoclast, or the persecuting prelate who causes rivers of blood to flow, that the souls of men be not endangered.

The war from its inception was waged with a spirit of malice and vindictive hatred, such as had been witnessed in modern warfare but once (during the French revolution) since the period of the religious wars of Europe, during the 16th and 17th centuries. The ancient animus was revived, the dial of time was turned back for centuries, and all the guarantees of constitutionalism which philosophic ages had secured, were madly and fanatically overturned in the wild and delusive hope of elevating to equality with the Caucasian, a race totally incapable of even sustaining the fruits of civilization. Negro liberation and elevation being the sole objects to be achieved by the fiery enthusiasts who gave life and soul to the Republican party, it would have been contrary to all experience had not vindictiveness ruled the hour. Were it to be expected that zealots, who esteemed the emancipation of four millions of negro slaves, the great blessing of the 19th century, would at all be lenient and tolerant in measures for the achievement of the result? Since the commencement of the civil war, the union of the States instead of being any longer *a league with death and a covenant with hell*, had become at length the great centre of their fondest hopes. Men of enthusiastic aspirations, had ascended the seats of power, bent upon wresting the ancient fabric of the Republic from its foundations; and fully determined upon breaking down all those parts of the Constitution that interposed obstacles to their designs. The legislation at the extra session of Congress in 1861, was chiefly confined to the granting of men and money to the Administration for the prosecution of the war of invasion against the South. But as "*out of the abundance of the heart the mouth speaketh*;" so from the utterances and conduct of Thaddeus Stevens, Sumner and other leading members of Congress, it was already clearly apparent to an observer, that the Federal Constitution, would be found to interpose slight resistance to the designs of these most extreme partisans and radical revolutionists, who now found themselves in position to so shape the laws of the nation, that their emancipating designs might be fully ultimated. The Constitution having conferred no authority upon the President or Congress to make war against the seceding States, was it to be anticipated that no further invasions of that instrument would take place?

The resolutions submitted by Members of Congress, and the majorities that endorsed these, exculpating the blockade of the Southern coast, the illegal arrests of innocent citizens and other unconstitutional acts of President Lincoln, clearly demonstrated that ulterior objects to the preservation of the Union and the Federal Constitution, were entertained by the leading men of both branches of Congress.

An initiative measure was enacted near the close of the session, which declared the confiscation of all the slaves employed with the consent of their masters to further the cause of the rebellion. The object of the war to a discerning eye was clearly portended in this enactment, but the people of the Border States and the Democrats of the North were assured that this was simply a military measure that the laws of war demanded. It was one, however, that Napoleon had disdained to make use of in his wars with Russia, although repeatedly solicited to employ it. But the European Emperor was fighting for conquest, the American Congress, though professing the same, for emancipation.

When the 37th Congress assembled in December, 1861, an advanced attitude on the slavery question, as we have seen in a former chapter, was presented; and fully matured plans seemed to have been agreed upon, by Sumner, Wilson, Stevens, Lovejoy and other leading radicals. There was nevertheless a number of conservative Republicans in Congress who strove to defend the Constitution to the best of their ability; but whom a deluded public opinion, either kept for the most part in radical traces, or democratic quarters ultimately gave them refuge. The Congressmen of this character were either reflective thinkers or sound constitutional statesmen, whose districts and States had become abolitionized; and they as politicians, must either yield to the current or retire from public life. Those chose the latter alternative with whom conscience ruled supreme.

On the 11th of December, 1861, Senator Trumbull, a Republican, offered the following resolution:

"*Resolved*, That the Secretary of State be directed to inform the Senate, whether in the loyal States of the Union any person or persons have been arrested or imprisoned, and are now held in confinement by orders from him or his Department; and if so, under what law said arrests have been made and said persons imprisoned."

In support of his resolution, and speaking of illegal arrests, the Illinois Senator said:

"The unconstitutionality of such action as this seems to be admitted by the Senator who comes to the defense of this despotic power. Why, sir, the power—without charge, without examination, without opportunity to reply, at the click of the telegraph—to arrest a man in a peaceable portion of the country, and imprison him indefinitely, is the very essence of despotism. What, sir, becomes of constitutional liberty, what are we fighting for if this broad ground is to be assumed and to be justified in this body, and any man is to be thanked for assuming an unconstitutional and unwarranted authority? What are we coming to, if arrests may be made at the whim or the caprice of a Cabinet Minister? Do you suppose he is invested with infalibility, so as always to decide aright? Are you willing to trust the liberties of the citizens of this country in the hands of any man to be exercised in that way? May not his order send the Senator from Connecticut or myself to prison? Why not?"

Most of the Republicans in the Senate opposed the above resolution of Senator Trumbull, many of them warmly justifying the President for all the arrests he had caused to be made; and as only *Democrats*, whom they chose to entitle traitors, had been made to suffer, they had no fault to find with the Executive Department of the Government. Senator Fessenden, of Maine, expressed the sentiments of the majority in the following language:

"Indeed, I know, that under the directions from the Secretary of State, certain individuals in the loyal States have been arrested and imprisoned. That is notorious; the whole country is aware of it. I will say here, that I do not believe there is the slightest warrant of law for any such proceedings, and I do not suppose that you will find a lawyer who does think there is any warrant of law for such proceedings, and yet I do not shrink from it. I justify the act, although it was against law. I justify it from the necessity of the case."

The resolution of Senator Trumbull was consigned by a vote of the Senate to its lethean tomb, the Committee on the Judiciary.

Besides the unconstitutional measures passed at this session of Congress, and clearly intended to advance the cause of emancipation, some of which have been detailed in a former chapter, others of the same character, both of a direct and indirect nature, and yet designed to effect similar aims were likewise enacted. A monetary crisis supervened with the close of the year 1861, in the general bank suspension, and the wheels of coercive government were likely to stop, unless the herculean might of despotic power could be invoked, also to relieve the financial condition. This crisis was enhanced, because of the constant delusion that had been practised upon the public mind, that the war would be of but from sixty to ninety days duration. Indeed, the men at the helm of government, dared not to disclose to public view the delusion* that had been perpetrated, although themselves well aware of it, through fear of the general alarm it would occasion. In that event, they feared that a peace party at the North would be likely to grasp the reins of power, and thus the aims of the revolutionists would be baffled. The public for a time had freely loaned of their money to support the Government, but Congress being as yet fearful to enact laws to tax the people, the sinews of war were at length exhausted.

But doubtless it had been from the first apparent to Salmon P. Chase, the Head of the Treasury Department, that the solution of the problem committed to his charge would necessitate a complete revolution in the financial affairs of the country, in order to enable the government to prosecute the war with success, against the seceded States; and for that length of time, which his discerning mind must have assured him, that it would

*Those who had the sagacity to perceive the delusion and the courage to expose it, were denounced by the intensely loyal hypocrites, as traitors and deserving of the severest punishment. It was incumbent upon one who desired to be esteemed a friend of the Union, that he be willing at all times to deceive his countrymen. As an illustration of the deception practised by the leading men, the following extract from a speech of Representative Morrill, of Vermont, of February 4, 1862, is cited: "We are urged by the gentleman from New York to pass this bill as a *war measure*, a *measure of necessity;* and to enforce this idea he gives you the figures of our probable requirements, if the war should be prolonged until July 1st, 1863. Sir, I have no expectation of being required to support a war for that length of time. The ice that now chokes up the Mississippi is not more sure to melt and disappear with the approaching vernal season, than are the rebellious armies upon its banks, when our Western army shall break from its moorings, and rushing with the current to the Gulf, baptise as it goes in blood the people to a fresher allegiance."—*Congressional Globe,* 2d Session of Thirty-seventh Congress, Part 1, p. 630.

be necessary to do so, to effect their subjugation. This was indeed a necessity, when our form of Government be taken into consideration. The principles upon which the States had united to form a union, based upon consent, had, as we have seen, been violated by the declaration of war to coerce those that had seceded. That in itself was the assumption of imperial power by the General Government, which had never been delegated to it. The war was at first pretended to be prosecuted upon republican principles, and by means of voluntary loans. For the first three months money was freely furnished to the Government, because the people expected its speedy termination; and for the next six months loans were with still increasing difficulty secured upon republican principles. The effort on the part of the Government to conduct a war, anti-republican in its character, by means of republican principles, was absurd, self-contradictory, and simply designed for the delusion of the Northern people. This, Secretary Chase and all the leading officials of his party, from the first must have clearly perceived, otherwise they were utterly incompetent for the positions they were chosen to fill.

But theirs was the party of revolution, and it behooved them to proceed with cautious steps, so as not to alarm the people, until the sections had become so far entangled in the conflict, and the Northern people so embittered in the carnage that the peace party would be impotent. The same sagacious shrewdness, therefore, was required by the Secretary of the Treasury and the revolutionary element in Congress to get the financial affairs so shaped as that the administration could control the national purse, as it was also designing to do with the sword.

The monetary crisis that took place at the close of the year 1861, was but the natural sequence, therefore, of the incongruous effort to wage a monarchical war upon republican principles. It was, in short, only circumstances necessitating the revolutionary monarchists to show their real designs; and with the greatest dexterity and adroitness was this essayed before the country. Secretary Chase, in his report of July 5th, 1861, and also in that of December 9th of the same year, suggested his plans by which he deemed it feasible that the national purse might be grasped in order to further the work of abolitionism. The great work to be achieved by his party for this purpose, was to obtain the overthrow of the principle of State Sovereignty, so far as the same in any wise conflicted with the central authority now fully resolved upon negro emancipation. For this purpose the currency of the country must undergo a radical change from what it had heretofore ever experienced. Mainly, therefore, in accordance with the suggestions of the Secretary in his reports, a bill was matured by the Committee of Ways and Means, of which Mr. Stevens was Chairman, and submitted to the House on the 30th of December, 1861. This bill proposed the issue of one hundred millions of Treasury notes, which with the fifty millions of demand notes already in circulation, should be a legal tender for all claims due the Government, and also, for all debts public and private within the United States, whether the same were already due, or to be collected in the future.

This was indeed a revolutionary movement of revolutionary men; but many of the conscientious adherents of the Republican party refused to give it their sanction, because of its utter violation of all justice and equity and of the whole spirit of the Federal Constitution. A cardinal principle of that fundamental charter which the legal tender clause of this measure proposed to repudiate, was that which declared that *no State shall pass any law impairing the obligation of contracts;* and it was one, the denial of which up to this period no American statesman had been bold enough as to conceive. But because this prohibition had not been applied in express terms to the Government of the United States, the Republican majority in Congress, had the audacity to introduce and sustain a measure plainly void and unconstitutional. Secretary Chase, in his letter of January 29th to Mr. Stevens, also gave his approbation to the legal tender feature of the Treasury Note Bill,* but at the same time ex-

*Afterwards, when success had crowned the Abolitionists, and Salmon P. Chase had been elevated to the most honored seat upon the Supreme Bench of the United States Court, he could speak in language that in 1862 would have been denounced by the loyal as treason. Speaking of the prohibition imposed by the Constitution upon the States to "pass any law impairing the obligation of contracts," Chief Justice Chase said: "It is true this prohibition is not applied in terms to the Government of the United States. Congress has express power to enact bankrupt laws, and we do not say that a law made in the execution of any other express power, which incidentally only impairs the obligation of a contract, can be held to be unconstitutional for that reason.

"But we do think it clear that those who framed and those who adopted the Constitution, intended that the spirit of this prohibition should pervade the entire body of legislation, and that the justice which the Constitution was ordained to establish, was thought by them to be incompatible with legislation of an opposite tendency. In other words,

pressed his loathing for such legislation. On this point he said:

"It is not unknown to them (the Committee) that I have felt, nor do I wish to conceal, that I now feel a great aversion to making anything but coin a legal tender in payment of debts."

Much, however, as conscience interposed, so great was his zeal in the cause of negro emancipation that he did not have the moral courage to utter his protest against a measure for which he well knew there was no warrant in the Federal Constitution. The necessity for such legislation was even insisted upon by him, as a means of prosecuting the war with success against the South.

The Democrats in both Houses of Congress, and some of the ablest Republicans opposed the passage of the Legal Tender Bill, with a stubborn resistance that no radical measure since the inauguration of Abraham Lincoln had encountered. It was shown to be entirely revolutionary in its character, and in conflict with the universal legal thought of the country, from the foundation of the Government. The opinion of no jurist, publicist or statesman was able to be cited by the advocates of the measure favorable to their position; but the declarations and writings of the most eminent men were adduced, combatting the views of the revolutionists. Daniel Webster, the great expounder of the Constitution, in his speech upon the renewal of the charter of the United States Bank in 1832, spoke as follows:

"Congress can alone coin money. Congress can alone fix the value of foreign coin. No State can coin money. No State, not even Congress can make anything a tender but gold and silver in payment for debts." *

Webster again expressed the general thought of the country on this question, in his speech in the Senate on the *Specie Circular* in 1836, in which he held the following language:

"Most unquestionably there is no legal tender, and there can be no legal tender in this country under the authority of this Government, or any other, but gold and silver—either the coinage of our own mints, or foreign coin at rates regulated by Congress. This is a Constitutional principle, perfectly plain, and of the highest importance. The States

we cannot doubt that a law not made in pursuance of an express power, which necessarily and in its direct operation impairs the obligation, is inconsistent with the spirit of the Constitution."—Hepburn vs. Griswold, in *American Law Register*, 1870, pp. 187–8.

The Supreme Court of the United States, in the above case of Hepburn vs. Griswold, decided that the clause in the acts of 1862 and 1863, making United States notes a legal tender in the payment of all debts, public and private, is, so far as it applies to debts contracted before the passage of these acts, unwarranted by the Constitution.

*Webster's Speeches. Vol. 2, p. 81.

are prohibited from making anything but gold and silver a payment of debts; and although, no such prohibition is applied to Congress, yet as Congress has no power granted to it in this respect, but to coin money and regulate the value of foreign coin, it clearly has no power to substitute paper or anything else for coin as a tender in payment for debts, and in discharge of contracts."*

An array of intellectual men in Congress, of both parties, as before stated, placed themselves in opposition to the passage of the Legal Tender Bill, and strongly argued that the measure was unconstitutional; and one that would launch the country on a sea of irredeemable paper currency, amidst whose billows the ship of free government might ultimately submerge. Roscoe Conkling, a Republican Representative from New York, spoke as follows on the constitutionality of the question:

"The proposition is a new one. No precedent can be urged in its favor; no suggestion of the existence of such a power can be found in the legislative history of the country; and I submit to my colleague, as a lawyer, the proposition that this amounts to affirmative authority of the highest kind against it. Had such a power lurked in the Constitution, as construed by those who ordained and administered it, we should find it so recorded. The occasion for resorting to it, or at least referring to it, has, we know, repeatedly arisen; and, had such a power existed, it would have been recognized and acted on. It is hardly too much to say, therefore, that the uniform and universal judgment of statesmen, jurists, and lawyers, has denied the constitutional right of Congress to make paper a legal tender for debts to any extent whatever. But more is claimed here than the right to create a legal tender, heretofore unknown. The provision is not confined to transactions *in futuro*, but is retroactive in its scope. It reaches back and strikes at every existing obligation."†

The same gentleman depicted the moral effect of such legislation, in the following words:

"But, sir, passing as I see I must from the constitutional objections to the bill, it seems to me its moral imperfections are equally serious. It will, of course, proclaim throughout the country a saturnalia of fraud, a carnival of rogues. Every agent, attorney, treasurer, trustee, guardian, executor, administrator, consignee, commission-merchant, and every debtor of a fiduciary character, who has received for others hard money, worth a hundred cents on the dollar will forever release himself from liability by buying up, for that knavish purpose, at its depreciated value, the spurious currency which we will have put afloat. Everybody will do it, except those who are more honest than the American Congress advises them to be."‡

George H. Pendleton, a distinguished Democratic Represen-

* Webster's Works. Vol. 4, p. 271.
† *Congressional Globe*, 37th Congress, part 1, pp. 634–5.
‡ *Congressional Globe*, Second Session, 37th Congress, Part 1, pp. 634–5.

tative from Ohio, argued the unconstitutionality of the measure, and the intrinsic inequity of a law that would attempt to unsettle all fixed values and unjustly confiscate, as it were, the credits of every man in the community. He predicted the calamitous consequences of such legislation as follows:

"You send these notes out into the world, stamped with irredeemability. You put on them the mark of Cain; they will go forth to be fugitives and vagabonds on the earth. What then will be the consequence? It requires no prophet to tell what will be their history. The currency will be expanded; prices will be inflated; fixed values will depreciate; incomes will be diminished; the savings of the poor will vanish; the hoardings of the widow will melt away; bonds, mortgages, notes, everything of fixed value will loose their value; everything changeable will be appreciated; the necessaries of life will rise in value; the Government will pay two-fold—certainly largely more than it ought—for everything that it goes into the market to buy; gold and silver will be driven out of the country."*

The radical republicans supported the Legal Tender measure of their party, believing it to be a matter of necessity to enact the same, to accomplish the subjugation of the Southern people. Belonging to that school of interpretation which professed to be able to find in the Constitution, any power that they deemed necessary for the national weal, it was not difficult for the leaders to find support in that instrument for any species of legislation which they desired. They, however, favored the measure because it was germinated in monarchical principles, and because such were needed upon the financial arena, and such as already had been and were to be introduced into the other avenues of the Government.

The measure was of a monarchical character, as it relied upon force for the circulation of the notes to be issued, looked to the direct and despotic coercion of arms, over-rode both the letter and spirit of the Constitution, shocked every principle, not only of justice between the Government and the citizens, but also between the citizens themselves, and of all sound political philosophy. That the Legal Tender Bill was simply a part of the financial scheme of Secretary Chase and the influential men of his party, to subsidize to their control the monied interests of the country, C. L. Vallandigham, of Ohio, had the clearness of vision to perceive. In his speech of February 3d, 1862, this patriotic and sagacious statesman uttered the following words:

*_Congressional Globe_, Second Session, 37th Congress, Part 1, p. 551.

"The notes are meant to circulate generally and permanently as currency, at least till the Secretary's grand fiscal machine, his magnficent *national paper mill,* founded upon the very stocks provided for by this bill, can be put in operation, when this sort of bills of credit are to become the sole currency of the country, and to drive all gold and silver and ordinary bank paper out of circulation."

The main argument urged in behalf of the bill was its necessity, and that no express words in the Constitution forbade such an enactment.

The friends of the measure denied that more than one hundred and fifty millions of legal tender bills would need to be issued by Congress; and in these denials we have another example of the deceptious method pursued by the Republican leaders to conceal the magnitude of the rebellion; and it was one whose Janus-faced visage was ever presenting itself during the whole progress of the war. Thaddeus Stevens, who was a warm friend of the Treasury Note Bill, in reply to a question propounded to him on the 6th of February, 1862, said:

"But my distinguished colleague from Vermont, fears that enormous issues would follow to supply the expenses of the war. I do not think any more would be needed than the $150,000,000."

But this assurance proved, like most others emenating from radical sources and made with reference to the duration and the expenses of the war, simply deceitful; and especially so in this case; it having been uttered by a man who had the sagacity from the commencement of hostilities to somewhat clearly measure the magnitude of the rebellion, and the length of time and the vast expenditures that would be required to overthrow it. Instead of one hundred and fifty millions being found sufficient, very many additional hundred millions of legal tender notes were necessary to be issued to perfect the great work of emancipation, and allow the tide of war to fully inundate and deluge in blood the States of South.

Another necessary feature of the financial scheme was that which imposed the requisite taxes upon the people to support the Government demands. The imposition of these was, however, made with the greatest caution; for it was perceived that nothing would so surely open the eyes of the masses as the infliction of onerous taxation. The Republicans steadily resisted the enactment of a sufficient internal revenue law as long as possible; and acquiesced in supporting such a bill only when circumstances forced them into the measure. By the Act passed August 5th, 1861, it was estimated that twenty millions of revenue could be raised; but that sum was by no means adequate to support the wants of the Government.

During the second session of the Thirty-seventh Congress, the question of revenue became a pressing one, upon the attention of Congress, and all schemes were resorted to in order to press off the consideration of so unpleasant a concern. The elections of 1862 were nearing themselves, and the agricultural interests of the country required to be handled with the greatest caution that political managers could employ. A revenue bill was at that time of all things most needed to sustain the wants of the administration, as Secretary Chase in his reports had undissemblingly shown. Congress at length found itself compelled to take up the consideration of this question. Mr. Stevens, the Chairman of the Committee of Ways and Means in March, 1862, submitted a complicated tax bill, which the members of the Committee had for nearly two months been busily engaged in elaborating. In the bill, as submitted, almost every conceivable tax was imposed upon manufactures, the profits of trade and industry, and the incomes of individuals. The most studied effort was made in the preperation of this system of revenue, so as to allow the agriculturists seemingly to escape from the burdens imposed. But the escape was only apparent, for upon the consumers ultimately fall the taxes of the community. The fallacious, hypocritical scheme, however, served as the blind to hide the enormous burdens that the revolutionary party was necessitated to impose upon the people, in order to carry through their designs of emancipation and negro elevation; and which was but a part of the centralizing plan they had in view in their war against the South.

This revenue bill met in Congress with no steady party opposition, for, although its whole features had a centralizing tendency, yet the Constitution clothed the law making body with the power to raise taxes. It is evident from the discussions in Congress, that a decided aversion was felt by all real Democrats to the passage of the bill, inasmuch as they were conscious that the money to be raised by it was to be expended for an unconstitutional and altogether anti-republican purpose. William H. Wadsworth, a Representative from Kentucky, made no concealment of his opposition to the measure, on account of the known objects to be achieved in the prosecution of the war against the seceded States. The bill, after a long deliberation in both Houses of Congress, became finally a law on the 1st of July, 1862.

This Internal Revenue Bill was very long and minute in its details, almost every transaction of business being obliged to submit to the imposition of stamp duty. This repulsive feature of British rule, that had aroused our revolutionary ancestors to resistance against the Crown of the mother country, was imposed by the radical Congress, and was submitted to by the people, because large armies and dictatorial satraps compelled obedience to the Federal Administration. But it was very unwillingly obeyed by a large body of the people, who somewhat faintly realized the objects to be promoted by the money wrung from the people by relentless partisans professing humanitarianism, yet rioting in the overthrow of Constitutionalism. A tax of three per cent. was levied upon all manufactures, and upon all incomes upwards of six hundred dollars. All professional gentlemen and men engaged in various departments of industry, were additionally taxed by means of licenses, and compelled either to pay the same for the advancement of abolition ideas, or withdraw from the occupation of their lives.

But as abolitionism and all other fanaticisms must necessarily accompany each other, it would have been remarkable had not the total prohibition influence, made itself felt in the internal revenue legislation of Congress. Representative Morrill, of Vermont, one of the first to explain the features of the bill, declared that the object of its framers was to impose upon the liquor trafic as heavy a tax as possible, so as to repress that trade to the utmost of their power. As a member of the American monarchical party, he could cite British precedent for such discrimination, with regard to duty on liquors, and said:

"In England, the duty on spirits is ten shillings and five pence, or about $2.52, per gallon."

Another Representative, a Member from Maine, a Mr. Rice, true to the principles of his State fanaticism, spoke as follows:

"I would not discriminate, partially, against any citizen engaged in any honest and reputable business ; but I would to the fullest extent impose excise duty on liquor and tobacco, let it come from whatever source it may, or let it injure whom it may. If men are driven out of this business, it will be all the better for the country. I was in favor of the amendment proposed by the gentleman from Kentucky, because I understood it, though not so intended by him, to be an absolute prohibition against distillation. If Congress would only put down, either by direct or indirect means, these distilleries that pour out fire and death over all the land, I think it would be performing a good work. It would be doing more good to the people than any other enactment it can pass.

"I hope the day will come when a prohibition will be put upon all distillation; when such a tariff will be placed on spirituous liquors as will exclude their importation. That will be a glorious day for the country."*

In the author of the last cited extract, we hear one of the ancient holy Pharisees and hypocrites, who would seem to have arisen from the dead; and who sets himself up as more pure and righteous than all other men; and whose opinions must be accepted as the whole rule of rectitude and moral probity. His doctrines admirably harmonized with the hidden monarchical sentiments of his party, but were altogether in disharmony with the principles he professed to advocate, that is to say: the freedom of all men. His own and the principles of his party would allow all to be free to the extent that his infallible judgment and despotic will would permit. Delightful freedom indeed was it that he and his fanatical Maine law compeers advocated.

A tax of about one hundred per cent. was imposed by this act upon spirituous liquors, which, by subsequent acts, was largely increased, all with the design of indirectly excluding by a species of Maine liquor law legislation, all kinds of spirituous, vinous and malt liquors from circulation in the community. The article of tobacco was likewise highly taxed in the Revenue Act of July 1st, 1862, because this article had also been condemned as unworthy of trafic in Puritan estimation.

The revenue to be raised by this act, estimated as about to yield $150,000,000, was a burden greater than was borne by the citizens of the most despotic governments of Europe; and yet so thoroughly deluded were the masses of the people by abolition fanaticism, that they seemed to yield their necks with pleasure to the burdens. But after submitting to the load, they ever afterwards were unable to relieve themselves; and the despots only continued to further lade the servilely adapted beings who had so ignobly yielded to their sway. They had unwittingly assumed a constantly accumulating load of debt, which, as Wen-

*_Congressional Globe_, Second Session, 37th Congress, Part 2, p. 1309.

dell Phillips, one of the task masters, had the candor to admit, would weigh down themselves, their children and descendants, to remote generations. A happy thought, indeed; possibly endurable, had the compensation therefor only been of an adequate character. But it is doubtful if fanaticism be competent to grasp that idea. Probably the conception is too logical, save for minds rarely seduced by fanatical delusions.

An inquisitorial spirit also displayed itself in the radical legislation of almost every character. The bill passed by Congress and approved July 1st, 1862, which stamped the Mormon matrimonial unions as criminal violations of social polity that deserved severe punishment, especially evinced this spirit in a marked degree. Lack of logical perception allowed the law-givers in this instance to forget that they were the boasted champions of liberty, both civil and religious, and being such, Mormondom was equally entitled with themselves to enjoy that privilege. But like their prototypal predecessors of the Hildebrandian and Cromwellian cast, they reserved to themselves the right to dictate what should be esteemed liberty. And in this they were not inconsistent with themselves, for fanaticism ever assumes the holiest mantle, much as it tramples, as in this case, upon the plainest constitutional guarantees.

But whilst trampling upon the Constitution of their country, it behooved the Republican leaders likewise to bid for popular support at the expense of governmental traditions, and by the most lavish and prodigal expenditures. After the enactment of the Homestead Law in 1862, an Act in conflict with the conservative teaching of early legislators, they must annul the well settled internal improvement principles of former Presidents and statesmen, in the passage of the Union Pacific Railroad and Telegraph Line, from the Missouri River to the Pacific Ocean. Indeed, a seemingly malicious zeal appeared to animate Mr. Stevens and the leading radicals in Congress, to effect in every particular as complete an overthrow and removal of the rubbish of the old constitutional edifice of the fathers, as was possible to be conceived. The existing Constitution, with its spirit and traditions, had been the work of slave holders and their allies; and all this must be remodelled, lest some foul taint might soil the new superstructure.

An oath to support the Federal Constitution, the only pledge heretofore required of the American citizen or ruler, was no longer deemed a sufficient guarantee of official incumbents, that they would discharge their functions with that fidelity which duty required. Pretended dread of future turbulence induced the revolutionary Congress to exact of *every person elected or appointed to any office of honor or profit under the Government of the United States* an oath of office, to which no conscientious Southern resistant of the abolition tyranny would be able to subscribe. This unwise effort to exclude from public trusts the participants in the so-called rebellion in the event of their overthrow, was still further proof that the advocates of such measures lacked the capacity of far-seeing statesmen, who always strive to harmonize, rather than provoke conflicting opinions. But artifice and craft were the large ingredients that influenced the partisan legislation of the last named character, and which was designed chiefly to exclude in future from power, those most competent to combat and circumvent the designs of the revolutionary legislators themselves.

A legal principle of universal application that had been coined in the jurisprudence of the mother country; and which in essence was made a part of the Constitution of 1787; and also of all the different States of the Union, that every offender shall be tried by a jury of his peers, was next to be wiped from the statute book of the nation. By the Act of July 16, 1862, Congress, fearful to run in open violation of the plain letter of the Constitution, which declared that in treason the "*trial shall be held in the State where the said crimes shall have been committed,*" nevertheless repealed the Act of 1789, which required, in cases punishable with death, that twelve jurors be summoned from the county where the offense was committed. In the repeal of that act, the spirit of the Constitution was equally violated, as had the enactment directed, that a jury drawn from a different State than that in which the offense was committed, should be intrusted with the trial of criminals. Such legislation was also the product of necessity, as the revolutionists clearly foresaw that no convictions for treason could be secured in any of the Southern States, unless under a species of packed jury system, which this law of July aimed to establish.

During the second session of the Thirty-seventh Congress, the confiscation of the property of rebels, became a question of leading importance; and one that was discussed in both Houses at some length. The ardent advocates of confiscation were impelled solely by the desire to secure the emancipation* of the negro slaves by an indirect measure of this character; as no other so feasible a plan presented itself to the revolutionists to secure, under the guise of legislation, objects not warranted by the Constitution. Senator Wilson, of Massachusetts, had the candor to confess, during the discussion of this question, that emancipation was the main feature of the confiscation movement that especially interested him. Sufficient laws were already in existence to punish treason of every grade; and it would have been time to enact further penalties when the rebellion was overthrown and the national authorities in condition to determine of what crime the Southern rebels were guilty.

But as the freedom of the Southern slaves was the grand object of the war, and as the Constitution of the United States forbade Federal interference with the affairs of the States, some kind of legislation must be excogitated to gratify abolition aspiration. The punishment of treason was within the power of Congress to determine; and this body was free to fix penalties, however severe, provided that "no attainder of treason shall work corruption of blood and forfeiture, except during the life of the person attainted." The framers of the instrument which interposed this check upon national legislation, had witnessed in history the cruel excesses of sanguinary despots from the days of William the Norman, to Oliver Cromwell; and they were unwilling that the innocent descendants of convicted traitors should be made to suffer for the crimes of their ancestors. Whilst, however, this restraint was the result of the molifying current of a refined civilization that had gradually obliterated the asperities of earlier epochs, it was this same obstacle that produced such anxiety in the Republican party to devise means, notwith-

*Senator Saulsbury, of Delaware, addressing the Abolition Senators, June 24th, 1862, said: "Your purposes are known,—your motives are understood. The present knows them and history will record them. Did not slavery exist in the Southern States, you would never have thought of a confiscation bill. Your design is to make this a war for the destruction of slavery. You desire to destroy the domestic institutions of the States. Abolitionism will be satisfied with nothing less than universal emancipation; and abolitionism would not prosecute this war another day or another hour, were it not for the hope that these objects may be accomplished."—*Congressional Globe*, Second Session, 37th Congress, Part 4, p. 2901.

standing this, to accomplish their main purpose, emancipation.

To this end, one bill after another was prepared by abolition members of both Houses of Congress, all having the same fond object in view. C. A. Wickliffe, of Kentucky, spoke in the following manner of these bills:

"The Chairman of this Committee, to whom had been referred all the wild, mad and unconstitutional bills, twenty in number, has given to the House the two bills under consideration. I have carefully collected all of these bills. I shall have them bound, and with an appropriate title-page preserved, that they may remain and be read after the excitement of the day shall have subsided; that those who may survive me shall take warning from the evidences which they afford, of an utter disregard of the Constitution of the country, and the danger to civil liberty which such disregard threatens. And if our liberty and constitutional Government shall survive the assaults made upon it at this hour, or if it should fail, then they may find among the many causes of its overthrow, these evidences of the reckless efforts of legislators to substitute passion for patriotism, as a rule of action, in the exercise of official duties and powers." *

Horace Greeley, in his history of "*The American Conflict*," speaks of the cautious method by which the Republican party approached the question of confiscation:

"The policy of confiscating or emancipating the slaves of those engaged in the rebellion, was very cautiously and timidly approached at the first or extra session of this (37th) Congress. Very early in the ensuing session, it was again suggested in the Senate by Mr. Trumbull, of Illinois, and in the House by Mr. Elliott, of Massachusetts."†

The position which first secured a somewhat unanimous approval amongst the revolutionary leaders in both Houses of Congress, was that which asserted for the military arm of the Government, the right to break the shackles from the limbs of the Southern slaves in order to weaken the cause of their masters. This bold and sweeping advance of the extreme Abolitionists was altogether too radical a change for timid and conservative Republicans; and the proposition besides encountering the united opposition of the Border State Congressmen and Northern Democrats, also met a warm resistance from Senators Cowan, of Pennsylvania, Browning and Collamer, of Vermont, who denounced it as in glaring antagonism with the Federal Constitution. Out of the boiling caldron of radical Senatorial views, a bill was prepared which proposed to clothe President Lincoln with

* Appendix to *Congressional Globe*, Second Session, 37th Congress, p. 260.
†Greeley's Conflict, vol. 2, p. 262.

discretionery power to proclaim free, the slaves of all persons who should be found in arms after a definite period.

In the House, a similar vehement contest was fought, over the question of confiscation of rebel property; and finally, two bills were reported from the Judiciary Committee that seemed to accord in the main with the known sentiments of radical Senators. The one provided for confiscating the real and personal property of rebels against the government; and the other for the emancipation of their slaves. In vain did the Democrats, Border State Representatives, and certain Conservative Republicans, argue the unconstitutionality of these measures; and to no purpose were they shown to violate all the principles of modern warfare among civilized nations. Judge Thomas, of Massachusetts, a Conservative Republican, spoke of these bills as follows:

"That the bills before the House are in violation of the law of nations and of the Constitution, I cannot—I say it with all deference to others—I cannot entertain a doubt."*

But though unconstitutional and violative of all modern international codes, the revolutionists must of necessity enact laws of the most extreme rigor against the rebels and their property; so that under the pretence of wholesale confiscation, they would be enabled to secure the great prize, the freedom of the slaves. No doubt many members of Congress, such as Thaddeus Stevens, Owen Lovejoy, and others, would ardently have desired to see the most extensive confiscation of rebel property that was possible to be secured; but the honest Abolitionists, who were influenced by moral principle, rather viewed the proposed severity in the confiscation movement as a feint to cover the real object to be grasped, emancipation. At least it was never seriously believed by any great number of Abolition Congressmen, that they would be able to inflict upon the South any general system of property confiscation. The measure, however, proved admirable for agitating purposes, and in the preparation of public opinion for partisan objects.

Both the Confiscation and Emancipation Bills introduced into the House, passed that body but failed to meet the approbation of the Senate. Although this latter body contained a large number of the most radical Abolitionists, still a majority were unwilling to go to the extreme length of enacting that all kinds

*Greeley's Conflict, vol. 2, p. 264.

of property should be wrested from rebel control without judicially action, and by the mere force of Executive fiat. The bills which had received the approbation of the one body of Congress, were upon a conference between the Senate and House of Representatives, so modified as to form one act providing for both confiscation and emancipation. In this shape the bill became a law and received the Presidential assent.

The main feature which the Senate impressed upon the confiscation scheme, was that which contemplated the conviction and punishment of traitors by due legal process, before their property could be legally sequestered. And yet little credit seems due to Senators who preferred to have the enactment in conformity with the Constitution in one particular, when in another they were not at all careful to regard it. For it was alone the knowledge that the assent of President Lincoln would otherwise be withheld from the bill, that induced Congress, very reluctantly, to declare by resolution that the act was only intended to operate upon the life interest of convicted traitors.

CHAPTER XVIII.

GOVERNMENTAL CONSOLIDATION REACHED.

When the Thirty-seventh Congress met on December 1st, 1862, the Government had thrown aside all disguise that its future policy should embrace emancipation as a means of weakening the rebellion. President Lincoln had seemingly permitted himself to be dragooned, by his active abolition partisans, into fulminating the proclamation of September 22d, which, by the beginning of the new year, should set all the slaves in the rebellious States in absolute freedom; and yet a more unwise measure for the accomplishment of that object was scarcely conceivable, as the President himself expressed it, in his interview with the Chicago divines, a few days prior to its promulgation. It could scarcely be believed, even by the most enthusiastic champions of negro liberation, that a paper proclamation, issued by the Executive of one of the contesting sections of the country, would be able to emancipate the slaves of the other more rapidly than the progress of arms warranted. But fanaticism reasons not, it sympathises, agitates, and runs counter to the rules of ratiocination: and in this instance, having engulphed philosophical forecast in clamor, it could do what at another time would have been utterly impossible.

The enactment of a few measures were still demanded of the American Congress, in addition to the numerous unconstitutional encroachments already made, in order that the consolidating programme of the revolutionary party might have a finished and symmetrical contour. The union of the purse and sword, a necessity of despotism, was the grand desideratum yet to be accomplished in the subversion of the rights of the States and of the immunities of the people. The traditionally recognized power of the States must be overthrown by every possible means, and no conceivable method seemed to promise greater results in this direction than the establishment of a national banking system. A national bank was one of the darling projects of Alexander Hamilton, the idol of Federalism and its successors; and in the history of American politics it proved one of the onerous burdens that always weighed upon the shoulders of those who favored its establishment.

And although a National bank had ceased to be a question in American politics since the period of John Tyler's administration, yet with the advent of Republicanism to power, the new brood soon betrayed their parentage in the advocacy of the old measures which Webster himself had declared obsolete. So thoroughly grounded, however, had become the opposition of Americans towards a bank of the United States, that the establishment of an institution of this character was deemed hazardous; and was only attempted after the leaders had discovered that the will of the people could with safety be defied, with large armies in the field from which all information dangerous to party success, could easily be excluded. And again, for the purpose of avoiding the popular objections which stood coined in the general mind against the establishment of a national bank, the scheme was varied by proposing a bill to incorporate banks in all sections of the country. A very captivating variation, indeed, was it, and one promising popular advantages to business circles. The danger of a national bank proving a political engine in the hands of whatever party might happen to control the Government, the main evil foreseen by President Jackson was equally great, whether one central establishment were created or thousands of banks with national privileges, because the latter, equally with the former, would be subordinate to federal control.

The establishment of a system of national banks, was believed by the revolutionary leaders to be one of the most efficient means to subvert the rights of the States, and draw all authority into the hands of the General Government. In this manner it was hoped that objects could be grasped by a species of monarchical encroachment, which otherwise were unattainable; and that a grand central government, nearly resembling that of Great Britain, could be established in the midst of the turbulence and excitement of the rebellion. Indeed, Alexander Hamilton himself had predicted that the Federal Government would prove a failure; and that it would only, after a time, be molded into consistency when it should have experienced the shock of war.

That Federal aspirations prompted the warm advocates of the national banking scheme, seems disclosed in the following extract from the speech of Elbridge G. Spaulding, a Republican Representative from New York, of February 19th, 1863. Mr. Spaulding said:

"It is now most apparent that the policy advocated by Alexander Hamilton, of a strong central government, was the true policy. A strong consolidated government would most likely have been able to avert the rebellion; but, if not able to prevent it entirely, it would have been much better prepared to have met and put down the traitorous advocates of secession and State rights, who have forced upon us this unnatural and bloody war. A sound national bank upheld and supported by the combined credit of the Government, and rich men residing in all the States of the Union, would have been a strong bond of union before the rebellion broke out, and a still stronger support to the Government in maintaining the army and navy to put it down."

The national banking system deduced its whole genealogical descent from monarchical principles. Its successful inauguration depended upon the suppression of the State banks, which existed constitutionally, as the Supreme Court of the United States had authoritatively declared; and which the General Government had no delegated power, either directly or indirectly, to suppress. But, when men could be found that had the boldness openly to declare that Congress had the right to appoint a dictator, as Thaddeus Stevens had already done, it is not strange that any kind of bill could be enacted depriving the States of their clear and constitutional authority to establish banks with State charters. During the discussion on the National Bank Bill, the right of the States to create banks was not questioned; but a sufficient tax was imposed in the bill upon the circulation of the State banks, as would compel them to exchange their notes for the new ones to be issued by the General Government. It was, in brief, simply a new method of indirectly doing that which the Constitution, as interpreted by the highest judicial tribunal of the country, had forbidden to be done.

The National Banking Bill met the approval of the most revolutionary Republicans of both Houses of Congress; and received the sanction of President Lincoln February 25th, 1863. It encountered, however, the united opposition of the Democracy and of a considerable number of the more conservative Republican Members of Congress, in the Senate and House of Representatives. In the Senate, such Republicans as Collamer, Cowan,

Grimes, Howard and Trumbull, refused to support the measure.

The Democrats in general viewed the bill as one of the consolidating measures designed to wrest power from the States and strengthen the central authority. Senator Powell, in his speech of February 10th, 1863, said:

"It is a grand scheme of consolidation; one that, in my judgment, will become dangerous to the public liberties, and I believe that it should not be forced upon the people of the States, particularly when it is forced there to destroy their banking institutions."

Senator Davis, in his speech of February 11th, said:

"This is a bold and daring attack upon the State banks. * * * I think it is the most stupendous and most dangerous scheme of policy that was ever introduced in a deliberative body."

That the National Bank Bill was of an altogether revolutionary character, Senator Howard contended in his speech of February 11, 1863, in which he used the following language:

"It contemplates a general revolution in the banking and currency system in this country; and it is admitted by its advocates as being intended to bring about an extinguishment of all the State banks by means of the machinery which is to be employed under the provisions of the bill."

The unconstitutionality of the bill was argued by Senator Collamer as follows:

"In the case of Kentucky, the Supreme Court decided, that the long continued usage in this country in States to make banks was constitutional, and that a State had a right to make a bank of issue. * * * Now, sir, if a State has that right, it has the right certainly, independent of the consent of Congress. Does it hold it at the will of Congress? Certainly not. The United States, in making a United States Bank, held it independent of State action, and it was so decided. If the State has this right and has it independent of the consent of Congress, it cannot have that right if the United States can tax it out of existence. Hence, I say, the United States have no more power to tax a State institution out of existence, than a State has to tax a United States institution out of existence."

The Federal Government, by the passage of the bank bill, had become the keeper of the people's purse; the sword must next be grasped, and then the power of the States and the citizens thereof could with impunity be defied. Men, as well as money were in abundance for a period, after the inauguration of the war, in answer to the calls of the President; but time disclosing the great deception that had been practised, neither could any longer be had in such quanties as the exigency demanded.

Congress, at its extra session in 1861, had given authority for raising vast armies; and all the soldiers whose services could be secured were enlisted under various proclamations of the President, but still more were in demand to end a rebellion whose resistance had far surpassed the popular expectation. But the Republican method of filling monarchical armies raised for monarchical purposes, soon displayed its incongruity as had been witnessed on the financial arena, and new plans were necessary to be adopted to save the revolutionary party from disintegration, and its aims from failure, should a majority of the Northern people discover the delusion that had been inflicted upon them.

By the middle of 1862, Northern patriotism was greatly flagging, because enlisting for the war was already discovered to be no holiday recreation, but a stern reality that few cared to encounter, save those whom fancied sympathy for the negro had blinded into the espousal of the abolition cause. It was now perceived that the war steed of Northern patriotism must experience a slight goad from the spur of his furious rider, in order to enable him any longer to penetrate to the front of the battle, and grapple with his rebel combatant upon the field of Southern conflict. This slight prick was essayed in the passage of the Act of Congress of July 17th, 1862, which authorized the calling out by draft of the militia of the loyal States for nine months, for the suppression of the Southern armies, and the restoration of the national authority.

But the rebellion against abolition domination, notwithstanding this, stood up in all its mighty strength and colossal magnitude. The enlisted legions of the North, from Maine to California, were sinking before the shafts of Southern resistance; and the invading armies had become so attenuated by the close of 1862, that more stringent means than had as yet been made use of, must be employed if the administration of Abraham Lincoln was to triumph over its stubborn foe. The might of Herculean despotism must be invoked to the rescue, or the flag of abolitionism must lower its folds on the field of battle. Neither the war cry of freedom for an enslaved race, nor the peans of the victorious soul of the felon of Charlestown, marching to victory, were sufficient any longer to arouse martial ardor in the breasts of the enrolled soldiers of Northern fanaticism.

The loathsome beast of despotic innovation now reared a more hideous aspect than it had as yet presented. An act was passed in both Houses of Congress ignoring all authority of the States over their own militia; and subjecting all able-bodied men of the North, between certain ages, to a merciless conscription, which found sanction neither in constitutional warrant nor in prior Anglo-Saxon history. Britain's Annals were scanned in vain for a model to subject to Presidential control the independent freemen of the North; and resort was necessarily had to the continental despotisms of the old world, which alone were able to supply a genuine copy. Charles J. Biddle, a Member of Congress from Pennsylvania, in his speech of February 23, 1863, grouped the Conscription Bill as one of that concatenation of measures which changed the whole fabric of the Government from a Republic into a consolidated despotism. In his speech he said:

"This (the Conscription Bill) is a part of a series of measures, which to my mind seem materially to alter the structure of the Government under which we live. The bill to transfer to the President, without limitation of time or place, our power over the writ of *Habeas Corpus;* the bill of indemnity which, to use the words of the Senate's Amendment, secures for all wrongs or trespasses committed by any officer of the Government, full immunity, if he pleads in the courts of justice the order of the President, and which also deprives State Courts of their jurisdiction in such cases; the bank bill, which puts the purse strings in the same hands with the sword; these bills, to my mind, couple themselves with this bill, and they seem to me, taken together, to change the whole framework of this Government; and instead of the Constitutional Government, which was originally so carefully devised for this country, they leave us a system which does not materially differ, according to any definition I can frame, from the despotism of France or Russia."

The passage of the Conscription Bill was found to be indispensable, because the abolition leaders perceived that the prosecution of the war, by means of enlisted soldiers, would surely prove a failure. Thaddeus Stevens, the Corypheus of abolition impulse, in the House of Representatives already had declared on the floor of Congress, that no more volunteers could be had from the North; and that other methods of filling the Union armies must be adopted. Vast numbers of soldiers who had voluntarily entered the Northern armies, afterwards deserted; some because they believed the Administration had forsaken the principles upon which the war was originally prosecuted; others did so, infected by the corrupt influences already everywhere prevalent.

Benjamin F. Thomas, a Republican member of the House,

from Massachusetts, submitted his reasons for the necessity of enacting the Conscription Bill, in the following language. He said:

"The policy inaugurated on the 1st of December, 1861, has been fruitless of good. It has changed the ostensible, if not the real issue of the war. That policy, and the want of persistent vigor in our military counsels, render any further reliance upon voluntary enlistments futile. The nostrums have all failed. Confiscation, emancipation by Congress, emancipation by proclamation of the President, compensated emancipation, arbitrary arrests, paper made legal tender, negro armies will not do the work. Nothing will save us now but victories in the field and on the sea; and then the proffer of the olive branch, with the most liberal terms of reconciliation and re-union. We can get armies in no other way, but by measures substantially those in the Bill before us, unless the Administration will retrace its steps and return to the way of the Constitution."*

The Democrats and Border State men of both Houses of Congress combatted the Conscription Bill with a zeal and ardor worthy of Charlemagne's paladins, and the knights of feudal history. But the conflict waged by these chivalric friends of their country in behalf of liberty and the Constitution, was nevertheless hopeless; yet, impelled by motives of uncalculating patriotism, they rushed within the breach and yielded themselves, sacrifices worthy of immortal glory. Senator Bayard, of Delaware, in his speech of February 28, 1863, used the following language concerning the Conscription Bill:

"From the foundation of the Government to this day, no attempt has been made in this country to pass a law of this character, by any Congress of the United States; no such bill has been introduced; no such doctrine as is involved in this bill has been contended for—that under the power to raise armies, you can raise them in any other mode than by enlistment or recruiting, or by the acceptance of volunteers. Has this power ever been attempted to be exercised by the Parliament of Great Britain, with all its omnipotence? No!"

Senator Kennedy, of Maryland, in the debate on this bill, said:

"As to the bill itself, I look upon it as odious and despotic. It goes further to subjugate the people of a free country than any I have ever read of in history."

Senator Saulsbury, of Delaware, during the same debate, uttered the following sentiments:

"I regard it as the crowning act, in a series of acts of legislation, which surrender all that is dear to the private citizen into the keeping and at the mercy of the Executive of this nation. * * * I assert, that under the law governing this administration, under the law

---

**Annual Cyclopedia*, 1863, p. 286.

as declared by the highest law officer of this Government, this bill not only authorizes the calling into the service of every able-bodied white man, but it authorizes the calling into the service of every able-bodied free negro, between the ages of twenty and forty-five, in the land. I say this because the Attorney-General of the United States has expressed the opinion, in writing, that the free negroes are citizens of the United States. * * * Sir, if the theory of this bill be the theory of your Government, if this be the power conferred upon Congress by the Constitution of the United States, tell me where is the difference between your form of Government and the most absolute and despotic form upon the face of the earth."

The Conscription Bill received the assent of President Lincoln March 3d, 1863, and contrary to the patriotic wish of the older statesmen, the power of the purse and the sword was united. The passage of the National Bank and Conscription Bills effected a complete revolution in the workings of the General Government, and though retaining the name of a Republic, no Empire in Europe now exerted a more absolute and despotic control over its citizens.

Absolutism had been reached in the passage of these two last named bills; but to round the figure more in harmony with Asiatic despotisms, all the unconstitutional excesses that had been committed since the advent of the Republican party to power must be condoned, and unlimited authority granted to the Federal Executive to trample in future upon civil liberty. It was not enough to satisfy the abolition appetite that the Constitution had been ignored, the reserved rights of the States overthrown, and the liberty of the citizen set aside; all these flagrant violations of right must be justified by an American Congress, intoxicated with the fumes of fanatical zeal and revolutionary incendiarism. It was a dark period in our history, when an assemblage of enthusiastic emancipationists had under deceptious colors stolen their way into the seats of representation in the National Capitol, and at length had it in their power to repudiate all the traditions of the anterior epochs of the Republic, and desecrate the holiest sanctuaries of the people.

Thaddeus Stevens, the cool, calculating demagogue, like his prototype, Cardinal Wolsey, paying hypocritical adoration at the shrines of zealous humanitarianism, on the 8th of December, 1862, brought into the Lower House of Congress a bill to indemnify the President and other persons for suspending the privilege of the writ of *Habeas Corpus*, and acts done in pursuance thereof. Up to this period it would have been difficult to have discovered in the utterances of the real or pretended emancipation zealots, with a few exceptions, that anything had been done by the President and Cabinet, or by any of their numerous subordinates throughout the country, that was not in strict accordance with the Constitution and the laws of Congress heretofore enacted. Had not an obsequious Attorney-General convicted the Chief-Justice of the Supreme Court of the United States of error, when the latter decided that the suspension of the *Habeas Corpus* was the perogative alone of the Federal Congress? Had not the revolutionary party by their representatives in both the United States Senate and House fully endorsed that view of constitutional interpretation, and acted in entire conformity therewith? Had not, again, a partisan press throughout the North, echoed the above sentiments to the eclat, and hurled anathemas and opprobrium upon the heads of those, who had the boldness and honesty to stand up and question the right of the President and his subordinates to suspend the *Habeas Corpus*, and do whatever else they might deem advantageous in furtherance of the abolition cause? Tomes would be required to contain all the labored arguments that filled to satiety the Northern press, designed to prove the entire constitutionality of the many violations of civil liberty, that were inflicted upon the citizens of the loyal States, and which would have driven to revolution the people of the most despotic governments of Europe; and could only have been perpetrated with impunity upon degraded serfs by the Ghengis Khans and Tamerlanes of history.

But the introduction and party support of the Indemnity Bill to a philosophical mind, was clear and palpable proof of the conscious falsity of the abolition reasoning, which claimed to find support for the infractions of the Constitution in that instrument itself. Mr. Stevens was far too clear in his perceptions to be deluded into the belief, that any sanction could be found in the Constitution for many acts to which he himself had freely given his adhesion. In supporting the admission of West Virginia, he had declared that there was no constitutional warrant for such action; but contended that the measure was justified by the exigency of the times. On many other occasions he had expressed similar sentiments, defending his views nevertheless by political necessity, and not by any authority to be found in the Federal

Constitution. At the beginning of the session of this Congress, he even had the boldness to declare upon the floor of the House, that he "had grown sick of the talk about the Union as it was, and the Constitution as it is."

The bill of indemnity, as it passed the lower House of Congress, led by Mr. Stevens, was too open a repudiation of the Constitution to receive the unqualified approval of a more cautious Senate. This body, the majority of whom were equally desirous to enact a bill of general oblivion for all the illegal and unconstitutional acts of the President, Cabinet, and all the inferior subordinates of the administration, was nevertheless more guarded in endeavoring to have its legislation apparently to conform with the words of the Federal Constitution, so far as the same could be made to do so. Senator Collamer, of Vermont, took grounds of opposition to the constitutionality of the Indemnity Bill, passed by the House, and prepared a substitute for it, which was reported by the Judiciary Committee of the Senate on the 27th of January, 1863. The main feature of the Senator's Substitute was that it provided for the removal to the Circuit Courts of the United States of all actions commenced, or to be commenced in the State Courts against persons who had violated the individual rights of their citizens. This was simply an indirect method of reaching, as far as possible, the same objects sought by the Indemnity Bill of Mr. Stevens, that is to say, absolute immunity for all the past and future unconstitutional acts of the Federal administration and its satellites. It was perceived that were authority granted to remove actions from a State into a Circuit Court of the United States, the judges and jurors of which were the menials of Federal power, the absolute oblivion of these actions was well nigh reached. Whilst this bill was before the Senate, James A. Bayard, of Delaware, expressed his views of the measure in the following language:

"With the solitary exception of an amendment, proposed by the Honorable Senator of Ohio, which was originally rejected and afterwards adopted, there is nothing in the bill that does ought than advance us towards a despotic exercise of power. It refers not only to the past, but to the future action of the Executive of the United States, and it throws a shield over every act of aggression that he can commit against the rights of an American citizen ; and interposes a bar, in point of fact, to the right of recovery against even the individual who is the agent for the purpose of infracting those rights. * * * They (the friends of the measure) will have, by the passage of this bill, brought the legislative power into accord with the Executive, so as to prevent for past action and for future action of the Executive, any redress on the part of an American citizen, however great the outrage may have been. In my judgment, it would have been better to pass the House Bill. That is a plain, open, manly defiance of the Federal Constitution. This is more indirect. It is in some respects sustainable; but I trust that in others, when it comes to the criterion of the Courts, it will be adjudged to be void and of no effect. It is useless to particularize now; but whether it be done under cover of law, and whether it be sustained or not, it is, in my belief, equally true that the passage of the bill is but an advance towards a centralized despotism in this country."*

The Senate bill having passed that body, came up in the House on the 18th of February, for consideration. Mr. Voorhees, of Indiana, spoke at considerable length in opposition to the measure. He said:

"SIR:—The bill now before the House has no parallel in the history of this or any other free people. It is entitled '*An Act to indemnify the President and other persons for suspending the privilege of the Writ of Habeas Corpus, and acts done in pursuance thereof.*' But it embraces even more than its startling title would indicate. It gives to the Executive and all his subordinates, not merely security for crimes committed against the citizen in times past, but confers a license to continue in the future the same unlimited exercise of arbitrary power, which has brought disgrace and danger to the country. I propose, to the best of my ability, this day to show that neither indemnity for the past nor impunity for the future can be bestowed on those who have violated, and who propose further to violate the great and fundamental principles of constitutional liberty."

After an extended debate in the House, the Senate's Substitute was rejected, and a Committee of Conference was appointed. This Committee reported a bill, which embodied a compromise of views between the two Houses; but which to the unobservant seemed to embrace new matter. One section of this Compromise Bill authorized the President, at any time during the rebellion, and when in his judgment required, to suspend the privilege of the writ of *Habeas Corpus* throughout the United States or in any part thereof. In another section, provision was made for removing into a Circuit Court of the United States any action "commenced in a State Court against any officer, civil or military, or against any other person for any arrest or imprisonment made, or other trespasses or wrongs done or committed, or

**Annual Cyclopedia*, 1863, p. 252.

any act omitted to be done, at any time during the present rebellion, by virtue or under color of any authority derived from or exercised by or under the President of the United States, or any Act of Congress."

The bill, as submitted by the Committee of the Senate and House of Representatives, met the approbation of the majority in both these bodies; and receiving the sanction of President Lincoln March 3d, 1863, became a law. This act completed the series of measures which completely changed the character of the Government from a confederation of States, into what history should entitle *the monarchically consolidated American Union.* With the enactment of this series, the legislative revolution was completed. The party of fanaticism had at length introduced their principles into the workings of the General Government; it next behooved them to sustain these upon the battle field, and thus carry forward and complete the social revolution, towards which they looked with anxiety.

The purse and the sword had now been grasped in one hand, and civil liberty, the birth-right of every American freeman, was wrested from its deposit, the Constitution, and committed to the keeping of Abraham Lincoln. This Chief Magistrate, whose oath demanded obedience to the Constitution and a faithful execution of the laws, though a guilty participant in the sacrilege of robbing his country's *Magna Charta,* became by the act of his criminal compeers, the repository of the sacred emblems of civil right, which anterior ages had bequeathed. Freedom ceased to be any longer what its name signified. From that period forward every American citizen possessed only such liberty us the Federal executive saw proper to accord him. The President had it in his power, by virtue of the act of Congress, to order the arrest and incarceration of any citizen in the broad arena of the Union; and no authority in the States or in the Federal Judiciary could withstand the dictator. His will, though feeble, was absolute, and that of the fiendish Nero and the tyrants of the French revolution was no more. These earlier despots were able to deprive of liberty whomsoever they chose; so could the American President.

Abraham Lincoln and his guilty associates in crime were voted by the Rump Congress entire immunity for all offences that any of them, under the guise of authority, had perpetrated, since the commencement of the rebellion, upon the persons and property of innocent and unoffending citizens; against whom no accusation could be preferred, save that they believed the abolition war policy to be unconstitutional and inimical to the principles of republics. But fortune, in her grant of imbecility, compensated for the grave error that a maddened and intoxicated people, in the midst of an appalling revolution, had committed. That beneficient goddess either had other duties for the American Union, or she wished in future to witness on the Western Continent, a chivalric combat of crown worthy heroes; for had Napoleonic will and ambition conjoined themselves with the powers of the Federal President, the days of the great occidental republic in name, even, would have been chronicled amongst the things of the past. The name was retained, however, because fear forbade its abandonment; but governmental consolidation in its fullness had been reached.

CHAPTER XIX.

DEMOCRATIC ANTI-WAR ATTITUDE.

Party ties, for a time, after the inauguration of hostilities against the South, seemed * to the unreflecting almost to have disappeared; but this was so in appearance, rather than in reality. A wave of deceived love for the Union swept over the North, and washed into the war current the masses of all political organizations, and large numbers of the Democratic leaders were also carried by the flood into an antagonism of sentiment to that which they and their party, prior to the attack on Fort Sumpter had advocated. In this rapid transit, from one school of political opinions to the opposite, we have a fair illustration of the manner in which modern pretended leaders are ready to abandon their principles and creed, when a storm of popular favor carries their opposing party bark into the port of triumphant victory.

But all those competent to think for themselves, and whose principles harmonized with the opinions that had been uniformly entertained by the representative men of the Democratic party, notwithstanding the popular clamor, remained attached to their sentiments; but from the necessity of the situation, they were either compelled to conceal their thoughts or run the risk of political martyrdom. Owing to the large desertion that had taken place in their ranks, the Democratic leaders that remained true their principles had become too few to be able to rally their followers into an opposition to the coercion doctrine of the abolition party. The cry for the Union drowned all the patriotic

* "There is, or has been quite a general impression, backed by constant and confident assertions, that the people of the free States were united in support of the war, until an Anti-Slavery aspect was given to it by the administration. Yet that is very far from the truth. There was no moment wherein a large portion of the Northern Democracy were not at least passively hostile to any form or shade of 'coercion;' while many openly condemned and stigmatised it as attrocious, unjustifiable aggression. And this opposition, when least vociferous, sensibly subtracted from the power and diminished the efficiency of the North."—Greeley's Conflict. Vol. 2, p. 513.

expostulation of those who endeavored to prove that a war against the South found no warrant in the Federal Constitution, or in the principles of an enlightened republican confederacy.

It soon seemed as if the war current was irresistible, and the large and cautious portion of those who believed the coercion policy to be unconstitutional, deemed it prudential to refrain from the utterance of their opinions, and thus the flood gates of war fury were permitted to open to their fullest extent. A small and resolute band, however, of bold and courageous freemen, members of the Democratic party and others antagonistic to ultra-abolitionism, declined to surrender all their sense of manhood and independence, and, without any hypocritical concealment of their opinions, steadfastly combatted the doctrine of coercion as wicked, anti-republican and unconstitutional, and one pregnant with future evils for the perpetuity of the free institutions of America. That war and bloodshed could unite in fraternal concord the two sections of the Union, now become inharmonious from a sectionalized antagonism of conflicting principles, appeared to this class of citizens as madness in the extreme. This class of Democrats was the only one deserving to be recognized as the followers of that party, which from the first endorsed the sentiments of the Virginia and Kentucky resolutions; and had such doctrines found no supporters even in the darkness of revolution, human nature on this occasion would have been convicted of a perfidy to principle unheard of in the annals of all anterior epochs.

The disintegration that had nearly penetrated to the core of the Democratic party, displayed itself in unmistakable colors when the war cry of abolitionism was heard throughout the length and breadth of the Republic. Men, who up to this period, had in words staunchly defended the cardinal principles of the old party of Jefferson, which denied to the General Government any power to compel by arms the people of a State to remain in a Union distasteful to them, at once changed their position and planted themselves under the banner of the coercionists.

And although the American people in appearance had divided the Northern against the Southern, a division, however, not of sections, obtained as the true one. On the one side were arrayed all those who, deducing their lineage from Federal and Tory ancestors, favored the employment of the war-power for the enforcement of the national will against the States and their people; and on the other were found those who denied that the General Government had ever been clothed by its framers with such august authority. The rebels in battle array were marshalled, ready to dispute the right of the Government to coerce by arms the people of any of the States, and they, like the anti-war party of the North, based their opinions upon the often endorsed Virginia and Kentucky resolutions of 1798–'9.* Dissemble the situation, therefore as we may, truth demands of the impartial historian the fair admission, that during the war of the rebellion but two real parties existed in the nation; the Southern Confederates and the Northern anti-coercion Democrats forming the one of these, and the unconcealed Abolitionists, who sincerely strove for the emancipation and elevation of the negro race, the other.

In former chapters, the hypocritical guise assumed by the political abolitionists, has been discussed at length; it now remains to be presented the false attitude likewise maintained, for selfish ends, by Democratic leaders, during the war; and to this deceptious position are due, in a large measure, the vast calamities that have been entailed upon the country, from an unholy and fiendish crusade of one section of the Union against the other. Had the influential Democrats of the Northern States boldly faced their political enemies upon the question of Southern subjugation, and sternly demanded that no men should be taken from any of the States for the wicked and unconstitutional purpose of crushing a kindred people, the demoniacal purpose of the fanatical party of Lincoln would have been foiled. Such a demand would have paralysed the power of the abolition administration, and prevented it from securing recruits for the vile object it was secretly plotting to accomplish, under the pretense of defending the Union. But, instead of asserting what justice and the principles of the Federal compact demanded, and resisting

* "From a period as early as 1798, there had existed in all the States a party almost uninterruptedly in the majority, based upon the creed that each State was in the last resort the sole judge, as well of its wrongs, as of the mode and measure of redress. * * * * The Democratic party of the United States repeated, in its successful canvas of 1836, the declaration made in numerous previous political contests, that it would faithfully abide by and uphold the principles laid down in the Kentucky and Virginia resolutions of 1798 and 1799, and that it adopts those principles as constituting one of the Main foundations of its political creed."—Special Message of Jefferson Davis of April 29, 1861.

the war and its prosecution; false and treacherous leaders within the Democratic organization, pretended that they were in favor of defending the national authority by arms, and compelling the obedience of the Southern States to the General Government. They confined their open opposition to contending that the war must be waged upon constitutional principles; whereas, it was clear to the mind of every conscientious and intelligent member of the Democratic party, that such a thing as a constitutional war against the Southern States was an utter absurdity; for the General Government possessed no further power than was conferred upon it by the Federal Constitution; and this instrument was silent as regarded any such authority.

The campaigns of 1861 were contested, seemingly without a political difference, both parties in the North advocating a most vigorous prosecution of the war against the South, in order that the restoration of the national authority might be effected. In some sections, certain Republicans united with the Democrats under the name of the Union party, and the resolutions of these in conventions, called for vigorous measures against the seceded States. The small party that found itself within the Democratic organization, was too feeble to make its voice heard in the party resolutions of county and State conventions.

In the resolves of Democratic conventions, the sentiment of the party might reasonably be supposed to have been indicated; but it was far from being so at this period. Like by its opponent, the Republican party, a false attitude was assumed by the Democratic party before the country, induced by a fear of popular opinion, which unmistakably had committed itself in favor of the war for the Union. The Republicans found it necessary to disguise the sentiments of all those in their party who sought to make the emancipation of slavery the direct object of the war against the South; and the Democrats deemed it also expedient for partisan effect to preserve as much as possible from disclosure the opinions of their independent men, who resisted from principle the prosecution of the war against the South. Both parties were thus false to their known creeds and antecedents, as was well understood by shrewd discerners of partisan opinions. From the first the political leaders of each party were able to detect the real sentiments of their adversaries. The Democrats accused the Republicans of designing negro emancipation, as their ultimate aim, which the latter stoutly denied; and on the other hand, the Republicans charged upon their opponents that they were in reality opposed to the war, though pretending to favor its prosecution; and this latter accusation was likewise vehemently denied. These accusations were indeed both well founded, as truthful history will be obliged to determine.

The Democrats of principle were opposed to the war, because it was an assumption by the General Government of an authority that had never been delegated to it. The States, as they viewed matters, having been originally Sovereign Commonwealths by their successful revolt against Great Britain, and their recognition as such in the family of nations, afterwards agreed to unite for commercial and other purposes in a general confederacy, in order that they might the better be enabled to defend their independence, and advance their happiness amongst the other nations of the earth. But the powers delegated by the States were clearly defined in the Constitution, and embraced only certain matters of a civil nature, which as the framers of the Government believed, could be better discharged by Federal than by State officials. The General Government, in this manner constituted, was simply as designed, the representative agent of the States, and in no wise clothed with authority to originally dictate to its component factors, the States themselves, the independent sovereignties, over all matters of government not clearly enumerated in the Federal bond of Union, the Constitution. The framers of the Federal Compact had discussed the question of granting the right to the central authority to coerce by force of arms the States, but this power they expressly refused to confer. In democratic eyes, therefore, what else could the war be, but an unwarranted exercise of unconstitutional authority.

Another reason that induced Democratic opposition to a war of subjugation, arose from the belief that all efforts of that kind, instead of cementing the antagonistic portions of the country, would simply widen the breach that had for years been forming between the people of the North and those of the South; and render a permanent Union of the two sections upon republican principles impossible. The history of the rise and fall of republics, and the philosophy of human nature, were sufficient to satisfy reflecting Democrats that the preservation of Governments, such as the American Union, must ever rest upon the free and unconstrained consent of the controlling minds of every community. This consent can alone be retained by that government which metes out equal and exact justice, according to the letter and spirit of its institutions, to all its component sections and their citizens. The Democratic party had ever done so whilst the reins of power were in their hands; and no serious revolt of any State ever raised its head during their administration of public affairs; and when dissatisfaction upon any occasion manifested itself, wisdom dictated to their representatives to remove the same, and this having taken place, peace instantly returned.

Again, the Democratic party could not approve of the war begun against the South, under the pretence of restoring the Union, when fully satisfied that other reasons formed the motives for its inauguration. Had they not read the declarations of Seward, Giddings, Burlingame, and other leaders, whose words clearly proved that negro emancipation, and that alone, was the secret that urged the Abolitionists to take up the cause of that same Union, which before this period had in their eyes been contemptible? If, argued the Democrats, the preservation of the Federal Union alone, influenced the Republican party in its movements, why did its representative men refuse all terms of compromise when offered by Southern statesmen; and at a time when this, as was admitted upon all sides, would have rescued the country from the bloody chasm into which abolition obstinancy and fanaticism were driving it? The party of reason and reflection could not be ignorant of all these facts; and when the war was made and prosecuted in violation of rectitude and a true and enlightened policy, was their approbation of the governmental iniquity to be expected? Not unless error and madness were to be canonized as truth. And would even true philanthropic motives have called for the emancipation of the Southern bondmen, the demand, nevertheless, would have forbidden war and bloodshed for the accomplishment of their freedom. For as Caucasian serfdom had perished in the different countries of Europe, before the advancement of a refining and Christian intelligence, without any revolutionary uprising; so also should the same influence, penetrating the Southern States themselves, have been permitted to remove African slavery without any obtrusive Northern intermeddling. Was then the Democratic party required to give its support to a war commenced in violation of all the principles of modern civilization? If it was not, what else, to be obedient to conscience, could sincere and intelligent members of the party of Jefferson in the North do, except to oppose to the utmost of their ability, the abolition war, as unconstitutional, unchristian, and altogether anti-republican in its aims and tendencies?

As the war against the South progressed, one occurrence after another revealed more clearly the changing programme of the administration party. The legislation of the first regular session of the Thirty-seventh Congress, disclosed to the eyes of thinking men that the overthrow of negro slavery, under the pretence of devotion to the Union, was fully resolved upon, by Republican leaders assembled at Washington and throughout the North. And as abolition approval became enthusiastic in its endorsement of the war and its changing schedule, so in like ratio did the Democratic party unite in a more solid phalanx of opposition to the anticipated designs of abolitionism.

In the different States of the North, an organized opposition in the Democratic party to the war, began first to display itself with intensity in the political campaigns of 1862; and yet no important convention of that party fully committed itself to an open denunciation of the war for the Union. The politicians who are ever upon the lookout for political ascendancy rather than for the success of principle, held in check those Democrats who would have had the party in its conventions to declare openly against the war, and brave to the utmost abolition malignity. An avowal by the Democratic party of its open repudiation of the war of invasion against the South, would have released it from its hypocritical attitute, and placed it in a position where its blows would have been more felt by its adversary. But in the base and ignoble condition in which it was placed by false leaders, men of honor and courage were unable to grapple successfully with their political opponents. How could men, thoroughly imbued with the belief that the war was unconstitutional, give a hearty support to candidates nominated upon a platform which called for the restoration of the Union by bloodshed, and for vigorous hostilities against the seceded States? They only did so as a choice of évils, convinced at the same time that the spirit of the Democratic party was repugnant to all coercive measures; and although the latter had been endorsed in their conventions, yet they felt that a cowardly policy alone had been instrumental in inducing their leaders to approve of such undemocratic principles.

The Democratic party went into the several State canvases, animated by hostility to the war, and thoroughly imbued with the conviction that the theory of the administration for the restoration of a Confederated Union was baseless and chimerical. The contest already having proved one of longer continuance than popular expectation had anticipated, was calculated to induce most of those who had originally favored compromise to support the principles and candidates of the Democratic party. A strong Northern tide of antipathy to the movements of abolitionism, had indeed been rising since the meeting of Congress, in December, 1861; and which continued to flow the more rapidly as the curtain of disguise continued from time to time to be lifted. The Presidential proclamation of September 22d, 1862, might seem to have produced a crisis of popular revulsion against the abolition policy, which showed itself in the anti-administration victories of the autumn of that same year.

The victories of this year, in the Northern States, recuperated somewhat the prostrate Democracy, and inflicted a slight blow upon the Republican administration, which was fruitful of benefit. Horatio Seymour, of New York, and Joel Parker, of New Jersey, were elected Governors of their respective States by considerable majorities. Pennsylvania, Ohio, Indiana and Illinois, were carried by the Democrats by small majorities on their State tickets. All these States sent heavier Democratic delegations to the Lower House of National Representatives, than were found in the Thirty-seventh Congress. Michigan, Wisconsin, and most other Western States, showed a decided falling off in administration strength.

It was natural that the result of the elections of 1862, should infuse a buoyancy of spirit into the breasts of the Northern Democracy; and many of them, forgetful of the platforms upon which their victory had been won, credited the growing anti-war sentiment of the people of their different States as the chief cause of their success. No doubt this sentiment was largely instrumental in keeping up the compact organization of the party; but the time had elapsed when the subjugationists, with vast armies in the field and the whole machinery of the National

Government at their command, could successfully be resisted. But the Peace Democrats of the Western States and elsewhere, emboldened, nevertheless, by the late successes, believed that the party could now be brought into an attitude of open resistance to the war; and, impressed with this conviction, they deemed it their duty to make the effort.

Besides, the Thirty-seventh Congress would have seemed to an indifferent spectator as if desirous of adding additional incentives to the Peace party, to resist the war of subjugation. For if ever a people should rebel against an ungodly and wicked faction having control of a Government, then the Northern people would have been fully justified in doing so at this period. But, notwithstanding the odious and unconstitutional legislation of this Congress, the people were found to be as slaves, utterly incapable of resisting the tyrannous despots, and the old party of law and order was still compelled to muzzle its utterances and stigmatize those resisting with arms the national tyranny, as traitors and assassins of liberty.

The anti-coercion sentiments of Benjamin Wood, one of the outspoken and independent peace Congressmen of the the North, which will ever reflect increasing lustre and glory upon his name throughout distant ages, are here given at considerable length; and this because they are typical of the views of those who from the first opposed the inauguaration of hostilities, and who ever afterwards continued to advocate a cessation of arms in order that reason might be left free to restore what fanaticism had disrupted. Mr. Wood, in his speech of February 27th, 1863, said:

"We can never by force of arms control the will of a people, our equals in the attributes of enlightened manhood; and while the will of that people remains adverse to political companionship with us, political companionship is impossible. Bloodshed, destruction of property and occupation of lands are possible; much suffering, grief and folly are possible; we have too sadly proved it; but a constrained union of Sovereign States is an impossibility, which if omnipotence could accomplish, omniscience would not attempt.

"I feel that upon the fresh, pure soil of the New World, we have thrown the seeds of discord, and they will take root. But while my experience and the testimony of our fathers through eighty-seven years of prosperity and progress, have well established my faith in the beneficence of a union of the States, I cannot understand that its blessings are of a nature to be enjoyed upon compulsion.

"But granting it possible, the question arises of equal moment, is it desirable? Has not the struggle already been too fierce to admit of unity and cordial feeling between a conquering and a conquered section? Sir, I fear it has; I believe that while the memory of this war exists, the people of the North and South, united by constraint, would not sufficiently forgive the past years' record to admit of kindly relationship in the same politcal household. Right or wrong, men will cling to their own impressions of a great and sanguinary struggle, in which they or their sires have been participants. As the living fathers of future generations this day feel, so will they bequeath to their children, and in natural course, the North and South will nurse their own seperate views of this unparalleled epoch of carnage and contention."

"Will the text book of history, conned by the boys of Massachusetts, serve hereafter in the school rooms of the Carolinas? Will the stories of Manassas, of Shiloh, of Antietam, of Fredericksburg, and of a hundred other battle fields, be told in the same spirit, Northward and Southward from the banks of the Potomac? Will the winter tales be similar when the youth of either section gather about the hearthstone, and feel the young blood tingle in their veins at the words of white haired heroes? Will the matrons of Louisiana train their offspring to venerate the name of Butler? Will the remembrances of Davis, Lee and Johnston be identical in New England and Virginia? No, sir, unless mutual consent should re-unite us, the pages of history and the words of tradition will breathe of the sympathies that now exist; and the generations to come will as surely be educated to distinct and opposite prejudices. The school-room, the pulpit and the press, would then, as now, inculcate doctrines that cannot assimilate; and in this Capitol, the representatives of the people would be the representatives of sectional antipathies. Sir, to avoid this, we must avoid inflicting the sting of submission, or engendering the pride of conquest.

"Our fathers gave us a Union founded on mutual consent, concession, and reciprocal attachment; we would entail upon our children, a political connection based upon hatred, suspicion, and opposing prejudices. A Nationality thus constituted, would be a mockery of republicanism and its bane; a political prostitution; the joining of hands before an altar whose divinity could attest the heart's irrepressible loathing and disgust. Had I the faculty to crush with one blow the material power of the South, I would not strike. My pride as an American would revolt at the thought of dragging them reluctant, hopeless, and spirit-broken into a fellowship that they abhor. Union restored by subjugation would be but the prelude to increasing altercation. It is not enough to affirm that I would not enforce the unnatural connection; sir, I would not consent to it. I would oppose it as a degredation to ourselves, an insult to our institutions, and a violation of the priciples of self-government. I would oppose it as an impediment to our national progress; as a perpetuation of discord and contention between States, and as involving either its own future dissolution, or the assumption by the General Government of military and despotic functions, fatal to republicanism. I confess, sir, that I apprehend no difficuities or misfortunes in the event of a separation at all commensurate with those that must inevitably prove the sequences of reunion by mere force of arms.

"I cannot conceive a happy, prosperous and republican Union, cemented by blood, remolded in repugnance, and prolonged by the submission of the weak to the dictation of the strong.

"A partnership in our Confederacy should be granted as a boon, and only to those that seek it; not enforced as an obligation upon those that ask it not. It should be held a privilege to be proud of, not an imposition to shrink from and protest against. Were I certain that, in a military sense, this war would prove successful, nevertheless I would oppose it; for with the destruction of the resisting power of the South, would vanish every hope of their existence as equal and contented members of one household.

"In my view this war, nominally for the Union, has actually been waged against it.

"But upon what foundation was the structure (of the Union) built? Sir, upon the free will of the people. Not of one State, or of one section, but of all the States and of all the sections. While that free will existed, the temple was of a nature to withstand the ravages of time. That free will has ceased to exist, and the temple has crumbled into dust. It is no more. It is a glory of the past. What you conceive to be the structure is but a memory, so intense that it seems reality; but the substance is not there. Rebuild it if you can; but you must first obtain the free will of the South which your armies and navies cannot secure.

"I have never voted a dollar for the war. As a legislator, as a citizen, and as a man, I claim to be absolved from all participation in this murderous strife. With all my humble abilities I have endeavored to arrest it. I shall still endeavor, and if in vain, let my efforts attest before God and man, that I am unstained with the blood of my countrymen.

"Sir, you may have observed that I have spoken without regard to the views of other men or the doctrines of political organizations. If I stand alone, my isolation conjures up no phantoms of doubt or fear. While my country groans beneath the stroke of her own dagger, I forswear all allegiance to party Whatever proposition in my mind shall enhance the prospect of peace shall have my vote. Peace is the goal of my political course—the haven of my hopes. I care not by whose chart I steer, or whose hand shall guide the helm, so that the compass shall guide thitherward. Whosoever shall raise its standards, shall find me ready to serve beneath its folds. Whosoever shall blazon the olive branch for his devise, shall have me his adherent. In whatever shape the demon of destruction shall appear, I will oppose him. In whatever garb the spirit of peace shall clothe her radiant form, I will embrace her. Conciliation, compromise or seperation, each shall be acceptable to me, if as its consequence, we shall be spared the scourge of war. Let the most zealous emancipationist suggest a cessation of hostilities, and I am with him. Let the staunchest member of the opposition uphold the war, and I am against him. I have no sympathies with those who denounce the Administration, and yet call for vigorous hostilities. In my view, the Abolitionist is a more honest politician and a more conscientious citizen. He is a fanatic—not a mere time server; wrong, but consistent in his wrong; the worshipper of a false God, but earnest in his adoration. Would that all who denounce him, were as sincere and as bold in the expression of their opinions." *

During February and March, 1863, the Peace Democracy began to assume a bolder position than they had as yet done; and the slurring epithet of *Copperheads*, from this period, was currently applied to them by their political enemies. Meetings of the Peace men were held in different sections of the country; and a large one in Mozart Hall, New York, was addressed by Fernando Wood and others of similar sentiments. Resolutions strongly denunciatory of the war were adopted by the Mozart Democracy.

The Democratic party of Connecticut, in the spring of 1863, placed in nomination for Governor, Col. Thomas H. Seymour, an early, consistent and outspoken opponent of the Abolition war; and the Convention which nominated him, adopted the following resolution:

"*Resolved*, That while we denounce the heresy of secession, as undefended and unwarranted by the Constitution, we as confidently assert, that whatever may heretofore have been the opinion of our countrymen, the time has now arrived when all true lovers of the Constitution are ready to abandon the "*monstrous fallacy*" that the Union can be restored

*Appendix to *Con. Globe*, 3d Session of 37th Congress, Part 2, pp. 134–5.

by the armed hand alone; and we are anxious to inaugurate such action, honorable alike to the contending sections, as will stop the ravages of war, avert universal bankruptcy, and unite all the States upon terms of equality as members of one Confederacy."

The war party now became more bitterly denunciatory of their political antagonists, than before, accusing them of a desire either to establish slavery throughout the North, or to disrupt the Union in the interest of the rebellion. It soon became evident that such abuse and vilification would be able to detract timid men from the support of the Peace party; and neutralize their strength by detaining them from the polls, or attract them to the support of those boasting themselves the Union party of the Nation. That the Peace Democracy would not be able successfully to contest with the party that already had seized the National purse and sword, become evident in the Connecticut campaign. Thomas H. Seymour was defeated and the peace movement crippled.

CHAPTER XX.

THE NEW ERA.

A new era of American affairs began with the 1st of January, 1863; this being the date of the emancipation edict, which proclaimed freedom to the negro slaves of the South. In this famous proclamation, President Lincoln boldly avowed the falsehood of his own former assurances of his constitutional inability and also his disinclination to interfere with the institutions of the seceded States*; and without any further disguise he declared that the future policy of the Government should embrace not alone the non-extension, but the entire removal of African Slavery. In more senses than one, therefore, did this constitute the commencement of a new era. It was impossible but that this proclamation emenating from the Chief Magistrate of the Nation, and clearly disproving his own former utterances and that of his party, should sanctify perfidy and breach of faith; and tend to enoble every form of treachery and corruption of which mankind are capable.

*"Apprehension seems to exist among the people of the Southern States, that by the accession of a Republican administration, their property and their peace and personal security are to be endangered. There has never been any reasonable cause for such apprehensions. Indeed, the most ample evidence to the contrary has all the while existed, and been open to their inspection. It is found in nearly all the public speeches of him who now addresses you. I do but quote from one of those speeches when I declare that I have no purpose, directly or indirectly, to interfere with the institution of slavery in the States where it exists. I believe I have no lawful right to do so, and I have no inclination to do so. Those who maintained and elected me did so, with full knowledge that I had made this and similar declarations, and had never recanted them. And more than this, they placed in the platform for my acceptance, and as a law to themselves and to me the clear and emphatic resolution which I now read.

"*Resolved*, That the maintenace inviolate of the rights of the States, and especially the right of each State, to order and control its own domestic institutions, according to its own judgment exclusively, is essential to the balance of power on which the perfection and endurance of our political fabric depend; and we denounce the lawless invasion by armed force of the soil of any State or Territory, no matter under what pretext, as among the grossest crimes."—Lincoln's Inaugural of March 4, 1861.

The new era being thus inaugurated in the promulgation of the final emancipation proclamation, the 37th Congress by the time of its termination, had so welded the chains of despotism, as to render the revolution complete and irreversible. The principles of the radical revolutionists, Sumner, Stevens, Lovejoy and others, which at first were seemingly repudiated utterly in Congress, now came forward and found party recognition, being sustained by a pretended popular opinion in the Northern States. The new era was especially significant in this, that legislation came to be molded by what showed itself, from a despotic suppression of opposing opinion, as the will of the majority.

The revolutionary leaders were sagacious and far seeing, and from an early period of the war, little doubt, even prior to its commencement, had planned the entire future policy of their party, which was to remodel the whole social system of the South as also of the North, should the might of numbers finally triumph over the defenders of the Constitution, and the principles of free government. Did not Charles Sumner offer his famous resolutions in the United States Senate, which declared the forfeiture of statehood by all the seceded members of the Southern Confederacy? and did he not do so at so early a day that his senatorial friends deemed it impolitic that they should commit the Republican party to their endorsement? Did not the radical Congressmen, from the first, oppose the admission of Representatives from the reclaimed sections of the South, out of fear for their favored State-suicide doctrine, which would territorialize the revolted States, and place them fully beneath the heel of their despotic power? Did Thaddeus Stevens, Bingham, of Ohio, Eliot, of Massachusetts, and certain other radicals in the House, vote for the admission of Flanders and Hahn as Representatives from the First and Second Districts of Louisiana, after the capture of the Crescent City by the Union army? Henry L. Dawes, himself a Republican, in his speech of February 17, 1863, showed the motive for the opposition to the admission of the Louisiana Representatives. He said:

"My own colleague (Mr. Eliot) has another remedy. These States, according to him, have destroyed themselves, and can re-enter the Union through the preparatory stage of Territorial Governments."

Again, the new era gave fresh impetus to the movement already begun of enrolling colored soldiers into the Northern armies. A few enthusiastic Union Generals had in the latter part of 1862, done everything in their power to impel the Washington authorities to determine to accept slaves and free negroes into the military service of the country; but President Lincoln and his advisers did not yet deem it prudent to take so important a step. until its entire safety in Northern public opinion might be premised. Fugitive slaves, had however, been accepted by several of these federal commanders, and at the same time with the knowledge of the Washington Administration. No express warrant to do so had as yet been given, and nevertheless negro regiments were recruited and daily drilled without any fear of rebuke from Abraham Lincoln or his Cabinet. These officers, however, well understood the spirit and tone of the Administration, and hence had no dread of any reprimands that might be inflicted, for they were fully assured that none such would be given by the President, unless in deference to opinions which he himself by no means cherished.

The revolutionary abolitionists had for some time been advocating the enrollment of negroes into the Union armies, and mainly in behalf of the future political equalization which they intended to advocate, should the overthrow of the rebellion be effected. With the new era, therefore, negro enrollment may be said to date its open approval by the National Administration. The President, in his Emancipation Proclamation, declared in language still somewhat guarded, that negroes should henceforth form a part of the military forces of the nation. He said:

"And I further declare and make known, that such persons of suitable condition will be received into the armed service of the United States to garrison forts, positions, stations and other places, and to man vessels of all sorts in said service.

The Abolitionists now conceived their victory as almost complete, since they, at length, had succeeded in having the Executive to declare before the nation that negro soldiers might be taken into the federal service. And, notwithstanding, in the cautious language which the President had made use of, he had scarcely committed himself beyond what was already granted in the Act of Congress of July 17, 1862. This Act had authorized the employment of negroes in constructing intrenchments, and in performing camp and other naval and military service, for which they might be found competent. Full equality in the military service, however, was not therein conceded, and Abraham Lincoln, though designing this equality, guarded his language so carefully, as that he should not appear before the country to be extending what in reality he meant to grant. His intentions, nevertheless, were fully understood by those of his friends and enemies, who were not deceived by words alone. But his ambiguous expressions admirably served the purpose of his political partisans, who were thus enabled to interpret them as exigencies might require.

The enrolling of negroes into the Union armies, which was so discouraged by the administration during the first and second years of the war, soon came now to be everywhere allowed. It was in accordance with what might readily have been surmised, that Massachusetts, the home of revolutionary republicanism, should be found to be the first place in the North to open its doors for negro recruiting. And the earliest upon record that invoked the privilege of doing so, was Governor Andrew, the prophetic Executive of the Bay State, who foresaw the streets and highways of his own Commonwealth crowded with soldiers, rushing to the battle's front, when the Presidential bugle of freedom should sound its blast throughout the land. This highly coveted privilege was accorded to the enthusiastic Chief Magistrate of the Old State of the Pilgrims, by Edward M. Stanton, Secretary of War, on the 20th of January, 1863.

And lest his characteristic timidity should deter Abraham Lincoln from allowing negro recruiting to be prosecuted with sufficient zeal in all sections of the Union, Thaddeus Stevens deemed it his duty to exert his utmost efforts to strengthen the Presidential nerves. It was the policy that Mr. Stevens had long desired to see inaugurated; and one which his fellow-members in Congress credited him as being the first to advocate upon the floor of the House. Long delay interposed, though wit and scorn gave frequent admonition of Presidential duty; but finally hesitation relaxed its hold. The decree had gone forth. And now others, perchance, might carry off the glory in equalizing the human races, should the leader of the House not conspicuously show himself the ardent champion of that movement which he had labored so faithfully to inaugurate.

His amendment of the 27th of January, to the bill before the House, to raise additional troops for the service of the Government, placed Mr. Stevens in full accord with the new era; and none need seek, after that exhibition of desire for negro equality, to snatch from Vermont's son the laurels he had so fairly won. From this period the name of *commoner* was fitly applied to the Lancaster statesman. But as the great orator of Kentucky, Henry Clay, also bore the same appellation, for distinction's sake in history, it will be well to entitle the younger statesman the *negro commoner*.

But this effort of Mr. Stevens, to raise negro soldiers, though it received the approbation of the Lower House of Congress, already quite obedient to his dictation, was deemed altogether needless, in the estimation of sagacious Senators. This highly learned body were unable to see any necessity for legislation, additional to what had been enacted in the preceding July. Senators contended that ample power had already been conferred upon the President to enable him to recruit negroes for any department of the land or naval service for which he might consider them competent. It might have been thought matter of surprise that these two *loyal* bodies should differ so widely as to the powers granted to the President, in regard to the enrollment of the negroes into the Union armies. Had no fears, however, been entertained as to the consequences of adopting the policy of the new era, it is apprehended that much greater harmony of sentiment would have prevailed between the Senate and House of Representatives. A clearly avowed negro equalizing and enlistment policy was yet dreaded by leading Republicans. Accordingly, the Thirty-seventh Congress adjourned, having its *role* of despotism finished and complete, but leaving as the mission of the new era to accomplish what reason discouraged, viz: *to equalize as soldiers and citizens the people of every race and clime.*

In view of the popular antipathy to the enrollment of African soldiers into the army, by far the most prudential method for the Government to pursue, was to permit the War Department to accord the privilege of raising colored troops, and thus elude public scrutiny to better advantage. Indeed, the wide spread contempt and hatred of the colored race, was turned to practical account by the philantrophic reformers, who argued that these despised men should be taken into the public service, in order to spare the lives of free white men of the North. The white soldiers of the North became at once very dear to the enthusiastic negro equalizers, when an object gratifying to their malicious souls was to be served. It had not before occurred to them that the lives of the poor white men should have been considered, at a time when the war could have been averted by a slight concession of principle to confederate allies, whose conscience and judgment were equally deserving of regard as their own. But they were the infallible conscience guides of the races, and the least swerving from the pre-arranged programme might have been fatal to their darling hopes of sable elevation.

The new era, with its despotic phases and Africanizing evolutions, was now fully installed. The qualm of loathing that had been rising for some time in democratic sentiment, was sufficient almost to produce a counter rebellion in the North to resist equally, what the Southern Confederates were battling. But much as any rebellion would have been justified, under the circumstances, in resisting the most consummate traitors and despots that had ever disgraced the principles of free government; a successful one was utterly impossibe at a time when all the governmental machinery was in the hands of the enemies of the Confederacy of the fathers, and when vast armies of the youthful men of the country were under arms, enlisted in the belief that they were called into to the service of their country to defend the Union and the Constitution; whereas, every stroke they inflicted was a stab at that Constitution they adored, and the civil liberty of their countrymen.

It was the principle of rule or ruin that spurred onwards the revolutionary men (though a minority of the American people) who had, under the guise of law, snatched control of the reins of Government; and which they determined either to remodel to suit their wild and delusive ideas of right, or to perish in the struggle. And so has it ever been in the world's history; and the Western revolutionists differed little from their elder brethren across the waters. Thaddeus Stevens, Charles Sumner and Horace Greeley varied but triflingly in spirit and sympathy from Robespierre, Danton and Marat, the men who were willing to subvert church and State, constitutional and social order, and overwhelm in one universal vortex of ruin everything that interposed obstacles to their mad designs and ambition.

The negro enrolling of the new era, was prosecuted with steady continuity in face of all the protests of the people of the Border, and the Democrats of the Northern States. Soldiers of African descent henceforth were enlisted into the service throughout the North, and likewise in those parts of the South which had been rescued from the control of the Confederates. Fugitive slaves were all the time making their way into the Union lines, and being speedily metamorphosed into regiments and *corps d' Afrique*, were steadily drilled by white officers. By the 22d of May, 1863, a special Bureau of colored troops was found necessary to be organized in the War Department for the management of this branch of the Federal army. President Lincoln, in his Message of the 8th of December, following, was able to speak of the colored recruits as follows:

"Of those who were slaves at the beginning of the rebellion, full one hundred thousand are now in the United States military service, about one-half of which number actually bear arms in the ranks."

The new era, again, was not alone revolutionary in the movements originated by the radicals for placing the negro in the Union armies, in order to pave the way for his future political equalization. It was the product of and pregnant with revolution. The old stable land marks of law and order must be removed to further the views of men who regarded neither the will nor interests of the people, further than they could make the same subserve their own purposes. Had public interests influenced them, would not their conduct from the first have been different? Should not the opinions and sentiments of the Southern people, being a part of the United States, have been consulted as to their demands and the conditions upon which they would have been willing to remain in the Union? Did not justice and reason so dictate? Did not the Northern Democratic party, in its conciliatory policy, demand this consideration in behalf of the rights of the Southern people? Were not the united South and the Democrats of the North a great majority of the citizens of the Union? It follows, then, as a sequence, that the Abolitionists,* a vast minority of the American people, despising the constitu-

*The word Abolitionists will be seen to have been employed at times to designate the Republican party, for the reason that though all Republicans were not Abolitionists, yet all Abolitionists were Republicans. And besides, it is difficult from the period of the Emancipation Proclamation, to conceive how any save Abolitionists could act with the Republican party.

tional guarantees of their Southern brethren, drove the latter into rebellion in defence of their inherited rights.

Permission for the soldiers to vote in the army was one of the instrumentalities seized upon by the revolutionists as an admirable means for the perpetuation of their power. And as a phase of the movements of the new era, it deserves to be considered. The defeat of the Republicans in the Autumn of 1862 in the North by the Democratic party, came upon them as a clap of thunder from a clear sky, and they were puzzled to devise plausible excuses for the disaster they had sustained. Their shrewd leaders fully comprehended the reasons that influenced the popular verdict that had been pronounced against them. But born of dissimulation, it was not to be expected that they would admit the real causes which they were aware had contributed to the result. The main excuse urged by them was, that it was owing to the absence of such vast numbers of their voters in the army, that the elections had resulted in their overthrow. It was a plausible pretence that crafty leaders could employ to good advantage; for it was reasonable to suppose that all who had enlisted in the Federal armies would be favorable to the prosecution of the war for the restoration of the Union. And, therefore, the presumption seemed probable that the majority of the enrolled men in the different Union armies could be relied upon to sustain by their votes the war in which these same soldiers were enlisted.

Immediately after the Republican reverses of 1862, movements were set on foot to amend the law, so as to secure the political aid of the soldiers in the field, in order that all future efforts of the Democracy to snatch power from Abolition hands might be thwarted. A purely deceptious method was instituted to change the law as it stood, in favor of soldier suffrage. Most of the Constitutions of the Northern States contained provisions adverse to the right of any indivividual voting, except he was prepared to tender his ballot in the district or the precinct where he resided. Well matured reasons had induced the framers of the different State Constitutions to demand of every voter that he be a resident citizen in that place where he offers to vote. A voting army has never been deemed a safe phenomenon by pure patriots who had no interests to subserve, save those of civil liberty and free representative government.

The method adopted by the Republican leaders, was simply to obtain the passage of a law by the Legislatures of the different States, permitting their soldiers in the army to vote; and that this result should be remitted and computed with the home vote. Laws to this effect were passed by the Legislatures of Pennsylvania, Connecticut, Iowa, and other States, which were declared unconstitutional. A bill also passed both Houses of the New York Legislature, which was promptly vetoed by Governor Seymour. It seemed madness to enact laws clearly in violation of the fundamental charter of a State, but an object was to be gained in so doing. The Democrats, as consistent men and as friends of their State Constitutions, could not support a measure in plain violation of these instruments. The opposition of Horatio Seymour, of New York, George W. Woodward, of the Supreme Court of Pennsylvania, and of other constitutional men in the different States, was made use of as an electioneering argument to induce the soldiers and their friends to believe that the Democrats of the North were disinclined to granting them the right of suffrage.

The Democrats did not meet the demand for soldier voting with that prompt opposition which duty required; but they temporized by showing their readiness to acquiesce in the change sought for, by supporting, in 1863, in the New York Legislature, Judge Dean's Bill for an amendment to the Constitution, providing for soldier suffrage. Instead of the evasive resistance to what they must have felt to be a violation of fundamental principle, an open and manly resentment of the political wrong contemplated, would have obtained strong support, even amongst intelligent soldiers themselves. But in none of the States was united party opposition made by the Democrats to the voting of the soldiers in the army, when it once came to be a question of amending the Constitution for that purpose. There can, however, be but little doubt, that from the time when the question of voting in the army was first mooted, it was viewed by all sound constitutional Democrats with dislike, because based upon unsound principles; but they saw the disadvantage under which they would be placed in attempting to combat it. But the Republican party, under the captivating pretence of equality, continued zealously to press the right of all citizens to vote, even when in the service of their country; and by 1864, fourteen

States had authorized their soldiers in the field to deposit their ballots in all elections of the people.

But, until the State Constitutions could be changed, the Republican party was necessitated to resort to the desperate expedient of sending home from the armies, as many of their partisans as were necessary to turn in their favor the election in any State in which a canvass was pending. This was done in the New Hampshire and Connecticut elections in the Spring of 1863, before alluded to; and in the succeeding elections in other States, steadily repeated. Indeed, the army from this period was manipulated into an engine of omnipotent power in the hands of unscrupulous partisans, who were willing to do any thing to perpetuate their hold of the machinery of Government. The most daring and high handed excesses and violations of all moral principle were resorted to by bold and bad men, instigated without doubt, by the highest officials, to counteract the will of the people through the instrumentality of the ballot. It was an easy matter for the officers of the army, the great majority of whom were favorites of the Administration, to send home to any election the Republican soldiers, and such others as were known to be in sympathy with the professed objects of the war party. Those known to be of contrary opinions, could easily be detained upon a thousand frivolous excuses, the enumeration of which would fill a volume. No excuse might be able to detain from his home on election day, a bold and intelligent Democrat like Lieutenant Edgerley, of New Hampshire, who knew that thousands of Republican soldiers had been sent to their States to vote; but, it was easy to cashier one of such independence, (as was done in this case*) for distributing Democratic ballots at his own home.

It was easy for Louis Napoleon, by means of his beautiful snare of universal suffrage, to carry away the liberty of his native France; and so in like manner it was no difficult task for the Republican party, by aid of the soldiers, from whom all information was excluded, to turn any election in their favor that they desired. The despotism required for the purpose was of course equally as perfect as that which enabled the French aspirant across the waters to seize the reins of absolute power. When no newspapers were allowed to circulate in the army, except such as the President and his officers were pleased to allow, and when

*New York *Herald* of April 27, 1863.

soldiers were not permitted to discuss public questions and freely canvass the acts of the Administration, what else could be expected than that the great majority of them would vote in favor of that same Administration?

The very constitution of an army makes it an available engine in the hands of that Administration by which it is directed, and hence arises the danger of allowing the right of suffrage to be exercised by its soldiers. The officers of the army are dependent upon the Administration and its agents, for their original positions, for assignments to duty suitable to their wishes, for leaves of absence, and for chances of appointment in the regular army, when mustered out as volunteers. As a consequence, the more submissively they act, the more probabilities exist for such advancements and other favors which they are desirous of obtaining. Upon these officers, in turn, the soldiers are dependent for the promptness of their pay, for humane treatment, for furloughs, for relief from exhausting duties and exposure, for considerate forbearance, in view of the petty breaches of discipline, and for numerous other mitigations of the hardships of military service.

In addition to the official, the sutler influence is of vast weight in making an army a machine, as it were, subject to the control of that political party, which for the time, has in its hands the power of the government. The sutlers are a class of men usually destitute of all moral principle, and such as have secured through official friends, their privilege of fleecing the ignorant soldiers; they, as a consequence, become serviceable adjuncts in the hands of unscrupulous politicians, to influence the will of the soldiers in the army. In view, therefore, of the subordinated relationship and dependence between the governing party in a country and its armies, what more potent instrumentality of despotism can be thought to exist than a voting army machine?

Another phase of the new era was the management of the freed negroes of the South after their liberation from bondage. The propriety of the emancipation of the slaves was made to rest upon the assumption of the equality of men of all races; and that all men are worthy of freedom, and capable of enjoying its fruits and advantages. The truth of this assumption being accepted, it should have seemed needless to resort to additional pains in behalf of the negro after his emancipation had been secured. But not so; for when this was once accomplished, the freedman (whose inferiority was felt by all) must next be taken under society and governmental tutelage; first, for his subsistence and secondly in order to fit him for that position in society which his liberators were secretly but busily carving for him. The young, the aged and the infirm negroes of those districts, rescued from the Confederates, must be supported by that Government which had effected their emancipation. The families of those who had enlisted in the Union armies, were at least, as was argued, become the especial wards of their *charitable liberators*. In a word, all the freedmen were the especial objects of abolition care and attention; and their education and preparation for all the functions of manhood, were inaugurated with unparalled zeal and enthusiasm.

Schools were established amongst the freedmen; and industrious teachers entered upon the work of communicating to the emancipated slaves the rudimentary elements of an English education. As citizenship was the goal of all these efforts, a preliminary question for consideration should have been to have inquired into the nature of modern civilization; and ascertained the requisites of the American citizen. It should have been borne in mind that with all the developments of modern progress and enlightenment, it still remained a question of great doubt whether good government can long endure the strain of the universal suffrage of even the Caucasion race alone. If a large proportion of the civilized race have been found utterly incapable of wielding the ballot in the furtherance of individual views, could it reasonably be supposed that the lowest barbarian race should be able to do so? Might it not have been well to have remembered the axiom of philosophic thinkers, that a race can sustain that form of civilization alone, which it was originally able to germinate? And especially did it seem inconsistent that the ardent advocates of negro education and elevation, should come from that same party of Americans, who had heretofore criticised democratic extension of the right of suffrage to the foreign emigrants who landed upon our shores. A large proportion of these foreigners possessed a much higher order of education than it was possible for the freed negroes to attain. But the principles of these anti-foreign suffragists, at once seemed to undergo a sudden change, and the emancipated Africans appeared to loom up in their imaginations as the idea. Americans of future ages.

The crop of corruption that so luxuriantly sprung up with the new era, and also proved one of its features, was evidence that an enemy had entered the fields of the republic, and scattered impurities baneful to representative government. How could it be otherwise when men were honored with the highest trusts of of the nation, who had coiled their way to power by means of the basest appliances of debauchery and political prostitution? At no period before in the history of government had men been honored with the highest appointments by the Executive of the nation, and by Congress, whose whole former career had been one continued succession of villainy and fraud from their first entry upon the career of public life. One man, Simon Cameron, had been selected to a seat in the Presidential Cabinet, and afterwards transferred to a ministerial position abroad, who with a blasted reputation had secured, as was generally charged, a Senatorial chair in the Congress of the United States by the means of filthy lucre, and the basest strategy that could be employed. Another, Thaddeus Stevens, a man long reputed as one of the most corrupt politicians of his State, by the selection of his political associates, had been made Chairman of the Committee of Ways and Means, the most important and responsible position in the Lower House of Congress.

In the distribution of governmental favors, no discrimination was made between men of corrupt antecedents and those of unblemished reputations. This in itself was to cast away entirely the scales of moral scrutiny. It was essentially the introduction into the workings of government of that thoroughly debasing norm of social life, which treats that individual with most consideration who possesses the largest sum of money, whether the same be the acquisition of honorable effort or otherwise. Besides, what other but an augmenting demoralizing influence could the breach of plighted Presidential faith produce upon the minds of the masses of society, who are always more ready to imitate the vices of their rulers rather than their virtues?

Indeed, the Republican party seemed in a large measure to be the fountain from which political corruption flowed. In different Northern Legislatures accusations of bribery and all other corrupting influences were charged in the newspapers of both political parties. It was ventilated in the partisan sheets, that the sum of $25,000 had been tendered a member of the Legislature of Pennsylvania in the Winter of 1863, for the vote that would determine the election of a leading Republican to the United States Senate.* Stalking corruption had also raised its filthy head in the New York Legislature. It was publicly charged in the newspapers that Callicott, a corrupt democratic representative of the State of New York, in consideration of the Speakership of the Assembly, had allowed himself to be bribed by the Republicans to support their measures, and assist them in the election of a United States Senator. The following extract from the *Tribune*, depicts the corruption of the New York Legislature, both branches of which were Republican:

"If we are to credit information that reaches us from most respectable sources, the Legislature now sitting at Albany, is fast earning a reputation for profligacy. We are well assured that there are committees of either branch, that levy regular assessments on bills passing through their hands, demanding $100 to $500 for those of considerable importance, but taking $50, or even $20 each, when the measure is of secondary consequence, and no more can be had. '*How much money is in this bill?*' is the first inquiry when a proposition is submitted. '*Have they got the money here in Albany?*' comes next. Promises to pay when the bill becomes a law, or at the close of the session, are scouted; and offers of interests in the enterprise to be promoted very rarely command attention.

"A friend who recently spent a day at the Capitol, represents the prevalent corruption as more general and shameless than was ever before known. How much has been or must be paid for this or that report or vote; how many members are 'interested' in the passage of this or that bill; how A or B was 'fixed' as to this robbery, or by whom C was seen in behalf of that gauge, is discussed as cooly and openly as the time made in the last notable race, or the cost of double locks on the Erie canal. And the lobby is represented as more numerous, more impudent, and more shameless than ever before."†

From the inauguration of the new era, was witnessed in an especial manner, a weakness of republican government; and this because of the truckling subserviency of political leaders to policy, for the masses, even in educated communities, just as in ancient times, think only as their leaders advise them. The chains of despotism had been forged in great abundance, and every political right was virtually withdrawn from citizens, and

* New York *World*, January 24, 1863.
†Quoted in New York *World*, of April 18, 1863.

placed in the keeping of the President of the United States. But for the falseness of the majority of the leaders, a cry for vengeance would have resounded throughout the land, and the Abolition traitors that had subverted liberty and the Constitution of their country would have been driven into speedy exile, or exalted to gallows high as those upon which Haman swung.

As before remarked, but two consistent parties existed in the North—the outspoken abolitionists who sought the overthrow of the system of Southern slavery, and the elevation of the emancipated negroes to equality with their former masters; and the unconcealed peace men, who opposed the prosecution of the war against the South as a violation of the Constitution, and an infraction of the principles upon which republican government is based. Properly speaking, these two parties, which were purely consistent, were simply the antagonistic extremes of the respective organizations with which they operated, and neither the peace men nor the Abolitionists could enlist full Democratic or full Republican endorsement. It must have been clear, however, to every penetrating Republican, after the commencement of the new era, that the measures sustained by his party could lead to no other result than that which was desired by the revolutionary Abolitionists. In sustaining the prosecution of the war, then, what else was he doing save perpetuating the delusion that the war was waged for the restoration of the Union?

The masses of the people of the North, of both political parties, cared little whether slavery lived or died in the struggle that was being waged between the sections. Indeed, slight doubt can exist that in the abstract, Northern Democrats as well as Republicans, were disinclined in sentiment to the institution of slavery: and that as a choice, they preferred in their own minds to see an end to the system of Southern bondage rather than its perpetuation. Republicans who were not confirmed Abolitionists, very nearly agreed in their views of slavery with the most of the Democrats themselves; and yet all these were devotedly attached to the Union of the States, and in its preservation they considered their future liberty and happiness to be involved. The Democrats, who were in favor of peace at any price, were those who viewed the war as an utter violation of the Constitution; and these, as before noted, formed the only consistent opponents of the Abolitionists, who from the first designed the destruction of slavery, and all the constitutional guarantees upon which it was based.

The great attachment of the Northern people to the Union, was the result of pure delusion, the product of prejudice and popular fancy; which could see liberty and republican happiness alone in its preservation. In this particular the Northern people differed little from the ancient Romans, who were so devoted to the name of the Republic that they were unable to perceive the loss of their freedom, whilst the naked form of that which they adored was preserved; and whilst the name of king would have driven them to revolt, that of *imperator* (emperor,) a more despotic title, was by no means discordant to their sensibilities.

Reflecting men, after the full installation of the new era, saw that the shadow of the old Union alone remained; but that its substance had fled. The number, however, of those who perceived the popular delusion, as regards the Union, and were sufficiently honest and courageous to attempt to dispel it, were too few to accomplish the mighty task. It is always easier to accompany currents than to attempt to strive against them. A boldness is demanded of the man, who dares to question popular opinions, that is not possessed by a large portion of mankind. Only true freemen are competent for this undertaking; and whilst these pass through the fires of martyrdom, hypocritical demagogues gather applause and honors amidst popular ruin and governmental shipwreck. Owing to the original yielding of the Democratic party to the false demands of fanaticism, the whirlpool currents obtained too strong a hold upon the vessel of State any longer to be resisted; and all was now rapidly sinking in one common vortex of destruction.

The New York and other riots of 1863, were simply the natural reaction against the tyrannical despotism that had encircled its coils around the American Republic; and which, like Laocoon, was dying encompassed in serpentine folds. But for the delusive devotion to the Union which had blinded the people so that they were unable to perceive civil liberty, save as an efflux from their favorite idol, instead of unorganized resistance to Federal conscription, the flames of Northern revolution would have burst from their confines and quickly consumed the gilded fabric of despotic tyranny, which abolition fanaticism had erected. The thunders of denunciation which, but for the above delusion, would have advised the administration of Abraham Lincoln of its criminal violation of the Constitution, in the arrest of Clement L. Vallandigham, the patriot of Ohio; instead of inducing replies of attempted justification from the daring usurper, would have hushed him into the silence of contempt, and admonished him of the volcano of revenge that was ready to overwhelm all who dared to repeat the foul deed which his servile minion had perpetrated.

In the latter part of the year 1863, the political parties again began to prepare their platforms for the Autumn elections. The Republican leaders, conscious of the unpopularity of the different unconstitutional acts that had been passed by the Rump Congress, and enacted by the Presidential dictator, deemed it politic to conceal from the public that such measures received party endorsement. This was simply to continue the same hypocritical method pursued by Republican leaders from the first organization of their party in 1855. That method consisted in the enunciation of a platform of principles, and after power had been grasped to steadily act disregardful of pledges. The New York *Herald* spoke of the Republican State Convention, held in September, 1863, at Syracuse, as follows:

"The Emancipation Proclamation, the Confiscation Act, arbitrary arrests, the suppression of the freedom of speech and of the press in the loyal States, the Indemnity Act and the Conscription Act, have not been endorsed. The Emancipation Act received only a qualified endorsement. All reference to it was omitted in the regular series of resolutions, as reported by the Committee and adopted by the Convention. But a radical, having moved its endorsement, this was adroitly evaded by an amendment endorsing it simply as a war measure."

The revolutionary Republicans, before this time, had clearly mapped out the boundaries they intended to traverse. Charles Sumner, Thaddeus Stevens, and other leaders of the same sentiments, had already indicated clearly that their aim was the territorialization of the seceded States; and that their re-admittance into the Union should be fully interdicted until the total prohibition of slavery within their borders could be secured. The conservative policy advocated by the political Republicans, with whom, for popularity sake, President Lincoln pretended to sympathize, simply demanded the restoration of the Union, and of the States *in statu quo ante bellum.* Sumner and Stevens represented the real, the Republican manipulators the ostensible policy of abolitionism. The one formed the line of attack, the other the protecting columns that came upon its flanks and formed its steady support. The preparation of the State and other platforms was the work of that crafty body of politicians, whose principal object was party success. Even the Republican convention of Massachusetts, in 1863, only endorsed the Emancipation Proclamation as a war measure.

The Democratic party, eqally with the Republican, permitted its platforms to be drafted by its politic men. Mozart Hall was necessitated to yield to Tammany; and the popular sails were again unfolded to the breeze, in order to still further perpetuate the delusion that cowardice and craft had originally permitted. The *Herald* spoke of the Albany Democratic State Convention, and as compared with the Syracuse Republican, as follows:

> "They are both entirely conservative. They both return thanks to our brave soldiers, who are now risking their lives in defense of the Union. They both pledge their supporters to sustain the Government and the Administration in all necessary measures for the suppression of the rebellion. They both express the desire of the people of the North for an honorable peace. They both oppose disunion and maintain the integrity of the Union. They differ in this: the Democrats condemn the Emancipation Proclamation, Confiscation, Conscription and the Indemnity Acts; while the Republicans shuffle out of the responsibility of these acts, and only endorse the Emancipation Proclamation as a war measure."*

In other States, the war policy of the Government for the restoration of the Union, was also approved, in words, by the Democratic party. Its ambiguous conduct was illustrated in the States of Maine, Ohio, and Pennsylvania, during the campaigns of 1863. In these States war platforms were adopted and peace men nominated in each of them as the candidates for Governor. In Pennsylvania, George W. Woodward, a conspicuous peace man, whose opinions and sentiments were known to harmonize with the cardinal principles of the old party of Jefferson, permitted himself to be induced to write a letter, a few days before the October election, in which he expressed his approbation of the war policy for restoring the Union. This was enough to destroy all the enthusiasm felt in behalf of his election; for no others, save peace men, could be enthusiastic supporters of the Democracy.

*New York *Herald*, September 13, 1863.

The result of the elections of 1863, were Waterloo defeats in the States where peace men were the candidates. C. L. Vallandigham, the Democratic candidate for Governor, was defeated in Ohio by over one hundred thousand majority; and George W. Woodward, in Pennsylvania, by upwards of fifteen thousand. The entire North, with the exception of New Jersey, was swept by a hurricane of administration victories. The Democratic party was utterly overthrown; and far more weakened and demoralized than had it fought the battle beneath its real colors, by opposing the abolition war upon principle; and though defeated, its moral integrity would have been rescued; and, like the young giant of the past, which it was, it would have returned to the combat with renewed strength, ready to grapple with its hated foe. Vallandigham and other peace men were signally defeated, because their cowardly compeers lacked the courage to follow honest leaders and urge their comrades to the onset. They permitted the enemy to be the attacking party and to crown their banners with victory.

CHAPTER XXI.

THE MILITARY SATRAPS.

The utter inconsistency of making war for the preservation of a republican Union was clearly exemplified in every effort that was made by the coercion party, from the outbreak of hostilities between the sections. The first error having been committed, it was necessary, as a sequence, that a train of inconsistencies should follow. When the principle of military force was once brought into requisition to compel the seceded States or the people thereof to obey the behests of a central authority, the principle of republicanism died and that of monarchy took its place.

The principle of making war to coerce the people of the South being thus anti-republican, all the means required to sustain the war policy must necessarily be of the same character. It was the principle of domination, which was the reverse of consent, that upon which republican government is based. And yet so great was the clamor for coercive measures that all who denied to the Government the right to exert the strong arm of military power, were denounced as traitors and enemies of the Republic. The preservation of the Union being once determined, then, to depend upon the employment of force, it became altogether needless in coercionist opinion to consult the will of the people further than necessities required. And so far, therefore, as the aims of the revolutionists were attainable, success alone was considered.

Instead of endeavoring to effect the conciliation of the disaffected people of the South, as sound judgment would have dictated, one despotic advance after another was made by the men who shaped the abolition counsels of the nation. Besides those before this enumerated, another of the unconstitutional means made use of to retain the power already grasped, was the suppression of the freedom of the ballot in the States of Delaware, Maryland, Kentucky and Missouri; and also in those parts of the other Southern States, over which the arms of the Federal Government had been successful.

The Democratic party had aimed at compromise for the settlement of the difficulties between the North and the South; and the people by the adoption of their policy would have prevented the rebellion from breaking out, as it did, and drenching the land in blood. Indeed, the acceptance of their policy at any time during the rebellion, would have stayed the tide of blood and led to a settlement of the sectional troubles. All the Southern rebels at any time demanded, was that their fair and constitutional rights as equals in the Confederate Union, should be recognized; and to this they were justly and honorably entitled. For, even after the rebellion broke out and blood had been shed, though rebels, they did not cease to be American citizens and men; and their rights were equally as deserving of being considered as before any acts of secession had taken place. And their rights were respected by all who loved the Union of the fathers as it had existed from the origin of the Government, and for the preservation of which, a hypocritical party pretended to have made war. But other objects than its preservation were to be secured, and any compliance with the principles which true republicanism demanded, would have been fatal to the objects that Abolitionism, through the pretence of devotion to the Union, sought to obtain.

Fanatics were not now likely to permit the suspension of a strife which they had succeeded in enkindling, in order to allow the sections to adjust their disputes by any peaceful method, And, as Anti-Republican war had been made against the rebels. something of a similar nature also must be inaugurated against the peaceful citizens of those Southern States that remained in the Union. Many rights had already been wrested from the Northern Democrats, and others who disapproved of the war policy of the Government, in the suspension of the *Habeas Corpus* and in the suppression of freedom of speech, and of the press and other unconstitutional proceedings. But, because of the infatuated delusion that had seized control of the minds of the Northern people, a greater excess in the despotic overthrow of civil rights by the Administration, was permissible in the Southern unseceded States, than in any portion of the loyal North. For it was undeniable that the people of the whole South, as a unit, almost, believed that the party of Abraham Lincoln, was a revolutionary one; and that its principles would produce lasting disorder and the destruction of the Confederate union of the States. Entertertaining these sentiments, could the body of the border people, after the unconstitutional proclamation of war, do else than sympathize with their Southern brethren, whose guaranteed rights were to be obliterated in the fiendish conflict that was being waged against them?

Instigated by the proclamation of freedom and the succeeding measures allied to it, were those which were framed to carry forward by the might of despotism the principles of emanicipation, and firmly fix them in the legislation of the States and nation. The Government of the several border Slave States must be controlled by one or other means by the party of emancipation, and skillful plans were devised by which this could be accomplished. A small and insignificant body of voters* in Delaware, Maryland, Virginia, Kentucky and Missouri had supported Mr. Lincoln for President, and in this was found the nucleus for the party of emancipation in these States, after the edict of January 1st, 1863. The balance of the citizens of these States who had cast their votes either for Douglas, Breckenridge or Bell, were considered by the rulers as more or less unsound advocates of the war policy of the Government, and of the freedom of the slaves designed by it to be accomplished.

The masses of a people, during periods of turbulence, like ours, seem always ready to lick the feet of power. By the wholesale arrests of Legislatures, and of influential citizens, effective resistance to the administration in the border Southern States was soon broken; and the hands of truckling hypocrites, who sought to better their worldly condition at the expense of honor and integrity, were strengthened. Shrewdly conceived oaths were prepared both for the voters and the officials of these States, so as to exclude from the polls and stations of trust, all those who had heretofore been the respected citizens and ruling men of their several States and localities. And these oaths were so skillfully framed as to exclude from the polls, by virtue of apparent right, all voters who had extended aid or even cherished any sympathy for the cause of the rebellious South. That they

* In Delaware only 3,815 voters supported Lincoln for President in 1860, 2,294 in Maryland, 1,929 in Virginia, 1,364 in Kentucky, and 17,028 in Missouri.

should have cherished none such, was to suppose an entire reversal of reason, and of the instincts of an enlightened humanity. Large numbers of the people of these States, being thus unable to accept the wholly unconstitutional oaths, were disfranchised; and the States, as a consequence, fell under the control of the few original Abolitionists, and of those perfidious and dishonorable classes who are ever ready, servilely, to bend their necks to the yoke of might, in order to grasp the thrift that fawning secures. Those who do so, however, are the ignoble souls of life, who are fitted for servitude, but unworthy of freedom, because unendowed with the traits needed for its maintenance.

In one election in the city of Baltimore, after the inauguration of the new schedule, full two-thirds of the citizens refused to go to the polls to tender their votes. They chose rather to preserve their honor, than sacrifice it in a vain effort to resist the authority of that unreasoning party, which wielded the sword of an arbitrary despotism.

The method which the revolutionists made use of to control the elections in these States, and defeat those who, in spite of unconstitutional oaths, dared to press their rights of freemen, was to send their military satraps, with soldiers, under the pretence of guarding the polls and preventing invasion and domestic violence. But the President of the United States had no right to send his military subordinates into any State to control or interfere with the elections, unless first requested so to do by the civil authorities. As in other matters, however, the Constitution, in this particular, was likewise violated with impunity. In some cases, then, the citizens were intimidated from appearing to vote their sentiments, inasmuch as proclamations had been issued by the satraps which threatened seizure of the property of the disloyal. And voting against the Government was declared to be conclusive evidence of this disloyalty. In other instances, the citizens who were known to entertain democratic opinions, as they appeared to vote were arrested and detained in custody until the election was closed, and then they were discharged.

In the Winter of 1863, a convention of the Democratic party of Kentucky, assembled at Frankfort, for the purpose of making nominations for State officers, was dispersed by a Colonel Gilbert, who commanded a regiment of troops. And when one of the Senators from this State afterwards demanded of the United

States Senate, that the conduct of the officer who interfered with that political assemblage of his State should be investigated, the demand was refused. The majority of this body, as then constituted, seemed to regard naught save partisan success, whether achieved by constitutional overthrow or otherwise.

The following extract from the speech of Senator Powell, of Kentucky, of March 3d, 1864, gives an illustration of the conduct of the military satraps in his State:

> "In many counties the name of the whole Democratic ticket was stricken from the poll book by the military authorities. In many voting places, and in entire counties of Kentucky, no man was allowed to vote for the ticket. In the county in which I live, the names on the Democratic ticket were stricken from or not allowed to go into the poll books of three or four of the voting precincts. It is asserted that in one precinct of that county sixteen votes were cast, all for the Wickliffe ticket. The military then came there, took the poll books from the judges and clerk, returned them to head-quarters and stopped the election.
>
> "Sir, there is abundant evidence of the facts that I have indicated. Since the beginning of time there never was a more atrocious assault on free elections, than took place in many counties of Kentucky. In many places the candidates were arrested. In the First Congressional District Judge Trimble, the candidate for Congress, as loyal a man and as true to the Constitution and Union of his fathers as lives in the Union, was arrested by military authority. He was brought to the City of Henderson, a town just without his district, and there he was kept in military confinement near a month until after the election was over. They told him if he would decline being a candidate for Congress they would release him. He would not so degrade his manhood as to decline the canvass at the bidding of military tyrants and usurpers, and he was kept in prison. They found that he would be elected by a large majority, notwithstanding his imprisonment, and then they sent the military over his district, and had his name stricken from the polls in almost every voting precinct in the district. The gentleman who beat him got some four thousand votes in a district that polls about twenty thousand."

The pretended excuse for the interference of the military authorities in the election of Kentucky in 1863, was found in the declaration of martial law, in that State, by Gen. Burnside, the jailor of Vallandigham. This satrap of the Administration, assumed the right to subordinate civil to military authority, because, forsooth, one thousand rebels were yet found within the borders of that State. The true reason was, that in this manner, it was conceived a plausible excuse would be offered to his subordinates and their justifiers for their unlawful and outrageous conduct. The excuse, however, was lame and impotent, for at the time, the small remaining number of rebels were leaving the State, and General Burnside had fifty thousand soldiers under his command to confront them.

But Federal soldiers were also sent to the polls in Maryland, and interfered with the elections in this State, although no pretext therefor could be found in the existence of rebel soldiers in the old Commonwealth. The freedom of elections was likewise overthrown by military interference in the other border Southern States. Governor Bradford, of Maryland, in his protest against military interference with a free ballot in his State, speaks as follows:

> "On the day preceding the election, the officer in command of the regiment, which had been distributed among the counties of the Eastern shore, and who had himself landed in Kent County, commenced his operations by arresting and sending across the bay some ten or more of the most estimable and distinguished of its citizens, including several of the most steadfast and uncompromising loyalists of the shore. The jail of the county was entered, the jailor seized, imprisoned, and afterwards sent to Baltimore, and the prisoners confined therein, under indictment, were set at liberty. The commanding officer referred to, gave the first clue to the character of the disloyalty, against which he considered himself as particularly commissioned; by printing and publishing a proclamation, in which, referring to the election to take place next day, he invited all the truly loyal to avail themselves of that opportunity to establish their loyalty, '*by giving a full and ardent support to the whole Government ticket, upon the platform adopted by the Union League Convention*;' declaring that, '*none other is recognized by the Federal authorities, as loyal or worthy of the support of any one, who desires the peace and restoration of the Union.*'"

When these outrageous proceedings were reported in the United States Senate, and referred to the Military Committee, instead of condemnation they received the approval of the committee in a long report, which set up a full justification for all that had been done. The tyrant's plea of necessity was the prolific repository, whence all excuses were drawn for the violation of the Constitution and the laws of the States. The Senators of the revolutionary party, in general, defended all the unconstitutional acts of the military satraps; and thus granted to the Administration and its subordinates full license to trample upon the freedom of elections in the Southern States.

By such means, this freedom was destroyed; and the revolutionary party, calling itself *Union*, obtained the control of Maryland, West Virginia and Missouri. For a time, also the freemen of Delaware and Kentucky were defeated by the revolutionists. It was not astonishing, then, that conventions elected under the dictation of the military satraps; and when large numbers of the best citizens of these States were disfranchised by means of unconstitutional test oaths, should be ready to do the work of abolitionism. In West Virginia, Maryland and Missouri, conventions were elected under military dictation; and these bodies proceeded to decree the emancipation of slavery within their borders.

CHAPTER XXII.

THE GREAT CONSPIRACY REVEALED.

As events progressed, during the period of the rebellion, the conspiracy to overthrow slavery, change the status of Southern society, and elevate the negro race to equality with the white, more and more displayed itself. Upon the assembling of the Thirty-eighth Congress, in December 1863, President Lincoln craftily submitted a plan for the restoration of the rebellious States to unionship, when the armed resistance should be so far overcome as to warrant measures for this purpose. As the chief representative of the nation, it was expected of him that some method would be pointed out, by which the seceded States should again be numbered amongst the Commonwealths of the Federal Union.

The President fully understood the disharmony that reigned in his party upon the question of Southern reconstruction, and in view of this, greater caution was needed to be observed by him, in submitting a plan for the restoration of the seceded States. He was well aware that the State suicide theory of Charles Sumner, was that which received the approval of Thaddeus Stevens, Salmon P. Chase, Wendell Phillips, and the other radicals of the Republican party; and at the same time he was sufficiently astute to perceive that this policy was as yet too extreme to meet public approval.

In the submission of his method of restoration for the Southern States, it is not to be believed, that the President meant to fix any definite mode; but it was rather enunciated and designed to serve as a toy for conflicting sentiment, and to be molded to suit public opinion as the same became more developed. Indeed, the President declared his plan as not intended to exclude others in the following words of his proclamation of December 8th, 1863:

"And while the mode presented, is the best the Executive can suggest, with his present impressions, it must not be understood, that no other possible mode would be acceptable."

That the President or his party should at all be trammeled by obligations of governmental compacts, was not to be expected after the entire repudiation of plighted faith, on their part, that had already been witnessed. Firm adherence to any promise or obligation would have been fatal to the principles of the revolution, for the accomplishment of which, the Republican party had been originally organized and brought into power; and a studied caution, as a consequence, therefore, was required to be observed in the submission of any plan of reconstruction, so as to permit any change of policy which ever varying circumstances might require. The President, in truth, had in his mind no fixed mode of restoration that he esteemed more than another, save as it might aid Abolition views; and his only object in submitting the one which he did, was to answer public expectation on that point.

The plan proposed by the President for restoring the Southern States to their former relationship in the Union, was in entire harmony with the prior Abolition programme. It was the embodiment of the principles of monarchy and revolution; such as we have discovered to have given tone to so-called Republicanism, from its earliest advent to power. The fears that induced the slave States to rebel in defense of their constitutional rights, were entirely overlooked. No tender of assurance was made, that the anticipations on their part had been groundless; but the attitude assumed by the President, still more clearly proved that Southern Statesmen had not been mistaken, in their conceptions of the danger that threatened their institutions. Like a conqueror, on the contrary, and despot which he was, utterly regardless of the fears and anticipations of those contesting his power, the President announces his plan of forcing all the armed resistance under his dominion and authority. He declares in explicit terms that slavery must be abandoned in all the rebellious States; and even in those sections of them in which he himself had made an exception in his Emancipation Proclamation of January 1st, 1863. Treating the Southern Confederates as traitors and outlaws, he compels them before they shall be permitted to secure again for their several Commonwealths, the right of Statehood, to accept an oath not demanded by the Constitution; and which no democratic freeman of the North, with a sense of manhood, would have subscribed. This odious oath, required of all voters, before being re-clothed with citizenship, to swear to abide by and support all acts of the Federal Congress, passed during the rebellion with reference to slaves; and also to support all proclamations of the President, made or to be made during the rebellion, which had reference to the same. A delusive exception, it is true, was inserted, should these laws and proclamations at any time be modified by Congress or the Supreme Court. The President, however, too well understood the designs of Congress, to fear aught from that quarter; and as to the Supreme Judiciary, it had been for some time a topic of discussion to so remodel this tribunal, as to render it harmless to Abolition progress, should any danger in that direction be seriously apprehended.

What an entire disregard of republican principle did the Presidential mode of reconstruction manifest? It was a plain violation of the Constitution, which clothed the Chief Magistrate with no power to dictate the qualifications of suffrage in any State or Territory. It was an entire reversal of the cardinal principle of Democracy in essaying to found government upon the will of a small minority of the people of a State, rather than upon that of the majority. Again, the method proposed by the President seemed strongly to imply his own disbelief in the current assertion of his party, that in all the rebellious States a majority of the people were loyal and attached in feeling to the Federal Government. He, himself, upon any other hypothesis, had condemned the war against the South as an outrage and a crime. But when he comes to find voters who shall bring back the rebel States into the Union, this majority of Southern patriots would seem to have escaped his recollection, inasmuch as his restoration plan was so framed, as did he think that it might be necessary, in some cases, to be satisfied with one-tenth of the citizens of a rebel State, out of whom his loyalists should be manufactured. And that a smaller number than the one-tenth of the people should constitute the basis of citizenship for reconstructing a seceded State, would scarcely have been proposed by the most radical revolutionist of the North.

But, admitting even a modicum of truth in the Abolition assumption of the loyalty of a majority of the Southern people; the policy of restoration proposed by President Lincoln, claimed the right to do what the Constitution in express terms forbade. This instrument precluded the taking of the private property of any citizen for public purposes or otherwise, unless ample compensation therefor should be made. And yet the President, in the plan submitted by him, proposed, without any recompense, to cancel the value, and destroy all the slave property in the rebel States, whether the same belonged to loyal or disloyal individuals. By this high-handed exercise of despotic might, the fears entertained by the Southern people of the designs of Northern fanaticism were fully sustained; and the rebellion from this period, at furthest, must ever stand justified in history. The rebels, anticipating the designs of abolitionism, from the collected utterances of the leaders of that party, originally revolted against its rule in behalf of their constitutional rights and privileges; and now, when their surmises had been verified in the action of the Federal President and the congressional radicals, what was to condemn the rebellion? Instead of rebels arrayed, striving to destroy the Union and the Constitution, the Confederates stood before the world as patriots, defending within their States, in essence, that same Constitution and the principles of republicanism guaranteed by it.

But despotic and unconstitutional as was the Presidential plan of reconstructing the seceded States, it by no means met the approbation of the radicals in Congress and throughout the North. Negro suffrage from this period, began to peer forth as one of the measures that must be secured in the revolution that was being urged forward. This, indeed, was a part of the great conspiracy that was now daily revealing itself.

The doctrine of human equality, being that which lay at the foundation of abolitionism, it was not to be supposed that the fanatics should halt with the achievement of simple emancipation. The more evidence the progress of arms gave the hopeful enthusiasts that the rebellion would probably, in the end, be overcome, the more effort was made by them to shape legislation in the interests of race equality. All the conflicting views regarding the restoration of the States to Federal autonomy, hinged therefore upon this question. Hitherto, emancipation was the principal result of equality, that was presented before the people in the agitating crusades that had been waged against Southern slavery. But shortly after the meeting of the Thirty-eighth Congress, and the submission of the Presidential plan of reconstruction; revolutionary leaders come forward and took open grounds in favor of extending the right of suffrage to the emancipated slaves of the seceded States. From this period the revolutionary party may be considered as composed of avowed negro and of anti-negro suffragists. And of the latter, many were such, simply because they deemed it impolitic as yet openly to avow their principles.

There can be little doubt even that President Lincoln agreed with the negro suffragists, and that his characteristic hypocrisy alone deterred him from avowing the principle in his reconstruction scheme of December 8, 1863. He was very solicitous, however, to shift the avowal of the doctrine of negro suffrage upon others,* whose position more securely guarded them from the assaults of public opinion. Owen Lovejoy, a man equally radical with Thaddeus Stevens, seemed to have fully understood the President's motives and feelings. In his letter of February 22d, 1864, to William Lloyd Garrison, he speaks of the President in the following language:

"I write you, although ill health compels me to do it, by the hand of another, to express to you my gratification at the position you have taken in reference to Mr. Lincoln. I am satisfied, as the old theologians used to say in regard to the world, that if he be not the best conceivable President, he is the best possible. I have something of the facts inside during his administration, and I know that he has been just as radical as any of his Cabinet. And, although he does not do everything that you or I would like, the question recurs whether it is likely we can elect a man who would. It is evident that the great mass of Unionists prefer him for re-election; and yet it seems to me certain that the Providence of God during another term will grind slavery to powder." †

---

* The following letter to Governor Hahn, of Louisiana, discloses the President's double dealing course of action:

"EXECUTIVE MANSION,
"Washington, March 13, 1864.

"HON. MICHAEL HAHN.

"*My Dear Sir*;—I congratulate you on having fixed your name in history as the first Free State Governor of Louisiana. Now you are about to have a convention, which, among other things, will probably define the elective franchise. I barely suggest, for your private consideration, whether some of the colored people may not be let in, as for instance, the very intelligent, and especially those who have fought gallantly in our ranks. They would probably help in some trying time to come, to keep the jewel of liberty in the family of freedom. But this is only a suggestion, not to the public, but to you alone.

"Yours truly,
"ABRAHAM LINCOLN."

† *Annual Cyclopedia* of 1864, p. 486.

The State suicide doctrine of Charles Sumner was inspired by the desire to secure in the Southern States for the negro, full equality with the Caucasian race. And all the efforts of Thaddeus Stevens and the other unconcealed revolutionists, to establish the principles of State destruction, the confiscation of Southern property, and the exclusion of Southern Representatives from the halls of Congress, were influenced by the same desire. These men, the soul and spirit of their party, were compelled, however, to await the developments of time, whilst the treacherous hypocrites within the same, were enabled still further to lure their countrymen into the snares that were set for them. The suicidal resolutions when first offered by Sumner, in 1862, met the cold reception of silence; and the Congressmen from Louisiana, and other military reconstructed States, were welcomed to the National Halls of the Thirty-seventh Congress, in spite of the opposition of Mr. Stevens and others, who were keen-sighted enough as to see the logical effect of such admission. But Mr. Stevens and others who agreed with him, were able to exclude from the Thirty-eighth Congress A. P. Field and the other Representatives of Louisiana and other subjugated States of the South. In their exclusion of Southern Representatives, additional evidence of the great conspiracy was presented.

The belief of the equality of all races of mankind, having germinated the movement of abolitionism, the fanaticism must run its full length, the control of the Government being now, as believed, firmly grasped. Nothing less than the complete political and social equality of races, would satisfy zealots who allow feeling rather than reason to guide them. And, as if to prove that their enthusiastic visions of human equality, could controvert logic and all the experience of anterior ages, they set themselves to work to elevate a race, fitted alone for barbarism or subordination.

The education of the colored race in the District of Columbia having been determined upon, after the act of Emancipation had passed, every other step must be taken in order to elevate the newly liberated man up to the full measure of perfect equality. As the Africo-American freedman had been introduced into the Northern armies, his standing in that position must be guarded; and all offences to his lately achieved dignity, resented by a Congress, desirous of obliterating the repugnant decrees of eternity.

And when a shoulder-strapped member of the enfranchised, race found himself forcibly ejected from the cars in the City of Washington, the elevators of the colored men were aroused to the utmost; and a law was speedily enacted by Congress which precluded the officers of the railroad companies of the City of Washington and Georgetown, from determining what regulations should be observed with regard to their passengers. No negro dare in future be ejected from any railroad cars in the District, under a severe penalty. It was not enough for the colored American that he be provided by the railroad companies with equal facilities for travel, and cars of equal quality with white people, he must be allowed to obtrude himself into white company, where his presence was offensive. This kind of legislation was an attempt to undo what God had done; that is, to obliterate the distinctions which he had made. Herein another evidence of the great conspiracy was disclosed.

Equalizing the compensation of all the soldiers in the armies, whether of African or Caucasian descent, was a part of the schedule that radical legislation must complete. And, as no Member of Congress seemed to long more ardently for this form of equality than Henry Wilson, of Massachusetts, and he who stood the acknowledged leader of revolutionary radicalism in the House, Thaddeus Stevens, it was appropriate and fitting that these distinguished representatives should be the first to propose the desired legislation. Accordingly, on the 8th of January, 1864, Mr. Wilson introduced into the Senate a bill to promote enlistments, which provided that all persons of African decent, who may have been mustered into the military service of the United States shall receive the same uniform, clothing, arms, equipments, camp-equipage, rations, medical and hospital attendance, pay and emoluments, as other soldiers of the regular and volunteer forces of the like arm of the service. After a spirited contest in the Senate, the bill as above proposed in substance was adopted in that body; and on the 30th of April, Mr. Stevens called it up in the Lower House of Congress. The measure likewise met the approbation of the House, and colored soldiers were placed on an equality with white from January 1st, 1864. "The Attorney-General has finally decided, that colored soldiers are in all respects entitled to the same compensation as white soldiers." *

* Henry Wilson's Anti-Slavery Measures in Congress, p. 312.

The most persistent efforts were made by the radicals in the first session of the 38th Congress, in both the Senate and House of Representatives, to allow the negro to grow to the full stature of free manhood, with which he, however, was but simply in the process of being endowed. He was clothed by Act of Congress with the right of appearing in all the courts of the United States as a witness, not so much because this privilege was then especially demanded, but rather because it was believed that it would aid in the final extirpation of slavery, the first grand object of the revolutionists. The repeal of the law, which precluded negroes from carrying the mails, was also strongly urged during this session, chiefly for the same reasons.

In this session of Congress, a Bill was prepared in the House, providing for the organization of the Territory of Montana, and having passed the same in the usual form, was remitted to the Senate for its approval. When the Bill came up for consideration in this body, Senator Wilkinson, of Minnesota, moved to strike out of section five, of the organizing Act, which prescribed who should be voters, the words "white male inhabitant," and insert "male citizen of the United States, and those who have declared their intention to become such." The undenied object of this amendment, was to secure the organization of the new Territory in accordance with the principles of the avowed Abolitionists, who already were beginning to urge that the right of suffrage should be extended to the negro race. Prominent members of the party in different sections of the North, had already given utterance to this recent demand of Abolitionism.

The amendment met with a considerable opposition from Republicans themselves, chiefly because they feared to encounter in the coming Presidential canvass the opposition that would array itself against the principle of negro suffrage. The majority of the Senators, however, all Republicans, showed themselves as favorable to universal suffrage by supporting the amendment. It was carried in the Senate by 22 yeas to 17 nays. Several of the Senators who supported the amendment made no concealment that they heartily favored the principle which it expressed; its adoption by the Senate, however, was admitted to be a pure abstraction, as not one negro inhabitant at the time was found in the new Territory. And of those also, who deemed it impolitic to agitate the question of suffrage at the time, in view of the approaching Presidential election, were some who declared themselves as not opposed to granting negroes the right of voting.

The submission and support of the amendment in the Senate, was the first clear proof that the Republican leaders were ready, when a fair opportunity would present itself, to extend the right of suffrage to all races of men. Up to this period they had studiously sought to elude the avowal of this principle, and positively averred that no such design was at all entertained by them. In the most solemn assurances, they declared that the emancipation of the negroes from the chains of slavery, would be the ultimate limit of humanitarian effort in behalf of the degraded race. It was even resented, as offensive, that they should be accused of the design of intending to open the ballot to ignorant African menials. But before the inauguration of the war, and for a time afterwards, had not they in equally strong terms resented the imputation, that the emancipation of slavery in the Southern States was designed by them?

The House of Representatives, however, declined to concur in the Senate's Amendment, because they saw clearly that negro suffrage would be too heavy a burden to carry in the Presidential contest of 1864. But enough was disclosed, from its adoption by the Senate, and from the sentiments that were beginning to be uttered by conspicuous radicals, favorable to this principle, to satisfy reflecting men, that it formed the main part of the great conspiracy that was rapidly revealing itself in its fullest extent.

The full completion of the conspiracy required the repudiation of the Fugitive Slave Laws, and also of that provision of the Federal Constitution which supported the Acts of 1793 and 1850. A bill for this purpose having been referred to the Judiciary Committee of the Senate, was reported back adversely. Repeated efforts were made, prior to January 11th, 1864, to effect the repeal of the Act of 1850, and also that of 1793. At the latter date, on motion of Charles Sumner, the question of the repeal of the Fugitive Slave Laws was referred to a committee of seven Senators, the majority of whom reported favorable to the measure. The Repealing Act received the approbation of the members of the revolutionary party in Congress, and was approved by President Lincoln, June 28th, 1864.

The bill was stubbornly resisted by the Democrats of both Houses of Congress, because of the violation which the repeal inflicted upon the Federal Constitution. The passage of the Repealing Act, in Democratic opinion, was an open and palpable infraction of the bond of covenant, according to the terms of which the States had united to form the Union; and for the preservation of which the radicals claimed that the war was being waged by the General Government. It was also argued by the Democrats that no practical good could result from the repeal at that time, as the slaves in the Border States were already in such a state of insubordination that they were free to go where they chose. All State control over the slaves had for months, prior to this period, almost entirely ceased in the Border States; and it was only in these States that the law could be considered as of any avail. But, besides, the Northern people at that time would not have permitted any fugitive slave to be reclaimed in their midst by any Southern master, however loyal to the General Government he may have been.

But in truth, the repeal of the Fugitive Slave Acts was simply a part of the programme which the revolutionary leaders, from the origin of their party, had designed, viz: to destroy slavery regardless of every guarantee which the Constitution contained. The report was really nothing, save an Act of the purest despotism and revolution, of which history affords an instance. It was utterly unwarranted and unjustified; and altogether as great a violation of civil right as would communism be guilty of, should it ultimately assume to wrest all property from its possessors, and distribute the same as its principles would dictate.

The plan of reconstruction, submitted by President Lincoln, in December, 1863, although in entire accord with the principles hitherto acted on and approved by every branch of the Federal Government, could not, as we have already observed, meet with the approval of the radical leaders of his party. It was not upon its face, sufficiently revolutionary to meet the approbation of men, utterly regardless of all constitutional restraint whatsoever. Members of Congress who were ready to avow that the war was carried on *outside of the Constitution*, as they viewed it, were not likely to agree with the Presidential plan of restoring the seceded States, to their Federal status in the Union.

The main reason why the Executive plan of reconstruction did not meet radical approval, was as before remarked, because the principle of negro suffrage had been entirely ignored. Salmon

P. Chase, a member of the President's Cabinet, in his letter to Gerrit Smith, of March 2d, 1864, speaking of the plan submitted by the head of the Nation, said:

"The Amnesty Proclamation seems to fail. I don't like the qualification in the oath required, nor the limitation of the right of suffrage to those who take the oath, and *are otherwise qualified*, according to the State laws, in force before the rebellion. I fear these are fatal concessions. Why should not all soldiers who fight for their country vote for it? Why should not the intelligent colored man of Louisiana have a voice, as a free citizen, in restoring and maintaining loyal ascendency."

From the identity of sentiment that pervades this letter of the Secretary, and that of President Lincoln, to Michael Hahn, of Louisiana, before quoted, they would both seem to have flowed from the same school of abolition thought. And, although the Executive preserved himself before the country as the apparent conservative, his views permitted him to drift beneath the current as an unseen revolutionist and a radical amongst his brethren.

The question of reconstruction during the first session of the Thirty-eighth Congress, was viewed as a favorable one for agitating purposes. It was regarded as very different when Mr. Ashley introduced the same question in the early part of the Th rty-seventh Congress. The revolution, however, had now advanced so far that but little fear was entertained to discuss in Congress the most radical topics. The most extreme revolutionists were able, at length, to promulgate their views on the question of suffrage; and so long as both Houses did not agree upon a measure of this kind, the leaders had it in their power to deny that such opinions would ever be adopted by the Administration.

On the 4th of May, 1864, Mr. Davis, of Maryland, Chairman of the Committee of the House, to whom had been referred the President's views upon the restoration of the rebel States, submitted a Bill, embodying a fixed and elaborate plan of reconstruction. This also, like the President's plan, was revolutionary as it assumed, without warrant and contrary to the former avowed policy of the Government, that the statehood of the seceded Commonwealths were altogether overthrown. The war for the repression of the rebellion, from its outbreak, had been waged upon the principle that the rebellious States were still in the Union; and that no act of secession could loosen the cords that held together the members of the old Confederacy. And the policy of the Government, for a long time after the outbreak of the war, was so shaped, lest something might be done or omitted, which would operate as an admission that the rebel States had in law seceded.

The bill prepared by the Reconstruction Committee of the House, provided for the appointment of a Provisional Governor by the President in each State declared to be in rebellion, to serve until a State Government should have been organized and recognized by the General Government. On the suppression of military resistance to the authority of the United States in any such State, an enrollment of white male citizens was to be made, and a convention was to be called, when a majority of them should have taken the oath of allegiance, to act upon the re-establishment of a State Government. All persons having held any office in the rebel service, civil or military, State or Confederate, and all those having borne arms in such service, were to be prohibited from voting for, or being elected as delegates to the State Convention. The convention was required by the bill to insert in the new Constitution to be formed by it, provisions disfranchising those who "held or exercised any civil or military office, (except offices merely ministerial, and military offices below the grade of colonel) State or Confederate under the usurping power;" also, prohibiting slavery, and repudiating all debts created by or under sanction of the usurping power, State or Confederate. The State Government, thus created, was to be recognized by the President after obtaining the assent of Congress, and only after such recognition was it allowed for the State to be represented in Congress and in the Electoral College. Slavery was further formally declared to be abolished in all the States in question, with remedies and penalties to give this declaration effect. Those rebels, holding any civil or military office with the conditions above stated, after this bill should become a law, were declared not to be citizens of the United States.*

The bill having passed the House of Representatives, was sent to the Senate for its concurrence, and after some debate and interchange of sentiment between the two Houses, was finally adopted by the latter body. The President could not approve the reconstruction plan of Congress, without too openly exposing

*Barrett's Life of Abraham Lincoln, p. 562.

himself to the charge of puerile vacillation and breach of plighted faith; for he was already fully committed to the recognition of the new State Governments of Louisiana and Arkansas. These States, in accordance with his own plan, had chosen Governors, changed their State Constitutions, and done whatever else was enjoined upon them to regain their lost Statehood in the Union. He had likewise appointed Military Governors for other Southern States. Besides, no essential abolition advantage would be gained, even should the President append his signature to the Reconstruction Bill. He, therefore, shrewdly withheld it.

The culminating movement in the great conspiracy, was that instituted to effect the final overthrow of Southern slavery, under the appearance of an apparent amendment to the Federal Constitution. This was an adroit, well-planned scheme of the revolutionists, to obtain in the midst of and by means of revolution, the object of abolition zeal, the eradication of the hated institution. The Constitution provided for an amendment, when the same having been proposed by the two-thirds of each House of Congress and submitted to the States, should be ratified by three-fourths of these.

Shortly after the assembling of the Thirty-eighth Congress, with other revolutionary measures, an amendment to the Constitution abolishing slavery in all the States was proposed by James M. Ashley, the super-serviceable member of the Lower House of Congress from Ohio. And as evincing concert of action, a proposition with like design not long afterwards was also submitted in the Senate, and referred to the Committee on the Judiciary.

After a time, the amendment having been matured, a joint resolution was offered that the same be submitted to the States for ratification. The resolution aroused a spirited opposition upon the part of the Democrats, who saw nothing in it save a subtile and crafty method of subverting that very Constitution which the revolutionists, hypocritically, were preparing in name to amend. For did not the amendment propose to interfere with the social economy of the States, even of the unrebellious States, and with affairs over which the General Government had no authority to legislate or interfere? It was in violation even of that resolution of the Chicago Convention of 1860, which declared that "the maintenance, inviolate of the rights of the States and especially the right of each State, to order and control its own domestic institutions, according to its own judgment exclusively, is essential to that balance of power on which the perfection and endurance of our political fabric depends."

The Democrats took the position that changing the fundamental charter of a country, was an action demanding so great solemnity that it should never be undertaken during a period of effervescence and civil commotion. Besides, no such pressing haste required an amendment to the Constitution to obliterate slavery, as the institution would prove well nigh invulnerable, so long as Southern armed resistance was not overcome upon the battle field. But slavery being the mark of abolitionism, it was not to be expected that men deeply indoctrinated with its fanatical views could rest, save in exerting to the utmost their strength in one or other method for the extinction and destruction of their hated foe. Statesmen of balanced minds, saw however, the inutility of all such maddened legislation, provided the restoration of the Union was the object to be achieved.

It was also argued that as the amendment proposed to interfere with social interests, its character was revolutionary. It was the introduction of a principle antagonistic to that which underlies all republican government. The Union was made for the political government of its members; and only for certain specified objects of a very general nature. The management of domestic affairs, according to the letter and spirit of the compound system of the United States Government, was remitted entirely to the States and to their people. The General Government, by the Constitution, was entrusted with no control over the marital or religious relations of the people of the States, or with the right of eminent domain within their limits. All these were social and State relations; so also was the institution of slavery.

Again, the Democrats viewed the effort to destroy slavery by an amendment to the Constitution, as at variance with its spirit, as a breach of good faith, and wholly unjust in its method. It was a breach of faith, because the war had been prosecuted upon the assumption that the seceded States yet formed integral parts of the Union; and being such, the Government was bound to see that the private property, at least of all loyal citizens, be preserved unharmed. For even in a pure monarchical government, it is deemed due to all adherents of the crown, that they suffer no loss in person or estate by reason of others in their midst having rebelled. How then, in the republic of the United States, could such be deprived of their property, unless a fair compensation were first made to them by the Government?

The leading Democrats of both Houses firmly contended that the Constitution, could not legally be so amended, as to destroy slavery in the States without the unanimous consent of those States. Senator Saulsbury, of Delaware, in his speech of March 31st, 1864, spoke as follows:

"I firmly believe in the truth, that if the Senate of the United States were to adopt this joint resolution, and were to submit it to all the States of this Union, and if three-fourths of the States should ratify the amendment, it would not be binding upon any State whose interest was affected by it, if that State protested against it."

"I know that the popular theory is that a convention can frame a Constitution, and if three-fourths of the States ratify it, it is obligatory in reference to everything and anything they do. * * * * If that be so, then I ask you, could three-fourths of the States say that you should have no manufactories, that you should plant no corn, that you should not have property in anything else which is the subject of property.

"Sir, property is not regulated, and was not intended to be regulated by the Constitution of the United States. Property is the creature of the law of the State, and whenever this Government undertakes either by legislative enactment, or operating through and by three-fourths of the States to say to the people of any State, "*we will what shall be property and what shall not be property in your midst; that subject shall be regulated by a Federal Constitution or by a Federal law*," they violate the purposes and objects for which the Constitution was framed; and do that which, if they had proclaimed had been their object in the beginning, would have prevented the formation of that Constitution, and of the Union.

"Can Congress propose an amendment to the Constitution which, being ratified by three-fourths of the States, shall become the supreme law of the land, by which there shall be an equal distribution of property throughout the United States?"

Senator Hendricks, of Indiana, on the same subject, in his speech of April 7th, 1864, said:

"I am not satisfied that this proposed amendment is one that can be made to the Constitution. The institution of slavery is a domestic institution. It exists not by virtue of the Federal Constitution, not by virtue of any law passed pursuant to the Constitution of the United States, but it had its existence before the formation of the Federal compact, before the establishment of the Federal Constitution. It was the Constitution of the Colonies."

George H. Pendleton, of Ohio, a member of the House, in his speech of June 15th, 1864, said

"There is in three-fourths of the States neither the power to establish nor to abolish slavery in all the States. The Federal Government has power over the relations of the States with foreign nations, and over the relations of the States as between and among themselves. It has no power over the purely internal affairs of the State. This principle was as familiar as household words three years ago. Every power delegated to the Federal Government, relates either to the inter-national or the inter-State relations of the United States. The domestic internal affairs of a State having no connection with the Federal Government, or with foreign nations or with the other States, are reserved to the absolute, exclusive, sovereign power of the States respectively, and to the people thereof. The other States are not affected by them, and have no interest in them. The Federal Government has no cognizance of them. The power of amendment, which is confided to three-fourths of the States, does not reach them nor the power to regulate them, but is limited to the subjects and powers delegated to the United States."

The resolution proposing the submission to the States of the constitutional amendment, which should abolish slavery throughout the Union, passed the Senate April 8th, 1864, by the strong vote of 38 yeas to 6 nays. The question was also considered in the House and a vote taken upon it June 15th; but there was a failure to secure two-thirds of this body in its favor. The vote in the House was 95 yeas to 66 nays, the Democrats in general opposing the resolution. Four Democrats, however, believing a further defence of the Constitution hopeless, voted with the majority.

CHAPTER XXIII.

THE POLITICAL CAMPAIGN OF 1864.

The Presidential campaign of 1864, was an anomalous one in the history of the American Union. It was to be conducted during the existence of the most gigantic revolution which free government had ever experienced, since the commencement of time. The sectional party which had grasped the reins of Administration in 1860, had as before shown, been the result of the long period of agitation which had cemented together the fanatical elements of the North, and made the ruling aggregation of this section, a somewhat homogenous compound.

But the long period of turbulence and civil war which had separated the sections of the country, had proved an eliminating process which had more and more strongly placed fanaticism and reason in opposition to each other. From the time when it was discovered, after the secession of the Cotton States, that the Republican leaders would not consent to settle the difficulties between the North and South by fair and honorable compromise, the reasoning classes began to enter their protests; and, although this protesting was chiefly in silence, it nevertheless had its influence in molding the aspect of the parties of the country. From that period, reflective men* began to drop their connection with the Republican, and become quietly absorbed in the Democratic party. And from the beginning of the war, during its whole progress, this process of separation was going on, and a counter elimination was likewise all this time taking place, which was drawing the most corrupt and selfish material from the Democratic into the so-called loyal party of the country. Fanaticism had at length become profitable; and it was not unusual to find men who had figured as conspicuous friends of peace and compromise,

*It is not meant, however, to assert that all the reflecting men deserted the Republican party; but that many did so is undeniable. Interest and other motives detained sagacious men in the Republican party who could not be ranked as Abolitionists.

turn out to be the most blatant advocates of the war and Southern subjugation.

When the time approached that candidates should be selected for a Chief Magistrate of the United States to succeed Abraham Lincoln, the two parties of the country had become more diametrically antagonistic than had ever before been witnessed in the country. The boiling caldron of war had stirred society to its foundation; and its sedimentary dregs that heretofore had remained quiescent, were cast to the surface, and were exerting an influence not felt on former like occasions. The enthusiastic mob, the fanatical agitators, and the intolerant clergy of the North, found themselves in the so-called Republican party, which was bent upon crushing out all resistance to the Federal despotism reared by them; and against these were arrayed the calm, considerative classes, who could only see destruction to free government in the policy and movements of the party that sustained the war and its further prosecution.

Never in the history of the country did the people's government exhibit itself in such odious features. Its like had alone been seen during the dark and bloody epoch of the French revolution. The preservation of republicanism had ever, to thinking men, seemed problematical; and the old Federal Union was believed to have afforded the most perfect illustration of a representative Republic which was anywhere to be found upon the globe. But all through the representative system of the American Union, a necessary substratum of intellectual and cultivated society, from the formation of the Constitution, had firmly held the helm of State; and cautiously guided it amidst the rocks and quicksands of social disorder, upon which like forms of government had been wrecked. An intelligent and polished class of society existed in the Southern States, from the peculiar race subordination of that section, which produced a succession of clear-headed statesmen, in whose estimation honor and integity formed guiding stars. The plan of the Federal Union itself was the conception of these eminent men; and its unclouded prosperity, until 1860, was owing to the influence they exerted in the maintenance of order and the repression of corruption.

But, whilst Southern statesmen formed a Union with slavery, it remained as the task of the intelligence of New England and the North to form a more perfect Union, where men of all races should be equal, both socially and politically. Northern fanaticism, by means of the free school system, conceived this to be attainable, although in direct contravention to all anterior political philosophy. Sound reason would rather have dictated a method of instruction, which would render each individual better fitted for the task and station of society, for which God and nature had chosen him; for the statesman and the religious preceptor, the highest grade of moral and scholastic culture, but for him chosen to fill the humble walks of life, the plainest elements of knowledge.

Human equality was first promulgated by the Redeemer of men, in a spiritual sense, and by Thomas Jefferson, in the Declaration of Independence, as the deduction of the thought of the seventeenth and eighteenth centuries* in an ethical and philosophical sense; yet contradistinguished from a natural and political sense. For no man of the keen sagacity, and intuition of the Virginia statesman would have been willing to stultify himself in the eyes of the scientific and philosophical world by asserting what his unclouded reason must have assured him was untrue, viz: That all men are created equal; as he could not but see that all men are created unequal, intellectually, physically and politically. The Hyder Alis and Pontiacs of their times are born unequal to any of their subjects; and though devoid of all save nature's education, exert a political power that their innate superiority alone accord them. Could it be proven that the author of the declaration meant to teach the entire equality of men, he would forever stand in the light of reason and common sense, as the purest demagogue that ever attempted to delude mankind. Such a conclusion is not, however, to be assumed, without the clearest evidence to sustain it. Natural and political inequality obtains amongst all men, because of the original endowment of creation; and it does not disappear in a representative republican government, when it is abstractly said, that all men are born equal. Democratic equality is purely speculative, and brings to the great body of the people no greater power than the same class enjoy under a monarchy. Power in an inertial condition, inheres, it is true, in the mass of society, but like the human body, it is ever exerted by the head of the body politic, those possessing the capacity

*Speech of R. M. T. Hunter, at the University of Virginia, on the 30th of June, 1865, p. 16.

to direct the social organism. It is so in all society, monarchical, aristocratical and democratical; and this was as clearly seen by Aristotle, the philosopher, over two thousand years ago, as at the present day. But for the men whose thought controls communities, eternal anarchy would reign. Political power is simply the effort of intellect directing society; and a few thinkers perform the task in every subdivision of government. The very superior minds control the aggregated whole of society, and the body of voters exert no more authority than the same number in the purest despotism of Asia. All the people can have, is the liberty for each individual to fill up and enjoy the full measure of his being. Good government does not depend, therefore, upon the general intelligence of the masses, but upon the superior intellect, culture and virtue of the few, who are by nature fitted for rulers.

The first successful effort of the abolitionized North, independent of the cultured South, to select a President, had resulted in a concession to the equalizing ideas of that section. Instead of an erudite, high-toned and honorable scholar, a tricky, jocular, village politician of mediocre capacity, was chosen to fill the seat that the most eminent citizens and educated Statesmen alone had heretofore graced. A boorish President was acceptable to partisans, who believed in the full equality of all men; and, although men are necessitated to qualify themselves for the ordinary avocations of life, a rail-splitter and flat boatman was deemed equally as competent for President of the United States, as the most acute logician and finished Statesman. Indeed, it may be averred, as a political axiom, that modern fanaticism can neither produce nor secure the services of a Statesman of Hamiltonian or Websterian calibre. This declaration finds support, when reference is made to the class of men elevated by the revolutionary party to Congress, and to other governmental trusts. Charles J. Ingersoll, a modern thinker, says:

> "We know, and only a great public change can account for it, that in the Revolution of 1776, a country of some three millions of people produced illustrious men; and in that of 1860 the same country, ten times as populous, did not produce one." *

The unnatural, equalizing tendency of the Republican party, having originally secured a President of ordinary ability and low

---

* Fears for Democracy, p. 121–2.

tastes, and a Congress likewise of nearly the same grade; it was not to be expected that higher aspirations would guide the party in 1864; inasmuch as the whole social structure was in a condition of turbulence and revolution. But, common and revolutionary as Abraham Lincoln had exhibited himself during his administration, he yet lacked some of the qualities that were considered at that time desirable to be possessed by the President of the United States. He did not have the lightning celerity of movement, and that utter disregard of the whole spirit of the Constitution which the radicals desired. His common sense assured him that *too great haste spoils the work;* and he waited to see the currents of opinion, before too clearly disclosing his own views. The radicalism of the President was intense, in the highest degree; but he caused it to be tempered with a greater degree of caution than the extreme revolutionists desired.

In pursuance of a movement inaugurated, in the winter of 1863–4, a convention of extreme radicals, who were opposed to the re-nomination of Abraham Lincoln, for President, met at Cleveland, May 31st, 1864; and after the adoption of a platform of principles, named John C. Fremont, as their candidate for the Presidential Chair. And in order, the more fully, to place themselves, in direct opposition to the President's policy, they announced the doctrine, that the reconstruction of the Southern States, was a question for the consideration of Congress, rather than the Federal Executive. The extreme revolutionary character, of the sentiments of the members of this convention, was also displayed in the endorsement of the principle of confiscating the lands of the rebels, regardless of law and the express words of the Constitution. In this convention, Thaddeus Stevens, Charles Sumner, and men of their revolutionary principles, if true men, should have been found, either in person, or by letters. Being deceivers however, they waited the assembling of another convention, which feared to avow, what its real leaders intended to carry into execution.

Great numbers of the radicals, no doubt, strongly sympathized with the Cleveland convention movement; and wished it success, but were too timid, openly to commit themselves to it. They altogether doubted that it could accomplish any potent result, inasmuch as the popular current in the Republican party seemed too strong in favor of Abraham Lincoln to be diverted from him by any effort that could be made. They surmised correctly, for the Cleveland Convention scarcely produced more than a passing ripple upon the surface. The President had a large army of subordinates, who were all interested in his re-nomination; and besides his skillful knowledge of the politician's art had enabled him to appear before the country as the man of all others, who was believed to be fitted to carry his party onwards to victory. His own remark, that it is never safe to change horses in crossing a stream, served to coin an impress upon the public mind that was now craftily utilized by him.

The Republican politicians assembled at Baltimore, June 7th, 1864, to make Presidential nominations for their party, and amongst these Thaddeus Stevens appeared as a delegate to the convention. And, in order to appear consistent before the country, in view of the contemplated plan of reconstruction, which was now the kernel of radical policy, Mr. Stevens strove to the utmost of his power to exclude all delegates to the convention from any of the rebel States. "He declared that he had never recognized Virginia as being in the Union, since she passed the Ordinance of Secession; and the applause which had greeted the delegates from those States that had spoken in the convention to-day, was to him a more dangerous element than armed rebels in the field."* In spite of the commoner's protest, the delegates from Tennessee, Louisiana and Arkansas, were admitted to seats in the convention, and accredited the full privileges of members from other States.

The Republican representatives in the Baltimore Convention, announced their platform as demanding the unconditional abandonment of all resistance to the Government, without any tender of compromise, and that slavery should no longer be tolerated by the Federal authorities as an institution of the country; the Emancipation Proclamation of the President, and the employment of African soldiers were also approved by the party leaders. An amendment to the Constitution was likewise recommended, so as finally to put an end to slavery in all of the States. But, although President Lincoln had made the subject of reconstruction, the capital topic of his message in December, 1863, and, although his plan was already scouted and derided by a large section of his party, a cowardly hypocritical silence was main-

*New York *World*, June 8th, 1864.

tained upon this most important point. This was the cardinal question of the time, which underlay all others, and which treading close on the heels of military success, was first in the order of importance. It especially deserved to be unfolded by honest men, who desire nothing but the advancement of justice. The truth, however, was that the Republicans were so divided on this subject, that any attempt to define a policy would have cleft the party asunder, and fixed a great gulph between the two segments, the warm adherents of Lincoln, and the Stevens and Sumner extremists.

The nomination of Abraham Lincoln, as Robert Breckenridge, the temporary Chairman of the Baltimore Convention substantially expressed it, was *une fait accompli*, even before the assembling of that body. It simply registered the party determination, as it had generally been arranged and understood throughout the North; inasmuch as no other candidate could be substituted, who would so heartily unite all classes of Republicans in his support. Being a man of no positive ideas, he could permit his opinions to be shaped to suit the popular gale. He, therefore, admirably suited as the Presidential foot-ball to be played by the revolutionists, who could propel him in whatever direction they chose. A man of fixed principles was by no means a suitable instrument of the existing emergency. Besides, Abraham Lincoln had the sobriquet of "*honest*" * appended to his name, which was well calculated to catch the unthinking herd of voters.

The nomination of a candidate for Vice-President, was a matter that likewise called for shrewdness at the hands of the Republican managers in the Baltimore Convention. Three men of early democratic faith—Andrew Johnson, of Tennessee, Hannibal Hamlin, of Maine, and Daniel S. Dickinson, of New York—were the prominent candidates for this position. The first named of these received the endorsement of the convention, in the face of the protest of Thaddeus Stevens, who saw in the

*Dr. Orestes Brownson, the clear-headed thinker and philosopher, himself a member of the Republican party, had the sagacity to perceive what the title of "*honest*" in American politics indicates. In a speech made by him, June 27th, 1864, he remarked that he had no confidence in any man who had the appendage of "*honest*" to his name, as he will invariably be found to be "a cunning man, a canny man, a foxy man." He also added, "There is not a more cunning man in this country than Abraham Lincoln."—*New York World, June 28th*, 1864.

nomination of this candidate a stab at his favorite theory of reconstruction. But the valuable services to the cause of abolitionism, rendered by the Military Governor of Tennessee, could not be overlooked by party manipulators, who more highly prized the ignoble surrender of life cherished principles than the manly performance of honorable duty. This nomination was but in keeping with the promotion of Callicott* and others of like antecedents, who were rewarded in proportion to the low obeisance they had made to the corrupt beast of infamy that had been set up for universal homage.

The selection of rulers by universal suffrage, to govern mankind, is a republican process. It is the result of modern thought, in opposition to the principles of monarchy; and designed to bestow upon all classes of men as large an amount of liberty and power as may be compatible with moral and governmental integrity. Philosophical reflection, in its desire for the elevation of general humanity, up to the period of the French revolution, had concurred in the justice of the effort to equalize men as much as possible in their social and political relations. The boiling, however, of the French caldron, upset the hopes of many calm European thinkers in the capacity of man for self-government; and from that period absolutism in the old world has been surrounding itself with strong barriers, so as to prevent further outbreaks of incendiary madness and lawless revolution.

But the Federal Union was the product of modern thought, as it was molded prior to the French revolution. This Confederacy, having been early grasped from the hands of the monarchical faction, that for a time controlled it; under the administrations of wise rulers it was rendered the model republic of both the ancient and modern world. The extraordinary prosperity which it enjoyed under the principles of Democracy, was because wisdom kept in harmony the complicated machinery of the whole system, based upon tacit, universal consent. During all this time, the turbulent, lawless and fanatical elements of society, were kept in due subordination by that succession of wise and eminent Statesmen who stepped to the helm of Government in 1800, and held the ship steady for sixty years. But the violent

*Salmon P. Chase appointed ex-Speaker Callicott to official position, little doubt in consideration of his base desertion of democratic principles.—*New York World, April 25th*, 1864.

rocking of the vessel began almost instantaneously to show itself with the departure of the great helmsmen, Clay, Webster and Calhoun. The false doctrine of equality had become so impressed upon the popular mind, that with the retirement of these distinguished Statesmen, nearly every newspaper reader conceived himself as equally competent to rule the nation as the elected representatives of the people. Free schools in the North had done their fancied work; they had educated a nation of Statesmen; and the millennial days of freedom were yet in store for the republic.

With such thoughts, the Northern people having originally elevated Abraham Lincoln to the Presidency, not because of his intellectual superiority, but because of his representing the ruling sentiments of his section; it was not to be expected that another than he or his like, would be the Presidential nominee of the Republican party in 1864. Reason had been discomfited in the election of 1860, and being fully dethroned, was in banishment in 1864. Popular election being the mode during pacific times, which wise men in State and Federal compacts had agreed upon for the choice of rulers, to whom the reins of power were to be entrusted, would this same method promote liberty and equity when these Constitutions were overthrown, and a period of disorder had seized the country?

Such was the condition of affairs, when Lincoln and Johnson were nominated at Baltimore, as candidates for President and Vice-President of the United States. Republican success in 1860, was due to the political prostitution of former Whig and Democratic leaders to the abolitionized sentiments of the North, already pregnant with revolution and constitutional downfall. But as the pretended foes of slavery extension, and the courtiers of popular opinions, had been exalted to high seats in the temple of Mammon, was it probable that in 1864, they would abandon their seats, after having caused hundreds of thousands of deluded soldiers to be drowned in seas of blood and carnage, to sustain the non-compromise policy of knaves and madmen. Again, the party that had grasped power in 1860, under the watchwords of economy and reform, was now necessitated to defend, not the annual expenditure of seventy millions of dollars for the support of the Government, but of one thousand millions. Delightful economists and reformers in truth! The party also, that had through the thousands of utterances of its leaders, proclaimed that no danger was to be apprehended from the secession of the Southern States, was now compelled to face an unsubdued rebellion of near four years duration. And the men who came into power vituperating and vilifying Democratic Administrations as having been dishonestly conducted, were since their advent to place, busily engaged in rearing a pagoda of fraud, iniquity and corruption, such as the civilized world had never before contemplated.

The Republican party, although boasting itself of its Christian designs and moral purposes, was the great destroyer of principle amongst the American people. Its organization rested upon the perversion of man's moral nature, the basis of which is truth. Its secret, but unavowed objects, had attracted to its folds, the infidel clergy and statesmen of the North, whose numbers are legion and whose God is humanity. The party from its origin, was the embodiment of conscious untruth in pretending that its only object was to prevent the extension of slavery into free territory; whereas, from its organization, it aimed at the complete extirpation of the institution, even where it had a constitutional existence. The personal liberty bills also had been enacted upon the pretence that these were for the protection of the citizens of the free States; yet, the sole object of these, though violating the Constitution, was to prevent the return of fugitive slaves. During the war again, the Republican party pretended to regard the emancipation of the slaves as a military necessity, when in truth it only meant to take advantage of the war to accomplish its original object. It also pretended to regard Democrats as traitors; but this was assumed simply to render them odious, and drive them from power. This method of ostracism, proved indeed a valuable aid to the revolutionists. During the whole war, indeed, falsehood colored the utterances of the Republican press, so as to delude the people concerning the progress and movements of the national arms. Oaths were not binding upon the consciences of the President, Cabinet Ministers, Senators or Congressmen, who subscribed to a higher law than the Constitution. Plighted faith was no longer required to be observed, according to the principles of those who sought by all means the eradication of the hated Southern institution. From the head of the nation, therefore, to the lowest party subaltern, almost, deception and fraud were employed to further the cause for which war had been made against the South. These and other influences necessarily germinated the festering corruption and demoralization, that arose all over the North in gigantic forms, after the installation of the Republican party; and which threatened to bury humanity in a night of universal gloom.

But the deluge had come; the foundations of the great deep of society were broken up, and constitutional ruin and prostration were everywhere visible. The anarchical mob of the North was ruling the nation, both in the Cabinet and upon the field. The Baltimore Convention was its selection, and the candidates its choice. Law, liberty and order were subordinated to the dictates of fanatical propagandism and revolutionary freedom. And it even militated nothing adversely to Abraham Lincoln, the favorite of the social dregs, that he had the courage at length to avow his infamous conduct in violating the Federal Constitution. In his letter of April 6th, 1864, to Colonel Hodges, he said:

"I felt that measures, otherwise unconstitutional, might become lawful by becoming indispensable to the preservation of the Constitution, through the preservation of the nation. Right or wrong, I assumed this ground, and now avow it."

Society being at this time, in a condition almost of chaotic anarchy and tumultuous disorder, public opinion was no fair index of the intelligent reflection of the reasoning classes, who must always guide the ship of government, or ruin invariably ensues. And as occurred in the French revolution, in the change of attitude by Mirabeau, La Fayette and others, the thoughtful men of the North, who could descry the maelstrom of social overthrow that the vessel of State was approaching, left (as before remarked) the Republican party in considerable numbers, after the commencement of the war; but for every one of this character that deserted the organization of fanaticism, two of an opposite kind came to it from the Democracy, now likewise become imbued with the spirit of revolution. A bitter partisan press was all the time fanning the flames of hatred against the South, and urging onwards the Northern armies to finish the work of destruction in which they were engaged. The anti-war Democrats were pointed out as sympathisers with the Southern rebels, who were drenching the fields of the Republic in the best blood of its citizens, patriotically fighting in defence of the life of the nation. The unreflecting democrat, whose son had fallen at Chancellorsville or Getttysburg, was stirred to rage when told that his party friends were opposed to the war against the people's enemies. He could not see that it was the wicked refusal of the Republican leaders to compromise the difficulties with the Southern people, which had impelled the sections into deadly conflict, and the same which had prolonged it, and flooded the land with blood.

In this state of sentiment, there existed but little probability that the Democrats could do more than protest against the acts and policy of the Administration party. But that they should resist, was in the nature of things; for do not all oppose those injuring them, if they have the power to do so? The Democratic party perceived that war was anti-republican and suicidal to the principles of free government; and they should have been false to the instincts of humanity not to have expressed their disapprobation of a further prosecution of the war. Accordingly, on the 29th of August, 1864, the National Convention of this party assembled in Chicago, and resolved in favor of a cessation of hostilities, in order that peace and the Union might ultimately be restored by pacific remedies. And as the dictate of reason and true republican sentiment, this resolution must ever stand justified before the world and the intelligence of coming ages.

The large majority of the members of this convention, were decided peace men, and made but little concealment of their views. But a portion of the delegates viewed the platform as entirely too strong a committal in favor of peace; and to counterbalance this, they insisted upon the expediency of nominating a war Democrat, as the party candidate for the Presidency. The name of General George B. McClellan was presented to the convention, amidst great applause; and being known to be very popular with the masses of the party, he received the nomination. This candidate was, however, by no means the choice of the avowed peace men, and was accepted by them with considerable reluctance. Could the reverse of that have been expected, when the peninsular hero's participation in the illegal arrest of the Maryland Legislature was as yet unforgotten. George H. Pendleton, a peace man, was settled by this convention as the Democratic candidate for Vice-President.

General McClellan's letter of acceptance had the effect of

deadening Democratic enthusiasm in his support. The military chieftain carried his martial autocracy with him in his letter accepting the nomination; and laid down an interpretation of the platform of his party which was agreeable to himself. But his letter evinced a base truckling to the corrupted war sentiment of the North; and the party should at once have repudiated him as its nominee, and selected a true representative of Democratic principles, who could have aroused warm enthusiasm in his support. There were indeed mutterings heard; but the Democracy had become too far demoralized under the guidance of selfish leaders to be capable of bold action. There were yet Spartan bands in its ranks in abundance, but competent leaders were wanting to unite and lead them to victory, or even honorable defeat.

But even the apparent united array of the old party, that had so long borne victory upon its banners, was terrifying to the enemy. A closing up of ranks was at once ordered. Fremont and his retiring followers deemed it also prudential to return to the fold in order that fanaticism united, might be able to grapple with the common foe. The campaign was short and spirited upon one side alone. Genuine enthusiasm was lacking in the breasts of the Anti-war Democracy. The candidate was tarnished in the eyes of true men, having fought the battles of the wicked despotism that was overthrowing the liberties of the country.

The Republican leaders, on the contrary, were buoyant with enthusiasm in anticipation of the victory of might over right. The legions of infidelity, malice and rapine, were moving their serried columns to the battle that was to crown them victors over equity and plighted compact. The spirit of intuition appeared to the Democratic freemen of the North, and audibly whispered in their tents, before the onset began, "*I will meet the at Phillippi.*" On November 8th, 1864, the battle was fought, and constitutionalism was prostrated upon the Western continent.

Abraham Lincoln was again elected President, carrying the electoral vote of every State considered in the Union, except three—New Jersey, Delaware and Kentucky. Over four hundred thousand of a popular majority endorsed his election. The anarchical mob-spirit of the North had again triumphed over reason and reflection; and the party, which was regardless of law and order, had anew seized the helm of Government. The exhausted youth of the South, now alone stayed, the oppressor's advance. Should their resistance at length be fully overcome, the Juggernaut of Northern incendiary fanaticism, would then roll its hideous figure over the prostrate form of constitutional government.

CHAPTER XXIV

FANATICISM TRIUMPHS.

The tide of warfare and invasion still continued to swell, and was rapidly submerging in a sea of blood, section after section of the Southern States. The available military strength from the old Dominion to Texas, had been conscripted to repel the hated Yankee invaders; the chivalric armies of defense were greatly reduced in numbers, and still further melting away in daily collisions with the enemy; and no avenues now remained open that promised replenishment to the rapidly exhausting Confederacy. The spirit and courage that had shown themselves upon a hundred battle-fields were yet unconquered, but the rolling waves of fresh levies from the North were advancing with steady move, and promised to prostrate in a general overthrow the still struggling remnants of the Southern armies. Cut off from the outside world, the Confederate defensive strength must alone be raised upon their own soil, and their armies replenished from their own citizens.

The American sectional struggle, being the commencement upon the Western Continent of the great battle of Communism with capital and stable government, the Red Republicans of the old world lent all their influence to the cause of the revolutionists, throwing their weight into the abolition scale by enlisting themselves in tens of thousands in the Northern armies. Europe imported its exuberant *sans culotte* population upon our shores; fanaticism turned the negro slaves of the South into conscripting fields; and from these two sources, the Northern military strength in a large measure was steadily replenished. But the conquest of the Southern rebels had not taken place in sixty days, as had been promised. The negroes of the South now proved a valuable reserve, upon which the war party of the North could fall back, and red republicanism also arose in demand to assist in the completion of the work that had at first been sneered at as a matter of insignificance.

That abolitionism and communism should have united in our sectional struggle, was altogether natural, inasmuch as they had like aspirations, being sisters of a common patronage. Both followed the movement of modern free thought, which for ages had desired to reach in governmental spheres, the practical equalization of humanity. To strive, however, for full human equality was to endeavor to remove what the inscrutable wisdom of Diety, for certain reasons, had implanted in nature. And those who did so, influenced by logical reasoning, were they for the most part, who were unwilling to recognize the existence of a Supreme Creator and ruler of men ; and their desire was to remove all the inequalities, which the creative mind had left upon the face of universal being. They were those who officiously set themselves up as wiser than the Divine Lawgiver, and as competent to rectify the work of His hands.

Freedom itself has been the conception of the philosophical thought of the world; and an attribute of those alone who have been able to comprehend and enjoy it. It has been the birthright of the few in all ages and countries; and so will it ever remain. The great mass of mankind are born either tyrants or slaves, both being endowed with like characteristics. For the slave becomes the most unrelenting task-master, when circumstances have elevated him from his former menial condition; and the tyrant, in turn, readily sinks to a state of servitude, when reverses of fortune have overtaken him. It is only he whom nature has endowed with the principles of freedom, who stubbornly resists the condition of slavery, in which his birth may have placed him; and who makes incessant effort to relieve himself from the chains of bondage. The great bulk of mankind do not realize the bondage of their creation; and hence thay make no effective effort to relieve themselves from it. Freedom does not consist in being relieved from the necessity of manual labor, but in the right to think, speak and act as a moral intelligence. Esop and Epictetus, the philosophers, were free men, though occupying the condition of slavery. He alone is a free man, whom his moral and intellectual qualities make free. And he is one, again, who only asks from others what he would be willing to extend were circumstances changed; but seeing the inequality implanted upon the face of creation, wisdom admonishes him to permit the laws of destiny to remain unquestioned as they are fixed.

Free government, likewise being the product of philosophical thought, has hitherto sunk, because too large a proportion of mankind have ever permitted themselves to be made the slaves of designing tyrants, who care alone for their own promotion and success. The ancient Republics of Greece and Rome disappeared, because their freemen were too few in numbers to defend them against the natural foes of their existence. Centralization, the antipodal force to freedom, from the origin of government, has been active and has always succeeded in submerging free institutions in the abyss of despotism. During the middle ages, also, the Teutonic intellect succeeded in establishing free republics and an enlargement of freedom in different parts of Europe; but all these were overthrown in the centralizing movements that reared absolute monarchies in France, Spain, England and elsewhere, about the close of the fifteenth century. The tyrants pretended to enlarge the liberties of the lower classes, in order to entice them to their support; and by means of the aid thus obtained they were enabled to prostrate freedom in one common ruin, and ride in triumph over those whose services they had so treacherously subsidized.

And in the alliance between abolitionism and the communistic element of Europe, free government in the Western world was again assailed by enemies who appeared in the habiliments of Confederates. These foes stood forth as the friends of freedom and universal humanity; and professed the most sincere love for America and her institutions. The attitude, however, which these assumed, clearly demonstrated that their zeal outstripping their wisdom, rendered them like Matthison and John of Leyden, the enemies of social order and constitutional law; and that their efforts to extend freedom beyond its natural limits, would in the end turn out to be labor in vain and purely abortive. And worse than this would follow, as it was perceived, that these superserviceable efforts would prove the suicidal, and destroy even liberty of those worthy of it; and as had happened in other ages, aid in centralizing all the power of the government, and ultimately lead to the establishment of an empire where the peaceful and prosperous Republic of America had flourished.

A tendency to centralization, as before observed, had existed from the origin of the Federal Union; and it was one, which of all others, distinguished the Federal party and its successors from their opponent, through all the periods of our history. Against this trait of Federalism, the Democratic party early arrayed itself, and steadfastly adhered to this position; and, although it was the party of the humble classes, and the one which might have been supposed most likely to sympathize in all efforts to elevate mankind; yet comprising in its ranks a body of philosophical thinkers, whom principle alone detained, it was not strange that it ever remained the Constitutional party of the country, which was opposed to all useless aims of fanatical zeal. The Democratic party was indeed, from its origin, the exponent of the most enlarged freedom of which men are capable. It was the one that made our country the home of the oppressed of all nations, and which strove by means of constitutional law to afford them all the means by which they might uninterruptedly work out their own destiny. It, however, never accepted the theory of the universal equality of all races of men. But Caucasian equality, in a certain sense, having been the established theory upon which the government was framed, this was accepted as the embodiment of the largest practical liberty that was attainable. The Democratic was, therefore, simply the Constitutional party of the nation.

Having been such, then, rather than a *sans culotte Democracy*, which its name might have implied; when the fanatical and revolutionary element of the country had developed itself to strength, and, like the tyrants of Europe, sought to subvert the fundamental theory of government, under the hypocritical cry of universal Democracy, it was natural that the party of Jefferson should stand by the constitutional institutions of the Republic. It thus exhibited itself as consistent with its early record, and opposed to the destructive principles of fanaticism and communism; both of which ever lie in wait for the overthrow of all established government when an opportunity presents itself. The uneasy, agitating and revolutionary elements of Europe, led by Victor Hugo, Garibaldi, and others of like character, were very naturally, therefore, in sympathetic accord with American fanaticism. The British Red Republican classes were so gratified with the re-election of Abraham Lincoln, that a large body of them in a letter, promptly congratulated the successful candidate upon his political success.

Fanaticism in America, fortified as it was, therefore, in the affections of the unreflecting millions of Europe, was a force of nearly invincible power. It is ever such in its nature, being propelled by the emotions rather than by the reason of mankind. What else furnished the crusaders the material, that prolonged for centuries their struggles for the conquest of the holy land? The thirty years' war of Germany was inspirited by that ever living principle of the human breast; and the blood that flowed on Saint Bartholomew's night, and which moistened the soil of France, Spain and the Netherlands for ages, was shed by this active enemy of human repose. Did not, indeed, leading Abolitionists openly declare that nothing could justify the flooding of American fields with crimson gore, except the principle which had produced the war? And what was that principle, as they themselves confessed it, but that urging of the equality of all mankind? In behalf of this, then, European and American fanatics were united. This union could not, therefore, be but almost omnipotent and resistless.

Fanaticism was the ruling force during the middle ages, and down to the peace of Westphalia. But philosophic reason rose to the helm about this period. The principles of Des Cartes and Bacon, taught men that when two religious parties of antagonistic principles live in the same country, it is the dictate of wisdom, that the one do yield to the other, so far as that they can live together in peace, rather than in a state of perpetual warfare. It was perceived that conquering a people does not lead to the change of their opinions, but rather intensifies them in their former notions. Fanatical and religious wars disappeared as the consequence of such views, from the face of Europe; and the adjudication of questions of this nature, was remitted to the forum of reason and sound judgment. The peace of Munster inaugurated in government the era of religious toleration. Compromise, from this period, settled what before had been referred to the arbitrament of arms.

But as christianity, the religion of peace, had been perverted by fanaticism into one of enthusiastic zeal and bloodshed, so was the philosophy of the seventeenth and eighteenth centuries changed by the like influence into revolution and governmental ruin. The same classes of men who, upon the religious arena, had converted the divine love of the master into bloody fervor, now entered the department of social life, and corrupted the principles of pure thought in the furnace of the French revolution. Excessive zeal and fanatical ardor, threatened during this eventful period, to overturn all sound government in an abyss of social destruction; and it was simply owing to the sagacious wisdom of European Statesmen, that the current of fanaticism, now found in the new channel, was able to be successfully stemmed. The stream of fury, crime and madness was at length stopped, but numerous lessons were written by the hand of destiny for the edification of future ages.

Fanaticism ever performs acts of kindred character. Doing the bidding of emotion, it never consults reason, and hence its work is hastily and imperfectly executed. Being the quality of feminine minds, it moves without the guidance of reflective thought, which is needed to direct human action. American abolitionism being of like quality with other fanaticisms, its movements in the war against the South must likewise be similar. And so indeed did it show itself. Having refused all tenders of amicable settlement and compromise between the sections, before the outbreak of hostilities, it was not to be supposed these pacific modes would be embraced after the demon of battle had lit up the flames of sectional strife. Death must continue his work of destruction, or the zeal of the invaders would not be satisfied. Instead of terms of adjustment being considered, the car of revolution pressed onwards to its final goal.

Sherman's invading hosts, by means of fire and sword, cut their way through South Carolina and Georgia; and Columbia, the capitol of the Spartan State of the Southern Confederacy, sunk amidst the cracking of hostile flames and the bombs of Northern artillerists. The shade of the brave Count Pulaski, from his honored monumental summit in the City of Savannah, was next compelled to view the old flag of the Republic, carried as a despot's banner, for which ignoble service the heroic Pole, in his devotions to constitutional liberty, had never consecrated it. Torn up railroads, burnt bridges, and plundered residences, marked the path of General Stoneman and his followers through South-western Virginia and Western North Carolina. Alabama and Western Georgia received rude experience in the severities of war. Captured cities and the remains of burned locomotives, cars and cotton, attested the presence of Wilson and his raiders. The beautiful and fertile valley of the Shenandoah, meandered by the river of its own name, was made memorable in modern warfare, because of the fiendish and Attilla-like destruction of property by General Sheridan and his devastating soldiery. The flouring mills and barns * of this large valley district of Virginia were consumed in the flames of Federal atrocity, an act of barbarity that finds no parallel in the annals of civilized war. And upon the flimsy pretext that a Northern engineer had been killed by some unknown rebel, the Federal Haynau confesses that "all the houses, within an area of five miles, were burned." † Destruction and desolation spread their ravages in all directions, as the armies of the North meandered in tortuous courses, through the barren fields of the South; and the black and smoking ruins that marked the invaders paths, presented sad evidence of the love that held together in fraternal union the Northern and Southern people.

Whilst the blows which fanaticism dealt, were falling thick and fast upon the Southern Confederacy; and whilst its walls already breached, upon all sides, were showing unmistakable signs of yielding to the assaults of the enemy, the valleys began to resound with shouts of joy for the nearly grasped victory. The mask that had so long been worn to conceal the object of the war, was now laid aside by the boldest of the radical leaders. George W. Julian, a Member of Congress from Indiana, in his speech of February 8th, 1865, boldly avowed that the designs of his party never contemplated anything further in their war for

---

* General Sheridan reported the destruction effected by his soldiers, as follows:

"In moving back to this point, the whole country from the Blue Ridge to the North Mountain, has been made untenantable for a rebel army. I have destroyed over 2,000 barns filled with wheat and hay and farming implements, over seventy mills filled with flour and wheat; have driven in front of the army over 4,000 head of stock, and have killed and issued to the troops not less than 3,000 sheep. This destruction embraces the Luray Valley and Little Fort Valley, as well as the main valley."—Greeley's Conflict, Vol. 2, p. 611.

† Horace Greeley, in his History of the American Conflict, Volume 2, page 611, speaks as follows of the devastation of the Shenandoah Valley:

"It is not obvious that the national cause was advanced, or the national prestige exalted, by this resort to one of the very harshest and most questionable expedients, not absolutely forbidden by the laws of civilized warfare."

the Union, expect their triumph for human rights, that is the the emancipation of the negro race, and their elevation to equal, social and political rights with the whites. Characterizing the conflict as a war of the people, he said:

"They (the people), expect that Congress will pass a bill for the confiscation of the fee of rebel landholders, and they expect the President will approve it. They expect that Congress will provide for the reconstruction of the rebel States, by systematic legislation, which shall guarantee republican governments to each of those States, *and the complete enfranchisement of the negro.* * * * They expect that Congress will provide for parcelling out the forfeited and confiscated lands of the rebels in small homesteads, among the soldiers and seamen of the war, as a fit reward for their valor, and a security against the ruinous monopoly of the soil in the South."

In the same speech Mr. Julian even admitted that "the whole policy of the Administration had been revolutionized." But this was an acknowledgment that would not have been made at a much earlier period. It had been the standing accusation of the Anti-war Democrats, but was steadily resented by the men themselves who had produced the revolution. Now, however, when their hold of the Government for the next four years was fully established, and when the rebellion seemed to be nearing its close, the men that had hitherto averred, in the most solemn language, that the war was alone prosecuted for the defense of the Union, could step forward, the success of their ideas being assured, and confess their hypocrisy and the deception that had been practiced upon the country.

In the second session of the 38th Congress, fanatical hopes were buoyant beyond what had before been witnessed. The Presidential election that crowned the Republican party with victory; and had dispirited, in a corresponding measure, large numbers of Democrats who felt that for the time being, their party was utterly prostrated. The car of radical destruction had obtained such velocity that it seemed to many as labor in vain to attempt any longer to resist it. And when Representative Ashley on the 6th of January, 1865, called up in the House his favorite joint resolution to submit to the States, the Constitutional Amendment abolishing slavery throughout the Union, several Democrats who, in the former session of Congress, had opposed the Amendment, now co-operated with the Republicans and gave it their support. Those who now for the first time supported the measure, had become fully convinced that though violative of the Constitution, it would be finally carried; and that longer resisting it would be attended with no beneficial results. And notwithstanding, duty to principle and obedience to their oaths, demanded of all sincere Democrats, that they defend with their votes the Federal Constitution; and that they allow the responsibility for its violation and overthrow to rest upon other shoulders than their own. After a heated controversy of three weeks on the floor of the House, the joint resolution was adopted by 119 yeas to 56 nays. When this result was announced, fanatical zeal as it ever does, burst all the barriers of order, and filled the Hall of Congress with loud and continued demonstrations of joy. One historian, himself a Republican, says: "Never was such a scene before witnessed in any legislative hall."*

At this session of Congress, the establishment of a Freedmen's Bureau was considered. A measure of this character was found necessary to be established, when the authority of the Southern master had been broken by the Presidential edict; and the negro slaves set adrift as freemen. And the demand for governmental protection came from the same classes of the people, who had ever claimed for the negro the highest rights; and that they were fully competent to take care of themselves if freedom was granted to them. The request for such a bureau came from the Freedmen's Aid Societies of Boston, New York, Philadelphia and Cincinnati; and from men who were the most ardent friends of emancipation and negro equality. As soon, however, as this equality had been proclaimed by the Government, these same people instinctively shrunk, as it were, from allowing the negro unaided to make his future way through life. They were fully conscious that he was incompetent to cope with the superior white man in the struggle for existence, much as they had boasted of his ability. But their emotional natures, driving them without rudder or compass, they had looked to emancipation as the long sought haven of hope; and as soon as this had been reached, a gleam of reason seemed to signify to them that the freed African was incompetent to retain, if left to him self, what he had grasped. George H. Pendleton, of Ohio, when this matter had been discussed, at the former session of Congress,

*Barrett's life of Abraham Lincoln, p. 686.

turned the argument against the Abolitionists in the following words:

"Nor need I remind gentlemen, that this very difficulty was frequently foretold, that the incapacity of the negro to take care of himself, was often alluded to, and that you always ridiculed the idea. What will you do with the negro when you shall have emancipated him? was frequently asked; and as often your virtuous indignation boiled over at the bare intimation that he was not thoroughly competent to take care of himself."*

The Freedmen's Bureau Bill was the subject of a long and heated discussion in both Houses of Congress. It was contended by those opposed to the measure, that the Constitution conferred no authority upon the General Government to establish such a bureau of African affairs; but it was become necessary, that stronger arguments should be urged against the passage of a bill, than its unconstitutionality. The faction whose aim was resisted by that instrument of compact, was not likely to heed arguments drawn from it. This was particularly so now, when the revolutionists believed that they were about to triumph in the near future over the armed combattants of the South. Some of the Republicans of both Houses, besides the Democrats, opposed the passage of the Freedmen's Bureau, as a measure not contemplated within the purview of the General Government. John P. Hale, of New Hampshire, and others, argued that as the negro was now freed, he should be left to manage his affairs to the best of his ability. The measure, however, passed both the Senate and House of Representatlves, and having received the assent of President Lincoln, became a law March 2d, 1865.

The act embraced the management of the affairs of freedmen refugees, and abandoned lands in the South. The bureau created by it was attached to the War Department; and its friends, doubtless wishing to excite no inquiry as to the expense that would be required to sustain it, made no appropriation for carrying out its purposes. But E. M. Stanton, the Secretary of War, exhibited his humble obeisance to his masters; and greatly endeared himself with them in the service he rendered their project by his illegal action. He assigned army officers to take charge of the new bureau's concerns, provided buildings for its accommodation, and furnished the supplies required by requisitions on the Quarter-Master's Department. By this method the

*Speech of March 1st, 1864.

expense needed to sustain the newly created bureau, could not easily be known, as the War Department was able to cover the whole with its ample wings.

The proceedings of the second session of the Thirty-eighth Congress, evinced a spirit of malignity and vindictiveness on the part of the revolutionary men who shone conspicuous in those bodies, that even supassed in intensity the worst exhibitions that the war fury had as yet produced. Indeed, this spirit in a measure animated the breasts of the war patriots from the commencement of hostilities. Bloody conquest and destruction of the Southern people, was the motto imprinted upon the banners of the braves, led by the hyena captains of the North, and inspired by the infidel clergy of New England; the hypocrites who pretended to be the followers of the meek and lowly man of Nazareth; but who were simply the exponents of the principles of Voltaire, Condorcet and Rousseau, and visionary propagandists of the murderous creed of the leaders of the French revolution.

Universal extermination of the Southern whites, wholesale seizure of their property, and its distribution amongst the emancipated negro slaves, were the proclaimed doctrines of Stevens, Wade, Sumner, and the other stars of the first magitude that sparkled in the firmament of fanatical glory. Rather than compromise with traitors, Thaddeus Stevens, early in the war, had announced himself as willing "*to see the Union shattered into ten thousand fragments.*" One revolutionary scheme after another had been from the first proposed in Congress by the most violent of these men, all designed to destroy the Southern whites and elevate barbarians to political equality with them. A retroactive spirit, antipodal to the destructive, during the first stages of the war, had the ability to hold the demoniac force in more circumscribed bounds than the French Girondists had been able to do, in the old world. The spirit was the same, however, but no vast American city afforded equal opportunities for its development, as existed across the waters.

The closing session of the Thirty-eighth Congress, supplemented former acts of negro elevation, by opening, at last to the new American, the privilege of carrying the United States mails. This was done at a period when demoralization and corruption, had made such inroads into the Republican party, that it was, perhaps, difficult for the *pure government of fanaticism*, to find enough of loyal whites, of sufficient honesty to perform even the menial service of carrying the mails. But, if negro purity was even at that time above par, the leaders had unfortunately omitted to consult their great Apostle, Jean Jacques Rousseau, who would have advised them that the African's morality would sink in the proportion as culture was thrust upon him.

The leading revolutionists, during this session of Congress, had a fine opportunity to inflame the minds of the Northern unthinking people, by accusing the rebels of cruelty towards Federal prisoners of war. It was not at all sincere sympathy for the Northern soldiers lying in Southern prisons, that excited these complaints, but the desire to intensify Northern hate against the rebels, which was the sole food that sustained the revolutionary Republican party. Generous breasts were equally touched with pity for prisoners of war, whether confined in Northern or Southern prisons. But the party that had it in their power to end the captivity of all the Northern prisoners by an exchange for Southern in their possession, and refused to do so, could not be supposed to entertain very ardent sympathy for their captives languishing in the enemy's custody. At this time, the North held twice as large a number of Southern prisoners, as the Confederates had in their keeping. Besides, real sympathetic men, would not have spurned the generous tender of Lord Wharncliffe, a British Nobleman, to mitigate the miseries of Federal prison life, as William H. Seward, the representative of the Administration, had the audacity to do.

Retaliation, confiscation and extermination were the current watch-words of fanatical feeling; and no measures of Congress received ardent support, save as they approximated the attainment of these *righteous* standards of intemperate zeal. Even the patriot daughters, the Sanitary and Christian Commissions, and the other charitable agencies of the North, could raise their five hundred millions of dollars to support Congress in its unconstitutional advances; and to aid in sending the demon of war upon his fiendish mission to the South. Another Madame Roland upon the American continent might have cried aloud: "*O, Christianity, what crimes are committed in thy name!*" An infidel priesthood had deluded the people into the belief, that the bible meant what its words contradicted; and an oligarchy of maddened enthusiasts, at the dictation of an atheistic Congress, sought to canonize the overthrow of constitutional rights as the highest attainment of humanitarian effort. Passionate hatred of slaveholders was esteemed by all these as the holiest inspirations of Divinity.

The 38th Congress closed its session March 3d, 1865, having expended their every effort to pour out the full vial of their demoniac wrath upon the heads of the Southern people. Measures of almost every character, were considered to complete the work of destruction. The leaders, however, were unable to secure the passage of their bill of retaliation, which should permit them to inflict vengeance upon the rebel prisoners in their hands, although the same was pressed for a time with great earnestness. Full confiscation of rebel property, as Mr. Stevens would have desired, was also too daring a project to run the gauntlet of public criticism in the North. Its pressure was left in abeyance. The great question of reconstruction, although considerably debated, was likewise left for future discussion when fanaticism had fully grasped its victory.

But the tide of war moved onwards, and speedily prostrated one embankment of opposition after another. The battle of the Five Forks was lost by the Confederates; and the long and heroic defense of Richmond and Petersburg, was ended. The Capitol of the resistant States was evacuated, and General Robert E. Lee and his depleted army were compelled to surrender themselves prisoners of war to the Northern invaders. The sun of the Confederacy sunk at Appomattox; and the night of fanatical despotism covered with its mantle the thirty-six States of the American Union.

The old Whig party had been prostrated by fanaticism; the Democracy had been rent and overthrown by it; and now, after four years of the bloodiest strife that civilization had ever contemplated, the united South was forced to lower her standards from the Potomac to the Rio Grande, and do repentant homage for daring to defend the inherited rights of her people. The Roman Republic was buried on the field of Phillippi; American Free Government was also gathered to its fathers, in the land of its birth, beneath the soil of Virginia. The social cataclysm that the founders and friends of the Republic had foreseen and dreaded, with pensive awe, had come at last in all its direful reality.

The windows of a wrathful heaven had opened wide upon their hinges; and the foundations of the great deep of constitutional liberty were broken up and destroyed.

Victory, however, had fully perched upon the banners of the revolutionists, and their triumphant armies were receiving the plaudits of a deluded people. Rivers of blood had been shed, and near a million of America's youth had perished in the terrific confict of arms which madness had provoked. Besides the enormous expenditure of several thousand millions of dollars which were required to prosecute a four years' war, a debt of almost three thousand millions of dollars, and a large pensionary list were entailed as a legacy upon the country, for the *benefit* of coming ages. But the fanatics knew no bounds to their ecstasy, when victory finally crowned their banners. The gain was so incalculable, in their estimation, that their shouts of applause almost rent in twain the whole Northern heavens. They had wrested, without compensation, four millions of negro bondmen from the ownership of their Southern masters, and they had done nothing more. What was this, however, save the equity and justice which robbers exhibit? But had they not (as history will inquire) also preserved the Union from destruction and dismemberment? The old Union, the product of mutual consent and compromise, needed no defenders before the rise of the Abolition party of the North; and but for this baneful organization no defense should have been at all necessary. The free government of the Constitution had been metamorphosed into a despotism under the name of a Republic. Such is the government which Abolitionists preserved for Americans. And their service in behalf of the Union simply resembled, therefore, the aid of those *generous* banditti, who enroll their names as a municipal constabulary, to protect the city against their own secret robberies.

CHAPTER XXV.

THEORIES IN CONFLICT.

The rebellious armies, after their long and valorous resistance, finally stocked their arms in submission to the Federal Administration. Iniquity and crime were now permitted to take their seats as conquerors, and dispense justice to their humbled vassals. But vengeance, one of the compensating furies of humanity, turned her hand and snatched the figure-head of conquest from its exalted seat, which left a void to be filled by another. The rancor of Marat, and the revenge of Charlotte Corday, had crossed the ocean, and were again confronting each other. In the moment of despair a victim is sacrificed. The American President was shot in Ford's Theatre, in the City of Washington, by the furious J. Wilkes Booth. The apparent embodiment of the victory, as usually happens, rather than of the crimes committed, was the one consigned by the fates to the eternal shades.

But Abraham Lincoln, the representative of the Abolition party, was by no means the worst man in its ranks; and vengeance missed its mark when he was selected to bear into the wilderness the sins of fanaticism. The Marat of the revolution had escaped, and was still breathing forth slaughter against the objects of his venom. But the act of canonization performed over the manes of the deceased President, will fail to rescue his name from the odium that must ever rest upon it as the representative despot who, in violation of his oath, trampled upon the Constitution of his country. Saintship in this case was too hastily conferred; and, it is to be feared, that in after years the adversary will yet rise and read so long a list of charges, that a re-hearing being granted, the verdict of fanaticism may be rescinded. Will not the enemy be tempted to cite even the place of the assassination, as an unbecoming one, in which saints and martyrs should be congregated, when the blood of their countrymen was moistening many a battle field. The assassin's poniard drank the life-blood of Saint Thomas a'Becket, in a spot more holy than the theatre. But Nero is said to have fiddled whilst Rome was burning, which was of a piece with visiting the theatre when death in every shape was stalking the land.

The mantle of the assassinated President fell upon Andrew Johnson, the Vice-President, who, after qualifying himself, entered upon the discharge of his official functions as the Chief Magistrate of the United States. Mr. Johnson was a Southern citizen; and as a Senator in Congress from Tennessee, had resisted the secession movement of his people with all the ability he could command. Even after his State had seceded he remained firm in his attachment to the Government; and for so doing had been burned in effigy in nearly every village of Tennessee. Although elected to high positions by his countrymen, no cordial sympathy had ever existed between the ruling classes of the South and himself. The former viewed him as a *sans culotte* of ability, who had risen to position without wealth, culture or social standing. A natural antagonism, in turn, repelled him from these; and allied him in feeling with the humble classes of his State and of the whole country. And again, though a member of the extreme Southern State Rights party, yet having lacked that cultured training needed to produce the finished statesman, he never fully accepted the ultimate deductions of the Jeffersonian and Calhoun theory of constitutional construction; and when secession came, his repugnance to the slave-holding classes of the South, induced him to take his stand with the representatives of the General Government, as being the surer embodiment of freedom and popular democracy.

A hurricane of rage and vindictive fury swept over the Northern States, as the news of the assassination of Abraham Lincoln sped over the telegraphic wires of the country. It was the period of the highest intensity of public feeling that had manifested itself since the announcement of the attack on Fort Sumpter in April, 1861. Freedom of opinion disappeared absolutely for a time, and it was expected that a sad melancholy should clothe the countenances of all in sorrow, for the misfortune that had befallen the Union. A philosopher would hardly have expected that all should be wrapped in sadness for the death of one who had permitted himself to be the leading representative of the fanatical classes of the country; who, in order to carry out their wild and chimerical ideas, had overthrown all the embankments of constitutional liberty, and flooded in a sea of blood the one-half of the States of the Federal Union. A sort of compensation, however, always obtains in the affairs of men and nations. Such may have happened in this case, in the divine order of omnipotence. Fanaticism had triumphed. A check was required; and a subservient President would by no means supply the demand. Destiny had selected one of stern material for the performance of the service she required. Andrew Johnson, with unquailing firmness, had already passed through the furnace of opposition, which had steeled him with the courage that enabled him to grapple successfully with the boldest assailant he might be compelled to encounter.

But to comfort themselves for the removal of their President, the Abolitionists pretended to believe that they recognized the finger of Providence in what had occurred. The kind hearted, charitable and humane Abraham Lincoln, as they effected to believe him to have been constituted, was not the man to dispense full and exact justice to rebels and traitors, who had maliciously exerted themselves, to the best of their ability, to destroy the Union, and establish a new one with slavery as its corner stone. The man who, as Military Governor of Tennessee, had shown himself relentless towards traitors, was the one to fill the Presidential Chair which the times demanded. Such expressions as the following were everywhere current: "*The traitors have killed their best friend; Andrew Johnson will show no mercy to traitors; Jefferson Davis and Robert E. Lee will now swing high on a sour apple tree.*"

The new President in his expressions and conduct, at first gave seekers of blood some verbal assurance that the mantle of authority had fallen upon *suitable* shoulders. Delegations of citizens from different States waited upon the Chief Magistrate, and tendered him their hearty support. To one of these from New Hampshire, shortly after his installation, he used the following language:

"Treason is a crime and must be punished as a crime. It must not be regarded as a mere difference of political opinion. It must not be excused as an unsuccessful rebellion, to be overlooked and forgiven. It is a crime before which all other crimes sink into insignificance; and in saying this, it must not be considered that I am influenced by angry or revengeful feelings."*

Not only did President Johnson express himself in the strongest terms, that *treason must be made odious;* but as an adroit dissembler he humored public sentiment, and moved with the current as it drifted. Deferring to public opinion, which came to suspect that Booth and his accomplices, were simply instruments in the hands of the President of the defunct Confederacy, and other prominent men of the South, on the 2d of May, 1865, he issued a proclamation offering large rewards for the arrest of certain prominent characters, whom suspicion had designated. In this proclamation, one hundred thousand dollars were offered for the capture of Jefferson Davis; and twenty-five thousand each, for Clement C. Clay, Jacob Thompson, George N. Sanders and Beverly Tucker; and ten thousand for William C. Cleary, the late clerk of Mr. Clay.

It was not long, after the President's accession to the Chair of State, that one remark after another began to disclose his real sentiments; and show that he was not in sympathy with the revolutionary element of the party to which he owed his election. In an address to a delegation from Indiana, April 21st, 1865, he touched the cardinal question of the time, that of reconstruction, in the following words:

"Some are satisfied with the idea that States are to be lost in territorial and other divisions,—are to loose their character as States. But their life-breath has only been suspended, and it is a high constitutional obligation we have to secure each of these States in the possession and enjoyment of a republican form of government. * * * While I have opposed dissolution and disintegration on the one hand, on the other I have opposed consolidation or the centralization of power in the hands of the few."†

Such language disclosed the fact that Andrew Johnson was neither an advocate of the State suicide theory of Sumner and Stevens, nor a consolidationist of the school of Alexander Hamilton. To reconcile, however, the above and other utterances of like character, with expressions made whilst he was Military Governor of Tennessee, is a somewhat difficult problem, but which time perhaps may aid in solving. But a Maurice of Saxony, was needed to figure upon the arena of American history. In Andrew John-

**Annual Cyclopædia* for 1865, p. 801.
†*Annual Cyclopædia.* for 1865, p. 801.

son, it may have been that the gold of constitutional democracy was again beginning to gleam through the sedimental filth of fanaticism, which had flooded it since the advent of the revolutionists to power.

The President for a time was very guarded in his expressions, and only an occasional sentence dropped from him, that (as time disclosed) indicated his genuine opinions. The excitement aroused by the assassination of Abraham Lincoln, upon the close of the rebellion, caused almost the firmest defenders of principle to vacillate somewhat in their political action, and bend before the terrific blasts of vindictive fury that were coursing all sections of the country. President Johnson would have required well-nigh super-human endowments to have resisted all the demands which fanaticism exacted of him; and to have steadily opposed every effort which the revolutionists made to utterly crush with the merciless heel of oppression, the conquered people of the Southern States. On the first of May, 1865, the President, following the advice of his Attorney-General, appointed a military commission to try the conspirators for the assassination of the murdered President. This officer pretented to find in the law of nations, authority for trying the culprits by military rather than by civil law. It was not difficult for that law officer of the Administration to invent excuses for the appointment of a military commission, when, after the close of the war he could, as chief legal expositor of the Government, declare that the wearing of Confederate uniforms was a fresh act of hostility.

The military commission, charged with the trial of the conspirators, sat from May 13th until June 29th, 1865; and, after having heard the evidence, sentenced the accused to punishments which the civil law had no power to inflict. Four of those charged as conspirators, David E. Harold, George S. Atzerodt, Lewis Payne and Mary E. Suratt, were sentenced by the Commission to be hung, which sentence was approved by President Johnson, and the 7th of July was fixed for their execution. A writ of *Habeas Corpus*, sued out in behalf of Mrs. Suratt, was suspended by the President; and strenuous efforts were made in the interests of this individual, in order to shield her from the doom of legal murder to which the American officials had condemned her. Even President Johnson, on the morning of the execution, refused to meet the suppliant daughter of the devoted woman, whom the furies were about to immolate to the manes of Abraham Lincoln. A dark cloud must ever rest upon the memory of the President who permitted fanaticism to exult in the sacrifice of this innocent female. Indeed, the execution of these four victims will ever stand in American history as one of the darkest blots upon its pages. The four victims were virtually murdered, inasmuch as they were tried and condemned by a tribunal unauthorized by the Federal Constitution. This governmental compact declares that:

"No person shall be held to answer for a capital or otherwise infamous crime, unless on the presentment or indictment of a Grand Jury, except in cases arising in the land or naval forces, or in the militia when in actual service, in time of war or actual danger."

On the 29th of May, 1865, the President instituted measures for the re-establishment of Federal authority in the subjugated States of the South. On this date he issued his Proclamation of Amnesty and Pardon, granting general forgiveness for past offenses to all those engaged in the rebellion, with fourteen exceptions, which included the most influential and intelligent of the Southern Confederates. And following in the wake of his predecessor, President Johnson, as a Roman Emperor, would have selected his pretors, named one after another, Military Governors for the States of North Carolina, South Carolina, Alabama, Georgia, Florida, Mississippi and Texas; but none were appointed for Virginia, Tennessee, Arkansas and Louisiana. The measures already taken by Abraham Lincoln for the re-organization of these last named States, were regarded by his successor as having placed them *rectae in curia*. William M. Holden, the first appointed of these, was named Governor of North Carolina the same day on which the afore mentioned edict of amnesty had been promulgated. In this *pronunciamento* it was ordered, as regards all voters in the South, before being re-clothed with the elective franchise, that they should take and subscribe an oath which the Constitution did not prescribe; and which required them to abide by and support all laws and proclamations, which had been made during the rebellion, with reference to the emancipation of slaves. All such demands made of the people of the South, were utterly inconsistent with the principles of the Federal Government. In the appointment of the Governors, and in the forced dictation of terms for the restoration of authority in the subjugated section, whilst the States were still named as such, they, nevertheless, were treated simply as conquered provinces; and governed by the laws of military dominion, which obtained during the middle ages.

Revolutionary as was the method pursued by President Johnson, for restoring the rebel States to their autonomy in the Union, it was not sufficiently so to meet the approval of the radical Abolitionists. It was clearly understood before the avowal of any plan of restoration by the President, that unless his views coincided with the radicals, his policy would be combatted by them. The unconcealed Abolitionists no longer demanded emancipation alone for the negro, but they now insisted likewise upon his social and political equality with the whites. Wendell Phillips, one of the early and consistent leaders of the Abolition party, in a speech delivered at the Cooper Institute, May 12th, 1865, gave utterance to the following sentiments:

> "Abolitionists secured liberty for the black man; he achieved but half of his work, which he had pledged half his life to effect during thirty years. I shall never relax my efforts till an amendment to the Constitution is passed, declaring that no State shall make any distinction between persons born on our soil, and those residing on it, on account of race, color or descent." *

No sooner, therefore, had the President avowed his plan of restoring the Southern States in the appointment of William W. Holden, as Military Governor of North Carolina, than the conflict with him was commenced. By his method, which was simply pursuing that inaugurated by Abraham Lincoln, the Southern whites would have had in their hands the sole power to re-shape their Constitutions, and mold the legislation of their respective States. Two antagonistic theories were striving for the ascendancy in the work of reconstruction. The Presidential plan was reprobated at once by Wendell Phillips, Salmon P. Chase, Horace Greeley, Thaddeus Stevens, Charles Sumner, and other shining lights of radicalism. A division in the Republican ranks was imminent; but it was the work of the tacticians to keep it from spreading to any further extent than could be avoided.

The Military Governors appointed by the President, issued proclamations to the people of their different States, calling

---

*New York *World*, May 13th, 1865.

upon them to elect delegates to conventions to revise their several Constitutions; these being now viewed by the conquerors as entirely defunct. All the proceedings, however, which looked to the restoration of the Federal authority in the Confederate States, were deemed necessary to be employed in order to complete the first measure of radical desire. The plan of revising the several State Constitutions, was a more modest method of getting fully rid of the institution of slavery, than any other that might have been devised. Abolition aspiration from the inauguration of the war, aimed at this as the first object to be accomplished; and no method promised for this result absolute surety, save the suppression of the institution by the Southern States themselves, after having been brought under Federal control. And the task was no difficult one upon the downfall of the rebellion. The great object of the war being well understood by all intelligent classes, whether Northern or Southern; when resistance to the Government was abandoned, the Confederates, with one consent almost, gave up any further defense of their institution.

Prominent statesmen throughout the South, declared their readiness to acquiesce in the overthrow of the institution of slavery, deeming the further advocacy of it nugatory. It was altogether as they conceived, ready to be ranked amongst the things of the past. There were many, however, who viewed the amnesty oath, which the citizens were obliged to subscribe before being clothed with the elective franchise, as a despotic trampling upon the rights of free men born in a republican government; but the current of popular opinion in the South, notwithstanding this, turned strongly in favor of resuming, at the earliest practicable moment, and by the only method proposed, amicable relations with the people of the Northern States. Officers were authorized in all places to administer oaths of amnesty to the citizens, and furnish them such certificates thereof, as would enable them to participate in the elections to be held for delegates to the conventions to revise their several State Constitutions. Before taking the oath, the applicant was required to make affidavit that he did not belong to any of the fourteen excepted classes. Having subscribed this, he was then allowed the oath of amnesty, which operated as a pardon for all past political offenses, and restored him fully to the rights of citizenship.

Public meetings were held throughout the entire South, and candidates of talent and character were nominated, and in many instances pledged to the repeal of the Ordinances of Secession and the abolition of slavery; and also, in favor of such amendments to the State Constitutions, as might seem necessary, under the new condition of affairs.

All the time, from the announcement of the Presidential plan of reconstruction, public opinion in the North was in a condition of ebullition. Political lines began at once to divide somewhat upon the new issues. Prominent radical papers began to endorse the ideas of Sumner, Stevens and other leaders, who had expressed themselves as favorable to universal suffrage. Democratic newspapers, on the contrary, soon after the appointment of William W. Holden as Governor of North Carolina, began to view the new President, although elected by Republicans, as a man who was not dominated by fanatical ideas, and who desired a fair and honorable restoration of the Southern States to their place in the Federal Union, and with all their rights save slavery unimpaired. Early in June, 1865, Democratic Committees recorded their endorsement of the President's reconstruction policy. In endorsing the President's plan of reconstruction,* the Democrats did so, however, simply as a choice of evils, and not because it was a method which they, as rulers, would have devised. A considerable number of prominent Republicans also ranked themselves under the Presidential banner. Many of those who did so, were anxious to preserve harmony in the Republican party. Even as strong a radical as Gov. Andrew, of Massachusetts, thought the effort to force negro suffrage in the South, was premature; and that the Government should

*President Johnson's plan of reconstruction, was the same as that which Abraham Lincoln and his Cabinet had originated. William H. Seward, the Secretary of the State, under both administrations, in his speech of October 20th, 1865, at Auburn, New York, said: "We are continually hearing debates concerning the origin and the plan of restoration. New converts, North and South, call it the President's plan. All speak of it as if it were a recent development. On the contrary, we now see that it is not specially Andrew Johnson's plan, nor even a new plan in any respect. It is the plan which abruptly, yet distinctly, offered itself to the last Administration, at the moment, I have before recalled, when the work of restoration was to begin; at the moment when, although by the world unperceived, it did begin, and it is the only plan which thus seasonably presented itself; and, therefore, is the only possible plan which then, or ever afterwards, could be adopted."—*New York World, October 24th*, 1865.

simply retain its military grasp of the rebel States, and universal suffrage would in time follow. The Governor was very anxious to avoid a breach with the President. General Cox, the Republican candidate for Governor of Ohio, came out in a letter early in 1865, opposing negro suffrage.

The fissure between President Johnson and the radicals once formed by the announcement of his plan of reconstruction, continued steadily to grow wider and develope itself. It soon became apparent in the Summer of 1865, that the leaders of the conflicting theories of State restoration had taken their posttions, and that no retreat was contemplated by either party. The New York *World* spoke of this party schism as follows:

"The split in the Republican party has made too much progress to be arrested. Several of the most eminent Republican leaders, with a majority of the party to back them*, stand against negro suffrage and they will not recede. Chief Justice Chase, Senators Sherman, Wilson, Sumner, and others of equal influence and distinction, are ardent negro suffrage men, in declared opposition to the policy of the President; and the first Republican State Convention held since Mr. Johnson's avowal of his policy on this subject (that of Iowa on June 14th, 1865), adopted negro suffrage as a plank in their platform. * * * The quarrel will be likely to culminate in the next Congress, when the radical members will assume to revise the Constitutions of the reconstructed States, that do not admit negroes to the elective franchise."†

In a public speech, Senator Wilson had already been bold enough as to warn the President that the radicals in Congress would reject every State Constitution, which did not come up to their mark on the slavery question. Radical meetings were held in different sections of the North, favoring negro suffrage. The Republican Convention of the State of Maine, held in 1865, took exception to the President's reconstruction policy, and by implication condemned it; the Democratic Convention of the same State, on the contrary, endorsed it without reservation. The representative party bodies of other States, placed themselves in about the same attitude towards the President's policy as did those of the States already named.

*This clause of the *World's* statement, that the majority of the Republican party stood with those leaders who opposed negro suffrage was clearly overdrawn. The majority of the party at this time were favorable to universal suffrage. Negro suffrage was made a party question in the State of Connecticut in 1865, and only defeated by 6272 votes. No Democrat supported it.

†*New York World*, June 21st, 1875.

The confiscation and extermination theory of reconstruction, also found its advocates along with the others that were advocated in 1865. The leading representative of this theory was Thaddeus Stevens, who upon the close of the war, loomed up as the great beacon of radicalism; and the man who was destined to exert a potent influence upon the reconstruction policy of the nation. Since the commencement of the war he had stood before the country as the most radical abolitionist in the lower House of Congress; and the representative of all others, who determined that no constitutional barriers should interpose between him and his party in their race towards the goal of universal liberty and equality. Being the extreme leader of the extreme wing of his party, crowned at length with victory over their opponents, Mr. Stevens was now able to bear a weight upon his political arms that none other could pretend to carry. He could with impunity, therefore, dare to advocate a policy that would have been unsafe for any other leader of his party to have urged. Regarded as the unconcealed opponent of the principles that had triumphed in the overthrow of the rebellion, he was free to claim their legitimate fruits; and with unabashed effontry, he assumed as the dictator of his party, to demand them.

In September, 1865, Mr. Stevens delivered a speech in the City of Lancaster, in which he advocated the confiscation of the property of all the leading rebels whose estate was worth ten thousand dollars, or whose land exceeded two hundred acres in quantity. He estimated that one-tenth of the whites only would loose their property by such a proceeding; yet that most of the real estate would be confiscated, it being held by the few. Of the property thus to be taken from the wealthy rebels, he declared that justice demanded that forty acres of it should be given to each freedmen, and the balance sold to liquidate the national debt. He calculated that by this process the sum of three thousand five hundred millions of dollars would flow into the public treasury, enough to pay off the debt contracted in the subjugation of the Southern people. The alliance between abolitionism and communism was proven in the demand of this intellectual leader. A more wholesale confiscation of the property of the discomfitted resistants of fanaticism, was urged by Mr. Stevens, than had taken place in England under William the Norman. The real *animus* of abolitionism, however, was shown in the position of this bold champion of his party.

The elections for the constitutional conventions took place at the times determined upon in the different States of the South. The delegates to these promptly convened and proceeded to organize, as the conquerors prescribed. Many of the prominent men of these States, and those even who had figured in the rebellion, appeared and took seats as members of the constitutional conventions. A dictatorial oath was likewise imposed upon every member of these several conventions, that they would support all laws and proclamations which had been made during the war with reference to slaves. These bodies adopted resolutions rescinding the acts of secession which their several States had enacted and abolishing slavery; and they framed Constitutions for their respective Commonwealths in conformity with the altered situation of affairs. After the adoption of the new Constitutions, elections were held in these different States for Governors, Members of Congress, Members of State Legislatures, and other officials. When the Legislatures convened, they in general adopted the amendment to the Constitution proposed by Congress, abolishing slavery. President Johnson strongly urged upon the Legislature of South Carolina, that it ratify the newly submitted amendment, as an example for the imitation of the other States. It did so, by an almost unanimous vote. But the representative assemblies of these States were for the time being, pure automata,* subject to the dictation of those who controlled opinion at the seat of the National Government; and their acts in no wise represented the free and independent sentiments of their people.

* Thaddeus Stevens was fully conscious that the Constitutions already forced upon the Southern States, in 1865, were altogether the result of Northern domination. Speaking of the Confederates, when once restored to their place in the Union and become masters of their own affairs, in his speech of December 18th, 1865, he said: "That they (the Southern people) would scorn and disregard their present Constitutions, forced upon them in the midst of martial law, would be both natural and just. No one who has any regard for freedom of elections, can look on those governments, forced upon them in duress, with any favor."—*Congressional Globe, 39th Congress, First Session, Vol. 1, p. 74.*

CHAPTER XXVI.

ANTI-REPUBLICAN RECONSTRUCTION.

The unconstitutionality and anti-republican character of the war for emancipation and negro elevation, under the pretense of defending the Union, were fully displayed after the close of the national conflict; when efforts were inaugurated to re-cement "the broken and dishonored fragments of a once glorious Union." The appalling spectacle in all its horror was in full view, which New England's ablest statesman, with ardent love of country, had wished never to contemplate. The prayer of the patriot had been heard, but the drama was being witnessed of "States discordant, belligerent, a land rent with civil feuds," and but lately "drenched in fraternal blood." The glorious ensign of the Republic was no longer waving over the peaceful fabric of the American Union; but what remained of it, typified an anarchical despotism, more ignoble and tyrannous than could be found outside of the dominions of Asia.

The principle of monarchy had mailed the batallions that prostrated constitutional government on the American continent. The harmonious people of the States had been hurled into sectional strife by mischievous intermeddling, induced by the monarchical conception which assumed in essence to declare, "*I am holier than thou.*" Instead of a free and happy Union, whose yearly governmental expenditure did not require over seventy millions of dollars, the unrighteous war of the emancipationists entailed upon it an annual expense of nearly five hundred millions, in order to meet the interest upon the Northern debt and other attendant demands. A highly oppressive tariff, enhanced for the consumers the value of the articles of every day necessity, and yielded for the liquidation of current expenses, over one hundred millions of dollars; where prior to the struggle less than half that amount had been raised through this politic method of indirect taxation. Interest on the national debt of three thousand millions, was to be collected from the labor of a highly taxed people. A pension list of Northern soldiers required the annual sum of thirty millions.* A Freedmen's Bureau had been created for a population which, in its natural condition of subordination, was comfortable and happy before the intermedlers appeared. This newly framed Bureau required for its support as large a sum of money as the whole Government during the Administration of John Q. Adams had consumed. Besides, the expense of a considerable standing army to watch the movements of the Southern people, was added to the burden of the citizens.

Anti-republicanism, after the close of the struggle of arms, dominated more strongly than ever in the counsels of both wings of the conquering party of the North, in the efforts made to adjust the sectional strife. It was attempted to be settled upon the principle of might dictating to right; and by means of the basest pandering to the uncultured ideas of the mob, that ever was witnessed in any country. All justice was ignored and the equality of the States repudiated. The refusal to consider the question of adjusting Southern loss in the unjust emancipation of their slaves; the forced obliteration of the Confederate debts; and the pensioning of Northern soldiers to the exclusion of Southern, simply added new fuel to the flames of strife between the sections, intensified existing hate, and made republican union upon such a basis an impossibility. Henry S. Lane, a Republican Senator from Indiana, seeing these difficulties in the way of an amicable settlement, spoke as follows:

"Do you suppose they (the Southern people) will willingly tax themselves to pay the interest upon the immense debt, created for their subjugation and overthrow?

"There are other questions you will be called upon to decide. You will have to provide a fund for the payment of your invalid pensioners. Think you they will vote willingly to raise money to pay the pensions of your invalid soldiers, when their own invalid pensioners are excluded? Can you hope for any cordial co-operation between the rebels and yourselves, upon any of these great subjects of national legislation? * * * I tremble in view of the evil consequences which would result from the admission of rebel members to your national debt, to the national credit, the plighted faith of the nation, to your bondholders, the plighted faith of the nation to your living and dead heroes."†

* Annual Report of Commissioner of Pensions for 1874, p. 8.
† *Annual Cyclopædia*, in 1866, p. 151.

But it was only the faith of fanatics that was plighted in the North, and that for base political purposes. And faith was not plighted upon one side alone. Southern faith had been plighted in defense of the rights guaranteed by the Constitution. And Confederate honor was equally sensitive with Federal; and was never dimmed when compared with any of which the North could boast. Equity, therefore, had demands in behalf of Southern wrongs, equally as for Northern. And Confederate soldiers felt their weakness and wounds, quite as keenly as did those who had been maimed under McClellan at Antietam or Meade at Gettysburg. The God of Justice demanded that the poor and wounded Confederate be treated by a generous and Christian nation with equal tenderness as the Federal who had exhausted his strength, to do what his hypocritical masters denied that they meant to accomplish. The poor Confederate was not even accused by his savage conquerors, of having sinned in conscience, in fighting for his section and people, and in defense of their inherrited and constitutional rights. If the soldiers of either of the contestants deserved to be pensioned, they surely, with equal right, deserved this favor who fought for constitutionalism and the inheritances of their countrymen. But a pretended and pitiful amnesty was all the boon accorded the crippled Southern soldier to soothe his declining years, and soften the hard pillow of advancing days. It was generous and humane to pension the wounded Federal soldiers, who had risked their lives upon the fields of battle, fought between the sections of our country. But no holier zeal inspired them than animated the Confederate soldiers to hazard all in the service of their States. The Federals obeyed what they conceived to be lawful authority; so did the Confederates. When the former in the great settlement were deemed by a kind government deserving of being pensioned, the latter were entitled to the same consideration. In addition to this, it was the only method for the Government to pursue, it it meant to harmonize in one pacific Union, the Northern and Southern States. The needy and crippled Confederate was, however, contemptuously cast aside, as not even deserving the sympathy of the people of his own native South. An opening ear of justice will yet meet his troubles and compensate him for what the obdurate heart of fanaticism denied him. But the widow and orphan, and thousands equally innocent, whose all was treasured up in Southern capital, which sunk at the dictate of the revolutionists, were likewise overlooked by men who madly expected to cement a peaceful Union, by means of war, rapine and robbery.

Wise and philosophica. statesmen, desirous of restoring the Union, would not have demanded of the Southern people, that they abandon all the rights for which they fought; and acquiesce wholly in the imperious behests of the conquerors. None, save a wicked and demented tyrant, refuses to consider the causes which have induced his subjects to rebel. If the Union of the States was to be reformed, this could alone be done by a general and free convention of the representative minds of the conflicting sections; and upon such terms as would be acceptable to all parties and interests. It was fully dissolved by the war of the rebellion; and if a new Union were to be constructed, it must of necessity be the work of compromise, and effected in the same manner as it had originally been organized. But to a thinking mind, the destruction of the Union was final and complete the moment that war fired up the passions and fury of the people of the North and South against each other. The antagonism of two powerful, warring nations, as were the Federals and Confederates, can never afterwards be eradicated; and humanity and civilization both demanded a peaceful separation, in preference to the wicked four year conflict, that was cruelly waged to subjugate a free people, and give freedom to barbarians, who are incapable of appreciating its fruits.

But the base spirit of tyranny and monarchy, which inspirited the crazy madmen of the North to inaugurate and wage with their own people a bloody war of several years, still rode triumphant, and animated the revolutionists to further victory. The weakness of democratic government fully unfolded itself, during the fierce struggle of arms, and afterwards in the forum of legislation. Its infirmity arose from the multitude of foes within its own household. Its foes are the tyrants and slaves, that ever produce the festering and corruption of humanity which ends in monarchy and despotism. In all the efforts of President Johnson to restore the seceded States, the virus of despotism was blighting instead of giving life to the branches of the Republic. What else was the unconstitutional test oaths, which Southern citizens were required to accept, before being permitted to exercise the rights of franchise? What, besides that, was it that induced the arrest and incarceration of Jefferson Davis, Alexander H. Stephens, and other prominent citizens of the South, who had with their people been recognized as belligerents in the family of nations? What, but despotism, was it that required the Southern legislators to adopt the amendment to the Constitution, abolishing slavery, and repudiate all the debts contracted in resisting the Abolition Administration? In assuming to pardon rebels, President Johnson simply deferred as a demagogue to the popular ideas of the North; there being in a strict constitutional view, nothing to be pardoned, as the intelligent revolutionists themselves well understood.* The experiment, at least, was never hazarded to determine, whether any treason had been committed by the rebellious men of the South. The mongrels knew that to be dangerous ground, and never had the courage to venture upon it. In the forum of law and reason, they themselves might have been convicted of all the treason that was committed, and shown to have been the wicked deceivers who caused all the blood to be shed that flowed in the unhappy struggle. The future has this judgment yet in store for them, and to be gibbeted in infamy with England's regicides. But in executing the pretended power to pardon the rebels, Andrew Johnson acted as a despot, rather than the President of a Republic. A wise and liberal policy demanded that rebels and Federals be treated as equals, and that they freely and without constraint be permitted, through their Representatives, to determine whether they would live together in one government, or organize separate ones.

But despotic as was the policy of Andrew Johnson, for the restoration of the rebel States, which had been coined for his use by President Lincoln and his counsellers, it was not such a one as suited the purposes of the extreme revolutionists. The radical leaders perceived the disadvantage they would sustain, should the Southern States be restored to their places in the Union; and they sought by every means in their power to delay the restoration of those States until negro suffrage could be forced upon them, and

*Gerritt Smith, the fanatic but honest abolition pioneer, delivered an address at Cooper Institute, New York, to prove that "the government has neither the legal nor the moral right to try the rebels." He contended that the Government had absolved them from the crime of treason by acknowledging them as belligerents.—*New York Times*, June 10, 1865.

the rebel strength neutralized by barbarian Africans. These States, during the Autumn of 1865, under the plan of reconstruction presented for their acceptance by President Johnson, had elected Senators and Representatives to the Thirty-ninth Congress, which was to meet in December, 1865. To prevent the admittance of these was the work of Thaddeus Stevens and the crafty leaders of his party. When Congress assembled, December 4th, it was shrewdly arranged that the names of the Senators and Members of Congress elected from the eleven Southern States, should be omitted from the rolls of the respective Houses until after the organization of both bodies.* This was the turning point of the scheme. It was determined upon in conclave, that but few, if any, from those States should be admitted until they would be reconstructed upon the basis of negro suffrage.

In accordance with what had been planned, and before President Johnson's Message had been presented to Congress, Thaddeus Stevens submitted his famous resolution, which had been approved in a secret caucus of the revolutionists. This resolution called for the appointment of a joint committee of fifteen—six Senators and nine Members of the House—whose duty it should be to inquire into the condition of the Southern States, and report whether any of them are entitled to be represented in either House of Congress; and until such report shall have been submitted, no member from any of these shall be received into either of the representative bodies.

Mr. Stevens secured the passage of his resolution in both Houses of Congress, and was made Chairman of the "Revolutionary Committee." Of all the men who might have been named, he was most deserving of that honor. The work to be performed by this dark tribunal, was of such a character as to

*That the omission of these names was part of a concerted plan, the following extract from a speech of George T. Curtis, in Brooklyn, seems to show: "The culminating point on which this matter is to turn, will be the action of the Clerk of the last House of Representatives in preparing the list of the members elect of the new House. It is given out—I know not on what authority—that the gentleman who held the office of Clerk of the last House. intends not to place upon the list, the names of any persons returned as members of the new House from any State that has been in rebelion. If the Clerk, Mr. McPherson, means to act wisely, I would advise him to seek the opinion of some constitutional lawyer, who is above being influenced in his legal opinions by his political affinities, and to act upon the opinion that may be given to him. It may save him much future tribulation,"—*New York Times*, Nov. 8, 1865.

require the services of an entrepid, reckless and daring man, such as Mr. Stevens had already shown himself to be. He was on all sides, even by his political enemies, acknowledged as the ablest and most influential leader of his party in Congress. This secret committee, being a conscience extinguisher, a man was required as its director, who in former years had desired no intrusive monitions from that unruly messenger of humanity; and who had the boldness to enjoin his partisans to consign the busy intruder to the custody of Pandemonium's master. The service to be performed by this ever to be remembered committee, was of a death-bringing nature to the principles of republicanism and free government; and such as Mr. Stevens and his intelligent party followers could not but have realized. The task of this despotic directory, was to disfranchise a sufficient number of the rebels; and, on the other hand, enfranchise the emancipated negroes, so as thereby to secure the permanent ascendancy of the revolutionary party, who might in after years rear monuments of glory to its intellectual creator.

Free government being the conception and product alone of the Caucasian race, the attempt in republican America to thrust its keeping into the hands of barbarian negroes, was one of the maddest and wickedest schemes that State-craft and perfidy ever devised for selfish, partisan purposes. It fully equalled the madness of the French revolution, as subsequent experience has clearly demonstrated. With the exception of a few bold and dangerous destructives, the Abolition leaders themselves believed that the Southern negroes were entirely unfitted to be entrusted with the right of suffrage. Senator Fessenden, himself an ardent Abolitionist, after the appointment of the above dangerous committee, and whose purpose was already planned, spoke of universal suffrage as follows:

"At this time no one contends that the mass of the population of the recent slave States, is fit to be admitted to the exercise of the right of suffrage."*

But the leaders were well aware that the Southern whites were almost a unit in opposition to the political theories of the Abolition party; and perceiving this, they saw that it was necessary to secure the aid of the negroes in the South, or their party would certainly be overthrown with Southern restoration.

---

* *Annual Cyclopædia*, 1866, p. 150.

They were well aware that the Northern Democrats and the Southern whites would again unite to resist the party of destruction; and that united, these would be able to seize control of the Government. And it was to avert this political calamity that negro suffrage was so strongly advocated by the revolutionists. It was not, therefore, the belief that universal suffrage was demanded as a right, or that the interests of republican government would be promoted by its bestowal upon the blacks, that prompted the negro suffragists in their movements; but base policy induced the support of it in order to prevent the disintegration of the most corrupt organization which ever controlled the affairs of any nation.

Thaddeus Stevens, the Chairman of the odious Committee, was a follower of Alexander Hamilton, and one who believed that Great Brittain exhibited the best form of government that the wisdom of man had ever yet devised.* In that country, a restricted suffrage prevailed. It would be very improbable to suppose that a believer in the perfection of the kingly govern, ment of England, could be induced to favor negro suffrage, unless he desired the more speedily to ruin republican institutions, in order that his favorite system of polity might be substituted. By far the most likely motive, however, which prompted Mr. Stevens, in his efforts to secure the right of suffrage for the freed blacks, was, as he himself confessed, to bolster up his party and forever weaken his political antagonists, the constitutional democracy. Base and ignoble were all such motives; and the men thus incited to act, deserve the execration of all future ages. The American Union had been pronounced the model republic of the ancient or modern world; and even to hazard its perpetuity or the principles it embodied, was more fiendish and diabolical than the darkest treason of midnight conclaves.

---

* During the trial of the Christiana rioters in Philadelphia, Mr. Stevens, who was one of the counsel in the celebrated case, in interviews which he had in the house of an old political companion, who had sat with him as a member of the Reform Convention of 1837–'8, expressed the opinion that the British form of government was the most perfect conception of man. Had he expressed this opinion after the ruin which fanaticism had brought upon the country he would be excusable, and could with justice be named a *monarchist from necessity;* but having entertained the belief before the deluge of social destruction came, is sufficient to entitle him to be enrolled as a *monarchist in principle,* and an Abolitionist from a desire to be odd and eccentric, which was somewhat in him a characteristic. His aspirations for fame are proof of this latter view.

The doctrine of Sumner and Stevens, which sustained the appointment of the Revolutionary Committee of fifteen, was endorsed by the extremists because it was the only one which would secure in their interest negro suffrage. This was the sole object sought to be accomplished in the reconstruction of the Union. If the plan of restoration, which Andrew Johnson adopted for the Southern States; and which came to be known as the Presidential policy, should be accepted, the question of suffrage would be left with the people of the States, where the Constitution placed it. Mr. Stevens and his allied revolutionary followers well knew that the people of the South were most intensely hostile to conferring the right of suffrage upon the ignorant negroes, who had lately been their slaves. These radical men perceived, however, that the subversion of the rebel States as organizations must be accomplished at every hazard, otherwise suffrage could not be secured for the emancipated slaves. President Johnson had already become an object of hatred with the leaders, because they had been unable to *water him** with that advantage which they had hoped. Mr. Stevens, who was a shrewd discerner of men, in the Baltimore Convention of 1864, seemed to have surmised a future difficulty of this character in the nomination of Andrew Johnson, a citizen of a slave State, for the Vice-Presidency. He no doubt felt that all native Southerners would oppose negro suffrage as a measure inimical to republican government.

The annihilation of the statehood of the seceded commonwealths, being the grand essential to be acknowledged in reconstruction, the Committee of Fifteen became the ready engine for this purpose. It was insisted that the States by their rebellion had ceased to be members of the Federal Union; were, by the overthrow of their armies, become conquered provinces; and that

*Wendell Phillips, the great moral leader of Abolitionism, remarked on a certain occasion: "Mr. Lincoln is a growing man; and why does he grow? Because we have *watered him.*" Garret Davis, of Kentucky, in his speech in the Senate of June 7th, 1866, having quoted the above words of the Abolition apostle, said: "There was a great deal of truth expressed in those few words. The Abolitionists in Congress, and out of Congress, *watered* the late President. They caused him to grow in the direction and shape that they wished him. They warped him from his own principles and policy to theirs. And what is the great sin of the present Executive of the United States? It is that he will not make himself the leader, the obedient tool of the majorities of the two Houses of Congress; that his judgment of his powers of his duties to the country is inconsistent with and may conflict with their party purposes."

their Senators and Representatives should be inhibited from seats in the National Congress, until their several State Constitutions were altered in conformity with the wishes of their Northern masters. In this demand, which was simply a part of the secret programme originally concerted, the revolutionists were disclosing their full purposes as yet, however, in a measure concealed as a party principle. During the campaign of 1865, the politic leaders of the Republican party, denied that negro suffrage was a principle of their organization, in order still further to play the old card of deception, in which experience had rendered them very skillful.* In supporting the annihilation of Southern statehood, the revolutionists were unable to determine at what period the act of State destruction had taken place. Had this most important event occurred when the State Ordinances of Secession were respectively adopted, or when they appeared in insurrection against the United States? If not at either of these periods, did it take place when they surrendered their arms to General Grant and Sherman, or when they dissolved their Confederate Governments, and acknowledged obedience to the Constitution and laws of the land?

*John Cessna, the Chairman of the Republican State Committee of Pennsylvania, denied in a public letter, in the campaign of 1865, that negro suffrage was a principle of his party.

CHAPTER XXVII.

BREACH WITH PRESIDENT JOHNSON.

After the Reconstruction Committee of Fifteen had been appointed by the Thirty-ninth Congress, other movements were instituted by the revolutionary leaders, one after another all designed to pave the way for negro suffrage. It was now become apparent to all observers, that this was the last grand act to be performed; and then the curtain would drop and the drama be ended. Fanatical aspiration aimed at this as its ultimate goal. Senator Stewart, of Nevada, an unconcealed Abolitionist, confessed this in his speech of January 18th, 1866. He said:

"If this question (negro sugrage) were out of the way, we could settle everything else in two weeks, at least, so far as a portion of the Southern States are concerned, and we could receive such Southern representatives that are loyal and none other. As the Senator from Ohio has said, there would be no difficulty in agreeing upon everything else, if it were not for the question of negro suffrage. We may as well meet this issue here and understand each other. This is the issue—the only issue before the country. * * * There are some who are determined to sacrifice the Union and the Constitution, unless they can achieve the right of suffrage for the negro."

It was determined by the managers, that an enlargement of the powers of the Freedmen's Bureau should be pressed as one of the means to elevate the negro to equality with the white race. The original bill for the creation of this bureau, became a law March 3d, 1865; and was to continue in force for one year after the close of the rebellion. Being a serviceable engine of military law to foster strife in the South, which was the nutriment of the Republican party, it could not with propriety be abandoned by the revolutionists at a period when the future was clouded with uncertainty. The conflict of arms, it is true, was ended; but the warfare was only transferred again from the field to the forum. The Southern people had been forced to renew their allegiance; the amended Constitutions of their States were framed in obedience to the dictates of the Executive and the radical rulers. But the whites were still masters of their State administrations, and would so remain unless Congress interfered.

A plausible pretext was afforded for the continuance of the Freedmen's Bureau, in the enactment, by some of the reconstructed Legislatures of the South, of vagrant, contract and apprentice laws for the government of the emancipated bondmen, which seemed to recognize the freed negroes as the inferiors of their late masters. All men of ordinary observation could not but see that the emancipated slaves were inferior to their former owners; and the necessity of laws to regulate their conduct in the new situation in which they were placed, was felt by all who had it in their power to rise above political prejudice. But any legislation, implying even, that a natural difference existed between the two races, was extremely offensive to men who had spent a life-time in securing the emancipation and liberty of the colored race. If these revolutionists did not as yet dare unitedly to proclaim the enfranchisement of the negro, they were able to do what was next to it, forbid all discrimination in State Legislation, so as to make him as far as possible the equal of the Caucasian in other particulars. And to accomplish this, the Freedmen's Bureau must be continued for a period, and made to embrace all that was possible to be grasped. In the early part of the first session of the Thirty-ninth Congress, therefore, a bill for this purpose was introduced into the Senate by Lyman Trumbull, of Illinois, and was supported by the great body of his party as an act which necessity imperatively demanded.

The working of the Freedmen's Bureau was already perceived to be in the interest of the fanatical party; and in view of the determination to exclude the Southern States from representation in Congress, until negro suffrage could be forced upon them, it must be continued yet for some years. Under it, a system of military law might be perpetuated, and this was an advantage not to be overlooked by the revolutionists. The great object to be achieved by them, was to thwart the State Legislation of the Southern whites, as far as the same conflicted with radical policy; baffle Presidential reconstruction, and endeavor to elevate the negroes at the expense of the discomfitted rebels. Already under color of the Act of March 3d, 1865, as originally passed, authority had been exerted far surpassing the tenor and words of the Statute, and transcending the bounds claimed for it. Even when Senator Sumner, during the discussion of the Freedmen's Bureau Bill had asked for an enlargement of power, his request was denied; and yet, so soon as the Act was passed, all which he had requested, was without law carried into practice. The law makers were too timid to concede, what they were well aware would be enforced.

Besides, victory had not completely crowned the banners of the revolutionists, when the novel bureau was first created. They now, however, were fully masters of the situation, and could dictate terms which prior to this, policy forbade. A communistic advance was no longer so dangerous, as before it would have been considered. The distribution of rebel property amongst the freedmen, could now be discussed with some safety; and the enlargement of the bureau's powers afforded an admirable opportunity for this purpose. It was urged, with boldness, by the friends of the bureau, that several millions of acres of *good land*, seized as the property of the Confederates, should be set aside for the new citizens; and that houses, schools and hospitals should be erected for them at public expense.

The Democrats resisted the enlargement of the Freedmen's Bureau, because of its perpetuation of military rule in the Southern States; and in that view they contended that it was violative of the Federal Constitution. The bill clothed the President with authority to appoint an army of officers in the South; and this they regarded as an unwarranted stretch of power. They further urged that the military jurisdiction thus indefinitely attempted to be extended over the eleven Southern States, and designed to embrace all questions that might arise concerning contracts, in which negroes were parties, was altogether anti-republican in its character. The creation of such a power, without any authority for revision by higher tribunals, was at variance with the fundamental principles of American jurisprudence. Such legislation, in their view, must in the nature of the case, be attended by acts of caprice, injustice and passion; and was without precedent in the former history of the country. The proceedings of trials so conducted for the punishment of offenders in civil life, and when no war was raging, were in no respect dissimilar from those in courts martial. The trials were to proceed without any previous presentment, contrary to what the Constitution required, an indictment not even being necessary to advise the defendant of the accusations to which he would be required to plead. Charges and specifications, in lieu thereof, were alone to be submitted. It was contended that this course would be an infringement of the Constitution, which declares that: "No person shall be held to answer for a capital or otherwise infamous crime, unless on the presentment or indictment of a Grand Jury, except in cases in the land or naval forces, or in the militia, when in actual service, in time of war or public danger." The trials to take place, were furthermore, in conflict with the Constitution, which prescribed that: "In all criminal prosecutions, the accused shall enjoy the right to a speedy and public trial by an impartial jury of the State and district wherein the crime shall have been committed."

After a warm debate in Congress, the enlarging Freedmen's Bureau Bill passed both Houses, and was remitted to President Johnson for his approval. This officer occupied as embarassing a position at the time, as could well be conceived. Having lent his influence to the extreme men, who had prosecuted the unconstitutional crusade against the people of the Southern States, he could expect little real sympathy from those who had resisted the war upon principle, should he break with his party. But with the subsidence of the rebellion, his early democratic ideas began to recur to him; and having now reached the highest seat of power in the nation, he thought himself competent to check the revolution in its mad career, which doubtless he had thus far accompanied rather as as demagogue than a patriotic statesman. He returned, therefore, February 19th, 1866, the bill to the Senate, in which it had originated, with his reasons for withholding his official signature. Andrew Johnson's reasons for his veto, were more sound than consistent with his prior conduct, as Military Governor of Tennessee and President of the United States. In objecting to the bill, because of its military character, the Executive was simply unconsciously, as it were, passing sentence upon his own conduct, in permitting up to that period and afterwards, the writ of *Habeas Corpus* to be suspended in the eleven States of the South. If opposed in principle, to the execution of military law by that part of the army, charged with the execution of the Freedmen's Bureau, why did he permit the same kind of authority to be carried into practice by the other divisions of the army? The fact is undeniable that military commissions up to that period, with the President's sanction, had been held all over the South; and these had consigned men to penitentiaries, and inflicted other odious punishments in violation of the plainest provisions of the Federal Constitution. But the breach between the President and the radicals was now rendered complete by his veto; and his impeachment from that period was one of the questions of discussion. Even before the open rupture memorials had been in circulation asking that he be impeached for official delinquency.

The Civil Rights Bill, which was simply complemental to the Freedmen's Bureau Bill; and part of a scheme for perpetuating military rule in the South, and subverting State sovereignty, was next the engrossing topic of Congressional discussion. It was also introduced by Senator Trumbull, Chairman of the Judiciary Committee, as part of the plan to govern the rebel States until his party should be able to reconstruct them upon the basis of universal suffrage. The essence of the Bill was contained in the first section, which declared that the emancipated slaves "shall have the same right in every State and Territory in the United States, to make and enforce contracts, to sue, be parties and give evidence, to inherit, purchase, lease, sell, hold and convey real and personal property; and to the full and equal benefit of all laws and proceedings for the security of persons and property as is enjoyed by white persons."

In support of the Bill, it was urged that several of the Southern States, since their reconstruction upon the Presidential plan, had enacted laws for the freedmen, which would practically reduce them to a condition of slavery. It was the same argument that had been produced in support of the Freedmen's Bureau. The friends of the measure believed that they would have the support of the President in its behalf, as he already in several instances had caused the legislative acts of these States, which discriminated against the blacks, to be set aside. He had done so, through General Sickles, declaring that "all laws shall be applicable alike to all inhabitants." By his own fiat, the President, through General Howard, set aside an Act of the Legislature of Mississippi; and by another order, through General Terry, an Act of the Legislature of Virginia; and forbade any magistrate or civil officer from attempting to execute it. He likewise ordered General Canby to cause the State Courts in his Department, to suspend all suits against persons charged with offenses for which white persons were not punished. From what source a President who was a believer in the doctrine of State Rights, could conceive that such arbitrary power as the above, was derived, is somewhat difficult to say. It was as plain an infraction of State Rights as could be committed. It was, however, no difficult matter for a President to act in this manner, who could so far forget himself as to have uttered the following declaration:

"Whenever you hear a man prating about the Constitution, spot him as a traitor."*

The Democrats in Congress resisted the Civil Rights Bill in all its phases, and portrayed with startling vividness the manner in which it undermined the independence of the judiciary. If Federal District Attorneys, Marshals, Agents of the Freedmen's Bureau, and other officials, shall have it in their power to arraign any State Judge, who may interpret a State law in a way unsatisfactory to some claimant of justice, of what use they insisted, can State laws and State Judges be? Better abolish both, without delay. But not only were these petty Federal officials empowered, under the Civil Rights Bill, to appear as accusers of the State judiciary; they even had a premium held out to them to prefer charges. For every case of alleged injustice to a freedman, a fee was fixed. Should the accused be declared innocent, the fee was to come out of the United States Treasury; but if found guilty, the convict was compelled to help to increase the store of the Federal informer.

If the colored race had been worthy of freedom, no such extreme measures, as the Freedmen's Bureau and the Civil Rights Bill, need have been resorted to by their emancipators to secure them in their liberty. No such legislation was ever required to bolster up and support the liberty of the serfs of Europe, when public opinion concurred in the propriety of according them their freedom. But the Northern anti-slavery zealots were aware that they had forced negro emancipation before its time; and had violated all precedent and history in their unconstitutional efforts to make freemen of barbarians. They knew that they had subverted the foundations of society in one-half of the Union, in

*Andrew Johnson was reported in the public journals to have made this remark whilst acting as Military Governor of Tennessee.

opposition to the cautionary protests of the wisest statesmen of America, and the universal intelligence of the South; and to sustain their unrighteous acts, laws must be enacted by Congress to counteract Southern revulsion, and practically enchain the educated and enlightened intellect of that section. If the Constitution had hitherto proved no barrier to the wild advances of fanatical legislators, could it be hoped that it would be such when the South was crushed beneath the heel of Jacobinical fury? And although the Statutes of the United States and the journals of Congress afforded no instance of such legislation ever having been proposed, the revolutionary leaders hesitated not to introduce and sustain in the Civil Rights Bill, a law, that invaded the reserved rights of the States, and trampled upon the compacts of the Constitution. The whole force of the party machinery was brought to the support of this bill, and it passed both Houses of Congress by heavy majorities. Even the unjust ejection* of legally elected Congressmen was resorted to for the purpose of having a two-thirds majority in each House, in order to counterpoise the Presidential veto, and prevent it from proving an insuperable obstacle in the way of radical advance.

But the President came again to the defense of the Constitution, and vetoed the Civil Rights Bill March 27th, 1866, basing his reasons therefor, upon sound democratic arguments. The demagogue, impelled by the monitions of duty, was endeavoring to throw aside his hypocritical robes, and array himself with the pure men of the country, with whom his reason allied him. As a vile politician, however, he had mingled with the social dregs against which his natural tastes revolted; and now, like his prototype, he was desirous of breaking with the repulsive alliance. He declared in his Message, vetoing the bill, that "it is another step or rather stride, towards the centralization and the

*John P. Stockton, a legally elected Democratic Senator from New Jersey, was debarred from his seat in the United States Senate, by the revolutionary men who controlled that body. The Committee of Seven, appointed to pass upon his case, five of whom were Republicans, reported in his favor; but partisan feeling and interest, both demanded the exclusion of every Democrat upon the most frivolous pretences. The Senator was, as a consequence, ousted from his seat. Daniel W. Voorhees, John D. Baldwin and James Brooks, Democratic Members of the Lower House, were likewise ejected from their seats in the Thirty-ninth Congress, for partisan purposes.

concentration of all legislative powers in the National Government." But he forgot that he, more perhaps than any other single individual, had helped to strengthen the party of centralization, which from their first seizure of power, had been invading the Constitution; and having up to this time been permitted unchecked to tread upon it, their regard for it could not be expected to revive at the dictation of one who, with themselves, had proved false to its most sacred mandates. Gamblers and thieves do not heed the pious monitions of one of their own number; sudden conversions being ever criticised with considerable scrutiny.

When the news of the veto by President Johnson, of the Civil Rights Bill, was spread over the North, a torrent of rage and vituperation poured forth more terrific and violent, even, than that which followed his first refusal to accompany the revolution in its late developments. He was denounced as a tyrant and usurper; and numerous were the demands made by the incendiary press to impeach and remove him from the high office, which he was accused of intending to prostitute in the interest of the discomfitted rebels. The veto was taken up on the 4th of April, 1866, in the Senate; and was defended in masterly arguments by Senators Johnson, Hendricks, Guthrie and other able men; and the unconstitutionality of the bill was particularly dwelt upon by these patriotic Statesmen. Being, however, a favorite measure of the revolutionary party, it obtained the requisite two-thirds majority of that body. It was next taken up in the House on the 9th of the same month, and secured a like majority; and thus became a law without the Presidential signature.

From the period of the President's veto of the Civil Rights Bill, a steady and persistent war was waged with the Executive Department of the Government. Indeed, from the commencement of this session of Congress, the whole of the legislation of almost whatever character it might consist, was made subsidiary by Thaddens Stevens and the other radicals, to the attainment of the one great object, universal suffrage. Henry J. Raymond,* Editor of the New York *Times*, himself a Republican Member of the House, spoke in his paper of the object of his party, as follows:

*Henry J. Raymond belonged to that wing of the Republican party which sustained President Johnson in his policy of restoration of the Southern States.

"Universal negro suffrage, as the condition *sine qua non*, of the restoration of the Union, is now and has been from the beginning of the session, the grand goal and objects of all their (the Republican revolutionists) efforts. They have cloaked it more or less, partly from policy and partly from fear; but the time is drawing nigh when they can cloak it no longer. The whole subject of restoration was first put into the hands of the Reconstruction Committee, there to await the manipulations necessary for success. Each House was pledged to admit no member from the South, until that Committee should have reported, and until final action should have been taken by both Houses on that report. This tied Congress hand and foot, and left the field perfectly clear for the grand campaign. Every attempt that has been made to draw attention to the case of Tennessee to the returns and qualifications of Southern members to the testimony reported to the Committee, or to any other general branch of this subject, has been temporarily squelched, by being sent under the Speaker's ruling, to the Committee of Fifteen, and under the injunct ion of secresy to this hour.

"Meantime all the talk and all the excitement that had been raised about constitutional amendments, equality of civil rights, status of the Rebel States, &c., &c., has been simply dust thrown in the eyes of the public to cover the approach to the grand fundamental, indispensable principle of universal negro suffrage, as the condition, without which no Southern State should ever be admitted to the Union. This is the secret of all the elaborate legal endeavors to prove that the Union is destroyed—that the States went out of it, and that they can get back only on such conditions as Congress may prescribe. This was the reason why Stevens entitled them conquered States, deprived of all rights, excluded from the protection of the Constitution, and to be dealt with as conquered subjects at the sovereign will and pleasure of the conquerors. This was the object of the studied legal argument of Mr. Shellaberger, in support of the doctrine of State suicide, and of his more recent effort to prove that if even, in the Union, they may rightfully be held to have forfeited all the rights of citizenship under the Constitution. The feeble but still more zealous efforts of Hart, Ward, Holmes and other radical members from this side, have all aimed at the same thing—namely, to lay a foundation for demanding, at the hands of the South, universal negro suffrage as the condition of restoration.

"The plan does not work quite to their liking; some of the more timid among them begin to doubt whether it is quite safe. Its strength with the people does not quite equal their anticipations. The President is more obstinate in his fidelity to the principles and platform of the Union party than they expected. The country is not convinced that the South is out of the Union, that their people are conquered subjects, or that Congress has the right to force universal negro suffrage upon them.

"Mr. Stevens announced, very early in the session, that he and the friends of universal negro suffrage were strong enough, by uniting with he Democrats, to defeat any kind of negro suffrage. * * * That radicals on the Reconstruction Committee, will follow the policy marked out by Wendell Phillips,* who is really the leader of the radical movement. They will report in favor of universal negro suffrage as the only basis on which the Union shall be restored—as the only condition on which the Southern States shall ever again be represented in Congress—and they will require these hesitating, halting gentlemen to walk up to the mark and vote with them in its support. * * * They have excluded Tennessee in spite of the conviction of three-fourths of the House, that her members ought to be admitted. They have repeatedly passed resolutions insulting the President, in spite of a professed desire for harmony between the Executive and Legislative Departments of the Government. And they have passed against the veto by overwhelming majorities, and with loud applause a bill (the Civil Rights Bill), which a majority of their own faction admitted by necessary implication to be utterly beyond the constitutional authority of Congress. And all this has been done by party drill and party menace."†

Senator Stewart condemned the inconsistency of his party in the following words:

"Do you think if you had avowed that negro suffrage was your ultimatum, that you knew the States were not in the Union, that your purpose was not to keep them in the Union, but to govern them as Territories, that you could have drawn the loyal masses of the North to this terrible conflict. Show me the platforms upon which this fight was made; show me the resolutions of Congress; show me the declarations that put in issue the question of negro suffrage, which is now delaying the peace and disturbing the country." ‡

The District of Columbia was the first place upon which the revolutionists determined to force negro suffrage. A bill was introduced into the House for this purpose in the first session of the Thirty-ninth Congress, and after a warm discussion received the approval of that body, and was remitted to the Senate for its concurrence. But the cautious Senatorial House, though equally radical as the representative assemblage, feared to concur in this measure until the elections of 1866 had been successfully tided over; although it had virtually committed itself to the same principle, when the organization of the Territory of Montana had been before it. But prudence deterred the political leaders of the revolutionary party from too openly committing themselves to negro suffrage, being well aware that too free a committal upon this question would jeopard their success, as partisans, in the coming political campaign. The eyes of the deluded North-

*President Johnson, in his speech to the citizens of Washington City, on the 22d of February, 1866, characterized Thaddeus Stevens, Charles Sumner and Wendell Phillips, as the three leaders of the radical party.

† New York *Times*, April 27th, 1866.

‡ Speech of January 18, 1866.

ern people must not be too fully opened to the designs of men, who only strove to rivet party chains at the expense of traditional institutions.

The Thirty-ninth Congress having delegated all authority over the admission of Senators and Members from the Confederate States, to the Committee of Fifteen, on reconstruction, awaited with humble submission the decrees of this Central Directory. In the meantime this Committee, under the Chairmanship of Mr. Stevens, now become the recognized leader of his party, busied itself in taking testimony concerning the condition of the Southern States, the temper of their people, the details of crime, the action of magistrates, and the general character and tendency of their officers. No member from any Southern State was admitted, or even allowed to bring his credentials to the notice and judgment of either the Senate or House of Representatives. Without the least courtesy of recognition, they were remitted with their passports to the august Sanhedrim of revolutionary domination. The local State Governments already in operation in the South, were ignored; and communications from the Governors elected by their people, under the authority of those appointed by the President, were not received; and these officers, themselves, were even denied receptions.

Whilst this Central Committee was engaged with its special labors, Congress was by no means idle. Numerous bills were introduced and referred to their respective committees; all of them as varied as the mental constitutions of their several proposers. Bills were submitted for erecting Territorial Governments in the Southern States; for confiscating the real estate and other property of the Southern people; for annulling the action of the President in granting pardons; for excluding from the exercise of political rights the great mass of the Southern citizens; for dividing among the freed slaves the lands of the Southern planters; for conferring the elective franchise upon the emancipated blacks of the South; and in general for accomplishing all such changes in the structure of the Government, as the authors of these measures respectively, found most consistent with their ideas of an Utopian Republic. Numerous amendments of the Constitution, some of them of the most sweeping character, were presented and pressed upon Congress and the attention of the country. Resolutions were adopted to hold the

Southern States under absolute military rule during the pleasure of Congress. The general scope of all the attempted action of that body, was to concentrate supreme authority over the States in the Federal Government; and all power in that Government in the hands of Congress.

After many long and heated discussions in Committee and in both Houses of Congress, an amendment* to the Constitution was at length agreed upon, and submitted for the consideration of the States on the 13th of June, 1866. This amendment conferred: First—an equality of civil rights. Second—Federal representation, based substantially upon voters instead of population. Declared—Third—the exclusion from office of certain classes of rebels. Proclaimed—Fourth—the public debt as inviolate, and forbade payment for emancipated slaves. Fifth—gave Congress power to carry these provisions into effect This amendment was by no means what the radicals desired. But they were doomed to the necessity of presenting something, and what they desired was as yet too extreme for the timid party slaves. Mr. Stevens made no concealment that the amendment failed to meet his views on the question of negro suffrage; but he declared it the best in his view that could then be secured. It was believed by many that the interest of the Southern people would overcome their prejudices to the negro, and that they would finally grant to him the right of suffrage. But if nothing else would have prevented the Southern States from accepting the proposed amendment, the known insincerity that accompanied its presentation would have been sufficient. Though endorsed by Congress as just and desirable, its adoption by any Southern State, or by the whole of them, was not presented as a condition of re-admission to representation in Congress; but that matter was left open as before to the constitutional discretion of each House. Wendell Phillips, the great moral leader of Abolitionism, in his speech of July 4th, 1866, disclosed the designs of the revolutionary leaders in submitting the amendment. He said:

"The Republican party to-day repeats the same experiment, and hopes it willbe successful. What the leaders in Congress think, is that the amendment will be rejected. * * * What then does Stevens, what does Boutwell, what does Wade, what does Sumner expect? When the elections are over and the amendment defeated, what do they expect? Why, they expect that the Republican party, victorious

*This is what was afterwards ratified as Amendment No. 14.

at the ballot-box, unfettered by the adoption of the amendment, will float back into Congress, able to pass an act that shall give the ballot to the negro and initiate an amendment to the Constitution which shall secure it to him. They hope, they expect, that after the defeat of the amendment in the fall elections, the party will return to Congress stronger than it stands to-day. They do not want the amendment accepted. The worst possible news that Thaddeus Stevens could hear, would be, that the amendment was adopted. The most unwelcome news you could carry to George Boutwell, of Groton, would be that the amendment had been ratified. They neither expect it nor wish it. It is a party move. I do not disgrace it when I say it is a party trick to tide over the elections and save time—nothing else; to serve a purpose—to get rid of an emergency—to tide over the summer—to get on the other side of the elections—that is all."*

On May 22d, 1866, in the House of Representatives, a bill was reported to continue in force the Freedmen's Bureau for two years. Some features of this measure had been altered from the last one, which had failed in its passage because of the Presidential veto; and it also embodied the provisions of the Civil Rights Bill. It passed both Houses with some modifications, after its introduction, but again failed to receive the signature of the Executive, and for very similar reasons to those which he had assigned as causing his disapproval of the former Freedmen's Bill. This time, however, the opposition to the President mustered in full strength, and the new bill excogitated out of pretended charitable regard for the negro race, was passed in both Houses over the veto, and enrolled upon the statute books of the nation.

But Congress, though recognizing Thaddeus Stevens as its intellectual leader, feared to follow him in his mad scheme for confiscating Southern property, and distributing it amongst the emancipated slaves. This stretch of communism was too nauseating for many who obeyed him as lord and master in every other particular. Many other propositions that found individual advocates in one or other House of Congress, failed likewise to receive such approval as to give them the character of laws. Although warmly urged, out of opposition to President Johnson, no enactments were passed for ignoring or superseding the local governments of the Southern States; for organizing Territories upon their soil; for disfranchising the white people, or for conferring the right of suffrage on the colored race. These were

*New York *World*, July 7th, 1866.

all regarded as too daring innovations to be as yet hazarded. Time must do its work before any of these bold measures could with safety receive strong party support. The Representatives to Congress from Tennessee were admitted just before the close of this session; but this right was simply extended to them as a blind to deceive the unwary in the coming Autumn elections.

The other action of this Congress, also portrayed its partisan predilection. The Internal Revenue Taxation, before the close of this session, underwent a modification at the dictation of the revolutionary rulers. An unheard-of excise of three cents per pound, was imposed upon cotton; and two dollars a gallon on whiskey. The Maine liquor law reformers were now in ecstasies. The millenium was surely advancing with rapid strides. No fair and equitable deduction, however, was made in the odious and unjust tariff, which special interests had originally procured to be enacted. Corporations and railroad monopolies came in with their sweeping demands; and an obsequious Congress hesitated not to donate vast tracts of the public domain in behalf of wild enterprises; which public property should rather have been husbanded with care, as a fund to help in the reduction of the public debt, and pay the expenses of the Government. The members of this Congress, whilst displaying an almost total disregard of the public interest, were by no means neglectful of their own affairs. As shrewd private financiers, they determined that a salary of five thousand dollars per annum would more swell their purses than the three thousand they already were receiving. A New York editor, himself a Member of the House, spoke of the partisan and financial action of this Congress as follows:

"Its general action, in matters of expense, has been lavish, where party interests were involved; and its general temper throughout the session has indicated a pretty close regard for securing the supremacy of the Union (*Abolition*) party in the future."*

*New York *Times*, July 30, 1866.

CHAPTER XXVIII.

THE POLITICAL CAMPAIGN OF 1866.

The break of President Johnson with the radicals, led to the belief that a new party, with the Executive as the central figure, might be organized, able to wrest power from the hands of the latter. The Democratic party was not in a condition to contest successfully upon the political arena with its old opponent. It had been decoyed by false leaders, in violation of its princlpies, and in opposition to the advice of its wisest members, into the endorsement of the war against the Southern people; and in doing so it played the *role* of duplicity, inasmuch as its leaders and thinkers were well known to entertain the belief that no constitutional warrant existed for making war against the seceded States of the South. Upon the close of the rebellion, it was no difficult matter, therefore, for the crafty demagogues of the Republican party to affix, as a stigma, the brand of seeming disloyalty upon the brow of the political opposition; who were vituperated as pretending to support the war for the Union, when they were known to be hostile in sentiment to its prosecution. It was not difficult to cite the utterances of representative Democrats, who, prior to the outbreak of hostilities and down to their close, had declared the war to have been an unconstitutional invasion of the rights of the Southern people. Might, nevertheless, triumphed over the Constitution; and its defense, of necessity, became treason. The Democracy had been quilty of no higher offense than defending in its letter and spirit the compacts of the fathers; but the revolutionists, having succeeded in overthrowing the old constitutional barriers, and being now in possession of the authority of government, towered aloft as the patriots of the new order of affairs. Those members of the Democratic party in the North, the most sincere and conscientious men in its ranks, who had been conspicuous from their opposition to the war, were after its close viewed by their fellows as dangerous leaders in the future political contests of the country. Men must henceforth lead the party to victory, who had either favored the war against the South, or who had been so cautious in their utterances as not openly to have committed themselves against it. The pure Democrats had martyred themselves upon the altar of principle; politic leaders now stepped forward, seized hold of the party reins, and marshalled the organization in accordance with the perverted ideas which the revolution introduced. It was fraud truckling to ignorance, and demonstrated the demoralizing tendency of politics when the moral and intellectual leaders of a people, from any cause, have been stricken down.

Early in the year 1866, a political association, called the National Union Club, was organized in the City of Washington, by Republicans, who coincided with the President in their views, and was designed to be the germ of similar organizations throughout the whole Union. The basis of the organization was expressed in a series of resolutions, denying the right of sesession; expressing confidence in the ability, patriotism and statesmanship of the President; endorsing the resolution of Congress of the 22d of July, 1861; asserting from the Chicago platform of 1860 the importance of maintaining the rights of the States; declaring the constitutional right of the several States to prescribe the qualifications of electors therein; that the war having closed, the rights of the States should be maintained inviolate; that the States were entitled to representation, and all loyal members should be admitted into Congress without unnecessary delay; that no compromise should be made by bartering "universal amnesty" for "universal suffrage;" and endorsing cordially the restoration policy of President Johnson as in harmony with that of President Lincoln.

This club was subsequently united with another of the same character in Washington; and a National Union Executive Committee likewise appointed. One of the first acts of the National Union Club, was to give an evening serenade, on the 23d of May, to the President and members of his Cabinet, in order to elicit an expression of opinion upon the existing political issues from the advisers of the President. A part of the Cabinet fully committed themselves to the Presidential plan of reconstruction, yet some of them declined to do so. William H. Seward, the Secretary of State, and Hugh McCullough, the head of the

Treasury Department, without reserve, endorsed the views of President Johnson.

Emboldened by the endorsement given to the President's policy by the Members of his Cabinet, itself the selection of his predecessor, his friends and admirers believed that the task of organizing a new party upon Executive popularity, would be no difficult one. A man who, in his own State, had resisted the waves of secession; had obtained the support of the Republican party; been elevated by the votes of the people to the second highest office in the nation; and now transferred by constitutional succession to the highest place of power; must unquestionably, as was conceived, have a strength with the people of considerable magnitude. The managers, therefore, with sagacious adroitness, untertook the task of organizing the Presidential followers into a political party that might strive with probability of success, before the Northern people, in the Congressional elections of 1866. A number of leading Republicans, Members of the Senate and House of Representatives, lent themselves to the undertaking, which aimed at nothing less than obtaining the control of the Government of the country. The Executive Committee of the National Union Club, issued on the 25th of June, a call for a National Convention, of at least two delegates from each Congressional District of all the States, and four at large from each of them, to meet in the City of Philadelphia, on the 14th of August.

The probability of building up a party that might be able to resist that one which sustained the revolutionary Congress, was based upon the belief that the Democracy would co-operate with any organization which promised the overthrow of radicalism. In this expectation, the friends of the President were not mistaken. Forty-one Democratic Members of Congress signed an address to the people of the United States, in which they declared their cordial approval of the call for the National Union Convention, and their endorsement of the principles which it enunciated. They urged the people of each State, Territory and Congressional District, to promptly select wise, moderate and conservative men to represent them in the Philadelphia Convention. The reasons alleged by the signers of this appeal, were that dangers threatened the Constitution; that the citadel of the public liberties was assailed; that it was essential to

National Union, that the rights, the dignity and the equality of the States, including the right of representation and the exclusive right to control their own domestic concerns under the Constitution should be preserved; that eleven States were unjustly excluded from the National Council, and that whilst denied representation, laws affecting their highest interests, have been passed without their consent, and in utter disregard of the fundamental principles of free government.

The action of President Johnson, with reference to the Freedmen's Bureau and the Civil Rights Bill, turned the Democratic party in his favor, as it was perceived that he exhibited a greater regard for the Constitution than did his enemies. And, although men of that organization could by no means justify the course he had pursued in sustaining the war against the South, and the other numerous breaches of the Constitution, which had been perpetrated with his acquiescence; yet the politicians were willing to ignore the past, in hope of a brilliant and successful future. But this was again, to repeat the original error, which the party had committed in endorsing the prosecution of the war for the restoration of the Union. The first error, from time to time, necessitated repetitions of the same; all of which would have been averted had the Democratic party from the first stood firmly by its cardinal principle of State Sovereignty, and refused to permit an armed blow to have been struck in behalf of the Federal Union. As the Union had died in secession, it should have been permitted to be resurrected by the same life-giving process of evolution, as it were, by means of which it had been created. That process was *consent*, the only one that can originate, preserve or reconstruct the republican government. Monarchical republicanism may, it is true, rest upon the sword; but it is impossible that any other kind should do so.

But, as the Democratic party by its desertion of principle, in supporting coercion as a means of restoring the Union, had rendered the war popular with the unreflecting masses of the North, how was it to regain power for a time upon old issues, save by the basest conceivable hypocrisy? It was necessary that its old tried and trusted leaders, who had never bowed the knee to the false gods of abolitionism should be ostracised, and new ones selected who had trampled upon the Constitution of their country, as if it were the waste paper of the highway.

Andrew Johnson, in the movement which culminated in the Philadelphia Convention, was viewed as a leader under whose banner, as it was believed, the Democracy might again ride to victory. In the estimation, however, of reflecting men, this hope seemed baseless and chimerical. If the war was justifiable, then the party that had prosecuted it to its close was the one to administer upon its effects, and gather the fruits of conquest. Was it to be supposed that the people of the country, who believed in the nationality of the Government, would entrust the adjudication of the affairs which the victory over the South placed within their power, to men who were suspected of having entertained sentiments of hostility to the war and its ultimate objects? A superficial knowledge of human nature alone, was sufficient to disprove such a supposition.

As the Democratic party, however, in 1866, was unable to retrieve its error, for the same reason that induced its original commission; it left this duty to be undertaken in the future, and to be accomplished during the same period when the republican union shall be in process of restoration (if this ever be possible,) out of the chaos of revolutionary despotism; and by the only method which modern Christian civilization recognizes; unless prior to the happening of this event the ship of State shall have been finally wafted within the whirpool gulph of a crushing absolutism. But the party of Jefferson and Calhoun, was led by false guides to the footstool of Executive power; and through hope of political triumph, made to endorse results which had been attained by means of the most iniquitous character. It was believed, nevertheless, by conservative Republicans and politic Democrats, that the convention to assemble in Philadelphia, on the 14th of August, would be able to unite an opposition against the revolutionary party, that had broken the Union into fragments; and which, in attempting to re-cement these by force, was only further pressing them into the lowest depths of social perdition.

The efforts that led to the holding of the Philadelphia Convention, were the first endeavors since the war, that were fairly made to bridge the chasm of blood that seperated the two sections of our country. Difficulties encompassed the situation upon all sides, and the work of civil war, only began to present its terrible visage to the reflective intellect of the nation, when the leaders set themselves to the task of bringing the people and sections upon a common platform. As the convention to assemble, was to represent the sentiments of all those who were hostile to the revolutionists, a difficulty presented itself as regards the delegates, who should be accredited as members to the harmonizing assemblage. Democrats and Conservative Republicans, both claimed the right of being represented in the convention. To obviate any misunderstanding that might exist, as to the parties entitled to be represented in that body, it was recommended by the Committee of the National Union Club, that two delegates from each Congressional District should be selected from the supporters of Lincoln and Johnson in 1864, and the same number from their opponents. In the Southern States, a corresponding number of delegates was permitted to be chosen by the people generally, who accepted the principles of the call. Both coercion and peace Democrats were elected as delegates; but it was feared by the politic manipulators, in view of the popular war sentiment which prevailed, that the presence of C. L. Vallandigham and other Northerners of his school, would injure the influence of the convention. This fear, however, was simply the result of that species of cowardice, of which republican governments are wonderfully prolific; and which doubtless germinates the demoralization that leads ultimately to their overthrow. If public opinion be wrong, that government which is sustained by it must submerge, or a power must exist somewhere, pure, free and independent, and one which is competent to denounce and correct the error. Can this ever be found of sufficent strength where leading men truckle to public prejudices, and only seek their own elevation at the expense of public prosperity and happiness?

Public attention for a time was almost entirely engrossed with the movement, which had for its object, the assembling of the Philadelphia Convention. It was believed that this convention would prove to be the line of demarcation, between the Executive and the Congressional modes of reconstruction; and that it, more than any other event, would nationalize the Presidential following. It occasioned the first rent in the Cabinet; and enabled President Johnson to surround himself with advisers, who sympathized, in the main, with his views of governmental policy. On the day preceding the assembling of the convention, W.

Dennison, Postmaster-General, tendered his resignation, which was accepted, and A. W. Randall appointed as his successor. James Speed, the Attorney-General, also tendered his resignation, and was succeeded by Henry Stanbery. Mr. Harlan, afterwards resigned the post of Secretary of the Interior, and O. H. Browning was substituted in his stead. The resigning members of the Cabinet retired from it mainly because, differing from the President, they were unwilling, when interrogated by a committee, to lend their sanction to the call for the convention.

When the delegates assembled in Philadelphia, Republicans and war Democrats were permitted to be the leading movers in the organization and manipulation of the representative body. General John A. Dix was made temporary Chairman, a former Democrat, but one who had sustained the war against the South with the most ardent enthusiasm. James R. Doolittle, a Republican Senator in Congress, from Wisconsin, was elected permanent President of the convention; and Edgar A. Cowan, a Republican Senator from Pennsylvania, was appointed as Chairman of the Committee on Resolutions. Henry J. Raymond, a Republican member of the House of Representatives, and editor of the New York *Times*, was the author of the address which was adopted by the convention, and which purported to be a succinct expression of the sentiment of that body.

In this convention, the earliest effort was made, since the war, to harmonize the conflicting sentiments of the people of the North and those of the South; and the difficulty of doing so, was for the first time fully realized. That the war had left two radically antagonistic peoples, loomed up into prominence in this convention; and in what manner to unite these, into an harmonious whole, was a question that quietly engaged the attention of the assembled representatives. The South appeared in the convention, through her delegates, and did so apparently by consent; but the coercive arm of the Government compelled this seeming acquiescence; for no representatives would have appeared from that section, if full freedom had been the privilege of her people. She had struck for independence, but the armed legions of the North baffled her in its attainment. How could her representative men, having supported the rebellion with the most enthusiastic earnestness, cherish another desire, save to be free from a people, who had sown the seeds of sectional strife in the land; and waged a godless and unconstitutional war against the rights, liberties and institutions of her people? But, though vanquished, the South nevertheless remained a separate, individual nation, whose feelings, sympathies and aspirations were discordant from those of the North, and will so remain throughout coming ages. Her inhabitants held in recollection a cause not to be forgotten; the memory of her heroes, martyrs, and fellow braves were imperishably inscribed upon her mental tablets; and her separate tombs and mausoleums were consecrated shrines, to which pious pilgrimages were wont to be undertaken.

The people of the North equally had their heroes and sympathies, which the struggle had engendered. A severance of boundary would no more have alienated the North and South from each other, than had the conflict done; and possibly the future may determine that wisdom, in the interests of free government, dictated that the metes and bounds of division even then, should amicably have been struck. One iniquity at least, with all its following evils, the nation and civilization would have been spared. That iniquity was reconstruction. But the two sections having met in the Philadelphia Convention, endeavored to evolve harmonious views. A series of resolutions were adopted, intended to meet Northern prejudice, some of which outraged Southern and honest democratic sentiment; and disclosed the difficulty that existed of ever again uniting the antipodes of American opinion in a common Republic. Could the Southern delegates endorse State coercion and the justice of a war that had beggarded their people? But policy demanded that they do so. Could they declare that the war had maintained the authority of the Constitution, when Thaddeus Stevens, the radical leader, made no concealment that that instrument had been repudiated by his party? Politicians, however, claimed this of them. Could they pronounce that the Confederate debt should be cancelled, and that of their conquerors liquidated? Honesty bore as weighty upon their consciences as upon those of the triumphant revolutionists. Again, must they forget their crippled soldiers, who had borne their colors upon many a crimsoned field; be denied the privilege of bestowing some legal alms for their relief; and be forced to contribute for the support of those who had overthrown the Constitution whilst carrying the false banner of Union and liberty. None, except cowards and deceivers, could exact all this of them. In extorting it, however, though in the house of their political friend, vassaldom and conquest, in all their vividness, loomed up before the assembled representatives of the conquered South. This itself was sufficient to assure thinking men that the republican government of the Fathers had ended its career.

Andrew Johnson and his reconstruction policy were endorsed by the Philadelphia Convention, which was one of the main objects that induced the politic managers originally to call it. As a present issue, the Presidential plan of restoring the Southern States to Federal autonomy, was far preferable to that advocated by the radicals. Being a fruit of conquest, however, it could by no means meet the full approval of the people of the South; but as their condition necessitated its acceptance, (in order, as they hoped, to attain Federal representation,) or have a worse than this forced upon them; they embraced it simply as a choice of evils. Andrew Johnson had not been elected President by the Southern people, nor by the Northern Democracy. But they both lent their support to his Administration, because the rebellion being ended, he more strongly than his enemies, defended the Constitution; and desired that no further invasions of State Sovereignty be permitted. In concurring with the President, the Southern people were able to do so, as conquered subjects; but not as freemen and equals in a Constitutional Republic.

In order to counteract the possible influence of the Philadelphia Convention, a number of persons styling themselves Union men of the South, were induced on July 4th, to issue a call for a convention of Southern Loyalists, to meet in the city of Brotherly Love in the month of September. Little doubt can exist, that the influence which prompted this movement, largely emenated from the radicals of the North, who believed that it would strengthen their influence with their political followers. The call evinced entire sympathy with the revolutionary Congress, and took decided grounds in opposition to the reconstruction of the Southern States upon the Presidential plan. Equality before the law was strongly urged; and also, that no State should be recognized as a legitimate government, until impartial protection would be incorporated in the organic law. The demand for negro suffrage was as yet withheld, as the revolutionary party was not quite prepared to carry this clearly printed upon their banners in the approaching campaign. But it was already inscribed in dark declarations, well understood by the initiated few, who directed thought, and managed in their interests the unindoctrinated masses.

A marked contrast as to Southern membership, was visible between the late Johnson Convention, and that of the Loyalists. The latter was made up in a great measure of self-appointed delegates,* who appeared neither having Southern homes nor constituencies to represent. In the former convention, on the contrary, the wealth and intelligence of the Southern States were represented. But a small proportion of the loyal delegates from the South were men of distinction or political influence. Ex-Attorney-General Speed, Governors Brownlow, of Tennessee, and Fletcher, of Missouri, John Minor Botts, of Virginia, A. J. Hamilton, of Texas and a few others, made up the notabilities of the assemblage. But the quintesence of ribaldry and fanaticism met together in the loyal body. The first illustration of universal equality, upon a conspicuous scale in America, was given on this occasion, in the parading of the whites and blacks, arm in arm, to this convention. They freely mingled together, as demonstrative of the doctrines meant, soon to be inaugurated in practice. Frederick Douglass, the mulatto orator of the North, first received full recognition as the representative of his race, in this ring streaked and speckled body of demagogues.

And although this convention of variegated hues was devoted in soul to negro suffrage, yet it feared so to declare itself. A considerable contest for a time raged in this mingled association, as to the propriety of crossing the Rubicon of their aspirations, without further delay. This party plunge was still dreaded by the Northern delegates, who had united with their loyalist friends; and also by those representing Southern constituencies, who were fully conscious that the white sentiment of their districts, was almost unanimous against the extension of the ballot to the negro. John Minor Botts, in the convention, expressed the belief that of thirty thousand white loyalists in Virginia, not

* "The Philadelphia Loyalist Convention of 1866, was composed of Freedmen's Bureau agents, ex-sutlers, discharged volunteer officers, New England schoolmasters, speculators and adventurers, who possibly have seen the South while they traveled in the track of war." New York *World*, September 17, 1866.

three hundred of them would sanction the bestowal of the right of suffrage upon the ignorant negroes. But for policy, such representatives as Mr. Botts would have been hissed by the infuriates from the rostrum; for it was the determination of these desperadoes to treat Southern opinion with the most studied indifference. Anna Dickinson, the Abolition oratrix of the North, in her chiding address, glowingly delivered in the presence of the motley assemblage, declared that she "*would tell the men of the convention that their great party from Maine to California was devoted to black suffrage.*"

But the majority of the Southern loyalists being equally devoted advocates of negro suffrage, as Mr. Stevens and his extreme congressional followers, were unwilling to allow the adjournment of the many colored convention, without an expression of sentiment on this question. Steadily continuing their pressure, the co-operative delegates from the North, being disinclined to committal on this issue, withdrew from all ostensible connection with the body. The more moderate loyalists from the South also followed these; and the infuriated madmen were now left masters of the situation, and allowed to wind up the proceedings of the convention. These prepared a series of resolutions, and adopted an address which contained the following language:

"We declare that there can be no security for us or our children; there can be no safety against the fell spirit of slavery, now organized in the form of serfdom, unless the Government, by national and appropriate legislation, enforced by national authority, shall confer on every citizen in the States we represent, the American birthright of impartial suffrage and equality before the law. This is the one all sufficient remedy."

Whilst declining to commit themselves to negro suffrage in 1866, the revolutionary party strove to make the submitted constitutional amendment appear before the country as the issue of the campaign. It was presented as a preferable reconstruction policy for the South, to that which had received the endorsement of President Johnson. The National Committee of the party declared "that Congress will restore the ten waiting States, if these States adopt the amendment." The Republican Convention of the State of New York made the same declaration in its enunciated platform of principles. The promises of these high authorities were uttered purely in the interest of party; and were calculated to attract voters who deemed the amendment as reasonable one for Southern acceptance. But the promises were altogether deceptious. Mr. Stevens and the leading men of his party in Congress, entertained no thought of admitting the Southern States to representation, even should the amendment be adopted by them. As if steering between Scylla and Charybdis, they had studied with care the temper of Northern sentiment; and framed an amendment which the people of their own section, owing to existing sectional hatred, would regard as fair and equitable; and which those of the South were sure to reject upon principle. Congress positively refused to declare, that Southern Representatives should be admitted to their seats, in the event of their States ratifying the amendment. Leading organs of the Republican party asserted in strong terms that the adoption of the amendment would not entitle the South to be rehabilitated in her ancient regalia. The New York *Independent*, one of the influential papers of the party, said:

"No leading Republican in Congress means to admit the ten waiting States, simply on the adoption of the amendment. These States are to be admitted on no conditions, short of the equal political rights of their loyal citizens without distinction of race. A reconstruction of the Union, on any other basis, would be a National dishonor. Until the rebel States can come back on this basis, they shall not come back at all."

George H. Boutwell, of Massachusetts, an influential Republican, in a speech, said:

"He did not intend to vote for the admission of either of the ten States, not at present represented in the Congress of the United States, until impartial suffrage was extended to all the people of those States."*

The composition of parties varied in this campaign very triflingly from what they had done prior to and during the rebellion. The Democrats of the North, with a slight sprinkling of Conservatives, made up the party which sustained the President; and the Republicans that which stood by Congress. The bulk of the latter sympathized with the radical leaders of Congress; and it was altogether natural that they should do so. They had favored the coercion of the South; and this policy had been ultimately crowned with triumph, notwithstanding the vast difficulties that were necessary to be encountered. The body of a party always go as their leaders dictate; and many of these unitedly must desert an organization before they can draw their

*New York *World*, October 24, 1866.

old party followers with them. It was not Luther alone, who carried the protestant columns into revolt to their former ecclesiastical leaders; but his schism became a success, because the professors of the Wittenberg University and the magnates of Saxony marched abreast with him. President Johnson had alone the approval of a few scattering Republican leaders, who with him, had sustained the war and its prosecution against the people of the South.

It was clear to observers, that President Johnson had mainly thrown himself into the arms of the Democratic party, the conscientious members of which had resisted upon principle the prosecution of the war against the seceded States. As Northern sentiment was at the time molded, this apparent change of attitude from one politcal extreme to the other, was itself sufficient to greatly damage the cause of the Executive. The revolutionary Congress was supported by the party which had returned as conquerors from the armed conflict; whilst the President had in the North, chiefly as his supporters, those whose political pennant had been lowered in the dust; and who were also begrimmed with standing accusations of having been the disloyal *confreres* of the defeated foe.

The campaign of 1866, in the different States, was a bitterly contested one. The memories of the war, as was natural, were dragged into the canvas, and made again to do their work of intensifying the hate of the people of the one section of the country against the other. The horrors of Andersonville, Libby, Bell Isle, Florence, and other Confederate prisons, were recalled in all their intensity, before the imaginations of the masses of the North; and the cannon of New Orleans, Vicksburg and Charleston, were once more subsidized, by clear toned demagogues, in the interest of the radicals, as if the rebellion had not as yet been fully ended. The President was accused by his political enemies of designing to aid the rebels to the disadvantage of the Union, by securing their representation in Congress, before they were fitted to serve the interests of a common country. He was denounced as endeavoring to accomplish, by traitorous usurpation, what Jefferson Davis and his enrolled legions had failed to secure upon the battle field. Was he not (as was asked by the Republican press) the betrayer of his associates, and the accepted advocate and defender of those who had sought to overthrow the liberty of their country? From being the pretended friend of the Union, he has gone over to the enemy, and now seeks to introduce the Trojan horse amongst his countrymen, in order the more surely to effect the destruction, which his rebel associates failed to accomplish. Tell us not that the President is not in sympathy with the defeated rebels. As evidence that he is, see the multitudes of blood-dyed traitors, to whom he has extended free and unconditional pardon for the crimes they have committed; and he is now striving by his plan of reconstruction to force these same rebels into the halls of Congress to outvote loyal men. See the Governors he has appointed; hear the sentiments of hostility they utter against the Congressional plan of reconstruction; learn the infuriate hatred which they and their people cherish towards the freedmen of the South, who buckled on their armor and fought your battles for the preservation of the Union and the Constitution. Again, do you not see, to-day, the President in close sympathy with the men, who resisted by their speeches and influence, the war for the Union? Are not the anti-war Democrats of the North, heartily supporting the President and his policy?

The above is a sample of the political abuse, which was heaped upon the President and those who sustained his reconstruction policy. Those supporting his views were stigmatized as the Johnson-Davis party. The New Orleans and Memphis riots of this year, the legitimate products of Northern intermeddling, were admirable subjects for misrepresentation, and did their full share in exasperating the North against the prostrate South.

Mr. Stevens, in this campaign, performed his share of service in clouding, by sophistry, the issue before the country In his speech of September 4th, at Bedford, Pa., and afterwards in Lancaster, he endeavored to defend his borrowed theory of State extinction; and in support of his view, demagogically perverted the argument of Chief Justice Ruffin, of North Carolina, against the legality of the Constitution of his State, which had been amended subsequent to the war at the dictation of President Johnson, and in obedience to revolutionary sentiment. Having used the argument of the Chief-Justice for a deceptious purpose, he next advocated a more thorough prostration of State authority, than that condemned, by advocating the reconstruction of the Confederate States, by means of so-called enabling acts; and in this manner secure the enfranchisement of the emancipated slaves in the South. But the burden of his discourses was the confiscation of Southern property, and the utterance of *ad captandum* appeals, calculated to inflame the passions of the unthinking classes, until the work of subverting the Statehood of the several excluded Commonwealths should be completed, and the clasps of partisan treachery so riveted as to be able to endure the adverse shocks of opposing opinion.

The preceding charges and appeals, as detailed, afford an illustration of the arguments made use of by the radical speakers and press during the campaign of 1866. Many of the accusations made against the President were wholly baseless; and those to which a deceptious representation gave plausibility, retired before the light of candor and reason. The following extract from the *Press*, a leading Republican paper of Philadelphia, discloses the character of the deceptious appeals spread before the country by the politicians in order to influence the unreflecting voters:

"On Tuesday next, the people of four States will decide at the ballot-box, who are to represent them in the National Congress; and in effect to pass upon the scheme of reconstruction as developed by the National Legislature. They are to decide whether they will accept the plan set forth by their representatives, or whether they will submit to that of Andrew Johnson; whether, in short, the loyal men shall govern the country, or whether the control of the Government shall be thrown into the hands of the traitors."*

In the next issue this same partisan paper contained the following utterance:

"The true issue of this campaign is the constitutional amendment."†

In a subsequent number, this political organ spoke as follows:

"The real question before the people, to-day, is whether traitors or loyal men shall rule the country."‡

The radical accusations that were hurled against Democratic opposition to the war, were most of all difficult to be answered. The party was placed by these charges, however, in a false attitude—that of hostility to the Government. Selfish leaders had led the Democracy so far astray, as to sanction State coercion in defense of the Union; and having veered thus from the ancient

*Philadelphia *Press*, October 3, 1866.
†*Press*, Oct. 5, 1866.
‡*Press*, Oct. 9, 1866.

land-marks, its orators and press were now. after the close of the rebellion, logically precluded from striking at the roots of the error, by showing who were responsible for the war; and demonstrating its iniquity and deplorable consequences. Crafty politicians, as a consequence, were the only men within the party, whose services were specially in requisition. Consistent Democrats were, therefore, hushed into silence as regards the war; and obliged to stand branded as traitors in unenlightened opinion. They had no choice left them, save to feign compliance with the new departure from principle, and support the Presidential mode of reconstruction, in opposition to the revolutionary Congress.

But the prospect of breaking the ranks of the revolutionary party, soon became doubtful after the issue had been made up between the two political organizations of the country. Early in the year, New Hampshire and Connecticut gave their usual party victories, which they had for years been wont to do. When Maine, in the beginning of September, came sweeping in with a majority of twenty-eight thousand for radicalism, the defenders of the Constitution again perceived that the omens were against them. The New York *Herald*, and other politic journals of the North, who had so far steadily sustained Andrew Johnson and his policy, in opposition to the revolutionists, broke when the news from the old Pine State was announced. They now advised the President to circumvent the radicals by accepting the amendment, and urging the Southern people to adopt it as a less evil than these were designing to inflict upon them. Its acceptance, they contended, would defeat the aims of the President's enemies, and leave the Southern people masters of their own State governments. But the Southern people stood upon higher ground than a desire simply to secure the representation of their States. They had fought for the right of self-government; and had the President been so fickle as to have followed the suggestions of these changeable counsellors, he would have found few Confederates who would have accepted his advice. The honor of the South was at stake; and though she had sunk upon the battle field, no power existed that could compel her to accept her own degredation.

It was only when the results of the October elections, in Pennsylvania, Ohio, Indiana and Iowa, were chronicled throughout the country, that it became clearly evident that President

Johnson had lost the battle, and was now at the mercy of the enemy. All these States gave sweeping majorities for the radical ticket. In the following November elections, the whole North was still found to be arrayed under the old banner of fanaticism; and the designs of the revolutionists were now fully assured. Save in the State of New York, the majorities that endorsed Congress through the North were almost overwhelming. Massachusetts was carried by near 70,000, Illinois by 40,000, Michigan 25,000, Wisconsin 20,000, and the other States by corresponding majorities. The only States that emancipated themselves from radical despotism, were Kentucky, Maryland and Delaware. By a system of disfranchisement, that drew its germs from Great Brittain's enslavement of the Irish Catholics, the revolutionists were enabled in this canvass to still hold, as in chains of bondage, the States of Missouri and West Virginia, the majority of whose people cherished for their destroyers as unquenchable a hatred as ever fired the breast of man.

CHAPTER XXIX.

RECONSTRUCTION, OR THE CLIMAX OF THE REVOLUTION REACHED.

The second session of the Thirty-ninth Congress assembled at the National Capitol on December 3d, 1866. In the preliminary caucus of the dominant party, which preceded the opening of the Senate and House of Representatives, Mr. Stevens still towered as the controlling dictator of his party, who appeared to give courage and enthusiasm to the timid and flagging members of the political conclave. The dauntless chieftain was returned to the field of conflict, panoplied as an Achilles, ready to combat with his hated foe, the Federal Executive. On his motion, a resolution was unanimously adopted in the caucus, requesting the Senate to reject all appointmonts made during the late recess, where the removals had been effected for political reasons. In this connection, he gave notice of his intention to introduce a bill to restrict the President as regards his right of removal from office. A committee, headed by Mr. Stevens, was likewise appointed to prepare the business programme of the session; and a resolution was adopted instructing this committee to consider the propriety of enacting a law, fixing the meeting of the next Congress before the time prescribed in the Constitution.

It was thus early exemplified, that the war against the President was to be prosecuted with unabating ardor. This officer was viewed by the revolutionists as the main obstacle in the way of their designs, the enfranchisement of the negro, and its concomitant results. For this purpose, it was resolved to deprive him as much as possible of all the power which his official station placed in his hands. Ever since his breach with the radicals, the President had been the subject of the most bitter and acrimonious abuse, of which history affords an example. From being the admired Southern patriot, after his veto of the Freedmen's Bureau bill, he sunk in radical esteem to the lowest depths of traitorous depravity; and henceforth no language was too intense to designate the foulness of the Presidential treason. Jefferson Davis, the arch-rebel of the Southern Confederacy, was never maligned with more vituperative denunciation, than was President Johnson, for daring to question the constitutionality of the enactments of the revolutionary Congress.

Since the opening of the Thirty-ninth Congress, in December, 1865, Mr. Stevens was looked upon by his partisan followers as the great champion of the revolution ; and the man of all others most fitted by age, intellect and effrontry, to lead the crusade for the overthrow of Confederate Statehood ; and, by means of negro suffrage, reverse the classes to be enslaved south of the Potomac. A bold man, and one of reckless daring, is ever needed to head revolutions, and lead them to the performance of deeds that dazzle the unreflecting, but which invoke cries of anguish from considerate observers. These latter, see in such men, the destroyers that devastate human effort, wreck progress, and overthrow the constructions, which time, talent and the skill of man have erected. They are the demons of earth, the infuriates of pandemonium, who ride in chariots of fire, drawn by steeds of fanaticism ; and they are sent on missions of woe to call the nations to halt in their careers, and enable them to see whither they are wending. The leader, around whom the revolutionists gathered, Mr. Stevens, was one of the bold, intrepid men of the Robespierrian cast, whose fame ever rests more upon their eccentricity than their philosophical intellectuality. Possessing more than ordinary ability, they astonish their inferiors, rather than overtop their equals.

A political desperado being required to lead the revolutionists to their desired goal, the managers stood aside and allowed Mr. Stevens to assume that lead, for which he had an inordinate ambition. As none had the same brazen audacity as himself, he was accorded a leadership which on no other occasion could he have commanded. His leadership, however, was simply that of the revolutionist, rather than of the dispassionate Statesman, who has the ability to control men by the strength of his logical reasoning. As a district politician, Mr. Stevens was able to exert the control of a despot, which his mentality had framed him ; but his power disappeared as he ventured into deeper fords. In the Reform, and in the political conventions of his State, he invariably sunk through lack of ability to cope as a strategist and

Statesman with his political compeers and equals. In his last struggle for the United States Senate, at a time when he seemed to be the recognized leader of his party, in the Lower House of Congress, he fell ingloriously in the conflict, with a man whom history can only regard as a dextrous and unprincipled politician.

Following the precedent inaugurated, at the opening of the first session of the Thirty-ninth Congress, the revolutionists, without waiting the Message of the President, as courtesy to the Chief Magistrate dictated, at the bidding of the American Robespierre, entered upon the performance of the programme which rancor and fanaticism had suggested. The Prince of destruction had, at length, enticed the Abolition Congress to the summit of their zeal's pagoda; and temptingly had shown them the deceptive glory that should crown their memories upon the completion of the work of political death, which he dictated. The prospect was enchanting; and, obeying the seductive deceiver, they advanced to the performance of the task assigned them.

The bestowal of the elective franchise upon the African race, would now crown, in abolition estimation, the four years' struggle of blood with appropriate satisfaction. In no place could the movement to this end, be inaugurated with more fitting propriety than in the District of Columbia, where Puritan instruction had for some time been busily elevating, as believed, the sable descendants of Africa to fancied equality with their former Caucasian masters. Accordingly, on the motion of Mr. Morrill, of Maine, the bill to grant suffrage to the freed negroes of the Federal District, was taken up in the Senate. Senators who had deemed it impolitic to concur in this project with the House at the former session, because an election was nearing itself, now laid aside their timidity and advocated the bill with the warmest enthusiasm. Republican Senators no longer made concealment that they viewed the battle for universal suffrage as already won; and that their party would not stop in its course, until the record of this victory was rgistered in the legislation of the nation. After a short discussion, the measure passed the Senate by a strict party vote. It was also taken up in the House, and obtained the like endorsement in that body.

The bill having passed both Houses, was remitted to the President for his signature; but this officer declined to approve the same; and returned it to the House in which it originated.

The President in his veto, dwelt upon the fact that the people of the District had almost unanimously in a special election,* declared their opposition to negro suffrage; and urged that the popular will should never be entirely disregarded, as was contemplated in the proposed bill. The incompatibility of forcing negro suffrage upon the people of the District, when the experiment was a novel one, and before the Northern States themselves were willing indiscriminately to accept Africans as voters, was adverted to in strong and emphatic language by the President. The unsettled condition of the country was also considered as unwarranting a change of the character proposed. But besides placing himself as a present defender of the Constitution, in opposition to the revolution, the President's arguments accomplished no result, as the bill was re-passed in both Houses of Congress and became a law over the Executive's veto.

But the conservative re-action to the revolution, inaugurated† by President Johnson, went on increasing as time elapsed after the close of the war. The Supreme Court in its decisions, appeared also as an embankment to the flood that was washing away one constitutional landmark after another. In 1866, in the ably argued case of Lambdin P. Milligan and his associates, who in 1864 had been sentenced to death by a military tribunal, this Court decided that such commissions had no authority, under the Constitution, for the trial of civilians. The nine Judges of the Supreme Bench agreed that the Court which had tried these citizens was illegally organized; that it had no jurisdiction in the case; and that its sentence was a nullity. Military courts for the trial of citizens were pronounced to be wholly unwarranted. But partisanship showed its dangerous influence on this occasion. Chief-Justice Chase, and other dissenters, whilst concurring with the majority of the Court, as to the illegality of the tribunal, declined to declare such trials as necessarily in conflict with the Constitution. The attitude their party had taken

*"In Washington, in a vote of 6,556—the largest with but few exceptions, ever polled in the city, only 32 ballots were cast for negro suffrage; while in Georgetown, in an aggregate vote of 813, a number considerably in excess of the average vote, at the four preceding annual elections—but one was given in favor of the proposed extension of the elective franchise."—Veto Message of President Johnson.

† An insensible Republican re-action had been progressing since the commencement of the war; but which only came fully into notice, when the President took position against the revolutionists. Senators Cowan, Dixon and Doolittle belonged to the reactionists.

during the war, seemed to require that this reservation should be made by Mr. Lincoln's appointees. But the decision amply justified the opposition that had been made to these tribunals by the Democratic party from the opening of the rebellion.

The Supreme Court afterwards, in *ex-parte* Garland, declared that the Act of 1862, and also that of 1865, (applicable to attorneys,) which exacted test oaths, were unconstitutional. This decision aroused the anger of Stevens, Boutwell, and their zealous followers. The latter of these two, introduced into the House a bill, to nullify this last decision of the Supreme tribunal, which was driven rough-shod through this body, over the rights of debate. The higher law, which was one of the fundamental principles of the revolutionary party, also showed its dangerous tendency in this movement of the Massachusetts Representative. If the decisions of the highest court of the nation were to be treated with contempt*; and threatening efforts be made to effect their reversal in an illegal manner by a fanatical Congress, then the days of constitutional government might be considered as nearly numbered. The section of the new Constitution of Missouri, which precluded ministers of the gospel, teachers and members of the bar, from officiating in their vocations, because they had been in the rebellion or had sympathized with the Confederates, was also pronounced by the Supreme Court as unconstitutional. The above decisions were emissions of sound

* The following extract from the Philadelphia *Press*, of January 19th, 1867, is adduced as showing the hypocritical partisan assaults that were made at this time upon the Supreme Court for its decisions :

"If it were not rather a violent presumption, a strong argument could be made, to show that a majority of the Supreme Court of the United States, had entered into a regular combination with the rebel State Judges and politicians. Certain it is that the effect of this combination, is to increase the argument, that is gradually and irresistably forcing Congress to establish republican governments all over the region in which the rebellion was begun and prosecuted. Justice Davis, in the case of the Indiana traitors, laid himself open to very general reprehension for injecting into a judicial statement, an almost open defense and apology for the rebellion."

Judges were not wanting at this period who were ready to stand with the revolutionary men of Congress ; and endeavor to throw contempt upon the decisions of the Supreme Court ; and even refuse to yield obedience to its mandates. Chief-Justice Carter, of the Superior Court of the District of Columbia, on the 12th of February 1867, pronounced the judgment of himself and his associates, Fisher, Olin and Wylie, denying the motion made by Mr. Bradley for the admission of Colonel A. B. McGruder, of the Confederate army as a practioner at the bar of the said Court. This decision was designed to invalidate that of the Supreme Court of the United States. The *iron clad* oath was as a serviceable political adjunct, and could not yet be dispensed with.

reason, and served to prove, as the Democrats from the first had contended, that the bulk of radical legislation was revolutionary and unconstitutional.

But notwithstanding Presidential and judicial reaction, the revolution had as yet such momentum, that its progress was irresistible. Negro suffrage for the Southern States, that fondly anticipated object was too dear in radical estimation to be abandoned at the dictation of the defenders of the Constitution. The first grand move for its attainment had been a fortunate one. The principle had been forced upon the Federal District; and a basis of operations now existed to make inroads into other quarters. The organization of the Territories of Nebraska and Colorado were taken up in this session of Congress, and their admittance into the Union conditioned upon their acceptance of universal suffrage. The imposition of this condition would be the forcible overthrow of the principle which had heretofore universally obtained, as regards the elective franchise. The determination of the question of suffrage had, up to this time, been universally deemed the province of the people of the States; but this republican principle was now about to yield to the current of the revolution that was flooding American soil.

The overthrow of this fundamental dogma, was strongly resented by the Democrats and the Republican Conservatives in both Houses of Congress; and the conscience of as violent a radical as Senator Wade, of Ohio, revolted at the attempt to reverse this cardinal principle of the Republic; and which had formed one of its corner-stones since the foundation of the Government. The Ohio Senator, in his speech on the Nebraska bill, used the following language:

"I do not know what right you have to say, that a State shall be admitted, not on an equality with every other State, and shall not be allowed to regulate her elective franchise as she pleases. I say to the gentleman who offers this amendment, that he has not under the Constitution, as yet declared anywhere, that the General Government can fix the status of the elective franchise. You have left it thus far with the States. The Constitutional Amendment that we passed last year left it to the States—even to the rebel States, to regulate it for themselves, the only restriction being, that they should not have political power for those of their population whom they excluded from the right of voting. Of course, I am as much for the principle of the amendment as anybody else. I wish the word *white* were excluded from the Constitution of my own State. But neither you, sir, nor I, nor this Congress can do it, under the Constitution of the United States. We have no power here to say to the State of Ohio, 'correct this error in your Constitution, or we will correct it for you.' Will any gentleman contend that we can do it?"*

The bills for the admittance of Colorado and Nebraska as States, passed the two Houses of Congress, and were sent to President Johnson for his approval, which he declined in both cases to extend. He vetoed these bills, basing his dissent largely upon the attempted enforcement of universal suffrage upon the people of these Territories, which he stigmatised as an infraction of the fundamental principles of republican government; yea, even as a violation of the Constitution. In the case of Colorado, the President opposed its admittance because the people of this Territory had themselves, through their House of Represetatives, entered their protest against it. He severely reflected upon the action of Congress, as regards the last named Territory, stigmatising it as partaking too evidently of a desire to admit new States, without regard to principle, for the political advantages that might thereby enure to the revolutionists. These vetoes were both reconsidered in the two Houses of Congress, but the President having disclosed the flimsy claims of Colorado for admittance into the Union, his views were sustained. Nebraska, however, was admitted as a State over the Presidential veto.

But the great work of reconstruction yet demanded the attention of the revolutionary Congress. The man to lead in what necessitated an utter repudiation of the Constitution, was the one who had heretofore in his utterances, been the most regardless of that instrument; and who had openly declared that the legislation of Congress regarding the Southern States, found its support outside of paper compacts. This man was Mr. Stevens, who, since the Thirty-ninth Congress, stood before the country as the leading radical in the Lower House; and who must ever figure as the Corypheus of revolutionary reconstruction, and the counterpart of Robespierre upon the American continent. As a skilled general, he began the last onset by a feigned movement in the submission of his North Carolina Bill, on the 13th of December, 1866; and which was simply designed to gain time, and allow public sentiment to develop itself in the direction he desired. Congress, in view of the popular apprehension, was pre-

* *Annual Cyclopædia*, for 1865, pp. 148–9.

cluded, as yet, from adopting any radical scheme of reconstruction; inasmuch as but four States of the South, Texas, Alabama, Florida and Georgia had up to this time passed upon the Constitutional Amendment. An observer at Washington was able to speak of the North Carolina Bill in the following words:

"The bill reported by Mr. Stevens, on Thursday last, is the beginning of the inevitable end"*

Different members of Congress, since the opening of this session, deeming the amendment too moderate, had introduced bills looking to reconstruction upon the radical basis; but all these were so variant that it was difficult to see how unity could be evolved from their conflicting views. Governor Holden and other North Carolinians, had conferred with Mr. Stevens, and aided him in the preparation of the bill he submitted for the legal rehabilitation of their State. But, although the bill assumed the entire overthrow of the constitutional government of the State, and proposed to confer a qualified suffrage upon all classes, without distinction of color, who could read and write, it was far from meeting the views of its proposer. The introduction of this bill created no enthusiasm in the breasts of those who cherished designs more revolutionary than it proposed. As a consequence, the bantling came dead-born into earth's sphere; and perished unwept, receiving neither the sorrow of its maternal progenitor, nor of the consanguineous fraternity.

But the real movement of Mr. Stevens, the arch revolutionist in Congress, to effect the reconstruction of the Southern States in accordance with his views, began fairly on the 3d of January, 1867. Disliking the bill which had been submitted by the Reconstruction Committee, he called up his own substitute which he sustained in one of his ablest speeches. This bill of Mr. Stevens admitted the temporary validity of the Government of the ten excluded States, and conferred upon all male citizens the right of suffrage; but excluded from citizenship, all those who being of full age, on the 4th of March, 1861, had held office under the Confederate States, or who had sworn allegiance to the said Government. It contained a plan of reconstructing the South, that did not meet the approbation of quite a number of the influential Abolitionists; but it served suitably as a subject of discussion before Congress and the nation. This bill of Mr. Stevens em-

*Philadelphia *Press*, December 18th, 1866.

bodied, as had also his North Carolina proposition, his leading conception, that the Confederate Commonwealths had lost their Statehood; and to regain vitality, required an emenation of power from the pleroma of the Rump Congress. This feature of his bill had the approbation of the revolutionists; and the discussion on their part, from this period, was mainly confined to the terms and franchise preliminaries to be adopted.

The Stevens Bill having been modified considerably by amendments and otherwise, again came up in the House on January 16th, 1867, when it was made the subject of a spirited discussion. Representative Paine, of Wisconsin, opened the debate in a very bitter attack upon Mr. Stevens for proposing to recognize as valid the existing State governments of the South. Mr. Bingham, of Ohio, also combatted the Stevens bill and the other radical modes of reconstruction that had been proposed; and declared that honor demanded of Congress, that it adhere to its proposition made to the South in its Constitutional Amendment. He moved the recommittment of the Stevens bill to the Committee on Reconstruction, in order that a better matured measure might be presented for the consideration of Congress. The bill, after having been modified, was referred to the Committee on Reconstruction.

On the 6th of February, Mr. Stevens, from this committee, reported a new "bill to provide for the more efficient government of the insurrectionary States." The revolutionists, by this time, were coming more into accord in their views; and time alone was needed to evolve the issue. The House entered, without delay, upon a debate on this bill, which lasted for several days. The last measure of Mr. Stevens, entitled the *Military Bill*, was intended to set aside the governments of the Southern States, and divide them into five districts, over each of which the General of the army should be authorized to appoint a subordinate, whose martial rule, in his special division, should be supreme. The bill proposed the complete subordination of the civil to military law; left the Southern States without representation; and was designed simply as a preparative for ulterior measures. It had been framed with the view of preparing the way for the Louisiana bill,* which

* The Louisiana Bill embodied the conclusions arrived at by the partisan committee appointed by the House of Representatives, to investigate the New Orleans riots of July 30th, 1866. Its clear object was to

enfranchised the negroes, but which virtually disfranchised the whites of the South. All this being secured, the coveted aim of the revolutionists would have been reached. But this was too extreme, for all except the Stevens radicals. On the 12th of February, James G. Blaine, of Maine, moved that the Military Bill be referred to the Committee on the Judiciary, with instructions to report back a provision admitting the Southern States, upon the adoption of the Constitutional Amendment, with suffrage for all, black and white. This amendment was to the effect that any rebel State adopting the Constitutional amendment, giving the elective franchise to its citizens without respect to color, and adopting a Constitution ratified by all its legal voters, should be declared entitled to representation in Congress; and that from the day of its admission, the military sections of the bill should be inoperative in such State. It did not strike out a single section of the Stevens Bill, but simply introduced a new issue of reconstruction. The Blaine Amendment was defeated in the House, upon the grounds that it did not disfranchise any of the rebel leaders, but accorded them the full privilege of participating in the work of reconstruction. The intense revolutionists supported the Stevens Bill, almost pure and entire; only the moderate Republicans favoring the amendment offered by Mr. Blaine. As a consequence, the amendment was defeated. The Military Bill of Mr. Stevens, then with slight alterations, on the 13th of February, obtained the sanction of the House, by a vote of 109 yeas to 55 nays.

The Military Bill, after this, came to the Senate and was debated in this body on February 16th, meeting with resolute opposition, chiefly on the ground that it proposed no solution of the question which for two years had been before Congress; and that it established in the South simply the rule of the sword, without containing any provisions for the restoration of civil governments. The first change proposed by the Senate, was the amendment which had been offered in the House by Mr. Blaine, but by that body rejected. This was also defeated in the Senate,

disfranchise as many of the Southern whites as pretexts could be urged for so doing. About nineteen-twentieths were proposed to be disfranchised by this measure. The bill was the production of Mr. Eliot, of Massachusetts, on whose motion the committee had been raised for the investigation of the said riot. It was introduced into the House on the 11th of February, and passed that body on the following day.

but rather, as it were, for parliamentary purposes. Senator Sherman submitted a substitute for the military bill of Stevens, which declared that no legal governments exist in the Confederate States, divided them into military districts, and prohibited State authority from interfering with military orders. The substitute differed from the Stevens Bill, in making it the duty of the President to appoint the military commanders, and in partially making the Blaine Amendment the basis of reconstruction. Military authority, by the Sherman substitute, was made supreme in the ten unrepresented States, and suffrage conferred upon all classes, without distinction of race or color.

The democratic resistance to the revolutionary movement, which aimed at negro suffrage in the Southern States, like as against a tide of destiny, was utterly powerless. Able and argumentative speeches were made by Senators Davis, Saulsbury, Hendricks, McDougal and others, showing the unconstitutionality of such legislation; but all logic and argumentation were vain, as the measure with but slight alteration passed as submitted by the Ohio Senator, and by the strong vote of twenty-nine yeas to ten nays. "Occasional," in the Philadelphia *Press* of February 17th, 1867, upon the passage of the Sherman Bill, wrote as follows:

> "This Sabbath morning found the Republicans of the United States Senate, after a session of eighteen hours, (except a rest from 4½ o'clock till 7 last evening) agreed in favor of the substitute of Sherman, of Ohio, for the various propositions that have been proposed and rejected."

The Sherman Bill, when it came to the House encountered a fierce opposition from Stevens, Boutwell, Stokes and other radicals, on the grounds that it provided too general an amnesty for the rebels, and that it would permit the State Governments in the South, after reconstruction, to fall into their hands. The object of these men was to secure the disfranchisement of as large a number of the Southern whites as possible, in order that their revolutionary party might be able to grasp and hold the sceptre in the South by means of negro suffrage. Hence, they greatly favored Mr. Eliot's bill for the government of Louisiana, which disfranchised the rebels, as it were, by wholesale. Mr. Stevens and his friends, as a consequence, united with the Democrats in opposition to concurring in the passage of the Sherman Bill as it came from the Senate, and carried a Committee of Conference.

The Senate refused a conference, and insisted on its amendments. The House now adopted two important amendments, the one offered by Mr. Shellaberger, and the other by Mr. Wilson. The first was to the effect, that until the rebel States were admitted to representation, the civil governments of the South should be purely provisional; and the latter declared, that no person excluded from office by the Constitutional Amendments, shall be permitted to take part in the re-organization of the rebel States. The Sherman Bill, with these amendments having passed the House, was sent to the Senate for its concurrence. This latter body accepted these amendments prepared by the House, and the bill was passed by thirty-five yeas to seven nays. Even Reverdy Johnson, of Maryland, as an acquiescent vicar of Bray, at the last hour deserted his colors for those of the enemy, and swelled the Senatorial roll of those trampling on the Constitution of their country.

The bill encountered the usual veto of the President, but was repassed by both Houses, and became a part of the unconstitutional, revolutionary legislation. As another Argonautic cruise, the great expedition of abolitionism was now ended; and the golden fleece of their hopes was grasped. This last act was also viewed as the philosopher's stone, which would transform as by magic, the emancipated slaves into American citizens, capable of preserving republican institutions. This, however, was simply the ostensible view entertained by the zealous, hair-brained fanatics, who had deluded themselves into the belief that education could metamorphose barbarian negroes into intelligent, virtuous citizens. The deep, crafty schemers of the Stevens type, entertained no such silly conceptions, but they bent with the popular communistic current of the age, and sought by means of fraud and hypocrisy to govern the unthinking by a more despotic tyranny than they assumed to have broken. During the discussion of the reconstruction measures, Mr. Stevens made no concealment that he favored the enfranchisement of the negroes, in order to strengthen his party, and politically enslave the Southern whites. This, in short, was the great object of the intelligent revolutionists. Stevens, while arguing for universal suffrage, said:

"The white Union men are in a great minority in each of those States. With them the blacks would act in a body; and it is believed that in each of said States, except one, the two united would form a majority, control the States, and protect themselves. * * * It would insure the ascendency of the Union party. For I believe, on my conscience, that on the continued ascendency of that party, depends the safety of this great nation. If impartial suffrage is excluded in the rebel States, then every one of them is sure to send a solid rebel representative delegation to Congress, and cast a solid rebel electoral vote. They, with their kindred copperheads of the North, would always elect the President and control Congress."*

The infamous, wicked and diabolical crime, which the sagacious revolutionists knew that they had committed against civilization and Southern society, fully assured them of the counter revolution of hate and retaliation, which would consign them to the bottomless pit of American rage and execration; unless by the votes of the ignorant negroes and whites, they should be able to embank with success against the recurrent flood. It was rule or ruin with the fanatical party. For they were too well aware, that, composing as they did, the great minority of the American people, a day of retribution would confront them in all its horrible solemnity. To hide, therefore, their guilt and escape merited detection, they preferred the downfall of constitutional republican government, with all its attendant calamities; and, as if to prevent forever its restoration, they re-opened all the flood-gates of ruin, which the wisdom of the world during many centuries had been engaged in closing.

But the climax of the revolution was now reached. The Republic of the fathers was fully prostrated in the Stevens-Sherman Reconstruction Enactment of the Rump Congress; the union of consent was transformed into one of antagonism, which arms and armies united; and the States were left in a condition of effervescence, from which the hand of the Napoleonic master may alone be able to rescue them. Hypocritical centralism had trampled over constitutionalism; but it was the creature of perfidy, fraud and dissimulation; and lacked the bold front that seizes the reins by manly entrepidity and moral heroism. As dastards and knaves, the revolutionists had subverted and trodden under foot the *Magna-charta* of their country, by pandering to the low insinuating sentiments of the time, and flinging sops to the multitude; and upon the ruins of constitutional government were rearing a despotism more odious and corrupt than the

**Annual Cyclopædia* for 1867, p. 207.

basest absolutism of Asia. The Southern States were consigned to military rule, until the new citizens should remodel the State Constitutions in conformity with the mandates of the Washington dictators. In the cataclysm that prostrated Southern society, constitutional government was wholly submerged; and the land of the Pinkneys, Rutleges and Randolphs was now ready to become a nest of unclean birds. The political buzzards and cormorants of the North had, for some time, been scenting the fields of putridity in which to gorge their insatiate maws.

In the wreck of society that befell the South at the hands of hypocrisy and fanaticism, honor and virtue, the two main pillars of free government were broken down, and chicanery and duplicity substituted. In the North, society had for years been bending to the blasts of fraud and dissimulation; and it was only preserved from overthrow by the high Southern tone* which diffused its influence from the Federal centre throughout the Union. This being mainly cut off in secession, the torrent of corruption began at once audibly to roar; and when the reconstructionists had ended their work, it was rushing with rapidity as a swelling stream. It was giving evident tokens that after uniting with the Southern flood, already rising from reconstruction, it would become the great river upon which all the communistic later-day craft should carry the soldiery to the last battle of Democracy, the Armegeddon of the new world.

The preliminary legislative work of reconstruction having been mainly completed† for the subversion of the State Governments in the South; the next question of pressing concern with the revolutionists, was how best to entrammel President Johnson, and circumscribe his official power by every means within their reach. Ever since his breach with them, they busied themselves in devising plans to overcome his opposition, and undermine his influence with the people. During this session of Congress, in accordance with his resolution in the preliminary caucus, Mr. Stevens, the great enemy of the President, introduced into the House a bill to regulate removals from office. A bill with similar purpose, introduced at the previous session, was also consid-

* Southern society, owing to its class subordination, naturally produced a higher tone of sentiment than the North has ever been able to exhibit.

† Two supplementary Reconstruction Bills were subsequently passed, which were designed for carrying into effect the provisions of the Stevens-Sherman Bill.

ered, and after having gone through the process of emendation, passed the House. Being taken up in the Senate, the concurrence of this body was likewise secured. It afterwards came to the President for his approval or dissent. The bill, as it passed both Houses, precluded the President from removing, of his own authority, officials; and requiring the assent of the Senate to render his removals valid, in like manner, as to confirm their appointments.

This was another unprecedented stretch of legislation, and of itself evinced the revolutionary character of the men who dominated, regardless of reason and law, in the Congress of the nation. The President vetoed the bill to deprive him of the authority legally vested in him as the Federal Executive; and the legitimacy of which had never been validly questioned since 1789, in the sitting of the first Congress, after the formation of the Constitution. But this onslaught upon Presidential authority, was the effort of pure partisans, who were bent upon wresting all power from their own Chief Magistrate, because they discovered that he entertained greater regard for his oath of office, than for the promotion of their revolutionary designs. President Johnson strongly disputed the right of Congress to abridge his power to dismiss, at his own option, any subordinate official for the performacne of whose duty he, as the head of the Government, was responsible. All his predecessors had exercised the power of dismissing authoritatively, and without question, any of their official subordinates; and it was one which the framers of the Government deemed the indispensable right of the officer who filled the Presidential Chair. The bill was, however, reconsidered; and having passed both Houses over the veto, was enrolled amongst the national statutes.

CHAPTER XXX.

THE AFRICANIZATION OF THE SOUTH.

The soul of the fanatics being fixed upon the total revolution of Southern Society, before the adjournment of the Thirty-ninth Congress, it was determined to convene at once the new one, in order to have the supervisory eye of radicalism over the Presidential occupant, and the working of the favorite legislation. Accordingly, the Fortieth Congress assembled on the 4th of March, immediately following the dissolution of the former representative bodies. It was soon apparent to the keen perception of the managers, that additional features must be impressed upon the Sherman-Stevens Reconstruction Act of March 2d, 1867, in order to secure the coveted objects of the friends of that measure. A supplementary bill was therefore prepared, and passed both Houses of Congress, directing the registration of the voters in the Southern States, and the other auxiliary particulars hitherto overlooked by the legislators. This supplement to the Reconstruction Act, also met the opposition of a Presidential veto, but on the 23d of March it became a law in the usual method as had its congenital associates.

President Johnson, although disapproving the revolutionary legislation, which was to subvert the State Governments of the South, and overturn the whole social system of that section, acquiesced, nevertheless, as the Executive representative of the nation, and took such action as the anti-constitutional enactments demanded. The ten States subjected to military despotism were divided into five districts,* over each of which the President

*The State of Virginia formed the *first* of these districts; North and South Carolina the *second;* Alabama, Florida and Georgia the *third;* Arkansas and Mississippi the *fourth;* and Louisiana and Texas the *fifth.* Considerable exchanging of the military commanders of these districts took place. General Hancock was substituted for General Sheridan, appointed a General of the army, as the law required of him. For the *first* of these districts, J. M. Schofield was selected; over the *second*, Daniel E. Sickles; in the *third*, General Pope; to the *fourth*, General Ord; and General Sheridan was assigned to the command of the *fifth* district.

The principles of republicanism were found altogether inadequate for the work which the revolutionists were determined to effect; and those of oriental empires were substituted by men striving for ideal equality, and the enlarged liberalism of socialistic Europe. But it was inconsistent, and wholly unphilanthropic, to find men, who professed to be the friends of republican liberty, entirely ignoring, as it were, the results of freedom; and even supplanting these by means of viler tyranny and more despotic usurpation than the people of America ever witnessed. Civil law all through the South was compelled to descend from its ancient seat, at the nod of military satraps, who were clothed with an authority, which no constitutional power in America was able to confer. The rule of the sword which modern civilization had laid aside, was substituted by legislators in order to force upon an unwilling people, measures against which, reason and the sensibilities of the Caucasian race, revolted.

A system of intolerance was inaugurated in the Southern States, under the pretence of law, which found no warrant, save in the enthusiastic zeal of despots, who, Gessler-like, could imprison their countrymen for differing with them in political opinions; and giving evidence of that difference by some unguarded remarks or incautious exhibitions of the feelings of freemen. It was but natural that the Southern people should resent treatment, designed to crush their free and independent spirit; render them down-trodden serfs of barbarian negroes; and enchain them to the car of revolutionary oppression, from which it should for years be impossible to rescue them. Governors of States, Judges of the courts, and other officials in the South, were removed

---

with great profit to the oppressed Southern people; General E. R. S. Canby for General Daniel E. Sickles, with some advantage; General McDowell for General Ord, with no loss, and General Meade took the place of General Pope, no special gain, however, being realized. General Schofield was honorably relieved by being invited to assume the higher post of Secretary of War. General Stoneman was then assigned to the command of the first district.

from their places by military dictators,* who were base enough as to sink their manhood in subserviency to arbitrary power; and in the execution of authority with which, as they were well aware, the Constitution of their country had never clothed them. Suppliant tools of despotism, whom the people of the South despised, were foisted into place and position by Generals Sheridan, Sickles and other appointees of the Federal Government.

A fermentation † of sentiment began in the South, with the appointment of the Federal satraps, and the inauguration of measures for the reconstruction of the Southern States. Meetings of the native whites assembled together for consultation all over the South. Assemblages of the negroes and of the unchivalric whites, inspired by the latter, soon commenced also to be held in different States, and resolutions were adopted at these, which were fully in accord with the views of the most extreme anti-slavery men of the North. No other result could be expected, than that the newly enfranchised race would sympathise with and attach itself, in a body to that party, to which it owed its freedom and the right of suffrage. The boon of liberty and American citizenship appeared to the untutored African, as of

*Gen. Sheridan removed Governors Throckmorton, of Texas, and Wells, of Louisiana. Gov. Jenkins, of Georgia, was removed by Gen. Meade; and Gov. Humphreys, of Mississippi, was removed by Gen. McDowell. The removal of other officers would near fill a volume.

† Movements were inaugurated, in April, 1867, in Georgia and Mississippi, to test before the Supreme Court of the United States the constitutionality of the reconstruction legislation, which would, unless checked, subvert the State Governments in the South. The Supreme Judicial Tribunal, was now become the last hope of the Southern people, to resist the flood of revolution, which was about to cover them with the putrid filth of negro supremacy. Applications were made on behalf of these States to file bills for injunctions to restrain the President, as the representative of the Government, from executing laws odious to himself and to the white people of the South. But the Supreme Court, before this period, had become a target of abuse for the revolutionary faction that held the reins of power; and its present existence depended upon the will of Congress. It was, therefore, impotent to resist the legislation, even though unanimously opposed to it. But besides, a minority of its members belonged to the political party, which favored the legislation offensive to the South. The Court, therefore, determined that it had no power to consider the reconstruction laws, and thence dismissed, for want of jurisdiction, the applications for the bills of injunction. It would seem not difficult to account for such a decision, or to estimate its value, when made by a Court that could decide the Legal Tender Bill unconstitutional; and in less than two years afterwards reverse that same decision, which it had so solemnly pronounced. The period, however, had arrived in the history of the country, when the fanatics were able to do what Daniel Webster predicted, that they would do after their advent to power: they were able to *set the Supreme Court at defiance.*

infinite consequence; and his devotion to his new masters became at once as servile and adulatory, as it had been in his former condition of slavery. He served therefore, admirably as the instrument in the hands of the dextrous politician to grasp what otherwise would have been impossible to obtain. Political manipulation in the South became a sort of mutual admiration school for corrupt office-seekers and ignorant negroes. The one could flatter the emancipated blacks upon the results of the war, and their great efficiency and aid in contributing to the same; whilst the other, in turn, could obsequiously acquiesce in the dictates of the new rulers, and help them to such posts of distinction as they especially coveted.

But the condition in which the Southern whites of the old ruling class now found themselves, was deplorable in the extreme. Bred in sentiments of honor and high-toned chivalry, they were unable to brook the reflection of universal suffrage in their midst; and that their former slaves, who were just released from servitude, should be recognized as equals with themselves upon the political arena. Investigation and observation had satisfied many persons, not only in the South but also in the North, that republican government ran a hazardous risk of loosing its equipoise even with unlimited Caucasian suffrage. But, to throw all the negroes into the political scale, without the least preparation for citizenship, was risking an extreme which conservatism would never have ventured. The plunge, however, having been made, large numbers of the people of the South were in the utmost quandary to know how to act in the altered situation of affairs. Many, impressed with the belief that republican government was fully ended, resolved to perform no part in the political drama, which was to be enacted for the restoration of civil government in the South, and in accordance with the revolutionary programme. They felt amply sustained in their views, when they called to mind the numerous predictions of the early statesmen of the Republic, who looked forward to a civil war, as the event which would end free government within the limits of the American Union. But, though these were the sentiments and opinions of a large and intelligent class of the Southern people, another portion of them, differing little from the former in many of their views, believed, nevertheless, that duty to themselves and to their section, demanded of them, that they should continue to struggle for their rights in the midst of all their difficulties; and that quiescence in the new movements inaugurated in their midst, would be fatal to all their hopes as citizens of a common country. This class of the Southern people resolutely placed their shoulders to the wheel, resolved to do their utmost to save their States from the deplorable fate, which negro suffrage had in store for all of those that should be submerged by the flood of filth ready to be let loose upon them.

The several military commanders, in accordance with their requirements, appointed Boards of Registration in their different districts, whose duty it should be, to cause an enrollment to be made of the old and new citizens, qualified to vote under the reconstruction schedule. They also, in general orders, named the times when elections should take place in the several States to determine upon the calling of conventions, to revise and alter the Constitutions of these States, and also to choose delegates to the said conventions, Auxiliary Boards of Registration were likewise appointed throughout every State of the South to be reconstructed; which boards were to act in subordination to the principal tribunal selected in each State by the military autocrats of the various districts. The registration of voters, which was made in all the Southern States, was purely a work of political partisanship,* engineered in the interests of that party which secured the passage of the laws, under which the proceedings were held. The negroes were enrolled as voters by wholesale, but the frown of power rested upon every applicant for registration, whose countenance indicated that suspicious descent, that was likely to revolt against any intimate contact with the suddenly elevated children of Ham. Every member of the suspected race, must either bear evident marks of soul-degredation, or prove his allegiance to the party of revolution, before he could have his name uncontestedly recorded as a legal voter in his State. All those making application for registration, and not possessing the characteristics agreeable to radicalism, were subjected to an ordeal of scrutiny, that was sufficient to deter all save the boldest from the undertaking.

* The Anti-Slavery standard confessed as follows: "The managers of the Republican party rely entirely on the rebel States to elect Gen. Grant. * * * It is planned to admit the Southern States on the well understood condition, that they vote the Republican ticket, no matter what name that ticket bears."—Quoted in the New York *Herald* of Jan. 9, 1868.

But registration being now the all important particular to be considered in the work of reconstruction, this matter was scrutinized and watched by the radicals with the all considerative care of devoted politicians. After the adjournment of the special session of the Fortieth Congress, in the Spring of 1867, danger was at once manifest, when the putting in force of the reconstruction laws became a question of Executive Administration. Certain doubtful points of the law were submitted by President Johnson to his Attorney-General, for an opinion that should form a guide upòn the matters in dispute. This officer, having thoroughly considered the questions in controversy, on the 12th of June gave an elaborate opinion upon the law, and one which aroused the fears of the revolutionists, and induced them again to buckle on their armor for a new contest with the Administration. If this opinion of the law officer of the Government were permitted to be accepted as the true intepretation of the law, they perceived that they would be unable to secure the reconstruction of the South in the interests of their party; and this desired result, in radical estimation, must be secured at all hazards. Altogether too small a number of Confederates would be excluded from the ballot-box, the official opinion being permitted to obtain as the interpretation of the Government. Clamor arose over the whole North, in opposition to the views of Mr. Stansberry, and no other remedy was feasible save in the re-assembling of Congress, and in the passage of another supplemental bill, that should nullify the newly submitted interpretation. On the 3d of July, 1867, therefore, both Houses of Congress assembled in overwhelming numbers, determined to give reconstruction a different turn from what the Administration, under the advice of the Attorney-General, was inclined to do. A declaratory act, as it was called, was passed at this special session of Congress, and became a law over the usual veto of the President. This act was declaratory, however, only in name, as additions, new in nature, character and effect, were clearly and palpably made to what had already been enacted on the subject of reconstruction. The principal points made more clear in the Act of July 19th, were the enunciation of the entire and complete suppremacy of the military power throughout the whole Southern country; the enlargement of the power of the military commanders; and that the Boards of Registration should have the fullest latitude of investigation, and the power of rejecting whomsoever they deemed proper. Senator Buckalew, afterwards speaking of this legislation and of the revolutionists, said:

"They carried on the whole proceeding of reconstruction with reference to party advantages." *

Registration, after the passage of this Act, proceeded with vigor; and the negroes were enrolled by the grossly partisan boards, with great satisfaction, as the individuals who should sanction by their votes the decrees of the revolutionary bodies. In many parts of the South, injustice of the most rank character was perpetrated upon the rights of the white people, who were fairly entitled to be registered and permitted to vote. Numerous classes of persons, by no means disqualified to register; such as sextons of churches, and petty officers of municipalities were rejected upon flimsy pretences, as disloyal and to be excluded from the rights of citizenship. After this part of the programme had been completed, it was found that the negroes upon the registry outnumbered the whites in nearly every one of the Southern States; and that thus the triumph of radicalism was assured. In two of these States the black population considerably exceeded the white, which gave the former the political control in them, even though none of the latter had been disfranchised for participation in the rebellion. Many of the whites refused to register, because they were unwilling to endure the ordeal, that was necessary to be encountered, before the partisan boards that were authorized to pass upon their qualifications as citizens of their States. The necessity imposed upon them, by the revolutionary Congress, seemed unjustly to require of them a degredation of their manhood, to which as freemen, educated in schools of honor, they were unwilling to submit. As chivalric members, therefore, of an overturned republic, they preferred to endure the injustice of political ostracism, rather than to be guilty of the meanness of crouching before the tribunals, which radicalism had set up; and ignobly struggling for the privilege of being re-clothed with that citizenship of which barbarian negroes were not deemed unworthy. Quite a number of the leading men were clearly disfranchised by the legislation of Congress; and many who were not, perceived that their registration could no longer save their States from the horrors of negro

* New York *World*, September 28th, 1867.

domination. Being unable, therefore, to interpose effective resistance, they were compelled to permit the Juggernaut of negro suffrage, unchecked, to take its course and prostrate the State Governments of the South in one common ruin. As doubts, also, were entertained as regarded the parties who were clearly entitled to register, these were seized upon by political mountebanks, as admirable means to deter large numbers of the white people from registering. It was given out from high quarters that all would be prosecuted whom the courts should afterwards determine not to have been entitled to be registered as voters. An oath was also exacted of all candidates for registration, which was designed to exclude from the polls as large a number as possible.

But the registration, such as it was, being at length completed by the boards having charge of the matter, the military commanders, by general orders, afterwards fixed the times when elections should take place in each State, to determine whether the novel yeomanry, would favor or disapprove of the calling of conventions to alter, according to the prearranged schedule, the several State Constitutions. It was likewise ordered, that delegates to the contemplated conventions should be voted for; and where conventions were carried, these bodies in due time should be convened in their respective States. In the elections thus fixed, the polls were directed to be kept open during several days, in order, as it was urged, to allow the new voters a fairer opportunity to express their desires for or against the conventions.

After the registration of the several Southern States had been completed, orders were then given that careful revisions should be made; and that the Registry Boards should strike from the lists, all whom they should determine to be unqualified to exercise the right of suffrage. This was an admirable safety-valve, in the control of expert politicians, by means of which to allow all the superfluous vapor, in the shape of white majorities, to pass off without endangering the carefully constructed machinery of radicalism, that was to carry the nation into the happy regions of African bliss. When this expunging process was with sagacious skill completed, the constitutional elections began to take place, one after another, with similar results. These elections were held in the different States from September, 1867, until

February in the following year. In most of the States, few voted at these elections except the negroes, and also a small number of whites, chiefly emigrants from the North. The negroes and their associate whites, voted almost without exception for the conventions.* A stronger conservative vote was polled in Virginia than in any of the Southern States. In this State, out of one hundred and sixty-nine thousand votes cast, sixty-one thousand opposed the calling of a convention to alter the Constitution. In most of the other States, only a comparatively small vote was cast against the conventions; in several of them, not over the one-tenth of the votes cast. The great body of the whites chose to absent themselves from the polls.

The delegates elected to these conventions were composed chiefly of unknown men, both white and colored. Neither character nor intellectual worth were considered in the selection of the individuals who were to re-frame the prostrated fabric of the American Union. Men of wealth and distinguished consideration were defeated in these elections; and obscure, corrupt personages were chosen to fill the seats, that had been honored by the ablest and purest patriots to whom America had given birth. As an example, Judge Alexander Rives, of Albemarle County, Virginia, a man of intelligence, wealth and position in society, was defeated as a delegate to the proposed convention of the State, by an ignorant negro. In Mecklenburg County, a negro, who was unable to read or write, and who had repeatedly been tarnished in his passage through Courts of Justice, was elected a delegate over a respectable citizen. A violent partisan named Hunnicutt, the corruptly accused Underwood, an Irishman by the name of Morrisey and two negroes, were the delegates elected from the City of Richmond. A class of leaders

* "The negroes were everywhere driven to the polls by the chiefs of the Union League Councils. The day before the election, radical agents traveled through Montgomery country, and summoned the blacks to come to the city and vote, telling them that General Swain had ordered them to do so, and would punish them if they did not. On the afternoon before the day of election, thousands of negroes marched into Montgomery in regularly organized regiments, each man bearing arms; and at night they camped around the city as a besieging army. The danger of a disturbace was so great that the military authorities ordered them to be disarmed. Ten per cent. of the negroes who voted could not now tell, and indeed never knew, the name on the ballot which they deposited in the box; they acted simply in obedience to the instructions of the Bureau agents, without the faintest glimmering of an idea of what they were doing."—*Correspondent from Alabama to N. Y. World, Nov. 11th, 1867.*

were thrown to the surface over the whole South, such as had been only the product of the raging sea of French *sans culottism.* The Parson Brownlows, and others of like revolutionary principles, took the places that had been occupied by the Washingtons, Jeffersons, Madisons, Clays and Calhouns of the pure days of the Republic. A considerable number of the delegates chosen to these conventions, were, as one correspondent declared, "black as Nox and Erebus." In more than one State the sable delegates were able to count a majority.

But the great Webster himself had now been outstripped, in the school of modern communistic progress. His eagle vision had never discerned the coming millenium of negro government, which should render perfect the weakness of Caucasian rule. When anticipating the downfall of the Republic, he had been unable to see the future made happy, by the contrivances which Stevens, Sumner, Phillips, and their allies devised. His soul-solicitous inquiries, however, were answered in the constitutional elections that had taken place in the South. The men were already chosen who, in fanatical estimation, were to supplement the deficiencies of the framers of our Government, and do what, as the expounder of the Constitution declared in the following words, to be the difficult problem. "Who," said he, "shall reconstruct the fabric of demolished Government? Who shall rear again the well-proportioned columns of constitutional liberty? Who shall frame together the skillful architecture which unites National Sovereignty with State Rights, individual security and public prosperity? Now if these columns shall fall they will be reared not again. Like the Coliseum and the Parthenon, they will be destined to a melancholly and mournful immortality. Bitterer tears, however, will flow over them than were ever shed on the monuments of Roman and Grecian art, for they will be the remnants of a more glorious edifice than Greece or Rome ever saw, the edifice of constitutional liberty."

From the first arrival of the military commanders in their several districts in the South, a period of turmoil and confusion was experienced, which baffles all efforts of the pen fairly to depict. The demoniac spirit of intolerance exhibited by Generals Sheridan, Sickles, and other military rulers towards the people, over whom they were commissioned to bear sway, was sufficient to goad the most pacific populations to resistance; and implant in the breasts of all of them feelings of hatred and deep-seated rancor. Could a nation of people calmly stand by, and endure the removal of their own legally elected officials, from the highest almost to the lowest, and see their places filled by hated individuals, whose only merit consisted in their devotion to the principles that had deluged their soil in blood, and beggared them in the land of their fathers? Reflect upon the aggregated multitude of other injuries and abuse, heaped upon the Southern people by the men and their subordinates, who were illegally appointed to rule over them during this period of convulsion; and consider, if the perpetration of such was calculated to re-cement the bonds of fraternal union, upon which free government assumes to be based. Was it to be expected that freemen would, as curs, lick the hands of those who smote them? And yet ten thousand fold more than this, would seem to have been expected by those, who could conceive that the legislation of Congress and the action of the revolutionary party, would not intensify the rage of the Southern whites, and array them in bitter hostility towards the black race throughout all the Southern States.

By the time the Congo conclaves began to assemble in the different States of the South, a well united opposition of the native whites was organized in all these States; and prepared to do everything in their power to resist the deadly unconstitutional march of the revolutionary party, over the fair fields of their once happy and prosperous section. But as the youthful Sampson of the South, had been fatally shorn beneath the apple tree of Appomattox, he was now left to grind in the prison house of his misfortunes; while at the same time, the dulcimers and cymbals of fanatical joy were sounding hilarious tunes over his downfall; and none were now anywhere found ready to do homage to the former proud foeman of Northern abolitionism. The hated strains of his enemies' mirth, he was forced to hear; but all the the avenues of escape from the bitter thraldom being closed, he was compelled to bear what otherwise would have been unendurable.

On the 5th of November, 1867, the motley Convention of Alabama, the first of its species, assembled at Montgomery, the Capital of the State, in obedience to the call of General Pope; and proceeded to the work of framing a Constitution and Civil Government, in accordance with the requisitions of the Reconstruction Acts. A considerable number of the delegates to this convention were negroes, one-half of whom were unable to write their own names. All of them being, however, serviceable instruments in the hands of the revolutionary party, their presence was agreeable, and desired by men who cared more for their political success than for the perpetuity of constitutional government. Indeed, the whites who figured as members of this and the following mixed-race conventions in the Southern States, were the creatures of the social convulsions of the country. The convention of mongrels, that next met to imitate the proceedure of statesmen and skilled lawgivers, was that of Georgia; and so, one after another, the citizens of the old Commonwealths of the South, were compelled to witness in their midst the variegated assemblages that were authorized by unconstitutional legislation to subvert their State Sovereignties, and foist upon them spurious constitutions that were nauseous to the conceptions of their people. It was infinitely more offensive to the people of the South; and, as they viewed it, more unjust, that their State governments, by acts of Congress, should be made the victims of negro suffrage,* inasmuch as all attempts to fasten it upon the North (save in New England) had signally failed.

Whilst the hybrid conventions were engaged in changing the State Constitutions of the South, Congress again assembled in

*Negro suffrage in the North was steadily resisted by the people, although the number of negroes in this section was comparatively small as compared with those in the South. Even up to the period when it was forced upon the South, one Northern State after another defeated the attempts that were made to introduce it. In the State of New York, in 1860, (where qualified negro suffrage already was adopted), a vote was taken upon allowing negroes the right of suffrage without a property qualification. The result was, yeas—197,503; nays—337,984. In the City of New York, the vote was, yeas—1,640; nays—37,471. In 1864, a like effort was made in the same State, which was defeated, with the following result: yeas—85,406; nays—224,336. In Illinois, in 1862, a vote was taken on the absolute and total exclusion of all negroes from the State limits, when the yeas were 171,893; nays—71,306, On granting them the right of office and suffrage, the yeas were 35,649; nays—211,920. And for the enactment of prohibitory laws against their coming into or voting in the State, the yeas were 198,938; nays—44,414. In 1865, the question of negro suffrage was submitted to the people of Connecticut, and was defeated by a majority of 6,272. In the State of Ohio, in 1867, when all efforts were made to overcome the prepossessions of the people, it was defeated by about 50,000 majority. About the same time it was defeated by considerable majorities in Kansas and Minnesota. And the people of Michigan, a State heavily Republican, in the Spring of 1868, voted down a Constitution for no other reason than that it conferred the elective franchise upon negroes.

December, 1867. It was at once determined to do, by one or other method, what Congress had now the power to perform. This was to "*set the Supreme Court at defiance.*" The case of McCardle, an editor of Mississippi, was coming before that tribunal, and the constitutionality of the Reconstruction Acts would be distinctly raised in its argument. McCardle had been arrested by General Ord, and having been brought before Judge Hill, of the United District Court of Mississippi, on *Habeas Corpus*, was remanded into military custody. Judge Hill reviewed the law, in an elaborate opinion, and declared that no judicial tribunal, having cognizance of the offense charged against McCardle, existed in the State, which was not subject to General Ord; and he felt unable to pronounce the Reconstruction Acts unconstitutional. He deemed the offense of the Mississippi editor a breach of law, of which the military authorities had cognizance. From this decision, the case was brought before the United States Supreme Court.

Early in December, a bill was introduced into the Senate, to determine what should constitute a quorum of the Supreme Court. The Senate bill was amended and passed the House, so as to require two-thirds of the Judges of that Court to pronounce a law of Congress unconstitutional. But the assaults made upon the House proposition was so severe, that it was finally abandoned. The object of the contemplated legislation, was to prevent a majority of the Court from deciding in the McCardle case, that the reconstruction laws were unconstitutional. The great efforts of the revolutionists to prevent a decision of the Court upon these laws, evinced that they themselves feared judicial scrutiny. Of the eight Judges, of which the Court was then composed, it seemed generally to have been understood, that five of them viewed the Reconstruction Acts as unconstitutional, and if a fair opportunity were afforded they might so decide. Such a decision must be prevented. During the discussion of this matter before the House, Mr. Stevens, the revolutionary corypheus of that body, from the Reconstruction Committee, submitted as a substitute, a bill to declare that the jurisdiction of the Supreme Court should not extend to anything pertaining to the reconstruction legislation. This, although the direct way of reaching what Congress was aiming at, was in the estimation of radical politicians rather too unguarded an avowal of the object. An amendment, designed to accomplish the same result, was therefore proposed in the House, precluding appeals from the Circuit Court to the Supreme Court. This was adopted in the House, and concurred in by the Senate. It became a law over the Presidential veto. The Supreme Court was now unable to render a decision in the McCardle case, and the reconstruction legislation was freed from scrutiny.

The work of forming new constitutions for the Southern States, was steadily prosecuted as prescribed. The great object with the white and sable Statesmen of the conventions, was to frame constitutions which would exclude from the polls as large a number as possible of the white people of the South,* so as to insure the success of the radical party by means of negro votes. After constitutions had been framed, elections were ordered in the different States for their adoption or rejection. A majority of the registered voters was required to vote upon the ratification of a constitution before the same could be pronounced as ratified. This majority was lacking in the election held in Alabama, but in those held in Arkansas, North Carolina, South Carolina, Louisiana, Georgia and Florida, the constitutions were declared adopted by negro majorities.

Protests from the white people of every State of the South were sent to Congress, declaring their repugnance to being compelled to submit to the rule of barbarian negroes. These protests predicted the most deplorable consequences to their section and government, if they should be forced to acquiesce in negro domination. Deaf ears, however, were turned to all these remonstrances. Instead of hesitating in their career, the revolutionists in June, 1868, admitted into the Union the State of Arkansas over the veto of the President. A few days afterwards North Carolina, South Carolina, Louisiana, Georgia, Florida and Alabama were admitted as States by an Act entitled the *Omnibus bill.* The admission of Alabama was a plain breach of faith, as it forced upon the unwilling people of the

*As a sample of the oaths required by most of the new constitutions to be subscribed by every applicant for registration, that from Alabama is given: "I * * * do solemnly swear (or affirm) that I accept the civil and political equality of all men, and agree not to attempt to deprive any person, or persons, on account of race, color or previous condition, of any political or civil right, privilege or immunity, enjoyed by any other class of men."—Art. vii, Sec. 4 of New Constitution of Alabama.

State a Constitution which, under the reconstruction law as it stood when the election was held, had been clearly defeated. The reconstructed States in turn, speedily discharged their obligations by adopting the Fourteenth Amendment to the Constitution. Their admission as States thereupon was complete. Senators and Representatives from these States were shortly afterwards received with open arms in both Houses of Congress. But three States, Virginia, Texas and Mississippi proved laggards in revolutionary policy. But time only was now required to finish the uncompleted task. The President now being powerless and the Supreme Court shackled, the Rump Congress was at length clothed with the requisite legislative omnipotence. The Africanization of the South was now fully assured.

CHAPTER XXXI.

IMPEACHMENT OF ANDREW JOHNSON.

Notwithstanding the revolutionary Congress was able to pass laws over the Presidential veto, and set the Supreme Court at defiance, it was not satisfied. Being the product of the turbulent elements of the country, it must obey the impulses of those by whom it was sustained, or others would grasp its place and sceptre. A strong feeling of hostility to Andrew Johnson, animated the revolutionists from the period when the President broke with his party, in the Winter of 1866. The Chicago *Tribune*, the leading Republican paper of the West, on the last day of March of that year, in a vehement and acrimonious article, urged the impeachment and removal from office of President Johnson, because of his having vetoed the Freedman's Bureau and the Civil Rights Bills, and otherwise used his efforts to stem the radical tornado. The demand of this Western organ met the warm approbation of the infuriates of the party; which proposal was from time to time renewed, as Presidential opposition in one direction and another, strove to break the current that was still further prostrating the Constitution of the Republic.

Party rancor and political hate, from the period of the collision of the President with his party, selected him as the mark of venom, against which the shafts of rage and malice were directed. From that time he became the central figure for the most malicious partisan abuse which history has ever recorded; and all the epithets which vindictiveness was capable of manufacturing, were hurled at him, as if to bury him beneath showers of defamation. The man who allowed himself to be made the conspicuous Southern instrument of fanaticism; to inflame passion against his native people; as soon as he strove to check the unholy waves, became well-nigh the victim of the same flames, which for years he had with others been feeding. A misconception of the objects of radicalism, had seduced his adhesion to the wicked and unconstitutional war that was proclaimed against the Southern people; and now at length, when those objects plainly displayed themselves, it was too late to successfully resist the current that was become terrific; and he, with others, must yield before the blasts that were sweeping over the land. Instead of being the admired patriot of the South who filled the office of Military Governor of Tennessee, an office inimical to the Constitution of the nation, Andrew Johnson was maligned in the abusive sheets of fanatism, as the enemy of his country, the associate in crime with Jefferson Davis and the arch-fiend of liberty. Viewing the Presidential conscience in the mirror of their own souls, the fanatics gave the Executive no credit for present sincerity in his opposition to their revolutionary designs. He had bowed to their false gods, when his homage was a prize in their estimation. But their victory was now complete; and the fruits must be safely gathered. They now only wanted in their folds the sincere devotees, whose pupilage and training made them undissembling members of the faith they advocated. Neither had the revolution as yet spent its force. Its enemies must either retire before it, or be crushed beneath its wheels.

From the first proposal that was made to impeach the President, the clamor was kept up by the radical extremists, the cry becoming still the more intense as the strife between the Federal Executive and Congress developed itself. Mr. Stevens was one of the earliest and most bitter enemies of the President; and lacking all conscientious regard for his obligations to support the Constitution, he aided to the utmost of his power in fanning the flames that were rising between the two Departments of the Government. During the second session of the Thirty-ninth Congress, in 1867, the impeachment ball was set in motion by General Ashley, a member of the Lower House of Congress from Ohio. This officious gentleman was put forward by the crafty manipulators to do the work that even partisan hate was as yet timid to undertake. He charged the President with "high crimes and misdemeanors;" with usurpation of power and violation of law; and also, that he had made a corrupt use of the appointing, the pardoning, and the veto power; and had corruptly interfered in elections. A committee was appointed, and after a laborious research and collection of testimony, three separate reports were submitted by different members. These reports were made in the first regular session of the Fortieth Congress, in December, 1867. The current of political fury that was beating against the President had by this time swollen considerably, and in many places was overflowing its banks. A majority of the above named committee concurred in recommending the impeachment of Andrew Johnson; but the House still hesitated to sanction this extreme proceeding, which partisan rancor alone sustained. Party prudence, therefore, dictated that a more plausible pretext for impeachment should be awaited. The vote in the House on this question was, 56 yeas, all revolutionists, to 108 nays. The Democrats voted against this first, as all the following efforts of madness.

In the meantime, the struggle between Congress and the President had grown more bitter and impracticable, and had been carried even into the latter's official household. Edwin M. Stanton, the Secretary of War, being a warm partisan of Congress, was offensive to the President as a member of his select Council. He continued, however, to retain his office, despite the repeatedly expressed wish of the Executive that he would retire. At length the President expressed his desire in writing. On the 5th of August, 1867, he addressed Mr. Stanton as follows:

"SIR:—Public considerations of a high character, constrain me to say that your resignation, as Secretary of War, will be accepted."

To this message of laconic brevity, Mr. Stanton, in his reply, was equally brief:

"SIR:— * * * In reply, I have the honor to say, that public considerations of a high character, which alone have induced me to continue at the head of this Department, constrain me not to resign the office of Secretary of War, before the next meeting of Congress."

On the 12th of the same month, the President suspended Mr. Stanton from his office, and empowered General Grant, temporarily to act as Secretary of War.

At the time the President suspended Mr. Stanton, the Senate of the United States was not in session. Upon the assembling of the Senate, in December, 1867, the President, as required by the Tenure of Office Act, communicated to this body his reasons for the suspension of the Secretary of War. The Senate having considered the President's reasons, declared them on January 13th, 1868, as inadequate to justify the removal of Mr. Stanton, in the following words:

"*Resolved*, That having considered the evidence and reasons given by the President, in his report of December 12th, 1867, for the suspension, from the office of Secretary of War of Edwin M. Stanton, the Senate do not concur in such suspension."

As soon as this decision of the Senate was communicated to General Grant,* the latter vacated the office of Secretary of War, and Mr. Stanton took possession of the same without delay.

General Grant to this question, replied:

"*I shall, in that event, either hand you my resignation as acting Secretary of War, or let a mandamus be issued against me to surrender the office.*

On Saturday, January 11th, 1868, two days before the non-concurring action of the Senate took place, the President again called General Grant's attention to the matter, when the latter reiterated his previous promise, and added that the President should hear from him on Monday. He saw the President, as promised, but gave no intimation of any change in his views. Afterwards, when Mr. Stanton had again taken possession of the War Office, General Grant called upon the President, and was present at a Cabinet meeting, and being reminded by the President of his promise, admitted his having made such in the presence of the members of the Cabinet. The President after this, in a letter, accused General Grant of a violation of his promise, and was sustained in his assertion by five members of his Cabinet. General Grant, in turn, over his signature, denied the charges made by the President, but stood alone in his allegations, and wholly unsupported.

Owing tc the speedy surrender of the War Office, by the *ad interim* Secretary to Edwin M. Stanton, the President was frustrated in his design of making a test case for the courts to determine the constitutionality of the Tenure of Office Act; and whether or not Congress had deprived him of the power of changing his Secretary of War. Had General Grant intimated his intention of surrendering the office, the President would have named a Secretary in his stead, who would have declined to surrender to Mr. Stanton, until the courts would have determined to whom the office belonged. In the contest between the President and Congress, it was quite natural for every man

*President Johnson, being apprehensive of the action which the Senate would take. asked General Grant, his Secretary of War *ad interim*, what his course would be, in case the Senate should not concur in his reasons for the removal of Mr. Stanton.

to take sides; but it was dishonorable for the head of the army to deceive his superior by violating his engagement with him. If he meant to surrender the office, he should have advised the President of his intention so to do. Not having done so, he exposed himself to the charges of breach of faith and corrupt alliance with the party that was combatting the President; conduct wholly unchivalric, and unbecoming a man who filled the exalted position he occupied. His action and the surrounding circumstances, seemed to cast upon him a cloud of suspicion, inasmuch as he had for some time been rising into prominence as the Presidential candidate of the Congressional party. The New York Syracuse Convention of the Republican party, declared for General Grant for President, one day after the dispute between himself and President Johnson had been published in the public papers of the country.

Affairs remained in this condition until the 21st of February, following, when President Johnson undertook the responsibility of removing Edwin M. Stanton, and appointed Lorenzo Thomas, Adjutant-General of the United States Army, to take his place as Secretary of War, *ad interim*. He at once communicated, in a brief message to the Senate, the fact of the removal of Mr. Stanton and the appointment of General Thomas to take his place. Henry Wilson, of Massachusetts, submitted the following preamble and resolution:

"WHEREAS, The Senate has received and considered the communication of the President, stating that he had removed Edwin M. Stanton, Secretary of War, and had designated the Adjutant-General of the Army to act as Secretary of War, *ad interim*, therefore,—

"*Resolved*, By the Senate of the United States, that under the Constitution and Laws of the United States, the President has no power to remove the Secretary of War and designate any other officer to perform the duties of that office *ad interim*."

The radicals contended that under the Tenure of Office Act,* the President had no authority, without the consent of the

* The first section of the Tenure of Office Act, of March 2d, 1867, was that, by means of which Congress limited the power of the President over removals from office. The following is a copy of the first section:

"Be it enacted by the Senate and House of Representatives of the United States, in Congress assembled, that every person holding any civil office, to which he has been appointed by, and with the advice and consent of the Senate; and every person who may hereafter be appointed to any such office, and shall become duly qualified to act therein, is and shall be entitled to hold such office until a successor shall have been in like manner appointed; *Provided* that the Secretaries of State, of the

Senate, to remove the Secretary of War and appoint his successor. The Democrats and the Conservative Republicans, on the contrary, argued that under the words of the law, the President was not precluded from acting as he had done. After an animated discussion, the above resolution of Senator Wilson was adopted.

A grand opportunity was now presented to Mr. Stevens, the arch radical of the House, in the attempted removal of Edwin M. Stanton. It was water upon the mill of his political malice. The defeat of the impeachment movement, which had been headed by General Ashley, was galling to the Lancaster Statesman. He afterwards made a strong effort to have it renewed, but without success. When the essayed removal of Mr. Stanton was made known, Mr. Stevens was by general consent permitted to take the lead in the new impeachment undertaking, on account of the fierce hostility he was known to entertain towards President Johnson. He, accordingly, on the 22d of February, formally reported in the House, from the Committee on Reconstruction, the attempted removal of Mr. Stanton; and at the same time offered the following resolution:

"*Resolved*, That Andrew Johnson, President of the United States, be impeached of high crimes and misdemeanors."

This resolution was discussed until the 24th, when it was adopted by 126 yeas to 47 nays. The war against the President was purely partisan, the Republicans supporting and the Democrats opposing impeachment.*

After the adoption of the above resolution, the House selected Messrs. Stevens and Bingham to inform the Senate of their action. When they came to the Senate, Mr. Stevens said:

"MR. PRESIDENT:—In obedience to the order of the House of Representatives, we have appeared before you. In the name of the House of

---

Treasury, of War, of the Navy, and of the Interior, the Postmaster-General and the Attorney-General, shall hold their offices respectively for and during the term of the President, by whom they have been appointed, and for one month thereafter, subject to removal, by and with the advice and consent of the Senate."

* Considerable excitement pervaded the whole country, as the news concerning impeachment spread. John W. Geary, the radical Governor of Pennsylvania, telegraphed to Simon Cameron as follows: "The news to-day created a profound sensation in Pennsylvania. The spirit of 1861 seems again to pervade the Keystone State. Troops are rapidly tendering their services to sustain the laws. Let Congress stand firm." Similar tenders were made by leading Democrats to the President from different sections of the country.

Representatives, and of all the people of the United States, we do impeach Andrew Johnson, President of the United States, of high crimes and misdemeanors in office; and we further inform the Senate that the House of Representatives will, in due time, exhibit particular articles of impeachment against him, to make good the same; and in their name we demand that the Senate take due order for the appearance of the said Andrew Johnson to answer to the said impeachment."

Messrs. Bingham, Boutwell, Stevens, Wilson, of Iowa, Logan, of Illinois, Julian and Ward, were selected by the House to prepare the articles of impeachment. The committee at once entered upon the task, and in a few days was ready to submit the articles upon which it was determined to try the President. The committee reported in the House the series of impeachment articles, which, with those separately offered formed, in all, eleven. These were adopted by the House, March 2d, 1868. The first eight of these were based upon the attempted removal of Edwin M. Stanton, on February 21st. The ninth was based upon the instruction given by the President to General Emory, of Washington, on February 22d, 1868; and the tenth, upon the President's denunciation of Congress in his Chicago tour, during the year 1866. The last article accused the President of having, in the City of Washington, in his speech of August 18th, 1866, declared that the Congress of the United States was an illegal body; and in accordance with that view had, on the 21st of February, attempted, without the consent of the Senate, to remove from office E. M. Stanton, Secretary of War.

After the adoption of the Articles of Impeachment, the House of Representatives proceeded to choose the managers, who should conduct before the bar of the Senate, the prosecution against President Johnson. The managers chosen by the House were John A. Bingham, of Ohio; George S. Boutwell, of Massachusetts; James F. Wilson, of Iowa; John A. Logan, of Illinois; Thomas Williams, of Pennsylvania; Benjamin F. Butler, of Massachusetts, and Thaddeus Stevens, of Pennsylvanai. On March 4th, the Board of Managers, accompanied by the House as a Committee of the Whole, proceeded to the Senate in order to present the Articles of Impeachment. Mr. Bingham, the Chairman of the Board of Managers, then said:

"The Managers of the House of Representatives, by order of the House of Representatives, are ready at the bar of the Senate, if it please the Senate to hear them, to present Articles of Impeachment, in maintenance of the impeachment prepared against Andrew Johnson, President of the United States, by the House of Representatives."

Then followed Speaker Wade's order to the Sergeant-at-Arms, who now made proclamation as follows:

"Hear ye! Hear ye! All persons are commanded to keep silence on pain of imprisonment, while the House of Representatives is exhibiting to the United States Senate, Articles of Impeachment against Andrew Johnson, President of the United States."

After this Mr. Bingham proceeded to read to the Senate, the eleven Articles of Impeachment.

The Senate, on its part, moved in the matter, after Messrs. Stevens and Bingham on February 25th, had communicated the resolution of the House impeaching the President. On the same day a committee was appointed to take suitable action and report. Two of the members of this committee, Senators Howard and Edmunds, waited upon Chief Justice Chase, and informed him of the action of the Senate. They also stated, that their committee proposed to prepare rules for the government of the Senate during the impeachment trial; and the Chief Justice was politely informed that any suggestions from himself would be cheerfully received. But politeness precluded them from adding what their knowledge would have prompted; that his views would only be accepted, so far as they might agree with those of the impeachers. The committee proceeded to prepare the rules, which the Senate adopted in its legislative capacity. This method of adopting rules was objected to by the Democratic Members of the Senate, but without avail, being overruled by the majority, that was all powerful, as on former occasions. Chief Justice Chase addressed a letter to Senator Howard, likewise taking exceptions to the Senate's mode of adopting rules to govern in the impeachment trial. He agreed with the Democratic Senators, that the Senate had no right to prescribe rules for the trial, until constitutionally organized as a Court of Impeachment. The letter of the Chief Justice created considerable sensation among the impeachment Senators; but the Senate proceeded, as had it not been written, and appointed a committee to wait upon and advise him of the trial, and request his attendance as the presiding officer.

Steps were taken towards the organization of the Senatorial Court, on Thursday, the 5th of March. The Chief Justice entered and addressed the Senate on that day in the following words:

"Senators, I am here in obedience to your notice, for the purpose of proceeding with you in forming a Court of Impeachment for the trial of Andrew Johnson, President of the United States. I am now ready to take the oath."

Associate Justice Nelson then administered an oath to the Chief Justice:

"That in all things appertaining to the trial of Andrew Johnson, President of the United States, now pending, I will do impartial justice according to the Constitution and Laws, so help me God."

The same oath was then administered, separately, to each of the Senators. Objection was made, by Democratic Senators, to Senator Wade being sworn, and sitting as a member of the Court of Impeachment; inasmuch as he, being the President of the Senate, would, in case of the conviction and removal of President Johnson, succeed to his office. It was argued that one in his position was too much interested to be a competent judge to try the President, as the rules of equity demanded; but unblushing partisanship came to the rescue, and the revolutionists determined that as he was not excluded by the Constitution, he should be sworn and permitted to sit as a judge upon the trial.

After the Senators were sworn, the Chief Justice declared the organization of the Senate as a High Court of Impeachment. The rules adopted by the Senate in its legislative capacity, to regulate the trial, were upon the suggestion of the presiding officer, approved by it as a Court of Impeachment. The House managers being now advised of the organization of the High Court of the Nation, came before it; and the Chairman, Mr. Bingham, arose and demanded of the Court that it take cognizance as to the appearance of Andrew Johnson, to answer the articles of impeachment which had been preferred against him. It was then ordered that a summons be issued requiring the appearance of the President before the bar of the Senate, on Friday, the 13th of March.

On the day fixed, President Johnson appeared in the High Court of Impeachment, not personally, but by counsel. Henry Stansberry, B. R. Curtis, Thomas A. R. Nelson, William M. Evarts, and William S. Groesbeck, all intellectual legal gentlemen, appeared as the President's defenders. His attorneys asked the Court to allow their client forty days to prepare his answer; but because Benjamin F. Butler and others wished the trial to proceed "*at railroad speed*," only ten days were granted. March

23d was fixed for filing the President's answer. When this day arrived, it was submitted. It answered separately the whole of the eleven articles of impeachment. As to the first eight of these, the President contended that the Tenure of Office Act, of March 2d, 1867, which precluded him from removing subordinate officials, without the consent of the Senate, was unconstitutional. He further contended, that even under the words of that act, he was not prevented from removing Edwin M. Stanton, as he was charged with attempting; and that, in doing so, he had violated neither the Constitution nor the law of Congress. He also denied that he was guilty, as the ninth article accused him, of having been, in his interview with General Emory, of Washington, or, in any of the particulars, as he therein stood charged. He claimed, as a citizen of the United States, that he was fully warranted in expressing, as other men, his views on political affairs; and that, consequently, he was not culpable, as charged in the tenth and eleventh articles, for the cited speeches which he had made. A replication to the President's answer, was without delay prepared; and having been adopted in the House by 115 yeas, to 36 nays, was filed by the managers in the Court of Impeachment, March 24th. The legal pleadings being now completed, the ardent impeachers, Sumner and his associates, as they had from the beginning urged, wished the trial to proceed at once; but it was again postponed until March 30th, to allow the President a short time finally to prepare for his defense.

On Monday, March 30th, Benjamin F. Butler opened the case for the managers in a speech, in which he sustained his view of the law, and stated the evidence which they proposed to adduce. Witnesses were then called by the managers, to prove the facts as alleged in the several articles of impeachment. Both oral and documentary evidence were admitted. The presentation of the evidence was managed mainly by General Butler, who displayed great adroitness and legal ability in this particular. His dexterity, as a criminal lawyer, shone conspicuous on this occasion. The Chief Justice was allowed the right of having a casting vote, where the Senate should be equally divided, although the radicals, led by Senator Sumner, sought to deprive him of this privilege. He was also accorded the privilege of primarily deciding upon the admissibility of evidence; his decision, however, was subject to reversal, upon an appeal to the Senate. The production of testimony by the managers consumed one week, the prosecution resting upon April 4th. The court of impeachment then adjourned until Thursday, April 9th. This additional time was allowed to the President and his counsel, to enable them to prepare and arrange the evidence which they intended to adduce in behalf of the defense.

Upon the meeting of the Impeachment Court, at the time to which it stood adjourned, Judge Curtis opened for Andrew Johnson in a logical, learned and argumentative speech, presenting the President's defense in the manner he believed the evidence and the law would sustain him. He resumed and concluded his speech on the following day; April 10th. Witnesses were next examined for the defense, amongst whom Generals Thomas and Sherman were conspicuous. As to the motive of the President, in the attempted removal of E. M. Stanton, evidence of his statements to General Sherman was offered in evidence to repel what had been proven by the managers. Considerable dispute arose over the admission of General Sherman's testimony on this point, he being produced to detail remarks of the President, showing his intention in the removal of the Secretary of War. The admission of this testimony was strongly combatted and refused; but was afterwards somewhat admitted. Many strong legal conflicts, took place between the managers led by General Butler and the President's skillful attorneys. The hero of Fort Fisher, was the prominent champion on the side of the House Managers, in these encounters, and he was severely accused of attempting to bully the President's counsel. In that, however, he signally failed. Mr. Stevens was too prostrated during the whole proceeding, to take any but a subordinate part. In his younger years, on such a trial, he would have shone as a star of the first magnitude. On the 20th of April, the evidence on both sides was closed, and the Court adjourned until April 22d.

The evidence in this important trial was rather formal in its character, as the facts were in the main undisputed. The evidence adduced by the managers, was chiefly to prove the facts alleged in the articles of impeachment, as was likewise, that for the defense, in order to sustain the assertions contained in the President's answer. The statements and counter-statements must in law, of necessity be proven; but the dispute was more legal in its nature than dependent upon facts, charged upon one side and denied upon the other.

On Wednesday, April 22d, the legal discussion began in a well prepared speech, delivered by George S. Boutwell, which occupied the attention of the Senate that and most of the following day. Judge Nelson followed in an able discourse in behalf of the President, which he finished April 24th. William S. Groesbeck on the same side, addressed the Court in an argumentative and ornate speech, on that and the following day. Thaddeus Stevens, one of the managers, read a carefully prepared speech, on Monday, April 27th; and Thomas Williams, another manager, occupied the balance of that and the succeeding day in the delivery of his argument. William M. Evarts followed for the defense, making the star speech of the trial, which engaged the attention of the Senatorial Court from April 28th to May 1st, four days. Henry Stansberry began his speech May 1st, and ended it on the next day. Manager Bingham began the closing argument May 4th, which occupied him three days, concluding it May 6th.

The legal arguments being ended, the Senate sitting as a Court, now spent some time in discussing and determining upon the method of taking the vote upon the Articles of Impeachment. An adjournment was then carried until Monday, May 11th. When the Court re-assembled, in accordance with an adopted rule, fifteen minutes were granted to each Senator to express his views upon impeachment, and the guilt or innocence of the President. Four independent Republican Senators, Messrs. Grimes, Fessenden, Trumbull and Henderson, openly declared themselves against conviction. This was a frightful bomb in the radical camp. The impeachers became alarmed. The victory which the zealots, on account of partisan subserviency, had scarcely doubted, was already in extreme danger. They seemed to descry the finger of doom, writing the verdict of Presidential acquittal upon the walls of the Senate Chamber. Despair drove them to an adjournment until the 16th of May, in order to see if, in the meantime, the power of party tyranny would not be able to compel a sufficient number of unwilling Senators to obey those who claimed to be their political masters.

From this time up to the re-assembling of the Senatorial Court, the most unjustifiable means were resorted to by the bitter political enemies of the President, to influence Senators who were regarded as doubtful, to vote for conviction. The whole weight of abuse, of an intensely partisan press, was brought to bear upon Senators, in order to force them to yield to what was made to seem as a pressing public opinion. Senators were addressed by telegraph, letter,* and otherwise to stand by their party, and not desert it in the hour of its deepest distress. They were threatened by prominent party leaders with political ostracism, should they choose to exercise the freedom of their own judgment, and vote for the acquittal of Andrew Johnson. The assertion of Mr. Stevens was accepted as the gospel of radicalism, to which all the faithful must subscribe, viz: *that the failure of impeachment, would be the death of the Republican party.* The Republican Senators, therefore, who had expressed themselves as opposed to the conviction of the President, were for several days the targets of the most virulent and malicious vituperation, that ever emenated from a partisan press. Besides this unbounded abuse of the known and unknown recreant Senators, the most desperate expedients, for insuring the conviction of the President, were proposed by unprincipled journalists and others, amongst whom the editor of the Philadelphia *Press*,† had for years borne a super-eminent rank.

---

* The radical Congressmen from Missouri, addressed Senator Henderson, of that State, the following impertinent letter:

WASHINGTON, May 12th, 1868.

Hon. John B. Henderson, U. S. Senate:

SIR:—On a consultation of the Republican Members of the House of Representatives from Missouri, in view of your position on the Impeachment Articles, we ask you to withhold your vote on any Article, upon which you cannot vote affirmatively. This request is made, because we believe the loyal people of the United States demand the immediate removal of Andrew Johnson from the office of President of the United States. Respectfully,

GEORGE W. ANDERSON,
JOSEPH W. McCLURG,
WILLIAM A. PILE,
BENJAMIN F. LOAN,
C. A. NEWCOMB,
JOHN F. BENJAMIN,
JOSEPH J. GRAVELY.

† The Philadelphia *Press* of May 13th, 1868, contained the following sentiments: "The Senate sitting, for the trial of Andrew Johnson, is according to the argument of the counsel for the defense, purely a court, subject to all the incidents, and following in its actions and practice, all the analogies of a judicial tribunal. This declaration they insist on, and repeat every time one of them addresses the Chief Justice. They have prepared and carefully observed, a formula involving this theory. Now, the Court never dies. If one of the Judges, or all of them die, or if their terms expire, the Court still lives in their successors. The cases are not discontinued, or affected by the change. The outgoing of one

The Senatorial Court met, according to adjournment, on the 16th of May, and proceeded to vote on the eleventh article of impeachment, which many regarded as the strongest of the series. The result of the vote was, thirty-five for conviction to nineteen for acquittal. The Constitution requiring two-thirds of the Senate to pronounce the President guilty, he was declared by the Chief Justice as acquitted on this article. Seven Senators, who had up to this time co-operated with the revolutionists, voted with the Democrats for the acquittal of President Johnson. These were William Pitt Fessenden, of Maine; J. S. Fowler, of Tennessee: James W. Grimes, of Iowa; John B. Henderson, of Missouri; E. G. Ross, of Kansas; Lyman Trumbull, of Illinois; and Peter G. Van Winkle, of West Virginia. The impeachers now had but one hope left, and that lay in another adjournment, to see what additional party threats might yet be able to effect.

An adjournment took place, until May 26th. The powers of party terrorism were again subsidized with all the effort that fanatical despair could render. It was, without doubt, supposed that the Chicago Convention, which was about to assemble, would work some inner awe within those who aspired to be leaders in the party ranks; and some rebukes from that body may even have been anticipated. General Grant was to be nominated as the Presidential candidate of the Lake City Conclave. This occurred on May 21st. His august name, now almost hailed as *Imperator*, would lend additional sanction to his already expressed opinion, that the conviction of President Johnson was a necessity. The 26th of May arrived. The Congressional Court re-convened for the last time. A vote was taken upon the second article of impeachment, with the same result as on the eleventh. The third also was voted on, but with no change. The seven recreant Senators yet remained obdurate in their apostasy to the revolution, whose principles they had so long and so faithfully served. Impeachment had failed. The High Court

Judge, or the incoming of another, does not and cannot have any bearing on the decision of the cases on the docket. *Now, if the nation in this hour of her extremity, needs loyal votes in the Senate, let the loyal majority admit at once the Senators from the newly reconstructed and regenerated State of Arkansas. They are standing, waiting at the door. It is a superfluous caution that keeps them out. Bring in two, if there is need of them, patriot Senators from Florida, Georgia, Louisiana and the Carolinas.*

now adjourned *sine die;* and E. M. Stanton, on the same day, advised the President that he had relinquished charge of the War Department. The partisan trial to depose an American President was now become an *Ilium fuit* of history.

The revolution was first checked in the acquittal of Andrew Johnson. But the check was only of the same kind, though in effect superior to that produced by the conservative reaction, led by Senators Cowan, Dixon and Doolittle; and which the Presidential resistance served to concentrate. The revolutionary force was partially stemmed by the apparent conservatism of the seven Republican Senators, ranging themselves for once with the Democrats, who had earnestly striven against the current since first it arose; and with somewhat similar effect as regarded themselves. The Democracy had been exiled; and likewise the Conservative Republicans, who from time to time had joined them in their efforts to resist the storm of fury, were consigned to the same quarters to await the call of their countrymen, when repose should again have taught them the severe but truthful lessons of history and experience.

The revolution must of necessity find its martyrs; and those who contributed towards its development were quite as deserving of that lot as those who patriotically strove to prevent it. But are the seven Republican nominal conservatives, whose votes saved Andrew Johnson from being deposed as President of the United States, entitled to any especial honor because of their action? So far as they then contributed to defeat the objects of the revolutionists, in one particular, they acted a worthy part. They, however, only deserve honor so far as they were influenced by motives of pure patriotism. From the time the sectional party first organized, most of these men had steadily lent their adhesion to nearly all the views of that dangerous organization; and all of them, from the outbreak of the rebellion, endorsed most of the revolutionary principles of their party up to the impeachment of the President. In preventing the President's deposition, their alarm simply aroused them to the necessity of arresting this new current of the revolution that had far exceeded their anticipations; and which was threatening to prostrate all the land marks of constitutional government. Is that, however, patriotism, which forbears to strike further out of dread for retroactive consequences?

If fear, or other like motive, induced the action of the revolutionary Senators, who voted for the acquittal of the President, its effect was but of brief duration. The dog speedily returned to his vomit again. The pretended conservatives were soon in alliance with their old political associates. They were begotten to political fame of the revolution; and its children they must remain. Neither can the Ethiopian change his skin, nor the leopard his spots. Fit companions of revolutionists, the Republican anti-impeachers, as truants, returned to their camp to be guarded and court-marshalled for their insubordination; but faithfully to renew their service with their old masters. In consummating the unconstitutional legislation, by which it was pretended to restore the seceded States, to their normal rights of representation in the Union; who were more efficient actors than Trumbull, Fessenden and others of the non-convicting Senators? In one aspect, their recurring reason stemmed the revolution; in another their fanaticism was further accompanying it on its doleful mission of death.

CHAPTER XXXII.

DEATH OF MR. STEVENS, WITH CONCLUDING REFLECTIONS.

The present work carries the historic thread of the revolution up to August 11th, 1868. On that day Thaddeus Stevens, the coryphеus of the Congressional revolutionists, ended his earthly career, leaving the seeds which he and his associates had sown, to germinate and yield their natural fruit. Our subject died in Washington City, the scene of his most famous labors, after an llness of some months, which terminated in his demise. Having been brought to his home in Lancaster, he was buried in the cemetery of his own selection, because none were precluded from interment within its enclosure, on account of race or color. In his funeral procession, he received the especial homage of that race, for which he was believed to have devoted his crowning efforts. Considerable numbers of these with others, followed his remains to their last resting place. A handsome monument in Shreiner's Cemetery marks his sepulchre.

But in the selection of Mr. Stevens, as the man whose political career should span the development and progress of the revolution which has been sketched, he was in no wise chosen as a subject for eulogium or laudation; but simply as typical of those who have subverted pure republicanism in the wild and chimerical hope of reaching what is wholly unattainable under any form of government. His career as a citizen and lawyer, is left mainly for others to portray, who have taste for this species of literature. His benevolence and witticism, peculiar traits developed by him, have likewise been omitted. The former of these, was in his hands simply an instrument by which he engineered his way to power in a government, which his reason disapproved. Lacking pure purpose, he was ready to embrace any means to attain the objects of his ambitious aspirations; and his shrewdness assured him that nothing would so attach the unthinking to his standard, as the favors he bestowed upon them. Had unselfish benevolence influenced his seeming charities, he would in other respects also, have shone as a moral luminary of his age and nation; and he would have left behind him, an impress of virtue never to be eradicated. But he passed away, having simply towered as an able, adroit, skillful lawyer, and an extreme advocate of human equality, regardless of consequences. In his advocacy, however, of this equality, he evinced to the philosophic mind, the demagogue; as only sincere, honest fanatics could advocate a doctrine that reason, from the origin of recorded history, has disproved. But Mr. Stevens was no fanatic. His intellectuality raised him high above all fanaticism, and enabled him to scan its strength, and adroitly use it as a caparisoned charger to ride to the goal of his political ambition. He fully understood the fanatics of his age, and clearly perceived, that paying court to their sentiments, was the only method by which he and his party, could overthrow the Constitutional Democracy. This he did, originally impelled out of personal hatred to men, who for years had been instrumental in excluding him from coveted posts of honor to which he had aspired.* Thrown thus into antagonism with the chivalric spirits, who controlled the old political parties, he was compelled to find his supporters amongst the incongruous herd of discontented agitators, whom birth and position consign to subordination and vassalage, and who are ever eady to combat their own and the imaginary ills of others.

Some concluding observations and reflections upon the course of events since the demise of Mr. Stevens, will not be deemed, as is presumed, inappropriately appended in this, the last chapter of the work. Only in this way can the dangerous character of the revolutionary men of the Stevens type be fully understood. The American Government, up to the period of the advent of fanaticism to power, had justly acquired the reputation of being the model Republic of the world. The Union was the promised land of peace, plenty and happiness for the oppressed of Europe.

---

*His confidential friends say, that in the campaign of 1844, whilst pretending to be the supporter of Henry Clay for President, he visited New York and other Northern States, and urged the Abolitionists to support Birney, so as to abstract a sufficient number of votes from Clay to cause his defeat. A confidential friend of Mr. Stevens, a man of prominence, who was an Abolitionist, was heard to remark about that time, that his two-faced action in this particular, was deserving of commendation. Only an Abolitionist or an unprincipled knave could commend such conduct.

A succession of honorable Statesmen had risen to eminence in the United States, that were worthy to be compared with the noblest personages of ancient or modern times. The Senate, adorned by the intellects of the Clays, Websters and Calhouns, was fully the peer of that of ancient Rome in her palmy days. From its formation the Government, as a kind of foster mother, had been receiving new accessions of territory, casting her protecting folds around the acceding acquisitions; and was so enlarging her domain as if purposing ultimately to embrace the whole Western continent. All this development and prosperity was the fruit of Jeffersonian Democracy and State right equality.

But how soon was the mighty fallen. No sooner had the ideas of Seward, Sumner and Giddings triumphed in the election of Abraham Lincoln, than the peaceful and prosperous days of the Republic ended. The preliminary crusade that led to this event, had been subverting the principles of morality and sound Christian purity, the pillars of all stable government. The doctrine, that a higher law* than the Constitution should regulate human

---

*The prevailing dishonesty and corruption of our country, take their source in the principles of the "*higher law*," and in the growing disbelief in the old systems of morality, which recognized all property as sacred and inviolable. The "*higher law*" is itself an efflux of modern infidelity, which is rapidly spreading its deadening blight over the fair fields of modern civilization; and in no country are its effects so sad as in America, the boasted land of liberty. Where the most extreme doctrines of disbelief can with freedom be discussed and propagated, it is reasonable to find the natural results of such indoctrination. The United States are now suffering from consequences so produced, and will continue to suffer, until the causes themselves be eradicated and fully removed.

The "higher law" doctrine being the development of the infidelity of the age, finds its chief nourishment in the far-famed Puritan free school system of America. This system of instruction is producing its desolating effects in our country, because morality and biblical instruction are not made essential parts of the tuitional work. Archibald Alison, a philosophic author, says: "*Education, if not based on religious tuition, is worse than useless;* and every day's experience is adding additional confirmation to the eternal truth."—[Alison on Population, Vol. 2, p. 292.]

M. Cousin, another European writer of celebrity, uses the following language: "Religion is, in my eyes, the best—perhaps the only—basis of instruction. I know a little of Europe, and I have never witnessed any good popular schools where Christianity was wanting. The more I reflect upon the subject the more I am convinced with the directors of the *Ecoles Normales* and the ministerial counselors, that we must go hand in hand with the clergy in order to instruct the people and make religious education a special and large part of instruction in our primary schools. I am not ignorant that these suggestions will sound ill in the ears of some, and that in Paris I shall be looked upon as excessively devout; but it is from Berlin, nevertheless, not Rome, that I write. He who speaks to you is a philosopher, one looked on with an evil eye, and even persecuted by the priesthood; but who knows human nature and

action, was destructive of all governmental subordination; and set up each individual's opinion as the norm that should regulate his obedience as a citizen. The refusal of the Abolitionists to acquiesce in the requirements of the Fugitive Slave Law, was in itself revolutionary and destructive of all government. In placing themselves in opposition to the rendition of fugitive slaves, they became robbers of the property of their countrymen, equally guilty, in a moral aspect, as they who purloin or otherwise destroy what belongs to another. Each slave that escaped from his Southern master, was his legal property; and the men who aided him in his escape, and those who justified this action, were the detroyers of society, and responsible for all the ills that America has suffered since the commencement of the rebellion up to the present time; and also for those which destiny has in store for her. They were the infidel and wicked subverters of morality and rectitude of life; and were they who opened wide the flood-gates of demoralization, which permitted the current of corruption to flow forth with such impetuosity, that it

---

history too well not to regard religion as an indestructible power, and Christianity, when rightly inculcated, as an essential instrument for civilizing mankind, and a necessary support to those on whom society imposes hard and humble duties, uncheered by the hope of future fortune or the consolations of self-love."—[Rapport sur l' Instruction de l' Allemagne, p. 272.]

Democracy, under the non-religious free school system of our country, is as a vessel set adrift upon the stormy ocean of life without rudder or helmsman, and permitted to float as the storms of passion may beat upon it. A gloomy future is in store for free government, if some means be not devised to change the present morality-destroying system of popular instruction, by which the youth of our country shall be indoctrinated in the principles of honor, virtue and truth, as well as made familiar with the developments of intellectual culture. The church and the school-house must again be united, or corruption and demoralization will sink republican government in a vortex of social ruin.

The destruction now threatening our country, in the upheavals of immorality and national corruption that are arrising all over the land, unmistakably traces its origin to the free school system of instruction as at present conducted. For years the bible, the *vade mecum* of Christian communities, has been expelled from the schools of our country; and the flood of impiety which, on that account, has penetrated them, is now showing its results in every village and hamlet from Maine to California. Whilst it was retained, it was the flaming sword that guarded against the entrance of the evil influences that are now displaying their baneful fruits in the high places of the nation. Its return must be secured, or liberty, that solace of freemen, will expire in the night of gloom that is fast setting upon our country.

And, if a reason be sought why corruption is more highly rearing its head under revolutionary Republican, than under constitutional Democratic rule, it is found in the fact that the leaders of the former party, contra-distinguished from their opponents, profess not to square their opinions with the teaching of revelation nor with the moral maxims of

now threatens to wash away all the defences of truth, virtue and and honor.

These minions of Plutonic darkness, drove the defenders of truth and the Constitution off the field of conflict and captured the citadels of virtue. Under the hypocritical pretence of elevating universal humanity to absolute equality, by means of the far-famed free schools, from which all biblical and moral instruction, as far as possible, was excluded, they set out virtually to infidelize the world, and consign Christianity to the fabled deposits of past ages. Their crusade against slavery was an insidious but cowardly attack upon the truths and morality of the Christian system. The original founders of their school and political maxims, were French Encyclopædists and British free-thinkers; and the ease with which large numbers of the Christian clergy were seduced into the support of revolutionary abolitionism, either showed the latter's lack of discernment, or proved them to be wolves in sheep's clothing, who were simply fattening upon the stipends of their needy parishioners. Had

---

the ancient philosophers. Did not Anson V. Burlingame, one of the high priests of Republicanism, demand *an anti-slavery Bible and an anti-slavery God?* In his utterances the spirit of the "higher law" was speaking, in unmistakable words, the full demands of the infidel Sanhedrim. And we see all around us the results of the new teaching, in the steady decline of moral sensibility. A Republican author is forced to make the following admission: "The fact is humiliating that the tone of American life is lower since the war, which was supposed to be about to usher in a new era of national honor and culture, than it was before. It may be, indeed, that we are in a state of transition from lower to higher aims; but the transition is very bewildering and lasts a very long time. The promised light refuses to come. The days grow darker every day, and the thoughtful patriot can dimly see little more than a broad and dismal waste, crowded with men ravenous for gain; while those who desire and seek better things are trampled under foot like dogs."—[Dix's American State, p. 15.]

But, notwithstanding, it is apparent that the moral tone is steadily declining, do not Republican propagandists still vaunt their superior intelligence over their political partisans, and boast that their ranks are composed of the refinement and intelligence of the country? Do they not laud their superior devotion to the free school system of America; and point to the culture which their voters display? And do they not refer sneeringly to the masses of the Democratic party, and gibe them for lack of their kind of intelligence? The contrast between the two parties (the negroes being excluded) is palpable and conceded; and it is to the credit of the Democratic party, that its ranks do not possess the irreligious intelligence of their opponents. But they do have that which enrolls them far above their political enemies. They have superior moral training and a superior moral sense. Theirs is yet the moral sense of the olden periods, before corruption had made its desolating inroads, induced by a false training, that is eating out the vitals of purity and reverence for right. Plato declared that "General ignorance is neither

these clergymen and their followers looked around them, they would have found themselves marshalled by the bold, brazen infidels of the North; and every stroke these poor deluded slaves struck, in behalf of rationalistic abolitionism, fell with all its force upon biblical revelation and the revered truths of the Christian religion. But they struck, not then being able to distinguish their friends from their enemies.

And though, at length, conscious that the American body politic is suffering from excruciating pains, they are still unable to comprehend what has given rise to the national disease. They ignorantly impute all our disorders to the Southern rebellion; and accuse the people of the South as the guilty agents in producing that sorrowful struggle between the people of the two sections. The late civil war has been largely instrumental in causing the condition of affairs by which we are now surrounded; yet numerous other agencies must also be considered, for a full solution of the causes of our troubles. False doctrine has been the germinating source of our national calamities. The war

---

the greatest evil nor the worst to be dreaded." Ignorance, indeed, is a blessing, unless intelligence be imparted in schools of virtue and moral purity.

But by how much the vaunted intellectual intelligence of the Republican party surpasses that of its antagonist, by so much has the tone of American life declined since the advent of that *cultured* organization to power in 1861. And thus by contrast is seen the danger that menaces free government in sustaining a system of education, that aims simply to develop the intellect of humanity, whilst ignoring and leaving its moral sense to perish.

What else, save a corruption germinator, could a party be, the prominent leaders of which defiantly cast aside moral restraint, as inculcated in the bible and by the Christian church; and simply look to a higher law for the guidance that humanity requires? For it is an undeniable fact, that the infidel hordes of the North naturally found their home in the organization that named itself Republican. They were the advanced levelers of the races; and as full equality could not take place until property was also equalized, it was to be expected that they would use all their efforts to effect such equalization. The public corruption and dishonesty of the last fifteen years, are but part of the equalizing process that these leaders advocate. Having no moral regard for individual rights, like robbers they feel themselves warranted in plundering from others as far as they have the power to do so; and the only barrier to their advances is dread of detection. It is thus that the principle of communism is working in the body politic, and producing the loathsome festering in our social and official corporations.

Does it not evince almost a putrid condition of the moral sense, when the highest Court of the nation could make a decision in palpable violation of the Constitution of the country? And what communistic draughts these same judges must have imbibed, before they could have become so intoxicated as to render a decision ignoring the fundamental principles of justice? They must have been apt pupils of the higher law school; and have received with humble docility the new gospel of Seward, Bur-

itself, like the other evils, with which we have been and are afflicted, was produced by the dissemination of spurious principles, that were antagonistic to republican institutions. It was caused by the officious effort of Northern intermedlers, to pluck the mote out of their brother's eye, without being conscious of the beam that clouded their own visions.

The war being produced by the anti-constitutional interference of a party, whose corner-stone principle was sectional hate, it should not be supposed that the body politic of our country could ever recover its wonted strength, until all the deadly virus would be totally expelled from the system. The war upon the part of the Southern people, therefore, was but an effort of nature which the republic made to cast off the offensive matter, which was threatening death to constitutional liberty. The effort would have been successful, but for the fact that the vigor of healthy life was dissolved in the disease of fanaticism which had overtaken our country. And all the subsequent struggles undergone to overthrow the policy of the revolution, were made in the interest of republican government. The Democracy, being the natural party of the Republic, could not die as long as any hope for free government remained. But the principles of the party of revolution, being the efflux of despotism, must be overthrown, or the Republic can never again be restored to its normal condition. As it now exists, it is simply a Republic in name, its cardinal principles having perished. It is a mockery to call our government a republic, until the people of every section of our common country shall have amicably adjusted all their difficulties since the beginning of the war; framed a new Constitution, or remodled the old one so as to make it satisfactory to all;

---

lingame and their worthy *confreres.* No doubt they passed a creditable examination in communistic exegesis before the judicial ermine had fallen upon them. Even members of the Republican party are compelled to acknowledge that our prevailing corruption has been aided by the conduct of men in high places. W. G. Dix, an author who speaks in eulogistic terms of Lincoln and Sumner, says: "Who can wonder at the corruption which prevails in so many departments of the Government, and in every nook and corner of the land, when a judgment of the Supreme Court of the United States, however just or legal its intention, is universally understood to permit and sanction fraud? * * * The resignation of those Judges of the Supreme Court, who pronounced irredeemable greeenbacks lawful money for the payment of previous debts, contracted to be paid in gold or its equivalent, would do more than anything else to redeem the honor of our highest tribunal, and to bring public opinion back to its bearings on financial questions."—[*The American State.* pp. 34 and 35.

and afterwards in State conventions shall have freely adopted the same. Then, and not before, will peace, prosperity and happiness return to our united country; and, as before, gladness cover our land as the waters cover the sea. If, however, this be impossible to be reached, on account of the turbulent elements of our composition, then without further dissembling let the declaration be made, that republican government has proved a failure; that the irrational efforts to secure what God opposes, universal equality, have, instead of bringing liberty, only sunk the strugglers deeper in the slough of despotism; and then let the inevitable consequences be accepted; let constitutional monarchies arise where the republic, whilst governed by wisdom and virtue, flourished, and let the world-struggle forever end. Who is unable to see that our Government, as conducted by so-called Republicanism, since its advent to power has been infinitely worse than the constitutional monarchy of Great Britain?

The Abolition party being based upon false principles, it of necessity produced an entire disintegration of our whole republican system of government. The history of the past fifteen years has demonstrated its workings. Coming into power as the pronounced advocate of moral delinquency, could abolition rule do ought else than produce the miserable desolation of principle which now covers our country from ocean to ocean. No other result was possible to occur, when the moral lepers, who controlled the underground railroads and their tutors, had seized control of the reins of government. Men who made a boast of their dexterity in securing the safe passage of fugitives to Canada and elsewhere, were suitable instruments to degrade virtuous tone throughout the community; and produce from Maine to California, that condition of moral putrefaction which is rapidly eating out the vitals of truth, honor and upright manhood. Having no respect for the immutable laws, which God has implanted upon the face of being, they were ready to set aside all the instruction of past ages, and reconstruct society in accordance with their wild and unhallowed conceptions. Atheists in disguise, and infidels in profession, they had no regard for the Christian code, nor even for the moral maxims of the Greek and Roman philosophers. The felon of Charlestown was the exemplar they worshipped, and his maxims formed their guide as citizens and rulers.

It was easy for such men, to violate as they did, the Federal Consititution, first in making war against the South, and afterwards in its prosecution. No oaths were binding upon them, most of them entertaining no belief in a future state of existence. They came into power, therefore, determined to destroy Southern society, and make it in future conform with their ideas, drawn from the revolutionary schools of France, where belief in a Deity is scoffed to the *encore.* The passage of the Legal Tender Bill, which declared that all debts, whether contracted before or subsequent to its enactment, should be paid by the notes issued by the Government, was simply the work of men destitute of moral obligation, and displayed their dangerous character. Necessity, they plead, as justifying their action, thereby admitting, that the Constitution clothed them with no such authority. What worse do banditti, pirates and other public robbers, than did the American Congress, in the enactment of the unjust and unconstitutional law, which permitted all debtors to discharge their obligations with less sums of money than they owed their creditors. Robbers embark in a career, in which necessity compels them to seize the property of others, in order to support their existence. The Abolition Congress and President Lincoln did the same. They entered, in violation of the Constitution, upon a war to subjugate and ruin the Southern people. Necessity compelled them to enact the Legal Tender Bill in order, under guise of law, to be able to subsidize, by a false financial system, the wealth of the American people, or abandon their unrighteous undertaking. But for their violations of sacred obligation, in having done so, the compensater of human action, as an avenging Deity, will yet sing songs of infamy over the tombs of those, who trampled upon and desecrated her holy laws.

The inspired book advises us, that we are to judge the tree by its fruits. In the application of this test to the political parties of our country, what a verdict of doom, at this time, strikes the vision of the revolutionary party; that party which has almost sunk the Ship of State in the billows of misgovernment and social corruption? It is, as many of their shrewd leaders have already expressed it, enough to make them shudder at the thought of the Democracy returning to power. They see the tide of ignominy slowly rolling, that is to cover them forever, unless by perjury, bribery, and the perversion of the elective franchise they can successfully embank against it, as they have been able to do since the close of the rebellion.

The tree of corruption, sprung chiefly from the soil fertilized by those who proclaimed a higher law than the Constitution, has produced in our country its natural fruit. It seems even to be growing with fearful rapidity, and producing every year a fresh and more abundant crop than that of the preceding season. Its roots have penetrated every State of our monarchically consolidated Union, diffusing exhalations that have tainted the moral atmosphere in all departments of society. And the pestiferous fruit, though in itself noxious, has come to be the chief object of aspiration amongst the American people, and is sought after with the greatest possible avidity. What at an early period in our history, would have been rejected with scorn as dishonorable and degrading, is now coveted by large numbers of the community with the greatest zeal.

The moral disease displayed itself fully with the installation of the abolition party, in power in 1861. The men who appeared in, and those who were appointed to the chief places of trust and honor under the Government, were mainly those who were most sensibly tainted with the leprosy that had for years been diseasing the body politic of the North; and the subsequent development of the public corruption, which from this time disclosed itself to the eyes of the nation, was chiefly traceable to this class of public functionaries. Accusations followed accusations, from that period of our history, and public officials were accused of peculations and plunder of the public money, which would never have been committed at an earlier period of our history. These charges, numerous as they were, nevertheless were mostly unheeded by the men and the party that controlled the National Government. And even when investigations were ordered, those appointed to inquire into the charges of corruption, were usually the friends and companions of the guilty parties themselves. During the whole period of the civil war, this condition of affairs continued, the corruption all the while steadily increasing. And this, it has continued to do, up to the present time.

It should have seemed probable, that the moral organization of the body politic would have revolted against the hideous deformities that arose upon all sides; and have rebuked the corrupt men who perpetrated and those who sustained evil doers in their foul iniquities. But the false doctrines which had been propagated with success for years, had also taken firm hold of the opinions of the masses, and they no longer viewed public offences as their ancestors had done before them. Besides, they were assured by crafty leaders, that periods of turbulence, as civil wars, ever engender corruptions, and lead to such violations of principle as ever shock the moral sense of communities. As soon as the corrupt officials came to discover that the moral tone had lowered itself, their descent on the descending plane perceptibly increased, and still further gained in velocity as fresh license was granted. Action and reaction were thus plainly effective in the lowering of the moral tone.

The lobby rings of the different States and nation, first showed themselves in their utter deformity, after the accession of the Abolition party to power. In those States, fully under the control of this party, the lobby at the seat of government was a fixed and profitable institution; and many Democrats came to be participant in its doings. But though individual impurities were disclosed in the Democratic organization, its principal leaders placed themselves in opposition to the lobbyists, and strove to break up their calling. In Pennsylvania this was effected, under the new Constitution, adopted in the State in 1873, mainly by the Democratic party, against the votes of most of the opposition party. In Washington, the corrupt lobby only attained to notoriety after the majority of both branches of Congress had become Abolitionists.

The sinking of the moral tone, throughout the country, which took place after the Abolition party came into power, gave rise to the numerous scandals, which from time to time, blackened the memories of public men in their States and at the Federal Capital. In consequence of this moral fall, a more corrupt and less cultivated class of politicians were able, in their respective States and districts, to secure their elevation to Congress. Means were resorted to by the successful politicians, which men of honorable tone refused to adopt; and when these reached Congress, they were eager to make up by bribes, and other corrupt practices, what they had expended to procure their seats. The Credit Mobilier, Pacific Mail, and numerous other scandals that inflicted dishonor upon Vice-President, Senators and other

Members of Congress, are to be imputed to the lowering tone of moral purity that has pervaded the nation since the year 1861.

With corruption stalking in mid-day, unrebuked in the Federal and State Capitals, it was not surprising that it should react upon the body politic. This it has done; and for a decade in the North, elections have proved farcical in the extreme. Men, for years, have been declared as elected Governors of States, Members of Congress, State Legislators and other officers, who never received the majority of the legal votes of the people. Fraudulent repeaters, purchased voters, and altered returns of elections, were employed to secure the prolongation of that party in power, which originally opened the flood-gates of political corruption. To such a degree of boldness did the so-called Republican leaders advance, that they no longer hesitated to count their victories in advance, basing them upon their knowledge of what the money placed in the hands of the leaders for the canvasses would be able to effect. Politicians no longer seek for men best fitted for public positions; and only those are selected as nominees, who respond most freely to the financial demands made upon them. The nominee must liquidate his assessment, under pain of being stricken from the list of candidates, and another name substituted for his own by the committee that holds the party despotism in its hands. This corrupting and anti-republican system of political proceedure, originating in the fertile brains of Abolitionists, has also made its entry into the Democratic party. Corruption seems the all present attendant of modern American politics.

Besides, is to be mentioned, as abolition fruit, the shocking misgovernment which followed the accession of the revolutionary party to power in the South, by the aid of negro votes. Men were then elected as public officials, who were utterly unfitted for any other occupation, save that of cotton pickers upon the plantation of a Southern master. A large proportion of several of the Southern legislatures were composed for years, of freed negroes, who were no better fitted to legislate upon questions of government than the Chiefs of Soudan or Guinea. Many of those who were elected, had simply been barbers, waiters in hotels, or field laborers upon Southern plantations before the outbreak of the rebellion. A few of them had picked up a smattering of the elementary branches of an English education, which fitted them in their own and abolition estimation, to be the rulers and law-givers in their States and in the nation. But that eternal adaptation and fitness of things, which cause harmony and their contrary inharmony, soon displayed themselves in the workings of governmental affairs, after the South had become Africanized.

It soon became apparent that it is not elementary education that fits men for self-government. This kind of learning only furnishes the tools for the acquisition of that other instruction, that prepares men for government. It is alone, after men have become imbued with the principles of moral science and political philosophy, that they are qualified for taking part in governmental affairs, and not when they have simply mastered the rudiments of an education. The history of other nations and of former times should be studied by legislators, the nature of government be well examined, and reflected upon; and the experience of our own and foreign nations be dilligently observed, inferences drawn therefrom, and attentively weighed and considered. By such education alone, are men prepared for taking an intelligent share in the concerns of government.

The misgovernment of years, that oppressed several of the Southern States from the period of reconstruction, until one after another of these were grasped from the talons of the filthy cormorants that were feeding upon them, is known throughout the nation. And some of these States as yet remain to be snatched from the political vultures that have fattened upon their substance. South Carolina remains in the grasp of corrupt scoundrelism, which was fastened upon her by a party, whose leaders deserve the reprobation and contempt of coming ages. Their rotten system of negro government has been thoroughly tested in that State, and the late election of F. J. Moses and W. J. Whipper, the colored jurist, has almost satisfied their own corruptionists, that the eyes of an indignant nation are opening to their misdeeds.

But not only is the fruit of fanaticism exemplified in the flagrant corruption and misgovernment that are festering in the nation, but the business of the people has been ruined by the adoption of an unwise financial system, which may, perhaps, ultimately produce universal bankruptcy and entail ruinous consequences upon coming generations. The condition of affairs under which we are now laboring, was predicted as sure to follow, should Congress adopt the Legal Tender Bill and banish gold and silver from business circles. But all the predictions were unheeded, and the conquest of the South was prosecuted at all hazards. It was accomplished; and now the people are reaping the harvest of financial disaster, the seeds of which the fanatical men of the war epoch sowed. And when the hurricane of death has come, these same destroyers of the currency are striving to appear before the nation as the constitutional financiers of the country. Like the old ruler of darkness who, when sick, desired the Monkish Cowl, but when cured again, was soon ready to lay it aside. The destructive party is smitten with sickness; and it now desires to show its penitence.

Can the condition of affairs under which we labor be altered? Only one remedy appears to present the possibility of improvement. And that is the restoration of the constitutional Democracy to power, and the purification of their own ranks by a gradual elimination of the corrupt elements. Can more of reform be expected from this party than from their political opponents? Upon the affirmative determination of this question, depend the restoration of our Union back to a republican condition, and its future preservation as a free government. Under the management of the revolutionay party, the Union from being a comparatively pure Confederated Republic, has become a corrupt consolidation; and the demoralization of affairs threatens the general prostration of moral principles.

Can the Democracy remedy this condition? That they may do so, is hoped for the following reasons. The democracy are the national party of America, tracing lineal descent from the framers of the republic. They are the constitutional party, the one which ever abides by its own and the nation's legal obligations; opposes all fanaticisms, but is the tolerator and extender of equal liberty to all religions. It is composed mainly of the conservative elements of the country. Its long continued existence, as a party, has been owing principally to the elements of its composition; the ranks accepting as dogmatical truths, its cardinal fundamental principles finding their own, and the country's interest in so doing. The Democracy* are largely the party of the laboring people, who are not in possession of the wealth of the country. The leaders are men whom the just and constitutional principles of the party hold in its ranks; and whom otherwise, interest might in the North attract to the opposition. These men when elevated to power, will again diffuse a new moral tone throughout the nation; and if possible, restore the Union to its former republican purity. Is it not natural to suppose that a more healthy tone of morality will be established amongst the people, by leaders who observed their oaths to support the constitution, than by those who, relying upon a higher law, disregarded them? By the latter, as has been seen, the political corruption has been introduced, but this remains to be arrested by the former. If however, they be unable to arrest the political disorders of our country, the days of the republic have ended.

The bitter fruits that the American people have been compelled, by fanaticism, to gather from the tree of evil, should admonish them to forsake the leaders, who have so treacherously seduced them. Let them return and accept the leadership of men of true principles; men of the same principles as those who laid the foundation of the republic, and built up for it a peaceful and prosperous government. For if they continue to follow the blind guides of the past, then America has only begun her career of madness; and a magazine of destruction is yet in reserve for her. If a speedy return to the path of wisdom be not made, one collision after another is in store for our country, until the grand climacteric epoch arrives. That will, in due time, come in the career of republicanism; and fanaticism is hastening it with rapid steps. It will be the grand climacteric in the history of modern times, the French revolution being simply the minor. All the time the portents of the struggle are gathering. It will be the great world battle of Christianity and stable government against the infidel, anarchical hosts, who are striving for a total overthrow and reconstructien of civilized Society. Abolitionism has gained its first battle on the Western continent. The communistic forces of Europe are marshalling their battalions, and advancing them with steady steps towards the standards of

*In the South, the wealthy classes attached themselves to the Democracy to resist the unconstitutional movement of fanaticism, and they remain united with that party.

their allies, the American fanatics and agitators. Both will soon unite their legions on common ground; proclaim the holding of property to be robbery; and the preparation for the last conflict will commence. Senseless propagandists are blindly hastening towards the communistic centre. Wisdom can alone shield our nation from what destiny seems to be gathering for her final destruction.

www.ingramcontent.com/pod-product-compliance
Lightning Source LLC
LaVergne TN
LVHW021314110826
845150LV00003B/566
* 9 7 8 1 4 2 5 5 5 7 9 2 8 *